Review & Reteach

Skills and Concepts Review

Algebra 1, Geometry, & Algebra 2

PRENTICE HALL

MATHEMATICS

Needham, Massachusetts
Upper Saddle River, New Jersey

Cover Photo: Digital Imagery 2001 © PhotoDisc, Inc.

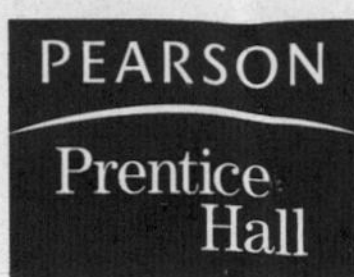

ISBN 0-13-068635-2
10 06

Table of Contents

Pre-Algebra Topics

Algebra 1 Topics

Table of Contents *(continued)*

Table of Contents *(continued)*

Geometry Topics

Table of Contents *(continued)*

Algebra 2 Topics

Table of Contents *(continued)*

Table of Contents *(continued)*

Answers

Name ____________________ Class ____________ Date ____________

Review 1

Variables and Expressions

OBJECTIVE: Identifying variables, numerical expressions, and variable expressions for word phrases

MATERIALS: None

Example

A *variable* is a letter that stands for a number.

Thomas needs \$2 to ride the bus to Videoland. How much can he spend on video games for each amount in the table?

Thomas has	Thomas can spend	
	Expression	Amount
\$5	$5 - 2$	\$3
\$7	$7 - 2$	\$5
\$10	$10 - 2$	\$8
d	$d - 2$	$d - 2$

The letter *d* is a variable that stands for the amount of money Thomas has. The expression $d - 2$ is a *variable expression*. It has a variable (d), a numeral (2), and an operation symbol ($-$).

Exercises

Videoland tokens cost one dollar for 4. How many tokens can Jennifer buy for each amount of money in the table?

	Jennifer has	Tokens Jennifer can buy	
		Expression	Amount
1.	\$5		
2.	\$8		
3.	\$6		
4.	*d* dollars		

Write a variable expression for each word phrase.

5. *h* divided by 7 ____________

6. *j* decreased by 9 ____________

7. twice *x* ____________

8. two more than *y* ____________

9. the quotient of 42 and a number *s* ____________

10. the product of a number *d* and 16 ____________

Name ______________________ Class ______________ Date ______________

Review 2

The Order of Operations

OBJECTIVE: Using the order of operations, including the use of grouping symbols

MATERIALS: None

Example

Simplify $\frac{18 + 4}{2} - 3(10 \cdot 2 - 3 \cdot 6)$

$\frac{18 + 4}{2} - 3(10 \cdot 2 - 3 \cdot 6)$	Work inside grouping symbols first.
$= \frac{22}{2} - 3(10 \cdot 2 - 3 \cdot 6)$	A fraction bar is a grouping symbol.
$= 11 - 3(10 \cdot 2 - 3 \cdot 6)$	Divide the fraction.
$= 11 - 3(20 - 18)$	Multiply within the parentheses.
$= 11 - 3(2)$	Subtract within the parentheses.
$= 11 - 6$	Multiply.
$= 5$	Subtract.

Exercises

Simplify each expression.

1. $8 + 2 \times 7$ ____________

2. $16 \div 2 - 5$ ____________

3. $\frac{8 + 12}{5}$ ____________

4. $4 - 24 \div 8$ ____________

5. $3 + 2 \cdot 5 - 4$ ____________

6. $15 - 2(5 - 2)$ ____________

7. $9 \cdot 3 + 2 \cdot 5$ ____________

8. $12 \div 4 - 6 \div 3$ ____________

9. $5(2 + 4) + 15 \div (9 - 6)$ ____________

10. $3 \cdot 2 + 16 \div 4 - 3$ ____________

11. $(18 + 7) \div (3 + 2)$ ____________

12. $3[8 - 3 \cdot 2 + 4(5 - 2)]$ ____________

13. $4 \cdot 9 + 8 \div 2 - 6 \cdot 5$ ____________

14. $[7 + 3 \cdot 2 + 8] \div 7$ ____________

15. $53 - [3(8 + 2) + 5(9 - 5)]$ ____________

16. $(20 + 22) \div 6 + 1$ ____________

17. $2[9(6 - 5)]$ ____________

18. $5 + 3 \cdot 4 - 8 + 2 \cdot 7$ ____________

Name ____________________ Class ____________ Date ____________

Review 3

Evaluating Expressions

OBJECTIVE: Evaluating variable expressions

MATERIALS: None

Example

Evaluate $a(b + 4) - c$, for $a = 2$, $b = 5$, and $c = 12$.

$a(b + 4) - c$

$= 2(5 + 4) - 12$ Replace the variables.

$= 2(9) - 12$ Work within grouping symbols.

$= 18 - 12$ Multiply.

$= 6$ Subtract.

Exercises

Evaluate each expression.

1. $2n - 7$, for $n = 8$ ____________

2. $4ab$, for $a = 2$ and $b = 5$ ____________

3. $\frac{x + y}{3}$, for $x = 7$ and $y = 8$ ____________

4. $2(m + n)$, for $m = 3$ and $n = 2$ ____________

5. $37 - 5h$, for $h = 7$ ____________

6. $\frac{6}{a} + b$, for $a = 3$ and $b = 7$ ____________

7. $4x + 5y - 3z$, for $x = 3$, $y = 4$, and $z = 2$ ____________

8. $15a - 2(b + c)$, for $a = 2$, $b = 3$, and $c = 4$ ____________

9. $7p + q(3 + r)$, for $p = 3$, $q = 2$, and $r = 1$ ____________

10. $\frac{36}{j} - 4(k + l)$, for $j = 2$, $k = 1$, and $l = 3$ ____________

11. $x + 3y - 4(z - 3)$, for $x = 4$, $y = 6$, and $z = 5$ ____________

12. $(4 + d) - e(9 - f)$, for $d = 7$, $e = 4$, $f = 8$ ____________

13. $3a - 2b + b(6 - 2)$, for $a = 4$, $b = 2$ ____________

14. $r(p + 3) + q(p - 1)$, for $p = 7$, $q = 4$, $r = 3$ ____________

Name ______________________ Class ______________ Date ______________

Review 4

Look for a Pattern

OBJECTIVE: Solving problems by looking for a pattern

MATERIALS: None

Example

Margarita learned to dig clams over her vacation and got steadily better at finding clams each day. On the first day she found 2 clams, on the second day 5 clams, and on the third day 8. If she continued to improve at the same rate, how many clams did she find on the sixth day?

Make a table to organize the numbers. Then look for a pattern.

Day	1	2	3	4	5	6
Clams	2	5	8	11	14	17
More than day before	0	3	3	3	3	3

Margarita found 17 clams on the sixth day.

Exercises

Phillipe got steadily better at playing ping pong on his vacation. The table shows the number of games he won the first three days. If he continued to improve at the same rate, how many games would he win on the sixth day?

1. Complete the table.

Day	1	2	3	4	5	6
Games Won	3	5	7			
More than day before	0					

2. Solve the problem.

____

Jennifer improved her bike riding distance steadily while preparing for a race. The table shows the distance in miles she rode during the first three weeks of training. If she continues to improve at the same rate, how many miles will she be able to ride in the sixth week? How many more miles did she ride in week 6 than she rode in week 5?

3. Complete the table.

Week	1	2	3	4	5	6
Miles Traveled	3	4	6	9		
More than week before	0					

4. Solve the problems.

____

____

Name ____________________ Class ____________ Date ____________

Review 5

Properties of Numbers

OBJECTIVE: Identifying properties of addition and multiplication and using them to solve problems

MATERIALS: None

Example

Properties of numbers help make mental computations easier.

Use mental math to simplify $1.84 + $.76 + $.16.

Since 0.84 + 0.16 = 1, it is easier to add $1.84 and $.16 first.

1.84 + 0.76 + 0.16	
= 1.84 + (0.16 + 0.76)	Use the commutative property of addition.
= (1.84 + 0.16) + 0.76	Use the associative property of addition.
= 2.00 + 0.76	Add within parentheses.
= $2.76	Add.

Use mental math to simplify 5 · 13 · 20 · 2.

Since 5 · 20 = 100, it is easier to multiply 5 and 20 first.

5 · 13 · 20 · 2	
= (13 · 5) · 20 · 2	Use the commutative property of multiplication.
= 13 · (5 · 20) · 2	Use the associative property of multiplication.
= 13 · 100 · 2	Multiply within parentheses.
= 13 · (200)	Multiply.
= 2,600	Multiply.

Exercises

Use mental math to simplify each expression.

1. 198 + 15 + 302 ____________

2. 16 + 27 + (−16) ____________

3. 4 · 7 · 25 ____________

4. 2 · 6 · 5 ____________

5. 18 + (−8) + 11 ____________

6. 5 · 9 · 8 ____________

7. 21 + 4 + (−1) ____________

8. 1,242 + 125 + 58 ____________

9. 50 · 13 · 2 ____________

10. (−209) + 576 + (−91) ____________

11. 17 + 9 + 13 + 6 ____________

12. 125 · 353 · 8 ____________

Name ______________________ Class ______________ Date ______________

Review 6

Mean, Median, and Mode

OBJECTIVE: Describing data by finding the mean, median, and mode

MATERIALS: None

Example

In 1995, eight states had pupil-teacher ratios that were close to the U.S. average of 17.3. Use the table at the right. Find the **a)** mean, **b)** median, and **c)** mode.

State	Pupils per Teacher
Arkansas	17.1
Illinois	17.1
Indiana	17.5
Louisiana	17.0
Mississippi	17.5
New Mexico	17.0
Ohio	17.1
Pennsylvania	17.0

a. Mean: $\frac{\text{sum of data items}}{\text{number of data items}}$

$= \frac{17.1 + 17.1 + 17.5 + 17.0 + 17.5 + 17.0 + 17.1 + 17.0}{8}$

$= \frac{137.3}{8} = 17.1625$

Rounded to the nearest tenth, the mean is 17.2.

b. Median: Write the data in order.

17.0, 17.0, 17.0, $\boxed{17.1, 17.1,}$ 17.1, 17.5, 17.5

$\frac{17.1 + 17.1}{2} = 17.1$ Find the mean of the two middle numbers. The median is 17.1

c. Mode: Find the data item that occurs most often.

Both 17.0 and 17.1 occur 3 times. The modes are 17.0 and 17.1.

Exercises

Find the mean, median, and mode. Round to the nearest tenth where necessary.

	mean	median	mode
1. 14.2 14.7 14.3 14.6	______	______	______
2. 8 7 3 5 9 2 4 7	______	______	______
3. 37 42 51 28 36	______	______	______
4. 1.1 1.8 2.6 1.8 1.9 2.6	______	______	______

The world's largest body of freshwater is formed by the Great Lakes of North America. Use the table of depths at the right. Find the following statistics. Round to the nearest tenth where necessary.

Lake	Depth (in ft)
Superior	1,333
Michigan	923
Huron	750
Erie	210
Ontario	802

5. mean: ______________________

6. median: ______________________

7. mode: ______________________

Name ______________________ Class ______________ Date ______________

Review 7

Simplify a Problem

OBJECTIVE: Solving problems by simplifying the problems

MATERIALS: None

Example

You have 12 meters of ribbon to cut into half-meter pieces. How many cuts do you need to make?

Simplify the problem. Suppose you only had 3 meters of ribbon. Use a diagram.

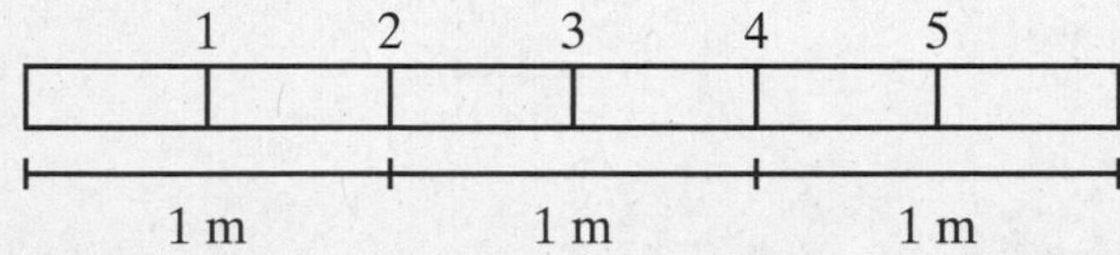

Although you will get 6 pieces of ribbon (2 · 3), you need to make only 5 cuts.

With 12 meters of ribbon, you would get 24 pieces with 23 cuts.

Exercises

Solve by simplifying the problem.

1. A plumber charges $25 to weld two pipes together. Pipe comes in 4-foot pieces and you need one piece 60 feet long. How much will it cost to have enough 4-foot pieces welded together? Fill in the table first.

Length of Pipe	Number of Welds
8	1
12	2
16	
20	
60	

____

2. How many digits are used to number the pages of a 425-page book? Fill in the table first.

Page Number	Number of Pages	Digits
1–9		
10–99		
100–425		

Total digits: ______________

3. You are serving fruit in small bowls at a luncheon. You decide to place one slice of melon and a spoonful of one type of berry in each bowl. You have three types of melon and four types of berries available. How many different combinations of melon and berries can you make?

____

Name ____________________ Class ____________ Date ____________

Review 8

Divisibility and Factors

OBJECTIVE: Using divisibility tests and finding factors

MATERIALS: None

Example

Find all the factors of 30.

Start with 1 and 30.
Is 30 divisible by 2? Yes, it ends in 0.
List 2 and 15.

Is 30 divisible by 3? Yes, the sum of the digits, 3, is divisible by 3.
List 3 and 10.

Is 30 divisible by 4? No, $4 \cdot 7 = 28$ and $4 \cdot 8 = 32$.

Is 30 divisible by 5? Yes, it ends in 0.
List 5 and 6.

When you list all the factors in order, the pairs with products of 30 form a symmetric pattern.

1, 2, 3, 5, 6, 10, 15, 30

Exercises

Fill in the boxes to find all the factors for each number.

1. 34

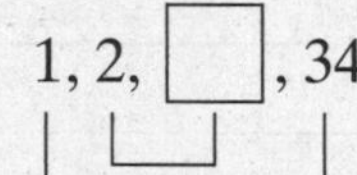

1, 2, ☐, 34

2. 50

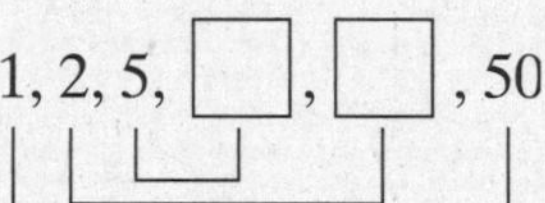

1, 2, 5, ☐, ☐, 50

3. 52

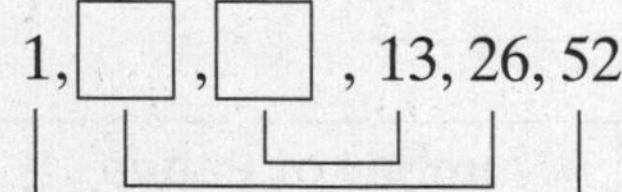

1, ☐, ☐, 13, 26, 52

4. 36

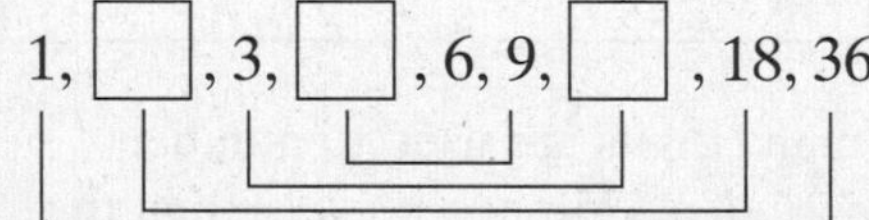

1, ☐, 3, ☐, 6, 9, ☐, 18, 36

Find all the factors of each number.

5. 55 ____________________

6. 40 ____________________

7. 42 ____________________

8. 48 ____________________

Name ________________ Class ________________ Date ________________

Review 9

Account for All Possibilities

OBJECTIVE: Solving problems by accounting for all possibilities

MATERIALS: None

Example

A taco shop serves beef, chicken, or bean burritos. You can have any burrito on a corn or a flour tortilla and with or without hot sauce. How many different burritos does the shop serve?

The different burritos are listed in the table at the right. To be sure all possibilities are counted, all the beef burritos are listed first. Within those, the two types of beef burritos on a corn tortilla are listed first. The pattern is continued with chicken and then bean burritos.

Filling	Tortilla	Hot Sauce
beef	corn	yes
beef	corn	no
beef	flour	yes
beef	flour	no
chicken	corn	yes
chicken	corn	no
chicken	flour	yes
chicken	flour	no
bean	corn	yes
bean	corn	no
bean	flour	yes
bean	flour	no

Exercises

Solve each problem by accounting for all possibilities.

1. Kara and Karl love steak, fried chicken, hamburgers, mashed potatoes, and french fries. They like green beans and peas. How many different meals including a meat, potatoes, and a green vegetable can they make from these choices? List all possibilities in the table to find the number of different meals.

   ____

Meat	Potato	Vegetable
steak	mashed	beans
steak	mashed	peas

2. What is the most money you can have in coins and not be able to make change for a dollar? Hint: You do not have to have each kind of coin.

   ____

Name ______________________ Class ______________ Date ______________

Review 10

Work Backward

OBJECTIVE: Solving problems by working backwards

MATERIALS: None

Example

Jody, Karl, and Kara want to buy a pizza. Jody said she can pay half the cost. Karl said he can pay $\frac{1}{3}$ of what was left after Jody paid half. Kara said she could pay the remaining $4. How much does the pizza cost?

Work backward.

Kara will pay $4. This is $\frac{2}{3}$ of what is left after Jody pays half, since Karl pays $\frac{1}{3}$ and $1 - \frac{1}{3} = \frac{2}{3}$. Let h equal half the cost of the pizza.

$\frac{2}{3}h = 4$

Use try, test, revise strategy to find $h = 6$.

Thus, Jody pays $6 and Karl pays $\frac{1}{3} \cdot 6 = \$2$.

The pizza costs $6 + 2 + 4 = \$12$.

Exercises

1. Steven, Lisa, and Mark want to buy a pizza. Steven said he could pay twice as much as Lisa. Mark said he could pay the remaining $3, which is $1 less than Lisa's share. How much does the pizza cost?

   a. How much is Mark paying? ______________

   b. How much is Lisa paying? ______________

   c. How much is Steven paying? ______________

   d. How much does the pizza cost? ______________

2. On Wednesday Olga's parents said she owed them too much money to borrow anymore. On Thursday, she paid her parents $15 she earned babysitting. On Friday she borrowed $5 to go to a movie. On Saturday, she paid them the $12 she earned babysitting. Then her debt was down to $22. How much did she owe on Wednesday?

   ____

3. Yuki, Mollie, Brandon, and Anna share an apple pie for desert. Brandon eats half the amount Mollie eats. Yuki eats four times as much pie as Brandon. Mollie eats $\frac{1}{4}$ of the pie. How much does Anna eat?

   ____

Name ______________________ Class ______________ Date ______________

Review 11

Transforming Formulas

OBJECTIVE: Solving problems involving formulas by solving for a specific variable

MATERIALS: None

Example

Solve the surface area formula $s = 2\pi r^2 + 2\pi rh$ for h.

$s = 2\pi r^2 + 2\pi rh$

$s - 2\pi r^2 = 2\pi r^2 - 2\pi r^2 + 2\pi rh$ — Subtract $2\pi r^2$ from each side.

$s - 2\pi r^2 = 2\pi rh$ — Simplify.

$\frac{s - 2\pi r^2}{2\pi r} = \frac{2\pi rh}{2\pi r}$ — Divide each side by $2\pi r$.

$\frac{s - 2\pi r^2}{2\pi r} = h$ — Simplify.

Exercises

Solve for the indicated variable.

1. $y = mx + b$, for x ______________

2. $y = mx + b$, for m ______________

3. $p = 6s$, for s ______________

4. $A = \frac{1}{2}h(B + b)$, for h ______________

5. $I = Prt$, for P ______________

6. $y = \frac{2}{3}x - 5$, for x ______________

7. $t = 0.05p$, for p ______________

8. $V = lwh$, for w ______________

9. $k = \frac{1}{2}mv^2$, for m ______________

10. $W = p(V - L)$, for V ______________

11. $F = \frac{Gm_1m_2}{r^2}$, for G ______________

12. $W = p(V - L)$, for L ______________

13. $V = \frac{h}{e}v - \frac{E}{e}$, for e ______________

14. $mv = (m + M)u$, for m ______________

Name ______________________ Class ______________ Date ______________

Review 12

OBJECTIVE: Determining whether a relation is a function using graphs and tables of values

MATERIALS: None

Example

Graph the relation. Is the relation a function? Explain.

x	y
3	4
−1	2
4	−3
−4	−2

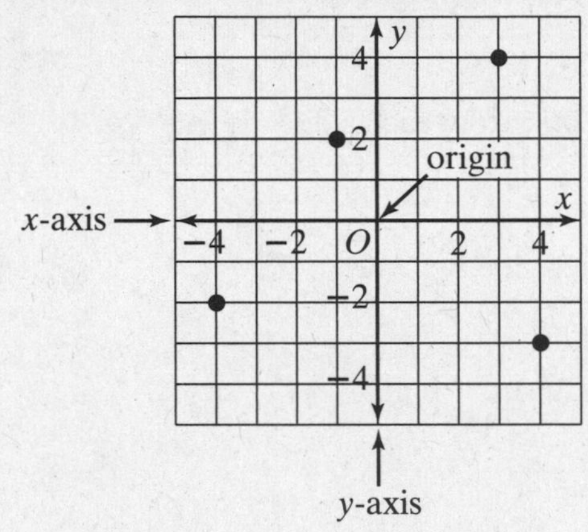

First, plot the point (3, 4). Start at the origin, where the x-axis and the y-axis cross. Go right 3 units and up 4 units.

To plot (−1, 2), from the origin go left one unit and up 2 units.

To plot (4, −3), from the origin, go right 4 units and down 3 units.

To plot (−4, −2), from the origin, go left 4 units and down 2 units.

Next, use the vertical line test. Hold a pencil vertically to the left of the graph. Slowly move it to the right. If you can find a vertical line that passes through two graphed points, then the relation is not a function. If you cannot find such a line, the relation is a function. This relation is a function because the vertical pencil does not pass through two points anywhere on the graph.

Exercises

Graph the relation. Is the relation a function? Explain.

x	y
−4	1
1	3
4	0
1	−2

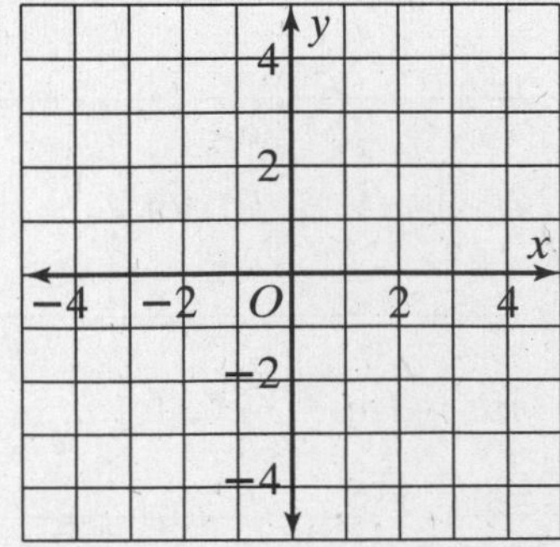

____

____

Name ______________________ Class ______________ Date ______________

Review 13

Writing Rules for Linear Functions

OBJECTIVE: Writing a function rule by analyzing a table or graph

MATERIALS: None

Example

Write a rule for the function.

x	$f(x)$
−2	−12
0	−2
2	8
4	18

As the x values increase by 2, the $f(x)$ values increase by 10. So $m = \frac{10}{2} = 5$. When $x = 0$, $f(x) = -2$. So $b = -2$. Substitute $m = 5$ and $b = -2$ into $f(x) = mx + b$.

$f(x) = 5x + (-2)$

$f(x) = 5x - 2$

Exercises

Write a rule for each function.

1. ______________

x	$f(x)$
−1	−7
0	0
1	7
2	14

2. ______________

x	$f(x)$
−9	−17
0	−8
9	1
18	10

3. ______________

x	$f(x)$
0	9
2	5
4	1
6	−3

4. ______________

x	$f(x)$
−6	7
−3	8
0	9
3	10

5. ______________

x	$f(x)$
−4	−6
0	−7
4	−8
8	−9

6. ______________

x	$f(x)$
−12	−83
−6	−47
0	−11
6	25

Name ____________________ Class ____________ Date ____________

Review 14

Scatter Plots

OBJECTIVE: Drawing scatter plots and using scatter plots for finding trends

MATERIALS: None

Example

Make a (U.S. Open wins, Wimbledon wins) scatter plot of the data in the table. Is there a *positive correlation*, a *negative correlation*, or *no correlation* between the two sets of data?

Player	U.S. Open	Wimble-don	French Open	Aust. Open
Andre Agassi	1	1	0	1
Jimmy Connors	5	2	0	1
Chris Evert	6	3	7	2
Steffie Graf	5	7	5	4
John McEnroe	4	3	0	0
Martina Navratilova	4	9	2	3
Pete Sampras	4	4	0	2
Monica Seles	2	0	3	4

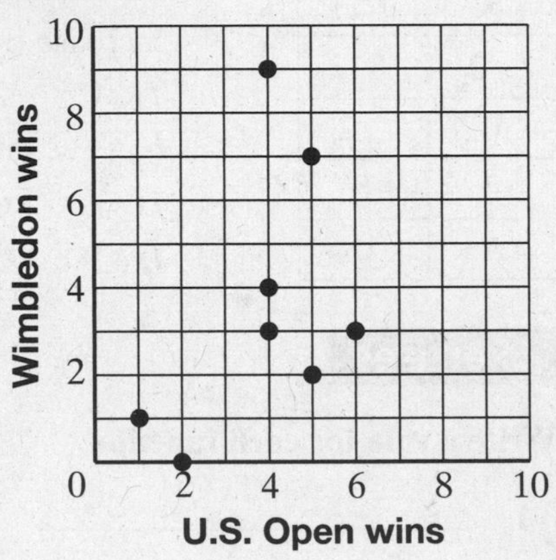

Plot each (U.S. Open wins, Wimbledon wins) ordered pair.

There does not seem to be a trend in the data. As the number of U.S. Open wins increase, the number of Wimbledon wins does not seem to increase or decrease. Thus, there is no correlation.

Exercises

1. Make a (U.S. Open wins, French Open wins) scatter plot using the data in the table above.

2. Make a (Wimbledon wins, Australian Open wins) scatter plot using the data in the table above.

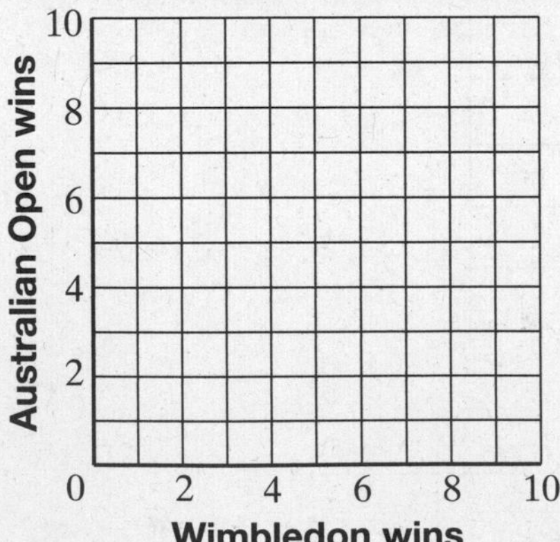

Is there a *positive correlation*, a *negative correlation*, or *no correlation* between the data sets in each scatter plot?

3. (U.S. Open wins, French Open wins) ____________________

4. (Wimbledon wins, Australian Open wins) ____________________

Name ______________________ Class ______________ Date ______________

Review 15

Solve by Graphing

OBJECTIVE: Solving problems by graphing **MATERIALS:** None

Example

The driver of a car slowed to a stop. After 3 seconds the car was traveling 41 mi/h. After 5 seconds it was traveling 30 mi/h and after 8 seconds it was traveling 12 mi/h.

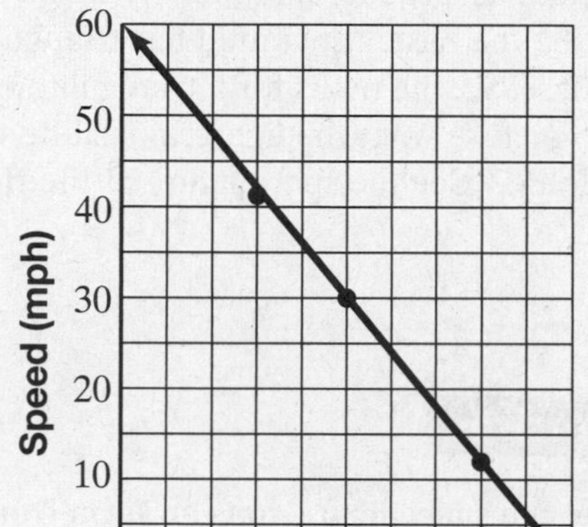

a. Make a scatter plot of the data and draw a trend line. Plot the points (3, 41), (5, 30) and (8, 12). Draw a line through (5, 30) and (8, 12).

b. About how fast was the car moving when the driver first applied the brakes?
When the time was 0, the speed was 60. So the driver was moving 60 mi/h.

c. Write an equation for your trend line. The y-intercept, b, is 60.
You can use the points (5, 30) and (8, 12) to find the slope.

$$m = \frac{\text{difference in } y\text{-values}}{\text{difference in } x\text{-values}} = \frac{12 - 30}{8 - 5} = \frac{-18}{3} = -6$$

Substitute $m = -6$ and $b = 60$ into $y = mx + b$.

$y = mx + b$
$y = -6x + 60$

d. Use your equation to find about how long it took for the car to stop.
When the car stops, the speed, y, is zero.

$y = -6x + 60$
$0 = -6x + 60$
$6x = 60$
$x = 10$

It took the car 10 seconds to stop.

Exercises

The water pressure at a depth of 100 ft in the ocean is 45 lb/in.^{2}. At a depth of 500 ft the pressure is 225 lb/in.^{2}.

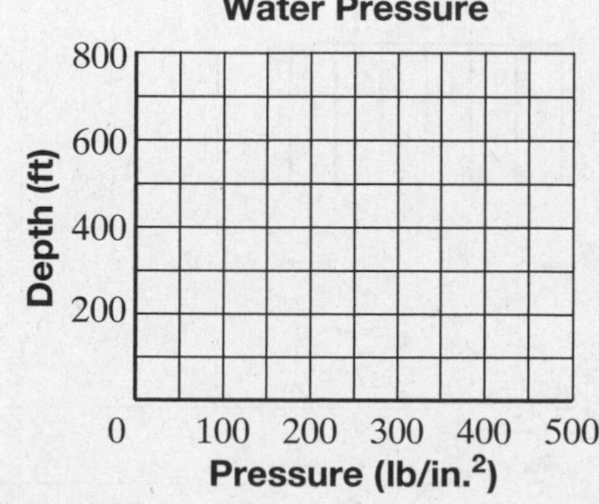

1. Make a (pressure, depth) scatter plot of the data.

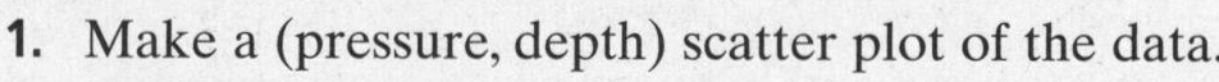

2. Draw a trend line.

3. Write an equation for your trend line.

____

4. Use your equation to find the approximate depth where the pressure is 180 lb/in.^{2}

____

5. Use your equation to find the approximate pressure at a depth of 800 ft.

____

Name ______________________ Class ______________ Date ______________

Review 16

OBJECTIVE: Identifying nets of common space figures

MATERIALS: None

Example

Name the space figure you can form from the net.

The net has a square and four triangles. So, the square must be the base. A pyramid has triangular sides and only one base. So, the net is for a triangular pyramid. You might try to picture what the figure looks like when it is cut out and folded. See the space figure at the right.

Exercises

Name the space figure you can form from each net. Start by naming the polygons in the net.

1.

polygons: ______________________

space figure: ______________________

2.

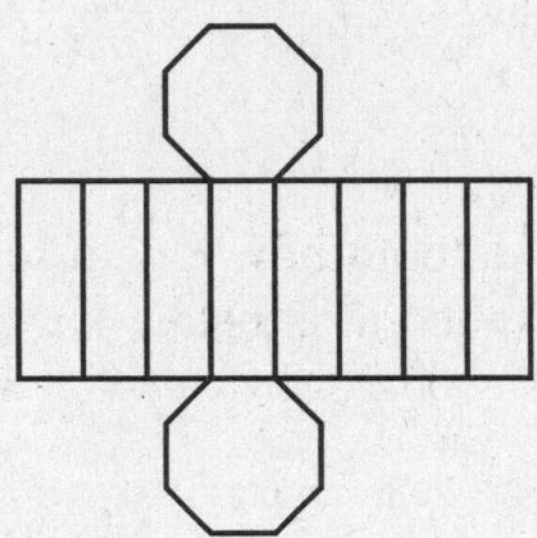

polygons: ______________________

space figure: ______________________

3.

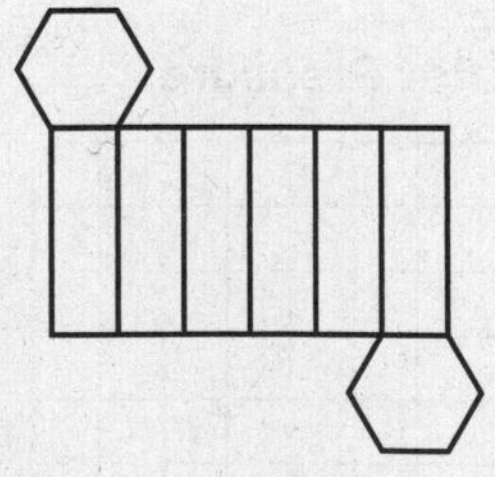

polygons: ______________________

space figure: ______________________

4.

polygons: ______________________

space figure: ______________________

Name ______________________ Class ______________ Date ______________

Review 17

Make a Model

OBJECTIVE: Solving problems by making a model **MATERIALS:** Graph paper

Example

Suppose you cut square corners off a piece of cardboard with dimensions 10 cm by 12 cm and fold up the sides to make an open box. To the nearest centimeter, what dimensions will give you the greatest volume?

Use a model to solve the problem. Cut out a 10 unit by 12 unit piece of graph paper. Cut a 1 by 1 square out of each corner. Fold to form a box.

The height of the box is the same as the length of the corner, 1 unit.

The length is 12 units minus the two corners or $12 - 2 = 10$ units. The width is 10 units minus the two corners or $10 - 2 = 8$.
$V = Bh = 10 \cdot 8 \cdot 1 = 80 \text{ units}^3$

Now cut 2 units by 2 unit squares out of the corners and fold the box.
$h = 2$
$l = 12 - 2(2) = 12 - 4 = 8$
$w = 10 - 2(2) = 10 - 4 = 6$
$V = Bh = 8 \cdot 6 \cdot 2 = 96 \text{ units}^3$

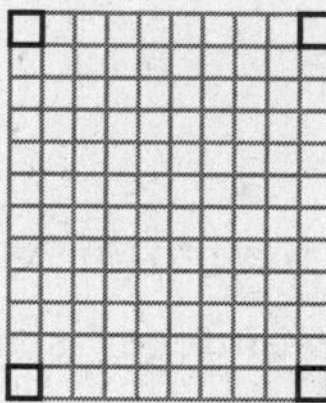

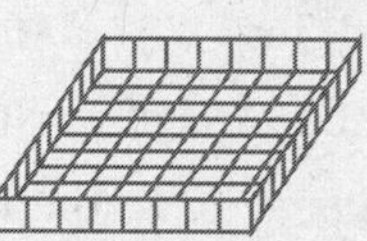

Now cut 3 unit by 3 unit squares out of the corners.
$V = (6 \cdot 4) \cdot 3 = 72 \text{ units}^3$

Then cut 4 unit by 4 unit squares out of the corners.
$V = (4 \cdot 2) \cdot 4 = 32 \text{ units}^3$

It is not possible to make a box by cutting 5 unit by 5 unit squares out of the corners. There would be no width.

So, to the nearest centimeter, a 2 cm by 6 cm by 8 cm box gives the greatest volume.

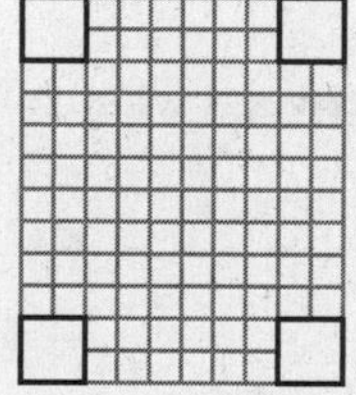

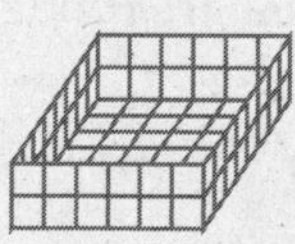

Exercises

Suppose you cut square corners off a piece of cardboard with dimensions 12 cm by 15 cm to make an open box. Use a model to find the dimensions, to the nearest centimeter of each box. Record your work in the table.

	Length of side of corner	Length	Width	Height	Volume
1.	1 cm				
2.	2 cm				
3.	3 cm				
4.	4 cm				
5.	5 cm				

6. Which dimensions give the greatest volume? ______________________

Name ____________________ Class ____________ Date ____________

Review 18

Square Roots and Irrational Numbers

OBJECTIVE: Finding square roots of numbers **MATERIALS:** None

Example

Estimate $\sqrt{27}$ to the nearest integer.

To estimate square roots, it is helpful to know the perfect squares in the following table.

n	1	2	3	4	5	6	7	8	9	10	11	12
n^2	1	4	9	16	25	36	49	64	81	100	121	144

Look at the n^2 row. These numbers are called perfect squares. Between which two perfect squares is 27?

$25 < 27 < 36$

so, $\sqrt{25} < \sqrt{27} < \sqrt{36}$

and $5 < \sqrt{27} < 6$

Since 27 is closer to 25 than to 36, $\sqrt{27}$ is closer to 5 than to 6.

Thus, $\sqrt{27}$ to the nearest integer is 5.

Exercises

Each square root is between what two integers? Circle the integer to which it is closer.

1. $\sqrt{18}$ ________, ________
2. $\sqrt{60}$ ________, ________
3. $-\sqrt{8}$ ________, ________
4. $\sqrt{90}$ ________, ________
5. $\sqrt{29 + 8}$ ________, ________
6. $-\sqrt{21}$ ________, ________
7. $\sqrt{133}$ ________, ________
8. $-\sqrt{118}$ ________, ________

Estimate to the nearest integer.

9. $\sqrt{48}$ ________
10. $\sqrt{80}$ ________
11. $\sqrt{119}$ ________
12. $\sqrt{141}$ ________
13. $\sqrt{67}$ ________
14. $\sqrt{95}$ ________
15. $\sqrt{6}$ ________
16. $\sqrt{20}$ ________
17. $\sqrt{12}$ ________
18. $-\sqrt{3}$ ________
19. $\sqrt{42}$ ________
20. $-\sqrt{22}$ ________
21. $-\sqrt{110}$ ________
22. $-\sqrt{31}$ ________
23. $\sqrt{45}$ ________

Name ______________________ Class ______________ Date ______________

Review 19

Frequency Tables and Line Plots

OBJECTIVE: Displaying data using frequency tables and line plots

MATERIALS: None

Example

Use the data in the rainfall table to make a frequency table and a line plot for Albuquerque.

Inches	0	1	2
Frequency	2	9	1

Average Monthly Rainfall (in.)

City	Month											
	J	F	M	A	M	J	J	A	S	O	N	D
Albuquerque, NM	0	1	1	1	1	1	1	2	1	1	0	1
Charleston, SC	4	3	4	3	4	6	7	7	5	3	3	3
San Francisco, CA	4	3	3	1	0	0	0	0	0	1	3	3
Wilmington, DE	3	3	3	3	4	4	4	3	3	3	3	4

The numbers of inches are 0, 1, 2, so these are listed in the top row. Since two months have 0 inches (less than 0.5 in.), the frequency is 2. Albuquerque has one inch of rainfall in 9 different months, so the frequency is 9. Similarly, the frequency for 2 inches is 1.

To draw a line plot, start with a number line. Label 0, 1, and 2 inches. Then make the appropriate number of X's above each number. Be sure to line up your X's across from each other.

Albuquerque Rainfall

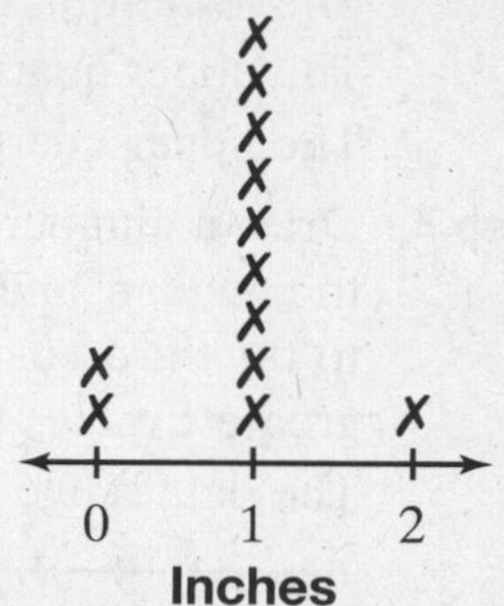

Exercises

Use the data in the rainfall table to make a frequency table and a line plot for each city.

1. Charleston, SC

Inches					
Frequency					

Charleston Rainfall

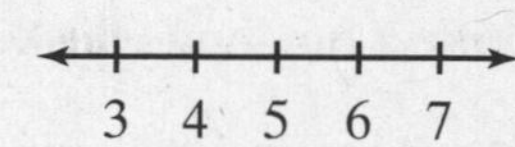

2. San Francisco, CA

Inches					
Frequency					

San Francisco Rainfall

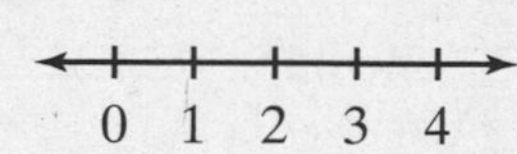

3. Wilmington, DE

Inches		
Frequency		

Wilmington Rainfall

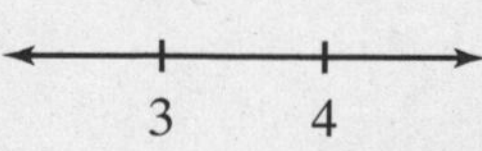

Name ______________________ Class ______________ Date ______________

Review 20

OBJECTIVE: Constructing box-and-whisker plots **MATERIALS:** None

Example

Make a box-and-whisker plot for the data set.

Percent of Federally Owned Land in Ten Western States				
45%	24%	52%	61%	28%
42%	34%	48%	63%	36%

Step 1: First list the data in order from least to greatest. Find the median.

24 28 34 36 42 | 45 48 52 61 63

Since there is an even number of percents (10), there are two middle numbers. Add them and divide by 2.

$\frac{42 + 45}{2} = \frac{87}{2} = 43.5$ The median is 43.5.

Step 2: Find the upper and lower quartiles.

The lower quartile is the median of the lower half. 24 28 [34] 36 42

The lower quartile is 34.

The upper quartile is the median of the upper half. 45 48 [52] 61 63

The upper quartile is 52.

Step 3: Draw a number line. Mark the least and greatest values, the median, and the quartiles. Draw a box from the first to the third quartiles. Draw whiskers from the least and greatest values to the box.

The data range from 24 to 63. A scale of 5 from 20 to 70 would have 11 marks.

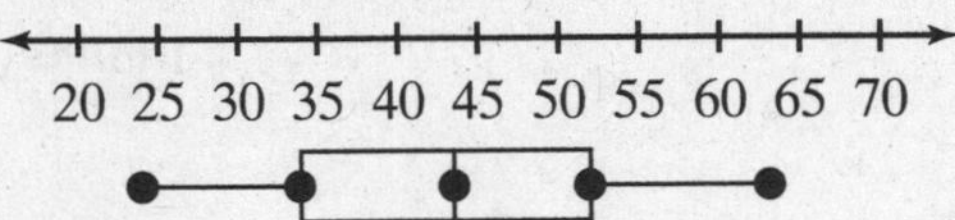

Exercises

Make a box-and-whisker plot for each data set.

1. Area in 1,000 mi^2 of 13 western states.

122	164	71	98	84	147	114
111	98	85	104	71	77	

median: ____________

lower quartile: ____________

upper quartile: ____________

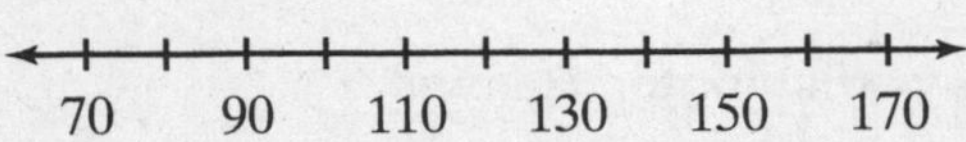

2. Percent of area that is inland water for 11 northeastern states.

13%	4%	26%	4%	32%	13%
15%	3%	21%	7%	21%	

median: ____________

lower quartile: ____________

upper quartile: ____________

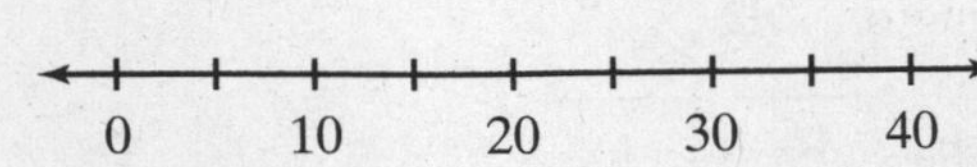

Name ______________________ Class ______________ Date ______________

Review 21

Using Graphs to Persuade

OBJECTIVE: Recognizing the use of different scales and breaks in scales of graphs

MATERIALS: None

Example

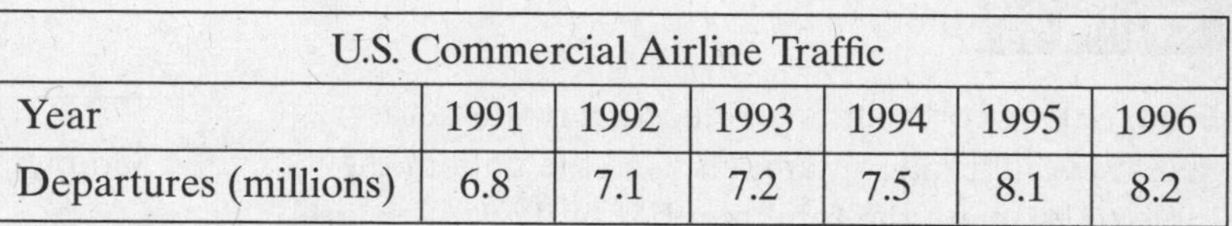

U.S. Commercial Airline Traffic						
Year	1991	1992	1993	1994	1995	1996
Departures (millions)	6.8	7.1	7.2	7.5	8.1	8.2

Use the data in the table. Draw a line graph on each grid at the right. Discuss the impressions given by the graphs.

The first graph gives the impression that airline traffic increased rapidly from 1991 to 1996. The second graph implies a much more gradual increase. The different impressions are given by the vertical scales. The vertical scale in the first graph is broken and increases by half millions. The vertical scale in the second graph is unbroken and increases by millions.

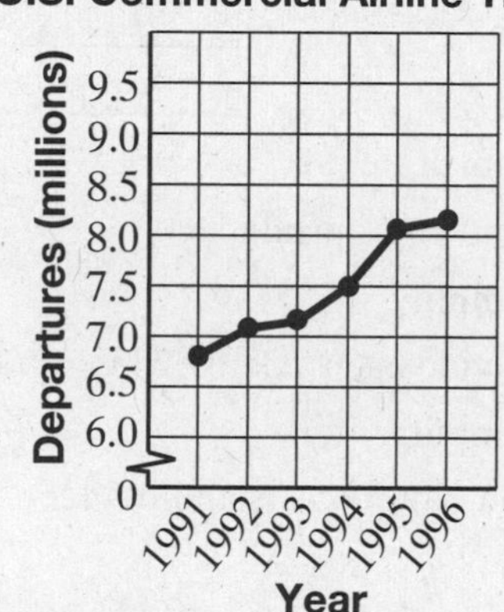

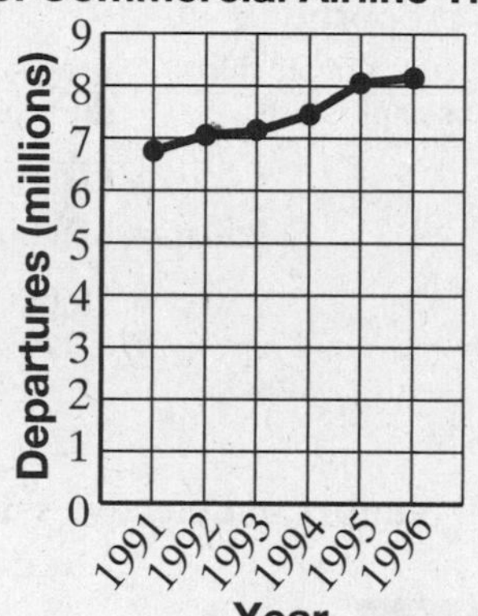

Exercises

U.S. City Average Gasoline Retail Prices						
Year	1991	1992	1993	1994	1995	1996
Price	$1.20	$1.19	$1.17	$1.17	$1.21	$1.29

1. Make a line graph of the data in the table using the grid below.

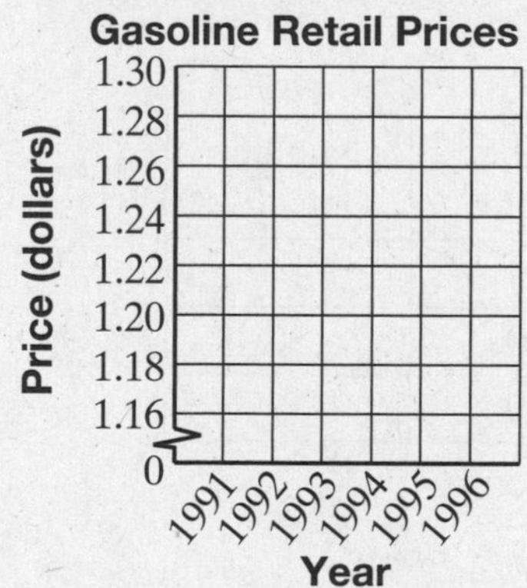

2. Make a line graph of the data in the table using the grid below.

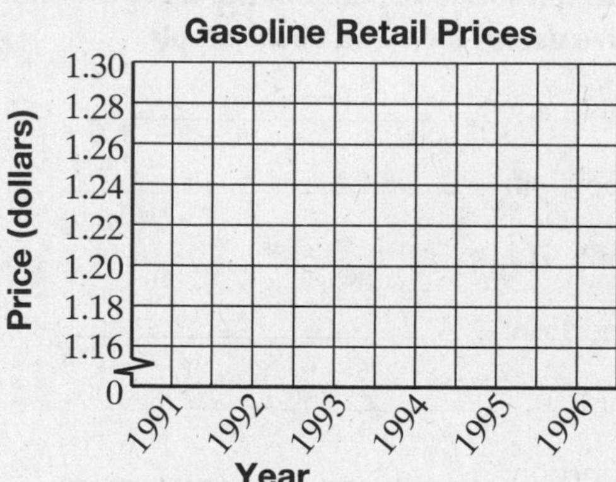

3. Compare the impressions given in the two graphs.

____

____

____

PRE-ALGEBRA TOPICS

Name ______________________ Class ______________ Date ______________

Review 22

Random Samples and Surveys

OBJECTIVE: Making estimates about populations using samples

MATERIALS: None

Example

From 8,000 sports shirts produced, a manufacturer takes several random samples. Use the data in the table to estimate the total number of defective shirts based on Sample A.

Sample	Number Sampled	Number Defective
A	250	6
B	400	8
C	500	9

Set up a proportion.

$$\frac{\text{defective sample shirts}}{\text{sample shirts}} = \frac{\text{defective shirts}}{\text{shirts produced}}$$

$\frac{6}{250} = \frac{x}{8{,}000}$ Substitute.

$250x = 6(8{,}000)$ Find cross products.

$250x = 48{,}000$ Simplify.

$\frac{250x}{250} = \frac{48{,}000}{250}$ Divide each side by 250.

$x = 192$ Simplify.

The total number of defective shirts based on Sample A is about 192.

Exercises

Use the data in the table above to estimate the number of defective shirts out of 8,000 based on each sample.

1. Sample B ____________ proportion used: ____________
2. Sample C ____________ proportion used: ____________

From 12,000 computer games produced, a manufacturer takes several random samples. Use the data in the table to estimate the total number of defective games based on each sample.

Sample	Number Sampled	Number Defective
A	400	16
B	800	30
C	500	19

3. Sample A ____________

   proportion: ____________

4. Sample B ____________

   proportion: ____________

5. Sample C ____________

   proportion: ____________

6. All 3 samples combined ____________

   proportion: ____________

Name ______________________ Class ______________ Date ______________

Review 23

Simulate a Problem

OBJECTIVE: Solving problems using simulations **MATERIALS:** None

Example

Each carton of monster yogurt contains a card with a monster cartoon character on it. Each of the 6 characters is equally likely. You purchase 8 cartons of yogurt. Find the probability that you get at least 5 different cards. Simulate the problem.

Since there are 6 characters, you can use a number cube to simulate the problem. A trial consists of rolling the cube 8 times. The results of 5 trials are shown in the table.

In trials 1, 4, and 5, four different numbers were rolled, representing 4 different cards. In trials 2 and 3, five different numbers were rolled, representing 5 different cards.

So, at least 5 different cards were found in 2 of the 5 trials and the probability is $\frac{2}{5}$ or 40%. Note that "at least 5" means 5 or 6.

Trial 1	6 6 1 5 1 6 6 4
Trial 2	1 6 2 4 4 2 6 5
Trial 3	5 6 3 1 1 6 2 1
Trial 4	6 2 1 2 3 3 2 6
Trial 5	3 5 4 4 3 4 2 4

Exercises

Use the table above combined with the one on the right to find each probability based on 10 trials. Write each probability as a percent.

Trial 6	5 6 1 1 5 1 1 3
Trial 7	2 4 4 6 5 6 2 6
Trial 8	2 4 4 2 2 6 6 4
Trial 9	1 4 6 4 4 2 3 4
Trial 10	4 4 4 2 4 5 3 6

1. Complete the frequency table for the ten trials.

2. Find the probability that you get exactly 4 different cards.

   ____

3. Find the probability that you get exactly 5 different cards.

   ____

4. Find the probability that you get at least 4 different cards.

   ____

5. Find the probability that you get at least 5 different cards.

   ____

6. Find the probability that you get no more than 4 different cards.

   ____

Number of Different Cards	Tally	Frequency (number of trials)
3		
4	III	
5	II	
6		

Name ______________________ Class ______________ Date ______________

Review 24

Use Multiple Strategies

OBJECTIVE: Solving problems using multiple strategies

MATERIALS: None

Example

A rectangular prism has length 5 cm, width $(x + 1)$ cm, height $(x + 3)$ cm, and volume 120 cm^3. Find the width and the height.

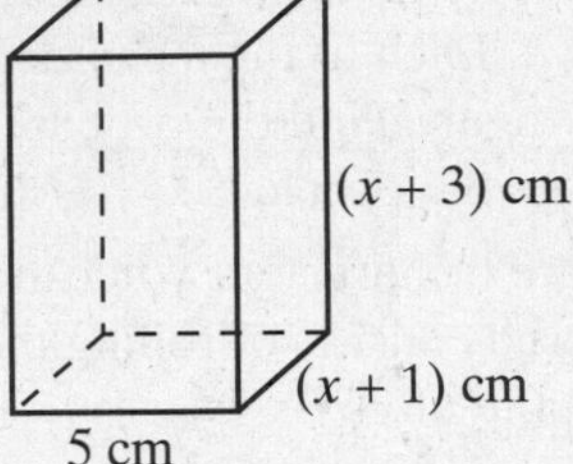

To get a visual picture of the problem, draw a diagram. Label the dimensions. Next, write an equation.

$V = Bh, B = lw$, so $V = lwh$ — Use the formulas for the volume of a prism and the area of a rectangle.

$V = lwh$

$120 = 5(x + 1)(x + 3)$ — Substitute 120 for V, 5 for l, $x + 1$ for w and $x + 3$ for h.

$\frac{120}{5} = \frac{5(x + 1)(x + 3)}{5}$ — Divide each side by 5.

$24 = (x + 1)(x + 3)$ — Simplify.

Use Try, Test, Revise to find x. Organize tests in a table.

x	$x + 1$	$x + 3$	$(x + 1)(x + 3)$	Comment
2	3	5	15	Too low
4	5	7	35	Too high
3	4	6	24	$x = 3$

If $x = 3, x + 1 = 3 + 1 = 4$
$x + 3 = 3 + 3 = 6$

The width of the prism is 4 cm and the height is 6 cm.

Check: $V = 5 \cdot 4 \cdot 6 = 120 \text{ cm}^3$ ✓

Exercises

Use multiple strategies to solve each problem.

1. The product of two whole numbers is 36. What is the greatest possible sum that the numbers can have?

____

2. The sum of two numbers is 14. What is the greatest possible product that the numbers can have?

____

3. A rectangle has length $k + 6$ and width $k - 6$. The area of the rectangle is 64. Find the length and the width.

____

Name ______________________ Class ______________ Date ______________

Review 25

Using Variables

OBJECTIVE: Using variables as a shorthand way of expressing relationships

MATERIALS: None

You often hear word phrases such as *half as much* or *three times as deep*. These phrases describe mathematical relationships. You can translate word phrases like these into mathematical relationships called *expressions*.

ALGEBRA 1 TOPICS

Example

Translate the following word expressions into algebraic expressions.

the sum of x and 15	seven times x
$x + 15$	$7x$
Remember that "sum" means to add.	Remember that "times" mean to multiply.

Example

Translate the following word sentence into an algebraic equation.

The weight of the truck is two times the weight of the car.

$=$ ← **Write an equal sign under the word *is*.**

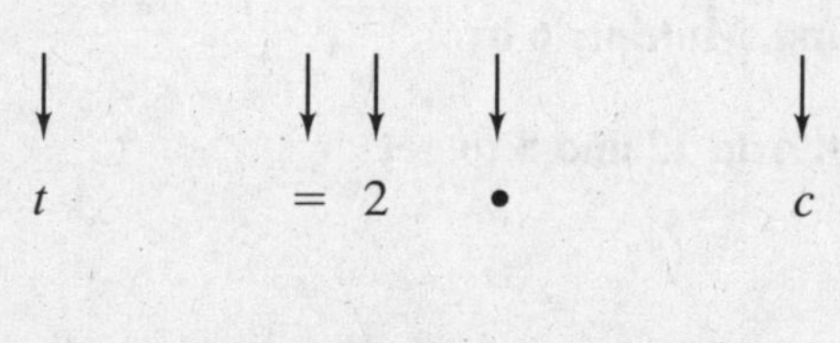

The weight of the truck is two times the weight of the car. **Whatever is written to the left of *is* belongs on the left side of the =. Whatever is written to the right of *is* belongs on the right side of the =.**

$t \quad = 2 \quad \bullet \quad c$ ← **Represent the unknown amounts with variables.**

$t = 2c$ ← **The translation is complete. Check to make sure you have translated all parts of the equation.**

Exercises

Translate the following word expressions and sentences into algebraic expressions or equations.

1. a number increased by 5
2. 8 subtracted from a number
3. a number divided by 9
4. 3 less than five times a number
5. A number multiplied by 12 is 84.
6. 7 less than n is 22.
7. 8 times a number x is 72.
8. A number divided by 3 is 18.

Name ______________________ Class ______________ Date ______________

Review 26

OBJECTIVE: Using the order of operations

MATERIALS: Three index cards or small pieces of paper

Review the order of operations to help you with this activity.

Order of Operations

1. Perform any operations inside grouping symbols.
2. Simplify any term with exponents.
3. Multiply and divide in order from left to right.
4. Add and subtract in order from left to right.

Example

Write + on the first index card, − on the second card, and × on the third card. Shuffle the cards and place them face down on your desk. Randomly pick cards to fill in the blanks with operation signs. Once you have filled in the operation signs, simplify the expression.

6___(9___7)___8	⟵	**Pick cards to fill in the blanks with operation signs.**
$6 \times (9 - 7) + 8$	⟵	**Subtract 7 from 9 inside the grouping symbols.**
$6 \times 2 + 8$	⟵	**Do multiplication and division first. Multiply 6 by 2.**
$12 + 8$	⟵	**Do addition and subtraction last. Add 12 and 8 to get the answer.**
20	⟵	**The answer is 20.**

Exercises

Randomly pick cards to fill in the operation symbols of the following expressions. Simplify the expressions.

1. 7____5____1

2. (3____9)____4

3. 8____2____(5____10)

4. (3____7____6)____1

Simplify each expression by following the order of operations.

5. $(5 \cdot 3) - 18$

6. $5 \cdot (3 - 18)$

7. $2 \cdot (27 - 13 \cdot 2)$

8. $2 \cdot 27 - 13 \cdot 2$

9. $18 \div (9 - 15 \div 5)$

10. $18 \div 9 - 15 \div 5$

11. $2 \cdot 8 - 6^2$

12. $2 \cdot (8 - 6^2)$

Name ____________________ Class ____________ Date ____________

Review 27

Exploring Real Numbers

OBJECTIVE: Classifying numbers **MATERIALS:** None

Review the following chart which shows the different classifications of real numbers.

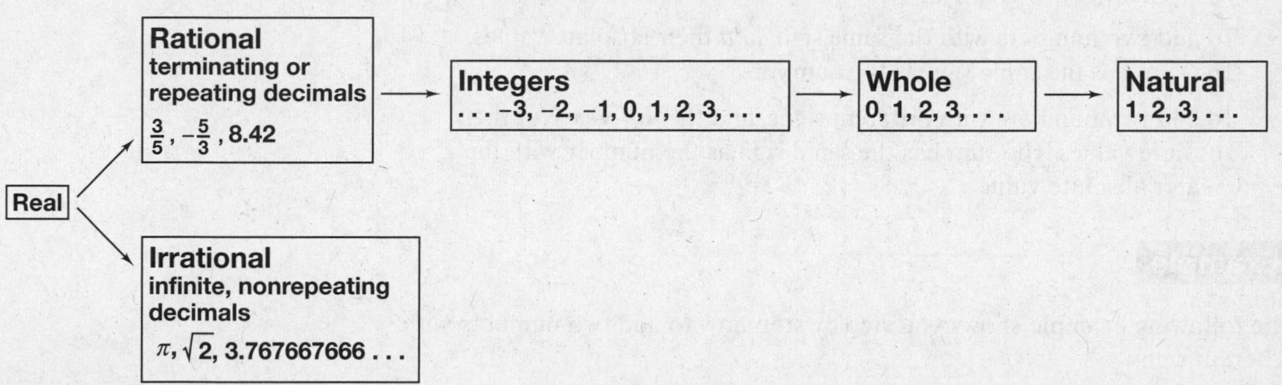

Example

Given the numbers $-4.4, \frac{14}{5}, 0, -9, 1\frac{1}{4}, -\pi$ and 32, tell which numbers belong to each set.

Natural:	32	numbers used to count
Whole:	0, 32	natural numbers and zero
Integers:	0, −9, 32	whole numbers and their opposites
Rational:	$-4.4, \frac{14}{5}, 0, -9, 1\frac{1}{4}, 32$	integers and terminating and nonrepeating decimals
Irrational:	$-\pi$	infinite, nonrepeating decimals
Real:	$-4.4, \frac{14}{5}, 0, -9, 1\frac{1}{4}, -\pi, 32$	rational and irrational numbers

Exercises

Name the set(s) of numbers to which each number belongs.

1. $\frac{-5}{6}$ **2.** 35.99 **3.** 0 **4.** $4\frac{1}{8}$

5. $\sqrt{5}$ **6.** −80 **7.** $\frac{17}{5}$ **8.** $\frac{12}{3}$

9. $\sqrt{100}$ **10.** $-\sqrt{4}$ **11.** 3.24 **12.** 3π

Give an example of each kind of number.

13. irrational number **14.** whole number

15. negative integer **16.** fractional rational number

17. rational decimal **18.** natural number

ALGEBRA 1 TOPICS

Name ______________________ Class ______________ Date ______________

Review 28

OBJECTIVE: Adding integers and decimals **MATERIALS:** None

Review the following addition rules.

- To add two numbers with the same sign, *add* their absolute values. The sum has the same sign as the numbers.
- To add two numbers with different signs, find the *difference* of their absolute values. The sum has the same sign as the number with the greater absolute value.

Example

The following example shows you step by step how to add two numbers with different signs.

$-6 + 2$

$6 - 2$ ⟵ **Find the difference of their absolute values.**

4 ⟵ **Subtract.**

-4 ⟵ **Since -6 has the greater absolute value, the answer takes the negative sign.**

Exercises

Simplify. Be sure to check the sign of your answer.

1. $-3 + (-4)$ **2.** $12 + 5$ **3.** $-5 + 8$ **4.** $-8 + (-2)$

5. $-2 + (-3)$ **6.** $9 + (-12)$ **7.** $-3 + 5$ **8.** $-4 + 3$

9. $-2.3 + (-1.5)$ **10.** $4.5 + 3.1$ **11.** $-5.1 + 2.8$ **12.** $13.9 + 7.3$

13. $1.3 + (-1.1)$ **14.** $-3.6 + (-6.7)$ **15.** $1.4 + (-21.4)$ **16.** $-9.8 + 3.5$

Evaluate each expression for $a = 5$ and $b = -4$.

17. $-a + (-b)$ **18.** $-a + b$ **19.** $a + b$ **20.** $a + (-b)$

Evaluate each expression for $h = 3.4$.

21. $2.5 + h$ **22.** $-2.5 + h$ **23.** $2.5 + (-h)$ **24.** $-2.5 + (-h)$

25. $h + 7.1$ **26.** $-h + 7.1$ **27.** $h + (-7.1)$ **28.** $-h + (-7.1)$

Name ______________________ Class ______________ Date ______________

Review 29

Subtracting Real Numbers

OBJECTIVE: Subtracting integers and decimals **MATERIALS:** None

Review the following subtraction rules.

- To subtract a number, rewrite the problem to add the opposite of the number.
- Follow the rules for addition of numbers.

Example

The following example shows you step by step how to subtract two numbers.

$5 - 11$

$5 + (-11)$ ⟵ **Rewrite the problem to add the opposite of the number.**

$11 - 5$ ⟵ **Find the difference of their absolute values.**

6 ⟵ **Subtract.**

-6 ⟵ **Since −11 has the greater absolute value, the answer takes the negative sign.**

Exercises

Simplify. Be sure to check the sign of your answer.

1. $7 - 12$	**2.** $6 - 9$	**3.** $4 - (-5)$	**4.** $7 - (-3)$
5. $-6 - 4$	**6.** $-7 - 2$	**7.** $-5 - (-4)$	**8.** $-3 - (-10)$
9. $-3.1 - (-5.4)$	**10.** $8.3 - 5.1$	**11.** $-7.8 - 6.6$	**12.** $-4.8 - 2.5$
13. $8.7 - 2.5$	**14.** $-4.6 - (-3)$	**15.** $-9.3 - (-8.1)$	**16.** $-9.9 - 3.8$

Evaluate each expression for $a = -4$ and $b = 3$.

17. $a - b$	**18.** $-a - b$	**19.** $a - (-b)$	**20.** $-a - (-b)$
21. $3b - a$	**22.** $-\lvert b \rvert$	**23.** $\lvert a - b \rvert$	**24.** $\lvert a \rvert - 3\lvert b \rvert$

Subtract. (Hint: Subtract corresponding elements.)

25. $\begin{bmatrix} -3 & -2 \\ 0 & 1 \end{bmatrix} - \begin{bmatrix} 3 & 1 \\ 2 & 4 \end{bmatrix}$

26. $\begin{bmatrix} \frac{1}{2} \\ -1 \end{bmatrix} - \begin{bmatrix} \frac{2}{3} \\ -3 \end{bmatrix}$

ALGEBRA 1 TOPICS

Name ______________________ Class ______________ Date ______________

Review 30

Multiplying and Dividing Real Numbers

OBJECTIVE: Multiplying and dividing integers and decimals

MATERIALS: A number cube

Review the following multiplication and division rules.

- The product or quotient of two positive numbers is always positive.
- The product or quotient of two negative numbers is always positive.
- The product or quotient of a positive and a negative number is always negative.

ALGEBRA 1 TOPICS

Example

Roll the number cube to determine the signs of the numbers in the following example. If you roll an even number (2, 4, or 6), write + in the blank to make the number positive. If you roll an odd number (1, 3, or 5), write a − in the blank to make the number negative. Decide what sign the answer will have before you calculate the answer.

____ 56 ÷ ____ 7 ⟵ **Roll the number cube to fill in the blanks.**

$-56 \div (+7)$ ⟵ **Suppose your first roll was a 3, so 56 is negative. Suppose your second roll was 6, so 7 is positive. Now that you have the signs of the numbers, decide what the sign of the answer will be. Dividing a negative number by a positive number results in a negative number.**

-8 ⟵ **The answer is −8.**

Exercises

Roll the number cube to determine the signs of the numbers in the following exercises. Remember to decide what sign the answer will have before you calculate the answer.

1. ____ 20 · ____ 8

2. ____ 3.2 · ____ 10

3. ____ 27 ÷ ____ 3

4. ____ 14 · ____ 4

5. ____ 120 ÷ ____ 12

6. ____ 45 ÷ ____ 9

7. ____ 1.4 · ____ 3

8. ____ 96 ÷ ____ 8

Simplify each expression.

9. $4(-2)$

10. $-6(12)$

11. $-2(-5)$

12. $-8(11)$

13. $(-7)^2$

14. $-10(-5)$

Name ______________________ Class ______________ Date ______________

Review 31

The Distributive Property

OBJECTIVE: Using the Distributive Property **MATERIALS:** None

You can compare the Distributive Property to distributing paper to the class. Just as you distribute a piece of paper to each person in the class, you distribute the number immediately outside the parentheses to each term inside the parentheses by multiplying.

Example

Simplify $3(2x + 3)$ by using the Distributive Property.

$3(2x + 3)$	⟵	**Draw arrows to show that 3 is distributed to the 2x and to the 3.**
$3(2x) + 3(3)$	⟵	**Use the Distributive Property.**
$6x + 9$	⟵	**Simplify.**

Example

Simplify $-(4x + 7)$ by using the Distributive Property.

$-1(4x + 7)$	⟵	**Rewrite using the Multiplication Property of −1.**
$-1(4x + 7)$	⟵	**Draw arrows to show that −1 is distributed to the 4x and to the 7.**
$-1(4x) + (-1)(7)$	⟵	**Use the Distributive Property.**
$-4x - 7$	⟵	**Simplify.**

Exercises

Draw arrows to show the Distributive Property. Then simplify each expression.

1. $2(5x + 4)$ **2.** $\frac{1}{4}(12x - 8)$ **3.** $4(7x - 3)$

4. $5(4 + 2x)$ **5.** $6(5 - 3x)$ **6.** $0.1(30x - 50)$

7. $(2x - 4)3$ **8.** $(3x + 4)7$ **9.** $8(x + y)$

10. $-(4x + 3)$ **11.** $-(-2x + 1)$ **12.** $-(-6x - 3)$

13. $-(14x - 3)$ **14.** $-(-7x - 1)$ **15.** $-(3x + 4)$

Name ______________________ Class ______________ Date ______________

Review 32

OBJECTIVE: Recognizing properties **MATERIALS:** None

The properties of real numbers allow you to write equivalent expressions.

The Commutative Properties of Addition and Multiplication allow you to add or to multiply two numbers in any order.

$a + b = b + a$ $\quad$ $a \cdot b = b \cdot a$

$3 + 6 = 6 + 3$ $\quad$ $12 \cdot 4 = 4 \cdot 12$

The Associative Properties of Addition and Multiplication allow you to regroup numbers.

$(a + b) + c = a + (b + c)$ $\quad$ $(a \cdot b) \cdot c = a \cdot (b \cdot c)$

$(1 + 3) + 6 = 1 + (3 + 6)$ $\quad$ $(1 \cdot 3) \cdot 6 = 1 \cdot (3 \cdot 6)$

The Distributive Property distributes multiplication over addition and subtraction.

$a(b + c) = ab + ac$ $\quad$ $a(b - c) = ab - ac$

$3(4 + 6) = (3 \cdot 4) + (3 \cdot 6)$ $\quad$ $5(9 - 3) = (5 \cdot 9) - (5 \cdot 3)$

Example

Name the property that each equation illustrates.

$72 + 56 = 56 + 72$ ⟵ **Commutative Property of Addition: The order of the addends is changed.**

$4(5 - 9) = (4 \cdot 5) - (4 \cdot 9)$ ⟵ **Distributive Property: The 4 is distributed.**

$30 \cdot (14 \cdot 5) = (30 \cdot 14) \cdot 5$ ⟵ **Associative Property of Multiplication: The numbers are regrouped.**

Exercises

Name the property that each equation illustrates.

1. $(17 + 4) + 9 = 17 + (4 + 9)$

2. $7(3 + 4) = (7 \cdot 3) + (7 \cdot 4)$

3. $84 \cdot 26 = 26 \cdot 84$

4. $(3 \cdot 6) \cdot 7 = 3 \cdot (6 \cdot 7)$

5. $8(6 - 3) = (8 \cdot 6) - (8 \cdot 3)$

6. $4.2 + 3.4 = 3.4 + 4.2$

Write the number that makes each statement true.

7. 27 + ____ = 12 + 27

8. (8 + 20) + 9 = ____ + (20 + 9)

9. 9(8 − 5) = (____ · 8) − (____ · 5)

10. 8 · 10 = 10 · ____

11. 3 · (9 · 6) = (3 · 9) · ____

12. 7(6 + 4) = (____ · 6) + (____ · 4)

Name ______________________ Class ______________ Date ______________

Review 33

Graphing Data on the Coordinate Plane

OBJECTIVE: Identifying coordinates on the coordinate plane

MATERIALS: Graph paper

Coordinates give the location of a point. To locate a point (x, y) on a graph, start at the origin, $(0, 0)$. Move x units to the right or to the left along the x-axis and y units up or down along the y-axis.

Example

Give the coordinates of points A, B, C, and D.

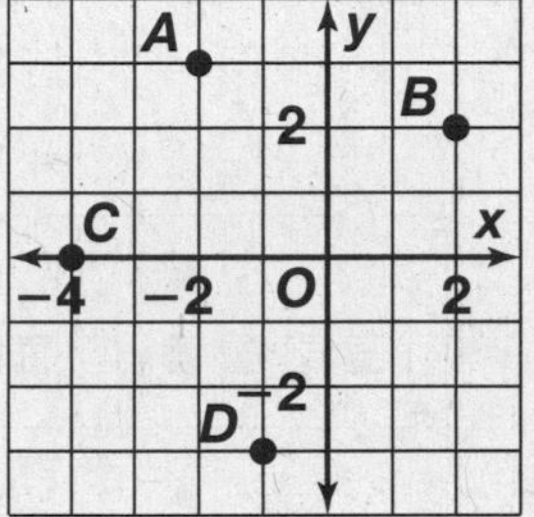

Point A is 2 units to the left of the origin and 3 units up. The coordinates of A are $(-2, 3)$.

Point B is 2 units to the right of the origin and 2 units up. The coordinates of B are $(2, 2)$.

Point C is 4 units to the left of the origin and 0 units up. The coordinates of C are $(-4, 0)$.

Point D is 1 unit to the left of the origin and 3 units down. The coordinates of D are $(-1, -3)$.

Exercises

Name the coordinates of each point.

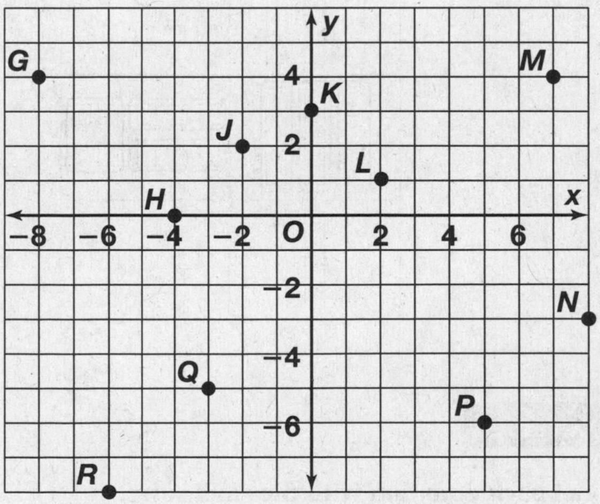

1. G

2. H

3. J

4. K

5. L

6. M

7. N

8. P

9. Q

10. R

Graph the points on the same coordinate plane.

11. $S\ (3, -5)$

12. $T\ (0, 0)$

13. $U\ (-1, -2)$

14. $V\ (4, 5)$

15. $W\ (0, 3)$

16. $Z\ (-5, 0)$

Name ______________________ Class ______________ Date ______________

Review 34

OBJECTIVE: Solving one-step equations **MATERIALS:** Tiles

As you model an equation with tiles, ask yourself what operation has been performed on the variable. With the tiles, perform the inverse operation on each side of the equation. Simplify by removing zero pairs.

Examples

Model each equation with tiles and solve.

1. $x + 4 = 6$

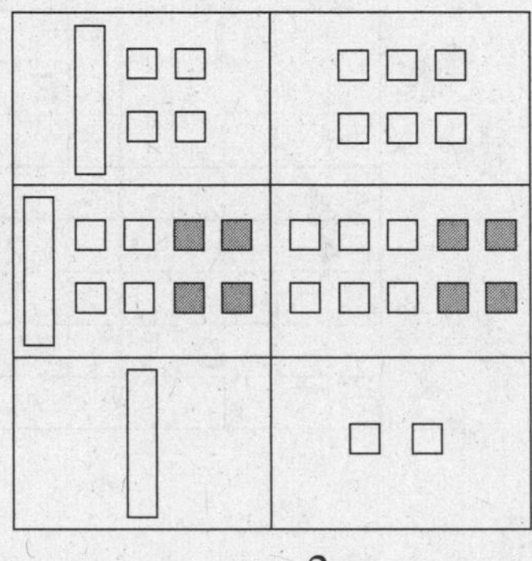

← **Model the equation with tiles.**

← **Subtract 4 from each side of the equation.**

← **Simplify by removing zero pairs.**

$x = 2$

2. $3x = 9$

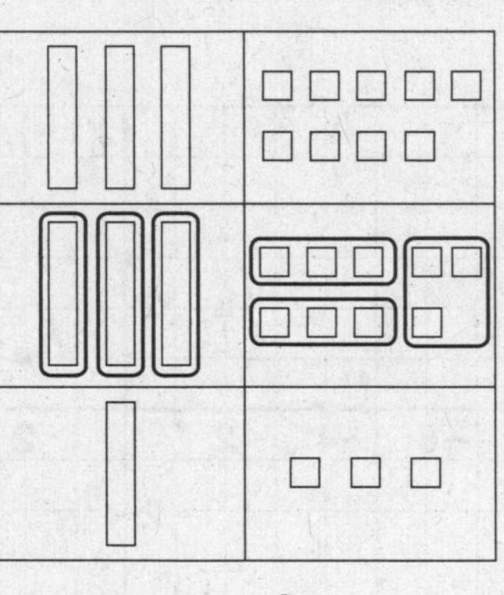

← **Model the equation with tiles.**

← **Divide each side into three identical groups.**

← **Solve for *x*.**

$x = 3$

Exercises

Model each equation with tiles and solve.

1. $x + 3 = 10$ **2.** $y - 4 = 2$ **3.** $-6 = 3y$

4. $2x = 6$ **5.** $y + 1 = 4$ **6.** $5y = 10$

7. $x - 5 = 4$ **8.** $12 = 4x$ **9.** $x + 4 = 2$

Solve.

10. $17 = -8 + x$ **11.** $-0.5 = \frac{d}{4}$ **12.** $0.8 = \frac{a}{5}$

13. $5.2 + h = 0.3$ **14.** $14 = x + 7$ **15.** $6x = 15$

Name ______________________ Class ______________ Date ______________

Review 35

Solving Two-Step Equations

OBJECTIVE: Solving two-step equations **MATERIALS:** None

The order of operations tells you to do multiplication and division before you do addition and subtraction. However, when solving two-step equations, you must first do any addition or subtraction necessary to isolate the variable on one side of the equation. Start by asking yourself, "Has any adding or subtracting been done to the variable?" If the answer is yes, perform the inverse operation. Then repeat this step for multiplication and division.

Example

Write the steps and solve the equation.

$3x + 4 = 10$	⟵	**Think: Is any adding or subtracting being done to the variable? 4 is being added. What is the inverse of adding 4?**
$3x + 4 - 4 = 10 - 4$	⟵	**Subtract 4 from each side.**
$3x = 6$	⟵	**Simplify.**
$3x = 6$	⟵	**Think: Is any multiplying or dividing being done to the variable? It is being multiplied by 3. What is the inverse of multiplying by 3?**
$\frac{3x}{3} = \frac{6}{3}$	⟵	**Divide each side by 3.**
$x = 2$	⟵	**Simplify.**

Exercises

Fill in the blanks to complete the steps and solve the equation.

1.

$\frac{s}{6} - 5 = -8$	⟵	**Think: Is any adding or subtracting being done to the variable? __________ is being __________. What is the __________ of subtracting 5?**
$\frac{s}{6} - 5 + 5 = -8 + 5$	⟵	**__________ 5 to __________ side.**
$\frac{s}{6} = -3$	⟵	**Simplify.**
$\frac{s}{6} = -3$	⟵	**Think: Is any multiplying or dividing being done to the variable? It is being ________ by 6. What is the inverse of ________ by 6?**
$6\left(\frac{s}{6}\right) = 6(-3)$	⟵	**Multiply each __________ by __________.**
$s =$ __________	⟵	**Simplify.**

Solve each equation.

2. $3x - 4 = 8$

3. $\frac{x}{4} + 3 = 10$

4. $4y + 5 = -7$

Name ______________________ Class ______________ Date ______________

Review 36

OBJECTIVE: Combining like terms **MATERIALS:** None

Example

Simplify $3a - 6x + 4 - 2a + 5x$ by combining like terms.

Ring each term that has the variable a. Draw a rectangle around each term that has the variable x, and a triangle around each constant term.

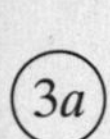

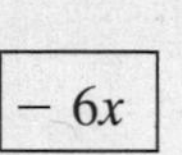

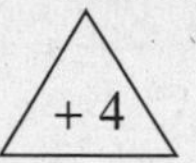

$+ 5x$

Group the like terms by reordering the terms so that all matching shapes are together.

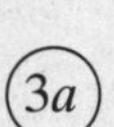

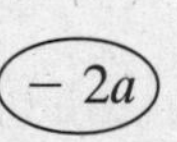

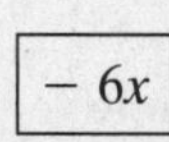

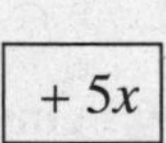

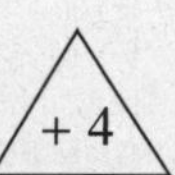

Combine like terms by adding coefficients.

$a - x + 4$

Exercises

Draw circles, rectangles, and triangles to help you combine like terms and simplify each expression.

1. $3a + 5 - x + 7x - 2a$

2. $2x - 5 + 3a - 5x + 10a$

3. $7b - b - x + 5 - 2x - 7b$

4. $-6m + 3t + 4 - 4m - 2t$

5. $2r + 3s - 5r$

6. $4 - p - 2x + 3p - 7x$

7. $3k - 2x + 6k + 5$

8. $3 + 2a - 7x + 2.5 + 5x$

9. $4a + 3 - 2y - 5a - 7 + 4y$

10. $c - 3 + 2x - 6c + 4x$

Simplify each expression.

11. $2b + 2 - x + 4$

12. $-5 - c - 4 + 3c$

13. $\frac{1}{2}a - 5 - \frac{1}{2}a$

14. $1.5y - 1.5 + 0.5y + 0.5z + 1$

15. $6a + 3b - 2a + 4$

16. $\frac{2}{3}a + 5 - \frac{1}{3}a - 7$

17. $-8 + x - 2 + 3x$

18. $x + y - z + 4x - 5y + 2z$

19. $\frac{7}{8}x + 5 - \frac{3}{8}x - 4$

20. $10y - 3x + 5 - 8 - 2y$

Name ______________________ Class ______________ Date ______________

Review 37

Equations with Variables on Both Sides

OBJECTIVE: Solving equations with variables on both sides	**MATERIALS:** None

To solve equations with variables on both sides, use these strategies:

- Rewrite the equation until all terms with variables are combined on one side and all constant terms are combined on the other side. As you rewrite the equation, use inverse operations and the equality properties.
- When you perform an operation on one side, you must do the same on the other.

Example

Solve $5a - 12 = 3a + 7$.

$\boxed{\text{○}}$ $(5a) - 12 = (3a) + 7$ ← **Circle all the terms with variables.**

$5a \boxed{-12} = 3a \boxed{+7}$ ← **Put rectangles around all constant terms. Plan steps to collect variable terms on one side and constant terms on the other.**

$5a - 12 - 3a = 3a + 7 - 3a$ ← **To get variables on the same side, subtract 3*a* from each side.**

$2a - 12 = 7$ ← **Combine like terms.**

$2a - 12 + 12 = 7 + 12$ ← **To get constants on the other side, add 12 to each side.**

$2a = 19$ ← **Combine like terms.**

$a = 9.5$ ← **To undo multiplication by 2, divide each side by 2.**

Check $5(9.5) - 12 \stackrel{?}{=} 3(9.5) + 7$

$47.5 - 12 \stackrel{?}{=} 28.5 + 7$

$35.5 = 35.5$ ✓

In what other ways could you solve for *a*? You could add 12 to each side, then subtract 3*a* from each side. Or, you could subtract 5*a* from each side, then subtract 7 from each side.

Exercises

Fill in the blanks to show a plan to solve each equation.

1. $9x + 4 = 6x - 11$ ________ $6x$ ________ each side; subtract ________ from each side.
2. $4b - 13 = 7b - 28$ Subtract ________ from each side; ________ 28 ________ each side.

Use circles and rectangles to mark the variables and constant terms. Write a plan that tells the steps you would use and then solve each equation.

3. $7c - 4 = 9c - 11$
4. $3 - 4d = 6d - 17$
5. $5e + 13 = 7e - 21$

Solve and check each equation.

6. $8f - 12 = 5f + 12$
7. $3k + 5 = 2(k + 1)$
8. $9 - x = 3x + 1$

Name ____________________ Class ____________ Date ____________

Review 38

Equations and Problem Solving

OBJECTIVE: Solving real-world problems involving equations with variables on both sides

MATERIALS: None

A table is useful in organizing information from a real-world problem. Below are examples of tables for several types of application problems.

	Rate × Time = Distance
Object 1	
Object 2	

	Length × Width = Area
Rectangle 1	
Rectangle 2	

Example

An airplane takes off from an airport at 7:00 A.M. traveling at a rate of 350 mi/h. Two hours later, a jet takes off from the same airport following the same flight path at 490 mi/h. In how many hours will the jet catch up with the airplane?

Define: Let t = the time the airplane travels.
Let $t - 2$ = the time the jet travels.

Set up table:

	Rate	× Time	= Distance
Airplane	350	t	$350t$
Jet	490	$t - 2$	$490(t - 2)$

Relate: distance traveled by airplane = distance traveled by jet

Write:

$$350t = 490(t - 2)$$

$$350t = 490t - 980 \quad \longleftarrow \text{ Use the distributive property.}$$

$$350t - 490t = 490t - 980 - 490t \quad \longleftarrow \text{ Subtract } 490t \text{ from each side.}$$

$$-140t = -980 \quad \longleftarrow \text{ Combine like terms.}$$

$$\frac{-140t}{-140} = \frac{-980}{-140} \quad \longleftarrow \text{ Divide each side by } -140.$$

$$t = 7 \quad \longleftarrow \text{ Simplify.}$$

Final answer: The jet will catch up with the airplane in 5 hours.

Exercises

Solve each problem.

1. Mary leaves her house at noon, traveling in her car at 45 mi/h. Later, Mary's brother Joe leaves their house and travels in the same direction at 60 mi/h. If Joe leaves at 2:00 P.M., at what time will he catch up with Mary?

2. Mike leaves school on his bike at 1:00 P.M., traveling at 12 mi/h. Janis leaves the same school one quarter of an hour later, traveling at 16 mi/h in the same direction. At what time will Janis catch up with Mike?

Name ________________ Class ________________ Date ________________

Review 39

OBJECTIVE: Solving a literal equation for one of its variables	**MATERIALS:** None

Variables are symbols used to represent numbers. Any symbol can be used. Notice how these literal equations have been rewritten using geometric symbols.

$a = b + c$	$\bigcirc = \blacktriangle + \square$
$xy = pq$	$\bigcirc \cdot \bullet = \blacktriangle \cdot \square$
$\frac{s}{t} = \frac{r}{q}$	$\frac{\bigcirc}{\bullet} = \frac{\square}{\blacktriangle}$

Example

Solve $\bigcirc \cdot \bullet = \blacktriangle \cdot \square$ for $\blacktriangle$ and then for $\square$.

Solving for $\blacktriangle$: $\bigcirc \cdot \bullet = \blacktriangle \cdot \square$

$\frac{\bigcirc\bullet}{\square} = \frac{\blacktriangle\square}{\square}$ ⟵ **Divide each side by $\square$, $\square \neq 0$.**

$\frac{\bigcirc\bullet}{\square} = \blacktriangle$ ⟵ **Simplify.**

Solving for $\square$: $\bigcirc \cdot \bullet = \blacktriangle \cdot \square$

$\frac{\bigcirc\bullet}{\blacktriangle} = \frac{\blacktriangle\square}{\blacktriangle}$ ⟵ **Divide each side by $\blacktriangle$, $\blacktriangle \neq 0$.**

$\frac{\bigcirc\bullet}{\blacktriangle} = \square$ ⟵ **Simplify.**

Exercises

Solve each literal equation for $\bigcirc$. Show your steps.

1. $\bigcirc + \square = \blacktriangle$
2. $\frac{\bigcirc}{\bullet} = \frac{\square}{\blacktriangle}$
3. Choose your own symbols (such as ❀, ✈, ★, ❤) and use them to write a literal equation. Solve for one of the symbols. Show each step.

Solve each equation for the given variable.

4. $5x + a = y; a$
5. $m = 6(p + q); q$
6. $2x + 3y = 8; x$
7. $xy = 3z; z$
8. $w = 3(x + y + z); y$
9. $2w - 8y = z; y$

Name ______________________ Class ______________ Date ______________

Review 40

Using Measures of Central Tendency

OBJECTIVE: Finding measures of central tendency **MATERIALS:** None

In working with statistical data, it is often useful to determine a single quantity that best describes the set of data. The best quantity to choose is usually one of the most popular measures of central tendency: the mean, the median, or the mode.

	Definitions
Mean	The **mean** is the sum of the data items in a set divided by the number of data items in the set.
Median	The **median** is the middle value in a set of data when the numbers are arranged in numerical order. If the set has an even number of data items, the median is the mean of the two middle data values.
Mode	The **mode** is the data item that occurs most often in a data set.

Example

Find the mean, median, and mode of the set of data: 34 46 31 40 33 40.

Mean: $\frac{34 + 46 + 31 + 40 + 33 + 40}{6} = \frac{224}{6} = 37.\overline{3}$ ← **Add the data items and divide by the number of data items in the set.**

Median: 31 33 34 40 40 46 ← **Arrange the data items in increasing order.**

$\frac{34 + 40}{2} = 37$ ← **Since there is an even number of data values, find the mean of the two middle data values.**

Mode: The mode is 40 since it occurs most often.

Exercises

Find the mean, median, and mode of each set of data.

1. daily sales of a store: \$834 \$1099 \$775 \$900 \$970
2. number of points scored in 8 soccer games: 0 10 4 11 7 6 3 2
3. number of days above 50°F in the last five months: 6 8 15 22 9
4. heights of players on a basketball team in inches: 72 74 70 77 76 72
5. resting heart rates in beats per minute: 76 70 64 70 72 68

Name ________________ Class ________________ Date ________________

Review 41

OBJECTIVE: Identifying solutions of inequalities **MATERIALS:** None

A sentence that contains the symbol >, <, ≥, or ≤ is called an **inequality.** An inequality expresses the relative order of two mathematical expressions. The sentence can be either numerical or variable.

Symbol	Description
>	is greater than
<	is less than
≤	is less than or equal to
≥	is greater than or equal to

Example

One way to determine whether a number is a solution of an inequality is to plot the number on a number line.

Is each number a solution of $x > -2.5$?

a. 3

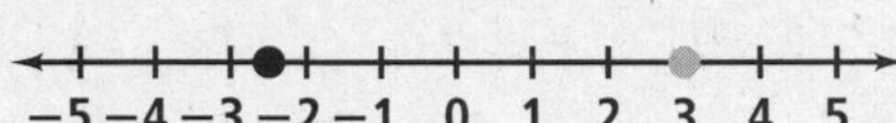

Since 3 is to the right of −2.5, it is greater than –2.5, so it is a solution. $3 > -2.5$

b. −5

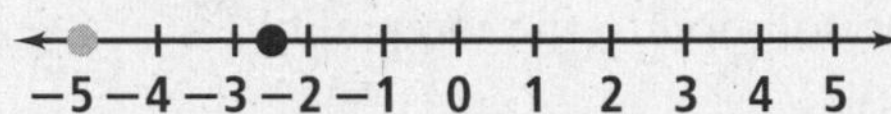

Since −5 is to the left of −2.5, it is less than −2.5, so it is not a solution. $-5 \ngtr -2.5$

c. −2

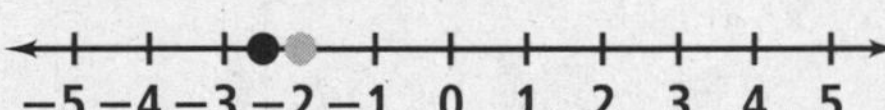

Since −2 is to the right of −2.5, it is greater than –2.5, so it is a solution. $-2 > -2.5$

d. −2.5

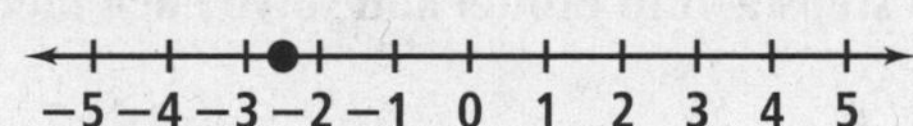

This is a special case: −2.5 is not greater than itself. Therefore, it is not a solution. $-2.5 \ngtr -2.5$

Exercises

Is each number a solution of $x \leq 8$?

1. −2 **2.** 7 **3.** −7 **4.** 8

Is each number a solution of $x \leq -9$?

5. 9 **6.** −14 **7.** −8.5 **8.** −6

Name ______________________ Class ______________ Date ______________

Review 42

Solving Inequalities Using Addition and Subtraction

OBJECTIVE: Using addition and subtraction to solve one-step inequalities

MATERIALS: Tiles

- To solve one-step inequalities, use the same strategies you use to solve equations. Apply the Addition and Subtraction Properties of Inequality.
- When you add or subtract the same quantity from each side of an inequality, the direction of the inequality symbol stays the same.

Example

Using tiles, solve the inequality $x - 3 < 4$.

a. Model the inequality with tiles. 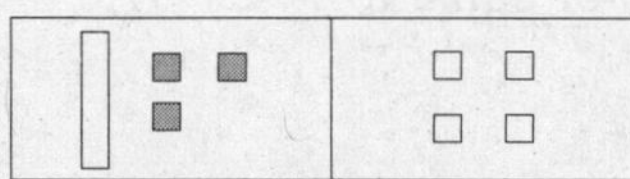 $x - 3 < 4$

b. Add or subtract the same quantity on each side to get the variable alone on one side of the inequality symbol.

For this example, add 3 to each side. $x - 3 + 3 < 4 + 3$

c. Simplify by removing zero pairs.

d. Write the solution to the inequality. $x < 7$

Note that even though you are adding the same quantity to each side of the inequality, the direction of the inequality symbol stays the same.

Exercises

Use tiles and steps a–d to model and solve each inequality.

1. $y - 2 < 4$ **2.** $x - 4 < 1$ **3.** $7 < w + 2$

4. $x - 6 > 10$ **5.** $10 \leq y + 8$ **6.** $a - 1 > 3$

7. $4 + h \leq 7$ **8.** $s - 3 > 2$ **9.** $b + 3 < 8$

Solve.

10. $x - 9 < 6$ **11.** $a - 7 > 5$ **12.** $b - 4 < 10$

13. $c + 5 > 7$ **14.** $6 + d < 11$ **15.** $f - 4 > 15$

16. The band must earn at least $75 for a trip. Band members already earned $35. Write and solve an inequality to find how much money they still need to earn.

Name ______________________ Class ______________ Date ______________

Review 43

Solving Inequalities Using Multiplication and Division

OBJECTIVE: Using multiplication and division to solve one-step inequalities	**MATERIALS:** Tiles, an index card or piece of paper with $<$ written on it

Example

Use tiles and the card to compare quantities as shown in these steps.

2 ______ 3

□□ $\boxed{<}$ □□□ ⟵ **Model the quantities with tiles and place your card to show how the quantities compare.**

$-2(2) \quad -2(3)$ ⟵ **Multiply each quantity by -2.**

$-4 \quad -6$ ⟵ **Write the results.**

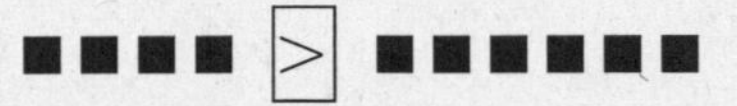

⟵ **Model the new quantities with tiles and place your card to show how the new quantities compare. Notice that you must rotate the card to make the new statement true.**

What happens to the direction of the inequality symbol when you multiply or divide an inequality by a negative number? The direction of the inequality symbol reverses.

Exercises

Model both lines of each exercise with tiles. Use your card to compare the quantities. Then fill in the blanks by writing $<$ or $>$.

1. 2 ______ 4

$-2(2)$ ______ $-2(4)$

2. -3 ______ -2

$-3(-3)$ ______ $-3(-2)$

3. 4 ______ -3

$\frac{4}{-2}$ ______ $\frac{-3}{-2}$

4. 3 ______ -1

$-1(3)$ ______ $-1(-1)$

5. -2 ______ 2

$\frac{-2}{-4}$ ______ $\frac{2}{-4}$

6. -1 ______ -3

$-3(-1)$ ______ $-3(-3)$

Solve and check.

7. $2.5a < 15$

8. $-3b > 21$

9. $6c < 24$

10. $\frac{x}{7} < -2$

11. $-\frac{y}{6} < \frac{2}{3}$

12. $8f > 56$

13. $-4.2d \geq 10.5$

14. $-\frac{2}{3}m \leq 10$

15. $-1.7x > -34$

16. $\frac{n}{8} \leq -2.5$

17. $-1.5k < 2.4$

18. $\frac{3}{5}p \geq -9$

19. $4t > -14$

20. $\frac{z}{15} > -\frac{2}{3}$

21. $-\frac{1}{2}w \leq -3.6$

Name ______________________ Class ______________ Date ______________

Review 44

Solving Multi-Step Inequalities

OBJECTIVE: Solving multi-step inequalities and graphing the solutions on a number line

MATERIALS: None

As you solve multi-step inequalities, keep these strategies in mind.

- Circle all the terms with variables. Then decide on which side of the inequality you are going to collect the variable terms. You may want to select the side that has the variable term with the greatest coefficient.
- Rewrite the inequality by using inverse operations in the same way you solve equations. If you multiply or divide both sides by a negative number, reverse the direction of the inequality symbol.
- Check three values on your graph: the number where the arrow starts, a number to the right of the starting value, and another to the left.

Example

Solve $3x + 2 < 5 + 2x$. Graph and check the solution.

$\textcircled{3x} + 2 < 5 \textcircled{+ 2x}$ ⟵ **Circle all the terms with variables.**

$3x \boxed{+ 2} < \boxed{5} + 2x$ ⟵ **Box all constant terms. Plan your steps to collect variable terms on one side and constant terms on the other.**

$3x + 2 - 2x < 5 + 2x - 2x$ ⟵ **To get variables on the left side, subtract 2*x* from each side.**

$x + 2 < 5$ ⟵ **Simplify.**

$x + 2 - 2 < 5 - 2$ ⟵ **To get constants on the right side, subtract 2 from each side.**

$x < 3$ ⟵ **Simplify.**

−2 −1 0 1 2 3 4 ⟵ **Graph your solution on a number line. Since 3 is not a solution, use an open circle.**

Check three values for the variable: 0, 3 (where the arrow starts), and 4.

$3(0) + 2 \overset{?}{<} 5 + 2(0)$	$3(3) + 2 \overset{?}{<} 5 + 2(3)$	$3(4) + 2 \overset{?}{<} 5 + 2(4)$
$2 < 5$ ✔	$11 \not< 11$ ✔	$14 \not< 13$ ✔

Exercises

Use circles and boxes to identify the variable and constant terms. Then solve, graph, and check your solution for each inequality.

1. $4x + 3 < 11$ **2.** $3x + 2 < 2x + 5$ **3.** $5x + 4 < 14$

4. $4x - 3 < 3x - 1$ **5.** $3x + 4 > 2x + 3$ **6.** $2x + 5 > -1$

Name ______________________ Class ______________ Date ______________

Review 45

Compound Inequalities

OBJECTIVE: Solving compound inequalities and graphing the solutions on a number line

MATERIALS: Two highlighting markers in colors that combine to make a third color, for example, blue and yellow or pink and yellow

Before you graph, practice making overlapping lines with your two markers. Notice, for example, that marks from a yellow marker and a blue one overlap to make a green line. A pink line and a yellow line combine to make an orange line. (If you have trouble seeing some colors, ask a partner to help you.)

Example

Solve and graph $-3 < x + 5 \leq 2$.

$-3 < x + 5$ and $x + 5 \leq 2$ ← **Rewrite the compound inequality as two inequalities joined by *and*.**

$-3 - 5 < x + 5 - 5$ and $x + 5 - 5 \leq 2 - 5$

$-8 < x$ and $x \leq -3$ ← **Solve each inequality.**

← **Graph the solutions separately on the same number line. Use a blue marker for one arrow (▨) and a yellow marker (▨) for the other. Notice that −8 is colored in only one of the graphs.**

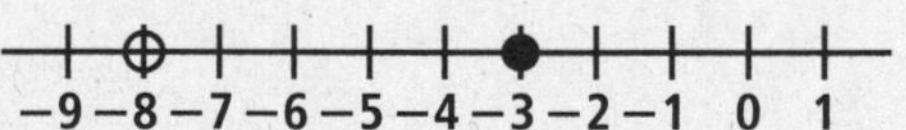

← **Graph the solution set of all the green points (▩). Think: *The green points are blue AND yellow.* This graph shows the solution set for the compound inequality.**

$-8 < x \leq -3$ ← **Write the solution set.**

Exercises

Solve each inequality and graph the solution. Hint: The solution set for *or* statements is all points that are blue or yellow or green.

1. $-3 \leq x - 5$ or $x + 5 \leq 2$

2. $x + 5 \leq 4$ or $-2x < -6$

3. $x - 2 \geq -6$ and $5 + x < 7$

4. $x - 2 \leq -6$ or $5 + x > 7$

5. $-3 \leq x + 1 < 3$

6. $3 \geq \frac{1}{2}x > -2$

7. $-5 \leq 2x - 1 < 7$

8. $3x < -6$ or $4x - 3 \geq 9$

9. $-5x < 15$ or $x \leq -5$

10. $-1 \leq \frac{1}{2}x + 1 < 0$

11. $1 - 2x \leq -5$ or $2x < -10$

12. $-9 < x - 7 \leq 1$

Name ______________________ Class ______________ Date ______________

Review 46

Absolute Value Equations and Inequalities

OBJECTIVE: Solving absolute value inequalities **MATERIALS:** None

The absolute value of a real number x, written $|x|$, is the distance of x from 0 on the real number line.

An inequality such as $|x| < k$, where k is a positive real number, is true for values of x that are less than k units from 0 on the number line. These are the numbers between $-k$ and k on the number line. Thus, x is a solution of $|x| < k$ whenever $-k < x < k$.

An inequality such as $|x| > k$, where k is a positive real number, is true for values of x that are more than k units from 0 on the number line. These are the numbers to the left of $-k$ and to the right of k on the number line. Thus, x is a solution of $|x| > k$ whenever $x < -k$ or $x > k$.

Example

Solve each inequality and graph the solution.

a. $|t + 3| < 4$ ← **The inequality is in the form $|x| < k$.**

$-4 < t + 3 < 4$ ← **Replace the form $|x| < k$ with the form $-k < x < k$. Here the expression $t + 3$ is in the place of x and $k = 4$.**

$-7 < t < 1$ ← **Subtract 3 from each part of the inequality.**

−8 −7 −6 −5 −4 −3 −2 −1 0 1 2

b. $|2y + 1| \geq 3$ ← **The inequality is in the form $|x| \geq k$.**

$2y + 1 \leq -3$ or $2y + 1 \geq 3$ ← **Replace the form $|x| \geq k$ with the form $x \leq -k$ or $x \geq k$. Here the expression $2y + 1$ is in the place of x and $k = 3$.**

$2y \leq -4$ or $2y \geq 2$ ← **Subtract 1 from each side of each inequality.**

$y \leq -2$ or $y \geq 1$ ← **Divide each side of each inequality by 2.**

−5 −4 −3 −2 −1 0 1 2 3 4 5

Exercises

Solve each inequality and graph the solution.

1. $|c| < 5$

2. $|u| \geq 1$

3. $|a + 1| \leq 2$

4. $|3m - 2| > 1$

5. $\left|\frac{1}{2}y - 3\right| \geq \frac{1}{2}$

6. $|2n + 1| < 7$

7. $|4 - 2u| \leq 8$

8. $|2g + 5| > 3$

9. $|1 - 2y| \geq 9$

Name ______________________ Class ______________ Date ______________

Review 47

Ratio and Proportion

OBJECTIVE: Solving proportions **MATERIALS:** None

An equation that states that two ratios are equal is called a proportion. In a proportion, the cross products are equal.

Example

Use cross products to find out if the proportion $\frac{2}{7} = \frac{10}{40}$ is true.

$\frac{2}{7} = \frac{10}{40}$

$2 \cdot 40 = 7 \cdot 10$ ⟵ **Write cross products.**

$80 = 70$ ⟵ **Simplify.**

$80 \neq 70$ ⟵ **Proportion is not true since 80 does not equal 70.**

Use cross products to write and solve equations involving proportions.

Solve: $\frac{5}{6} = \frac{25}{x}$

$\frac{5}{6} = \frac{25}{x}$ ⟵ **The cross products are 5*x* and 6 · 25 or 150.**

$5x = 6 \cdot 25$ ⟵ **Set cross products equal to each other.**

$5x = 150$ ⟵ **Simplify.**

$\frac{5x}{5} = \frac{150}{5}$ ⟵ **Use the Division Property of Equality.**

$x = 30$ ⟵ **Simplify.**

Exercises

Determine if the proportions are true. (Hint: the cross products should be equal.)

1. $\frac{6}{10} = \frac{12}{20}$

2. $\frac{4}{5} = \frac{7}{8}$

3. $\frac{33}{22} = \frac{24}{16}$

Solve each proportion.

4. $\frac{x}{5} = \frac{2}{10}$

5. $\frac{9}{180} = \frac{n}{60}$

6. $\frac{2}{x} = \frac{8}{36}$

7. $\frac{2}{6} = \frac{4}{x}$

8. $\frac{30}{125} = \frac{n}{100}$

9. $\frac{3}{18} = \frac{t}{6}$

10. $\frac{t}{5} = \frac{3}{5}$

11. $\frac{28}{8} = \frac{7}{x}$

12. $\frac{9}{n} = \frac{18}{2}$

Name ______________________ Class ______________ Date ______________

Review 48

Proportions and Similar Figures

OBJECTIVE: Finding missing measures of similar figures

MATERIALS: None

Setting up a proportion can help determine the missing lengths from similar figures. Remember the following:

- Always compare corresponding sides when writing the ratios.
- Be consistent by keeping sides of the same figure either in the denominators or numerators.

Example

$\triangle ABC \sim \triangle DEF$
Find the length of x.

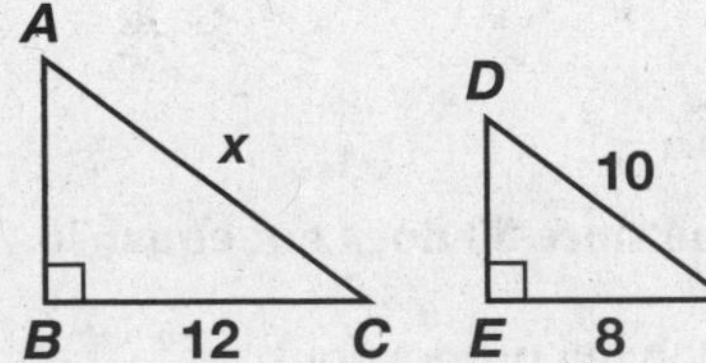

BC corresponds to EF
AC corresponds to DF

$\frac{AC}{DF} = \frac{BC}{EF}$ ⟵ **Notice the numerators, AC and BC, are sides of the same triangle.**

$\frac{x}{10} = \frac{12}{8}$ ⟵ **Substitute appropriate values.**

$8x = 10 \cdot 12$ ⟵ **Write the cross products.**

$\frac{8x}{8} = \frac{120}{8}$ ⟵ **Divide each side by 8.**

$x = 15$ ⟵ **Simplify.**

Exercises

Find the length of *x*.

1. $\triangle TUV \sim \triangle QUP$

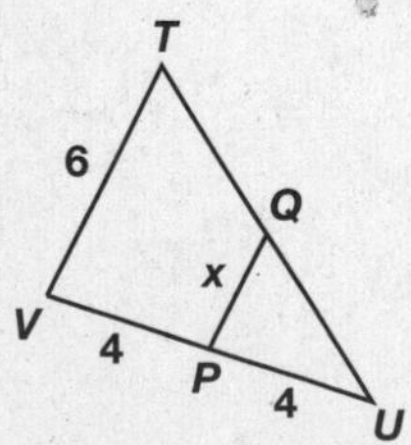

2. $\triangle KLM \sim \triangle KHJ$

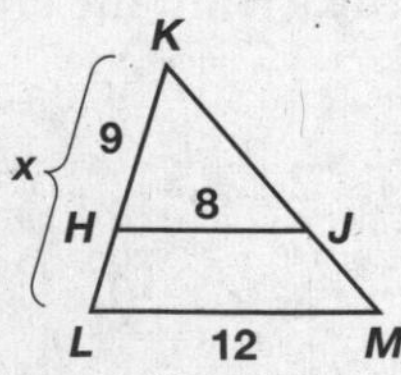

3. $\triangle PQR \sim \triangle MNP$

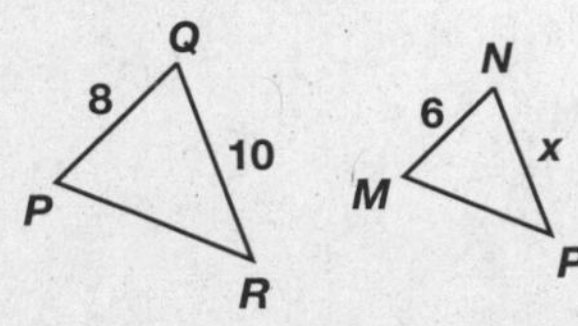

4. $\triangle ABC \sim \triangle DEF$

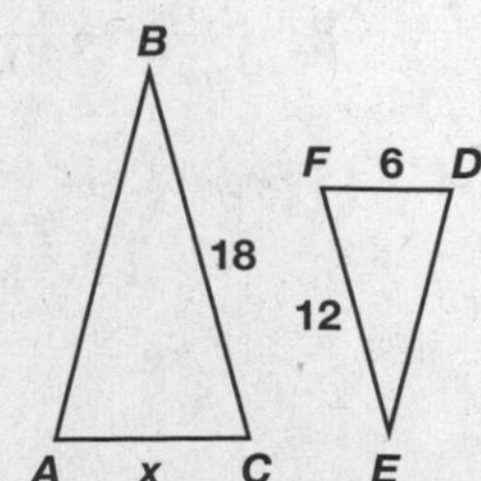

Name ____________ Class ____________ Date ____________

Review 49

Proportions and Percent Equations

OBJECTIVE: Using equations to solve problems involving percents

MATERIALS: None

To solve percent problems, you can often represent words with math symbols. This table shows some words and the symbols you can use to represent them.

word	what	is	of
symbol	*n* (or another variable)	=	×

ALGEBRA 1 TOPICS

Example

What is 30% of 20?

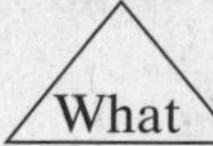

What is 30% of 20? ⟵ **Draw a triangle around the word that represents the variable. Draw a rectangle around the word that represents =. Circle the word that represents ×.**

30% 20? ⟵ **Copy just the shapes and numbers, including percent.**

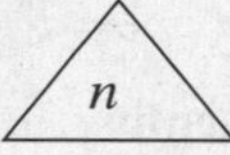

n = 0.30 × 20 ⟵ **Inside each shape, represent the word with the correct symbol. Rewrite percents as decimals.**

$n = 0.30 \times 20$ ⟵ **Write the equation.**

$n = 6$ ⟵ **Solve the equation.**

30% of 20 is 6. ⟵ **Answer the question.**

Exercises

Use rectangles, circles, and triangles to rewrite and answer each question.

1. What is 10% of 50?

2. 8 is 40% of what?

3. 25 is what percent of 100?

4. 7 is what percent of 35?

5. What is 30% of 50?

6. 3 is 25% of what?

7. 0.4 is what percent of 0.8?

8. What is 25% of 25?

9. What is 25% of $\frac{4}{7}$?

10. Kamala is 15 years old and her brother is 20. Kamala's age is what percent of her brother's?

11. Luis worked 12 h at the school library. That represents 25% of the total hours he has voluteered to work. How many hours has he volunteered to work?

12. The sales tax rate is 6%. What is the sales tax on $55?

Name ______________________ Class ______________ Date ______________

Review 50

OBJECTIVE: Finding percent of change

MATERIALS: About 35 counters such as beans or paper clips

Use this ratio to find the percent of change from an original amount to a new amount:

$$\text{percent of change} = \frac{\text{amount of change}}{\text{original amount}}$$

Example

Jana's pay changed from \$6/h to \$7/h. Find the percent of change in her pay and whether it is a percent of increase or of decrease.

original amount **new amount** ← **Divide your paper into two areas, labeled "original amount" on the left and "new amount" on the right.**

← **Place 6 counters to represent \$6 under the original amount and 7 counters under the new amount.**

← **Find the difference between the amount of counters on the left and on the right.**

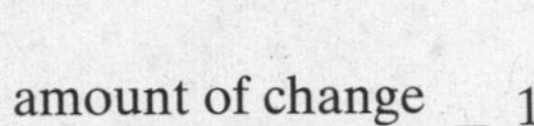

← **Put the counters representing the difference (amount of change) over the counters representing the original amount.**

$\frac{\text{amount of change}}{\text{original amount}} = \frac{1}{6}$ ← **Write the ratio represented by the counters.**

The percent of increase is 16.67%. ← **Write the ratio as a percent.**

More counters under the original amount represents a percent of decrease.
More counters under the new amount represents a percent of increase.

Exercises

Use counters to find each percent of change. Describe the percent as an increase or decrease. Round percents to the nearest integer.

1. 8 in. to 12 in.
2. 7 min to 5 min
3. \$3 to \$4
4. 2 lb to 4 lb

Find each percent of change. Describe the percent as an increase or decrease. Round percents to the nearest integer.

5. Today eight students leave your classroom.
6. You put 5 pencils in a box that already has 12 pencils.
7. The length of a shadow changes from 75 feet to 65 feet.

Name ______________________________ Class ____________________ Date ________________

Review 51

Applying Ratios to Probability

OBJECTIVE: Finding probability	**MATERIALS:** None

The possible results of an experiment are **outcomes**. If you want to find the theoretical probability of a particular event, or a **favorable outcome**, you use this formula.

$$P(\text{event}) = \frac{\text{number of favorable outcomes}}{\text{number of possible outcomes}}$$

Example

Twenty-four students in your homeroom placed lunch orders today. The list sent to the cafeteria is shown at the right. If a student is randomly selected from your class, what is the probability that the student ordered pizza or a hamburger?

Pizza	9
Taco	3
Hot dog	4
Hamburger	6
Tuna sandwich	2

$$P(\text{pizza or hambuger}) = \frac{\text{number of favorable outcomes}}{\text{number of possible outcomes}}$$

$$= \frac{9\text{ (number of pizza orders)} + 6\text{ (number of hamburger orders)}}{24\text{ (total number of orders)}}$$

$$= \frac{15}{24}$$

$$= \frac{5}{8}$$

Exercises

You are fishing in a pond stocked with fish. The table at the right shows a recent fish count. Find each probability.

Sunfish	90
Crappie	33
Smallmouth bass	15
Largemouth bass	12
Total	150

1. *P*(sunfish)
2. *P*(smallmouth bass)
3. *P*(largemouth bass)
4. *P*(sunfish or crappie)
5. *P*(catfish)
6. *P*(not a sunfish)
7. *P*(not a crappie or not a sunfish)
8. *P*(sunfish or smallmouth bass)
9. *P*(catfish or largemouth bass)
10. *P*(smallmouth or largemouth bass)

Name ______________________ Class ______________ Date ______________

Review 52

Probability of Compound Events

OBJECTIVE: Finding the probability of independent and dependent events

MATERIALS: Colored counters and a small bag

To find the probability of two events that are **independent** (the probability of the first **does not** affect the second), multiply the probabilities of the events.

$$P(A \text{ and } B) = P(A) \cdot P(B)$$

To find the probability of two events that are **dependent** (the probability of the first **does** affect the second), multiply the probability of the first by the probability of the second happening after the first.

$$P(A \text{ then } B) = P(A) \cdot P(B \text{ after } A)$$

Examples

A bag contains 6 white counters, 5 red counters, and 19 counters of other colors.

A. Find the probability of choosing a white and then a red counter if you **replace** the first counter before choosing the second counter.

$P(A) = P(\text{white}) = \text{total number} \ldots\ldots = \frac{6}{30}$ or $\frac{1}{5}$

$P(B) = P(\text{red}) = \text{total number} \ldots\ldots = \frac{5}{30}$ or $\frac{1}{6}$

$P(A \text{ and } B) = \frac{1}{5} \cdot \frac{1}{6} = \frac{1}{30}$

The probability of choosing a white and then a red counter (with replacing the first counter) is $\frac{1}{30}$.

B. Find the probability of choosing a white and then a red counter if you **do not replace** the first counter before choosing the second counter.

$P(A) = P(\text{white}) = \text{total number} \ldots\ldots = \frac{6}{30}$ or $\frac{1}{5}$

$P(B) = P(\text{red}) = \text{total number} \ldots\ldots = \frac{5}{29}$

$P(A \text{ and } B) = \frac{1}{5} \cdot \frac{5}{29} = \frac{1}{29}$

The probability of choosing a white and then a red counter (without replacing the first counter) is $\frac{1}{29}$.

Exercises

Choose counters of two colors, *A* and *B*. Write down the number of each, and put them in a bag.

1. Find the probability of choosing a counter of color *A* and then a counter of color *B* if you replace the first before you pick the second.

2. Find the probability of choosing a counter of color *A* and then a counter of color *B* if you do not replace the first pick.

Name ______________________ Class ______________ Date ______________

Review 53

OBJECTIVE: Interpreting and sketching graphs from stories

MATERIALS: None

When you draw a graph without actual data, the graph is called a sketch. A sketch gives you an idea of what the graph will look like. Use the description and the sketch to answer the questions.

Example

Kira rides her bike to the park to meet a friend. When she arrives at the park, Kira and her friend sit on the bench and talk for a while. Kira then rides her bike home at a slower pace.

Kira's Ride

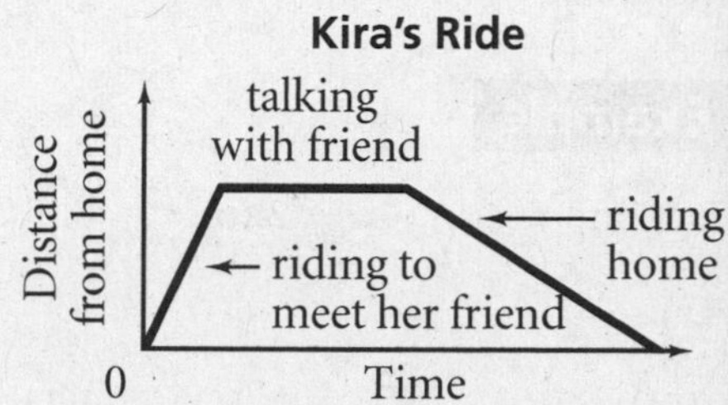

1. What does the vertical scale show?
   It shows distance from home.
2. What does the horizontal scale show?
   It shows time.
3. Why is the section of the graph showing Kira riding to meet her friend steeper than the section of the graph showing her ride home?
   Kira was riding faster on her way to meet her friend.
4. Why is the section of the graph flat when Kira is talking to her friend?
   Kira's distance from home is not changing, but time is still passing.

Exercises

To take photographs of the area where you live for a school project, you ride your bike to the top of Lookout Knoll. The road leading to the top is steep. When you arrive at the top, you rest and take some photographs. On the way back down the same road, you stop to take photographs from another location.

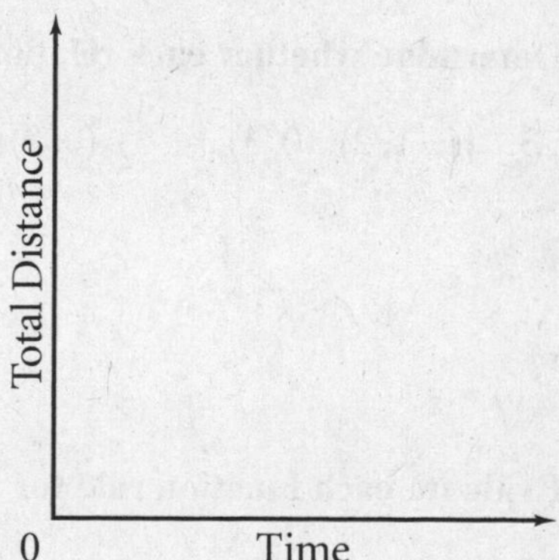

1. What does the vertical scale show?
2. What does the horizontal scale show?
3. Draw a sketch of the trip comparing the distance you traveled to time. Label the sections.
4. Which parts of the graph represent your taking photographs? Explain.
5. Which part of the graph is steeper, your ride to the top of Lookout Knoll or your ride down? Explain.
6. Suppose the vertical axis represents distance from the base of Lookout Knoll. With all other information remaining the same, draw a sketch of the trip comparing distance from the base of Lookout Knoll to time. Label the sections.

Name ______________________ Class ______________ Date ______________

Review 54

OBJECTIVE: Evaluating functions **MATERIALS:** None

A function is a relation that assigns exactly one value in the range to each value in the domain. A function rule may be given as an equation. The function $f(x) = 3x + 5$ will take a value x and change it into $3x + 5$. The function is read "f of x equals three x plus five," not "f times x." Evaluating a function means finding a value in the range for a given value from the domain.

Example

Evaluate $f(x) = 4x - 2$ for $x = 0, 1,$ and 2.

$f(x) = 4x - 2$

$f(0) = 4(0) - 2$ $\quad f(1) = 4(1) - 2$ $\quad f(2) = 4(2) - 2$ ← **Substitue each value for *x*.**

$f(0) = 0 - 2$ $\quad f(1) = 4 - 2$ $\quad f(2) = 8 - 2$ ← **Simplify.**

$f(0) = -2$ $\quad f(1) = 2$ $\quad f(2) = 6$

Exercises

Find the domain and range of each relation.

1. $\{(-4, 3), (-2, -1), (0, 0), (1, 4), (2, 6)\}$

2. $\{(-6, -4), (-3, -1), (1, 2), (2, 4), (3, 7)\}$

Determine whether each relation is a function.

3. $\{(-1, 2), (0, 3), (4, 3), (0, 5)\}$

4.

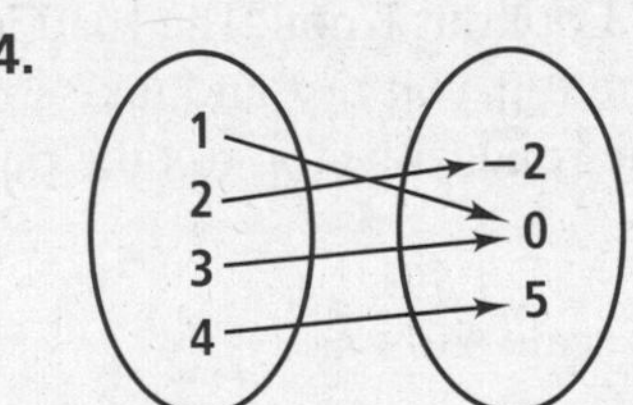

Evaluate each function rule for $x = -2$.

5. $f(x) = 4x$

6. $f(x) = -3x$

7. $f(x) = x - 2$

8. $f(x) = -2x + 1$

9. $f(x) = \frac{1}{2}x + 2$

10. $f(x) = -\frac{3}{2}x + 2$

Find the range of each function, given the domain.

11. $g(m) = m^2; \{-2, 0, 2\}$

12. $h(x) = -\frac{1}{3}x - 1; \{-3, 0, 6\}$

13. $h(n) = 3n^2 - 2n + 2; \{-1, 0, 1\}$

14. $g(n) = n^2 + n - 2; \{-2, 0, 2\}$

15. $g(x) = |x| + 2; \{-4, -2, 4\}$

16. $f(x) = -2|x| - 1; \{-3, -2, 3\}$

Name ______________________ Class ______________ Date ______________

Review 55

Function Rules, Tables, and Graphs

OBJECTIVE: Graphing a function **MATERIALS:** Graph paper

You can use a rule to model a function with a table and a graph.

Example

Graph the function $y = 2x + 3$.

Step 1: Choose four different values for x. Write these values in the first column of the table. Choose some negative values for x.

Step 2: Evaluate the function to find y for each value of x.

x	$y = 2x + 3$	(x, y)
-2	$y = 2(-2) + 3 = -1$	$(-2, -1)$
-1	$y = 2(-1) + 3 = 1$	$(-1, 1)$
3	$y = 2(3) + 3 = 9$	$(3, 9)$
5	$y = 2(5) + 3 = 13$	$(5, 13)$

Step 3: Plot the ordered pairs to graph the data.

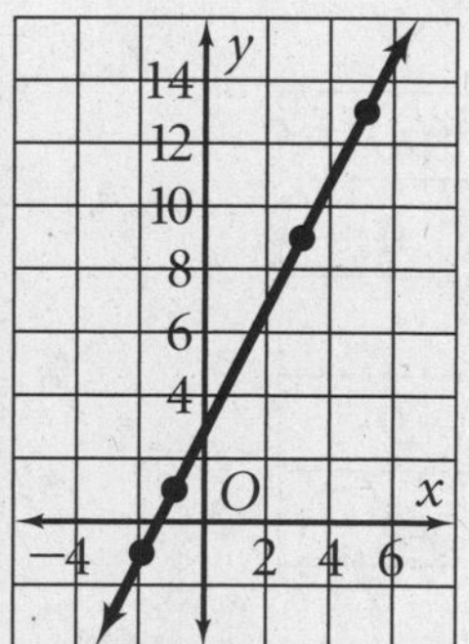

Exercises

Use a table to graph each function. Choose an appropriate number of values for x. Choose some negative values for x.

1. $y = 4x + 1$

2. $y = x - 2$

3. $y = x + 5$

4. $y = |x| - 3$

5. $y = x^2 - 4$

6. $y = 3x + 3$

7. $y = -|x| + 3$

8. $y = -x^2 + 4$

Review 56

OBJECTIVE: Writing rules for functions from tables and words

MATERIALS: None

You can write a rule for a function by analyzing a table of values. Look for a pattern in the data table. For each row, ask yourself, "What can I do to the first number to get the second number?" Write the patterns. Circle the pattern that works for all of the data in the table. This is the rule for the function.

Example

x	f(x)	
1	3	← **Add 2 or multiply by 3.**
2	4	← **Add 2 or multiply by 2.**
3	5	← **Add 2.**

The function rule must be $f(x)$ equals x plus 2. The statement can be written as $f(x) = x + 2$.

Exercises

Analyze each table and then write the function rule.

1.

x	f(x)
0	0
1	3
2	6
3	9

2.

x	f(x)
0	−1
1	0
2	1
3	2

3.

x	f(x)
0	0
−1	1
3	9
5	25

Write a function rule for each situation.

4. the length $\ell(w)$ of a box that is two more than four times the width w.

5. the width $w(\ell)$ of a sheet of plywood that is one half the length ℓ.

6. the cost $c(a)$ of a pounds of apples at $.99 per pound

7. the distance $d(t)$ traveled at 65 miles per hour in t hours

8. the value $v(q)$ of a pile of q quarters

9. a worker's earnings $e(n)$ for n hours of work when the worker's hourly wage is $8.25

10. the distance $f(d)$ traveled in feet when you know the distance d in yards

Name ______________________ Class ______________ Date ______________

Review 57

Direct Variation

OBJECTIVE: Using constant of variation to solve problems

MATERIALS: Graph paper and a straight piece of wire or pipe cleaner

Example

Is the equation of the line joining the points (2, 3) and (4, 6) a direct variation? If it is, find the constant of variation.

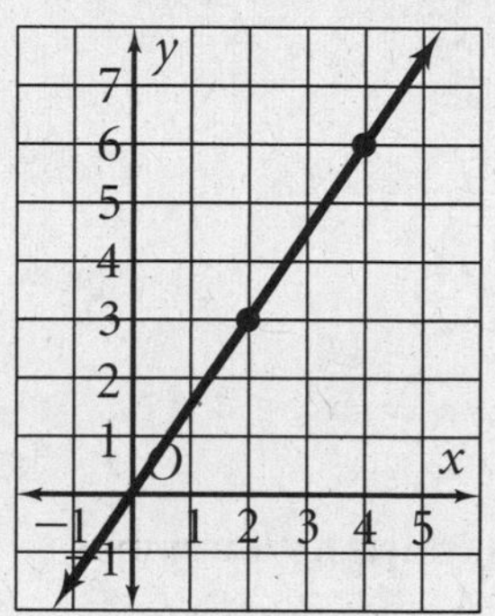

← **Graph the two points. Place the wire on the graph so that it passes through the two points given.**

a. Is the graph a straight line passing through the origin? Yes, it is.

b. Is the equation of this line a direct variation? Yes, since the line passes through the origin.

c. What is the constant of variation?

$y = kx$ ← **Write the general form of a direct variation.**

$3 = k(2)$ ← **Substitute the coordinates of either point.**

$k = \frac{3}{2}$ ← **Solve for *k*.**

The constant of variation is $\frac{3}{2}$.

Exercises

Work with a partner. Draw axes and label them and the origin on your graph paper. One partner places the wire on the graph so that it passes through the two points given. The other partner answers the questions. Exchange roles for each exercise.

Is the equation of the line joining each pair of points a direct variation? If it is a direct variation, what is the constant of variation?

1. $(-1, 3), (1, -3)$

2. $(0, 3), (-1, 1)$

3. $(1, -2), (4, -8)$

4. $(5, 5), (-5, -5)$

5. $(2, 4), (1, 2)$

6. $(2, 3), (3, 5)$

Name ____________________ Class ____________ Date ____________

Review 58

Describing Number Patterns

OBJECTIVE: Finding the common difference and writing the next several terms in a sequence

MATERIALS: None

When trying to determine the common difference of an arithmetic sequence or find the pattern, it is helpful to attempt to express each term in the sequence as an expression involving the same number.

Example

Find the common difference of the sequence: 4, 7, 10, 13, . . .

Let n = the term number in the sequence.
Let $A(n)$ = the value of the nth term of the sequence.

$A(1) = 4$

$A(2) = 7 = 4 + 1(3)$ ← **3 is the common difference.**

$A(3) = 10 = 4 + 6 = 4 + 2(3)$ ← **Notice that the 3 in each expression is multiplied by a number one less than the term number.**

$A(4) = 13 = 4 + 9 = 4 + 3(3)$

$$A(n) = 4 + \underbrace{3 + 3 + \ldots + 3}_{n\ -\ 1\text{ terms}} = 4 + (n - 1)3$$

The formula for the sequence is $A(n) = 4 + (n - 1)3$.

You could use the formula for the sequence to determine the next several terms simply by substituting a specific term in for n. For example:

Term:

5th term $A(5) = 4 + (5 - 1)3$
$A(5) = 16$

100th term $A(100) = 4 + (100 - 1)3$
$A(100) = 301$

Exercises

Find the common difference of each sequence.

1. 2, 9, 16, 23, . . .

2. 5, 1, −3, −7, . . .

3. −52, −41, −30, −19, . . .

Find the next two terms in each sequence.

4. 2, 0, −2, −4, . . .

5. −4, −1, 2, 5, . . .

6. −17, −22, −27, −32, . . .

Find a formula for the sequence in the exercise indicated and use it to determine the fifth and tenth terms of the sequence.

7. Exercise 1

8. Exercise 2

9. Exercise 3

Name ______________________ Class ______________ Date ____________

Review 59

Rate of Change and Slope

OBJECTIVE: Calculating the slope of a line **MATERIALS:** None

Example

Calculate the slope of the line shown in the graph.

a. Pick any two points on the line. Write their coordinates. Underline the x-coordinates and circle the y-coordinates. This example uses (0, 0), (2, 4).

b. The difference of y-coordinates shows the vertical change or *rise*. Find the rise of the line by subtracting the y-coordinates.
vertical change = rise = $4 - 0 = 4$

c. The difference of x-coordinates shows the horizontal change or *run*. Find the run of the line by subtracting the x-coordinates. Be sure to subtract the x-coordinates in the same order as the y-coordinates.
horizontal change = run = $2 - 0 = 2$

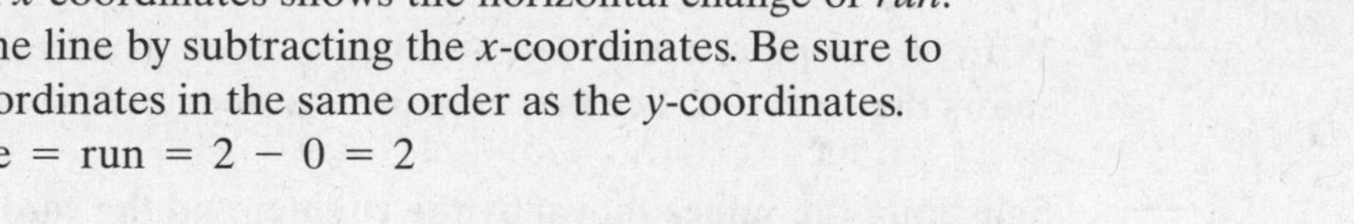

d. Find the slope of the line through the two points by forming the ratio of rise to run.

$$\text{slope} = \frac{\text{rise}}{\text{run}} = \frac{4}{2} \text{ or } 2$$

Exercises

Use steps a–d from the example to find the slope of each line.

1.

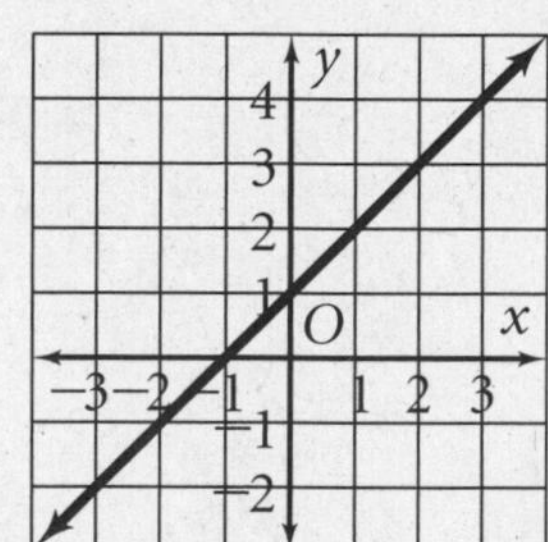

2.

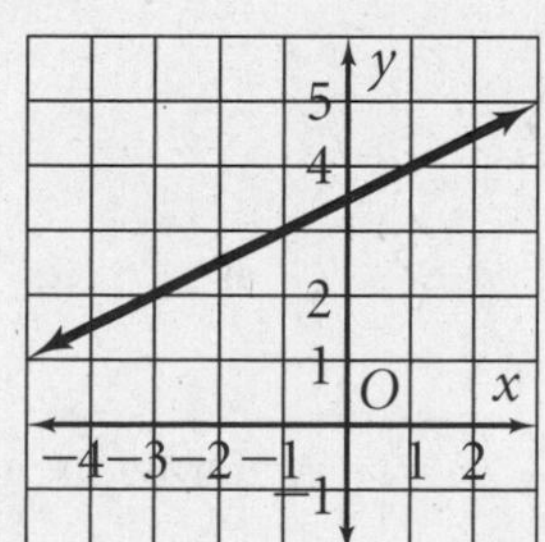

3.

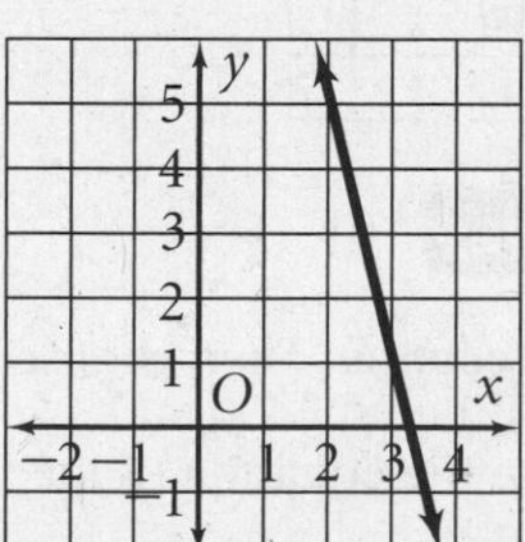

4. Draw a horizontal line. Find the slope of the line.

5. Draw a vertical line. Find the slope of the line.

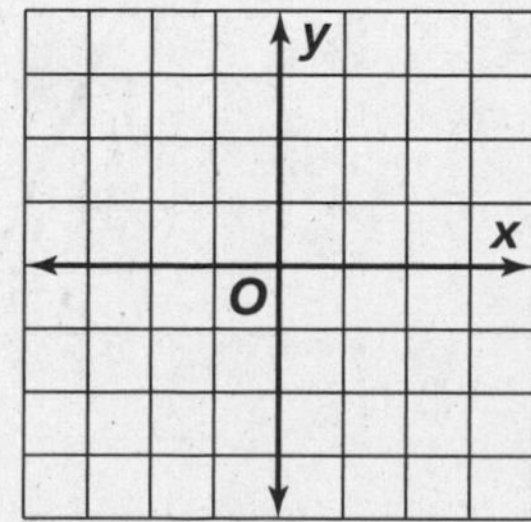

Name ______________________ Class ______________ Date ______________

Review 60

Slope-Intercept Form

OBJECTIVE: Using the slope and y-intercept to draw graphs and write equations	**MATERIALS:** Graph paper, counters, ten index cards

Write these numbers on the index cards, one number to a card: $1, -1, 2, -2, \frac{1}{2}, -\frac{1}{2}, 3, -3, \frac{1}{3}, -\frac{1}{3}$. These numbers represent different slopes.

- Draw a coordinate plane on the graph paper.
- Put a counter at any integer on the y-axis. Choose one of the index cards.
- Use the y-intercept shown by the counter and the slope shown on the card to write the equation of a line.
- Draw the graph of that line.

Example

Place the counter at -4. Choose the index card with the number 2.

$y = mx + b$ ← **Write the slope-intercept form of the equation of a straight line. The counter shows that $b = -4$. The first card gives a slope of 2, so $m = 2$.**

$y = 2x + (-4)$ ← **Substitute the values shown by the counter and the card.**

$y = 2x - 4$ ← **Write the equation of the line in simplified form.**

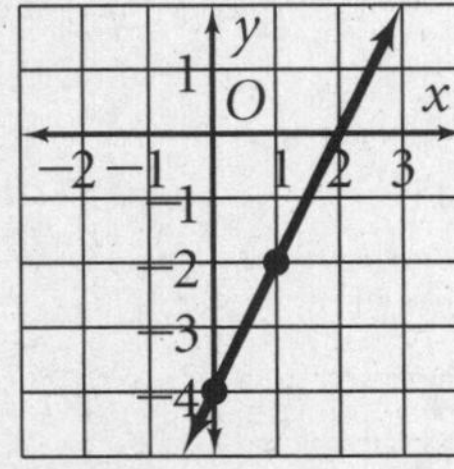

← **Slope $= \frac{\text{vertical change}}{\text{horizontal change}}$, so rewrite 2 as $\frac{2}{1}$. Starting at the counter, move 2 units up and 1 unit to the right and place a second counter. Draw a straight line joining the two points for the graph of $y = 2x - 4$.**

Exercises

Place the counter. Then choose an index card.

1. Write the equation of the line.
2. Draw the graph.

Write an equation for each line.

3. 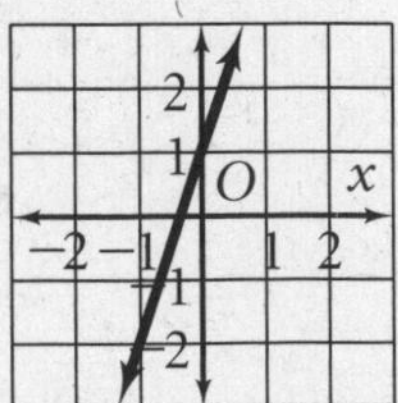

4. 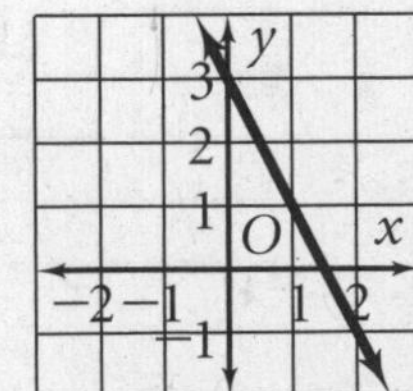

5. 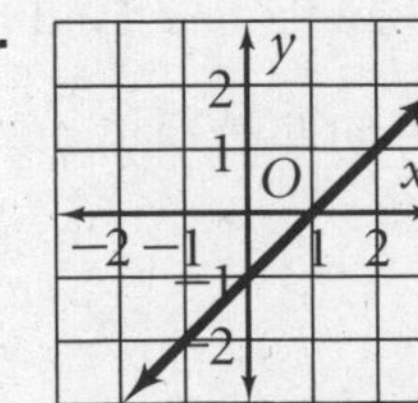

Name ______________________ Class ______________ Date ______________

Review 61

Standard Form

OBJECTIVE: Graphing equations using x- and y-intercepts	**MATERIALS:** Small self-stick removable notes

Example

Graph $4x + 5y = 20$ using x- and y-intercepts.

a. Write the equation in large figures so that each term is slightly smaller than a self-stick note.

b. Write a zero on a self-stick note.

c. Place the note over the $4x$. Solve the remaining equation.

$$0 + 5y = 20$$

$$5y = 20$$

$$y = 4$$

This gives us the point of the y-intercept: (0, 4).

d. Place the note over the $5y$. Solve the remaining equation.

$$4x + 0 = 20$$

$$4x = 20$$

$$x = 5$$

This gives us the point of the x-intercept: (5, 0).

e. Graph the two points. Draw the line between them.

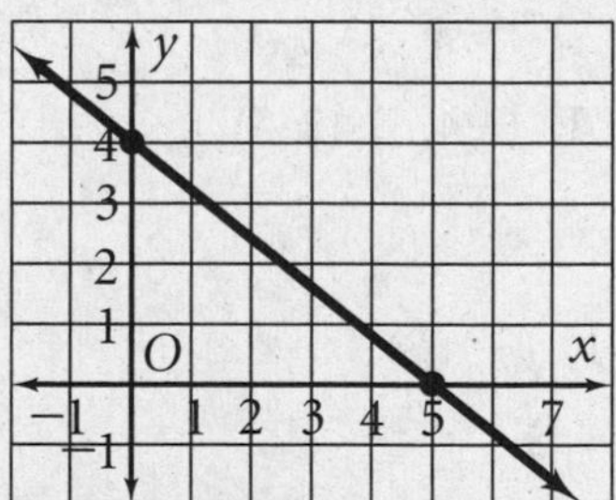

Exercises

Graph each equation using steps a–e.

1. $3x + 4y = 36$

2. $5x + 3y = 15$

3. $7x - 4y = 28$

4. $4x - 3y = 9$

5. $10x + 30y = 90$

6. $6x + 3y = 12$

ALGEBRA 1 TOPICS

Name ________________ Class ________________ Date ________________

Review 62

Point-Slope Form and Writing Linear Equations

OBJECTIVE: Writing an equation given the graph of a line or two points on a line

MATERIALS: Graph paper

Example

Write an equation for the line shown in point-slope form.

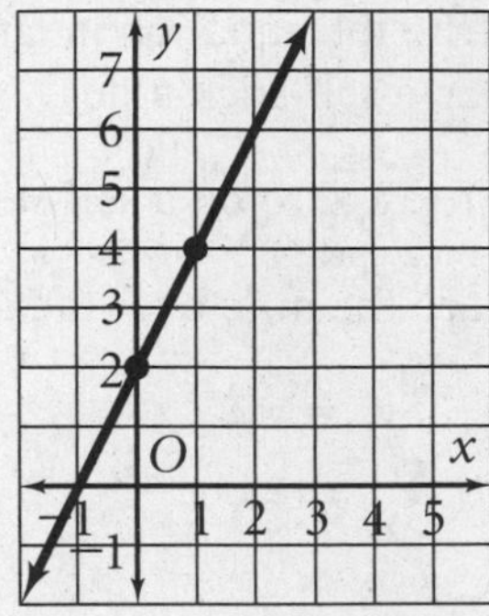

a. Select any two points on the line. It is a good idea to select points whose coordinates are integers.
(0, 2) and (1, 4) lie on the line.

b. Use slope $= \frac{\text{rise}}{\text{run}}$ to find the slope.
From (0, 2), move up 2 units (rise = +2) and right 1 unit (run = +1) to get to (1, 4). So, $\frac{\text{rise}}{\text{run}} = \frac{+2}{+1} = 2$.
or
Use $m = \frac{y_2 - y_1}{x_2 - x_1}$ to find the slope.
If $(x_1, y_1) = (0, 2)$ and $(x_2, y_2) = (1, 4)$, then $m = \frac{4 - 2}{1 - 0} = \frac{2}{1} = 2$.

c. Use the point-slope form to write the equation.
Substitute $m = 2$ and $(x_1, y_1) = (0, 2)$.
$y - y_1 = m(x - x_1)$
$y - 2 = 2(x - 0)$
$y - 2 = 2x$

or

Substitute $m = 2$ and $(x_1, y_1) = (1, 4)$.
$y - y_1 = m(x - x_1)$
$y - 4 = 2(x - 1)$

Note: If you rewrite $y - 2 = 2x$ and $y - 4 = 2(x - 1)$ in slope-intercept form, you get $y = 2x + 2$. Although the two equations look different, they do represent the same line.

Exercises

Graph the line through the given points. Then follow steps a–c from the Example to write the equation of the line passing through the given points in point-slope form.

1. (6, 4), (4, 3) **2.** (0, −18), (5, 2) **3.** (−2, −2), (−4, 2) **4.** (−4, 5), (2, 5)

Write an equation for the line through the given points in point-slope form.

5. (2, −5), (0, −7) **6.** (4, 3), (3, −2) **7.** (2, −1), (−1, 8)

8. (−3, 4), (3, 8) **9.** (4, −1), (−8, 2) **10.** (5, −2), (−4, −2)

11. (−2, −6), (8, 4) **12.** (−4, 1), (−2, 2) **13.** (6, −6), (−3, −12)

14. (0, 0), (8, 7) **15.** (0, −2), (8, −6) **16.** (2, 7), (−6, −5)

17. (−1, −10), (5, 2) **18.** (0, 7), (−5, 12) **19.** (0, 1), (4, −7)

Name ______________________ Class ______________ Date ______________

Review 63

OBJECTIVE: Writing equations for parallel and perpendicular lines

MATERIALS: Graph paper and two items that can be used to represent lines such as pencils, straws, or coffee stirrers

Example

Write an equation for the line that is parallel to $y = 3x$, and contains $(0, -2)$. Then, write an equation for the line that is perpendicular to $y = 3x$ and contains $(0, -2)$.

On a piece of graph paper, draw a grid like the one shown below. Comparing $y = 3x$ to $y = mx + b$, we see that the line has y-intercept 0 and its slope is 3 or $\frac{3}{1}$. This means that the graph contains $(0, 0)$ and a point 3 units up and 1 unit right from there, $(1, 3)$. Place a pencil or other object on the grid that joins the points $(0, 0)$ and $(1, 3)$.

Place a second pencil on the grid so that it is parallel to the first pencil. Notice that you can move your second pencil to many other places on the grid and still have it parallel to your first pencil. Now, place your second pencil so that it contains $(0, -2)$, keeping it parallel to your first pencil. You have only one correct placement. Count units to verify that the slope of the line represented by your second pencil is also $\frac{3}{1}$ or 3. This line has slope $m = 3$ and y-intercept $b = -2$. So, its equation is $y = 3x - 2$.

Leaving your first pencil in place, move the second pencil so that it is perpendicular to the first. Now, place your second pencil so that it contains $(0, -2)$, keeping it perpendicular to the first pencil. You have only one correct placement. Count units to verify that the slope of the line represented by your second pencil is $-\frac{1}{3}$. Recall that the product of the slopes of perpendicular lines is -1, so $3(-\frac{1}{3}) = -1$. This line has slope $m = -\frac{1}{3}$ and y-intercept $b = -2$. So, its equation is $y = -\frac{1}{3}x - 2$.

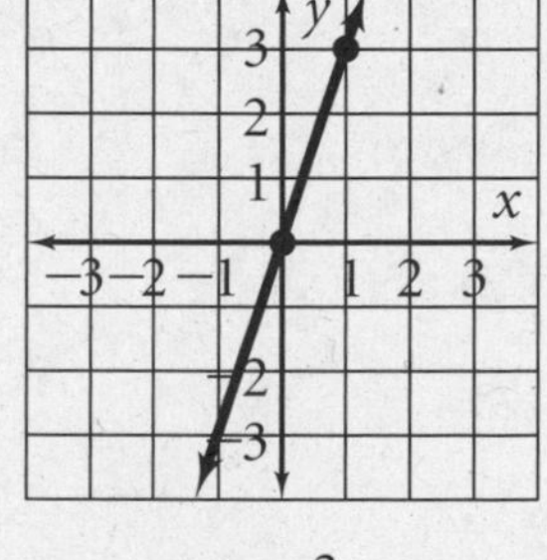

$y = 3x$

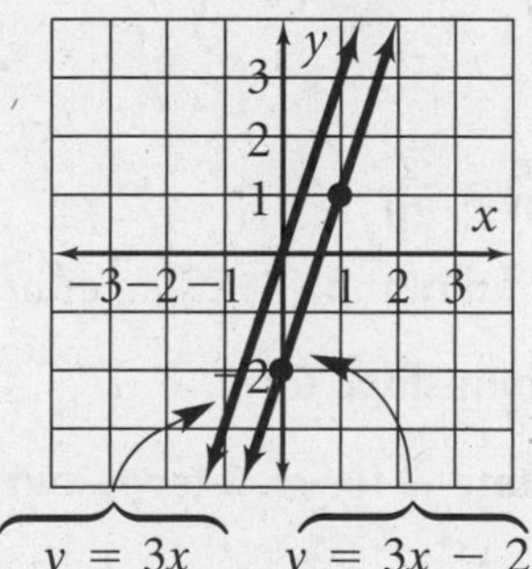

$y = 3x$ $y = 3x - 2$

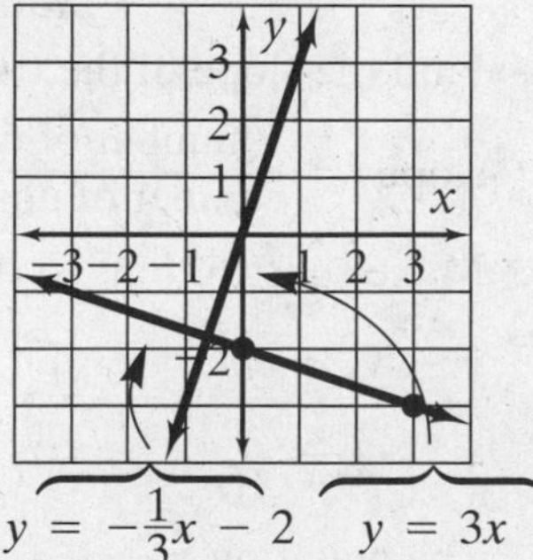

$y = -\frac{1}{3}x - 2$ $y = 3x$

Exercises

Follow the steps above to find an equation of the line parallel to the given line that contains the given *y*-intercept. Then find an equation of the line perpendicular to the given line that contains the given *y*-intercept.

1. $y = 5x; (0, -1)$

2. $y = -3x; (0, 4)$

3. $y = 2x + 1; (0, -3)$

4. $y = -\frac{1}{4}x - 2; (0, 2)$

5. $y = \frac{1}{2}x + 2; (0, -1)$

6. $y = -\frac{1}{2}x; (0, 2)$

7. $y = -3x - 1; (0, 2)$

8. $y = \frac{2}{3}x + 1; (0, -2)$

9. $y = 3x - 4; (0, 6)$

Name ______________________ Class ______________ Date ______________

Review 64

Scatter Plots and Equations of Lines

OBJECTIVE: Finding the equation of a trend line **MATERIALS:** None

Example

Rise in Minimum Wage

Year	Minimum Wage
1950	$.75
1963	$1.25
1975	$2.10
1980	$3.10
1991	$4.25
1996	$4.75
1997	$5.15

Source: *World Almanac 2001,* p. 150.

Find an equation of a reasonable trend line for the data.

a. Graph the points and draw a trend line. Let 0 correspond to 1950.

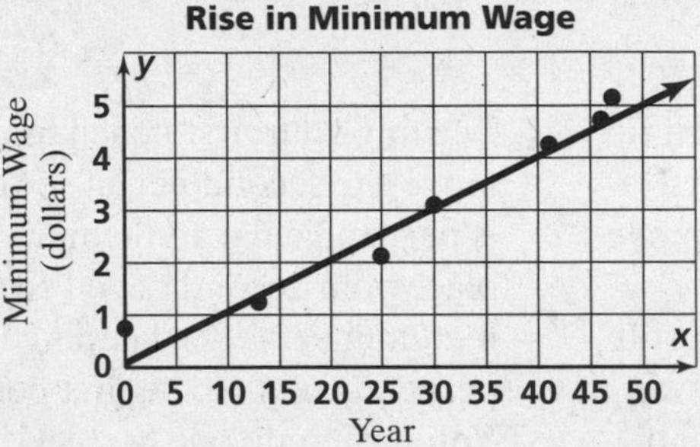

b. Pick any two points that appear to lie on the trend line, for example, (30, 3) and (50, 5).

c. On a new grid, graph the two points you selected. Draw the line through these two points.

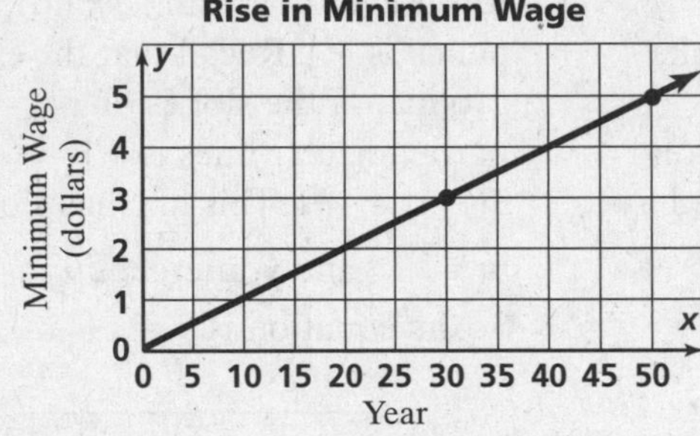

d. Find the slope of the trend line.

$$\text{slope} = \frac{\text{number of units up}}{\text{number of units across}} = \frac{\text{rise}}{\text{run}} = \frac{2}{20} = \frac{1}{10}$$

e. Make substitutions to obtain the equation of the line using either (30, 3) or (50, 2) as (x_1, y_1).

$y - y_1 = m(x - x_1)$ ← **Use point-slope form.**

$y - 3 = \frac{1}{10}(x - 30)$ ← **Substitute $\frac{1}{10}$ for m, 3 for y, and 30 for x.**

The equation $y - 3 = \frac{1}{10}(x - 30)$ models the rise in minimum wage.

Exercises

Find an equation of a reasonable trend line for each scatter plot.

1.

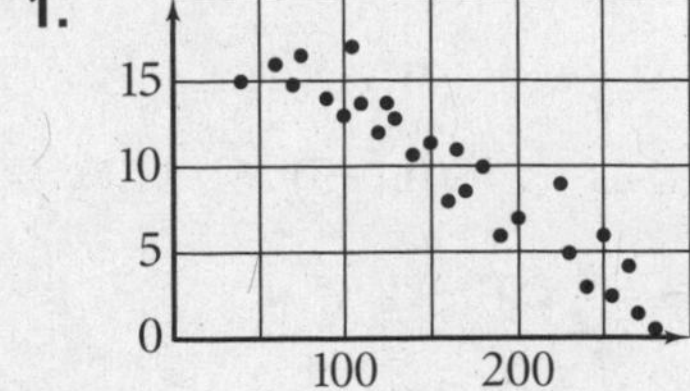

2.

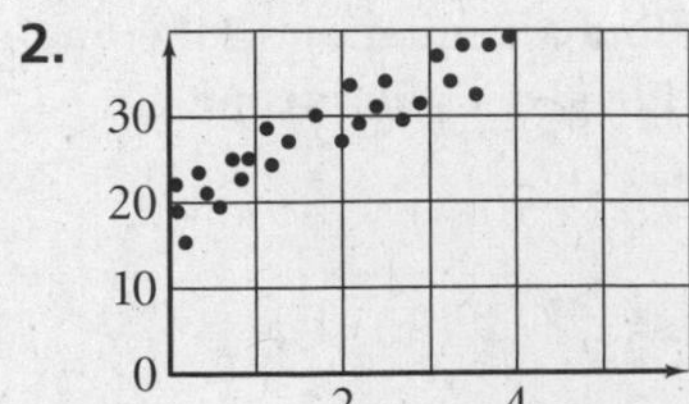

3.

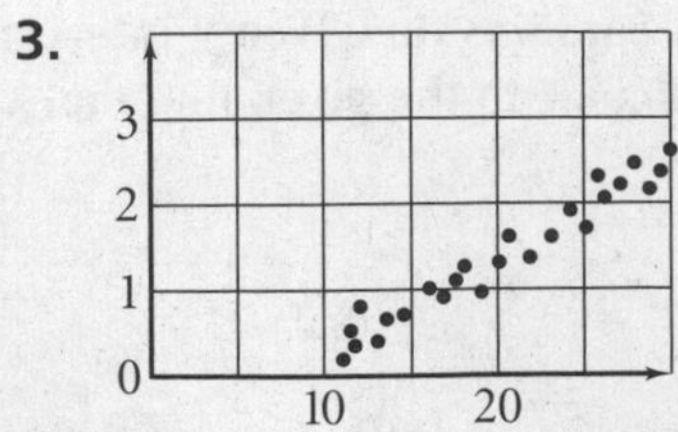

Name ______________________ Class ______________ Date ______________

Review 65

Graphing Absolute Value Equations

OBJECTIVE: To translate an absolute value equation	**MATERIALS:** None

An absolute value equation has a graph that looks like a *V* and it points either upward or downward.

A translation shifts a graph from its home position horizontally (left or right), vertically (up or down), or in some cases both. Translating a graph does not change its shape, but moves it to a different position.

Example

Graph $y = |x| + 1$.

Start with the graph of $y = |x|$.

Remember this is a *V*-shaped graph pointing upward with its vertex at the origin.
The $+ 1$ tells us that the the graph will be shifted up 1 unit.
If the equation were $y = |x| - 1$, then the graph would be shifted down 1 unit.
You could also make a table of values.

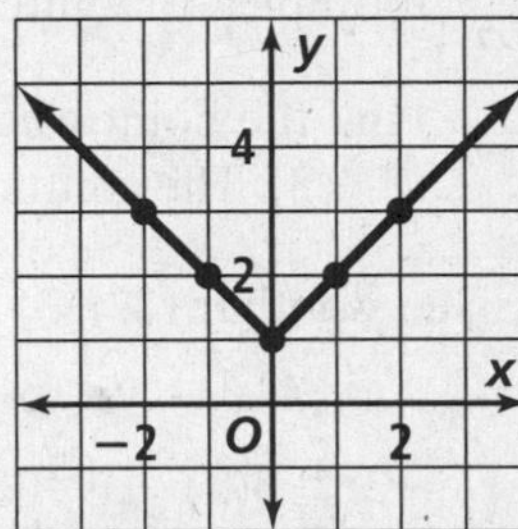

$y = \|x\| + 1$	
x	y
−2	3
−1	2
0	1
1	2
2	3

Substitute values for x and then plot the points.

Remember that an equation in the form $y = |x + 4|$ would be shifted horizontally. The shift would be the ***opposite*** of the sign inside the absolute value symbols.

For example, $y = |x - 3|$ would shift to the right (positive direction) 3 units.
$y = |x + 3|$ would shift to the left (negative direction) 3 units.

Exercises

In which direction would each absolute value equation shift and by how many units?

1. $y = |x| + 12$ **2.** $y = |x| - 15$ **3.** $y = |x + 13|$ **4.** $y = |x - 15|$

Graph each absolute value equation.

5. $y = |x| + 1$ **6.** $y = |x| - 2$ **7.** $y = |x - 3|$ **8.** $y = |x + 3|$

Name ______________________ Class ______________ Date ______________

Review 66

Solving Systems by Graphing

OBJECTIVE: Solving systems of linear equations by graphing

MATERIALS: Graph paper, two toothpicks

- When you graph two equations, the point of intersection is the solution.
- To graph each equation, apply the slope-intercept form, $y = mx + b$.

Example

Solve by graphing.

$y = 3x - 9$

$y = -x - 1$

a. In the first equation, $b = -9$ and $m = 3$. Therefore, place one toothpick so that it intersects the y-axis at -9 and has a slope of 3.

b. Graph the second equation with $b = -1$ and $m = -1$ by placing another toothpick that intersects the y-axis at -1 and has a slope of -1.

c. Find the point where the two lines intersect. The lines intersect at $(2, -3)$. The solution of the system is $(2, -3)$.

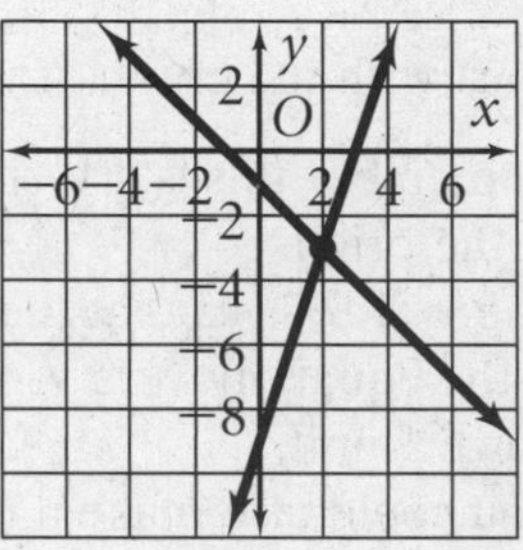

Check. See whether $(2, -3)$ makes both equations true.

$y = 3x - 9$		$y = -x - 1$
$-3 \stackrel{?}{=} 3(2) - 9$	← **Substitute $(2, -3)$ for (x, y).** →	$-3 \stackrel{?}{=} -(2) - 1$
$-3 \stackrel{?}{=} 6 - 9$		$-3 = -3$ ✓
$-3 = -3$ ✓		

Exercises

Use graph paper, toothpicks, and steps a–c above to model and solve each system.

1. $y = 5x - 2$
$y = x + 6$

2. $y = 2x - 4$
$y = x + 2$

3. $y = x + 2$
$y = -x + 2$

Solve each system.

4. $y = 3x + 2$
$y = 3x - 4$

5. $y = 2x + 1$
$2y = 4x + 2$

6. $y = x - 3$
$y = -x + 3$

7. $y = 5x + 1$
$y = x - 3$

8. $y = x - 5$
$y = 4x + 1$

9. $y = 3x - 1$
$y = 3x - 4$

Name ______________________ Class ______________ Date ______________

Review 67

Solving Systems Using Substitution

OBJECTIVE: Solving systems of linear equations by substitution

MATERIALS: None

Example

Solve using substitution.

$$-4x + y = -13$$
$$x - 1 = y$$

$y = 4x - 13$ ⟵ **Rewrite each equation in the form $y = mx + b$.**

$y = x - 1$

$y = \boxed{4x - 13}$ ⟵ **Circle the sides of the equations that do not contain y.**

$y = \boxed{x - 1}$

$4x - 13 = x - 1$ ⟵ **Since both circled parts equal y, they are equal to each other.**

$3x = 12$ ⟵ **Solve for x.**

$x = 4$

$y = 4x - 13$ ⟵ **Substitute 4 for x in either equation. Solve for y.**

$y = 4(4) - 13$

$y = 3$

The solution is (4, 3).

Check to see whether (4, 3) makes both equations true. If it doesn't, then the system has no solution.

$-4(4) + 3 \stackrel{?}{=} -13$ $4 - 1 \stackrel{?}{=} 3$

$-16 + 3 \stackrel{?}{=} -13$ $3 = 3$ ✓

$-13 = -13$ ✓

Exercises

Solve each system using substitution. Check your solution.

1. $-3x + y = -2$
$y = x + 6$

2. $y + 4 = x$
$-2x + y = 8$

3. $y - 2 = x$
$-x = y$

4. $6y + 4x = 12$
$-6x + y = -8$

5. $3x + y = 5$
$2x - 5y = 9$

6. $x + 4y = 5$
$4x - 2y = 11$

7. $2y - 3x = 4$
$x = -2$

8. $3y + x = -1$
$x = -3y$

9. $2x + y = -1$
$6x = -3y - 3$

Name ______________________________ Class ____________________ Date ______________

Review 68

Solving Systems Using Elimination

OBJECTIVE: Solving systems of linear equations using elimination

MATERIALS: At least 15 of each of three types or colors of objects, such as beans, colored cubes, or paper clips

When both linear equations of a system are in the form $Ax + By = C$, you can solve the system by elimination. You can use different objects (or, in the example below, symbols) to represent A, B, and C.

Example

Model each equation. Then solve the system of linear equations by elimination.

$$4x - 5y = -7$$
$$4x + y = -1$$

Use: ✱ for the coefficient of x, ■ for the coefficient of y, and ✦ for the constant.

a.

x		y		
✱✱✱✱	−	■■■■■	=	−✦✦✦✦✦✦✦
✱✱✱✱	+	■	=	−✦

b. Since there are an equal number of ✱s, subtract the second equation to eliminate x.

✱✱✱✱	−	■■■■■	=	−✦✦✦✦✦✦✦
(−)✱✱✱✱	+	(−)■	=	(−)−✦
	−	■■■■■■	=	−✦✦✦✦✦✦

c. Since there are six items on the variable side of the equation, divide by 6 on both sides to find that $y = 1$.

d. Now solve for the value of the eliminated variable in either equation.

$4x - 5(1) = -7$ ⟵ **Substitute 1 for y.**

$4x = -2$ ⟵ **Solve for x.**

$x = -\frac{1}{2}$

Since $x = -\frac{1}{2}$ and $y = 1$, the solution is $(-\frac{1}{2}, -1)$.

Check. See whether $(-\frac{1}{2}, 1)$ makes the other equation true.

$$4x + y = -1$$
$$4(-\tfrac{1}{2}) + 1 \stackrel{?}{=} -1$$
$$-1 = -1 \checkmark$$

Exercises

Use different objects that represent A, B, and C to model and solve each system by elimination.

1. $3x + 5y = 6$
$-3x + y = 6$

2. $2x + 4y = -4$
$2x + y = 8$

3. $y = x + 2$
$y = -x$

Name ______________________ Class ______________ Date ______________

Review 69

Applications of Linear Systems

OBJECTIVE: Writing and solving systems of linear equations

MATERIALS: Graph paper or graphing calculator

As you solve multi-step systems of linear equations, remember these strategies:

- Determine which form each equation is in:

  $Ax + By = C$ or $y = mx + b$
- If the equations are in the form $Ax + By = C$ and a variable can easily be eliminated, use elimination.
- If the equations are in $y = mx + b$ form, use graphing or substitution.

Example

Last year, Zach received $469.75 in interest from two investments. The interest rates were 7.5% on one account and 8% on the other. If the total amount invested was $6000, how much was invested at each rate?

Define x = investment in first account; y = investment in second account

Relate The total amount invested was $6000.

Write

$x + y = 6000$ ← **Determine the form of each equation:** $Ax + By = C$

$0.075x + 0.08y = 469.75$

$y = -x + 6000$ ← **Since a variable cannot easily be eliminated, rewrite one equation in the form** $y = mx + b$.

$0.075x + 0.08(-x + 6000) = 469.75$ ← **Substitute** $-x + 6000$ **for** y.

$-0.005x = -10.25$ ← **Solve for** x.

$x = 2050$

$2050 + y = 6000$ ← **Substitute 2050 for** x **in the first equation and solve for** y.

$y = 3950$

The amount invested in the first account was $2050. The amount invested in the second account was $3950.

Exercises

Model with a system of equations and solve using elimination, substitution, and graphing. Explain which is the best method, and why.

1. Mary ordered lunch for herself and several co-workers on Monday and Tuesday. On Monday, she paid $7 for five sandwiches and four sodas. On Tuesday, she paid $6 for four of each. Find the price of a sandwich and the price of a soda.

2. A local landscape company had a one-week sale. On Monday, Mrs. Jones had $82 to spend. After purchasing 5 trees, she had just enough money left to purchase 1 shrub. Later in that same week, she purchased 2 trees. She had $37 with her, so she again had enough money left to purchase 1 shrub. Find the cost of a

Name ______________________ Class ______________ Date ______________

Review 70

OBJECTIVE: Graphing linear inequalities **MATERIALS:** Graph paper

To graph inequalities, use the same strategies used to graph equations. Remember that the boundary line is solid if the inequality has an equal sign (indicating that the points on the boundary line are part of the solution) and dashed if the inequality does not have an equal sign (indicating that the points on the boundary line are not part of the solution).

Example

Graph the inequality $y - 3 < x$.

a. The equation of the boundary line is $y - 3 = x$. Rewrite the equation in the form $y = mx + b$.

$y = x + 3$

b. Graph the boundary line, $y = x + 3$. Since coordinates of points on the boundary line do not make the inequality true, graph a dashed line.

c. Use these guidelines for shading: If the inequality sign is less than (<), then shade the lower region of the graph (or the left region, for the vertical lines). Otherwise, shade the upper region of the graph (or the right region, for vertical lines).

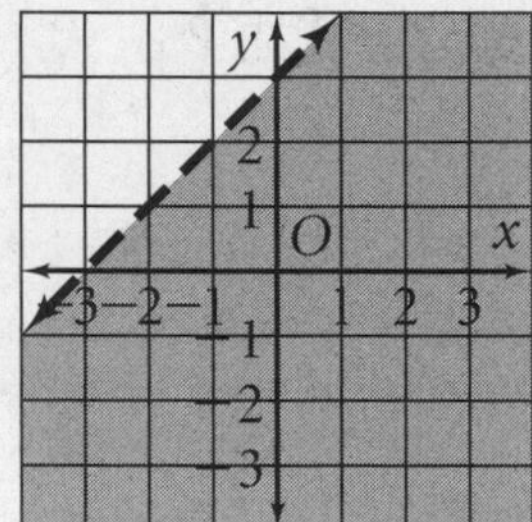

d. Test the point (0, 0) from the shaded region. See whether (0, 0) satisfies the original inequality.

$y - 3 < x$

$0 - 3 < 0$

$-3 < 0$ **True**

The inequality is true for (0, 0). So the shaded region is correct.

Exercises

Follow steps a–d above to graph each linear inequality.

1. $y < x + 2$ **2.** $y \leq 2x + 1$ **3.** $y > x$

Name ______________________ Class ______________ Date ______________

Review 71

Systems of Linear Inequalities

OBJECTIVE: Solving systems of linear inequalities by graphing	**MATERIALS:** Graph paper, two highlighting markers in colors that combine to make a third color (pink and yellow, for example)

- When you graph the first inequality, mark the solution area with one color. Then graph the second inequality and mark the solution area with the other color. The common solution for the two inequalities appears where the two colors combine to make a third color.
- To graph inequalities, use the same strategies you use to graph equations.
- The boundary line is solid if the inequality has an equal sign (indicating that the points on the line are part of the solution) and dashed if the inequality does not have an equal sign.

Example

Solve by graphing.

$y - x < 5$
$y + 6 \geq 2x$

a. Rewrite the inequalities in slope-intercept form.
$y < x + 5$
$y \geq 2x - 6$

b. Graph the boundary line, $y = x + 5$ using a dashed line.

c. Test the inequality $y - x < 5$ using the point (0, 0). Since the inequality is true for (0, 0), shade the region containing (0, 0) yellow.

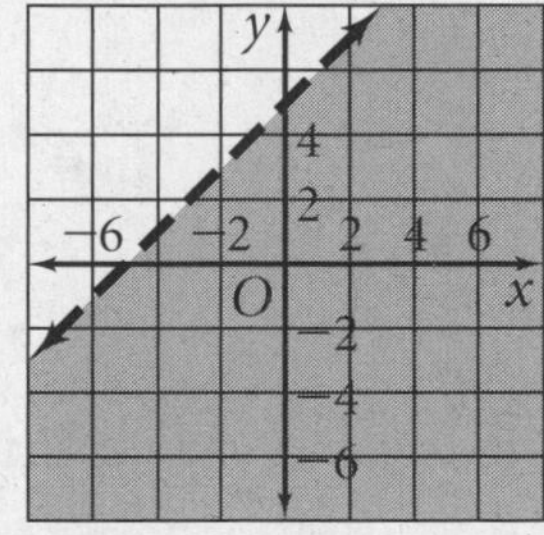

d. Graph the boundary line, $y = 2x - 6$ using a solid line.

e. Test the inequality $y + 6 \geq 2x$ using the point (0, 0). It is true; therefore, shade the region containing (0, 0) pink, including the boundary line.

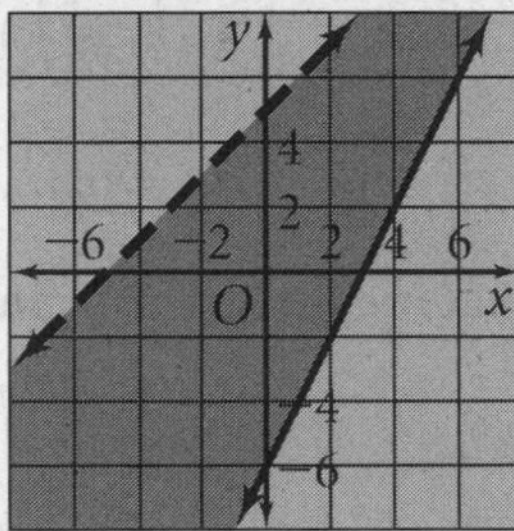

f. The region that appears orange is the solution region.

Exercises

Follow steps a–f above to graph each system of linear inequalities.

1. $y < 4x - 7$
$y > \frac{1}{2}x + 4$

2. $y - 4 < x$
$3y < x + 6$

3. $2x + 3y > 6$
$x - y \leq 0$

Name ______________________ Class ______________ Date ______________

Review 72

Zero and Negative Exponents

OBJECTIVE: Evaluating and simplifying expressions in which zero and negative numbers are used as exponents

MATERIALS: None

ALGEBRA 1 TOPICS

- When a nonzero number a has a zero exponent, then $a^0 = 1$.
- For any nonzero number a and any integer n, $a^{-n} = \frac{1}{a^n}$.

Example

Write each expression as an integer or a simple fraction.

a. 2.7^0

1 ⟵ **Rewrite, using the property of zero as an exponent.**

b. 5^{-2}

$\frac{1}{5^2}$ ⟵ **Rewrite as a fraction, using the property of negative exponents.**

$\frac{1}{25}$ ⟵ **Simplify.**

Exercises

Write each expression as an integer, a simple fraction, or an expression that contains only positive exponents. Simplify.

1. 10^{-3}

2. 1.67^0

3. 5^{-4}

4. 7^{-3}

5. $\left(-\frac{3}{2}\right)^{-2}$

6. $(5x)^{-4}$

7. 4^{-1}

8. 376.5^0

9. b^{-5}

Write each expression so that it contains only positive exponents.

10. $\left(\frac{2}{7}\right)^{-4}$

11. $3ab^0$

12. -4^{-3}

13. $a^{-3}b^{-4}$

14. $\frac{3x^{-2}}{y}$

15. $12xy^{-3}$

16. $\frac{8}{4^{-2}}$

17. $\frac{(3x)^{-1}}{4}$

18. $\frac{(2x)^{-2}}{3y^{-1}}$

19. $\frac{(4x)^{-2}}{2^{-3}}$

20. $\frac{(3a)^2b^{-3}}{b^{-2}}$

21. $\frac{4^0 5^3}{2^{-3}}$

Name ______________________ Class ______________ Date ______________

Review 73

OBJECTIVE: Writing numbers in scientific notation	**MATERIALS:** None

To write a number in **scientific notation**, follow these steps:

- Move the decimal to the right of the first integer.
- If the original number is greater than 1, multiply by 10^n, where n represents the number of places the decimal was moved to the left.
- If the original number is less than 1, multiply by 10^{-n}, where n represents the number of places the decimal was moved to the right.

Examples

Write each number in scientific notation.

a. 9,040,000,000 ⟵ **standard form**

9.040 000 000. ⟵ **Move the decimal to the left nine places.**

9.04×10^9 ⟵ **Drop all insignificant 0's. Multiply by the appropriate power of 10.**

b. 0.000 000 8 ⟵ **standard form**

0.000 000 8. ⟵ **Move the decimal to the right seven places.**

8.0×10^{-7} ⟵ **Multiply by the appropriate power of 10.**

Exercises

Write each number in scientific notation.

1. 420,000

2. 5,100,000,000

3. 260 billion

4. 830 million

5. 0.00075

6. 0.004005

Write each number in standard notation.

7. 6.345×10^8

8. 3.2×10^{-5}

9. 4.081×10^6

10. 2.581×10^{-3}

11. 3.07×10^{-2}

12. 1.526×10^6

13. 8.04×10^{-4}

14. 7.625×10^5

15. 6.825×10^4

16. 3.081×10^{-5}

17. 8.3847×10^2

18. 3.6245×10^{-2}

Name ______________________ Class ______________ Date ______________

Review 74

Multiplication Properties of Exponents

OBJECTIVE: Multiplying powers with the same base

MATERIALS: None

ALGEBRA 1 TOPICS

- A power is an expression in the form a^n.
- To multiply powers with the same base, add the exponents $a^m \cdot a^n = a^{m+n}$

Example

Simplify $4^6 \cdot 4^3$.

$4^6 \cdot 4^3$

$= 4^{6+3}$ ⟵ **Rewrite as one base with the exponents added.**

$= 4^9$ ⟵ **Add the exponents.**

So $4^6 \cdot 4^3 = 4^9$.

Exercises

Complete each equation.

1. $8^2 \cdot 8^3 = 8^{■}$
2. $2^{■} \cdot 2^6 = 2^9$
3. $a^{12} \cdot a^{■} = a^{15}$
4. $x^{■} \cdot x^5 = x^6$
5. $b^{-4} \cdot b^3 = b^{■}$
6. $6^4 \cdot 6^{■} = 6^2$
7. $3^4 \cdot 3^8 = 3^{■}$
8. $c^{■} \cdot c^{-7} = c^{11}$
9. $10^{-6} \cdot 10^{-3} = 10^{■}$

Simplify each expression.

10. $3x^2 \cdot 4x \cdot 2x^3$
11. $m^2 \cdot 3m^4 \cdot 6a \cdot a^{-3}$
12. $p^3q^{-1} \cdot p^2q^{-8}$
13. $5x^2 \cdot 3x \cdot 8x^4$
14. $x^2 \cdot y^5 \cdot 8x^5 \cdot y^{-2}$
15. $7y^2 \cdot 3x^2 \cdot 9$
16. $2y^2 \cdot 3y^2 \cdot 4y^5$
17. $x^4 \cdot x^{-5} \cdot x^4$
18. $x^{12} \cdot x^{-8} \cdot y^{-2} \cdot y^3$
19. $6a^2 \cdot b \cdot 2a^{-1}$
20. $r^6 \cdot s^{-3} \cdot r^{-2} \cdot s$
21. $3p^{-2} \cdot q^3 \cdot p^3 \cdot q^{-2}$

Name ______________________ Class ______________ Date ______________

Review 75

More Multiplication Properties of Exponents

OBJECTIVE: Using two more multiplication properties of exponents

MATERIALS: None

- To raise a power to a power, multiply the exponents.
- Every number and variable inside parentheses is being raised to the power to the right of the parentheses.

Example

Simplify $(4x^3)^2$.

$(4x^3)^2$

$(4^1x^3)^2$ ← **Rewrite each number and variable with an exponent.**

$(4^1x^3)^2$ ← **Draw arrows from the exponent outside the parentheses to each exponent inside the parentheses.**

$4^{2 \cdot 1}x^{2 \cdot 3}$ ← **Rewrite, showing the exponents to be multiplied.**

4^2x^6 ← **Multiply the exponents.**

$16x^6$ ← **Simplify.**

Exercises

Draw arrows from the exponent outside the parentheses to each exponent inside the parentheses. Then simplify each expression.

1. $(5^2)^4$
2. $(a^5)^4$
3. $(2^3)^2$
4. $(4x)^3$
5. $(7a^4)^2$
6. $(3g^2)^3$
7. $(g^2h^3)^5$
8. $(s^6)^2$

Simplify each expression.

9. $(x^2y^4)^3$
10. $(3r^5)^0$
11. $g^9 \cdot g^{-7}$
12. $(c^4)^7$
13. $(3.2)^5 \cdot (3.2)^{-5}$
14. $(8ab^6)^3$
15. $(x^2y^3)^2$
16. $(x^7)^2$
17. $(3x^2y)^2$
18. $(-2x^2)^3$
19. $(x^3y^4)^3$
20. $(3x^2y)^3$
21. $(-4x^2y^3)^3$
22. $(xyz)^0$
23. $x^5 \cdot x^{-7}$

Name ______________________ Class ______________ Date ______________

Review 76

Division Properties of Exponents

OBJECTIVE: Applying division properties of exponents	**MATERIALS:** None

To divide powers with the same base, subtract exponents.

Example

Simplify $\frac{4^3}{4^5}$.

Method 1

$\frac{4 \cdot 4 \cdot 4}{4 \cdot 4 \cdot 4 \cdot 4 \cdot 4}$ ← **Expand the numerator and the denominator.**

$\frac{\not{4} \cdot \not{4} \cdot \not{4}}{\not{4} \cdot \not{4} \cdot \not{4} \cdot 4 \cdot 4}$ ← **Draw lines through terms that are in both the numerator and the denominator.**

$\frac{1}{4 \cdot 4}$ ← **Cancel.**

$\frac{1}{4^2}$ or 4^{-2} ← **Rewrite with exponents.**

Method 2

$3 - 5 = -2$ ← **Subtract the exponents from the original equation. Compare this to the exponent in the first answer.**

So $\frac{4^3}{4^5} = 4^{3-5} = 4^{-2}$. ← **Subtract the exponents from the original equation. Compare this to the exponent in the first answer.**

$\frac{1}{4^2}$ ← **Write with positive exponents.**

To raise a quotient to a power use repeated multiplication.

Exercises

Use both methods shown in the example to simplify each expression. Use only positive exponents.

1. $\frac{z^6}{z^3}$ **2.** $\left(\frac{3^2}{4}\right)^3$ **3.** $\frac{m^{-3}}{m^{-4}}$ **4.** $\frac{5^3}{5^4}$

5. $\left(\frac{b^7}{b^5}\right)^3$ **6.** $\frac{5a^5}{15a^2}$ **7.** $\frac{2^2}{2^5}$ **8.** $\frac{d^8}{d^3}$

9. $\frac{x^7}{x^5}$ **10.** $\left(\frac{10^8}{10^2}\right)^3$ **11.** $\frac{14x^{11}}{7x^{10}}$ **12.** $\frac{8x^9}{12x^6}$

13. $\frac{x^{12}}{x^5}$ **14.** $\frac{6x^4}{4x^2}$ **15.** $\frac{x^3}{x^8}$ **16.** $\left(\frac{x^5}{x^3}\right)^4$

Name ______________________ Class ______________ Date ______________

Review 77

Geometric Sequences

OBJECTIVE: Finding the next terms of a geometric sequence	**MATERIALS:** None

- Multiplying a term in the sequence by a fixed number to find the next term forms a geometric sequence.
- The fixed number is called the common ratio.

Example

Find the next three terms of the sequence 3, −9, 27, −81, . . .

3, −9, 27, −81, . . .

$-\frac{9}{3} = -3$

The common ratio is −3.

Note that each term in the given sequence is −3 times the previous term.

Let A(n) = the value of the nth term in the sequence.

A(5) = −3 · −81 = 243 ← **the common ratio times the fourth term**

A(6) = −3 · 243 = −729 ← **the common ratio times the fifth term**

A(7) = −3 · −729 = 2187 ← **the common ratio times the sixth term**

The next three terms in the sequence are 243, −729, 2187.

Exercises

Find the next three terms in each of the following sequences.

1. 2, 8, 32, 128, . . .

2. −3, 6, −12, 24, . . .

3. 1, −1, 1, −1, . . .

4. 12, 6, 3, $\frac{3}{2}$, . . .

5. 20, −10, 5, $-\frac{5}{2}$, . . .

6. 100, 10, 1, 0.1, . . .

7. 3, 15, 75, 375, . . .

8. −8, −12, −18, −27, . . .

9. 1.5, 4.5, 13.5, 40.5, . . .

10. 8, $-\frac{8}{3}$, $\frac{8}{9}$, $-\frac{8}{27}$, . . .

11. 7, −14, 28, −56, . . .

12. 100, 50, 25, 12.5, . . .

13. 8, 32, 128, 512, . . .

14. 76, −38, 19, −9.5, . . .

Name ______________________ Class ______________ Date ______________

Review 78

OBJECTIVE: Examining patterns in exponential functions

MATERIALS: None

To express exponential changes as a function of a variable, follow these steps:

Step 1 Make a table of the data.

Step 2 Find the pattern.

Step 3 Write an equation with exponents.

Example

You have ten CDs. That number doubles every year. How many CDs will you have at the end of 5 yr?

Step 1 Make a table.

Time	No. of CDs
0	10
1 yr	$10 \cdot 2$
2 yr	$10 \cdot 2 \cdot 2$
3 yr	$10 \cdot 2 \cdot 2 \cdot 2$

Step 2 Find the pattern.

$10 \cdot 2 \longrightarrow$ After 1 yr

$10 \cdot 2^2 \longrightarrow$ After 2 yr

$10 \cdot 2^3 \longrightarrow$ After 3 yr

$10 \cdot 2^n \longrightarrow$ After n yr

Step 3 Write an equation with exponents and solve.

$y = 10 \cdot 2^n \longleftarrow$ **Write the equation.**

$y = 10 \cdot 2^5 \longleftarrow$ **Substitute 5 for n.**

$y = 320 \longleftarrow$ **Use a calculator.**

You will have 320 CDs at the end of 5 yr.

Exercises

Follow the above steps to write and evaluate the function.

1. Your science class is collecting cans. You start with 150 cans. Your collection triples every week. How many cans will you have collected after 7 wk?

2. A population of 2500 triples in size every 10 yr. What will the population be in 30 yr?

3. Your parents invested $2000 in a college fund for you when you were 4 yr old. It has doubled in value every 4 yr. If you are now 16, how much is in your college fund?

4. A bacteria culture doubles in size every 8 h. The culture starts with 150 cells. How many will there be after 24 h? After 72 h?

Name ______________________ Class ______________ Date ______________

Review 79

Exponential Growth and Decay

OBJECTIVE: Modeling exponential growth and decay

MATERIALS: None

To write an exponential function to find growth, follow these steps.

Step 1 Find the initial amount *a*.

Step 2 Multiply by the growth factor *b*, which occurs over *x* time periods. Remember that if your growth factor *b* is $0 < b < 1$, then *b* is your decay factor, and the function expresses negative growth, that is, a decay function.

Step 3 After the *x* time periods, the new amount will be $a \times b^x$.

The function is written $y = a \cdot b^x$.

Example

The cost of a car is $10,000. Suppose the price increases 5% each year. What will the cost be at the end of 10 yr? What if the price decreases 7% each year? Use the table below to find the amounts.

a (initial amount)	*b* (growth factor)	*x* (number of increases)	*y* (new amount)
10,000	100% + 5% = 105% = 1.05	10	$10{,}000 \cdot 1.05^{10} = y$
10,000	100% − 7% = 93% = 0.93	10	$10{,}000 \cdot 0.93^{10} = y$

The cost at the end of 10 yr with a growth factor of 5% will be $16,289; with a decay factor of 7%, it will be $4839.82.

Exercises

Write an exponential function to model each situation. Find each amount at the end of the specified time. Round your answers to the nearest whole number.

1. A town with a population of 5,000 grows 3% per year. Find the population at the end of 10 yr.

2. The price of a bicycle is $100. It increases 8% per year. What will the price be at the end of 5 yr?

3. A 2 ft-tall tree grows 10% per year. How tall will the tree be at the end of 8 yr?

4. $1,000 purchase
10% loss in value each year
5 yr

5. $5,000 investment
13.5% loss each year
8 yr

6. 20,000 population
12.5% annual decrease
10 yr

Name ______________________ Class ______________ Date ______________

Review 80

OBJECTIVE: Adding and subtracting polynomials **MATERIALS:** Tiles

Example

Using tiles, simplify $(2a^2 + 4a - 6) + (a^2 - 2a + 4)$.

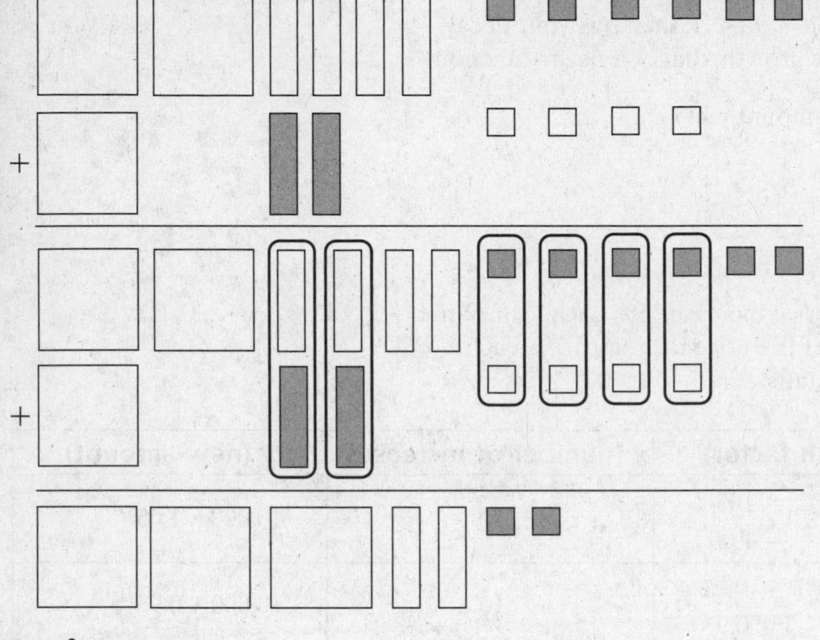

Use tiles to represent the terms of $2a^2 + 4a - 6$.

Use tiles to represent the terms of $a^2 - 2a + 4$. Align like terms vertically with the tiles in the row above.

Remove zero pairs.

Count the remaining tiles.

$3a^2 + 2a - 2$ ← **Solution**

Exercises

Use tiles to simplify each sum or difference.

1. $(4x - 5y + 3) + (2x + 7y - 7)$

2. $(3a^2 + 5a - 6) - (2a^2 - 3a - 9)$

3. $(6x^2 - 3x + 2) + (3x^2 + x - 5)$

4. $(4x^2 + 2x - 7) - (-3x^2 - 6x + 2)$

5. $(6z^3 - 5z^2 + 1) + (8z^3 + 7z^2 - 4)$

6. $(4x^2 + 2) - (-2x^2 + 5) + (x^2 + 4)$

Simplify. Write each answer in standard form.

7. $(2x^2 - 3x + 4) + (3x^2 + 2x - 3)$

8. $(7x^3 - 3x + 1) - (x^3 + x^2 - 2)$

9. $(3y^2 - 3y + 2) + (4y^2 + 3y - 1)$

10. $(5x^2 - 10) - (3x^2 + 7)$

11. $(2x^3 + x^2 + 1) + (3x^3 - x^2 + 2)$

12. $(4x^3 + 3x + 2) - (2x^2 - 3x + 7)$

13. $(3x^2 + 7x - 6) + (x^3 + x^2 - x - 1)$

14. $(4x^2 - x + 6) - (3x^2 - 4)$

Name ______________________ Class ______________ Date ______________

Review 81

Multiplying and Factoring

OBJECTIVE: Factoring a monomial from a polynomial

MATERIALS: None

- To factor a polynomial you must find the **G**reatest **C**ommon **F**actor. The **GCF** is the greatest factor that divides evenly into each term.

Example

Factor $18x^3 + 6x^2 - 12x$.

a. First find the GCF.

$18x^3 = (2)\ (3)\ 3\ (x)\ x\ x$

$6x^2 = (2)\ (3)\ x\ (x)$

$12x = (2)\ 2\ (3)\ (x)$

← **List the factors of each term. Circle the factors common to all terms.**

$2 \cdot 3 \cdot x = 6x$ ← **Multiply the circled terms together to get the GCF.**

b. Factor out the GCF from each term.

$\frac{18x^3}{6x} = 3x^2$ ← **Divide each term by the GCF.**

$\frac{6x^2}{6x} = x$

$\frac{-12x}{6x} = -2$

$6x(3x^2 + x - 2)$ ← **Solution**

Exercises

Use the GCF to factor each polynomial.

1. $21x - 14$

2. $5y^3 - 10y^2 + 15y$

3. $x^3 + 3x^2 + x$

4. $3x^2 + 6x^4$

5. $18x^3 - 6x^2 + 24x$

6. $z^3 - 3z^2$

7. $12k^3 + 6k^2 - 18k$

8. $6x^3 - 4x^2 + 8x$

9. $8p^4 + 12p^2 + 4p$

10. $36x^2 - 18x$

11. $6x^2 + 18x$

12. $6x^3 - 2x^2 + 8x$

13. $6x^3 + 6x^2 - 6x$

14. $5x^3 + 5x^2$

15. $3x^2 + 6x + 3$

16. $10x^2 + 35x$

17. $8x^5 + 16x^4 - 8x^3$

18. $9x^3 - 6x^2 - 15x$

Name ______________________ Class ______________ Date ______________

Review 82

OBJECTIVE: Multiplying binomials **MATERIALS:** None

To multiply two binomials, follow these steps:

- Multiply each term in one binomial by each term of the other binomial. Drawing arrows as a visual reminder of what to do is a helpful technique.
- Circle like terms and combine.

Example

Find the product $(x + 7)(x + 2)$.

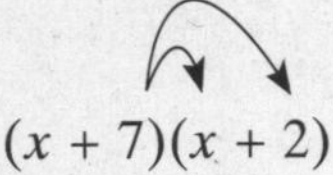

$(x + 7)(x + 2)$ ← **Draw arrows from the first term in the first binomial to both terms in the second binomial.**

$x^2 + 2x$ ← **Multiply each term of the second binomial by *x*.**

$(x + 7)(x + 2)$ ← **Draw arrows from the second term in the first binomial to both terms in the second binomial.**

$7x + 14$ ← **Multiply each term of the second binomial by 7.**

$x^2 + 2x + 7x + 14$ ← **Add the two expressions.**

$x^2 + \textcircled{2x} + \textcircled{7x} + 14$ ← **Circle like terms and combine.**

$x^2 + 9x + 14$ ← **Solution**

Exercises

Use arrows as shown above to simplify each product.

1. $(x + 6)(x - 2)$ **2.** $(x - 8)(x - 4)$ **3.** $(x - 3)(x + 9)$

4. $(x + 2)(x - 7)$ **5.** $(2x + 3)(x + 4)$ **6.** $(x + 4)(2x + 5)$

Simplify each product.

7. $(7x + 4)(2x - 4)$ **8.** $(3x + 2)(3x + 2)$ **9.** $(5x + 1)(x + 1)$

10. $(2x + 1)(x + 1)$ **11.** $(4x + 1)(2x - 1)$ **12.** $(3x - 1)(x + 2)$

Name ______________________ Class ______________ Date ______________

Review 83

Multiplying Special Cases

OBJECTIVE: Finding the square of a binomial and finding the difference of two squares.

MATERIALS: None

Examples

Finding the square of a binomial.

Remember:
- Square the first term.
- Double the product of the two terms.
- Square the last term.
- Write the sum of your three products.

$(x - 5)^2$	**Square the first term:**	x^2
	Double $(x)(-5)$:	$2 \cdot (-5x) = -10x$
	Square the last term:	$(-5)^2 = 25$
	Write the sum of your three products:	$x^2 - 10x + 25$

Finding the difference of two squares.

Remember:
- Square the first term.
- Square the last term.
- Write the difference of your first square and your second square.

$(3x - 2)(3x + 2)$	**Square the first term:**	$(3x)^2 = 9x^2$
	Square the last term:	$(2)^2 = 4$
	Write the difference of your first square and your second square:	$9x^2 - 4$

Exercises

Find each product.

1. $(x - 7)^2$

2. $(x + 1)^2$

3. $(x - 4)^2$

4. $(x - y)^2$

5. $(2x + 3)^2$

6. $(3x - 5)^2$

7. $(2x + 1)^2$

8. $(5x - 4)^2$

9. $(x + 7)(x - 7)$

10. $(x + 8)(x - 8)$

11. $(x - 3)(x + 3)$

12. $(x + y)(x - y)$

13. $(4x + 3)(4x - 3)$

14. $(2x + 5)(2x - 5)$

15. $(3x + 2)(3x - 2)$

16. $(7x - 1)(7x + 1)$

Name ______________________ Class ______________ Date ______________

Review 84

Factoring Trinomials of the Type $x^2 + bx + c$

OBJECTIVE: Factoring trinomials of the type $x^2 + bx + c$

MATERIALS: Tiles

Examples

Factor $x^2 + 6x + 8$.

$(x \quad)(x \quad)$ ← **Write factors of x^2, the first term of the trinomial, at the beginning of each set of parentheses. Note that the coefficient of x^2 is 1.**

+1 and +8 −1 and −8

(+2) and (+4) −2 and −4

← **List pairs of numbers that are factors of +8, which is the constant term of the trinomial. Choose the pair of factors that add to equal +6, the coefficient of the middle term of the trinomial.**

$(x + 2)(x + 4)$ ← **Write those two factors, with their signs, at the end of each set of parentheses.**

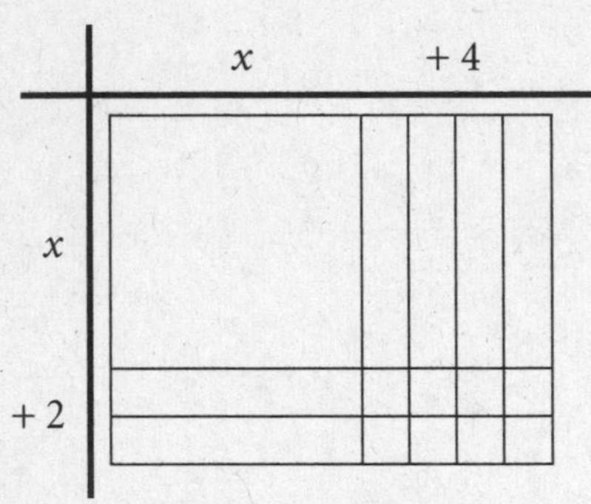

← **The trinomial $x^2 + 6x + 8$ represents the area of a rectangle with side of length $(x + 4)$ and $(x + 2)$.**

Factor $x^2 + 4x - 21$.

$(x \quad)(x \quad)$

−1 and +21 +1 and −21

−3 and +7 +3 and −7

← **List pairs of numbers that are factors of −21.**

$(x - 3)(x + 7)$ ← **Choose the pair of factors that add to equal +4.**

Exercises

Factor each expression.

1. $y^2 + 11y + 18$ **2.** $x^2 - 8x + 15$ **3.** $x^2 - 11x + 18$

4. $y^2 - 5y + 4$ **5.** $x^2 + 6x + 8$ **6.** $y^2 - 8y + 12$

7. $r^2 + 13r + 12$ **8.** $x^2 - 16x + 39$ **9.** $x^2 - 10x + 16$

10. $x^2 - x - 2$ **11.** $x^2 - 4x - 32$ **12.** $x^2 - 7x - 18$

13. $x^2 + 7x + 10$ **14.** $x^2 - 11x + 24$ **15.** $x^2 + 16x + 63$

Name ______________________ Class ______________ Date ______________

Review 85

Factoring Trinomials of the Type $ax^2 + bx + c$

OBJECTIVE: Factoring trinomials of the type $ax^2 + bx + c$; $a > 1$

MATERIALS: None

A table can be helpful when factoring trinomials of the type $ax^2 + bx + c$.

Examples

Factor $2x^2 + 13x + 20$.

Write the first term in the top left box of the table. →

$2x^2$	

Write the constant term in the bottom right box of the table. →

$2x^2$	
	20

Find the product *ac*. → Since $a = 2$ and $c = 20$, $ac = 40$.

Find two numbers whose product is *ac* and sum is *b*. → Since $ac = 40$ and $b = 13$, the numbers are 8 and 5.

These numbers are the coefficients of the *x* terms that are written in the remaining boxes of the table. →

$2x^2$	$8x$
$5x$	20

(Note: Try repeating these steps, exchanging the locations of $5x$ and $8x$.)

Now, find the greatest common factors of the terms in each row and column. Write these above and to the left of the table. →

	x	4
$2x$	$2x^2$	$8x$
5	$5x$	20

Read across the top of the table to find one factor. → $x + 4$

Read down the left of the table to find the other factor. → $2x + 5$

So, $2x^2 + 13x + 20 = (x + 4)(2x + 5)$.

You can check your answer using FOIL.

Factor $3x^2 - 2x - 8$.

$ac = 3(-8) = -24$

$b = -2$

The numbers whose product is -24 and sum is -2 are -6 and 4. Write $-6x$ and $4x$ in the table and find the GCFs of each row and column.

	$3x$	4
x	$3x^2$	$4x$
-2	$-6x$	-8

$3x^2 - 2x - 8 = (3x + 4)(x - 2)$.

Exercises

Factor each expression.

1. $2x^2 + 11x + 14$

2. $4x^2 - 12x + 5$

3. $6x^2 - 13x + 2$

4. $6x^2 + 7x - 20$

5. $3x^2 + 4x - 4$

6. $8x^2 - 13x - 6$

7. $2x^2 - 5x + 3$

8. $5x^2 - 26x - 24$

9. $6x^2 - 7x - 3$

10. $6x^2 + 7x - 3$

Name ______________________ Class ______________ Date ______________

Review 86

Factoring Special Cases

OBJECTIVE: Factoring the difference of two squares	**MATERIALS:** None

- The difference of two squares is written $a^2 - b^2$. Note that both terms must be perfect squares.
- The **factors** of the difference of two squares, $a^2 - b^2$ are $(a + b)$ and $(a - b)$. Once you have determined that the binomial you want to factor is the difference of two squares, you can factor by using the formula $a^2 - b^2 = (a + b)(a - b)$.

Examples

Factor $a^2 - 16$.

$a^2 - 16$ ← **Both terms are perfect squares.**

$a^2 - 4^2$ ← **Rewrite 16 as 4^2.**

$a^2 - b^2 = (a + b)(a - b)$ ← **Write the formula.**

$a^2 - 4^2 = (a + 4)(a - 4)$ ← **Replace b with 4.**

$(a + 4)(a - 4)$ ← **Solution**

Factor $3a^2 - 75$.

$3a^2 - 75$ ← **Both terms are *not* perfect squares.**

$3(a^2 - 25)$ ← **Both $3a^2$ and 75 are divisible by 3. Factor out 3.**

$3(a^2 - 5^2)$ ← **25 is a perfect square. Rewrite 25 as 5^2.**

$a^2 - b^2 = (a + b)(a - b)$ ← **Write the formula.**

$3(a^2 - 5^2) = 3(a + 5)(a - 5)$ ← **Replace b with 5.**

$3(a + 5)(a - 5)$ ← **Solution**

Exercises

Factor each expression.

1. $a^2 - 36$ **2.** $x^2 - 64$ **3.** $y^2 - 49$

4. $4x^2 - 25$ **5.** $9y^2 - 16$ **6.** $25x^2 - 64$

7. $3x^2 - 12$ **8.** $2x^2 - 18$ **9.** $4x^2 - 16$

10. $x^2 - 225$ **11.** $x^2 - 144$ **12.** $16x^2 - 49$

13. $6x^2 - 54$ **14.** $7x^2 - 112$ **15.** $5x^2 - 125$

Name ______________________ Class ______________ Date ______________

Review 87

Factoring by Grouping

OBJECTIVE: Factoring by grouping **MATERIALS:** None

To factor a polynomial with four terms, we can sometimes group pairs of terms together, find the GCF of each pair, then factor a GCF from the resulting terms.

Examples

Factor $2x^3 - 8x^2 + 5x - 20$.

Group pairs of terms together. ⟶ $(2x^3 - 8x^2) + (5x - 20)$

Factor the GCF from each pair. ⟶ $2x^2(x - 4) + 5(x - 4)$

(Note: To proceed with this method, both sets of parentheses must contain the same expression.)

Replace the expressions in parentheses with ▲. ⟶ $2x^2$ ▲ + 5 ▲

Now, factor the common factor ▲ from both terms. ⟶ ▲ $(2x^2 + 5)$

Lastly, replace the ▲ with the expression it represents. ⟶ $(x - 4)(2x^2 + 5)$

So, $2x^3 - 8x^2 + 5x - 20 = (x - 4)(2x^2 + 5)$.

You can check your answer using FOIL.

It is sometimes possible to use this method to factor trinomials by first rewriting the middle term as a sum.

Factor $2x^2 + 13x + 15$.

Find two numbers whose product is *ac* and sum is *b*. ⟶ Since $a = 2$ and $c = 15$, $ac = 30$. Since $ac = 30$ and $b = 13$, the numbers are 10 and 13.

Rewrite the middle term as a sum of two terms whose coefficients are the two numbers you just found. ⟶ $13x = 10x + 3x$

Replace the middle term with this sum. ⟶ $2x^2 + (10x + 3x) + 15$

Regroup the terms and proceed as in the first Example. ⟶ $(2x^2 + 10x) + (3x + 15)$

Factor the GCF from each pair. ⟶ $2x(x + 5) + 3(x + 5)$

Replace the common expression with ▲. ⟶ $2x$ ▲ + 3 ▲

Factor ▲ from both terms. ⟶ ▲$(2x + 3)$

Replace the ▲ with the expression. ⟶ $(x + 5)(2x + 3)$

So, $2x^2 + 13x + 15 = (x + 5)(2x + 3)$.

Exercises

Factor each polynomial by grouping.

1. $2x^3 + 4x^2 + x + 2$ **2.** $2x^3 + 6x^2 + 3x + 9$ **3.** $5x^3 - 25x^2 + 2x - 10$

4. $2x^3 + 12x^2 - 5x - 30$ **5.** $7x^3 - 4x^2 + 7x - 4$ **6.** $9x^3 - 12x^2 - 18x + 24$

7. $3x^2 + x - 2$ **8.** $2x^2 - x - 3$ **9.** $5x^2 + 34x - 7$

Name ______________________ Class ______________ Date ______________

Review 88

OBJECTIVE: Graphing quadratic functions of the form $y = ax^2 + c$

MATERIALS: Graph paper

$y = ax^2$	Comparison	$y = ax^2 + c$
It forms a parabola.	Same	It forms a parabola.
It opens up if $a > 0$.	Same	It opens up if $a > 0$.
It opens down if $a < 0$.	Same	It opens down if $a < 0$.
Its line of symmetry is the y-axis.	Same	Its line of symmetry is the y-axis.
The vertex is the origin	Different	The vertex is shifted up c units from the origin if $c > 0$, down c units if $c < 0$.

Example

Sketch the graph of the equation $y = -x^2 + 5$.

Gather some information about the graph by looking closely at the equation.

opens *downward*

$y = -x^2 + 5$

The vertex is shifted *up* five units from the origin.

Make a table of values

x	y
−3	−4
−1	4
0	5
1	4
3	−4

Graph.

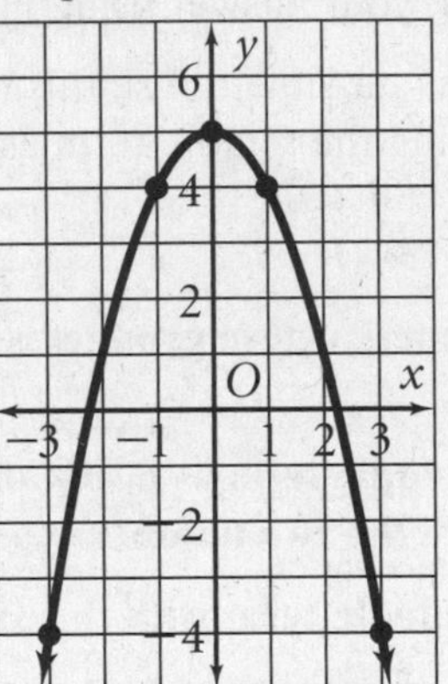

Exercises

Fill in the blanks for each equation. Make a table of values. Then graph each equation.

The parabola opens ______________.

The vertex is shifted ______________ unit(s) from the origin.

1. $y = x^2$
2. $y = 3x^2 + 1$
3. $y = -4x^2$
4. $y = \frac{1}{2}x^2$
5. $y = -\frac{1}{2}x^2 - 3$
6. $y = x^2 + \frac{1}{2}$
7. $y = 2x^2 - 4$
8. $y = -x^2 - 3$
9. $y = -4x^2 + 7$
10. $y = \frac{1}{4}x^2 - 2$

Name ____________________ Class ____________ Date ____________

Review 89

OBJECTIVE: Graphing quadratic functions of the form $y = ax^2 + bx + c$

MATERIALS: Graph paper

To graph the quadratic function $y = ax^2 + bx + c$:

- Find the axis of symmetry by substituting a and b values into the equation $x = -\frac{b}{2a}$. This is also the x-coordinate of the vertex.
- Find the y-coordinate of the vertex by substituting the x-value into the quadratic equation and solving for y.
- For graphs of inequalities, the curve is dashed for $<$ or $>$ and solid for $\leq$ or $\geq$.

Example

Sketch the graph of the equation $f(x) = -3 - 2x + x^2$.

Standard form: $y = x^2 - 2x - 3$

Axis of symmetry: $y = -\frac{b}{2a} = -\frac{(-2)}{2(1)} = \frac{2}{2(1)} = 1$

Vertex: Substitute $x = 1$ into the equation to get y.

$y = (1)^2 - 2(1) - 3 = -4$
vertex: $(1, -4)$

Table of Values		
x	$x^2 - 2x - 3$	y
-2	$4 + 4 - 3$	5
0	$0 - 0 - 3$	-3
2	$4 - 4 - 3$	-3

← y-intercept (row $x = 0$)

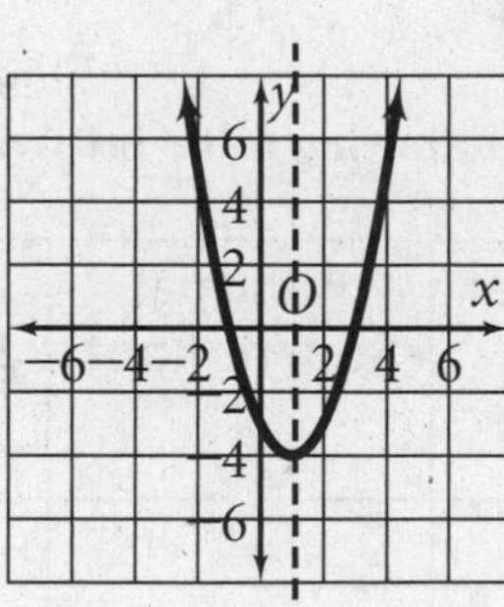

Exercises

Find the following to graph $y + x^2 = 16 + 4x$.

1. Standard form:
2. Axis of symmetry:
3. Vertex:
4. Table of values
5. Graph

Graph each function.

6. $y + x^2 = -1 + 2x$

7. $f(x) = -4x + 3 + x^2$

Name ______________________ Class ______________ Date ______________

Review 90

Finding and Estimating Square Roots

OBJECTIVE: Finding square roots **MATERIALS:** Calculator

- In decimal form, a rational number terminates or repeats.
- In decimal form, an irrational number continues without repeating.

ALGEBRA 1 TOPICS

Example

Complete the following table involving square roots.

Number	Principal Square Root	Negative Square Root	Rational/ Irrational	Perfect Square or $\sqrt{\ }$ Between Which Consecutive Integers
81	9	−9	rational	perfect square
0.25	0.5	−0.5	rational	perfect square
$\frac{4}{9}$	$\frac{2}{3}$	$-\frac{2}{3}$	rational	perfect square
7	2.645 . . .	−2.645 . . .	irrational	between 2 and 3
−17	undefined	undefined	undefined	undefined

Exercises

Complete the following table involving square roots.

1.

Number	Principal Square Root	Negative Square Root	Rational/ Irrational	Perfect Square or $\sqrt{\ }$ Between Which Consecutive Integers
$\frac{1}{64}$				
26				
23				
−36				
$\frac{81}{324}$				

Simplify each expression, and label it as rational or irrational.

2. $\sqrt{100}$

3. $\sqrt{12}$

4. $\sqrt{-14}$

5. $\sqrt{63}$

6. $-\sqrt{0}$

7. $\sqrt{\frac{1}{9}}$

Name ______________________ Class ______________ Date ______________

Review 91

Solving Quadratic Equations

OBJECTIVE: Solving quadratic equations in $ax^2 = c$ form

MATERIALS: Calculator

Quadratic equations written in the form $x^2 = c$ can be solved by finding the square root of each side.

Value of c	No. of Real Solutions	x-Intercepts
$c > 0$	2	$(+\sqrt{c}, 0)(-\sqrt{c}, 0)$
$c = 0$	1	$(0, 0)$
$c < 0$	0	none

Note: Every parabola has two roots, but they are not always real number roots; they could be complex or a double root.

Example

Solve $3x^2 - 48 = 0$.

$3x^2 - 48 + 48 = 0 + 48$ ← **Add 48 to each side.**

$3x^2 = 48$

$x^2 = 16$ ← **Divide each side by 3.**

$x = \pm\sqrt{16}$ ← **Find the square roots.**

$x = \pm 4$ ← **Simplify.**

$3(4)^2 - 48 = 0$ $\quad 3(-4)^2 - 48 = 0$ ← **Check the results in the original equation.**

$3(16) - 48 = 0$ $\quad 3(16) - 48 = 0$

$48 - 48 = 0$ $\quad 48 - 48 = 0$

Exercises

Fill in the following chart to find the solutions to each equation.

	1. $4x^2 = 100$	**2.** $2x^2 - 6 = 0$	**3.** $x^2 + 4 = 0$	**4.** $81x^2 - 5 = 20$
Rewrite in $ax^2 = c$ form.				
Rewrite in $x^2 = \frac{c}{a}$ form.				
Find the square roots.				
Solutions				

Name ______________________ Class ______________ Date ______________

Review 92

Factoring to Solve Quadratic Equations

OBJECTIVE: Solving quadratic equations by factoring

MATERIALS: None

The Zero-Product Property can be used when factoring quadratic equations. It states that if the product of two numbers equals zero, then one of its factors is zero. For example, if $(x - 2)(x + 1) = 0$, then either $(x - 2) = 0$ or $(x + 1) = 0$. This property allows you to solve a quadratic equation.

Example

Solve $2x^2 - x = 3$ by factoring.

$2x^2 - x = 3$

$2x^2 - x - 3 = 0$ ⟵ **Subtract 3 from each side.**

$(2x - 3)(x + 1) = 0$ ⟵ **Factor $2x^2 - x - 3$.**

$2x - 3 = 0$ or $x + 1 = 0$ ⟵ **Use the Zero Product Property.**

$2x = 3$ or $x = -1$ ⟵ **Solve for x.**

$x = \frac{3}{2}$ or $x = -1$

The solutions are $\frac{3}{2}$ and -1.

Check

Substitute $\frac{3}{2}$ for x.

$$\left(2\left(\frac{3}{2}\right) - 3\right)\left(\frac{3}{2} + 1\right) \stackrel{?}{=} 0$$

$$(3 - 3)\left(\frac{5}{2}\right) \stackrel{?}{=} 0$$

$$(0)\left(\frac{5}{2}\right) = 0 \checkmark$$

Substitute -1 for x.

$$(2(-1) - 3)(-1 + 1) \stackrel{?}{=} 0$$

$$(-2 - 3)(0) \stackrel{?}{=} 0$$

$$(-5)(0) = 0 \checkmark$$

Exercises

Solve by factoring.

1. $x^2 + 7x + 10 = 0$

2. $x^2 - x = 12$

3. $x^2 - 5x + 6 = 0$

4. $x^2 - 6x = -8$

5. $2x^2 + 5x + 3 = 0$

6. $3x^2 + 2x - 8 = 0$

7. $x^2 - 3x - 28 = 0$

8. $2x^2 - x - 10 = 0$

9. $6x^2 + 2x = 4$

Name ______________________ Class ______________ Date ______________

Review 93

Completing the Square

OBJECTIVE: Solving quadratic equations by completing the square

MATERIALS: None

Remember that to complete the square, the coefficient of the squared term is 1 and the constant term is moved to the right side of the equation.

Example

Solve by completing the square: $2x^2 - 16x - 40 = 0$

$2x^2 - 16x - 40 = 0$

$x^2 - 8x - 20 = 0$ ⟵ **Divide each side by 2.**

$x^2 - 8x = 20$ ⟵ **Add 20 to each side.**

$x^2 - 8x + 16 = 20 + 16$ ⟵ **Take $\frac{1}{2}$ the coefficient of x, square it, and add to both sides.**

$(x - 4)^2 = 36$ ⟵ **Write the left hand side as a square.**

$\sqrt{(x - 4)^2} = \sqrt{36}$ ⟵ **Take the square root of each side.**

$x - 4 = \pm 6$ ⟵ **Simplify.**

$x - 4 = 6$ or $x - 4 = -6$ ⟵ **Write as two equations.**

$x = 10$ or $x = -2$ ⟵ **Solve.**

Check by substituting $x = 10$ and $x = -2$ into the original equation.

Exercises

Tell what is done in each step of the solution.

1. $3x^2 + 6x - 45 = 0$

   a. $x^2 + 2x - 15 = 0$

   b. $x^2 + 2x = 15$

   c. $x^2 + 2x + 1 = 15 + 1$

   d. $(x + 1)^2 = 16$

   e. $\sqrt{(x + 1)^2} = \sqrt{16}$

   f. $x + 1 = \pm 4$

   g. $x + 1 = 4$ or $x + 1 = -4$

   h. $x = 3$ or $x = -5$

Solve each equation by completing the square. Express all radicals to the nearest hundredth.

2. $x^2 - 10x + 16 = 0$

3. $x^2 - 12x + 32 = 0$

4. $x^2 - 12x + 3 = 0$

5. $x^2 + 8x - 5 = 0$

Name ______________________ Class ______________ Date ______________

Review 94

Using the Quadratic Formula

OBJECTIVE: Using the quadratic formula to solve quadratic equations	**MATERIALS:** Calculator

- The quadratic formula can be used to solve any quadratic equation.
- When the quadratic equation is in standard form ($ax^2 + bx + c = 0$), where $a \neq 0$, the solutions are found by the quadratic formula

  $x = \dfrac{-b \pm \sqrt{b^2 - 4ac}}{2a}$.

ALGEBRA 1 TOPICS

Example

Solve $x^2 + 5x = 14$.

$x^2 + 5x = 14$

$x^2 + 5x - 14 = 0$ ⟵ **Rewrite in standard form.**

$\overset{a}{x^2} + \overset{b}{5x} - \overset{c}{14} = 0$ ⟵ **Write *a, b, c* above the appropriate numbers. (*a* = 1, *b* = 5, *c* = −14)**

$x = \dfrac{-b \pm \sqrt{b^2 - 4ac}}{2a}$ ⟵ **Use the quadratic formula.**

$x = \dfrac{-5 \pm \sqrt{5^2 - 4(1)(-14)}}{2(1)}$ ⟵ **Substitute 1 for *a*, 5 for *b*, and −14 for *c*.**

$x = \dfrac{-5 \pm \sqrt{25 + 56}}{2}$ ⟵ **Solve.**

$x = \dfrac{-5 \pm \sqrt{81}}{2}$ ⟵ **Simplify.**

$x = \dfrac{-5 \pm 9}{2}$

$x = \dfrac{-5 + 9}{2}$ or $x = \dfrac{-5 - 9}{2}$ ⟵ **Write two equations.**

$x = 2$ or $x = -7$ ⟵ **Solve for *x*.**

The solutions are $x = 2$ or $x = -7$.

Exercises

Use the quadratic formula to solve each equation. If necessary, round answers to the nearest hundredth.

1. $3x^2 + 7x + 2 = 0$

2. $x^2 + 3x + 2 = 0$

3. $4y^2 = 3 - 5y$

4. $2 = 11z - 5z^2$

5. $x^2 + 5x = 6$

6. $-3x^2 + x + 5 = 0$

7. $x^2 = 3x + 4$

8. $-4x^2 + x + 7 = 0$

Name ____________________ Class ____________ Date ____________

Review 95

OBJECTIVE: Using the discriminant to find the number of solutions of a quadratic equation

MATERIALS: Calculator

In the quadratic formula $x = \dfrac{-b \pm \sqrt{b^2 - 4ac}}{2a}$, the discriminant is the expression under the radical sign, $b^2 - 4ac$. The discriminant determines how many solutions, or x-intercepts, a quadratic equation has.

- If the discriminant is positive, there are two real solutions.
- If the discriminant is 0, there is one real solution.
- If the discriminant is negative, there are no real solutions.

Example

Find the value of the discriminant and the number of real solutions for each quadratic equation.

$ax^2 + bx + c = 0$	Discriminant ($b^2 - 4ac$)	Number of Solutions	Number of x-intercepts
1. $x^2 + 2x + 3 = 0$	$(2)^2 - 4(1)(3) = -8$	none	none
2. $x^2 - 2x + 1 = 0$	$(-2)^2 - 4(1)(1) = 0$	one	one
3. $x^2 - 2x - 2 = 0$	$(-2)^2 - 4(1)(-2) = 12$	two	two

Exercises

Find the value of the discriminant and the number of solutions for each quadratic equation.

$ax^2 + bx + c = 0$	Discriminant ($b^2 - 4ac$)	Number of Solutions	Number of x-intercepts
1. $2x^2 + 3x + 3 = 0$			
2. $x^2 - 2x + 4 = 0$			
3. $3x^2 - 6x + 3 = 0$			

Find the value of the discriminant and the number of solutions of each equation.

4. $-2x^2 + 4x - 2 = 0$

5. $-\frac{1}{2}x^2 + x + 3 = 0$

6. $5x^2 - 2x + 3 = 0$

Name ____________________ Class ____________ Date ____________

Review 96

Choosing a Linear, Quadratic, or Exponential Model

OBJECTIVE: Choosing a linear, quadratic, or exponential model

MATERIALS: None

When analyzing data to determine whether the model that best fits the data is linear, exponential, or quadratic, use the following guidelines.

Linear ($y = mx + b$)	The y-coordinates have a common difference.
Exponential ($y = a \cdot b^x$)	The y-coordinates have a common ratio.
Quadratic ($y = ax^2 + bx + c$)	The y-coordinates have a common second difference.

Example

Which kind of function best models the data below? Write an equation to model the data.

x	−2	−1	0	1	2
y	$\frac{3}{4}$	$\frac{3}{2}$	3	6	12

The y-coordinates have a common ratio, 2. Notice that each y-coordinate is equal to the previous y-coordinate multiplied by 2. The data is best modeled by an exponential function. To determine the function

$$y = a \cdot b^x,$$

let a = the value of y when $x = 0$;

let b = the common ratio, 2.

$$y = 3 \cdot 2^x$$

Exercises

Determine the function that best models the data. Write an equation to model the data.

1.

x	−2	−1	0	1	2
y	−7	−4	−1	2	5

2.

x	−2	−1	0	1	2
y	−8	−2	0	−2	−8

3.

x	0	1	2	3	4
y	2	$\frac{5}{2}$	3	$\frac{7}{2}$	4

4.

x	−2	−1	0	1	2
y	$-\frac{2}{9}$	$-\frac{2}{3}$	−2	−6	−18

5.

x	−4	−3	−2	−1	0
y	4	$\frac{9}{4}$	1	$\frac{1}{4}$	0

Name ______________________ Class ______________ Date ______________

Review 97

Simplifying Radicals

OBJECTIVE: Simplifying radicals involving products and quotients

MATERIALS: None

The following are three examples of simplifying radicals. Simplifying each radical makes it meet a condition that must be true to show that a radical expression is in its simplest form.

Example

Condition	Not in Simplest Form	How to Simplify	Simplest Form
The Multiplication Property of Square Roots is used to simplify the radical.			
The expression under the radical sign has no perfect square factors other than 1.	$\sqrt{20}$	Rewrite as a product of perfect squares and other factors. $= \sqrt{4 \cdot 5}$ $= \sqrt{4} \cdot \sqrt{5}$	$2\sqrt{5}$
The Division Property of Square Roots is used to simplify the radical.			
The expression under the radical sign is a fraction.	$\sqrt{\frac{16}{25}}$	Separate into two radical expressions. Simplify each separately. $\frac{\sqrt{16}}{\sqrt{25}}$	$\frac{4}{5}$
The denominator contains a radical expression that is not a perfect square	$\frac{3}{\sqrt{2}}$	Rationalize the denominator by multiplying the fraction by a radical expression equal to 1. $= \frac{3}{\sqrt{2}} \cdot \frac{\sqrt{2}}{\sqrt{2}}$	$\frac{3\sqrt{2}}{2}$

Exercises

Simplify each radical expression.

1. $\sqrt{2} \cdot \sqrt{12}$
2. $3\sqrt{5} \cdot 2\sqrt{5}$
3. $4\sqrt{80}$
4. $\sqrt{3} \cdot \sqrt{36}$
5. $\sqrt{18}$
6. $\frac{5}{\sqrt{3}}$
7. $2\sqrt{28}$
8. $2\sqrt{\frac{4}{5}}$
9. $\sqrt{\frac{14}{25}}$
10. $\frac{\sqrt{5}}{\sqrt{64}}$
11. $2\sqrt{\frac{3}{8}}$
12. $\sqrt{\frac{16}{9}}$

Name ________________ Class ________________ Date ________________

Review 98

OBJECTIVE: Finding the lengths of the sides of a right triangle

MATERIALS: None

As you solve problems using the Pythagorean Theorem, keep in mind these ideas.

- In the formula, a and b represent the *legs* of the right triangle.
- The *hypotenuse* is represented by c. This is the side *opposite* the right angle.
- Drawing a picture of the triangle each time is a good strategy for making sure you use the formula correctly.
- Writing a, b, and c on your picture with the values from your problem gives you a visual representation of your problem before you solve it.

Example

Find the length of the missing side: $a = 3$, $b = ■$, $c = 5$.

$c = 5$, $a = 3$, $b = ?$ ⟵ **Draw a triangle and include the values from the problem for *a*, *b*, and *c*.**

$a^2 + b^2 = c^2$ ⟵ **Use the Pythagorean Theorem.**

$3^2 + b^2 = 5^2$ ⟵ **Substitute 3 for *a* and 5 for *c*.**

$9 + b^2 = 25$ ⟵ **Simplify.**

$b^2 = 16$ ⟵ **Subtract 9 from each side.**

$\sqrt{b^2} = \sqrt{16}$ ⟵ **Take the square root of each side.**

$b = 4$ ⟵ **Use a calculator if necessary.**

Exercises

Draw and label a triangle. Find the length of the missing side to the nearest tenth.

1. $a = 6, b = ■, c = 10$

2. $a = ■, b = 4, c = 10$

3. $a = 5, b = 12, c = ■$

Find the length of the missing side to the nearest tenth.

4. $a = ■, b = 5, c = 7$

5. $a = 4, b = ■, c = 9$

6. $a = 7.5, b = 4, c = ■$

7. $a = 5, b = ■, c = 12$

8. $a = 8, b = ■, c = 17$

9. $a = 6, b = 8, c = ■$

10. $a = ■, b = 24, c = 25$

11. $a = 4, b = 3, c = ■$

12. $a = 9, b = ■, c = 15$

Name ______________________ Class ______________ Date ______________

Review 99

The Distance and Midpoint Formulas

OBJECTIVE: Finding the distance between two points in a coordinate plane; finding the coordinates of the midpoint of two points

MATERIALS: None

The following strategies may be used to help you apply the distance formula or the midpoint formula correctly.

- Underline the x-coordinates.
- Circle the y-coordinates.

Example

Find the distance between (2, 5) and (−1, −3). Round your answer to the nearest tenth.

$(\underline{2},⑤), (\underline{-1},\text{⊖3})$ ← **Underline the x-coordinates and circle the y-coordinates.**

$d = \sqrt{(x_2 - x_1)^2 + (y_2 - y_1)^2}$ ← **Write the distance formula.**

$d = \sqrt{(2 - (-1))^2 + (5 - (-3))^2}$ ← **Substitute the underlined numbers for x-coordinates and the circled numbers for the y-coordinates, in corresponding order.**

$d = \sqrt{3^2 + 8^2}$ ← **Simplify.**

$d = \sqrt{9 + 64}$

$d = \sqrt{73}$

$d = 8.5$ ← **Use a calculator. Round to the nearest tenth.**

Exercises

Find the distance between each pair of points. Round your answers to the nearest tenth.

1. (4, −2), (0, 4)
2. (2, 5), (−1, −3)
3. (4, −2), (−3, 5)
4. (−3, −2), (4, −1)

The midpoint of a line segment with endpoints $A(x_1, y_1)$ and $B(x_2, y_2)$ is $\left(\frac{x_1 + x_2}{2}, \frac{y_1 + y_2}{2}\right)$. Find the midpoint of $\overline{AB}$.

5. $A(2, 4)$ and $B(0, 6)$
6. $A(-6, -2)$ and $B(4, -1)$
7. $A(-2, 4)$ and $B(-6, 8)$
8. $A(-3, 6)$ and $B(-5, 0)$

Name ______________________ Class ______________ Date ______________

Review 100

Operations with Radical Expressions

OBJECTIVE: Simplifying radical expressions **MATERIALS:** None

- Underline radicals not in simplest form.
- Circle like terms. They can be combined.

ALGEBRA 1 TOPICS

Example

Simplify $\sqrt{27} + 2\sqrt{3}$.

$\sqrt{27} + 2\sqrt{3}$ ← **Underline radicals not in simplest form.**

$\sqrt{9 \cdot 3} + 2\sqrt{3}$ ← **Rewrite as a product of perfect squares and other factors. 9 is a perfect square and a factor of 27.**

$\sqrt{9} \cdot \sqrt{3} + 2\sqrt{3}$ ← **Use the Multiplication Property of Square Roots.**

$3\sqrt{3} + 2\sqrt{3}$ ← **Simplify $\sqrt{9}$.**

$3\sqrt{3} + 2\sqrt{3}$ ← **Circle like terms.**

$5\sqrt{3}$ ← **Combine like terms by adding the coefficients.**

Example

Simplify $\sqrt{5}(2 + \sqrt{10})$

$\sqrt{5}(2 + \sqrt{10}) = 2\sqrt{5} + \sqrt{50}$ ← **Use the Distributive Property.**

$= 2\sqrt{5} + \sqrt{25} \cdot \sqrt{2}$ ← **Use the Multiplication Property of Square Roots.**

$= 2\sqrt{5} + 5\sqrt{2}$ ← **Simplify.**

Exercises

Underline radicals not in simplest form and circle like terms. Simplify each expression.

1. $3\sqrt{24} - 2\sqrt{6}$

2. $6\sqrt{3} + 4\sqrt{3}$

3. $\sqrt{27} + \sqrt{3}$

4. $3\sqrt{12} - 2\sqrt{3}$

5. $10\sqrt{6} - 3\sqrt{6}$

6. $6\sqrt{7} - \sqrt{28}$

Simplify each expression.

7. $\sqrt{5}(\sqrt{5} + 2)$

8. $(\sqrt{2} + 1)(\sqrt{2} - 1)$

9. $\sqrt{2}(\sqrt{2} - \sqrt{3})$

10. $(2\sqrt{3} + \sqrt{5})^2$

11. $(3\sqrt{2} - \sqrt{5})(2\sqrt{5} + 4\sqrt{2})$

12. $(2\sqrt{3} + 1)(\sqrt{3})$

Name ______________________ Class ______________ Date ______________

Review 101

Solving Radical Equations

OBJECTIVE: Solving equations that contain radicals	**MATERIALS:** Index cards or pieces of paper of a similar size

A radical equation has a *variable* under the radical sign. The radical expression must be alone on one side of the equal sign before squaring.

Example

Jubal solved a radical equation, showing all the steps. He wrote each step on a separate index card. Then he dropped the pack of cards! Number each of his cards to show the correct order of his steps.

The number in the lower left corner shows the correct order for the steps.

$\sqrt{y} = 4$ **3.**	$3 + \sqrt{y} - 3 = 7 - 3$ **2.**	$y = 16$ **5.**
The solution of $3 + \sqrt{y} = 7$ is 16. **8.**	$(\sqrt{y})^2 = (4)^2$ **4.**	$3 + \sqrt{16} \stackrel{?}{=} 7$ **6.**
$3 + 4 = 7$ ✔ **7.**	$3 + \sqrt{y} = 7$ **1.**	

Exercises

Solve each radical equation.

1. $\sqrt{3a} - 9 = 0$ **2.** $\sqrt{n - 2} = 3$ **3.** $c = \sqrt{3c - 8}$

4. $\sqrt{b} - 6 = -2\sqrt{b}$ **5.** $s = \sqrt{24 - 10s}$ **6.** $\sqrt{5x - 1} = \sqrt{3x + 9}$

7. $\sqrt{3y + 1} = 6$ **8.** $\sqrt{5x} - 3 = 2$ **9.** $\sqrt{2x + 1} = 5$

ALGEBRA 1 TOPICS

Name ______________________ Class ______________ Date ______________

Review 102

Graphing Square Root Functions

OBJECTIVE: Graphing and exploring square root functions

MATERIALS: Graph paper

Make a table of the values for x and y. These values can be plotted as ordered pairs.

Example

Make a table and then graph the function $y = \sqrt{6 + x}$.

Step 1 Select a domain that makes the expression under the radical greater than or equal to zero.

$6 + x \geq 0$

$x \geq -6$

Domain $= -6, -5, -2, 3, \ldots$

Step 2 Make a table like the one below. Replace x with each member of the domain to find y.

Domain	Replace *x* to find *y*.	Range
x	$\sqrt{6 + x}$	y
-6	$\sqrt{6 + (-6)} = \sqrt{0}$	0
-5	$\sqrt{6 + (-5)} = \sqrt{1}$	1
-2	$\sqrt{6 + (-2)} = \sqrt{4}$	2
3	$\sqrt{6 + 3} = \sqrt{9}$	3

Step 3 Use the values for x and y from the table to graph the function.

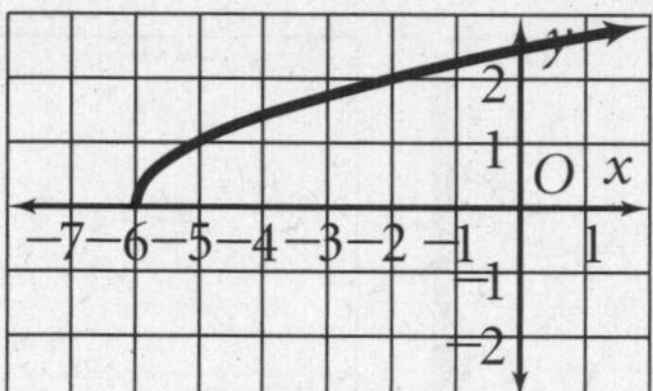

What do all of the y-values have in common? They are all positive.

Exercises

Graph each function using Steps 1–3.

1. $y = \sqrt{4 + x}$
2. $f(x) = \sqrt{x - 2}$
3. $y = \sqrt{x - 3}$

Graph each function.

4. $y = \sqrt{x - 1} + 2$
5. $f(x) = \sqrt{x} - 4$
6. $f(x) = \sqrt{5 - x} + 1$
7. $f(x) = \sqrt{x - 1} - 2$
8. $f(x) = \sqrt{x} + 3$
9. $f(x) = \sqrt{1 - x} + 3$
10. $f(x) = \sqrt{x + 5} - 1$
11. $f(x) = \sqrt{3x + 1} + 2$
12. $f(x) = \sqrt{3 - 2x} + 2$

Name ____________________ Class ____________ Date ____________

Review 103

OBJECTIVE: Exploring and calculating trigonometric ratios

MATERIALS: None

To make sure you are applying a trigonometric formula correctly, you should label the triangle's adjacent leg, opposite leg, and hypotenuse before you get started. Remember these key points:

- The *hypotenuse* is *opposite* the right angle.
- *Adjacent* means *next to.*
- Use a pencil when labeling sides so that your marks can be erased when the problem is for a different angle.

Example

For $\triangle ABC$ find the sine, cosine, and tangent of $\angle A$ and $\angle B$.

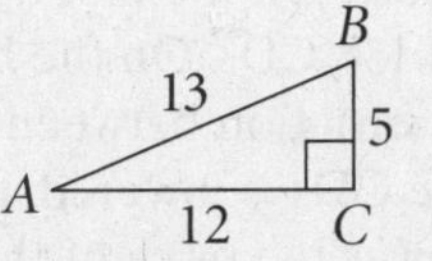

For $\angle A$

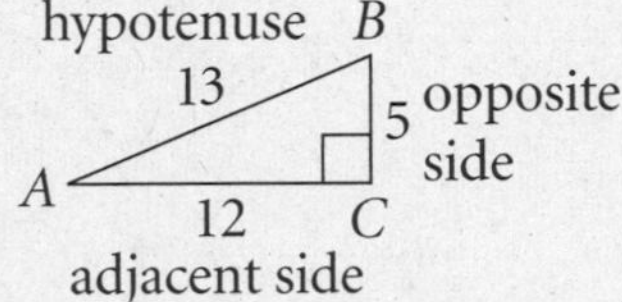

Redraw and label the sides of $\triangle ABC$ for sine, cosine, and tangent of $\angle A$ and $\angle B$.

For $\angle B$

hypotenuse B
13
5 adjacent side
A
12 C
opposite side

For ∠A	Trigonometric Ratios	For ∠B
$\sin A = \frac{5}{13}$	sine $= \dfrac{\text{length of opposite leg}}{\text{length of hypotenuse}}$	$\sin B = \frac{12}{13}$
$\cos A = \frac{12}{13}$	cosine $= \dfrac{\text{length of adjacent leg}}{\text{length of hypotenuse}}$	$\cos B = \frac{5}{13}$
$\tan A = \frac{5}{12}$	tangent $= \dfrac{\text{length of opposite leg}}{\text{length of hypotenuse}}$	$\tan B = \frac{12}{5}$

Exercises

Use $\triangle ABC$ to evaluate each expression.

B
15
9
A
C
12

1. $\sin A$ **2.** $\cos A$ **3.** $\tan A$

4. $\sin B$ **5.** $\tan B$ **6.** $\cos A$

Name ________ Class ________ Date ________

Review 104

OBJECTIVE: Solving inverse variations **MATERIALS:** None

- The relationship shown by the equation $xy = k$, where $k \neq 0$, is called an inverse variation.
- The two quantities x and y multiplied together result in a constant k. As one quantity increases, the other decreases.

Example

Two young graduates from the business school of the University of Texas decided to open a music store. On the first day of business, they charged \$12.00 for a CD. They sold 138 CDs. On the basis of their research, they believe there is an inverse variation between sales and price. If they are correct and the price of the CDs is lowered, the number sold should increase. They decide to lower the price of the CDs to \$11.50. How many CDs can they expect to sell?

Price	No. Sold
\$12.00	138
\$11.50	x

← **Put the data into a table.**

← **Let x represent the missing quantity.**

(Price 1)(No. sold at price 1) = (Price 2)(No. sold at price 2) ← **Write an equation showing the relationship of the variables.**

$(\$12.00)(138) = (\$11.50)(x)$ ← **Substitute the values.**

$1656 = 11.5x$

$x = 144$ ← **Solve for x.**

Dropping the price by \$.50 will result in selling 144 CDs. This is an increase of 6 CDs.

Exercises

Refer to the example to answer each question.

1. How many CDs can the owners expect to sell if they drop the price to \$11.00? What if they raise the price to \$12.50? (Round your answers to the nearest whole number.)
2. If the owners want to sell 162 CDs, what price should they charge for each?
3. Make a table with the data from Exercises 1 and 2.

Name ______________________ Class ______________ Date ______________

Review 105

Graphing Rational Functions

OBJECTIVE: Graphing rational functions	**MATERIALS:** None

A vertical asymptote occurs at a value for which the function is not defined. The function $y = \frac{2}{x + 1}$ is undefined at $x = -1$. Therefore, the vertical asymptote is $x = -1$.

Example

Graph the rational function $y = \frac{4}{x + 2} - 1$.

Step 1 Find the vertical asymptotes.

$x + 2 = 0$ ⟵ **Set the denominator equal to zero.**

$x = -2$ ⟵ **Solve for x.**

Step 2 Find the horizontal asymptotes.

From the form of the function ($y = \frac{a}{x - b} + c$) we know there is a horizontal asymptote at $y = -1$.

Step 3 Make a table of values using values of x near -2.

x	−6	−4	−3	−1	1	2	0
y	−2	−3	−5	3	$\frac{1}{3}$	0	1

Step 4 Graph the data.

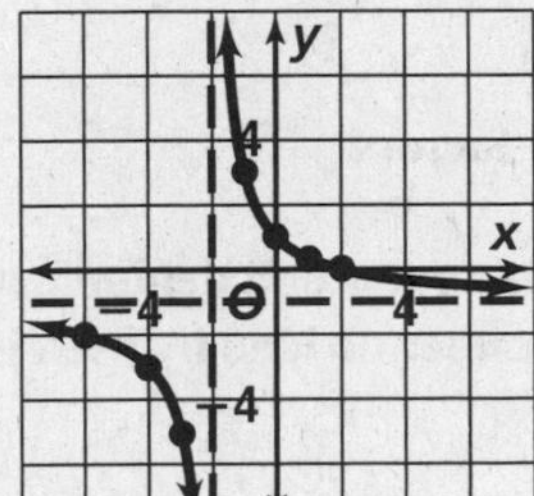

Exercises

Graph each rational function.

1. $y = \frac{4}{x + 2}$
2. $y = \frac{2}{x - 3} + 2$
3. $y = \frac{2}{x} + 5$
4. $y = \frac{1}{x} - 5$
5. $y = \frac{3}{x} + 2$
6. $y = \frac{2}{x + 2} + 1$

ALGEBRA 1 TOPICS

Name ______________________ Class ______________ Date ______________

Review 106

Simplifying Rational Expressions

OBJECTIVE: Simplifying rational expressions **MATERIALS:** None

ALGEBRA 1 TOPICS

Example

Simplify $\frac{3x + 6}{2x + 4}$.

$3x + 6 = 3(x + 2)$ ⟵ **Factor the numerator.**

$2x + 4 = 2(x + 2)$ ⟵ **Factor the denominator.**

$= \frac{3(x + 2)}{2(x + 2)}$ ⟵ **Rewrite the expression in terms of the factors.**

$= \frac{3\cancel{(x + 2)}}{2\cancel{(x + 2)}}$ ⟵ **Mark through common factors in the numerator and denominator. These two factors cancel because any number divided by itself equals 1.**

$= \frac{3}{2}$ ⟵ **Simplify.**

Example

Simplify $\frac{4x - 24}{x^2 - 9x + 18}$.

$4x - 24 = 4(x - 6)$ ⟵ **Factor the numerator.**

$x^2 - 9x + 18 = (x - 6)(x - 3)$ ⟵ **Factor the denominator.**

$= \frac{4(x - 6)}{(x - 6)(x - 3)}$ ⟵ **Rewrite the expression in terms of the factors.**

$= \frac{4\cancel{(x - 6)}}{\cancel{(x - 6)}(x - 3)}$ ⟵ **Mark through common factors in the numerator and denominator. These two factors cancel because any number divided by itself is 1.**

$= \frac{4}{x - 3}$ ⟵ **Simplify.**

Exercises

Simplify each expression.

1. $\frac{5x - 15}{3x - 9}$ **2.** $\frac{x + 7}{2x + 14}$ **3.** $\frac{2x - 2}{x - 1}$

4. $\frac{5x - 20}{x^2 - 16}$ **5.** $\frac{x^2 - 6x - 16}{x^2 - x - 6}$ **6.** $\frac{6x^2 + 3x}{2x^2 + 11x + 5}$

Name ______________________ Class ______________ Date ______________

Review 107

Multiplying and Dividing Rational Expressions

OBJECTIVE: Multiplying and dividing rational expressions	**MATERIALS:** None

When multiplying rational expressions, look for common factors.

Example

Multiply $\frac{3x - 6}{5x - 20} \cdot \frac{10x - 40}{27x - 54}$.

$$\frac{3x - 6}{5x - 20} \cdot \frac{10x - 40}{27x - 54} = \frac{3(x - 2)}{5(x - 4)} \cdot \frac{10(x - 4)}{27(x - 2)}$$ ⟵ **Factor each expression.**

$$= \frac{\cancel{3}\cancel{(x - 2)}}{\cancel{5}\cancel{(x - 4)}} \cdot \frac{\cancel{10}^{2}\cancel{(x - 4)}}{\cancel{27}_{9}\cancel{(x - 2)}}$$ ⟵ **Divide out common factors and reduce fractions.**

$$= \frac{2}{9}$$ ⟵ **Simplify.**

When dividing rational expressions, multiply by the reciprocal. The reciprocal of a fraction is the fraction with the numerator and denominator interchanged.

Example

Divide $\frac{x^2 + x}{3x - 15} \div \frac{x^2 + 2x + 1}{6x - 30}$.

$$\frac{x^2 + x}{3x - 15} \div \frac{x^2 + 2x + 1}{6x - 30} = \frac{x^2 + x}{3x - 15} \cdot \frac{6x - 30}{x^2 + 2x + 1}$$ ⟵ **Multiply by the reciprocal.**

$$= \frac{x(x + 1)}{3(x - 5)} \cdot \frac{6(x - 5)}{(x + 1)(x + 1)}$$ ⟵ **Factor the numerators and denominators.**

$$= \frac{x\cancel{(x + 1)}}{\cancel{3}\cancel{(x - 5)}} \cdot \frac{\cancel{6}^{2}\cancel{(x - 5)}}{\cancel{(x + 1)}(x + 1)}$$ ⟵ **Divide out common factors.**

$$= \frac{2x}{x + 1}$$ ⟵ **Simplify.**

Exercises

Simplify.

1. $\frac{x^2 - x}{2x + 4} \cdot \frac{x + 2}{x}$

2. $\frac{x^2 + x}{x^2 + 8x + 7} \cdot (x + 7)$

3. $\frac{x^2 - 1}{x^2 + 4x + 3} \div \frac{x - 1}{x^2 + 2x - 3}$

4. $\frac{x^2 - 9}{5x + 15} \div \frac{x - 3}{x + 3}$

5. $\frac{x^2 - x - 30}{6x - 36} \div \frac{5x + 25}{x}$

6. $\frac{x^2 - 9}{x^2 + 4x - 12} \div \frac{x^2 + 2x - 3}{x^2 + 5x - 6}$

Name ______________________ Class ______________ Date ______________

Review 108

Dividing Polynomials

OBJECTIVE: Dividing polynomials **MATERIALS:** None

The procedure for dividing two polynomials is similar to the one for dividing whole numbers.

If the dividend or the divisor has missing terms, remember to insert these terms with zero coefficients.

ALGEBRA 1 TOPICS

Example

$(x^2 - 5x + 8) \div (x - 3)$

$$\begin{array}{r} x \phantom{{}-5x+8} \\ x-3\overline{)x^2 - 5x + 8} \\ \underline{x^2 - 3x} \phantom{{}+8} \\ -2x + 8 \end{array}$$

← **Think $x\overline{)x^2} = \frac{x^2}{x} = x$.**

← **Multiply $x(x - 3) = x^2 - 3x$.**

← **Subtract $(x^2 - 5x) - (x^2 - 3x) = -2x$, and bring down the 8.**

Repeat the process.

$$\begin{array}{r} x - 2 \\ x-3\overline{)x^2 - 5x + 8} \\ \underline{x^2 - 3x} \phantom{{}+8} \\ -2x + 8 \\ \underline{-2x + 6} \\ 2 \end{array}$$

← **Think $x\overline{)-2x} = \frac{-2x}{x} = -2$.**

← **Multiply $-2(x - 3) = -2x + 6$.**

← **Subtract $(-2x + 8) - (-2x + 6) = 2$. The remainder is 2.**

The answer is $x - 2 + \frac{2}{x - 3}$.

Exercises

Divide.

1. $(x^2 + 5x + 6) \div (x + 3)$

2. $(2x^2 + 5x - 1) \div (2x - 1)$

3. $(x^3 - 8) \div (x + 2)$

4. $(x^3 - 2x + 1) \div (x - 1)$

5. $(x^2 - 8x + 16) \div (x - 4)$

6. $(6x^2 + 42x + 60) \div (x + 4)$

7. $(2x^2 - 2x - 24) \div (x + 3)$

8. $(2x^3 + 17x^2 + 38x + 15) \div (x + 5)$

9. $(x^3 + 7x^2 + 8x - 16) \div (x - 2)$

10. $(4x^3 + 22x^2 + 36x + 18) \div (x + 3)$

Name ______________________ Class ______________ Date ______________

Review 109

Adding and Subtracting Rational Expressions

OBJECTIVE: Adding and subtracting rational expressions

MATERIALS: None

Use the flowchart to add and subtract rational expressions.

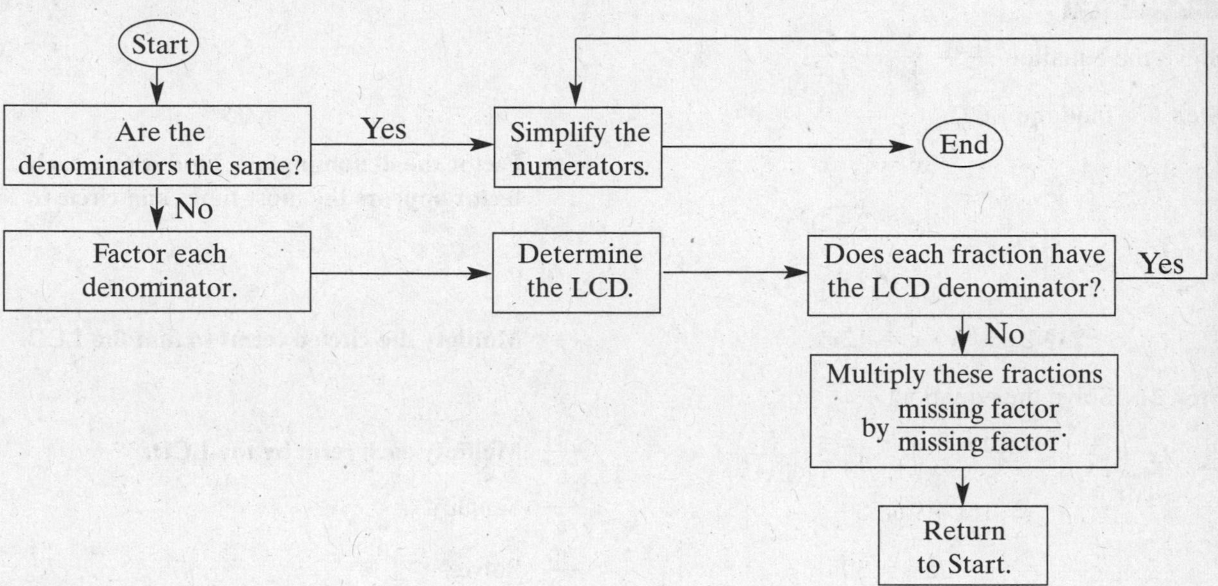

ALGEBRA 1 TOPICS

Example

Simplify $\frac{2x}{x^2 - 1} + \frac{3}{x - 1}$ by following the flowchart.

$x^2 - 1 = (x - 1)(x + 1)$ ← **Factor each denominator. If a denominator is already simplified, rewrite it in a set of parentheses.**

$x - 1 = (x - 1)$

$(x - 1)(x + 1)$ ← **Determine the LCD.**

$\frac{3}{x - 1} \cdot \frac{(x + 1)}{(x + 1)} = \frac{3x + 3}{x^2 - 1}$ ← **The first fraction already has the LCD for a denominator, but the second one does not. Multiply the second fraction by the factor it is missing.**

$\frac{2x}{x^2 - 1} + \frac{3x + 3}{x^2 - 1} = \frac{2x + 3x + 3}{x^2 - 1}$ ← **Simplify the numerators.**

$= \frac{5x + 3}{x^2 - 1}$

Exercises

Simplify the following using the flowchart.

1. $\frac{x + 1}{x^2 - 4} + 3$

2. $\frac{2x - 5}{x^2 + 3x + 2} + \frac{4}{x + 2}$

3. $\frac{3z + 2}{16 - z^2} + \frac{3}{z - 4}$

4. $\frac{x + 1}{x + 5} - \frac{5}{x^2 + 6x + 5}$

5. $\frac{1}{x^2 - 9} + \frac{4}{x + 3}$

6. $\frac{x + 1}{x + 3x + 2} + \frac{2}{x + 2}$

Name ____________ Class ____________ Date ____________

Review 110

Solving Rational Equations

OBJECTIVE: Solving equations involving rational expressions

MATERIALS: None

ALGEBRA 1 TOPICS

Example

Solve the equation $\frac{4}{3x} + \frac{3}{4x} = \frac{5}{2x^2}$.

Step 1 Find the LCD.

$3x = \textcircled{3} \cdot x$ ← **Factor the denominators. Find where each factor appears the most times and circle it.**

$4x = \textcircled{2 \cdot 2} \cdot x$

$2x^2 = 2 \cdot \textcircled{x \cdot x}$

$3 \cdot 2 \cdot 2 \cdot x \cdot x = 12x^2$ ← **Multiply the circled terms to find the LCD.**

Step 2 Solve the equation.

$12x^2\left(\frac{4}{3x}\right) + 12x^2\left(\frac{3}{4x}\right) = 12x^2\left(\frac{5}{2x^2}\right)$ ← **Multiply each term by the LCD.**

$16x + 9 = 30$ ← **Simplify.**

$25x = 30$ ← **Solve.**

$x = \frac{6}{5}$

Exercises

Solve each equation.

1. $\frac{3}{2x} + \frac{5}{6x} = \frac{4}{5x^2}$
2. $\frac{2}{3x} + \frac{4}{5} = \frac{3}{2x}$
3. $\frac{6x}{5} - \frac{1}{2} = \frac{2x}{3}$
4. $\frac{2}{5x} - \frac{5}{2x} = \frac{3}{5x^2}$
5. $\frac{3}{y-3} = \frac{3}{y^2-9}$
6. $\frac{5}{2x-2} = \frac{15}{x^2-1}$
7. $\frac{1}{m-1} = \frac{3}{m^2-1}$
8. $\frac{x}{x-2} = \frac{3x}{x+2}$
9. $\frac{4}{x} + 1 = \frac{6}{x}$
10. $\frac{x+2}{3} = x - 2$
11. $\frac{5}{x} - \frac{4}{x} = 8 + \frac{1}{x}$
12. $\frac{11}{x} + \frac{13}{x} = 12$
13. $\frac{x}{2x} + \frac{2}{4x} = \frac{5x}{x}$
14. $\frac{9}{x} + \frac{6}{5x} = \frac{6}{2x^2}$
15. $\frac{5}{3x} - \frac{x}{x^2} = \frac{1}{6x^2}$
16. $\frac{x}{x+1} + 2 = 5$
17. $\frac{2}{x-5} + 1 = \frac{5}{x-5}$
18. $\frac{21}{x^2} - \frac{10}{x} = \frac{15}{x^2}$
19. $\frac{3}{2x} - \frac{2}{x^2} = \frac{2}{x}$
20. $\frac{3}{x^2-9} = \frac{2}{x-3}$
21. $\frac{5}{x^2-4} + \frac{2}{x-2} = \frac{3}{x+2}$

Name ______________________ Class ______________ Date ______________

Review 111

OBJECTIVE: Using permutations to count outcomes

MATERIALS: Calculator

Think of the Multiplication Counting Principle as choices · choices · choices . . .

Example

You are hosting a New Year's party at which a total of seven people are present. You decide to distribute gag gifts in the following way: Guests will pick a number from a jar and will open a gift in order of their numbers. In how many possible ways can the gifts be distributed?

Person	No. of Choices
1	7
2	6
3	5
4	4
5	3
6	2
7	1

The number of possible ways in which the gifts can be distributed is $7 \cdot 6 \cdot 5 \cdot 4 \cdot 3 \cdot 2 \cdot 1 = 7! = 5040$

The next year, you decide to make your party more interesting. Now, Person 1 will open a present. Person 2 will choose between opening a new present or taking the present that person 1 opened. If Person 2 takes Person 1's gift, Person 1 gets to open another. Person 3 can open a new present or can take an already opened gift. In how many ways can the gifts be distributed now?

Person	No. of Choices
1	7
2	7
3	7
4	7
5	7
6	7
7	7

Now each person will have seven gifts to choose from, counting both opened and unopened gifts. The number of possible distributions of gifts is now

$7 \cdot 7 \cdot 7 \cdot 7 \cdot 7 \cdot 7 \cdot 7 = 7^7 = 823{,}543$.

Exercises

For each situation, make a table and calculate the number of possible gift distributions.

1. There are 11 guests. Each chooses in turn from the unopened gifts.
2. There are 11 guests. Each chooses any gift, opened or unopened.
3. There are 14 guests. Each chooses in turn from the unopened gifts.
4. There are 14 guests. Each chooses any gift, opened or unopened.

Name ______________________ Class ______________ Date ______________

Review 112

OBJECTIVE: Finding combinations **MATERIALS:** Calculator

The expression ${}_nC_r$ represents the number of combinations of n objects arranged r at a time. Your calculator allows you to calculate ${}_nC_r$ quickly.

Example

You have 12 CDs in your collection. You select 4 CDs at random to take to a party. How many different sets of CDs could you select?

${}_{12}C_4$ ← **Write the expression.**

= 12 MATH ◄ ▼ ▼ ENTER 4 ENTER ← **Use these calculator keystrokes to find ${}_{12}C_4$.**

= 495 ← **Write the answer.**

There are 495 different combinations possible.

Exercises

Use a calculator to solve each combination problem.

1. You are hosting a dinner party. You are making a salad for each guest from lettuce and three other ingredients. The other ingredients that the guests may choose from are tomatoes, cucumbers, mushrooms, croutons, and bacon bits. How many different salads can be made?

2. You have 12 players on your volleyball team. How many different combinations of 6 players can the coach choose?

3. There are 11 girls and 9 boys trying out for the cheerleading squad at the high school. The squad will contain 5 boys and 5 girls.

   a. How many different combinations of girls are possible?

   b. How many different combinations of boys are possible?

4. You have a list of 20 errands to do by the end of the day. By 8:00 P.M., you have completed 6 of the 20 errands. How many different combinations of errands could you have completed?

5. Five students are running for student council. Only three students can be elected. How many different combinations of students are possible?

Name ______________________ Class ______________ Date ______________

Review 113

Patterns and Inductive Reasoning

OBJECTIVE: Using inductive reasoning to make conjectures	**MATERIALS:** Pennies

Example

Describe the next two figures in the sequence.

, , , . . .

Each pile of pennies has two more than the preceding pile, so the next pile will have seven pennies, followed by a pile of nine pennies.

Exercises

Use pennies to model the next two figures in each sequence. Then draw a sketch of the two new figures. Show a maximum of ten coins in one stack.

1. 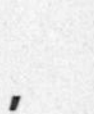, ,      , . . .

2. , , ,  , . . .

3. ,  ,  , . . .

4. , , , . . .

5. , , . . .

6. , ,  , . . .

GEOMETRY TOPICS

Name ______________________ Class ______________ Date ______________

Review 114

Points, Lines, and Planes

OBJECTIVE: Understanding basic terms and postulates of geometry

MATERIALS: Colored pencils or markers

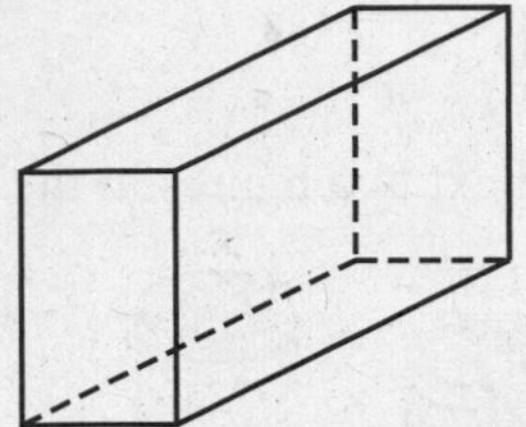

Example

Label the figure at the right as indicated.

a. Label three points that are coplanar as *A, B,* and *C.*

b. Label three points that are collinear as *X, Y,* and *Z.*

c. Trace two intersecting lines, and label their point of intersection as *T.*

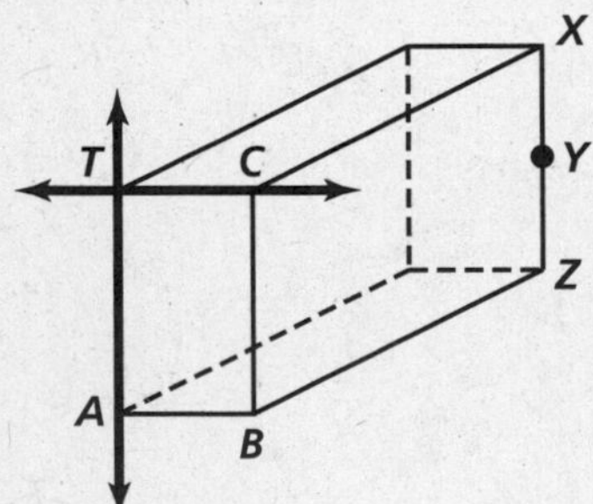

GEOMETRY TOPICS

Exercises

Using colored pencils, label and shade the figure at the right as indicated.

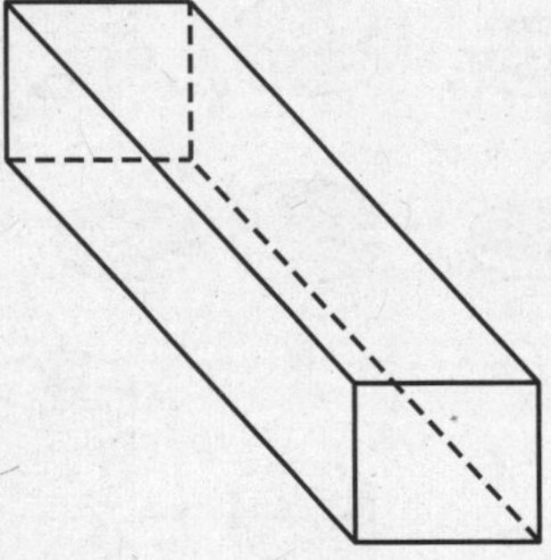

1. With a yellow pencil, shade a plane. Then label three noncollinear points on the plane as *R, S,* and *T.*
2. With an orange pencil, shade a plane that intersects the plane you shaded yellow.
3. Describe the intersection of the planes you shaded yellow and orange.
4. With a red pencil, label four points that are coplanar as *E, F, G,* and *H.*
5. With a blue pencil, label three points that are collinear as *P, Q,* and *R.*
6. With a brown pencil, label four points that are not coplanar as *W, X, Y,* and *Z.*

Use the grid at the right.

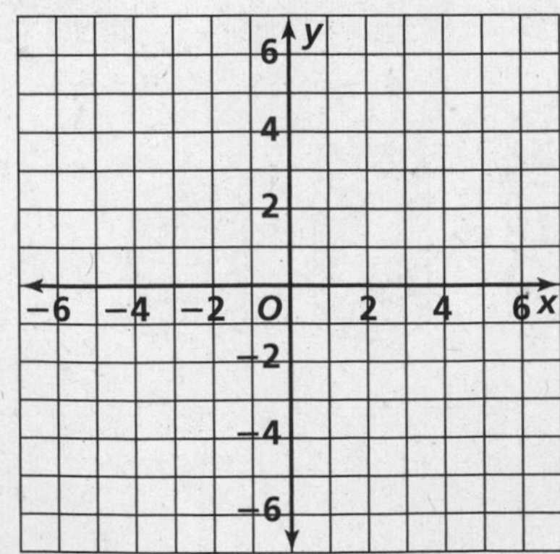

7. Graph the following points on the grid: $P(-1, -1)$, $Q(0, 4)$, $R(-3, -5)$, $S(2, 5)$, and $T(3, -4)$.
8. Name three noncollinear points.
9. Name three collinear points.
10. Name two intersecting lines.

Name ______________________ Class ______________ Date ______________

Review 115

Segments, Rays, Parallel Lines, and Planes

OBJECTIVE: Recognizing parallel lines and parallel planes

MATERIALS: None

Example

Name two pairs of parallel lines.

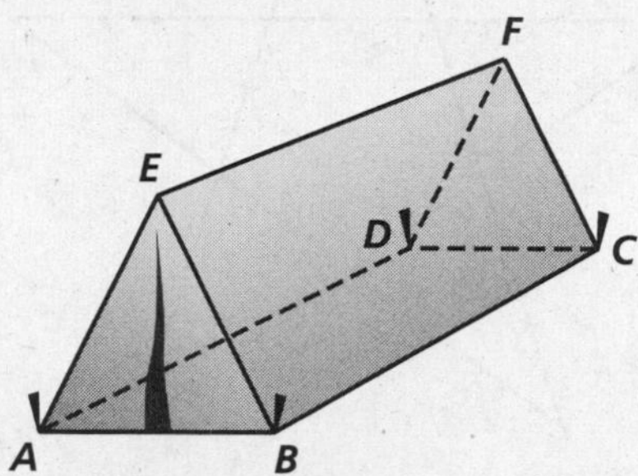

$\overleftrightarrow{EF}$ and $\overleftrightarrow{BC}$ are parallel because they are coplanar lines that do not intersect. So are $\overleftrightarrow{AE}$ and $\overleftrightarrow{DF}$.

Exercises

For Exercises 1–7, name the lines or planes indicated.

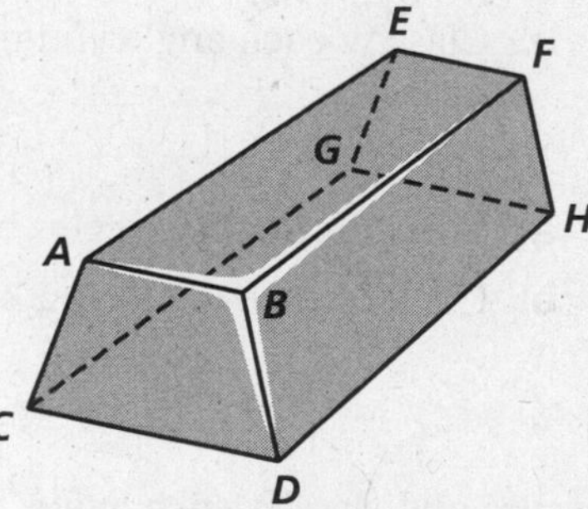

1. Name a pair of parallel lines.
2. Name a pair of skew lines.
3. Name a pair of lines that are neither parallel lines nor skew lines.
4. Name a pair of parallel planes.
5. Name a pair of planes that intersect in a line.
6. Name three planes that intersect at a point.
7. Name a pair of skew lines different from the pair named in Exercise 2.

Draw a sketch for each of the following.

8. three parallel lines
9. two skew lines
10. two intersecting planes
11. two parallel planes
12. three intersecting lines
13. two parallel planes intersected by a line

GEOMETRY TOPICS

Review 116

OBJECTIVE: Finding the measure of an angle **MATERIALS:** Protractor

Example

Measure and classify each angle formed by the five points of the star.

Measuring with a protractor shows that each angle is about 36°. Because each angle is less than 90°, each angle is an acute angle.

Exercises

The small stars illustrate which type of angle to measure. Use the large star when actually measuring the angles.

1. **a.** Measure the five angles on the inside of the pentagon that is formed.
   b. Classify each angle you measured.

2. **a.** Measure two of the angles on the outside of the pentagon that is formed.
   b. Classify each angle you measured.

3. **a.** Measure the five angles between two points of the star.
   b. Classify each angle you measured.

Measure and classify each angle.

4. 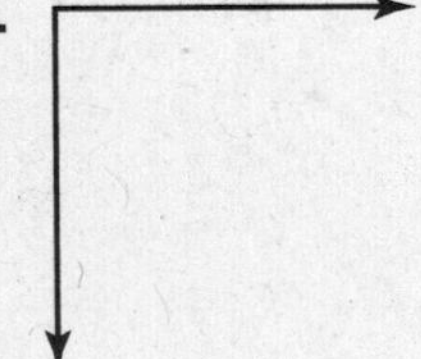

5. 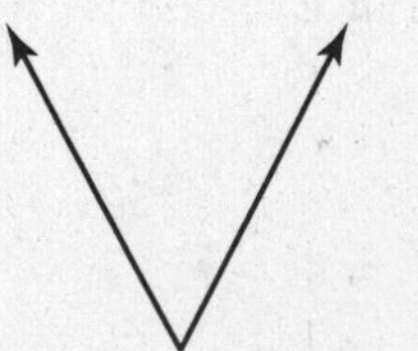

6. 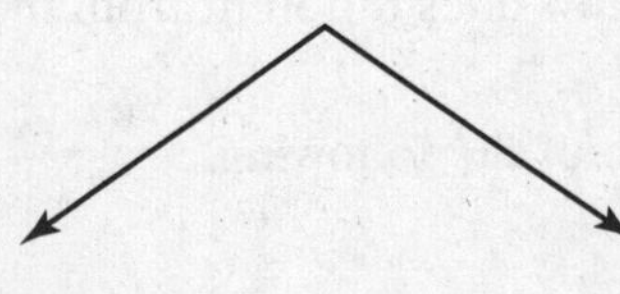

7. 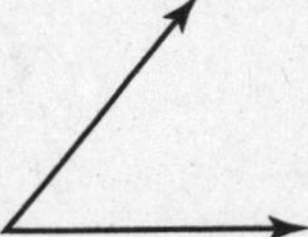

8. 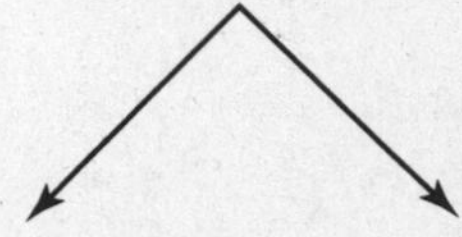

9. 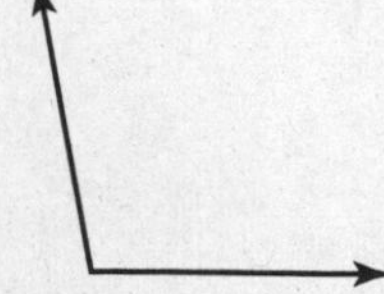

Name ______________________ Class ______________ Date ______________

Review 117

Basic Constructions

OBJECTIVE: Using a compass and straightedge to construct angles

MATERIALS: Compass, straightedge

Example

Construct $\angle TRQ$ so that $m\angle TRQ = m\angle X + m\angle Y$.

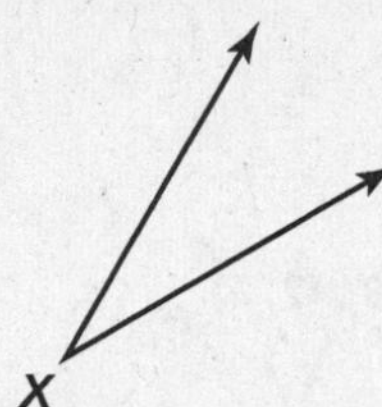

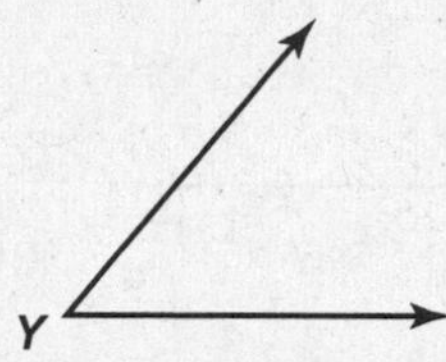

First, construct $\angle PRQ$ so that $m\angle PRQ = m\angle X$.

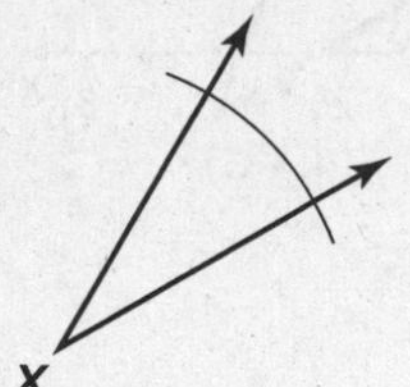

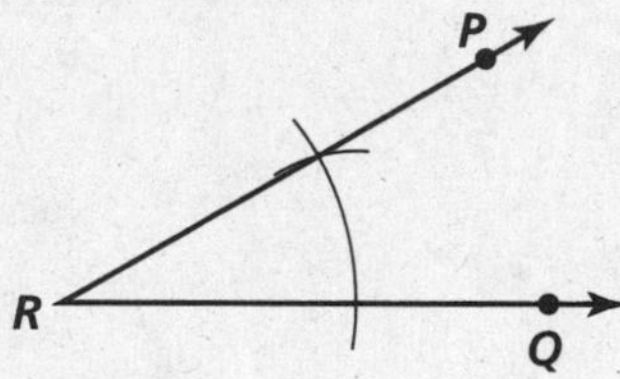

Second, construct $\angle TRP$ so that $m\angle TRP = m\angle Y$.

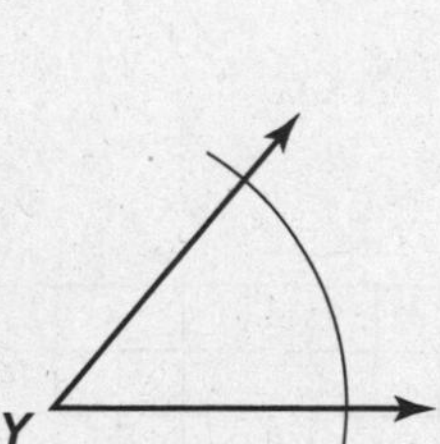

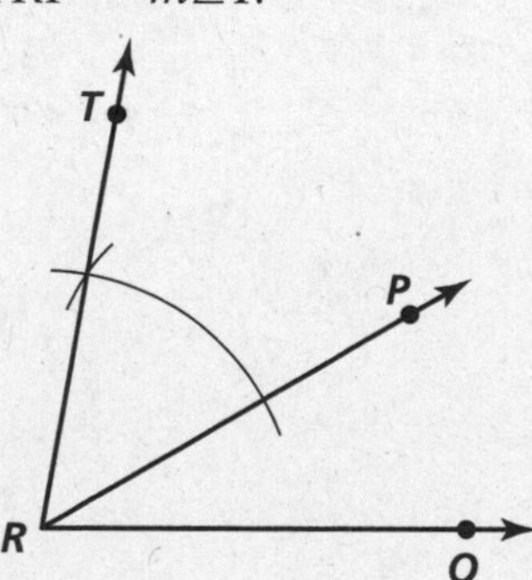

Then, $m\angle TRQ = m\angle PRQ + m\angle TRP$, so $m\angle TRQ = m\angle X + m\angle Y$.

Exercises

Use the diagrams at the right for the following constructions.

1. $\angle CAB$ so that $m\angle CAB = m\angle 1 + m\angle 2$
2. $\angle QRS$ so that $m\angle QRS = m\angle 2 - m\angle 1$
3. $\angle XYZ$ so that $m\angle XYZ = 2m\angle 1$

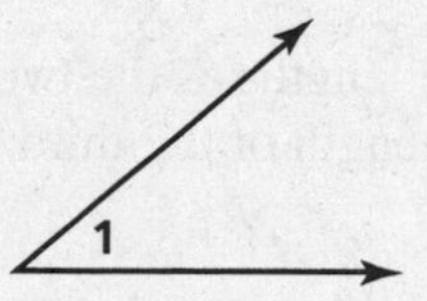

Use the diagrams at the right for the following constructions.

4. $\angle DEF$ so that $m\angle DEF = m\angle 3 + m\angle 4$
5. $\angle TUV$ so that $m\angle TUV = m\angle 3 - m\angle 4$
6. $\angle JKL$ so that $m\angle JKL = \frac{1}{2}m\angle 3$

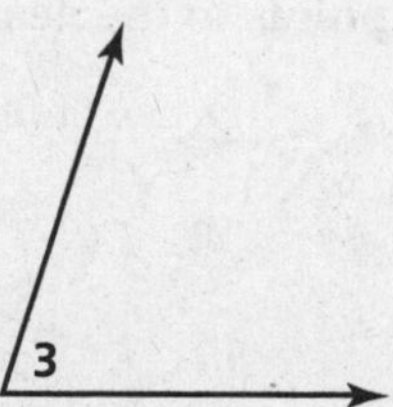

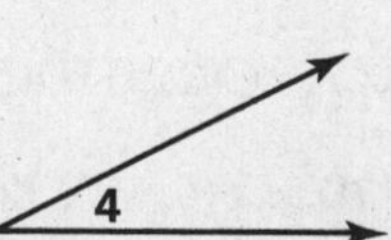

Name ______________________ Class ______________ Date ______________

Review 118

OBJECTIVE: Finding the distance between two points in the coordinate plane

MATERIALS: Graph paper, ruler

Example

Show that the sum of the lengths of the two shortest sides of the triangle is greater than the length of the third side.

Use the distance formula: $d = \sqrt{(x_2 - x_1)^2 + (y_2 - y_1)^2}$

$BA = \sqrt{(2 - (-1))^2 + (4 - 2)^2}$
$= \sqrt{3^2 + 2^2}$
$= \sqrt{9 + 4}$
$= \sqrt{13}$
≈ 3.6

$AC = \sqrt{(-1 - 4)^2 + (2 - (-1))^2}$
$= \sqrt{(-5)^2 + 3^2}$
$= \sqrt{25 + 9}$
$= \sqrt{34}$
≈ 5.8

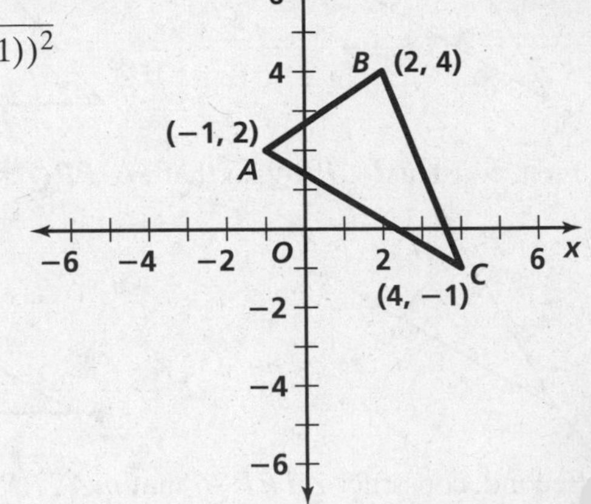

$BC = \sqrt{(2 - 4)^2 + (4 - (-1))^2}$
$= \sqrt{(-2)^2 + 5^2}$
$= \sqrt{4 + 25}$
$= \sqrt{29}$
≈ 5.4

$3.6 + 5.4 > 5.8$, so $BA + BC > AC$.

Exercises

Use the grid at the right.

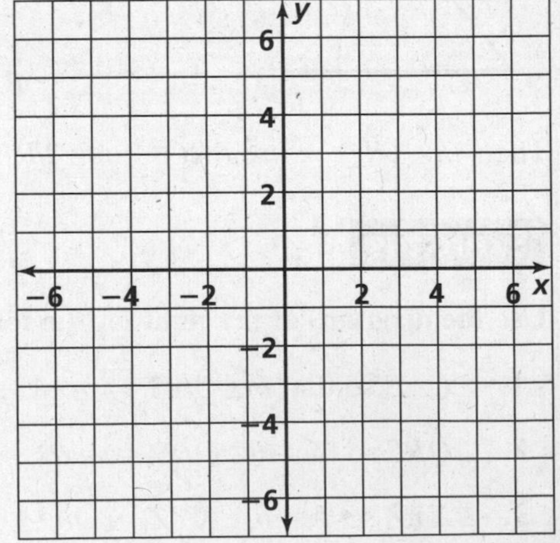

1. Graph the coordinates $X(-2, 4)$, $Y(6, -3)$, and $Z(2, -2)$. Connect the vertices to form a triangle.

2. Find the lengths of the sides $\overline{XY}$, $\overline{YZ}$, and $\overline{XZ}$ to the nearest tenth.

3. Show that the sum of the lengths of the two shortest sides is greater than the length of the third side.

Find the distance between the points to the nearest tenth.

4. $A(-2, -5), B(-4, 7)$
5. $R(3, -4), S(-1, 3)$
6. $G(-4, -5), H(3, 2)$
7. $C(2, 5), D(5, -6)$
8. $E(-7, 3), F(0, 9)$
9. $J(-11, -4), K(-3, -1)$
10. $X(0, 10), Y(-6, -7)$
11. $L(5, -6), M(8, 2)$
12. $U(9, 3), V(9, -14)$

Name ______________________________ Class ______________ Date ______________

Review 119

Perimeter, Circumference, and Area

OBJECTIVE: Finding area and perimeter of squares, rectangles, and circles	**MATERIALS:** Graph paper

Example

A rectangle has an area of 48 square units. Its base and height are integers. Use graph paper to determine possible dimensions of the rectangle.

Because the base and height are integers, they must be factors of 48.

List all the factors of 48: 1, 2, 3, 4, 6, 8, 12, 16, 24, and 48. Use the factors to draw possible rectangles on graph paper.

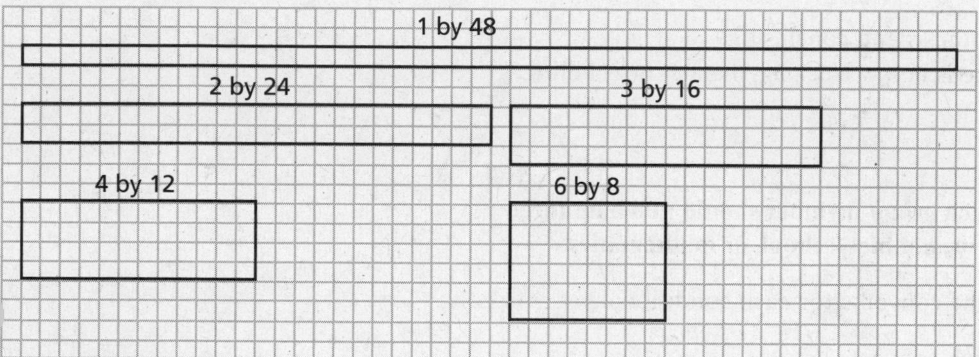

Exercises

Solve for the indicated perimeter or area.

1. **a.** A rectangle has an area of 60 square units. If its base and height are integers, what are its possible dimensions? Sketch each rectangle on graph paper.
   b. Find the perimeter of each rectangle.
2. **a.** A rectangle has an area of 36 square units. If its base and height are integers, what are its possible dimensions? Sketch each rectangle on graph paper.
   b. Which of the possible rectangles has the greatest perimeter?
3. Find the dimensions of a rectangle having the least possible perimeter when its base and height are integers and its area is 18 cm^2.

Draw a circle on graph paper so that the center is at the intersection of grid lines.

4. What is the diameter of your circle? What is the radius of your circle?
5. Estimate the area of the circle by counting the number of squares and parts of squares in the circle.
6. Calculate the area of your circle, using the formula. Round your answer to the nearest tenth.
7. How does your calculated result compare with your estimated result?

Name ______________________ Class ______________ Date ______________

Review 120

OBJECTIVE: Writing the converse of conditional statements

MATERIALS: None

Example

Write the converse of the following statement.

If snow is falling, then the temperature is below freezing.

If snow is falling, then the temperature is below freezing.

hypothesis: If snow is falling — conclusion: then the temperature is below freezing

Converse: Interchange hypothesis and conclusion.
If the temperature is below freezing, then snow is falling.

Exercises

Work in groups of three. Each group member should make up three conditionals relating to sports, hobbies, school, or mathematics.

1. Working alone, write the converse for each conditional.
2. Determine whether each converse is true.
3. Compare your answers with those of the other members of your group. Revise your work until you all agree.

Write the converse for each of the following conditionals. Determine the truth value of each conditional and its converse.

4. If you see lightning, then you hear thunder.
5. If your pants are blue, then they are jeans.
6. If you are eating an orange fruit, then you are eating a tangerine.
7. If a number is a whole number, then it is an integer.
8. If a triangle is an obtuse triangle, then it has one angle greater than 90°.
9. If $n = 8$, then $n^2 = 64$.
10. If you got an A on the first test, then you got an A for the quarter.
11. If a figure is a square, then it has four sides.
12. If $\sqrt{x} = 12$, then $x = 144$.

Name ______________________ Class ______________ Date ______________

Review 121

Biconditionals and Definitions

OBJECTIVE: Writing biconditional statements and identifying good definitions

MATERIALS: None

Example 1

Consider the true statement given below. Write its converse. If the converse is also true, combine the statements as a biconditional.

Conditional: If a pentagon has five equal sides, then it is an equilateral pentagon.

Converse: If a pentagon is an equilateral pentagon, then it has five equal sides.

The converse is true, so the two statements can be written as one biconditional.

Biconditional: A pentagon is an equilateral pentagon if and only if it has five equal sides.

Example 2

Show that this definition of isosceles triangle is a good definition. Then write it as a true biconditional. *An isosceles triangle has two sides of equal length.*

Conditional: If a triangle has two sides of equal length, then it is an isosceles triangle.

Converse: If a triangle is isosceles, then it has two sides of equal length.

Because the two conditionals are true, this is a good definition and can be rewritten as a biconditional.

Biconditional: A triangle is an isosceles triangle if and only if two sides are of equal length.

Exercises

Write the two conditional statements that make up each biconditional.

1. $|n| = 15$ if and only if $n = 15$ or $n = -15$.
2. Two segments are congruent if and only if they have the same measure.
3. You live in California if and only if you live in the most populated state in the United States.
4. An integer is a multiple of 10 if and only if the last digit is 0.

If the statement is a good definition, write it as a biconditional. If not, find a counterexample.

5. An elephant is a large animal.
6. Two planes intersect at a line.
7. An even number is a number that ends in 0, 2, 4, 6, or 8.
8. A triangle is a three-sided figure whose angle measures sum to 180°.

GEOMETRY TOPICS

Name ______________________ Class ______________ Date ______________

Review 122

Deductive Reasoning

OBJECTIVE: Using the Law of Detachment and the Law of Syllogism to draw conclusions

MATERIALS: None

Example 1

Use the Law of Detachment to draw a conclusion.

If a person goes to the zoo, he or she will see animals.	*conditional*
Karla goes to the zoo.	*hypothesis of conditional*

Both the conditional and hypothesis are given to be true. By the Law of Detachment, the conclusion is that Karla will see animals.

However, the Law of Detachment does not apply when a conditional and a *conclusion* are given. Consider the following:

If a person goes to the zoo, he or she will see animals.	*conditional*
Karla sees animals.	*conclusion of conditional*

The Law of Detachment cannot be used to say that Karla went to the zoo. In fact, Karla may have seen dogs in the park and not gone to the zoo at all. In this case, no conclusion is possible.

Example 2

Use the Law of Syllogism to draw a conclusion.

If a polygon is a hexagon, then the sum of its angles is 720.	*conditional 1*
If the sum of the angles of a polygon is 720, then it has six sides.	*conditional 2*

Both conditionals are given to be true. By the Law of Syllogism, if a polygon is a hexagon, then it has six sides.

Exercises

For each problem, tell which law may be used to draw a conclusion. Then write the conclusion. If a conclusion is not possible, write *not possible* and explain why.

1. If a person is driving over the speed limit, the police officer will give the person a ticket.
   Darlene is driving over the speed limit.

2. If two planes do not intersect, then they are parallel.
   If two planes do not have any points in common, then they do not intersect.

3. If the result of the arm X-ray is positive, then a bone is broken.
   The result of Landon's arm X-ray is positive.

4. If you live in Chicago, then you live in Illinois.
   Brad lives in Illinois.

5. If a figure is a circle, then its circumference is πd.
   Tony draws a circle with a diameter (d) of 1 inch.

GEOMETRY TOPICS

Name ______________________ Class ______________ Date ______________

Review 123

OBJECTIVE: Naming and ordering properties used in algebraic reasoning

MATERIALS: None

Example

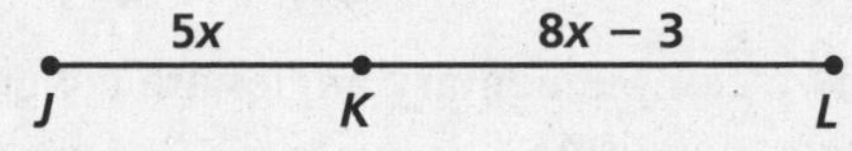

Use the figure to solve for x. Justify each step.

Given: $JL = 62$

$JK + KL = JL$	Segment Addition Postulate
$5x + (8x - 3) = 62$	Substitution Property
$13x - 3 = 62$	Simplify
$13x = 65$	Addition Property of Equality
$x = 5$	Division Property of Equality

Exercises

Name the properties that justify the steps taken.

1. $AB = EF$; therefore $AB + CD = EF + CD$.
2. $\angle ABC \cong \angle Q$; therefore $\angle Q \cong \angle ABC$.

Support each statement with a reason.

3. $5(y - x) = 20$	Given	**4.** $2x = m\angle C + x$	Given
$5y - 5x = 20$	?	$x = m\angle C$	?
5. $CD = AF - 2(CD)$	Given	**6.** $(q - x) = r$	Given
$3(CD) = AF$	?	$4(q - x) = 4r$	?
7. $m\angle Q - m\angle R = 90$	Given	**8.** $m\angle AOX = 2m\angle XOB$	Given
$m\angle Q = 4m\angle R$	Given	$2m\angle XOB = 140$	Given
$4m\angle R - m\angle R = 90$	?	$m\angle AOX = 140$	?

9. $m\angle P + m\angle Q = 90$ and $m\angle Q = 5m\angle P$. Order the steps given below to show that $m\angle Q = 75$.
   1. By the Distributive Property, $6m\angle P = 90$.
   2. By substitution, $m\angle Q = 5 \times 15 = 75$.
   3. By the Division Property, $m\angle P = 15$.
   4. Given: $m\angle P + m\angle Q = 90$, $m\angle Q = 5m\angle P$.
   5. By substitution, $m\angle P + 5m\angle P = 90$.

Name ______________________ Class ______________ Date ______________

Review 124

OBJECTIVE: Using deductive reasoning to solve problems and verify conjectures

MATERIALS: None

Example

Suppose that two complementary angles are congruent. Prove that the measure of each angle is 45.

Given: $\angle 1$ and $\angle 2$ are complementary.

$m\angle 1 = m\angle 2$

Prove: $m\angle 1 = 45$ and $m\angle 2 = 45$

By the definition of complementary angles, $m\angle 1 + m\angle 2 = 90$. By substitution, $m\angle 1 + m\angle 1 = 90$. Using the Addition Property of Equality, $2m\angle 1 = 90$. Using the Division Property of Equality, $m\angle 1 = 45$. By substitution, $m\angle 2 = 45$.

Exercises

In the diagram, $m\angle 1 = m\angle 3$. Order the steps given below to prove that $m\angle 2 = m\angle 4$.

1. By the Angle Addition Postulate, $m\angle 3 + m\angle 4 = 180$.
2. Prove: $m\angle 2 = m\angle 4$
3. By substitution, $m\angle 3 + m\angle 2 = m\angle 3 + m\angle 4$.
4. By the Angle Addition Postulate, $m\angle 1 + m\angle 2 = 180$.
5. Given: $m\angle 1 = m\angle 3$
6. $m\angle 1 + m\angle 2 = m\angle 3 + m\angle 4$ by the Transitive Property of Equality.
7. Subtract $m\angle 3$ from both sides, and you get $m\angle 2 = m\angle 4$.

In the diagram, $\angle 7$ and $\angle 8$ are congruent, and $\angle 10$ is a right angle. Explain why each statement is true.

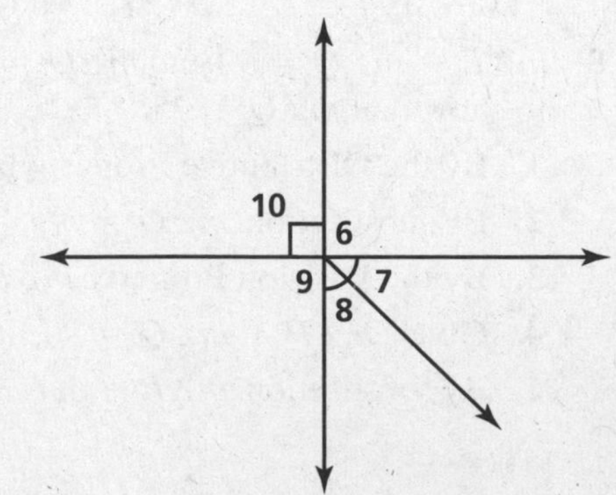

8. $m\angle 8 = 45$
9. $\angle 9$ and $\angle 10$ are supplementary.
10. $\angle 6$ is a right angle.

Name ______________________ Class ______________ Date ______________

Review 125

Properties of Parallel Lines

OBJECTIVE: Relating the measures of angles formed by parallel lines and a transversal

MATERIALS: Ruler, protractor

Example

If $m\angle 1 = 100$, find the measure of each of the other seven angles.

$m\angle 1 + m\angle 2 = 180; m\angle 2 = 80$	Supplementary angles
$m\angle 1 + m\angle 4 = 180; m\angle 4 = 80$	Supplementary angles
$\angle 1 \cong \angle 3; m\angle 3 = 100$	Vertical angles
$\angle 3 \cong \angle 5; m\angle 5 = 100$	Alternate interior angles
$m\angle 3 + m\angle 8 = 180; m\angle 8 = 80$	Same-side interior angles
$\angle 3 \cong \angle 7; m\angle 7 = 100$	Corresponding angles
$m\angle 6 + m\angle 7 = 180; m\angle 6 = 80$	Supplementary angles

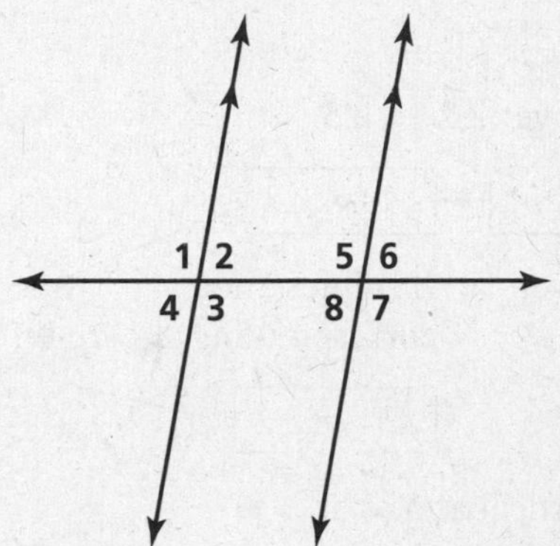

Exercises

Complete the following to find measures of angles associated with a pair of parallel lines and a transversal.

1. **a.** Draw a pair of parallel lines using lined paper or the edges of a ruler. Then draw a transversal that intersects the two parallel lines.

   b. Use a protractor to measure one of the angles formed. Record the measure on your drawing.

   c. Find the measures of the other seven angles without measuring.

   d. Verify the angle measures by measuring each with a protractor.

Find the measure of each angle in the diagram at the right.

2. $m\angle 1$
3. $m\angle 2$
4. $m\angle 4$
5. $m\angle 5$
6. $m\angle 6$
7. $m\angle 7$
8. $m\angle 8$

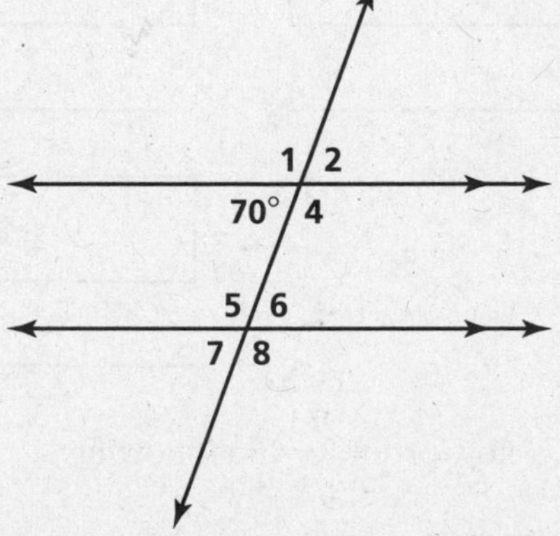

GEOMETRY TOPICS

Name ________________ Class ________________ Date ________________

Review 126

OBJECTIVE: Writing flow proofs **MATERIALS:** None

Example

Write a flow proof for Theorem 3-1: If two parallel lines are cut by a transversal, then alternate interior angles are congruent.

Given: $l \parallel m$

Prove: $\angle 2 \cong \angle 3$

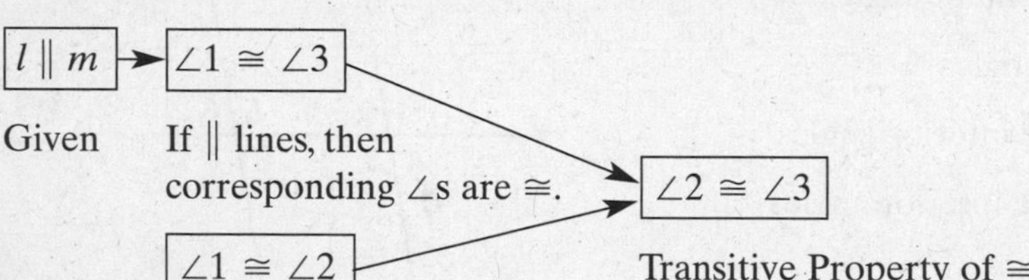

Exercises

Complete a flow proof for each.

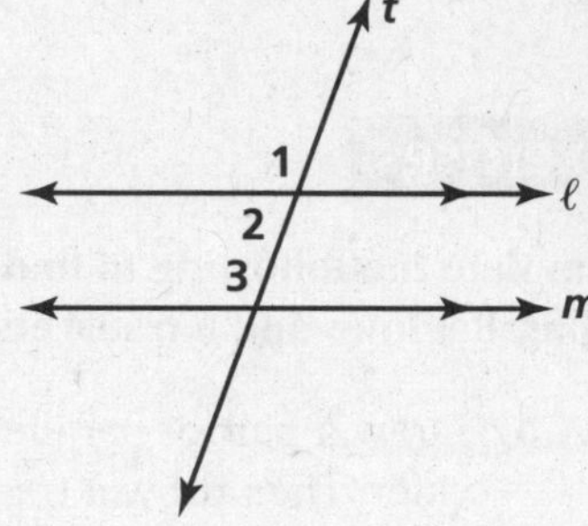

1. Complete the flow proof for Theorem 3-2 using the following steps. Then write the reasons for each step.

   a. $\angle 2$ and $\angle 3$ are supplementary. **b.** $\angle 1 \cong \angle 3$ **c.** $l \parallel m$
   d. $m\angle 1 + m\angle 2 = 180$ **e.** $m\angle 3 + m\angle 2 = 180$

   Theorem 3-2: If two parallel lines are cut by a transversal, then same-side interior angles are supplementary.

   Given: $l \parallel m$

   Prove: $\angle 2$ and $\angle 3$ are supplementary.

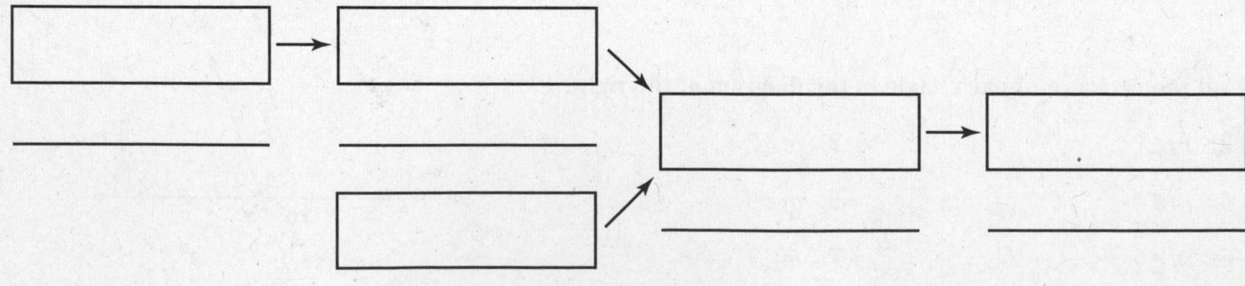

2. Write a flow proof for the following:

   Given: $\angle 2 \cong \angle 3$

   Prove: $a \parallel b$

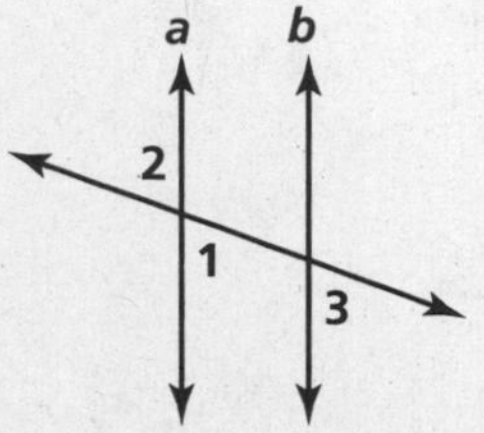

GEOMETRY TOPICS

Name ______________________ Class ______________ Date ______________

Review 127

Parallel Lines and the Triangle Angle-Sum Theorem

OBJECTIVE: Classifying triangles and finding the measures of their angles

MATERIALS: Ruler

Example

In the diagram at the right, *ACED* has four right angles. Find the missing angle measures in $\triangle ABC$, and classify them. Then classify $\triangle ABC$ in as many ways as you can.

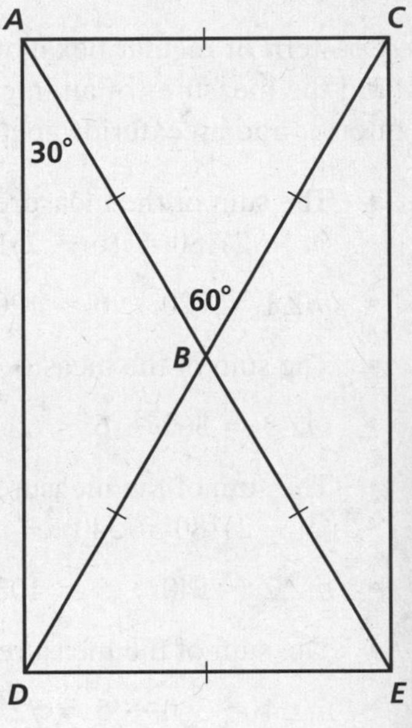

$m\angle CAB + m\angle DAB = 90$	Angle Addition Postulate
$m\angle CAB + 30 = 90$	Substitution
$m\angle CAB = 60$	Subtraction Property of Equality
$m\angle ACB + m\angle CAB + m\angle ABC = 180$	Triangle Angle-Sum Theorem
$m\angle ACB + 60 + 60 = 180$	Substitution
$m\angle ACB + 120 = 80$	Addition
$m\angle ACB = 60$	Subtraction Property of Equality

Because $m\angle CAB < 90$ and $m\angle ACB < 90$, $\angle CAB$ and $\angle ACB$ are acute.

Therefore, $\triangle ABC$ is equilateral, equiangular, and acute.

Exercises

Refer to the diagram above.

1. Find the missing angle measures in $\triangle ABD$, $\triangle CBE$, and $\triangle BDE$.
2. Name the eight triangles in the diagram. Then sketch the triangles, and classify them in as many ways as possible. ($\triangle ABC$ has been classified in the example.)

In the diagram at the right, $\angle RPT$, $\angle PTS$, $\angle TSR$, and $\angle SRP$ are right angles.

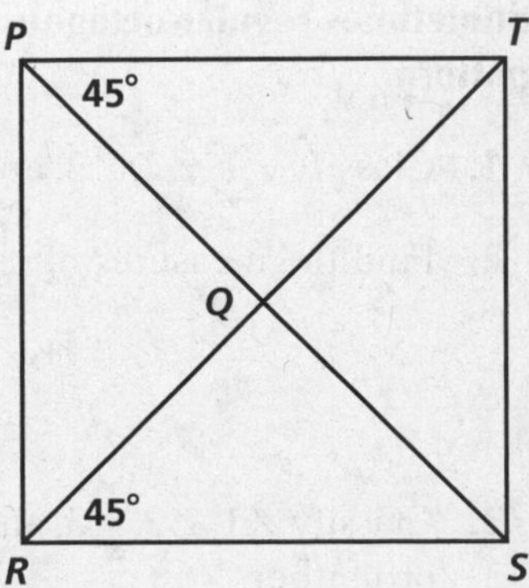

3. Find the missing angle measures in $\triangle PQT$, $\triangle PQR$, $\triangle RQS$, and $\triangle SQT$.
4. Measure the side lengths of $\triangle PQT$, $\triangle PQR$, $\triangle RQS$, and $\triangle SQT$ to the nearest millimeter.
5. List and classify each triangle. (*Hint:* There are eight triangles.)

Name ______________________ Class ______________ Date ______________

Review 128

OBJECTIVE: Finding the sum of the measures of the interior and exterior angles of polygons

MATERIALS: None

Example

A pattern of regular hexagons and regular pentagons covers a soccer ball. Find the measures of an interior and an exterior angle of the hexagon and an interior and an exterior angle of the pentagon.

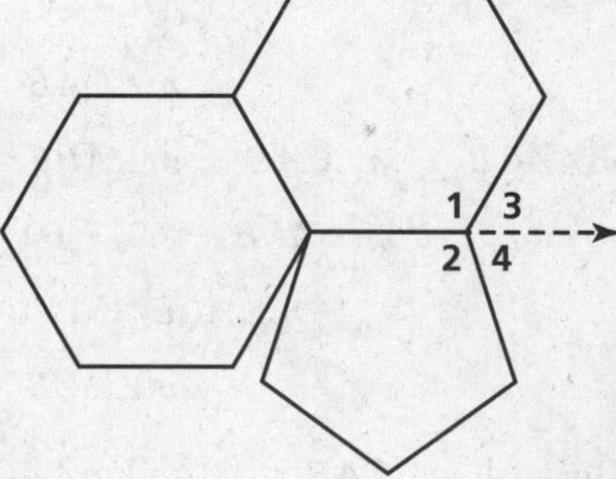

- The sum of the measures of the interior angles of a hexagon equals $(n - 2)180 = (6 - 2)180 = 720$.
- $m\angle 1 = 720 \div 6 = 120$.
- The sum of the measures of the exterior angles of a hexagon equals 360.
- $m\angle 3 = 360 \div 6 = 60$.
- The sum of the measures of the interior angles of a pentagon equals $(5 - 2)180 = 540$.
- $m\angle 2 = 540 \div 5 = 108$.
- The sum of the measures of the exterior angles of a pentagon equals 360.
- $m\angle 4 = 360 \div 5 = 72$.
- An interior angle of the hexagon measures 120, and an exterior angle measures 60.
- An interior angle of the pentagon measures 108, and an exterior angle measures 72.

Exercises

Sometimes regular octagons are pieced around a square to form a quilt pattern.

1. Classify $\angle 1$, $\angle 2$, $\angle 3$, and $\angle 4$ as interior or exterior angles.
2. Find the measures of $\angle 1$, $\angle 2$, $\angle 3$, and $\angle 4$.

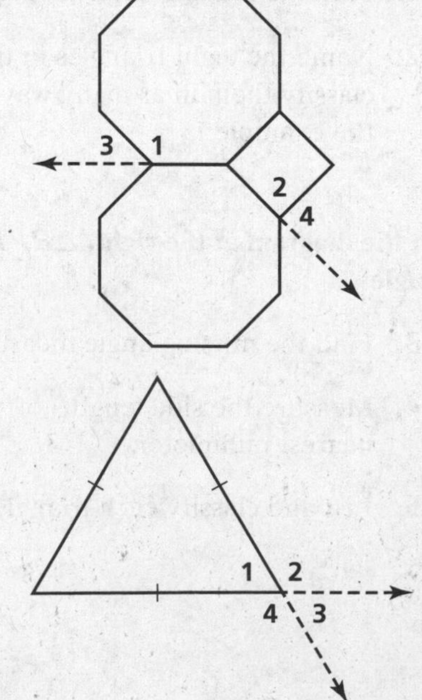

3. Classify $\angle 1$, $\angle 2$, $\angle 3$, and $\angle 4$ as interior angles, exterior angles, or neither.
4. Find the measures of $\angle 1$, $\angle 2$, $\angle 3$, and $\angle 4$.

GEOMETRY TOPICS

Name ______________________ Class ______________ Date ______________

Review 129

OBJECTIVE: Writing and graphing equations of lines

MATERIALS: Graphing paper

If you know two points on a line, or if you know one point and the slope of a line, then you can find the equation of the line.

Example

Write an equation of the line that contains the points $J(4, -5)$ and $K(-2, 1)$. Graph the line.

If you know two points on a line, first find the slope using $m = \frac{y_2 - y_1}{x_2 - x_1}$.

$$m = \frac{1 - (-5)}{-2 - 4} = \frac{6}{-6} = -1$$

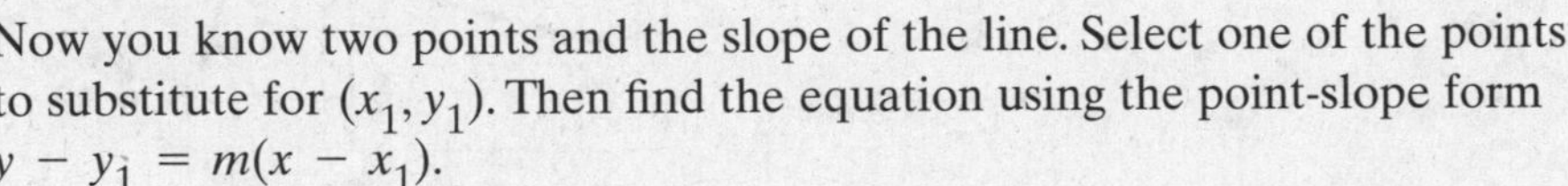

Now you know two points and the slope of the line. Select one of the points to substitute for (x_1, y_1). Then find the equation using the point-slope form $y - y_1 = m(x - x_1)$.

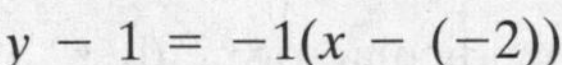

$y - 1 = -1(x - (-2))$ Substitute.

$y - 1 = -1(x + 2)$ Simplify within parentheses. You may leave your equation in this form or further simplify to find the slope-intercept form.

$y - 1 = -x - 2$

$y = -x - 1$

Answer: Either $y - 1 = -1(x + 2)$ or $y = -x - 1$ is acceptable.

Exercises

Write an equation for the line with the given slope that contains the given point. Graph each line.

1. slope 2, $(2, -2)$
2. slope $\frac{1}{3}$, $(-6, -2)$
3. slope -1, $(-3, 0)$
4. slope $\frac{5}{6}$, $(-6, -3)$
5. slope $-\frac{1}{2}$, $(-4, 3)$
6. slope 0, $(3, 1)$

Write an equation for the line containing the given points. Graph each line.

7. $(2, 3), (4, -4)$
8. $(-4, 5), (3, -2)$
9. $(0, 1), (-5, -1)$
10. $(1, 1), (6, 1)$
11. $(-3, 0), (-5, 4)$
12. $(-3, 4), (-3, -1)$

Write an equation for the line with the given information. Graph each line.

13. contains point $(4, -2)$, slope -3
14. contains points $(3, -1), (5, 5)$
15. contains point $(2, 1)$, slope $\frac{1}{4}$
16. contains point $(8, -2)$, slope $-\frac{3}{4}$
17. contains points $(-4, 5), (-3, 4)$
18. contains points $(1, 1), (2, 1)$

Name ____________________ Class ____________ Date ____________

Review 130

OBJECTIVE: Identifying and writing equations for parallel and perpendicular lines

MATERIALS: Graphing paper

Example 1

Write an equation for the line that contains $G\ (4, -3)$ and is parallel to $\overleftrightarrow{EF}: -\frac{1}{2}x + 2y = 6$. Write another equation for the line that contains G and is perpendicular to $\overleftrightarrow{EF}$. Graph the three lines.

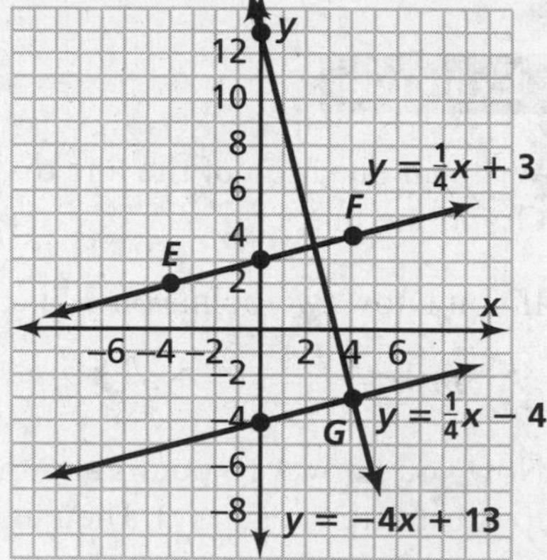

Step 1 Rewrite in slope-intercept form: $y = \frac{1}{4}x + 3$

Step 2 Use point-slope form to write an equation for each line.

Parallel line: $m = \frac{1}{4}$

$y - (-3) = \frac{1}{4}(x - 4)$

$y = \frac{1}{4}x - 4$

Perpendicular line: $m = -4$

$y - (-3) = -4(x - 4)$

$y = -4x + 13$

Example 2

Given points $J(-1, 4)$, $K(2, 3)$, $L(5, 4)$, and $M(0, -3)$, are $\overleftrightarrow{JK}$ and $\overleftrightarrow{LM}$ parallel, perpendicular, or neither?

$-\frac{1}{3} \neq \frac{7}{5}$ Their slopes are not equal, so they are not parallel.

$\frac{1}{3} \cdot \frac{7}{5} \neq -1$ The product of their slopes is not -1, so they are not perpendicular.

neither

Exercises

Find the slope of a line (a) parallel to and (b) perpendicular to each line.

1. $y = -2x$
2. $y = \frac{1}{4}x - 6$
3. $x = -3$

Write an equation for the line that (a) contains G and is parallel to $\overleftrightarrow{EF}$. Write another equation for the line that (b) contains G and is perpendicular to $\overleftrightarrow{EF}$. (c) Graph the three lines to check your answers.

4. $\overleftrightarrow{EF}: y = -2x + 5,\ G(1, 2)$
5. $\overleftrightarrow{EF}: 6y + 4x = -12,\ G(0, -4)$
6. $\overleftrightarrow{EF}: x - \frac{1}{3}y = 4,\ G(-3, -2)$

Tell whether $\overleftrightarrow{JK}$ and $\overleftrightarrow{LM}$ are parallel, perpendicular, or neither.

7. $J(2, 0), K(-1, 3), L(0, 4), M(-1, 5)$
8. $J(-4, -5), K(5, 1), L(6, 0), M(4, 3)$

9.

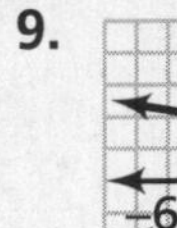

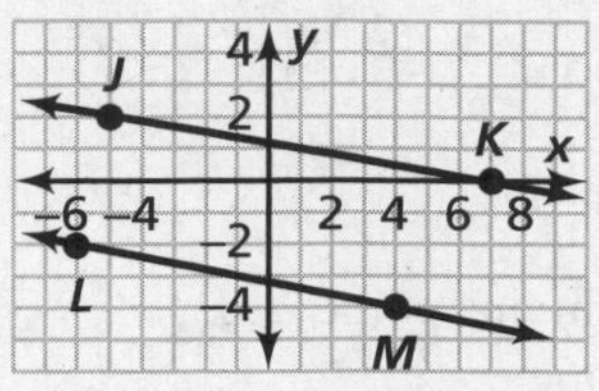

10.

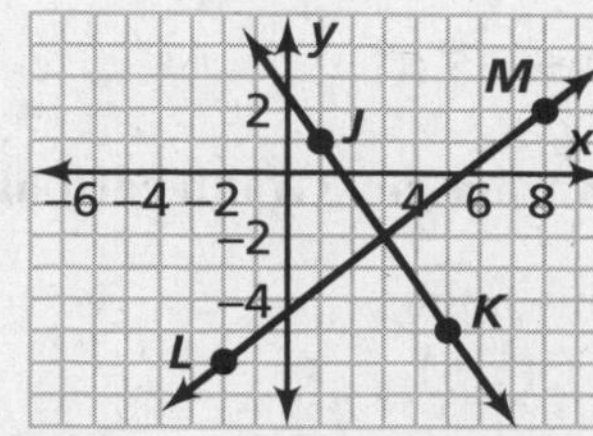

11.

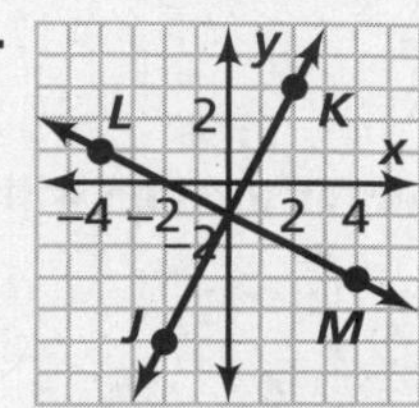

12. $\overleftrightarrow{JK}: y = \frac{1}{5}x + 2$
$\overleftrightarrow{LM}: y = 5x - \frac{1}{2}$

13. $\overleftrightarrow{JK}: 2y + \frac{1}{2}x = -2$
$\overleftrightarrow{LM}: 2x + 8y = 8$

14. $\overleftrightarrow{JK}: y = -1$
$\overleftrightarrow{LM}: x = 0$

Name ______________________ Class ______________ Date ______________

Review 131

Constructing Parallel and Perpendicular Lines

OBJECTIVE: Constructing perpendicular lines **MATERIALS:** Straightedge, compass

Example

Construct a right triangle in which the lengths of the legs are *a* and *b*.

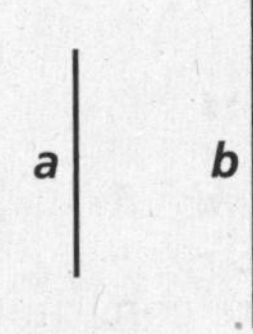

Step 1 Construct $\overline{BC}$ with length *a*.

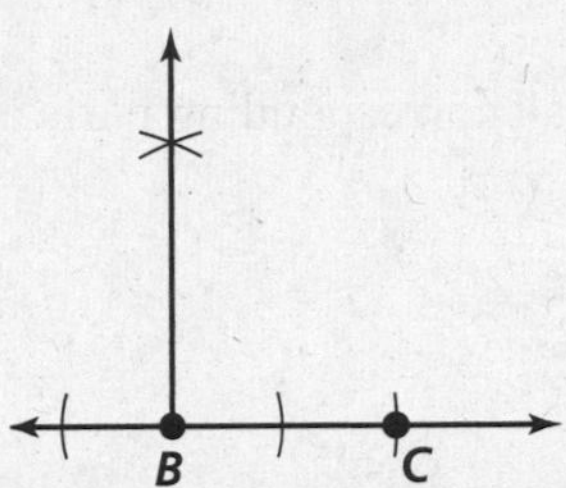

Step 2 Construct a line perpendicular to $\overline{BC}$ through *B*.

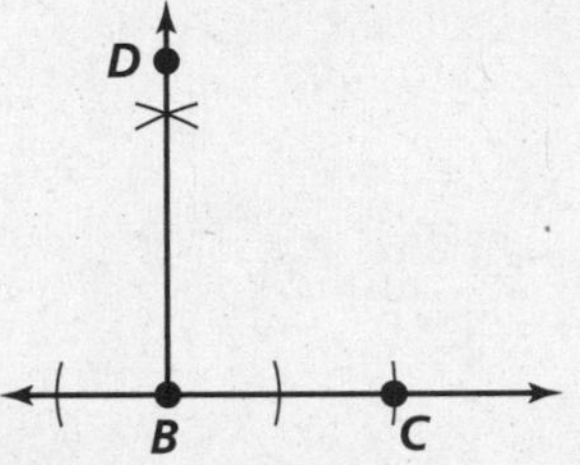

Step 3 Construct point *D* on the perpendicular line so that $BD = b$.

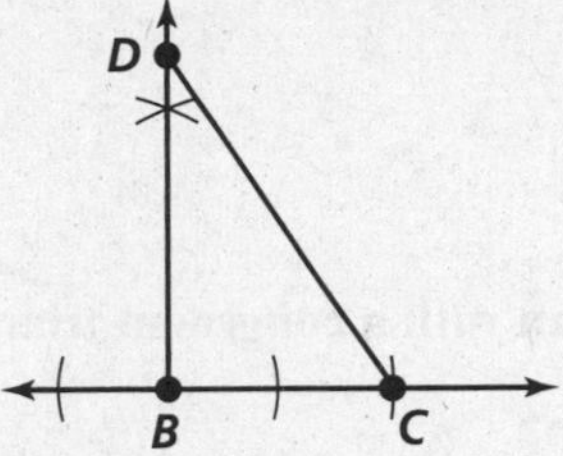

Step 4 Draw $\overline{DC}$.

GEOMETRY TOPICS

Exercises

Follow the given steps to construct a right triangle.

1. Construct a right triangle in which the length of one of the legs is *a* and the length of the hypotenuse is *b*. Use the following steps.

   Step 1 Construct $\overline{XY}$ with length *a*.

   Step 2 Construct a line perpendicular to $\overline{XY}$ through *X*.

   Step 3 Construct point *Z* on the perpendicular line so that $YZ = b$.

   Step 4 Draw $\overline{YZ}$.

For Exercises 2–4, use the lengths *a* and *b* given at the top of the page.

2. Construct a right triangle in which the length of each leg is *b*.
3. Construct a right triangle in which the length of one leg is *a* and the length of the hypotenuse is 2*a*.
4. Construct a right triangle in which the length of the hypotenuse is *b*.

Name ______________________ Class ______________ Date ______________

Review 132

Congruent Figures and Corresponding Parts

OBJECTIVE: Recognizing congruent figures and their corresponding parts

MATERIALS: None

Example

$\triangle ABC \cong \triangle XYZ$. Find $m\angle A$.

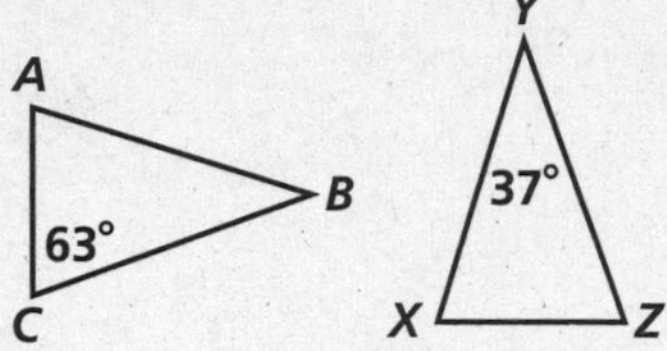

Because the triangles are congruent, all corresponding parts are congruent.

Sides: $\overline{AB} \cong \overline{XY}$, $\overline{BC} \cong \overline{YZ}$, $\overline{AC} \cong \overline{XZ}$

Angles: $\angle A \cong \angle X$, $\angle B \cong \angle Y$, $\angle C \cong \angle Z$

Because $\angle B \cong \angle Y$, $m\angle B \cong 37$.

Use the Triangle Angle-Sum Theorem to find $m\angle A$.

$$m\angle A + m\angle B + m\angle C = 180$$
$$m\angle A + 37 + 63 = 180$$
$$m\angle A + 100 = 180$$
$$m\angle A = 80$$

Exercises

Match each triangle in the first column with a congruent triangle in the second column.

1. 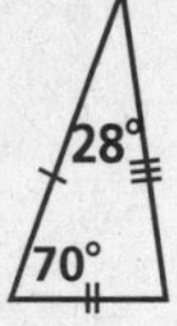

a. 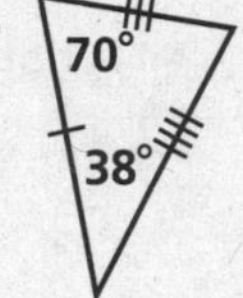

2. 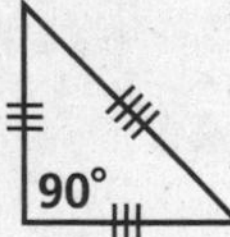

b. 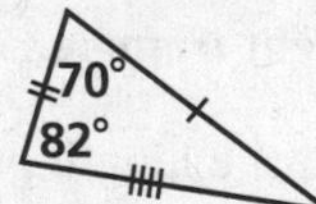

3. 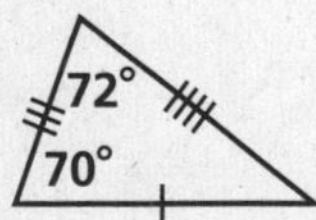

c. 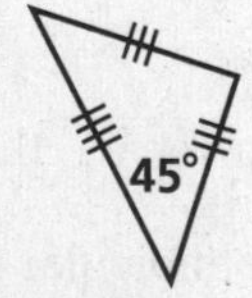

Find the measure of the indicated angle.

4. $\triangle PQR \cong \triangle STU$. Find $m\angle U$.

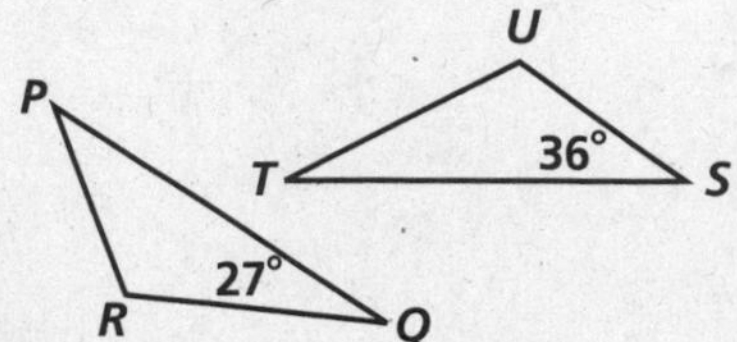

5. $EFGH \cong JKLM$. Find $m\angle M$.

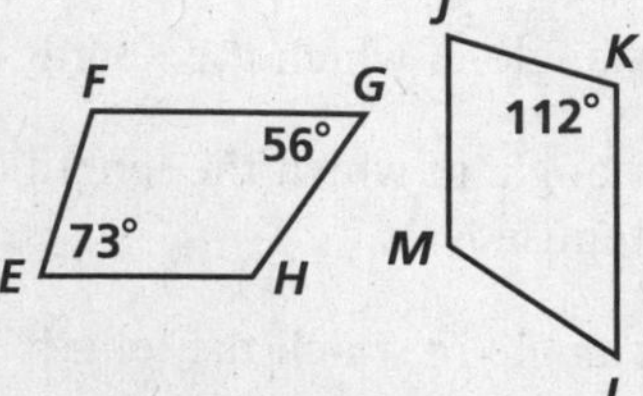

GEOMETRY TOPICS

Name ______________________ Class ______________ Date ______________

Review 133

Triangles Congruent by SSS and SAS

OBJECTIVE: Proving two triangles congruent using the SSS and SAS postulates

MATERIALS: Ruler, protractor

Example

Name the triangle congruence postulate you can use to prove each pair of triangles congruent.

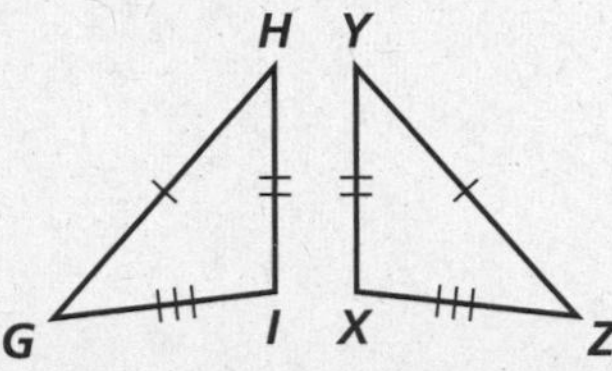

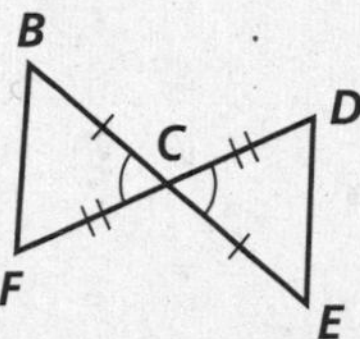

a. Because three sides of $\triangle GHI$ are congruent to three sides of $\triangle ZXY$, $\triangle GHI \cong \triangle ZYX$ by the SSS Postulate.

b. Because two sides and the included angle of $\triangle BCF$ are congruent to two sides and the included angle of $\triangle ECD$, $\triangle BCF \cong \triangle ECD$ by the SAS Postulate.

GEOMETRY TOPICS

Exercises

Refer to the triangles at the right.

1. Use a ruler to show that the top two triangles at the right are congruent by the SSS Postulate.
2. Use a ruler and a protractor to show that the two large triangles at the right are congruent by the SAS Postulate.

Name the triangle congruence postulate you can use to prove each pair of triangles congruent. Then state the triangle congruence.

3. 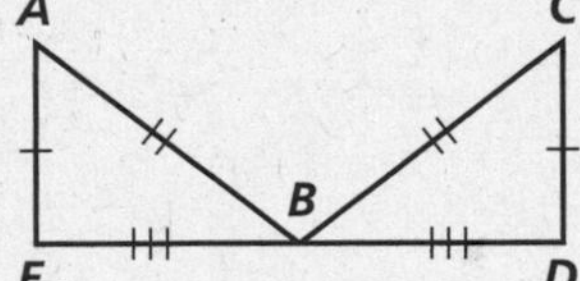

4. 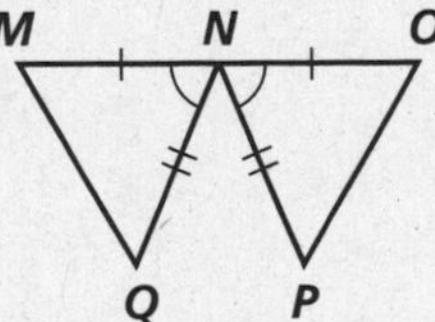

5. 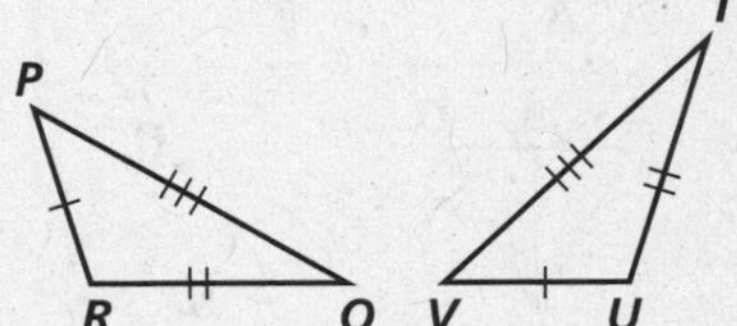

6. 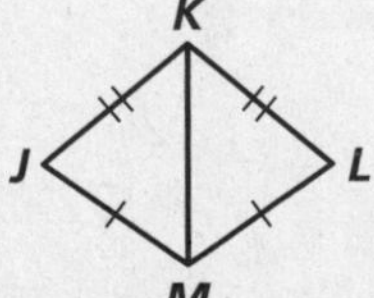

7. 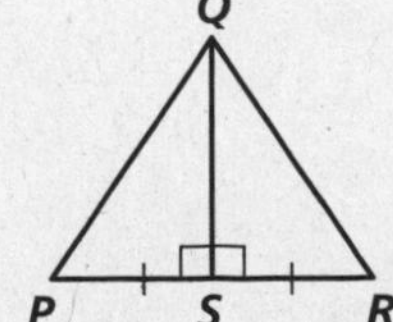

8. 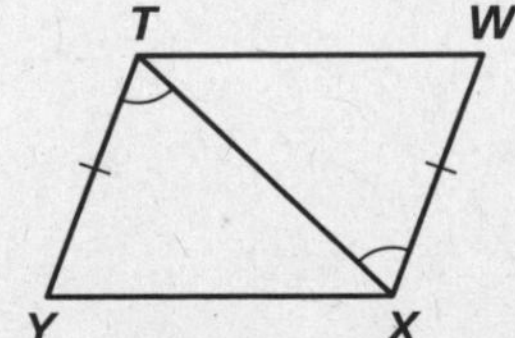

Name ______________________ Class ______________ Date ______________

Review 134

OBJECTIVE: Proving two triangles congruent by the ASA Postulate and the AAS Theorem

MATERIALS: Ruler, protractor

Example

Tell whether the ASA Postulate or the AAS Theorem can be applied directly to prove the triangles congruent.

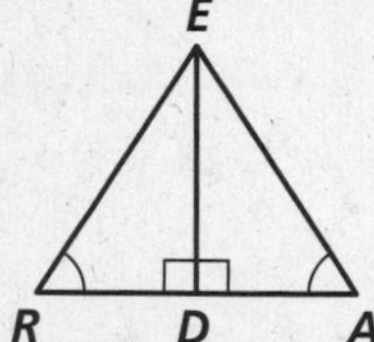

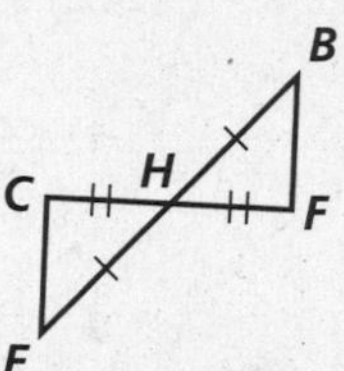

a. Because $\angle RDE$ and $\angle ADE$ are right angles, they are congruent. $\overline{ED} \cong \overline{ED}$ by the Reflexive Property of $\cong$, and it is given that $\angle R \cong \angle A$. Therefore, $\triangle RDE \cong \triangle ADE$ by the AAS Theorem.

b. It is given that $\overline{CH} \cong \overline{FH}$ and $\overline{EH} \cong \overline{BH}$. Because $\angle CHE$ and $\angle FHB$ are vertical angles, they are congruent. Therefore, $\triangle CHE \cong \triangle FHB$ by the ASA Postulate.

Exercises

Indicate congruences.

1. Copy the top figure at the right. Mark the figure with the angle congruence and side congruence symbols that you would need to prove the triangles congruent by the ASA Postulate.

2. Copy the second figure shown. Mark the figure with the angle congruence and side congruence symbols that you would need to prove the triangles congruent by the AAS Theorem.

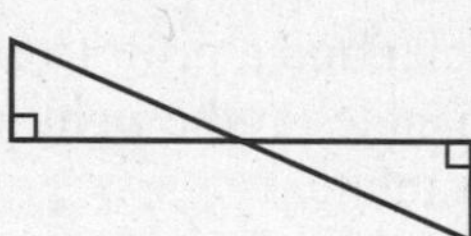

3. Draw two triangles that are congruent by either the ASA Postulate or the AAS Theorem.

What additional information would you need to prove each pair of triangles congruent by the stated postulate or theorem?

4. ASA

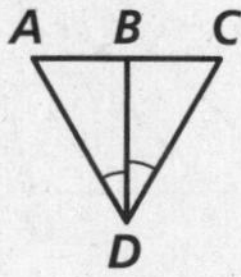

5. AAS

6. SAS

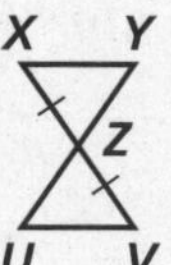

7. SSS

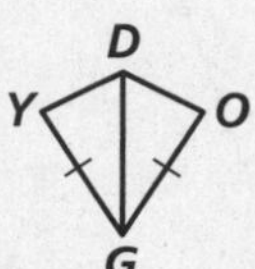

8. AAS

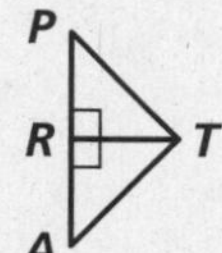

9. ASA

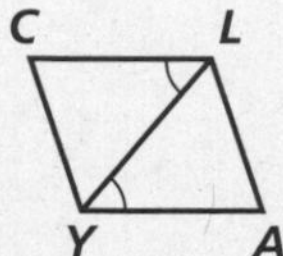

Name ________________________ Class ____________ Date ____________

Review 135

Using Congruent Triangles: CPCTC

OBJECTIVE: Using triangle congruence and CPCTC to prove that the parts of two triangles are congruent

MATERIALS: None

Example

Write a two-column proof.

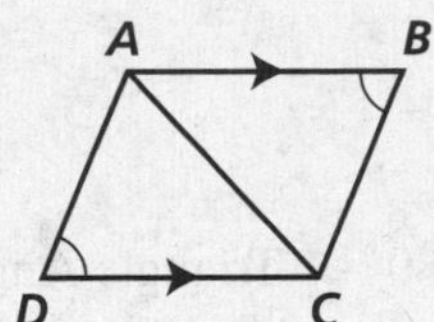

Given: $\overline{AB} \parallel \overline{DC}$, $\angle B \cong \angle D$

Prove: $\overline{BC} \cong \overline{DA}$

Statements	***Reasons***
1. $\overline{AB} \parallel \overline{DC}$	**1.** Given
2. $\angle BAC \cong \angle DCA$	**2.** If $\parallel$ lines, then alternate interior $\angle$s are $\cong$.
3. $\angle B \cong \angle D$	**3.** Given
4. $\overline{AC} \cong \overline{AC}$	**4.** Reflexive Property of $\cong$
5. $\triangle ABC \cong \triangle CDA$	**5.** AAS Theorem
6. $\overline{BC} \cong \overline{DA}$	**6.** CPCTC

Exercises

Complete the two-column proof.

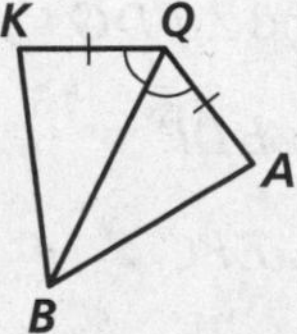

1. Given: $\overline{QK} \cong \overline{QA}$; $\overrightarrow{QB}$ bisects $\angle KQA$

Prove: $\overline{KB} \cong \overline{AB}$

Statements	***Reasons***
a. ?	**1.** Given
2. $\angle KQB \cong \angle AQB$	**b.** ?
c. ?	**3.** Reflexive Property of $\cong$
4. $\triangle KBQ \cong \triangle ABQ$	**d.** ?
5. $\overline{KB} \cong \overline{AB}$	**e.** ?

Write a two-column proof.

2. Given: $\overline{MN} \cong \overline{MP}$, $\overline{NO} \cong \overline{PO}$

Prove: $\angle N \cong \angle P$

3. Given: $\overline{ON}$ bisects $\angle JOH$, $\angle J \cong \angle H$

Prove: $\overline{JN} \cong \overline{HN}$

GEOMETRY TOPICS

Name ______________________ Class ______________ Date ______________

Review 136

OBJECTIVE: Using and applying properties of isosceles triangles

MATERIALS: None

Example

Find $m\angle ABE$.

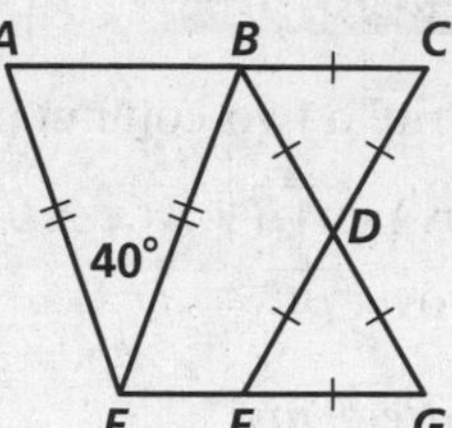

Because $AE \cong BE$, $m\angle EAB \cong m\angle ABE$.

$m\angle EAB + m\angle ABE + m\angle AEB = 180$	Triangle Angle-Sum Theorem
$m\angle EAB + m\angle ABE + 40 = 180$	Substitution
$m\angle EAB + m\angle ABE = 140$	Subtraction Property of Equality
$2m\angle ABE = 140$	Substitution
$m\angle ABE = 70$	Division Property of Equality

Exercises

Work with a partner to find the measures of the angles of quadrilateral *BDFE* in the diagram above.

1. Find the measures of the angles of $\triangle CBD$ and $\triangle FDG$.
2. Use the Angle Addition Postulate to find $m\angle BDF$.
3. Use the Angle Addition Postulate to find $m\angle EFC$.
4. Use the Angle Addition Postulate to find $m\angle EBG$.
5. Use the Polygon Interior Angle-Sum Theorem to find $m\angle BEF$.

Find the measure of each angle.

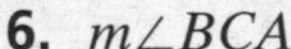

6. $m\angle BCA$
7. $m\angle DCE$
8. $m\angle DEF$
9. $m\angle BCD$
10. $m\angle BAG$
11. $m\angle GAH$

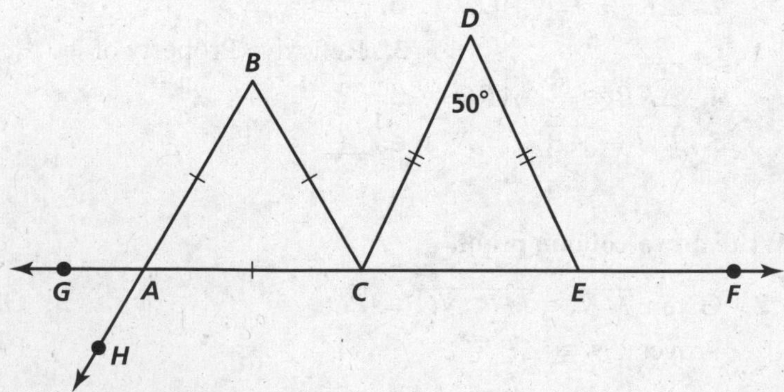

Name ______________________ Class ______________ Date ______________

Review 137

Congruence in Right Triangles

OBJECTIVE: Proving triangles congruent by the HL Theorem

MATERIALS: Ruler

Example

Explain why $\triangle GFD \cong \triangle EFD$ by the HL Theorem.

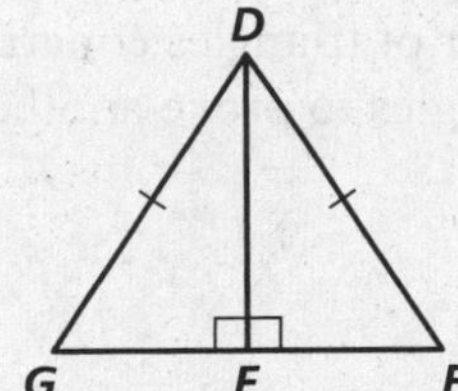

To prove two triangles congruent by the HL Theorem, prove that:

1. They are right triangles. — 1. $\angle GFD$ and $\angle EFD$ are right angles. Therefore, $\triangle GFD$ and $\triangle EFD$ are right triangles.
2. Their hypotenuses are congruent. — 2. $\overline{GD} \cong \overline{ED}$ is given.
3. One pair of legs is $\cong$. — 3. $\overline{DF} \cong \overline{DF}$ by the Reflexive Property of $\cong$.

Exercises

Measure the hypotenuses and the length of one pair of legs to decide whether the triangles are congruent by the HL Theorem. If the triangles are congruent, state the congruence.

1. 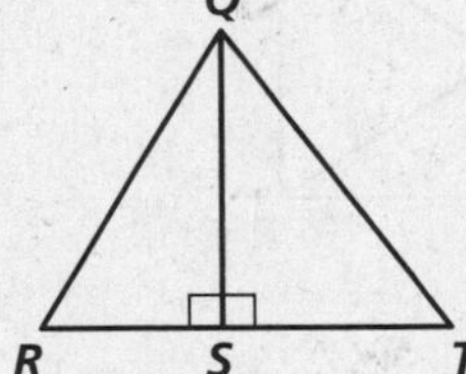

2. 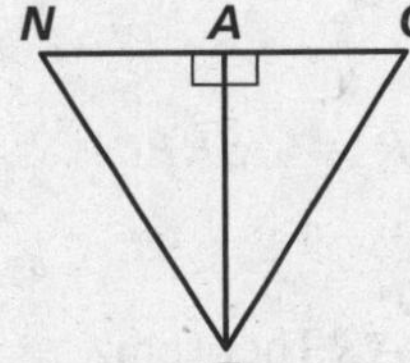

3. 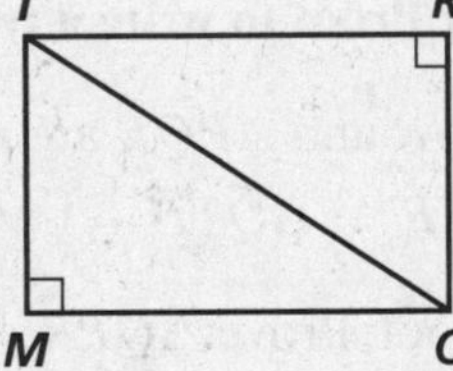

Tell whether the HL Theorem can be applied to prove the triangles congruent. If possible, write the triangle congruence.

4. 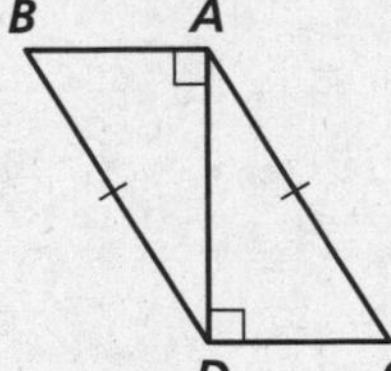

5. 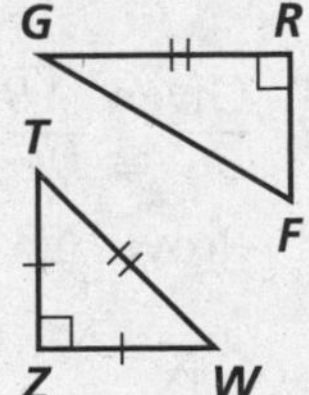

6. 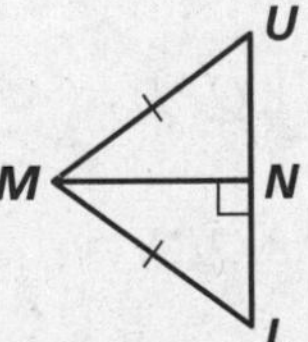

7. 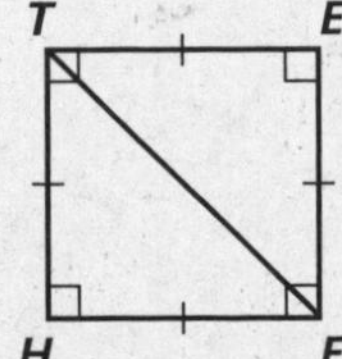

8. 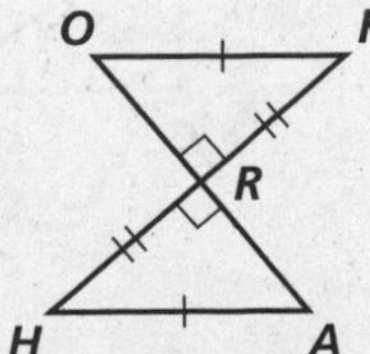

9. 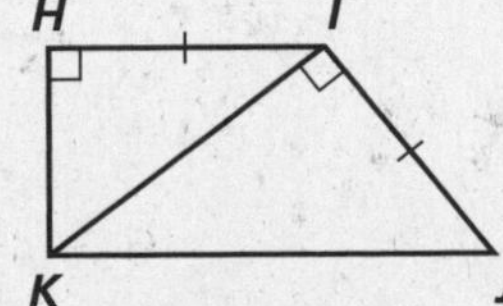

GEOMETRY TOPICS

Name ________________ Class ________________ Date ________________

Review 138

Use Corresponding Parts of Congruent Triangles

OBJECTIVE: Proving triangles congruent by first proving two other triangles congruent

MATERIALS: None

Sometimes you can prove one pair of triangles congruent and then use corresponding parts of those triangles to prove another pair congruent.

Example

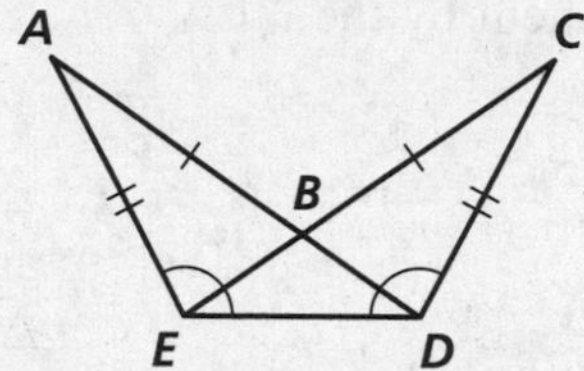

Write a paragraph proof.

Given: $\overline{AB} \cong \overline{CB}$, $\overline{AE} \cong \overline{CD}$, $\angle AED \cong \angle CDE$

Prove: $\triangle ABE \cong \triangle CBD$

$\overline{ED} \cong \overline{ED}$ by the Reflexive Property of $\cong$. It is given that $\overline{AE} \cong \overline{CD}$ and $\triangle AED \cong \triangle CDE$. Therefore, $\triangle AED \cong \triangle CDE$ by the SAS Postulate. $\angle A \cong \angle C$ by CPCTC. It is given that $\overline{AB} \cong \overline{CB}$. Therefore, $\triangle ABE \cong \triangle CBD$ by the SAS Postulate.

GEOMETRY TOPICS

Exercises

Use the Plan for Proof to write a two-column proof.

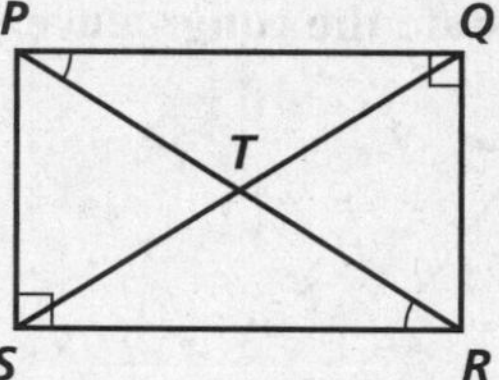

1. Given: $\angle PSR$ and $\angle PQR$ are right angles, $\angle QPR \cong \angle SRP$

   Prove: $\triangle STR \cong \triangle QTP$

   Plan for Proof: Prove $\triangle QPR \cong \triangle SRP$ by the AAS Theorem. Then use CPCTC and vertical angles to prove $\triangle STR \cong \triangle QTP$ by the AAS Theorem.

Write a Plan for Proof.

2. Given: $\angle MLP \cong \angle QPL$, $\angle M \cong \angle Q$

   Prove: $\triangle MLN \cong \triangle QPN$

3. Given: $\overline{AB} \cong \overline{ED}$, $\overline{BC} \cong \overline{DC}$

   Prove: $\triangle ABF \cong \triangle EDF$

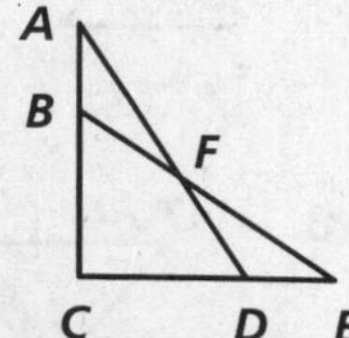

Name ______________________ Class ______________ Date ______________

Review 139

OBJECTIVE: Using properties of midsegments to solve problems

MATERIALS: Ruler

Example

$\overline{DE}$ is the midsegment of $\triangle ABC$. $\overline{FG}$ is the midsegment of $\triangle ADE$. $\overline{HI}$ is the midsegment of $\triangle AFG$. If $BC = 12$, find DE, FG, and HI.

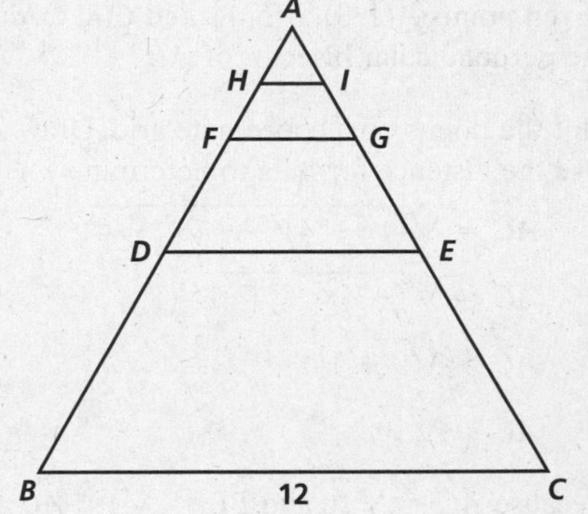

$$DE = \frac{1}{2}BC \qquad FG = \frac{1}{2}DE \qquad HI = \frac{1}{2}FG$$

$$= \frac{1}{2}(12) \qquad = \frac{1}{2}(6) \qquad = \frac{1}{2}(3)$$

$$= 6 \qquad = 3 \qquad = 1.5$$

Exercises

Follow the indicated steps to complete each exercise.

- Draw a triangle. Label it $\triangle XYZ$.
- Draw the midsegment of $\triangle XYZ$ parallel to $\overline{YZ}$. Label it $\overline{MN}$.
- Draw the midsegment of $\triangle XMN$ parallel to $\overline{MN}$. Label it $\overline{PQ}$.
- Draw the midsegment of $\triangle XPQ$ parallel to $\overline{PQ}$. Label it $\overline{RS}$.

1. If $RS = 4$, find the following lengths.

a. PQ **b.** MN **c.** YZ

- Draw a triangle. Label it $\triangle PUV$.
- Draw the midsegment of $\triangle PUV$ parallel to $\overline{UV}$. Label it $\overline{ST}$.
- Draw the midsegment of $\triangle PST$ parallel to $\overline{ST}$. Label it $\overline{QR}$.
- Draw the midsegment of $\triangle PQR$ parallel to $\overline{QR}$. Label it $\overline{NO}$.

2. If $QR = 5$, find the following lengths.

a. NO **b.** ST **c.** UV

3. If $NO = 2$, find the following lengths.

a. QR **b.** ST **c.** UV

Name ______________________ Class ______________ Date ______________

Review 140

OBJECTIVE: Determining whether a given point lies on the perpendicular bisector of a segment

MATERIALS: Graph paper

Example

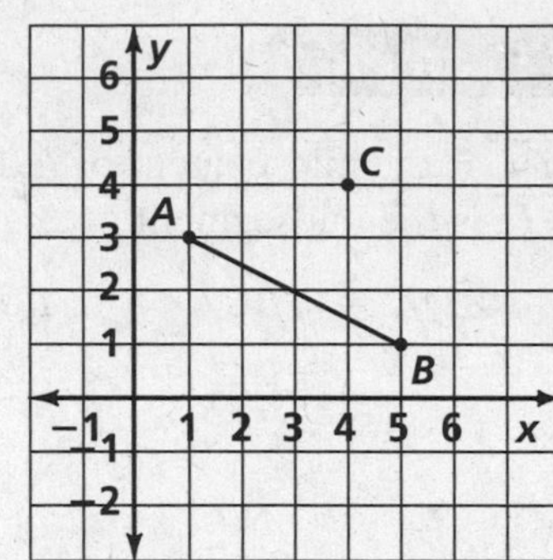

Given points $A(1, 3)$, $B(5, 1)$, and $C(4, 4)$, does C lie on the perpendicular bisector of $\overline{AB}$?

Plot the points on a coordinate grid. Draw $\overline{AB}$.
Use the distance formula to determine whether $AC = BC$.

$AC = \sqrt{(1 - 4)^2 + (3 - 4)^2}$ $\qquad$ $BC = \sqrt{(5 - 4)^2 + (1 - 4)^2}$

$AC = \sqrt{(-3)^2 + (-1)^2}$ $\qquad$ $BC = \sqrt{1^2 + (-3)^2}$

$AC = \sqrt{9 + 1}$ $\qquad$ $BC = \sqrt{1 + 9}$

$AC = \sqrt{10}$ $\qquad$ $BC = \sqrt{10}$

Because $AC = \sqrt{10}$ and $BC = \sqrt{10}$, $AC = BC$, and C lies on the perpendicular bisector of $\overline{AB}$.

Exercises

Complete these exercises on bisectors.

1. Given $D(3, 1)$, $E(7, 2)$, and $F(4, 5)$, does F lie on the perpendicular bisector of $\overline{DE}$?

2. Given $X(1, 2)$, $Y(7, 2)$, and $Z(4, 6)$, does Z lie on the perpendicular bisector of $\overline{XY}$?

3. Given $H(-4, 5)$, $I(-6, 2)$, and $J(-1, 3)$, does H lie on the perpendicular bisector of $\overline{IJ}$?

4. Given $P(-7, -7)$, $Q(-5, -2)$, and $R(0, -5)$, does Q lie on the perpendicular bisector of $\overline{PR}$?

5. Point $T(-9, 5)$ lies on the perpendicular bisector of $\overline{UV}$. If the coordinates of point U are $(-2, 1)$, which of the following are the coordinates of point V?

   A. $(-2, 7)$ $\qquad$ **B.** $(-1, 6)$ $\qquad$ **C.** $(0, 5)$

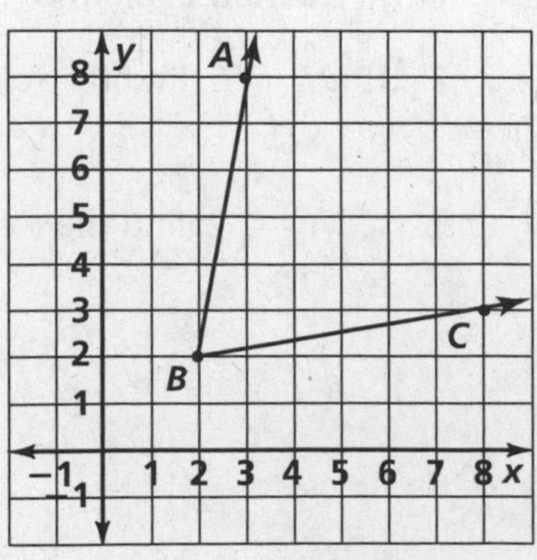

6. Use the diagram at the right. Which of the following points lies on the angle bisector of $\angle ABC$?

   A. $(6, 5)$ $\qquad$ **B.** $(7, 8)$ $\qquad$ **C.** $(4, 4)$

Name ______________________ Class ______________ Date ______________

Review 141

Concurrent Lines, Medians, and Altitudes

OBJECTIVE: Finding the point of concurrency of the altitudes of acute, obtuse, and right triangles	**MATERIALS:** Protractor, straightedge

Example

Draw an obtuse triangle. Find the point of concurrency of the lines containing its altitudes.

Draw obtuse triangle ABC.

Extend side $\overline{AB}$.

Move the straightedge on your protractor along $\overrightarrow{AB}$ until C lies directly under 90. Label the point lying directly under C on $\overrightarrow{AB}$ as point D.

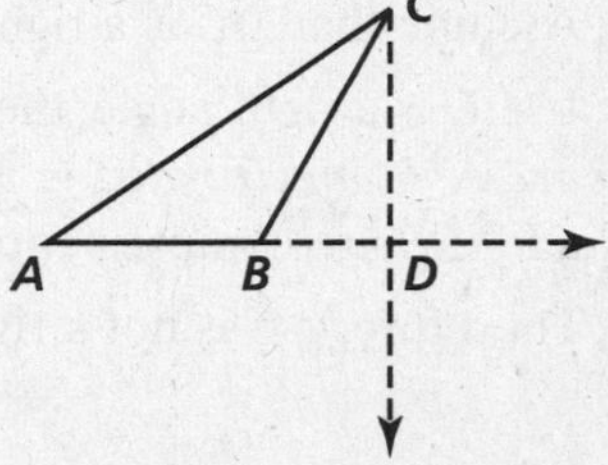

Draw $\overrightarrow{CD}$, the ray containing the altitude $\overline{CD}$.

Extend side $\overline{BC}$.

Move the straightedge on your protractor along $\overrightarrow{CB}$ until point A lies directly under 90. Label the point lying directly under A on $\overrightarrow{CB}$ as point E.

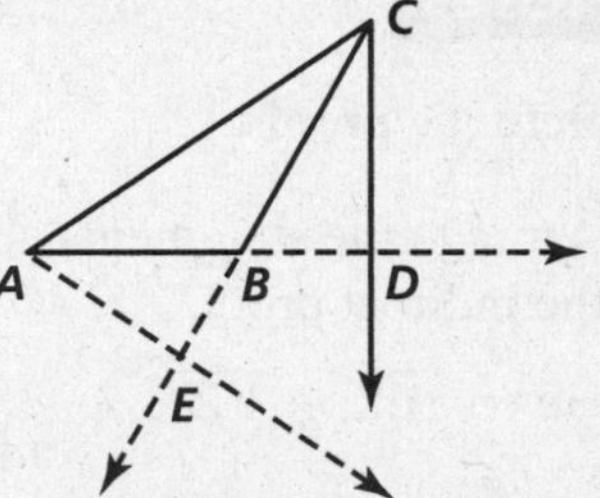

Draw $\overrightarrow{AE}$, the ray containing the altitude $\overline{AE}$.

Move the straightedge on your protractor along $\overline{AC}$ until B lies directly under 90. Label the point directly under B on $\overline{AC}$ as point F.

Draw $\overrightarrow{FB}$, the ray containing the altitude $\overline{BF}$.

The point of concurrency is G.

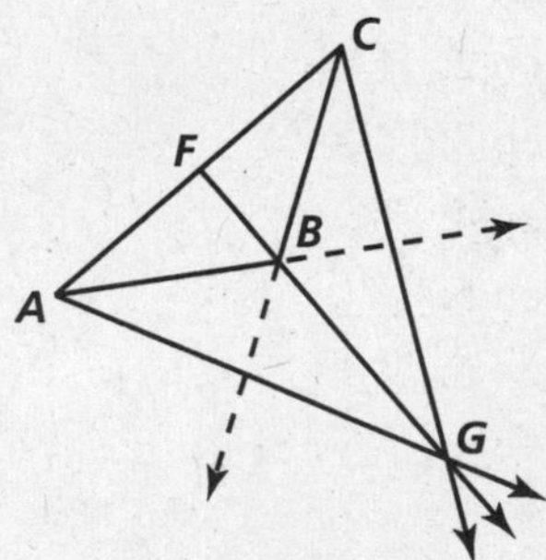

Exercises

Determine the point of concurrency.

1. Draw an acute triangle. Find the point of concurrency of the lines containing its altitudes.

2. Draw a right triangle. Find the point of concurrency of the lines containing its altitudes.

GEOMETRY TOPICS

Name ______________________ Class ______________ Date ____________

Review 142

Inverses, Contrapositives, and Indirect Reasoning

OBJECTIVE: Writing convincing arguments using indirect reasoning

MATERIALS: None

Example

Given: $\angle A$ and $\angle B$ are not complementary.

Prove: $\angle C$ is not a right angle.

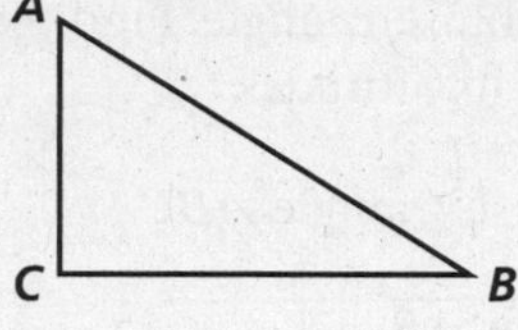

Step 1: Assume that $\angle C$ is a right angle.

Step 2: If $\angle C$ is a right angle, then by the Triangle Angle-Sum Theorem $m\angle A + m\angle B + 90 = 180$. So $m\angle A + m\angle B = 90$. Therefore, $\angle A$ and $\angle B$ are complementary. But $\angle A$ and $\angle B$ are not complementary.

Step 3: Therefore, $\angle C$ is not a right angle.

GEOMETRY TOPICS

Exercises

Complete the proofs.

1. Arrange the statements given at the right to complete the steps of the indirect proof.

Given: $\overline{XY} \ncong \overline{YZ}$

Prove: $\angle 1 \ncong \angle 4$

Step 1: ?

Step 2: ?

Step 3: ?

Step 4: ?

Step 5: ?

Step 6: ?

A. But $\overline{XY} \ncong \overline{YZ}$.

B. Assume $\angle 1 \cong \angle 4$.

C. Therefore, $\angle 1 \ncong \angle 4$.

D. $\angle 1$and $\angle 2$ are supplementary, and $\angle 3$ and $\angle 4$ are supplementary.

E. According to the Converse of the Isosceles Triangle Theorem, $XY = YZ$ or $\overline{XY} \cong \overline{YZ}$.

F. If $\angle 1 \cong \angle 4$, then by the Congruent Supplements Theorem, $\angle 2 \cong \angle 3$.

2. Complete the steps below to write a convincing argument using indirect reasoning.

Given: $\triangle DEF$ with $\angle D \ncong \angle F$

Prove: $\overline{EF} \ncong \overline{DE}$

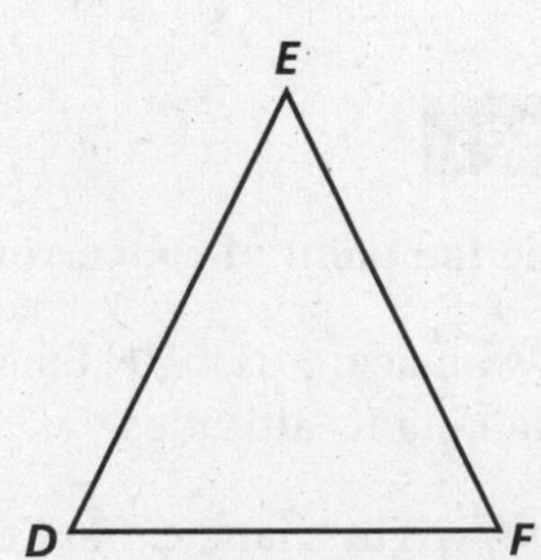

Step 1: ?

Step 2: ?

Step 3: ?

Step 4: ?

Name ______________________ Class ______________ Date ______________

Review 143

OBJECTIVE: Using inequalities involving triangle side lengths and angle measures to solve problems

MATERIALS: Straightedge

Example

Use the triangle inequality theorems to answer the questions.

a. Which is the largest angle of $\triangle ABC$?
$\overline{AB}$ is the longest side of $\triangle ABC$.
$\angle C$ lies opposite $\overline{AB}$.
$\angle C$ is the largest angle of $\triangle ABC$.

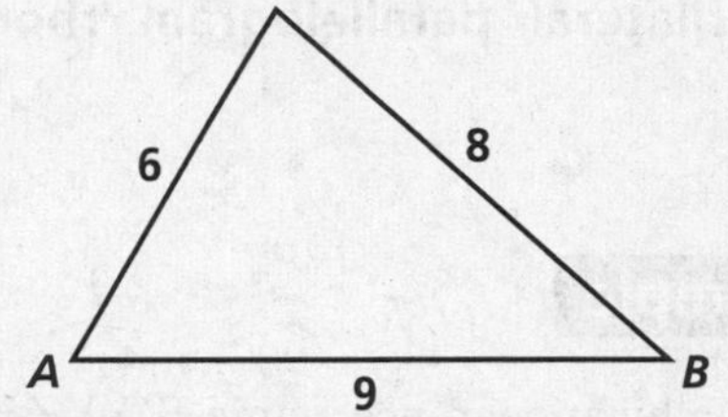

b. Which is the shortest side of $\triangle DEF$?
Find $m\angle E$.

$$\begin{aligned} m\angle D + m\angle E + m\angle F &= 180 && \text{Triangle Angle-Sum Theorem} \\ 30 + m\angle E + 90 &= 180 && \text{Substitution} \\ 120 + m\angle E &= 180 && \text{Addition} \\ m\angle E &= 60 && \text{Subtraction Property of Equality} \end{aligned}$$

$\angle D$ is the smallest angle of $\triangle DEF$.
Because $\overline{FE}$ lies opposite $\angle D$,
$\overline{FE}$ is the shortest side of $\triangle DEF$.

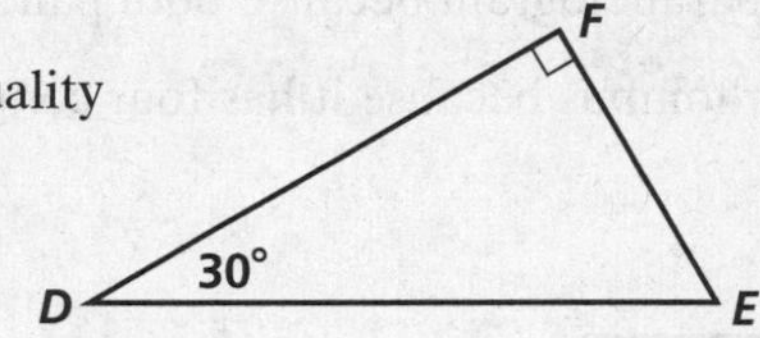

Exercises

Complete the following exercises.

1. Draw three triangles, one obtuse, one acute, and one right. Label the vertices. Exchange your triangles with a partner.

a. Identify the longest and shortest sides of each triangle.

b. Identify the largest and smallest angles of each triangle.

c. Describe the relationship between the longest and shortest sides and the largest and smallest angles for each of your partner's triangles.

Which are the largest and smallest angles of each triangle?

2.

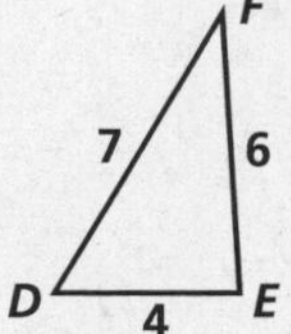

3.

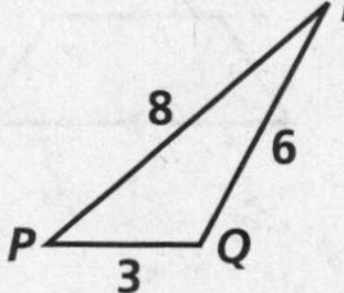

4.

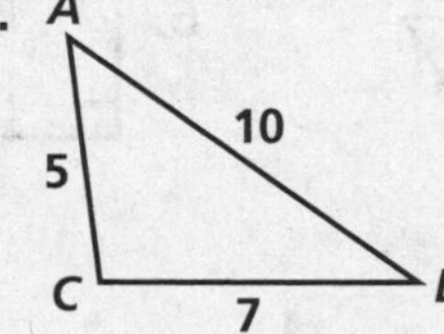

Which are the longest and shortest sides of each triangle?

5.

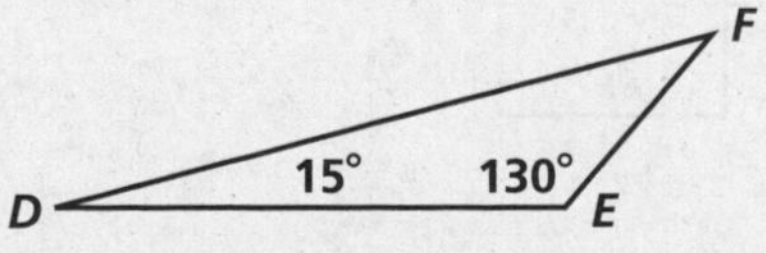

6.

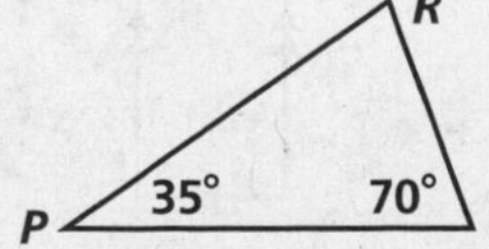

7.

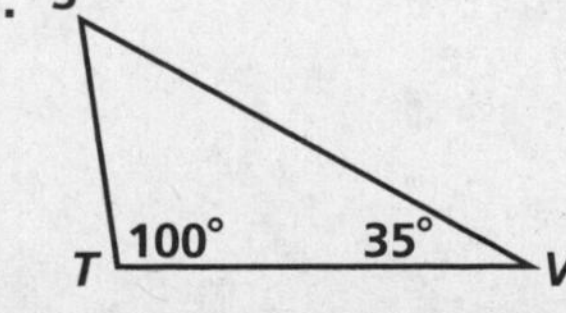

Name ____________________ Class ____________ Date ____________

Review 144

OBJECTIVE: Classifying special types of quadrilaterals

MATERIALS: Ruler, protractor

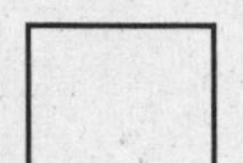
quadrilateral

parallelogram

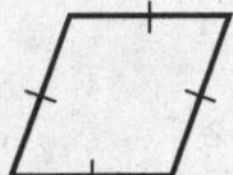
rhombus

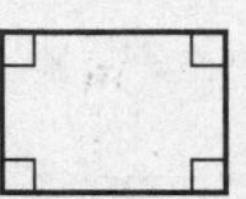
rectangle

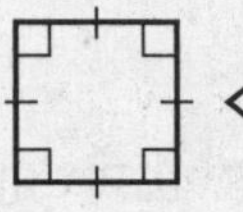
square

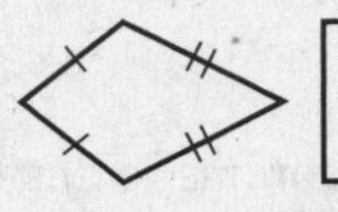
kite

trapezoid

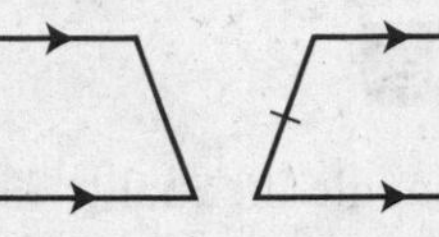
isosceles trapezoid

Example

Judging by appearance, name *WXYZ* in as many ways as possible.

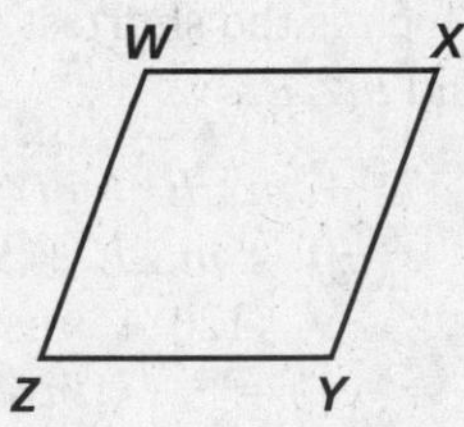

It is a quadrilateral because it has four sides.

It is a parallelogram because both pairs of opposite sides are parallel.

It is a rhombus because it has four congruent sides.

Exercises

Use a protractor and a ruler to sketch an example of each quadrilateral. Then name it in as many ways as possible.

1. a quadrilateral with exactly one pair of parallel sides
2. a quadrilateral with opposite sides parallel
3. a quadrilateral with four right angles
4. a quadrilateral with four congruent sides

Classify each quadrilateral by its most precise name.

5. 

6. 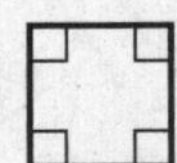

7. 

8. 

9. 

10. 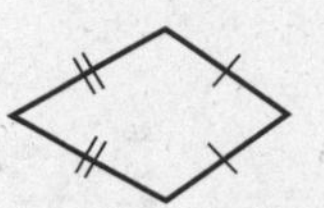

11. 

12. 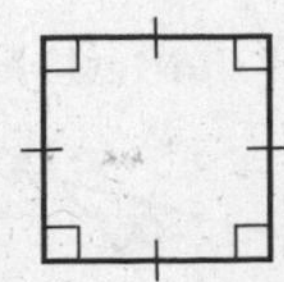

Name ______________________ Class ______________ Date ______________

Review 145

OBJECTIVE: Finding relationships among angles, sides, and diagonals of parallelograms

MATERIALS: None

Example

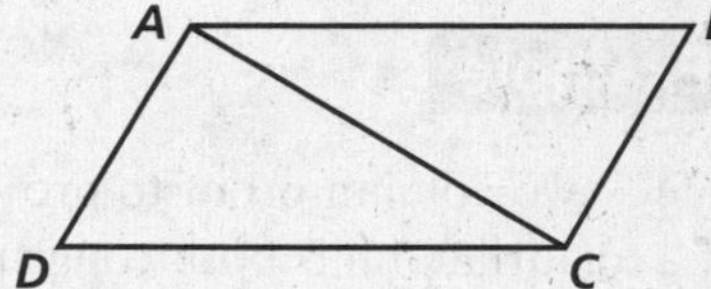

Use a two-column proof to prove Theorem 6-2: Opposite angles of a parallelogram are congruent.

Given: parallelogram $ABCD$

Prove: $\angle B \cong \angle D$

Statements	***Reasons***
1. parallelogram $ABCD$	**1.** Given
2. $\overline{AB} \cong \overline{CD}$, $\overline{BC} \cong \overline{DA}$	**2.** Opposite sides of a parallelogram are congruent.
3. $\overline{AC} \cong \overline{CA}$	**3.** Reflexive Property
4. $\triangle ABC \cong \triangle CDA$	**4.** SSS
5. $\angle B \cong \angle D$	**5.** CPCTC

Exercises

Use the figure to write a proof for each.

1. The proof in the example demonstrates that one pair of opposite angles is congruent. Prove that the other pair of opposite angles is congruent in parallelogram $ABCD$ above.

2. Given: parallelogram $ACDE$; $\overline{CD} \cong \overline{BD}$

Prove: $\angle CBD \cong \angle E$

3. Given: parallelogram $ACDE$; $\overline{AE} \cong \overline{BD}$

Prove: $\angle CBD \cong \angle C$

4. Given: parallelogram $ACDE$; $\angle CBD \cong \angle E$

Prove: $\triangle BDC$ is isosceles.

5. Given: isosceles trapezoid $ABDE$; $\angle C \cong \angle E$

Prove: $\overline{AE} \cong \overline{CD}$

Name ______________________ Class ____________ Date ____________

Review 146

Proving That a Quadrilateral Is a Parallelogram

OBJECTIVE: Finding characteristics of quadrilaterals that indicate that the quadrilaterals are parallelograms	**MATERIALS:** None

Example

Use a two-column proof to prove Theorem 6-6: If one pair of opposite sides of a quadrilateral is both congruent and parallel, then the quadrilateral is a parallelogram.

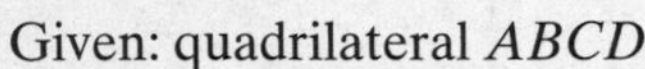

Given: quadrilateral $ABCD$

$\overline{AB} \cong \overline{CD}$

$\overline{AB} \parallel \overline{CD}$

Prove: $ABCD$ is a parallelogram.

Statements	***Reasons***
1. quadrilateral $ABCD$, $\overline{AB} \cong \overline{CD}$, $\overline{AB} \parallel \overline{CD}$	**1.** Given
2. $\angle BAC \cong \angle DCA$	**2.** Parallel lines form congruent alternate interior angles.
3. $\overline{AC} \cong \overline{CA}$	**3.** Reflexive Property
4. $\triangle ABC \cong \triangle CDA$	**4.** SAS
5. $\angle DAC \cong \angle BCA$	**5.** CPCTC
6. $\overline{AD} \parallel \overline{CB}$	**6.** If alternate interior angles are congruent, then lines are parallel.
7. $ABCD$ is a parallelogram.	**7.** Definition of parallelogram

Exercises

Determine whether the given information is sufficient to prove that quadrilateral *WXYZ* is a parallelogram.

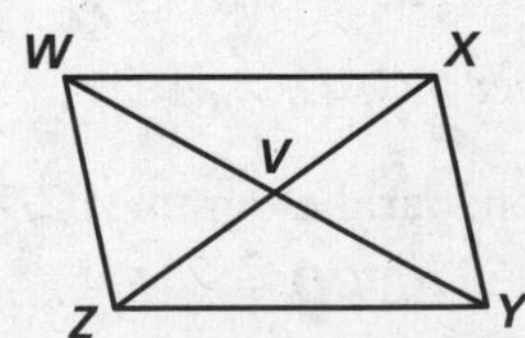

1. $\overline{WY}$ bisects $\overline{ZX}$

2. $\overline{WX} \parallel \overline{ZY}$; $\overline{WZ} \cong \overline{XY}$

3. $\overline{VZ} \cong \overline{VX}$; $\overline{WX} \cong \overline{ZY}$

4. $\angle VWZ \cong \angle VYX$; $\overline{WZ} \cong \overline{XY}$

Use the figure at the right to complete each proof.

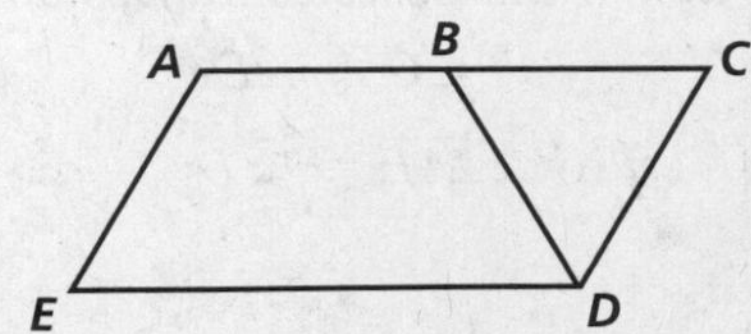

5. Given: triangle with $\overline{BD} \cong \overline{CD}$, $\overline{AE} \cong \overline{BD}$, and $\overline{AE} \parallel \overline{CD}$

Prove: $ACDE$ is a parallelogram.

6. Given: $\angle CBD \cong \angle C$, $\overline{AE} \cong \overline{BD}$, and $\overline{AC} \cong \overline{ED}$

Prove: $ACDE$ is a parallelogram.

Name ______________________ Class ______________ Date ______________

Review 147

Special Parallelograms

OBJECTIVE: Finding properties of rectangles and rhombuses

MATERIALS: None

Example

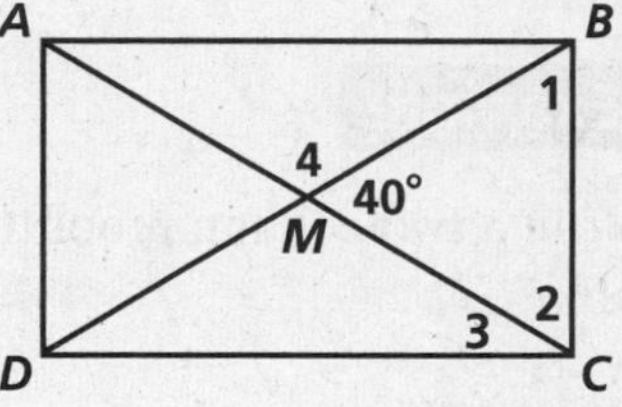

Find the measures of the numbered angles in the rectangle.

Because $\angle 4$ and $\angle BMC$ are supplementary, $m\angle 4 = 140$.

Because the diagonals of a rectangle are congruent, $AC = BD$. And because the diagonals bisect each other, $BM = CM$. Therefore, $\triangle BMC$ is isosceles with $BM = CM$.

So, by the Isosceles Triangle Theorem, $m\angle 1 = m\angle 2$.

$$m\angle 1 + m\angle 2 + 40 = 180$$
$$m\angle 1 + m\angle 1 + 40 = 180$$
$$2m\angle 1 = 140$$
$$m\angle 1 = 70$$
$$m\angle 2 = 70$$

Finally, because $\angle 2$ and $\angle 3$ are complementary, $m\angle 3 = 20$.

Exercises

Find the measures of the numbered angles in each rectangle.

1. 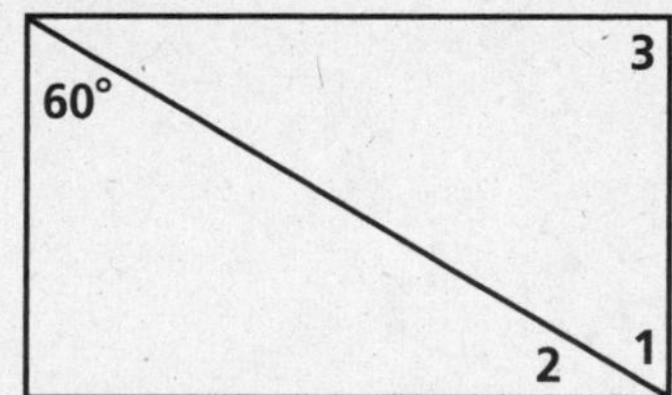

2. 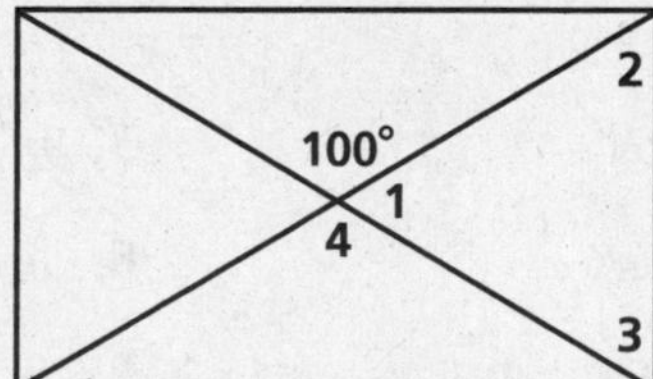

3. 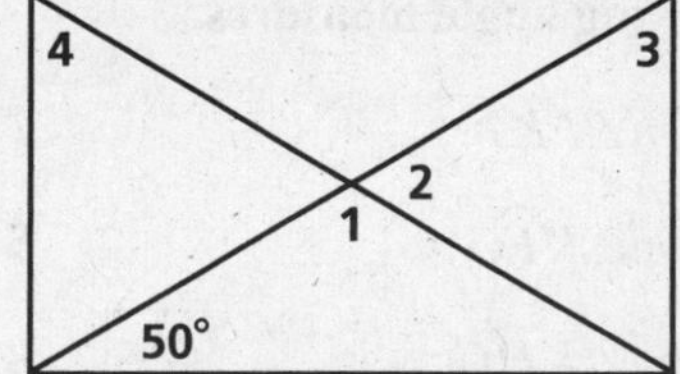

Find the measures of the numbered angles in each rhombus.

4. 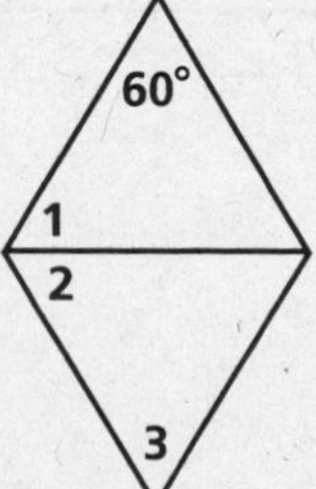

5. 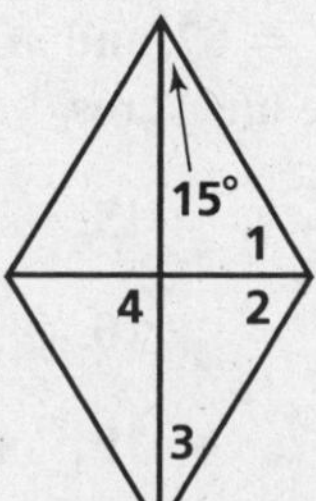

6. 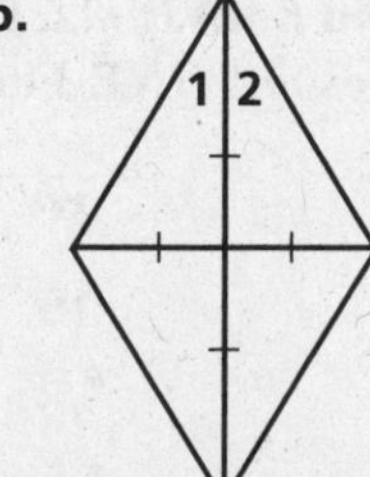

Name ______________________ Class ______________ Date ______________

Review 148

OBJECTIVE: Using triangle congruence and two-column proofs to find angle measures in trapezoids and kites

MATERIALS: None

Example

Write a two-column proof to identify three pairs of congruent triangles in kite *FGHJ.*

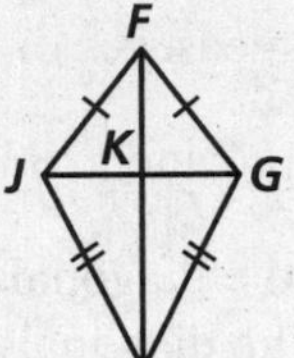

Statements	*Reasons*
1. $m\angle FKG = m\angle GKH = m\angle HKJ = m\angle JKF = 90$	**1.** Theorem 6-17
2. $\overline{FG} \cong \overline{FJ}$	**2.** Given
3. $\overline{FK} \cong \overline{FK}$	**3.** Reflexive Property of Congruence
4. $\triangle FKG \cong \triangle FKJ$	**4.** HL Theorem
5. $\overline{JK} \cong \overline{KG}$	**5.** CPCTC
6. $\overline{KH} \cong \overline{KH}$	**6.** Reflexive Property of Congruence
7. $\triangle JKH \cong \triangle GKH$	**7.** SAS Postulate
8. $\overline{JH} \cong \overline{GH}$	**8.** Given
9. $\overline{FH} \cong \overline{FH}$	**9.** Reflexive Property of Congruence
10. $\triangle FJH \cong \triangle FGH$	**10.** SSS Postulate

So $\triangle FKG \cong \triangle FKJ$, $\triangle JKH \cong \triangle GKH$, and $\triangle FJK \cong \triangle FGH$.

Exercises

In kite *FGHJ* in the example, $m\angle JFK = 38$ and $m\angle KGH = 63$. Find the following angle measures.

1. $m\angle FKJ$ **2.** $m\angle FJK$ **3.** $m\angle FKG$

4. $m\angle KFG$ **5.** $m\angle FGK$ **6.** $m\angle GKH$

7. $m\angle KHG$ **8.** $m\angle KJH$ **9.** $m\angle JHK$

10. Write a two-column proof to identify three pairs of congruent triangles in isosceles trapezoid *LMNP.*

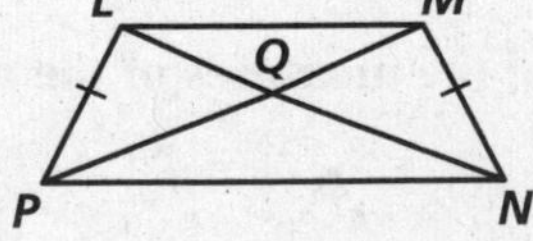

In isosceles trapezoid *LMNP*, $m\angle LPQ = 45$, $m\angle QMN = 87$, and $m\angle PQN$ is 12 less than 6 times $m\angle QNP$. Find the following angle measures.

11. $m\angle PLQ$ **12.** $m\angle LQP$ **13.** $m\angle MNQ$

14. $m\angle MQN$ **15.** $m\angle QNP$ **16.** $m\angle QPN$

17. $m\angle PQN$ **18.** $m\angle LMQ$ **19.** $m\angle LQM$

20. Use isosceles trapezoid *LMNP* to explain why in Chapter 4 you did not learn about an Angle-Angle-Angle Theorem to prove triangles congruent.

Name______________________________ Class__________________ Date______________

Review 149

OBJECTIVE: Choosing convenient placement of figures on coordinate axes

MATERIALS: None

Example

Use the properties of each figure to find the missing coordinates.

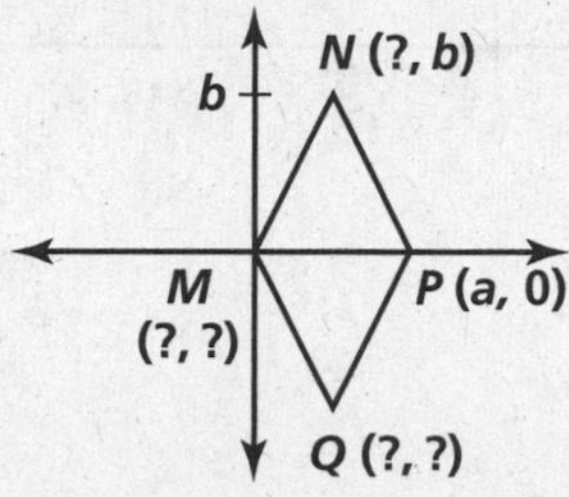

rhombus *MNPQ*

M is at the origin $(0, 0)$. Because diagonals of a rhombus bisect each other, N has x-coordinate $\frac{a}{2}$. Because the x-axis is a horizontal line of symmetry for the rhombus, Q has coordinates $(\frac{a}{2}, -b)$.

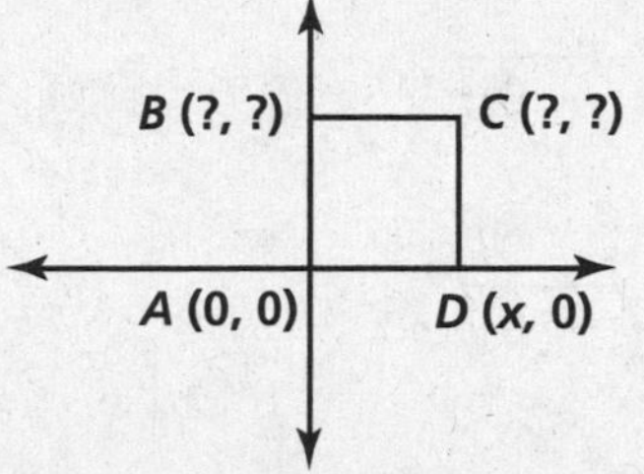

square *ABCD*

Because all sides are congruent, D has coordinates $(0, x)$. Because all angles are right, C has coordinates (x, x).

Exercises

Use the properties of each figure to find the missing coordinates.

1. parallelogram *OPQR*

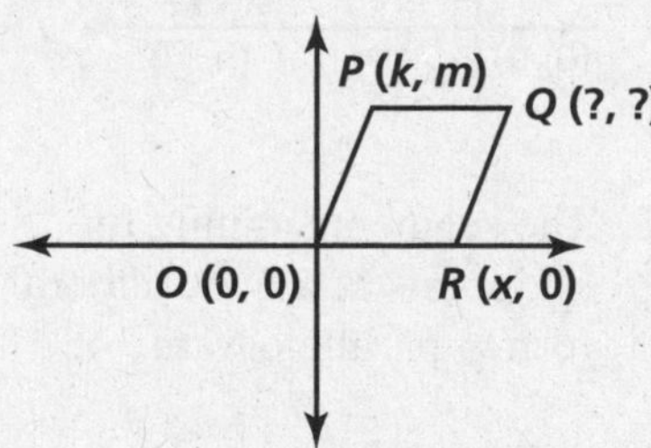

2. rhombus *XYZW*

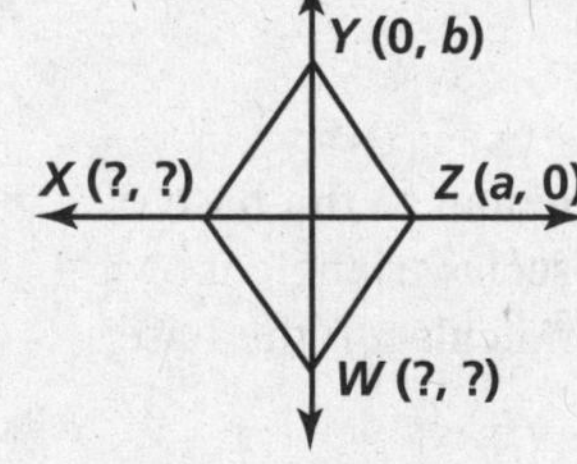

3. square *QRST*

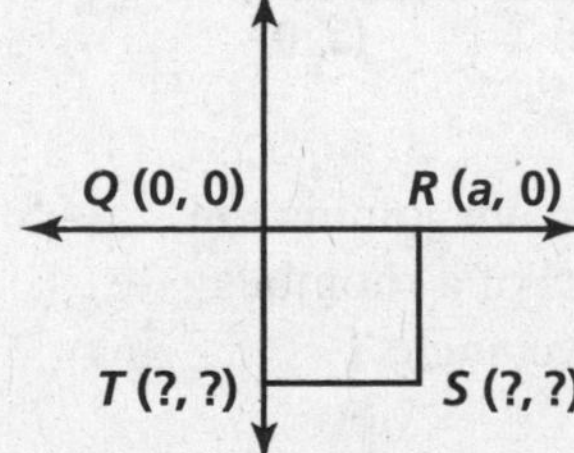

4. A quadrilateral has vertices at $(a, 0)$, $(-a, 0)$, $(0, a)$, and $(0, -a)$. Show that it is a square.

5. A quadrilateral has vertices at $(a, 0)$, $(0, a + 1)$, $(-a, 0)$ and $(0, -a - 1)$. Show that it is a rhombus.

6. Isosceles trapezoid $ABCD$ has vertices $A(0, 0)$, $B(x, 0)$, and $D(k, m)$. Find the coordinates of C in terms of x, k, and m. Assume $\overline{AB} \parallel \overline{CD}$.

Name ______________________ Class ______________ Date ______________

Review 150

Proofs Using Coordinate Geometry

OBJECTIVE: Proving theorems using figures in the coordinate plane

MATERIALS: None

Example

Use coordinate geometry to prove that the diagonals of a rectangle are congruent.

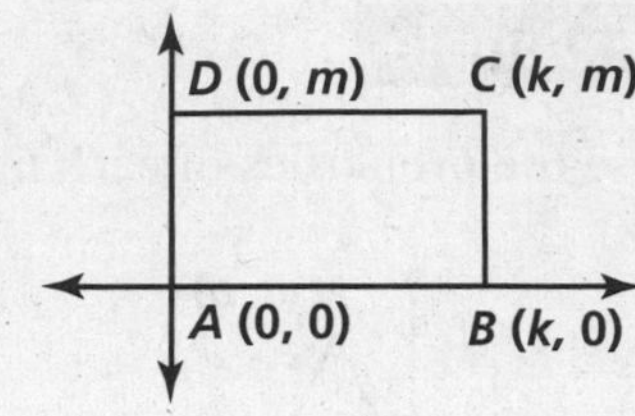

$$AC = \sqrt{(k - 0)^2 + (m - 0)^2}$$
$$= \sqrt{k^2 + m^2}$$
$$BD = \sqrt{(0 - k)^2 + (m - 0)^2}$$
$$= \sqrt{(-k)^2 + m^2}$$
$$= \sqrt{k^2 + m^2}$$
$$\overline{AC} \cong \overline{BD}$$

Exercises

Use coordinate geometry and the figures provided to prove the theorems.

1. Diagonals of an isosceles trapezoid are congruent.

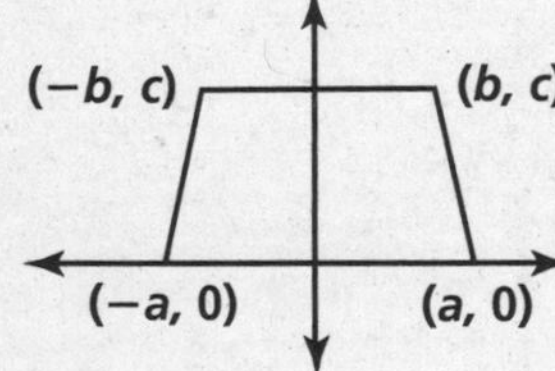

2. The line containing the midpoints of two sides of a triangle is parallel to the third side.

(b, c)
(0, 0)
(a, 0)

3. The segments joining the midpoints of a rectangle form a rhombus.

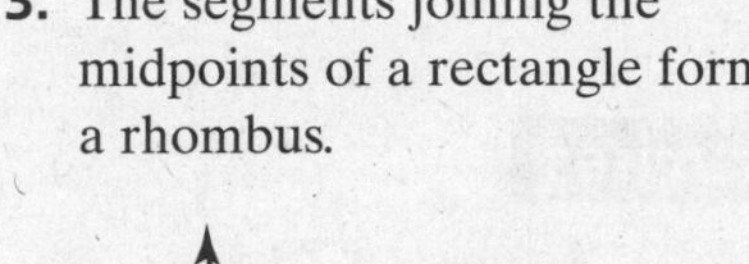

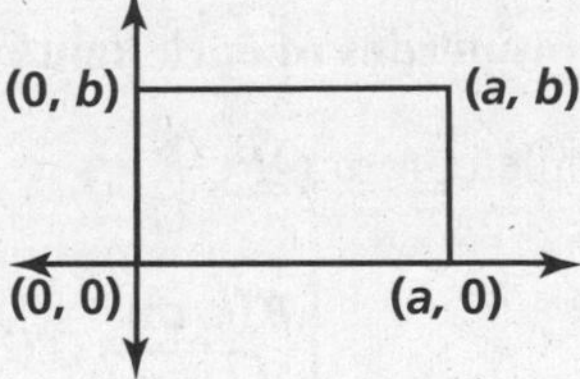

4. The segments joining the midpoints of a rhombus form a rectangle.

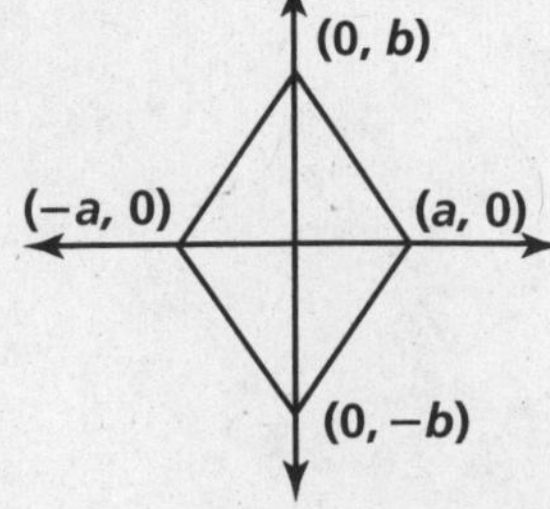

5. The median to the base of an isosceles triangle is perpendicular to the base.

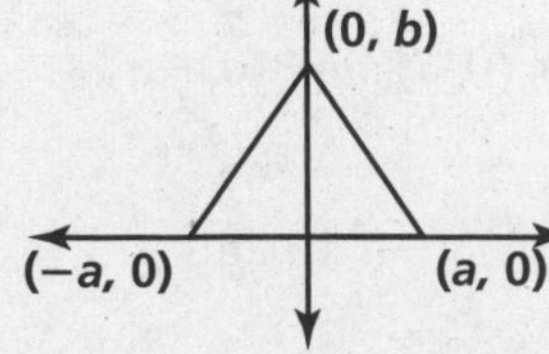

6. The segments joining the midpoints of a quadrilateral form a parallelogram.

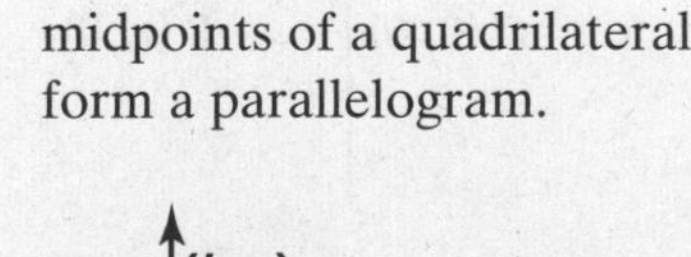

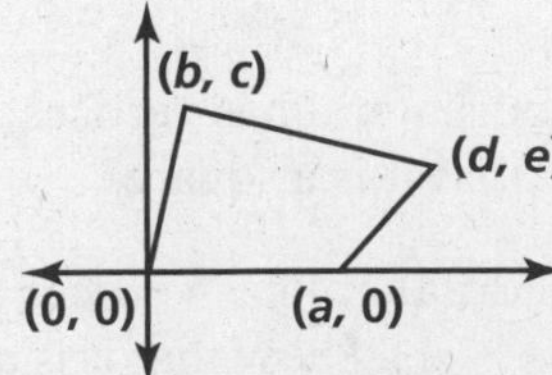

Name ____________________ Class ____________ Date ____________

Review 151

Areas of Parallelograms and Triangles

OBJECTIVE: Finding areas of triangles and parallelograms	**MATERIALS:** Graph paper

Example

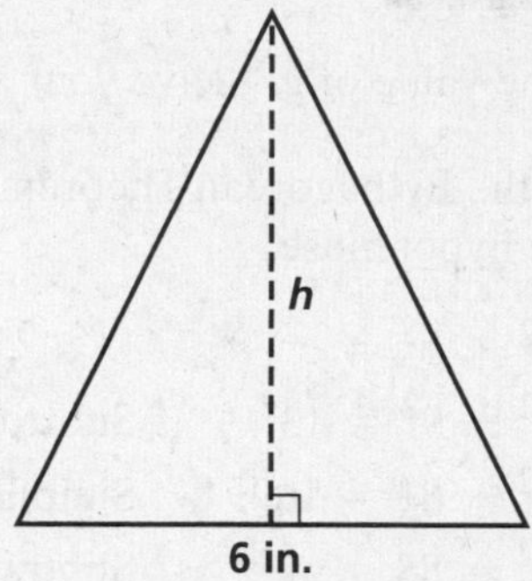

A triangle has an area of 18 in.^{2} The length of its base is 6 in. Find its corresponding height.

Draw a sketch. Then substitute into the area formula, and solve for *h*.

$A = \frac{1}{2}bh$

$18 = \frac{1}{2}(6)h$ Substitute.

$18 = 3h$ Simplify.

$h = 6$

The height of the triangle is 6 in.

Exercises

Complete each exercise.

1. Use graph paper. Draw an obtuse, an acute, and a right triangle, each with an area of 12 square units. Label the base and height of each triangle.
2. Draw a different obtuse, acute, and right triangle, each with an area of 12 square units. Label the base and height of each triangle.
3. A triangle has height 5 cm and base length 8 cm. Find its area.
4. A triangle has height 11 in. and base length 10 in. Find its area.
5. A triangle has area 24 m^2 and base length 8 m. Find its height.
6. A triangle has area 16 ft^2 and height 4 ft. Find its base.
7. A triangle has area 8 in.^{2} The lengths of the base and the height are equal. Find the length of its base.
8. On graph paper draw three parallelograms, each with an area of 24 square units. Label the base and height of each parallelogram.
9. A parallelogram has area 35 in.^{2} and height 7 in. Find its base.
10. A parallelogram has area 391 cm^2 and base 17 cm. Find its height.
11. A parallelogram has area 81 ft^2. The lengths of the base and the height are equal. Find the length of its base.

GEOMETRY TOPICS

Name ______________________ Class ______________ Date ______________

Review 152

The Pythagorean Theorem and Its Converse

OBJECTIVE: Using the Pythagorean Theorem **MATERIALS:** Graph paper

Example

Find the value of g. Leave your answer in simplest radical form.

Using the Pythagorean Theorem, substitute g and 9 for the legs and 13 for the hypotenuse.

9 g 13

$a^2 + b^2 = c^2$	
$g^2 + 9^2 = 13^2$	Substitute.
$g^2 + 81 = 169$	Simplify.
$g^2 = 88$	Subtract 81 from each side.
$g = \sqrt{88}$	Take the square root.
$g = \sqrt{4(22)}$	Simplify.
$g = 2\sqrt{22}$	

GEOMETRY TOPICS

Exercises

Complete each exercise.

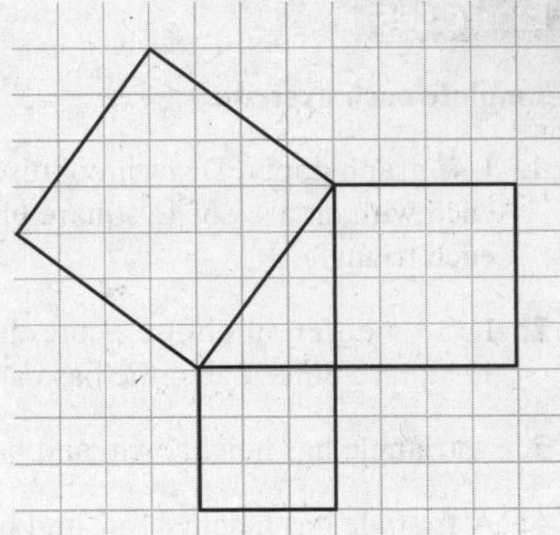

1. Draw a right triangle on graph paper so that the vertices are on the intersection of grid lines. Measure and label the lengths of the sides.
2. Construct a square on each side of the right triangle as shown.
3. Find the area of each square.
4. How does the sum of the areas of the two smaller squares compare with the area of the largest square?
5. What does this tell you about the relationship between the sides of the triangle?

Find the missing side lengths. Leave your answers in simplest radical form.

6. 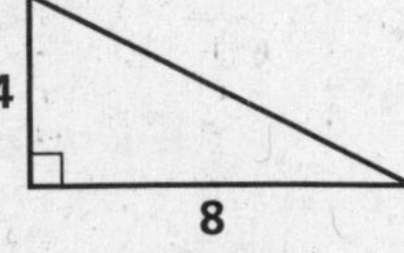

7. 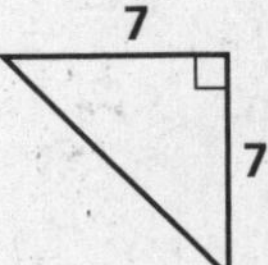

8. 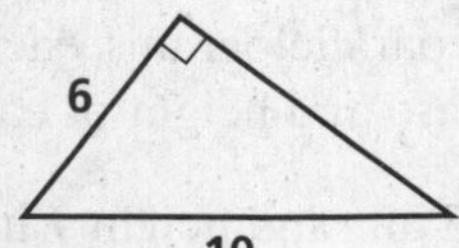

9. 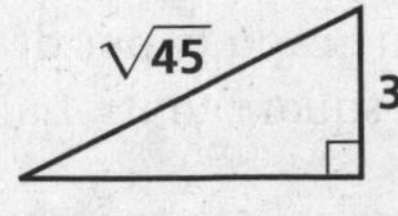

Name ______________________ Class ____________ Date ____________

Review 153

OBJECTIVE: Using the properties of a 30°-60°-90° triangle

MATERIALS: Centimeter grid paper, ruler, protractor

Example

Find the value of each variable.

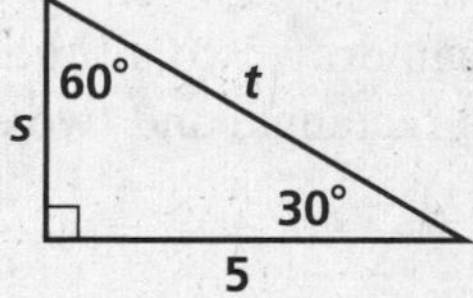

$5 = \sqrt{3}s$ — In a 30°-60°-90° triangle the length of the longer leg is $\sqrt{3}$ times the length of the shorter leg.

$\frac{5}{\sqrt{3}} = s$ — Divide both sides by $\sqrt{3}$.

$s = \frac{5}{\sqrt{3}} \cdot \frac{\sqrt{3}}{\sqrt{3}} = \frac{5\sqrt{3}}{3}$ — Rationalize the denominator.

The length of the hypotenuse is twice the length of the shorter leg.

$t = 2\left(\frac{5\sqrt{3}}{3}\right) = \frac{10\sqrt{3}}{3}$

Exercises

Complete each exercise.

1. Draw a horizontal line segment on centimeter grid paper so that the endpoints are at the intersections of grid lines.
2. Use a protractor and a straightedge to construct a 30°-60°-90° triangle with your segment as one of its sides.
3. Use the 30°-60°-90° Triangle Theorem to calculate the lengths of the other two sides. Round to the nearest tenth.
4. Measure the lengths of the sides to the nearest tenth of a centimeter.
5. Compare your calculated results with your measured results.
6. Repeat the activity with a different segment.

For Exercises 7–10, find the value of each variable.

7.

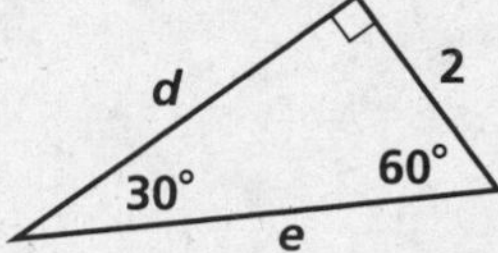

8.

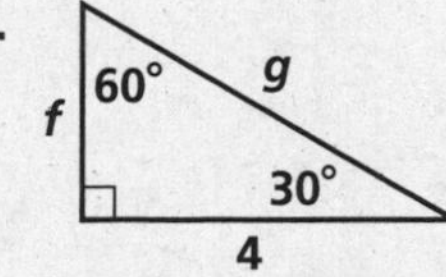

9.

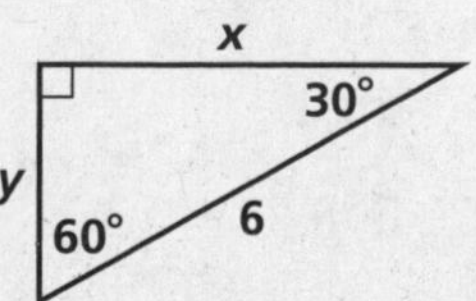

10.

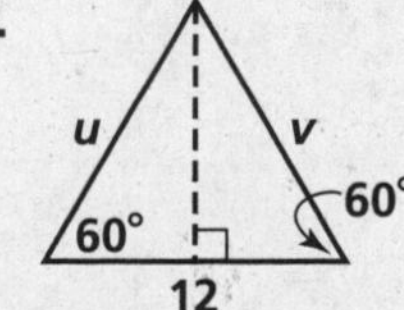

Name ______________________ Class ______________ Date ______________

Review 154

Areas of Trapezoids, Rhombuses, and Kites

OBJECTIVE: Finding areas of trapezoids and kites **MATERIALS:** Centimeter grid paper

Example

Find the area of trapezoid *EFGH*.

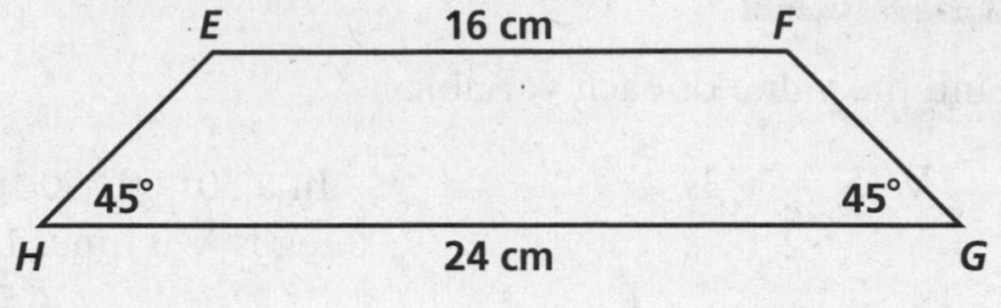

You can draw two altitudes that divide the trapezoid into a rectangle and two congruent 45°-45°-90° triangles.

$\frac{24 - 16}{2} = \frac{8}{2} = 4$ Find the length of the base of each triangle.

Because the legs of a 45°-45°-90° triangle have the same length, $h = 4$.

$A = \frac{1}{2}h(b_1 + b_2)$ Use the formula for the area of a trapezoid.

$= \frac{1}{2} \cdot 4(16 + 24)$ Substitute.

$= 80$ Simplify.

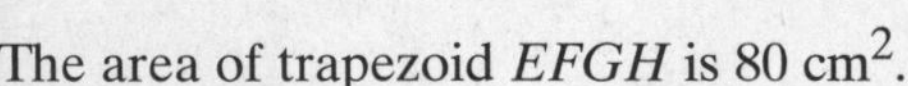

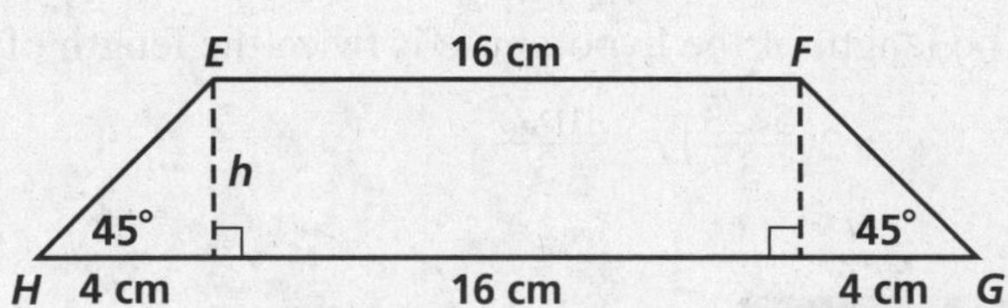

The area of trapezoid *EFGH* is 80 cm^2.

Exercises

Complete each exercise.

1. On centimeter grid paper, try to draw a trapezoid with area 48 cm^2.
2. Measure the bases and the height of the trapezoid.
3. Use the formula to calculate the actual area of the trapezoid.
4. Revise your figure until its area is 48 cm^2 or very close.
5. On centimeter grid paper, try to draw a kite with area 18 cm^2.
6. Measure the diagonals of the kite.
7. Use the formula to calculate the actual area of the kite.
8. Revise your figure until its area is 18 cm^2 or very close.

Find the area of each figure to the nearest tenth.

9.

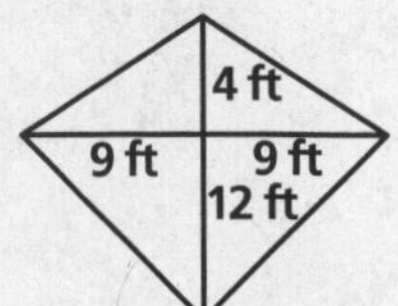

10.

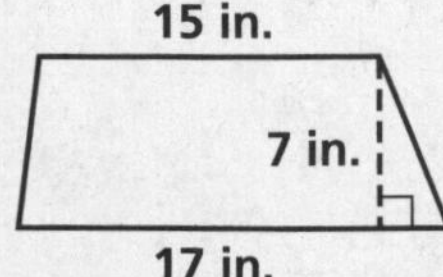

11.

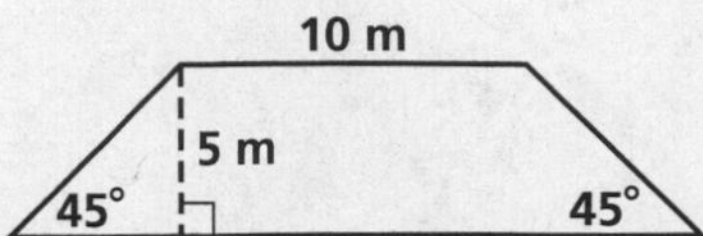

12.

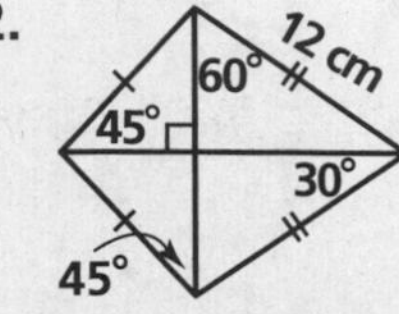

Name ____________________ Class ____________ Date ____________

Review 155

Areas of Regular Polygons

OBJECTIVE: Finding areas of regular polygons **MATERIALS:** Graph paper

Example

Find the area of a regular quadrilateral (square) inscribed in a circle with radius 4 cm.

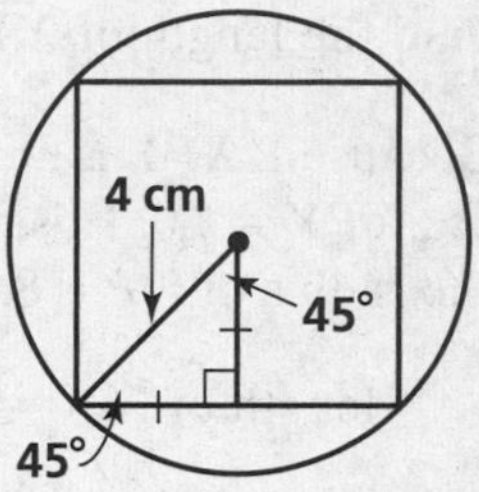

Draw one apothem to the base to form a 45°-45°-90° triangle. Using the 45°-45°-90° Triangle Theorem, find the length of the apothem.

$4 = \sqrt{2}a$ The hypotenuse = $\sqrt{2}$ · leg in a 45°-45°-90° triangle.

$a = \frac{4}{\sqrt{2}}$ Simplify.

$a = \frac{4}{\sqrt{2}} \cdot \frac{\sqrt{2}}{\sqrt{2}} = 2\sqrt{2}$ Rationalize the denominator.

The apothem has the same length as the other leg, which is half as long as a side of the square. So the length of a side of the square is $2(2\sqrt{2})$ cm or $4\sqrt{2}$ cm. To find the square's area, use the formula for the area of a regular polygon.

$A = \frac{1}{2}ap$

$= \frac{1}{2}(2\sqrt{2})(16\sqrt{2})$ $p = 4(4\sqrt{2}) = 16\sqrt{2}$

$= 32$

The area of the regular quadrilateral is 32 cm^2.

Exercises

Complete each exercise.

1. Draw a square on graph paper.
2. Draw and label an apothem and a radius.
3. Measure the lengths of the apothem, the radius, and a side.
4. Check that the apothem equals half the length of a side.
5. Use a calculator to check that the apothem times $\sqrt{2}$ equals the radius.

Find the area of each square.

6. 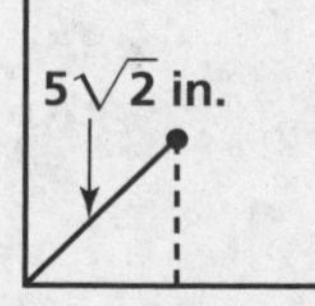

7. 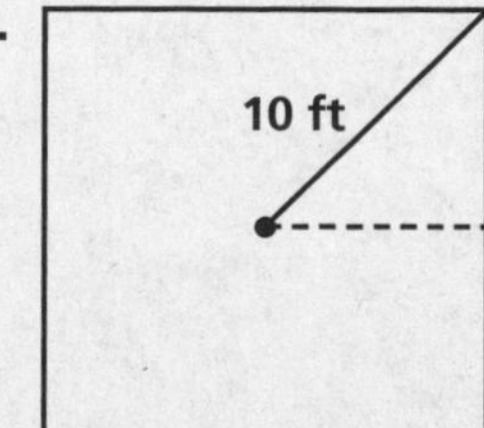

8. 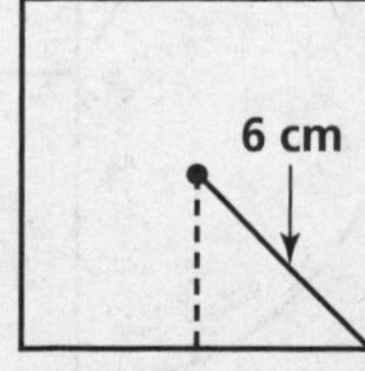

9. 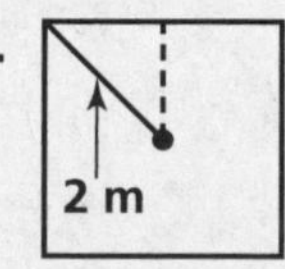

GEOMETRY TOPICS

Name ________________ Class ________________ Date ________________

Review 156

OBJECTIVE: Finding the length of an arc **MATERIALS:** Compass, protractor, string, ruler

Example

Find the length of $\overset{\frown}{XY}$. Leave your answer in terms of π.

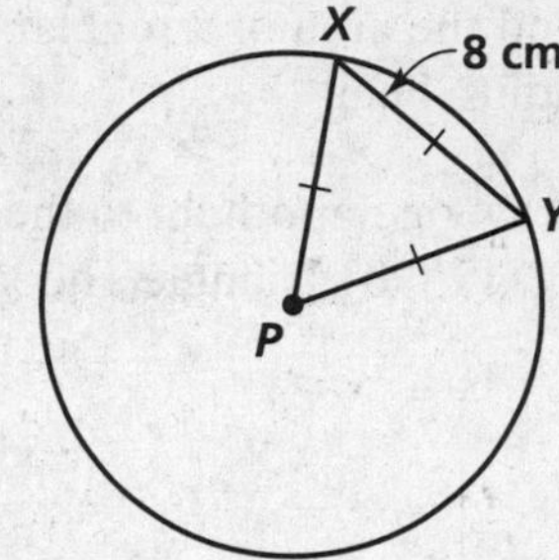

Because $\triangle XPY$ is an equilateral triangle and therefore equiangular, $m\angle XPY = 60$. This means that $m\overset{\frown}{XY} = 60$. Because $\overline{XY} \cong \overline{PY}$, the radius of $\odot P$ is 8.

$$\text{length of } \overset{\frown}{XY} = \frac{m\overset{\frown}{XY}}{360} \cdot 2\pi r \quad \text{Use formula for arc length.}$$

$$= \frac{60}{360} \cdot 2\pi(8) \quad \text{Substitute.}$$

$$= \frac{8\pi}{3} \quad \text{Simplify.}$$

The length of $\overset{\frown}{XY}$ is $\frac{8\pi}{3}$ cm.

Exercises

Complete each exercise.

1. Draw a large circle with a central angle less than 180°.
2. Use a protractor to measure the central angle.
3. Use a ruler to measure the length of the radius.
4. Use the formula for arc length to find the length of the arc intercepted by the central angle.
5. Lay a piece of string along the circle. Mark the string at the endpoints of the arc. Measure the length of string between the marks using a ruler.
6. How does your calculated result compare with your measured result?

Find the length of each arc. Leave your answers in terms of π.

7. $\overset{\frown}{SV}$
8. $\overset{\frown}{UV}$
9. $\overset{\frown}{SUT}$
10. $\overset{\frown}{UTV}$
11. $\overset{\frown}{UT}$
12. $\overset{\frown}{VT}$
13. $\overset{\frown}{UVT}$

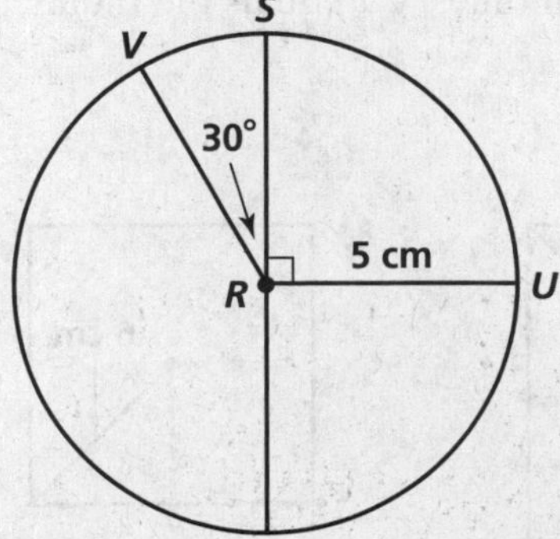

Name ______________________ Class ______________ Date ______________

Review 157

Areas of Circles and Sectors

OBJECTIVE: Computing the areas of circles	**MATERIALS:** Graph paper

Example

Find the area of a circle with circumference 24π cm. Leave your answers in terms of π.

Use the formula for circumference, and solve for *d*.

$$C = \pi d$$
$$24\pi = \pi d$$
$$d = 24$$

Because the radius is half the diameter, $r = 12$ cm.

$$A = \pi r^2$$
$$= \pi \cdot 12^2$$
$$= 144\pi$$

The area of the circle is 144π cm^2.

Exercises

Complete each exercise.

1. On graph paper, draw a circle whose center is at the intersection of grid lines.
2. Find and label the length of a radius.
3. Estimate the area of the circle by counting the number of squares and parts of squares in the circle.
4. Calculate the area of the circle using the formula. Round your answer to the nearest tenth.
5. How does your calculated result compare with your estimated result?
6. Repeat the activity with a different size circle.

Compute the area of the circle. Leave your answers in terms of π.

7. circle with radius 5 ft
8. circle with radius 2 in.
9. circle with diameter 16 m
10. circle with diameter 9 ft
11. circle with circumference 36π cm
12. circle with circumference 16π in.

In $\odot Q$, sector *PQR* has an area of 27.2π cm^2 and $m\widehat{PR} = 50°$.

13. What is the length of the radius to the nearest centimeter?
14. What is the area of the circle to the nearest square centimeter?

GEOMETRY TOPICS

Name ______________________ Class ______________ Date ______________

Review 158

OBJECTIVE: Using geometric models to find the probability of events

MATERIALS: Tacks, 3-in. by 5-in. index card, compass

Example

If a dart lands at random on the poster at the right, what is the probability that the dart will land inside one of the polygons?

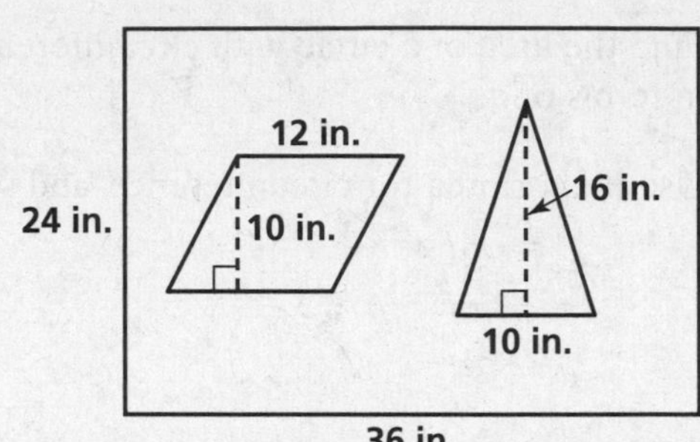

Find the sum of the areas of the polygons.

$$\begin{aligned}\text{Area of polygons} &= \text{Area of parallelogram} + \text{Area of triangle}\\ &= (12)(10) + \tfrac{1}{2}(10)(16)\\ &= 120 + 80\\ &= 200 \text{ in.}^2\end{aligned}$$

Find the total area of the poster.

$A = (24)(36) = 864 \text{ in.}^2$

Calculate the probability.

$$\begin{aligned}P(\text{polygon}) &= \frac{\text{area of polygons}}{\text{total area}}\\ &= \frac{200}{864}\\ &\approx 23\%\end{aligned}$$

Exercises

Complete each exercise.

1. Use a compass to draw a circle with radius 1 in. on an index card.

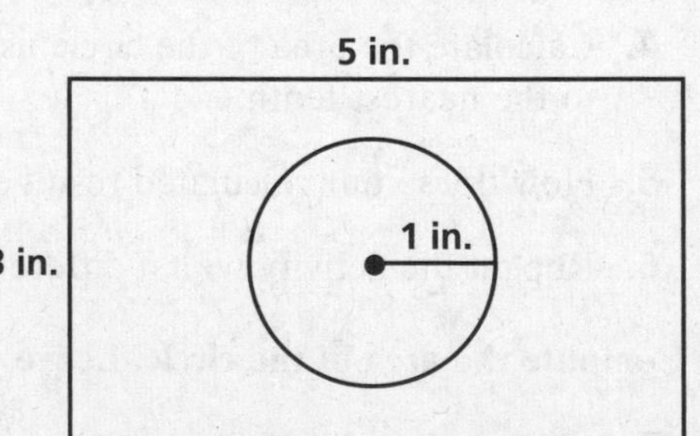

2. Calculate the probability that if a tack is dropped on the card, its tip will land in the circle.
3. Lift a tack 12 in. above the index card and drop it. Repeat this 25 times. Record how many times the tip of the tack lands on the circle. (Ignore the times that the tack bounces off the card.) Calculate the experimental probability:

$$P = \frac{\text{number of times tip landed in circle}}{25}$$

4. How do the probabilities you found in Exercises 2 and 3 compare?
5. If you repeated the experiment 100 times, what would you expect the results to be?
6. If a dart lands at random on the poster at the right, what is the probability that the dart will land in a circle?

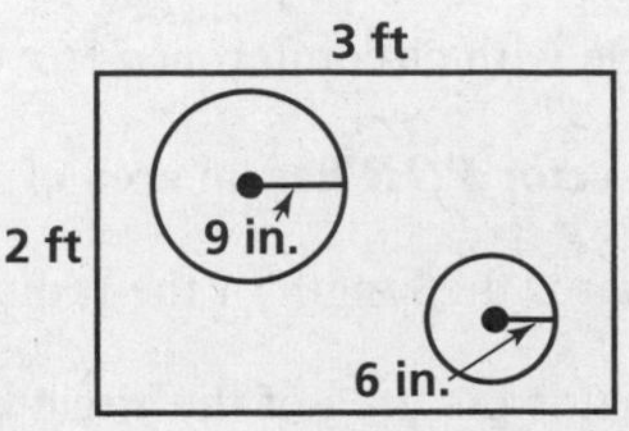

Name ______________________ Class ______________ Date ______________

Review 159

Ratios and Proportions

OBJECTIVE: Using proportions to solve problems involving large numbers

MATERIALS: None

Example

About 15 of every 1000 lightbulbs assembled at the Brite Lite Company are defective. If the Brite Lite Company assembles approximately 13,000 lightbulbs each day, about how many are defective?

Set up a proportion to solve the problem. Let x represent the number of defective lightbulbs per day.

$$\frac{15}{1000} = \frac{x}{13{,}000}$$

$$15(13{,}000) = 1000x \qquad \text{Use the cross-product property.}$$

$$195{,}000 = 1000x$$

$$\frac{195{,}000}{1000} = x$$

$$195 = x$$

About 195 of the 13,000 lightbulbs assembled each day are defective.

Exercises

Use a proportion to solve each problem.

1. About 45 of every 300 apples picked at the Newbury Apple Orchard are rotted. If 3560 apples were picked one week, about how many apples were rotted?

2. A grocer orders 800 gallons of milk each week. He throws out about 64 gallons of spoiled milk each week. Of the 9600 gallons of milk he ordered over three months, about how many gallons of spoiled milk were thrown out?

3. Seven of every 20 employees at V & B Bank Company are between the ages of 20 and 30. If there are 13,220 employees at V & B Bank Company, how many are between the ages of 20 and 30?

4. About 56 of every 700 picture frames put together in an assembly line have broken pieces of glass. If 60,000 picture frames are assembled each month, about how many will have broken pieces of glass?

Algebra **Solve each proportion.**

5. $\frac{300}{1600} = \frac{x}{4800}$

6. $\frac{40}{140} = \frac{700}{x}$

7. $\frac{x}{2000} = \frac{17}{400}$

8. $\frac{35}{x} = \frac{150}{2400}$

9. $\frac{x}{1040} = \frac{290}{5200}$

10. $\frac{x}{42{,}000} = \frac{87}{500}$

11. $\frac{x}{380} = \frac{180}{5700}$

12. $\frac{1200}{90{,}000} = \frac{270}{x}$

13. $\frac{325}{x} = \frac{7306}{56{,}200}$

Review 160

OBJECTIVE: Finding how to use ratio and proportion with similar polygons

MATERIALS: None

Example

Are the quadrilaterals similar? If they are, write a similarity statement, and give the similarity ratio. If they are not, explain.

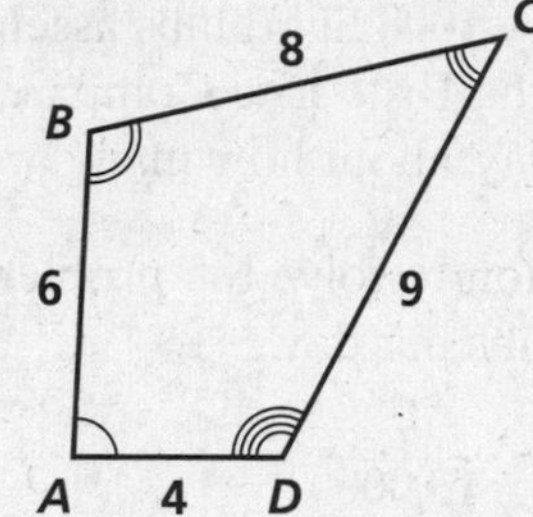

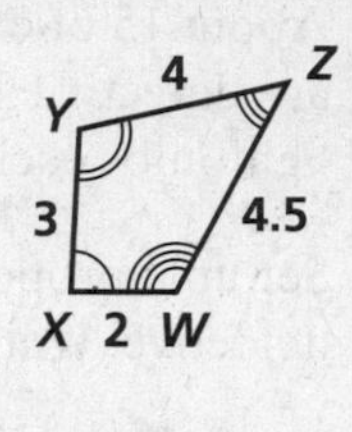

Compare angles: $\angle A \cong \angle X, \angle B \cong \angle Y, \angle C \cong \angle Z, \angle D \cong \angle W$

Compare ratios of sides: $\frac{AB}{XY} = \frac{6}{3} = 2$ $\quad \frac{CD}{ZW} = \frac{9}{4.5} = 2$

$\frac{BC}{YZ} = \frac{8}{4} = 2$ $\quad \frac{DA}{WX} = \frac{4}{2} = 2$

Because corresponding sides are proportional and corresponding angles are congruent, $ABCD \sim XYZW$.

The similarity ratio of $ABCD$ to $XYZW$ is 2 : 1.

Exercises

If the polygons are similar, write a similarity statement, and give the similarity ratio of the first figure to the second. If not, write *not similar.*

1.

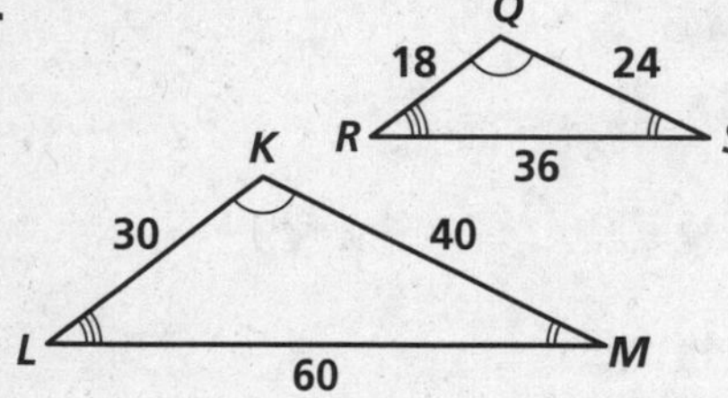

2.

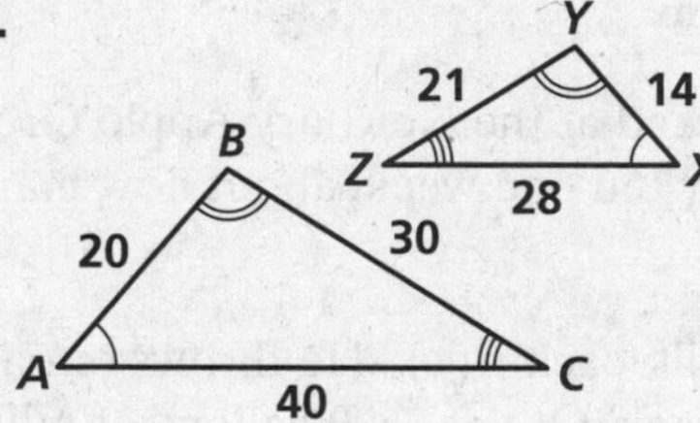

3.

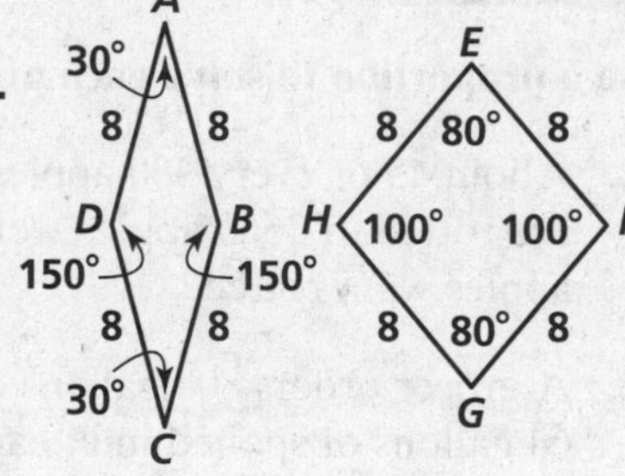

4.

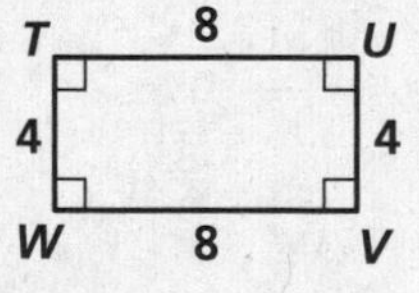

5.

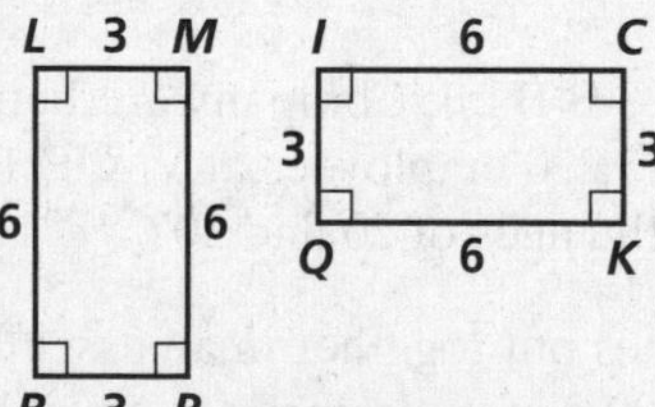

6.

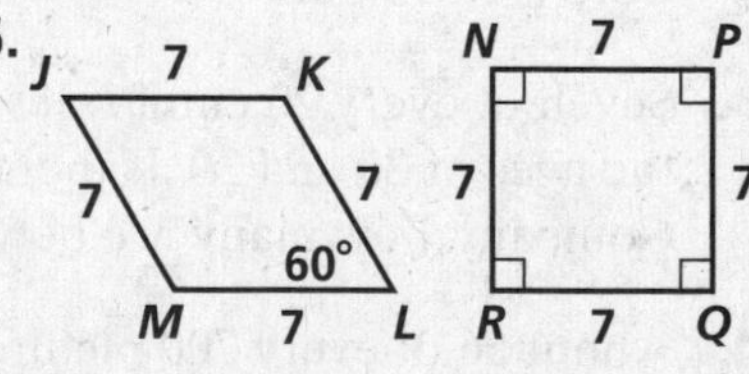

State whether the figures are similar. If so, give the similarity ratio.

7. a square with sides of length 10 and a square with sides of length 11

8. a rhombus with sides of length 4 containing a 30° angle and a rhombus with sides of length 4 containing a 40° angle

9. a rhombus with sides of length 4 containing a 50° angle and a rhombus with sides of length 9 containing a 130° angle

Name ______________________ Class ______________ Date ______________

Review 161

Proving Triangles Similar

OBJECTIVE: Proving two triangles similar using the AA ~ Postulate and the SAS ~ and SSS ~ Theorems

MATERIALS: None

Example

Explain why the triangles are similar. Then write a similarity statement.

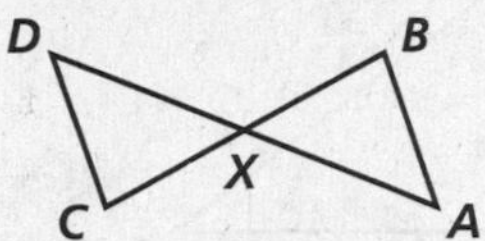

Given: $\overline{DC} \parallel \overline{BA}$

Because $\overline{DC} \parallel \overline{BA}$, $\angle A$ and $\angle D$ are alternate interior angles and are therefore $\cong$. The same is true for $\angle B$ and $\angle C$. So, by AA ~ Postulate, $\triangle ABX \sim \triangle DCX$.

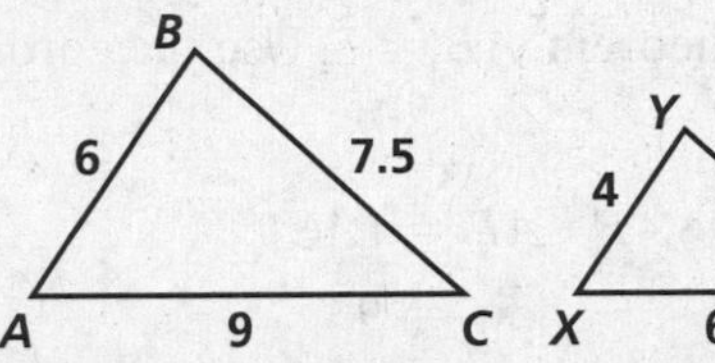

Compare the ratios of the lengths of sides: $\frac{AB}{XY} = \frac{BC}{YZ} = \frac{CA}{ZX} = \frac{3}{2}$

So, by SSS ~ Theorem, $\triangle ABC \sim \triangle XYX$.

Exercises

Are the pairs of triangles similar? If so, state which postulate or theorem allows you to conclude this, and write a similarity statement. If not, write *not similar*.

1. 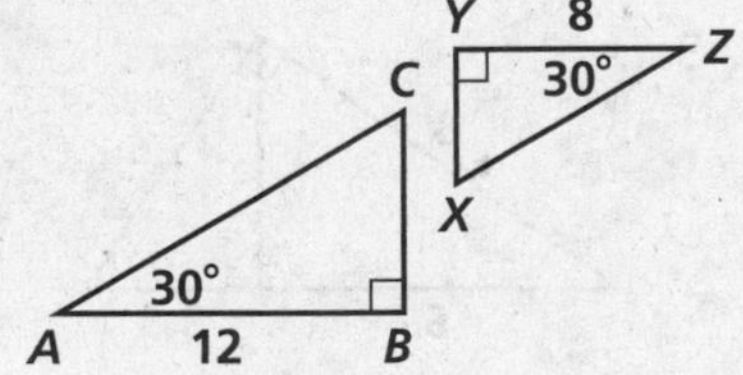

2. 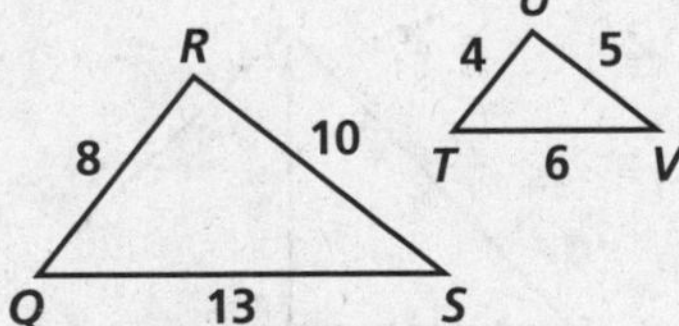

3. 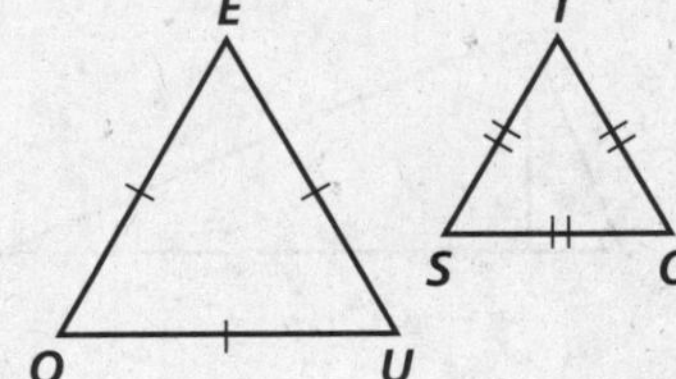

4. 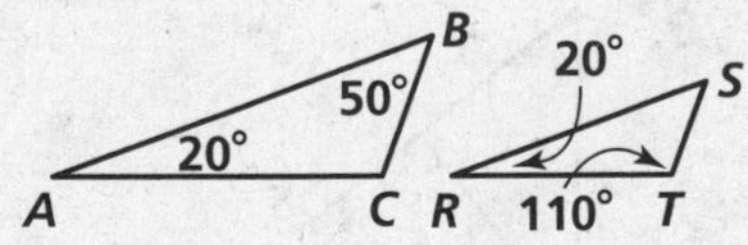

5. 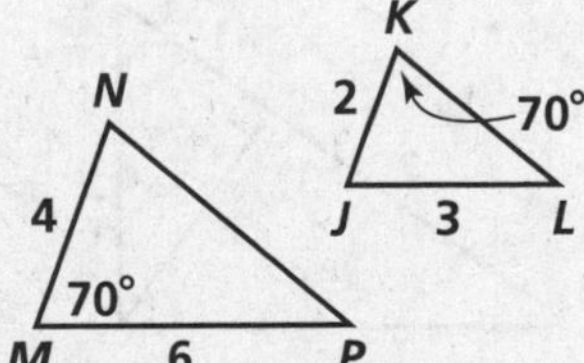

6. 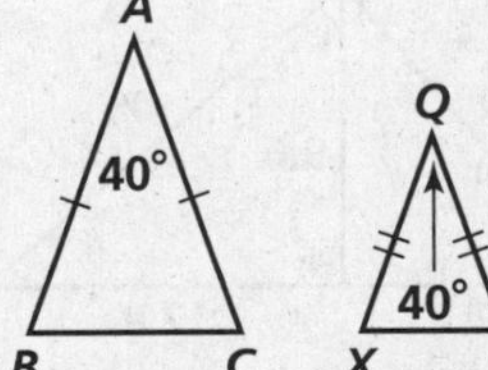

7. Are all equilateral triangles similar? Explain.

8. Are all isosceles triangles similar? Explain.

9. Are all congruent triangles similar? Are all similar triangles congruent? Explain.

GEOMETRY TOPICS

Name ____________________ Class ____________ Date ____________

Review 162

Similarity in Right Triangles

OBJECTIVE: Finding relationships between the lengths of the sides of a right triangle and the altitude to the hypotenuse

MATERIALS: Calculator

Example

Solve for *x*, *y*, and *z*.

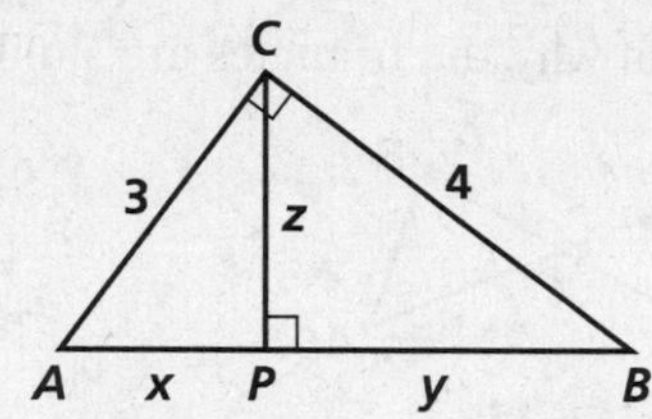

By the Pythagorean Theorem, $AB = 5$. Use the corollaries to Theorem 8-3 to find *x*, *y*, and *z*.

Corollary 2 gives you $AB \cdot AP = (AC)^2$ $\quad$ $AB \cdot BP = (BC)^2$

$5x = 9$ $\quad$ $5y = 16$

$x = 1.8$ $\quad$ $y = 3.2$

Corollary 1 gives you $(CP)^2 = AP \cdot BP$

$z^2 = (1.8)(3.2)$

$z^2 = 5.76$

$z = 2.4$

Exercises

Find the values of the variables in each right triangle.

1.

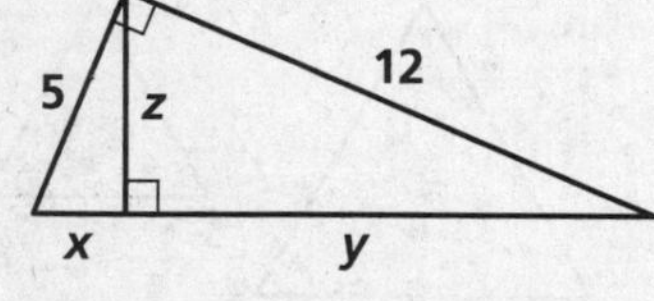

2.

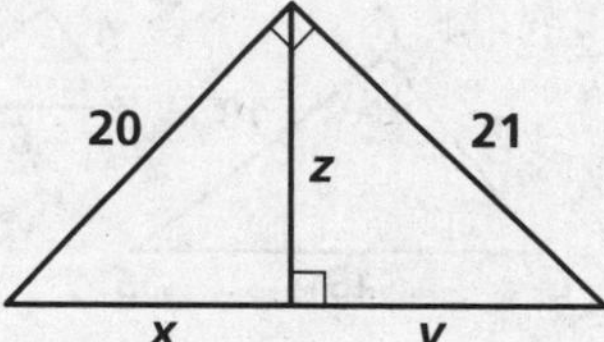

3.

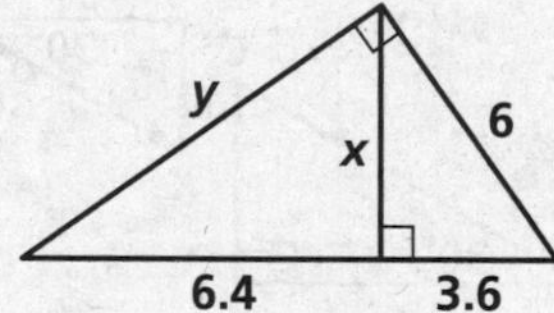

4.

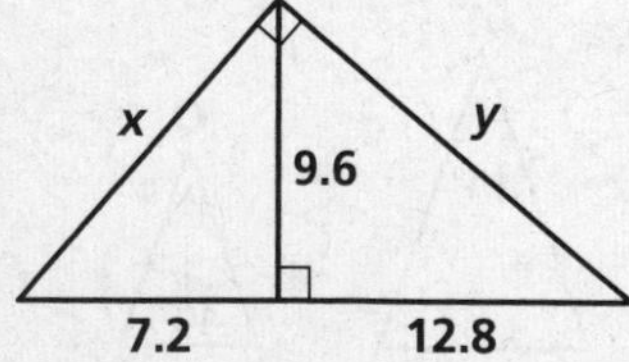

5.

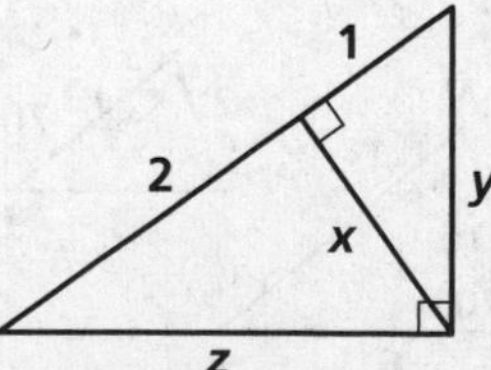

6.

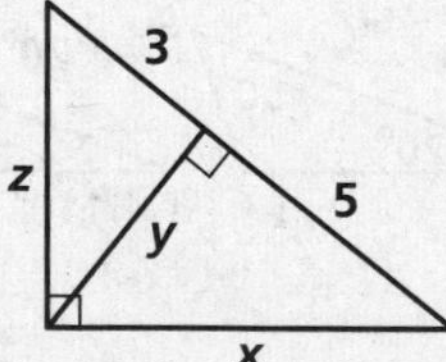

7. Find the length of the altitude to the hypotenuse of a right triangle whose sides have lengths 10, 24, and 26.

8. Find the length of the altitude to the hypotenuse of a right triangle whose legs have lengths 6 and 7.

9. Find a formula for the length of the altitude to the hypotenuse of a right triangle whose legs have lengths *a* and *b*.

GEOMETRY TOPICS

Name ______________________ Class ______________ Date ______________

Review 163

Proportions in Triangles

OBJECTIVE: Investigating proportional relationships in triangles

MATERIALS: Calculator

Example

Find the value of each variable.

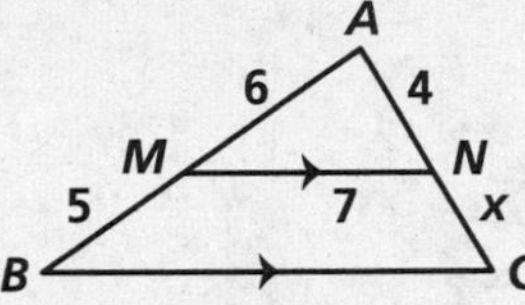

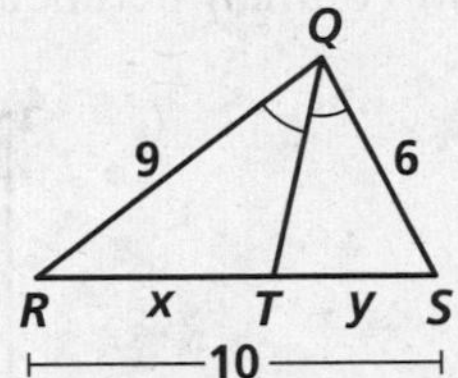

$\frac{AM}{MB} = \frac{AN}{NC}$ by the Side-Splitter Theorem

$\frac{6}{5} = \frac{4}{x}$ by substitution

$6x = 20$ by cross-multiplication

$x = \frac{10}{3}$

$\frac{QR}{QS} = \frac{RT}{ST}$ by the Triangle-Angle-Bisector Theorem

$\frac{9}{6} = \frac{x}{y}$ by substitution

$\frac{9}{6} = \frac{x}{10 - x}$ because $x + y = 10$

$9(10 - x) = 6x$ by cross-multiplication

$90 - 9x = 6x$

$90 = 15x$

$6 = x$

$4 = y$

Exercises

Find the value of each variable.

1. 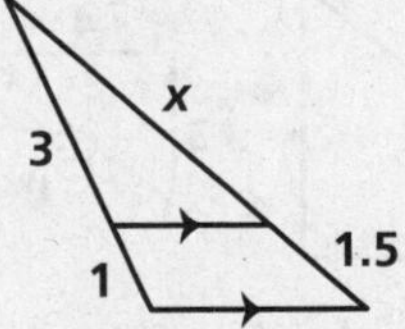

2. 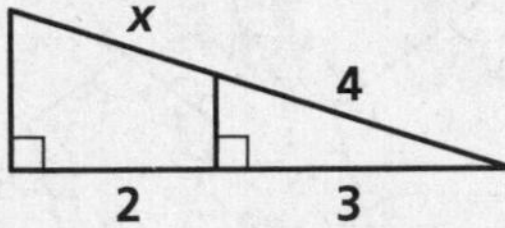

3. 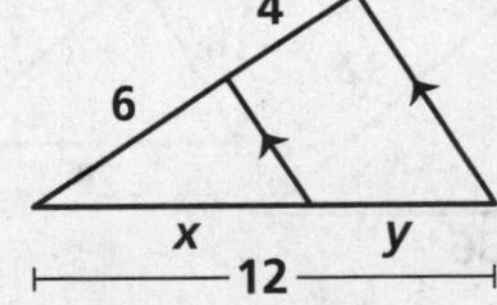

4. 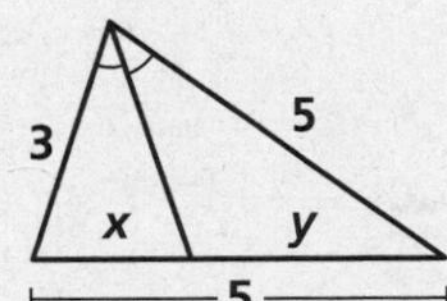

5. 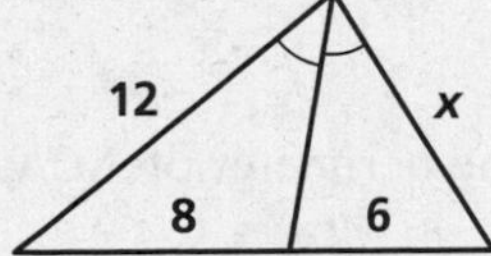

6. 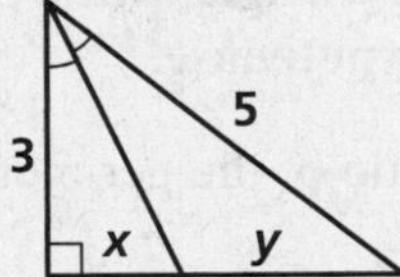

In $\triangle ABC$, $AB = 6$, $BC = 8$, and $AC = 9$.

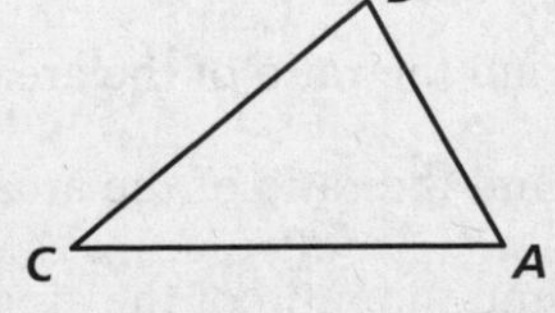

7. The bisector of $\angle A$ meets $\overline{BC}$ at point N. Find BN and CN.
8. $\overline{XY} \parallel \overline{CA}$. Point X lies on $\overline{BC}$ such that $BX = 2$, and Y is on $\overline{BA}$. Find BY.

GEOMETRY TOPICS

Name ____________________ Class ____________ Date ____________

Review 164

OBJECTIVE: Finding the relationships between the similarity ratio and the perimeters and areas of similar figures	**MATERIALS:** None

Example

Each pair of figures is similar. Find the ratio of their perimeters and the ratio of their areas.

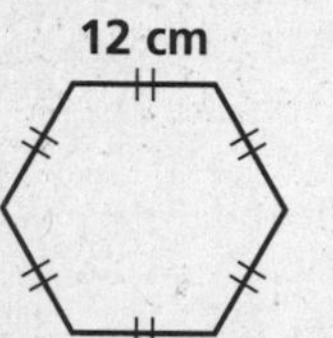

By Theorem 8-6, the ratio of the perimeters is $12 : 6 = 2 : 1$, and the ratio of the areas is $2^2 : 1^2 = 4 : 1$.

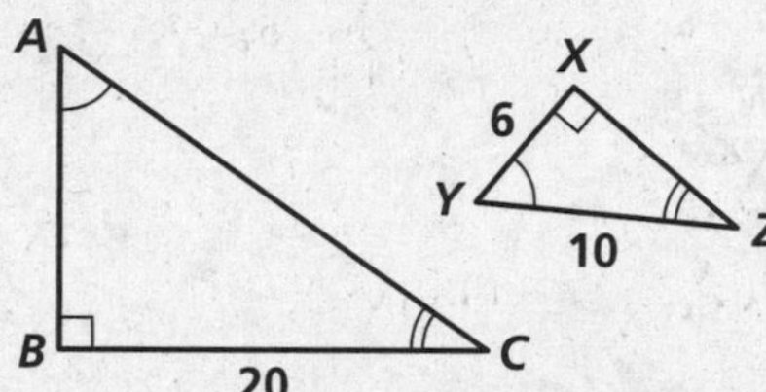

By AA ~ Postulate, $\triangle ABC \sim \triangle XYZ$ where $\overline{BC}$ and $\overline{XZ}$ are corresponding sides.
By the Pythagorean Theorem,

$$(XZ)^2 + (XY)^2 = (ZY)^2$$
$$(XZ)^2 + 6^2 = 10^2$$
$$(XZ)^2 = 64$$
$$XZ = 8$$

Therefore, by Theorem 8-6, the ratio of perimeters is $20 : 8 = 5 : 2$, and the ratio of areas is $5^2 : 2^2 = 25 : 4$.

Exercises

Each pair of figures is similar. Find the ratio of their perimeters and the ratio of their areas.

1.

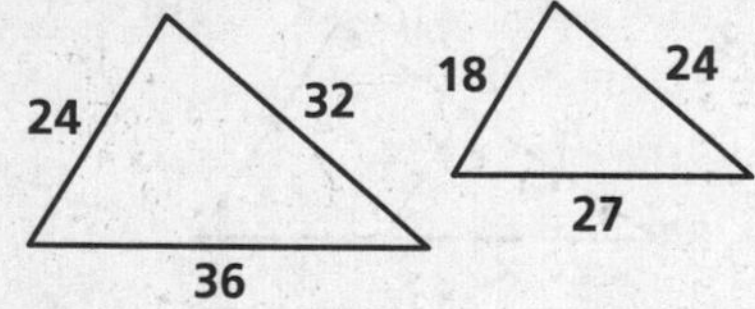

2.

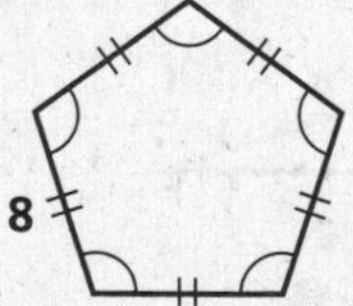

5

3.

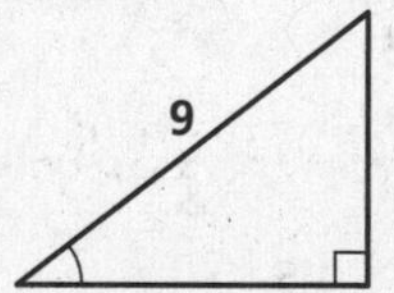

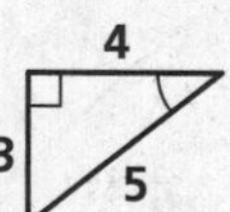

$\triangle ACB$ is a right triangle with $BC = 3$, $AC = 4$, and $AB = 5$. $\overline{CN}$ is the altitude to the hypotenuse.

C

B N A

4. Find the ratio of the perimeter of $\triangle ANC$ to the perimeter of $\triangle CNB$.

5. Find the ratio of the perimeter of $\triangle ANC$ to the perimeter of $\triangle ACB$.

6. Find the ratio of the perimeter of $\triangle CNB$ to the perimeter of $\triangle ACB$.

7. Find the ratio of the area of $\triangle ANC$ to the area of $\triangle CNB$.

8. Find the ratio of the area of $\triangle ANC$ to the area of $\triangle ACB$.

9. Find the ratio of the area of $\triangle CNB$ to the area of $\triangle ACB$.

Name ______________________ Class ______________ Date ______________

Review 165

OBJECTIVE: Using tangents to determine side lengths in triangles

MATERIALS: Calculator

Example

Find the measure of the acute angle that the line $y - \frac{3}{4}x = 2$ makes with the x-axis. Round your answer to the nearest tenth.

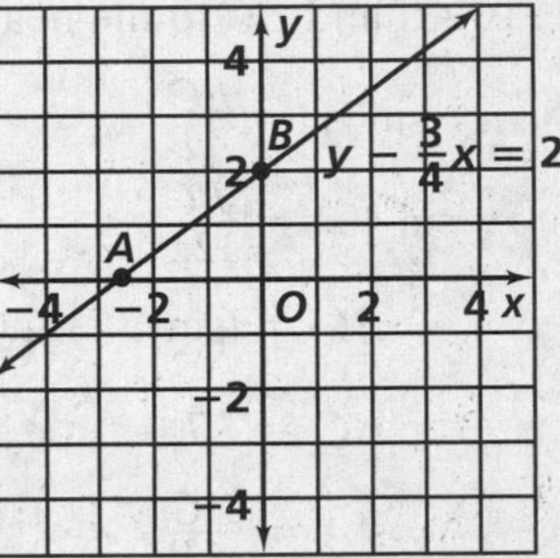

The line $y - \frac{3}{4}x = 2$ can be rewritten $y = \frac{3}{4}x + 2$. Therefore, its slope is $\frac{3}{4}$.

$$\text{slope} = \frac{\text{rise}}{\text{run}} = \frac{BO}{AO} = \tan A$$

Therefore, $\tan A = \frac{3}{4}$.

Therefore, $m\angle BAO = \tan^{-1}\left(\frac{3}{4}\right) \approx 36.9$.

Exercises

Find the measure of the acute angle that the given line makes with the *x*-axis.

1. $y = \frac{1}{2}x - 2$

2. $y + 4x = 7$

3. $y = 6x + 10$

Find the measure of the acute angle that the given line makes with the *y*-axis.

4. $2x + y = 1$

5. $y = 7x$

6. $y = 70x$

In $\triangle ABC$, find the measures of $\angle A$ and $\angle B$ where $m\angle C = 90$.

7. $AC = 3, BC = 4, AB = 5$

8. $AC = 5, BC = 12, AB = 13$

9. $AC = 1, AB = 3$

10. $AC = 6, BC = 12$

11. The vertices of $\triangle JKL$ are $J(-2, 6)$, $K(-2, 0)$, and $L(-5, 0)$. Find the measure of $\angle J$.

12. Find the measure of $\angle L$ in Exercise 11.

13. Find the measure of the acute angle formed by the intersection of the lines $2y - x = 4$ and $y = 4x + 2$.

Name ________________________ Class ____________ Date ____________

Review 166

OBJECTIVE: Using sine and cosine to determine unknown measures in right triangles

MATERIALS: Calculator

Example

Find AC and BC to the nearest tenth.

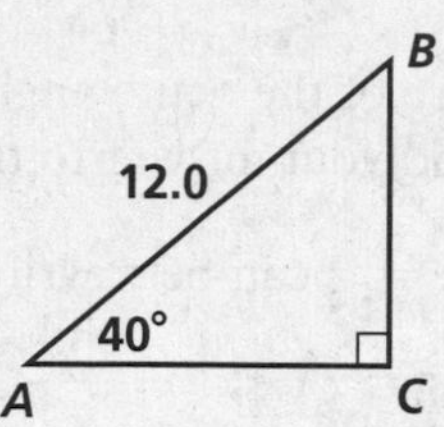

$\sin A = \frac{BC}{AB}$	Definition of sine
$\sin 40° = \frac{BC}{12.0}$	Substitute.
$BC = (\sin 40°)12.0$	Cross-multiply.
$BC = 7.7$	Use a calculator.
$\cos A = \frac{AC}{AB}$	Definition of cosine
$\cos 40° = \frac{AC}{12.0}$	Substitute.
$AC = (\cos 40°)12.0$	Cross-multiply.
$AC \approx 9.2$	Use a calculator.

Exercises

Find the missing lengths in each right triangle. Round your answers to the nearest tenth.

1. 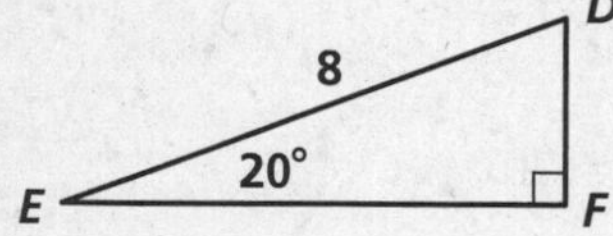

2. 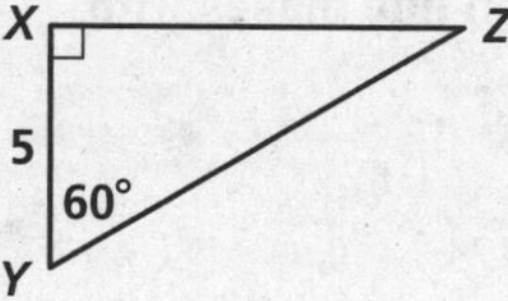

3. 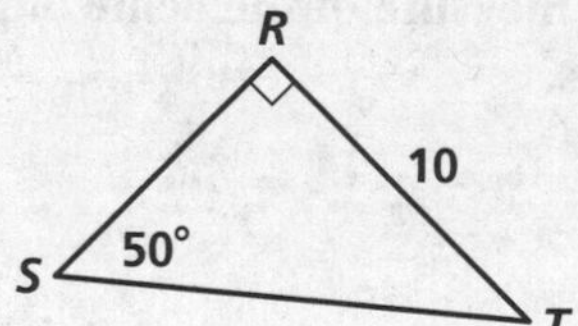

4. In $\triangle ABC$, $m\angle C = 90$, $m\angle A = 15$, and $AB = 6$. Find AC.

Find the measures of the acute angles of each right triangle. Round your answers to the nearest tenth of a degree.

5. 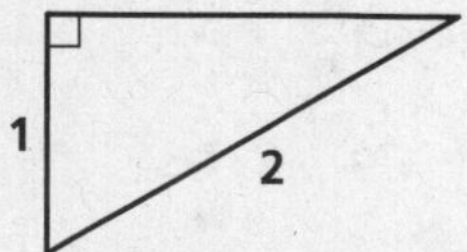

6. 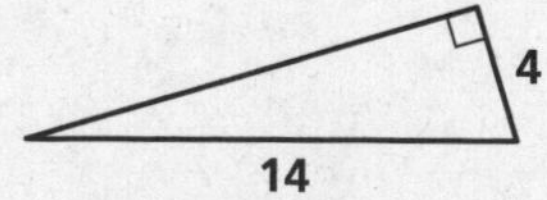

7. 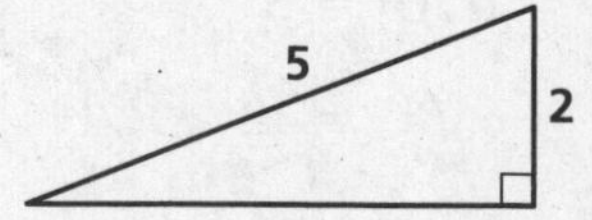

8. In $\triangle RST$, $\angle R$ is a right angle and $m\angle S = 32$. If the hypotenuse has length 4, find the lengths of the two legs.

9. A right triangle has a hypotenuse of length 10 and one leg of length 7.
   a. Find the length of the other leg using trigonometry.
   b. Find the length of the other leg using the Pythagorean Theorem.

Name ______________________ Class ______________ Date ______________

Review 167

Angles of Elevation and Depression

OBJECTIVE: Using angles of elevation and depression and trigonometric ratios to solve problems	**MATERIALS:** Calculator

Example

A man standing 100 ft from a tall building measures the angle of elevation to the top of the building from the point where he is standing. If that angle is 62°, approximately how tall is the building?

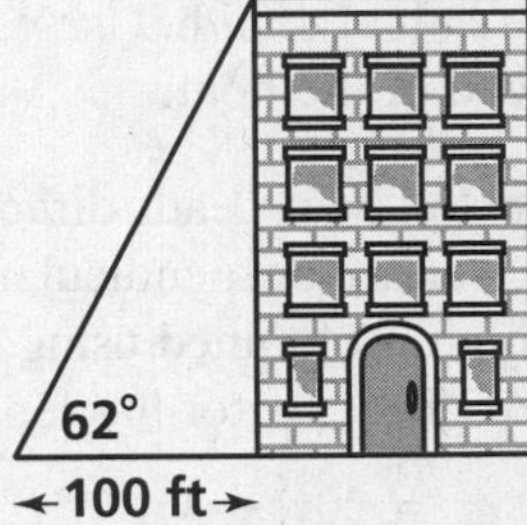

In the diagram at the right,

$$\tan 62^\circ = \frac{\text{height of building}}{100 \text{ ft}}$$

Cross-multiplying:

$$\begin{aligned}\text{height of building} &= 100 \cdot (\tan 62^\circ) \text{ ft} \\ &= 188.07 \text{ ft}\end{aligned}$$

The building is approximately 188 ft tall.

Exercises

Solve each problem. Drawing an accurate diagram will help.

1. You stand 40 ft from a tree. The angle of elevation from you to the top of the tree is 47°. How tall is the tree?

2. The angle of elevation to a building in the distance is 22°. You know that the building is approximately 450 ft tall. Estimate the distance to the base of the building.

3. An airplane is flying at an altitude of 10,000 ft. The airport at which it is scheduled to land is 50 mi away. Find the angle at which the airplane must descend for landing. (*Hint:* There are 5280 ft in 1 mi.)

4. A lake measures 600 ft across. A lodge stands on one shore. From your point on the opposite shore, the angle of elevation to the top of the lodge is 4°. How tall is the lodge?

5. A library wishes to build an access ramp for wheelchairs. The main entrance of the library is 8 ft above sidewalk level. If the architect recommends a grade (angle of elevation) of 6°, how long must the access ramp be?

6. Two buildings stand 90 ft apart at their closest points. At those points, the angle of depression from the taller building to the shorter building is 12°. How much taller is the taller building?

Name ______________________ Class ______________ Date ______________

Review 168

OBJECTIVE: Solving problems that involve vector addition

MATERIALS: Calculator

Example

A boat heads directly across a river at 20 mi/h. The river is flowing downstream at 4 mi/h. Use vector addition to find the resultant path and speed of the boat.

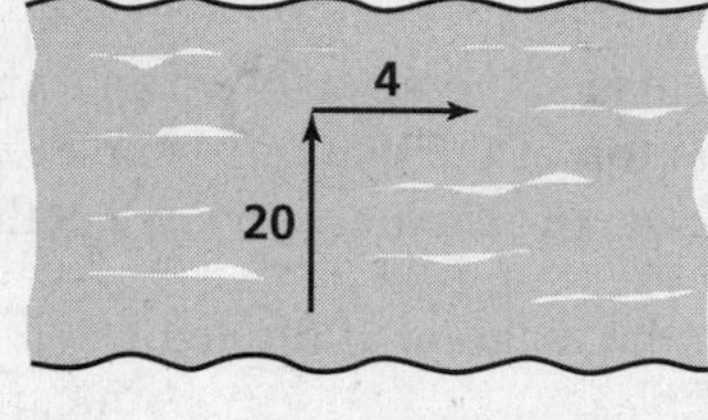

Because the boat heads directly across, its vector and the vector for the flow of the river are perpendicular. The vector that describes the resultant path of the boat is obtained using the head-to-tail method and the Pythagorean Theorem. That vector has length c where

$$c^2 = 20^2 + 4^2$$
$$c^2 = 416$$
$$c \approx 20.4$$

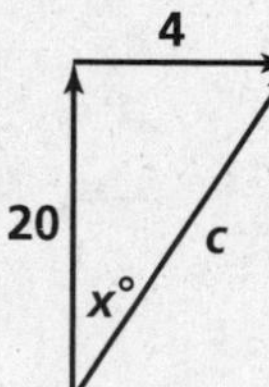

So the resultant speed is approximately 20.4 mi/h. In the diagram, the path is $x°$ east of north. Using trigonometry,

$$\tan x = \frac{4}{20} = 0.20$$
$$x \approx 11.3°$$

Exercises

Solve each problem. Drawing an accurate diagram will help.

1. A boat heads directly across a river at 8 mi/h. The river flows downstream at 10 mi/h. Find the resulting speed and direction of the boat. Round your answers to the nearest tenth.

2. A woman walks 6 mi due east from her home. She then walks 8 mi due south.
   a. How far is she from her home?
   b. In what direction should she walk to return home?

3. A bird heading directly south at 5 mi/h encounters a wind blowing due east at 3 mi/h. How would the direction of the bird be affected?

4. A boat heads directly across a river at 12 mi/h. The river is 3 mi wide. Upon disembarking, the boat's captain finds that the boat is 1 mi downstream from where he had intended to land. Find the speed of the river's current.

Name ______________________ Class ______________ Date ______________

Review 169

OBJECTIVE: Using trigonometry to find the areas of regular polygons

MATERIALS: Calculator

Example

Find the area of a regular hexagon with side 12 cm.

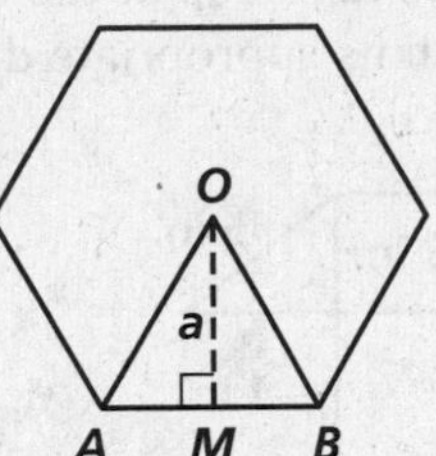

Area $= \frac{1}{2}ap$, where a = apothem

p = perimeter

$p = 6 \cdot 12 = 72$, because the figure is 6-sided.

Area $= \frac{1}{2}a(72) = 36a$

To find a, examine $\triangle AOB$ above. The apothem is measured along $\overline{OM}$, which divides $\triangle AOB$ into congruent triangles.

$$AM = \frac{1}{2}AB = 6$$

$$m\angle AOM = \frac{1}{2}m\angle AOB$$

$$= \frac{1}{2}\left(\frac{360}{6}\right)$$

$$= 30$$

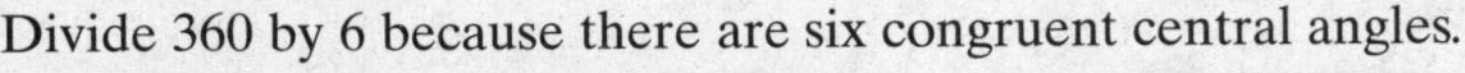

Divide 360 by 6 because there are six congruent central angles.

So, by trigonometry, $\tan 30° = \frac{AM}{a}$

$$\tan 30° = \frac{6}{a}$$

$$a = \frac{6}{\tan 30°}$$

Finally, area $= \frac{1}{2}ap = \frac{1}{2}\left(\frac{6}{\tan 30°}\right)(72) \approx 374.1 \text{ cm}^2$.

Exercises

Find the area of each regular polygon.

1. Find the area of a regular octagon with side 2 in.

2. Find the area of a regular decagon with side 4 cm.

3. Find the area of a regular hexagon with apothem 5 in.

4. Find the area of a regular pentagon with side 10 in.

5. Find the area of a regular pentagon with apothem 10 in.

6. Find the area of a regular 20-gon with perimeter 40 in.

7. **a.** Find the area of a regular quadrilateral with side 9 in.

b. What other method can be used to find the area?

Name ______________________ Class ______________ Date ______________

Review 170

OBJECTIVE: Drawing nets of various space figures **MATERIALS:** Graph paper, scissors, tape

Example

Draw a net for the doorstop at the right.
Label the net with its appropriate dimensions.

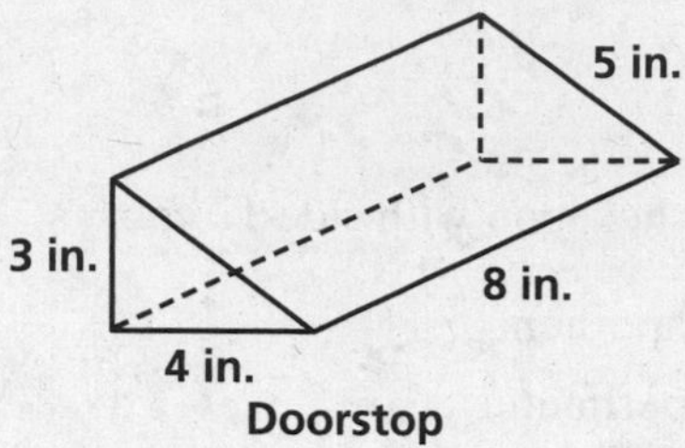

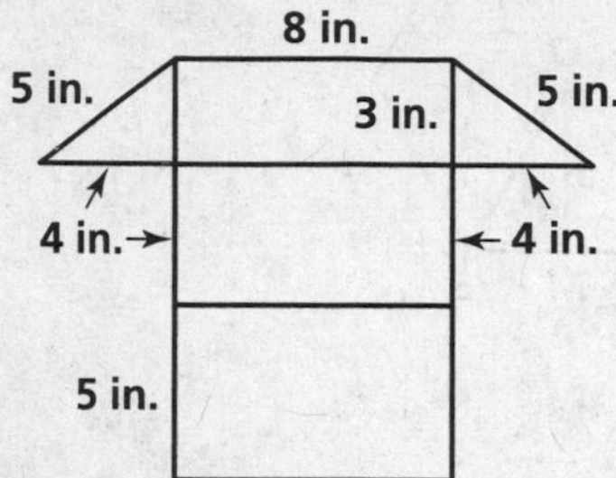

Exercises

Complete the following to verify Euler's Formula.

1. On graph paper, draw three other nets for the polyhedron shown above. Let each unit of length represent $\frac{1}{4}$ in.
2. Cut out each net, and use tape to form the solid figure.
3. Count the number of vertices, faces, and edges of one of the figures.
4. Verify that Euler's Formula, $F + V = E + 2$, is true for this polyhedron.

Draw a net for each three-dimensional figure.

5.

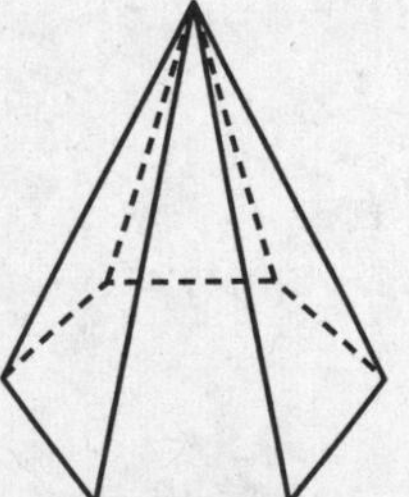

6.

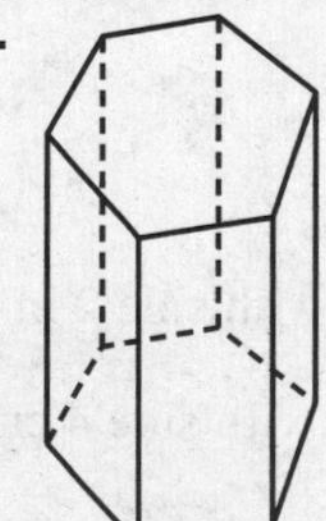

7.

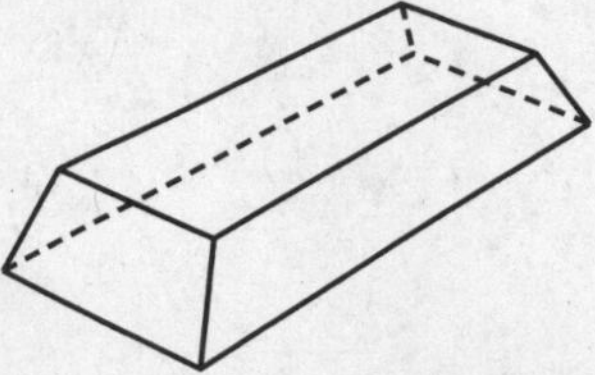

8.

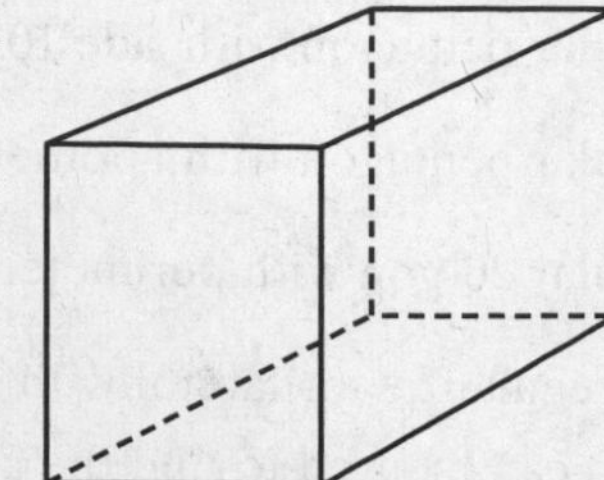

Name ______________________ Class ______________ Date ______________

Review 171

OBJECTIVE: Creating isometric and orthographic drawings

MATERIALS: Isometric dot paper

Example

Create an isometric drawing and an orthographic drawing of the cube structure at the right.

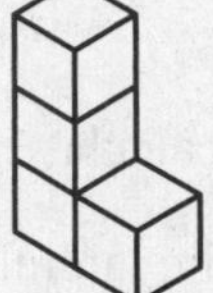

Isometric drawing:

First, draw the front edges of the figure.

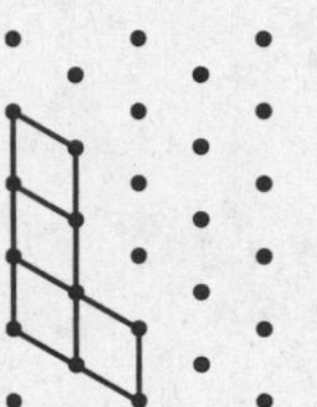

Next, draw the segments for the back edges of the figure.

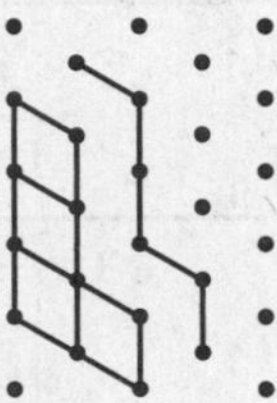

Complete by drawing the six segments joining the front and back edges.

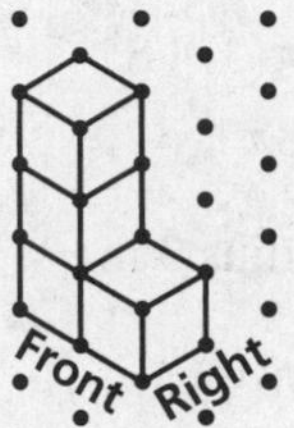

Orthographic drawing:

From the front view, four squares are visible.

From the top view, two squares are visible.

From the right view, three squares are visible.

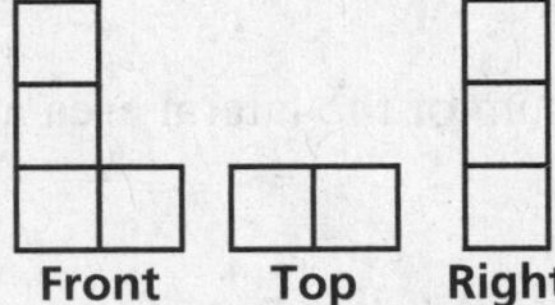

Exercises

Create (a) an isometric drawing and (b) an orthographic drawing of each cube structure.

1. 

2. 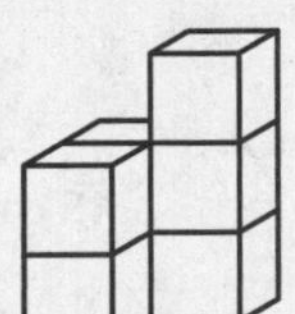

3. 

4. 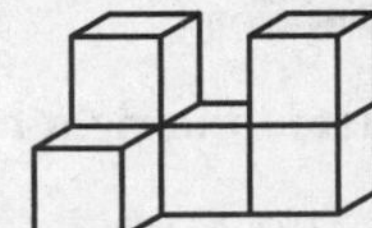

5. Use the isometric drawing to create an orthographic drawing.

6. Use the orthographic drawing to create an isometric drawing.

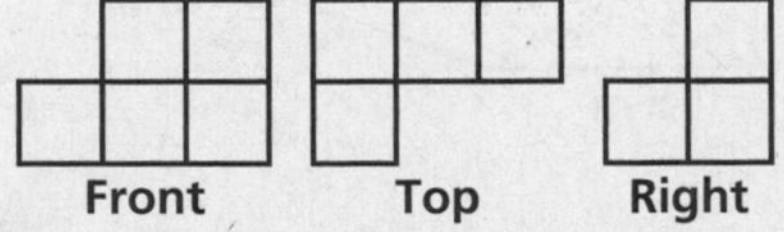

Name ______________________ Class ______________ Date ______________

Review 172

OBJECTIVE: Finding lateral areas and surface areas of cylinders and prisms

MATERIALS: Centimeter grid paper, scissors, tape

Example

Draw a net for the cylinder to calculate its surface area.

From the net, we can see that the lateral surface area is a rectangle with length equal to the circumference of the base of the cylinder.

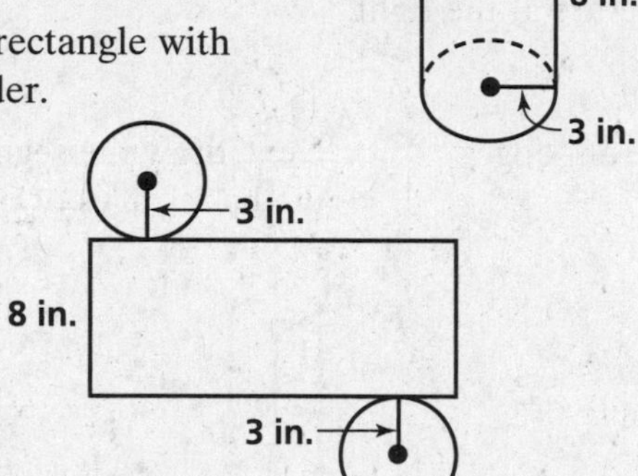

$$\begin{aligned}\text{Area of rectangle} &= b \cdot h \\ &= 2\pi r \cdot h \\ &= 2\pi(3) \cdot 8 \\ &= 48\pi\end{aligned}$$

Each base is a circle with radius 3 in.

$$\begin{aligned}\text{Area of base} &= \pi r^2 \\ &= \pi(3)^2 \\ &= 9\pi\end{aligned}$$

The surface area is the sum of the lateral area and the area of the two bases.

$$\begin{aligned}\text{S.A.} &= \text{L.A.} + 2B \\ &= 48\pi + 2(9\pi) \\ &= 66\pi \approx 207.3\end{aligned}$$

The surface area of the cylinder is about 207.3 in.^{2}

Exercises

Use the net at the right to complete the following.

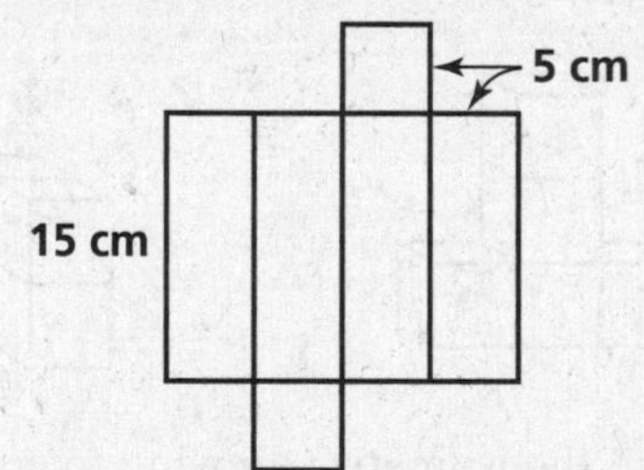

1. Draw the net at the right on centimeter grid paper.
2. Cut out the net, and tape it together to make a prism.
3. Find the lateral area and surface area of the prism.

Find the surface area of each figure. Round your answers to the nearest tenth, if necessary.

4. 18 cm, 5 cm

5. 12 in., 12 in., 12 in.

6.

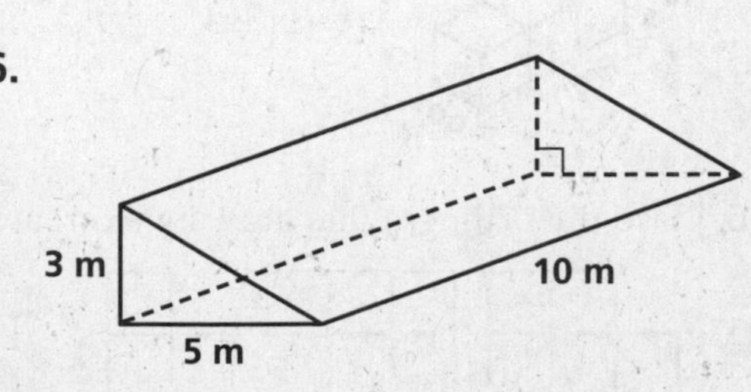

GEOMETRY TOPICS

Name ______________________ Class ______________ Date ______________

Review 173

OBJECTIVE: Finding lateral areas and surface areas of cones and pyramids

MATERIALS: Graph paper, scissors, tape

Example

Find the surface area of a cone with slant height 18 cm and height 12 cm.

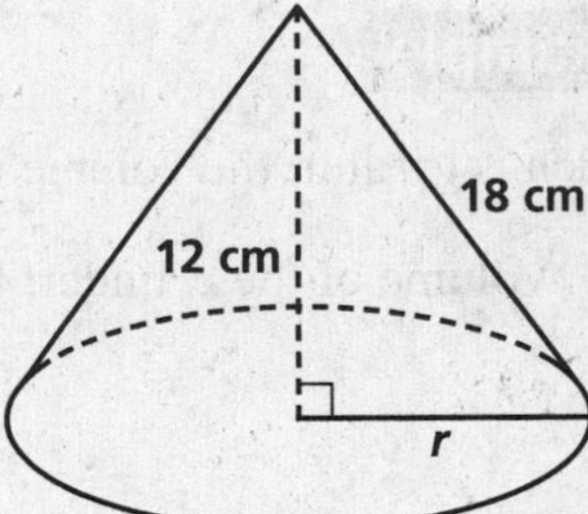

Begin by drawing a sketch.

Use the Pythagorean Theorem to find r, the radius of the base of the cone.

$$r^2 + 12^2 = 18^2$$
$$r^2 + 144 = 324$$
$$r^2 = 180$$
$$r \approx 13.4$$

Now substitute into the formula for the surface area of a cone.

$$\begin{aligned} \text{S.A.} &= \text{L.A.} + B \\ &= \pi rl + \pi r^2 \\ &= \pi(13.4)(18) + \pi(13.4)^2 \\ &\approx 1321.9 \end{aligned}$$

The surface area of the cone is about 1321.9 cm^2.

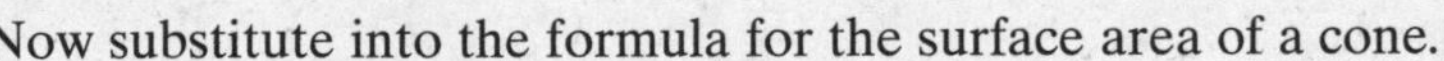

Exercises

Use graph paper, scissors, and tape to complete the following.

1. Draw a net of a square pyramid on graph paper.
2. Cut it out, and tape it together.
3. Measure its base length and slant height.
4. Find the surface area of the pyramid.

In Exercises 5–8, round your answers to the nearest tenth, if necessary.

5. Find the surface area of a square pyramid with base length 16 cm and slant height 20 cm.
6. Find the surface area of a cone with radius 5 m and slant height 15 m.
7. Find the surface area of a square pyramid with base length 10 in. and height 15 in.
8. Find the surface area of a cone with radius 6 ft and height 11 ft.

Name ______________________ Class ______________ Date ______________

Review 174

OBJECTIVE: Finding the volumes of cylinders and prisms

MATERIALS: None

Example

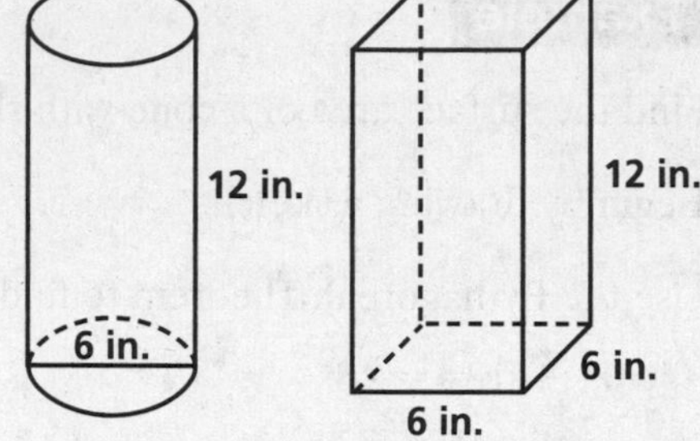

Which is greater: the volume of the cylinder or the volume of the prism?

Volume of the cylinder: $V = Bh$

$= \pi r^2 \cdot h$

$= \pi(3)^2 \cdot 12$

≈ 339.3

Volume of prism: $V = Bh$

$= s^2 \cdot h$

$= 6^2 \cdot 12$

$= 432$

The volume of the cylinder is about 339.3 in.^3 The volume of the prism is 432 in.^3 The volume of the prism is greater.

Exercises

Find the volume of each object.

1. the rectangular prism part of the milk container
2. the cylinder part of the measuring cup

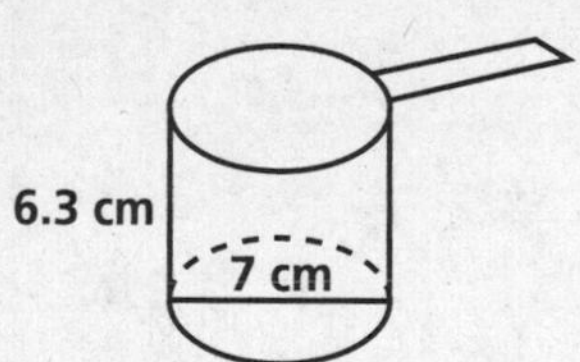

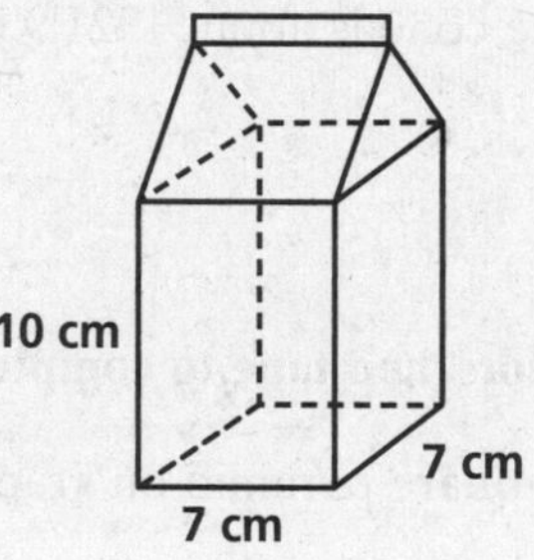

Find the volume of each of the following. Round your answers to the nearest tenth, if necessary.

3. a square prism with base length 7 m and height 15 m
4. a cylinder with radius 9 in. and height 10 in.
5. a triangular prism with height 14 ft and a right triangle base with legs measuring 9 ft and 12 ft
6. a cylinder with diameter 24 cm and height 5 cm

Name ______________________ Class ______________ Date ______________

Review 175

OBJECTIVE: Finding volumes of cones and pyramids

MATERIALS: None

Example

Calculate the volume of the cone.

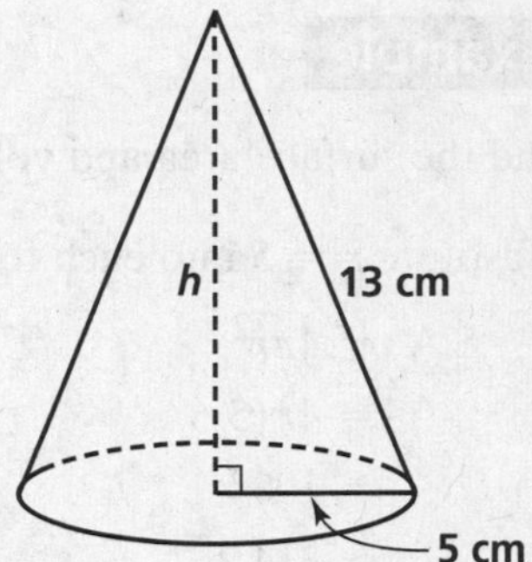

Find the height of the cone.

$13^2 = h^2 + 5^2$	Use the Pythagorean Theorem.
$169 = h^2 + 25$	Substitute.
$h^2 = 144$	Simplify.
$h = 12$	Take the square root of each side.

Find the volume of the cone.

$V = \frac{1}{3}\pi r^2 h$	Use the formula for the volume of a cone.
$= \frac{1}{3}\pi(5)^2 \cdot 12$	Substitute.
$= 100\pi$	Simplify.
≈ 314.2	

The volume of the cone is about 314.2 cm^3.

Exercises

1. From the figures shown below, choose the pyramid with volume closest to the volume of the cone at the right.

A.
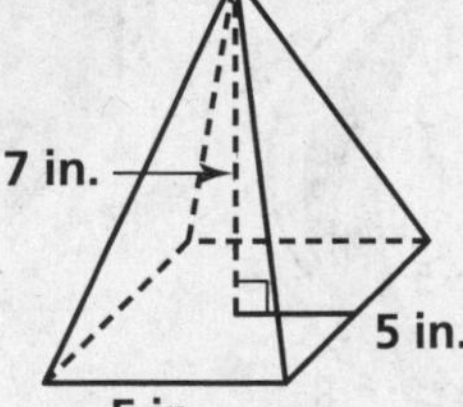

B.
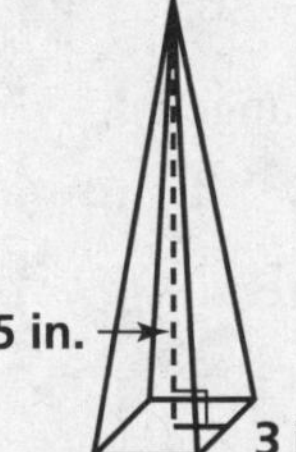

C.
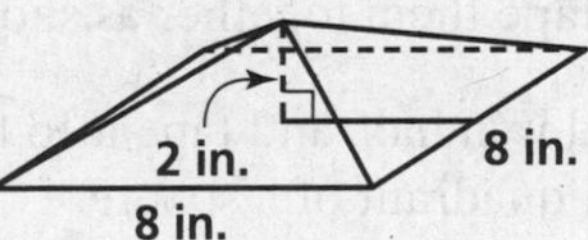

7 in.
2.5 in.

Find the volume of each figure. Round your answers to the nearest tenth, if necessary.

2.
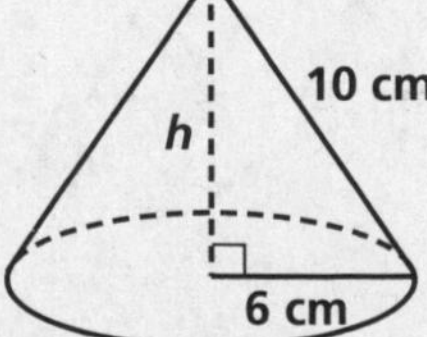

3.
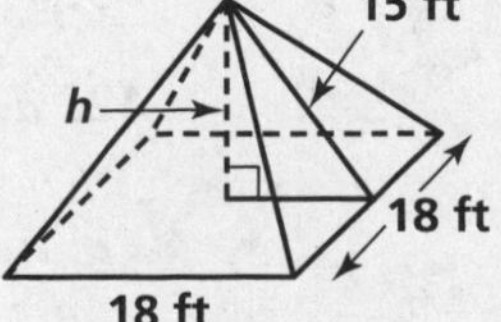

4.
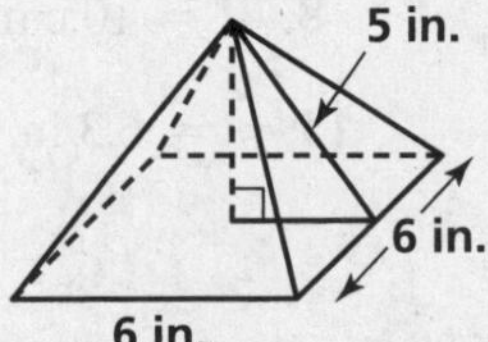

5.
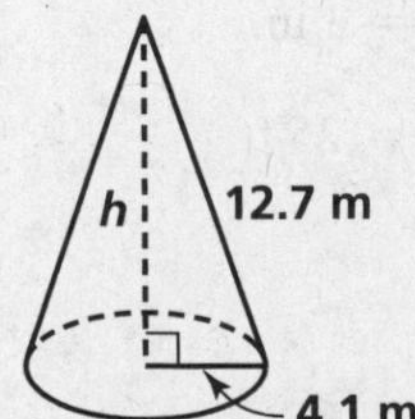

Name ____________________ Class ____________ Date ____________

Review 176

OBJECTIVE: Calculating the surface areas and volumes of spheres

MATERIALS: Compass, scissors, tape

Example

Find the surface area and volume of the sphere.

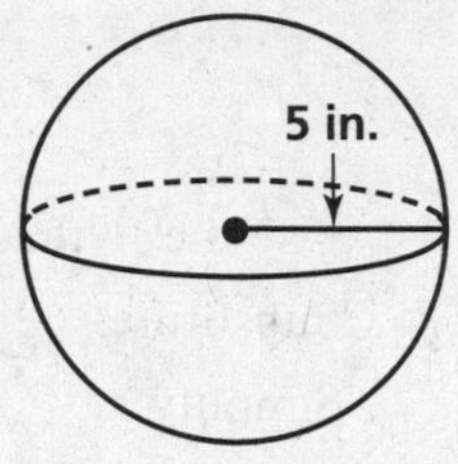

Substitute $r = 5$ into each formula, and simplify.

$$\begin{aligned} \text{S.A.} &= 4\pi r^2 \\ &= 4\pi(5)^2 \\ &= 100 \\ &\approx 314.2 \end{aligned} \qquad \begin{aligned} V &= \tfrac{4}{3}\pi r^3 \\ &= \tfrac{4}{3}\pi(5)^3 \\ &= \tfrac{500\pi}{3} \\ &\approx 523.6 \end{aligned}$$

The surface area of the sphere is about 314.2 in.^2 The volume of the sphere is about 523.6 in.^3

Exercises

Use the figures at the right to guide you in completing the following.

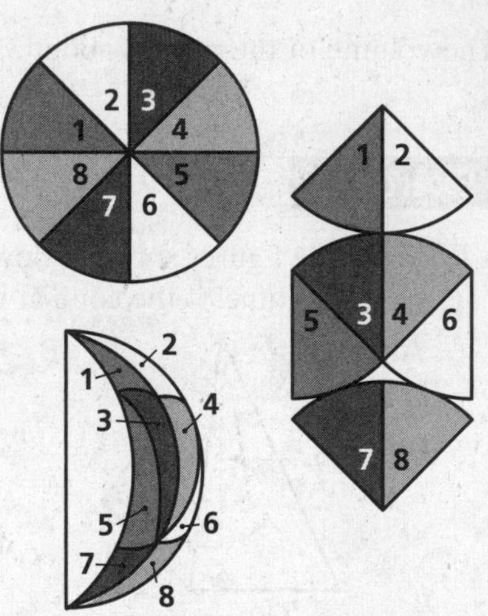

1. Use a compass to draw two circles, each with radius 3 in. Cut out each circle.
2. Fold one circle in half three successive times. Number the central angles 1 through 8.
3. Cut out the sectors, and tape them together as shown.
4. Take the other circle, fold it in half, and tape it to the rearranged circle so that they form a quadrant of a sphere.
5. The area of one circle has covered one quadrant of a sphere. How many circles would cover the entire sphere?
6. How is the radius of the sphere related to the radius of the circle?

Find the volume and surface area of a sphere with the given radius or diameter. Round your answers to the nearest tenth, if necessary.

7. $r = 3$ in.
8. $d = 10$ cm
9. $r = 12$ m
10. $d = 25$ ft
11. $r = 6.3$ in.
12. $d = 8.4$ mm

Name ______________________ Class ______________ Date ______________

Review 177

OBJECTIVE: Finding the relationships between the similarity ratio and the ratios of the areas and volumes of similar solids

MATERIALS: Calculator

Example

The pyramids shown are similar, and they have volumes of 216 in.^{3} and 125 in.^{3} The larger pyramid has surface area 250 in.^{2}

Find the ratio of their surface areas, and find the surface area of the smaller pyramid.

By Theorem 10-12, if similar solids have similarity ratio $a : b$, then the ratio of their volumes is $a^3 : b^3$. So

$\frac{a^3}{b^3} = \frac{216}{125}$

$\frac{a}{b} = \frac{6}{5}$ Take the cube root of both sides to get $a : b$.

$\frac{a^2}{b^2} = \frac{36}{25}$ Square both sides to get $a^2 : b^2$.

Ratio of surface areas $= 36 : 25$

If the larger pyramid has surface area 250 in.^{2}, let the smaller pyramid have surface area x. Then

$$\frac{250}{x} = \frac{36}{25}$$
$$36x = 6250$$
$$x \approx 173.6 \text{ in.}^2$$

Exercises

Find the similarity ratio.

1. Similar cylinders have volumes of 200π in.^{3} and 25π in.^{3}
2. Similar cylinders have surface areas of 45π in.^{2} and 20π in.^{2}

Find the ratio of volumes.

3. Two cubes have sides of length 4 cm and 5 cm.
4. Two cubes have surface areas of 64 in.^{2} and 25 in.^{2}
5. Similar pyramids have bases with areas of 50 in.^{2} and 9 in.^{2}

Find the ratio of surface areas.

6. Two cubes have volumes of 64 cm^3 and 27 cm^3.
7. Similar cylinders have volumes of 343π cm^3 and 125π cm^3.

Name ______________________ Class ______________ Date ______________

Review 178

Tangent Lines

OBJECTIVE: Finding the relationship between a radius and a tangent and between two tangents drawn from the same point

MATERIALS: None

Example

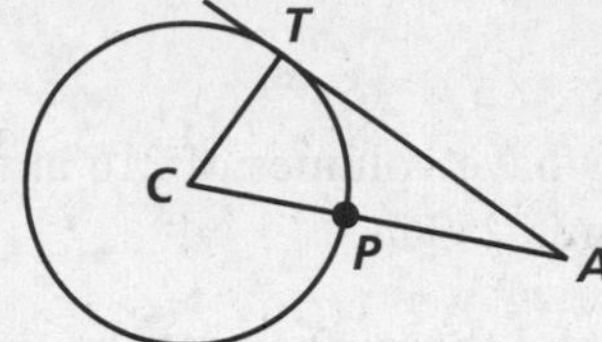

$\overline{AT}$ is tangent to $\odot C$ at T.
$\overline{AT}$ is twice as long as $\overline{AP}$.
$\odot C$ has radius 3.
Find AP and AT.

Because $\overline{AT}$ is tangent at T, $\angle ATC$ is a right angle. Therefore, by the Pythagorean Theorem,

$$AT^2 + CT^2 = AC^2$$
$$AT^2 + CT^2 = (CP + AP)^2$$

Because $AT = 2AP$, $(2AP)^2 + CT^2 = (CP + AP)^2$.

And because radius $= 3$, $(2AP)^2 + 9 = (3 + AP)^2$.

Now solve for AP.

$$4AP^2 + 9 = 9 + 6AP + AP^2$$
$$3AP^2 - 6AP = 0$$
$$3AP(AP - 2) = 0$$
$$AP = 0 \text{ or } AP = 2$$

Because $AP > 0$, $AP = 2$, and $AT = 4$.

Exercises

Find the measure of each segment.

1. $\odot C$ has radius 6. From point Q outside $\odot C$, a tangent is drawn meeting $\odot C$ at point T. $QT = 11$. Find QC.

2. Point X lies outside $\odot W$. $XW = 29$. $\odot W$ has radius 10. A tangent is drawn from X to $\odot W$, meeting the circle at point T. Find XT.

3. $\odot M$ has radius 4. From external point E, a tangent is drawn meeting $\odot M$ at T. $\overline{ET}$ has length $\frac{1}{3}$ the length of $\overline{EM}$. Find ET.

4. From point B, a tangent is drawn to $\odot C$, meeting it at T. $\overline{BC}$ meets the circle at X. $BX = 5$ and $BT = 10$. Find the radius of $\odot C$.

Name ____________________ Class ____________ Date ____________

Review 179

Chords and Arcs

OBJECTIVE: Finding the lengths of chords and measures of arcs of a circle

MATERIALS: Calculator

Example

In $\odot C$, chord $\overline{AB}$ has length 16 cm and is 6 cm from the center.

Find the radius of $\odot C$ and $m\widehat{AB}$.

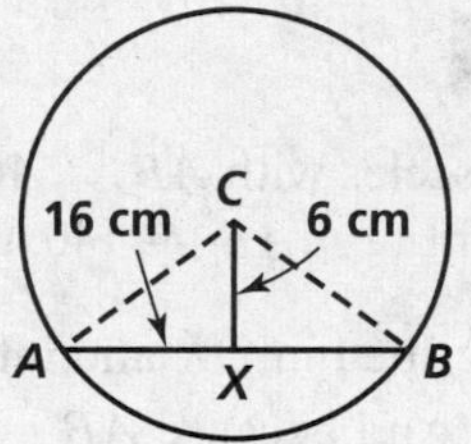

Draw $\overline{CX} \perp \overline{AB}$. By Theorem 11-6, $\overline{CX}$ bisects $\overline{AB}$. Therefore, $AX = 8$ cm. By the Pythagorean Theorem,

$$\begin{aligned} CX^2 + AX^2 &= CA^2 \\ 6^2 + 8^2 &= CA^2 \\ 100 &= CA^2 \\ 10 \text{ cm} &= CA \end{aligned}$$

To find $m\widehat{AB}$, first extend $\overline{CX}$, as shown at the right. By Theorem 11-6, $\overline{CM}$ bisects $\widehat{AB}$. So, $m\widehat{AB} = 2m\widehat{AM} = 2m\angle ACX$.

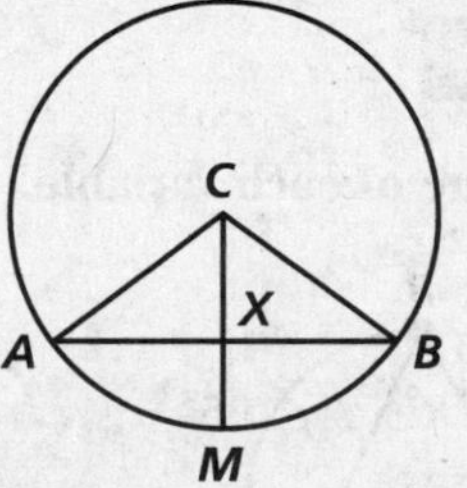

Then use trigonometry to find $m\angle ACX$.

$$\begin{aligned} \tan(\angle ACX) &= \frac{AX}{CX} = \frac{8}{6} = 1.3\overline{3} \\ m\angle ACX &= 53.1 \\ \text{So } m\widehat{AB} &= 106.2 \end{aligned}$$

Exercises

Find x using the information given. Leave your answers in simplest radical form.

1.

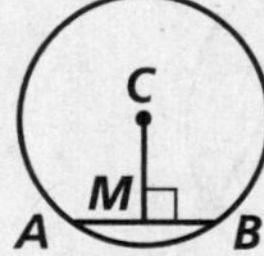

$AB = 20$
radius = 15
$CM = x$

2.

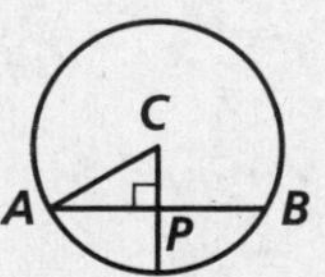

$AB = 24$
$CP = 12$
$CA = x$

3.

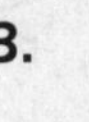

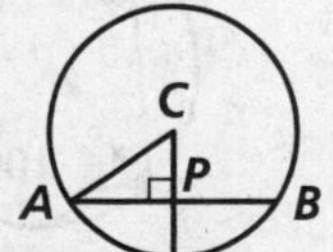

$CP = 5$
radius $= 9$
$AB = x$

Find the measure of each segment to the nearest hundredth.

4. Find the length of a chord that is 1 cm from the center of a circle of radius 6 cm.

5. Find the length of a chord that is 8 cm from the center of a circle of radius 8.1 cm.

6. For a circle of radius 10 in., find the distance from the center to a chord of length 10 in.

7. For a circle of radius 8 in., find the distance from the center to a chord of length 15 in.

GEOMETRY TOPICS

Name ______________________ Class ______________ Date ______________

Review 180

OBJECTIVE: Finding the measures of inscribed angles and the arcs they intercept

MATERIALS: None

Example

$\triangle ABC$ is isosceles with $AB = AC$ and is inscribed in $\odot X$. $\overline{CT}$ is tangent to $\odot X$ at point C. $m\widehat{AB} = 140$. Find $m\angle A$, $m\widehat{BC}$, and $m\angle BCT$.

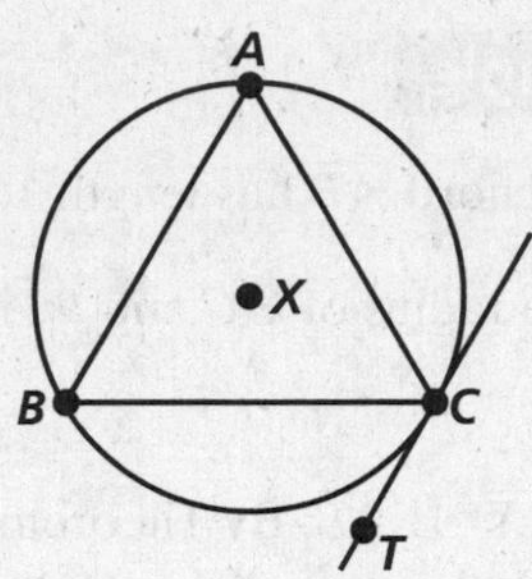

$\angle ACB$ is inscribed in $\odot X$ and intercepts $\widehat{AB}$, so $m\angle ACB = \frac{1}{2}m\widehat{AB} = \frac{1}{2}(140) = 70$. And because $AB = AC$, $m\angle B = m\angle ACB = 70$.
So $m\angle A = 180 - 70 - 70 = 40$, and $m\widehat{BC} = 2m\angle A = 80$.

Finally, $\angle BCT$ is an angle formed by a chord and tangent. Therefore, by Theorem 11-10,

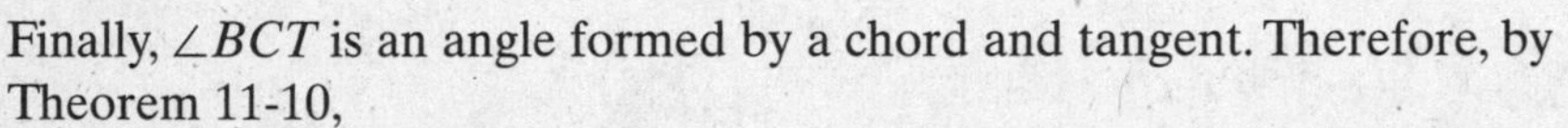

$$m\angle BCT = \tfrac{1}{2}m\widehat{BC} = 40.$$

Exercises

Find the value of each variable.

1.
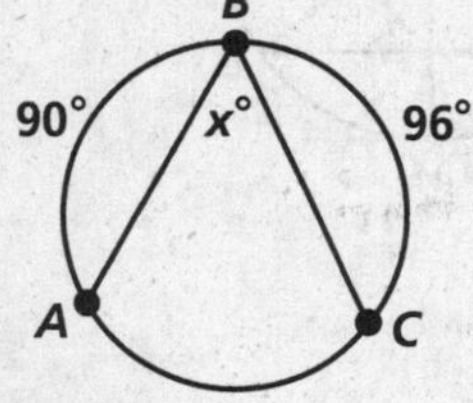

2.
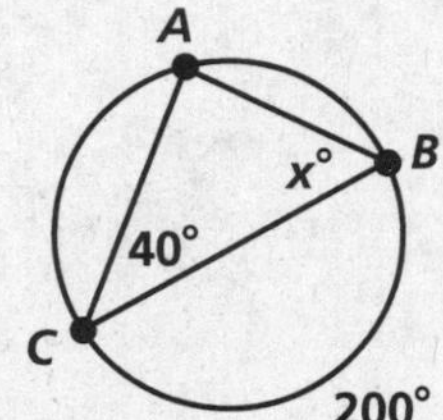

3.
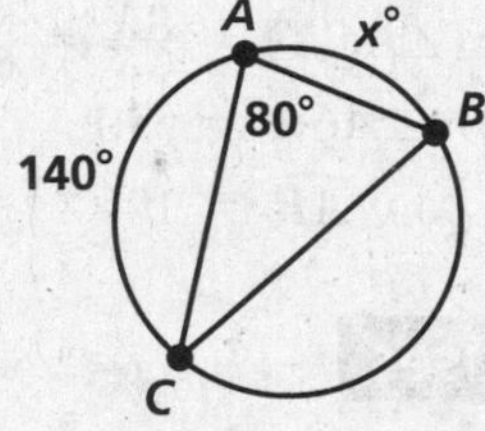

4.
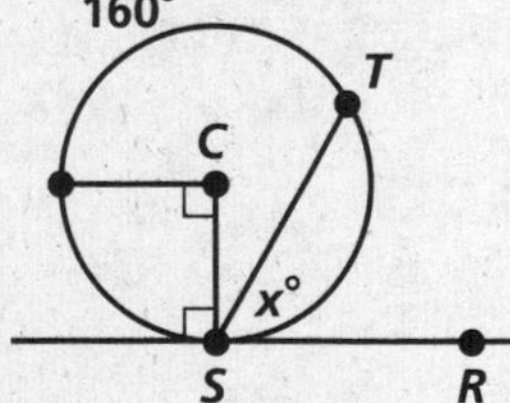

5.
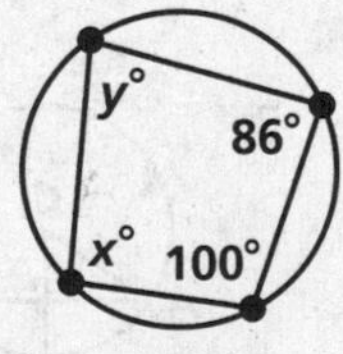

6.
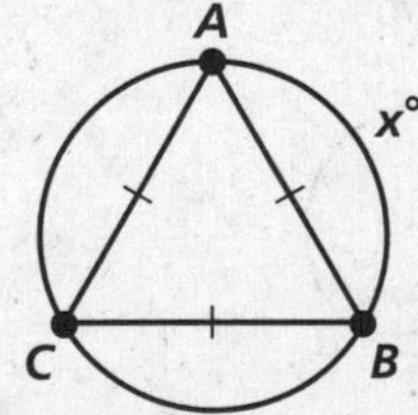

Points A, B, and D lie on $\odot C$. $m\angle ACB = 40$. $m\widehat{AB} < m\widehat{AD}$. Find each measure.

7. $m\widehat{AB}$

8. $m\angle ADB$

9. $m\angle BAC$

Name ______________________ Class ______________ Date ______________

Review 181

Angle Measures and Segment Lengths

OBJECTIVE: Finding the measures of angles formed by chords, secants, and tangents

MATERIALS: None

Example

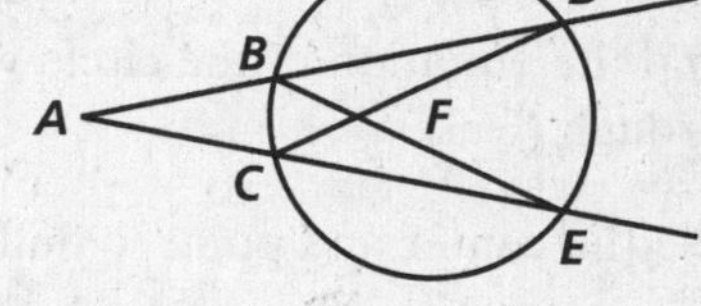

In the circle shown, $m\widehat{BC} = 15$ and $m\widehat{DE} = 35$.

Find $m\angle A$ and $m\angle BFC$.

Because $\overleftrightarrow{AD}$ and $\overleftrightarrow{AE}$ are secants, $m\angle A$ can be found using Theorem 11-11, part (2).

$$\begin{aligned} m\angle A &= \tfrac{1}{2}(m\widehat{DE} - m\widehat{BC}) \\ &= \tfrac{1}{2}(35 - 15) \\ &= 10 \end{aligned}$$

Because $\overline{BE}$ and $\overline{CD}$ are chords, $m\angle BFC$ can be found using Theorem 11-11, part (1).

$$\begin{aligned} m\angle BFC &= \tfrac{1}{2}(m\widehat{DE} + m\widehat{BC}) \\ &= \tfrac{1}{2}(35 + 15) \\ &= 25 \end{aligned}$$

Exercises

Find the value of each variable.

1.

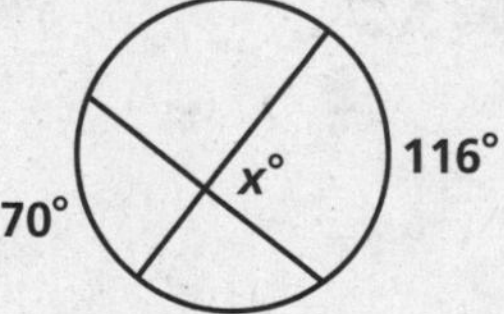

2.

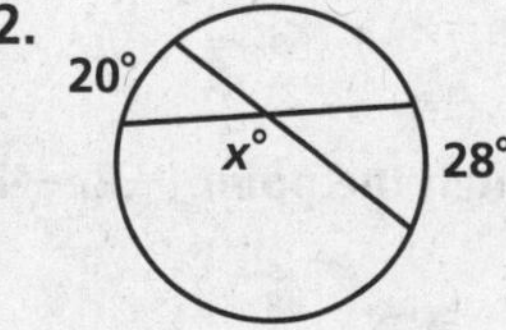

3.

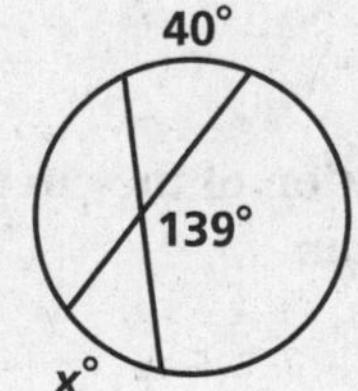

4.

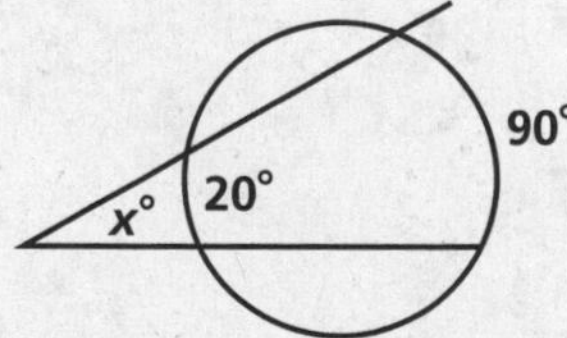

5.

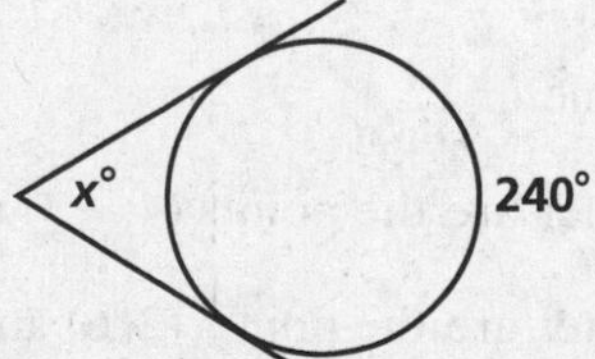

6.

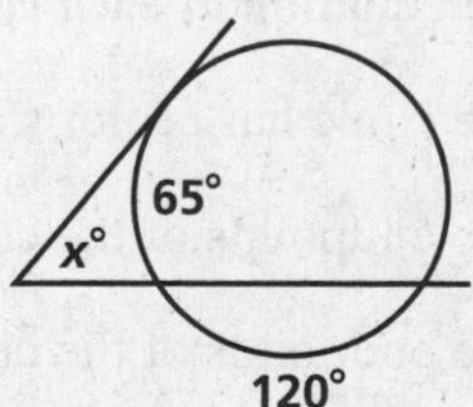

7.

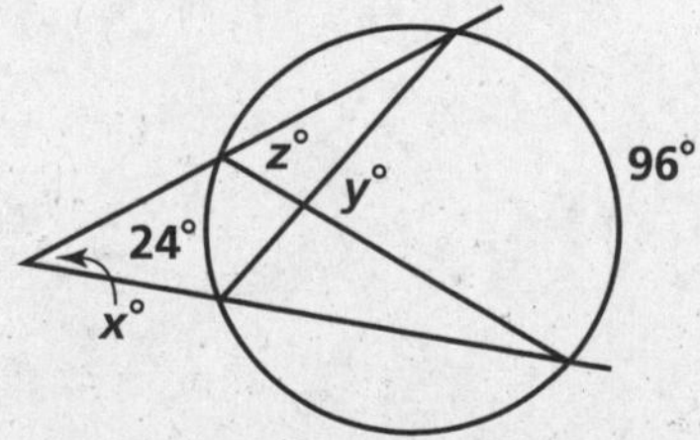

8.

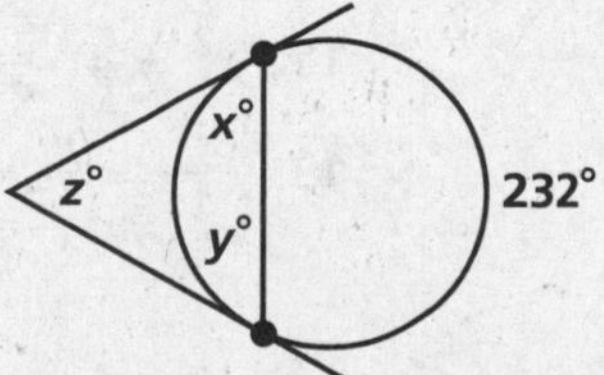

9.

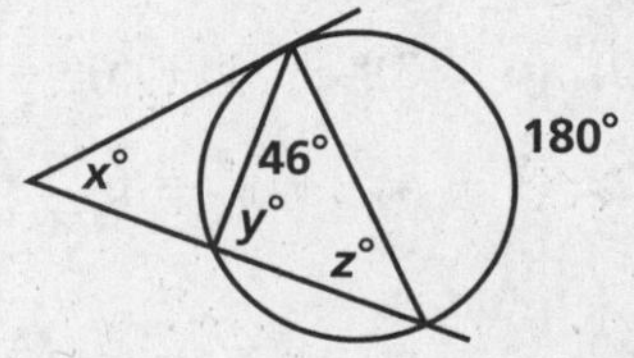

GEOMETRY TOPICS

Name ______________________ Class ______________ Date ______________

Review 182

OBJECTIVE: Writing the equation of a circle **MATERIALS:** None

Example

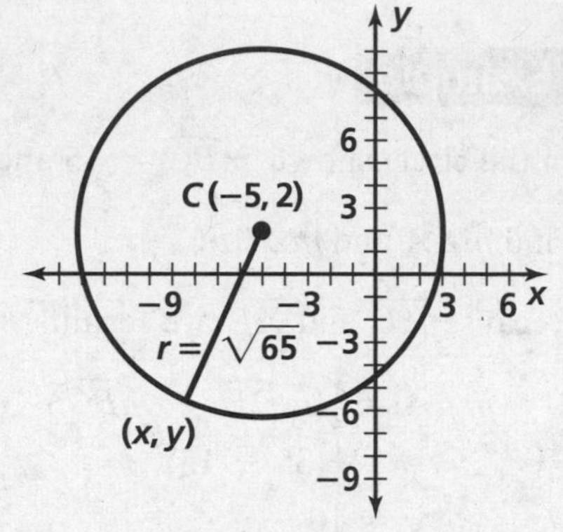

Find the equation of the circle whose center is $(-5, 2)$ and that passes through $(3, 3)$.

Use the center and point to find the radius.

$r = \sqrt{(-5 - 3)^2 + (2 - 3)^2}$ Distance Formula

$r = \sqrt{(-8)^2 + (-1)^2}$

$r = \sqrt{65}$

With $r = \sqrt{65}$ and center at $(-5, 2)$, the circle has the equation

$(x - (-5))^2 + (y - 2)^2 = (\sqrt{65})^2$.

Simplified, this becomes $(x + 5)^2 + (y - 2)^2 = 65$.

Exercises

Find the equation of the circle whose center and radius are given.

1. center $(3, 11)$ radius $= 2$
2. center $(-5, 0)$ radius $= 15$
3. center $(6, -6)$ radius $= \sqrt{7}$

Find the equation of the circle that passes through the point $(-2, -4)$ with the given center.

4. $C(0, 0)$
5. $C(-2, -2)$
6. $C(3, 1)$

Find the equation of each circle described.

7. The circle has center $(5, 2)$ and diameter 12.
8. The endpoints of the circle's diameter are the points $(4, -3)$ and $(4, 7)$.
9. The endpoints of the circle's diameter are the points $(2, 6)$ and $(-6, 0)$.

Identify the center and radius of each circle.

10. $(x + 3)^2 + (y + 5)^2 = 25$
11. $x^2 + y^2 = 0.04$
12. $(x - 4)^2 + y^2 = 6$
13. $\frac{(x - 3)^2}{2} + \frac{(y - 5)^2}{2} = 8$

Name ______________________ Class ______________ Date ______________

Review 183

OBJECTIVE: Using perpendicular bisectors to solve locus problems

MATERIALS: Compass, straightedge

Example

A family on vacation wants to hike on Oak Mountain and fish at North Pond and along the White River. Where on the river should they fish in order to be equidistant from North Pond and Oak Mountain?

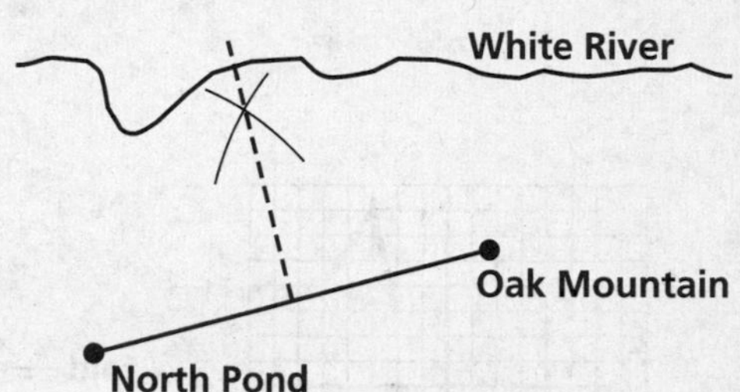

Draw a line segment joining North Pond and Oak Mountain.

Construct the perpendicular bisector of that segment.

The family should fish where the perpendicular bisector meets the White River.

Exercises

Describe each of the following, and then compare your answers with those of a partner.

1. the locus of points equidistant from your desk and your partner's desk
2. the locus of points on the floor equidistant from the two side walls of your classroom
3. the locus of points equidistant from a window and the door of your classroom
4. the locus of points equidistant from the front and back walls of your classroom
5. the locus of points equidistant from the floor and the ceiling of your classroom

Use points *A* and *B* to complete the following.

6. Describe the locus of points in a plane equidistant from points *A* and *B*.
7. How many points are equidistant from *A* and *B* and also lie on $\overleftrightarrow{AB}$? Explain your reasoning.

A •

• *B*

Name ____________________ Class ____________ Date ____________

Review 184

OBJECTIVE: Locating reflection images of figures **MATERIALS:** Scissors, graph paper

Example

Find the reflection images of $\triangle MNO$ in the x- and y-axes. Give the coordinates of the vertices of the images.

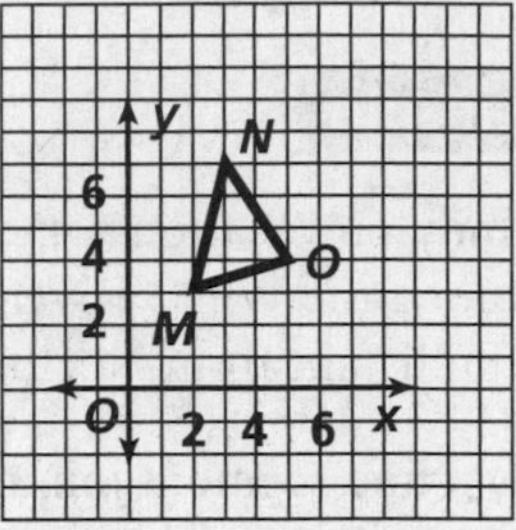

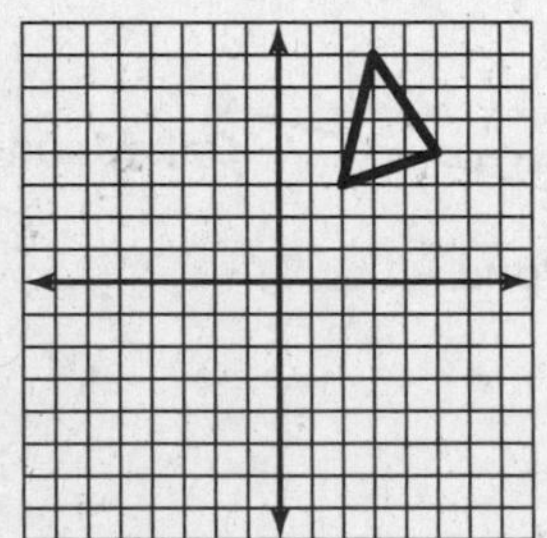

Copy the figure onto a piece of graph paper.

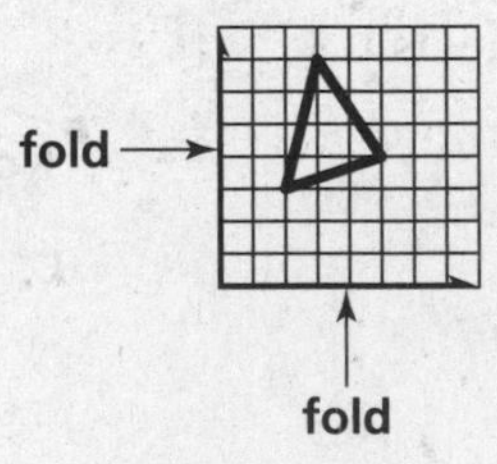

Fold the paper along the x-axis and y-axis.

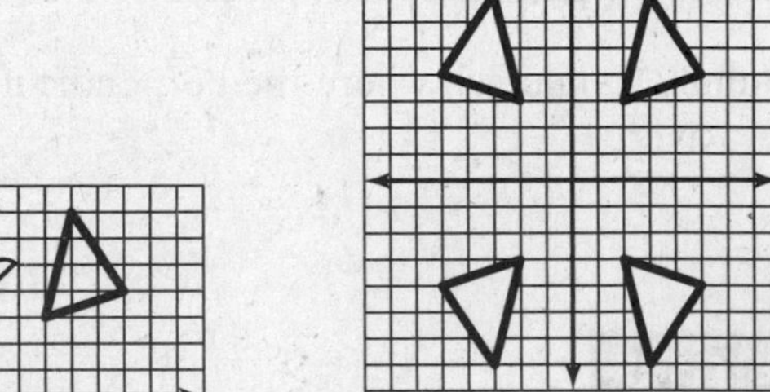

Cut out the triangle.

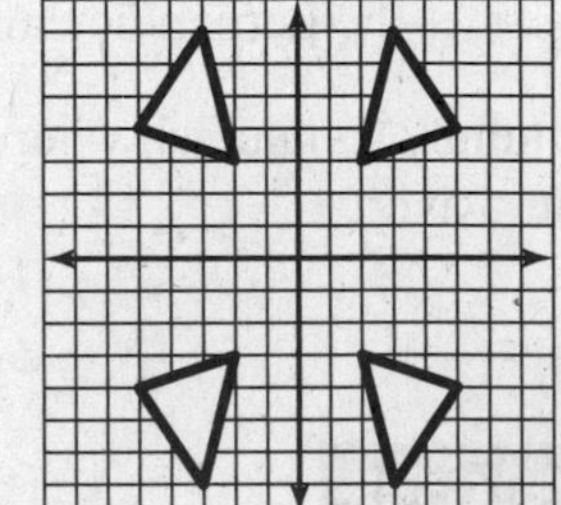

Unfold the paper.

From the graph we can see that the reflection image of $\triangle MNO$ in the x-axis has vertices at $(2, -3)$, $(3, -7)$, and $(5, -4)$. The reflection image of $\triangle MNO$ in the y-axis has vertices at $(-2, 3)$, $(-3, 7)$, and $(-5, 4)$.

Exercises

Use a sheet of graph paper to complete Exercises 1–5.

1. Draw and label the x- and y-axes on a sheet of graph paper.
2. Draw a nonregular triangle in one of the four quadrants. Make sure that the vertices are on the intersection of grid lines.
3. Fold the paper along the axes.
4. Cut out the triangle, and unfold the paper.
5. Label the coordinates of the vertices of the reflection images in the x- and y-axes.

Find the coordinates of the vertices for the reflection images of the triangle in the x- and y-axes.

6. $\triangle FGH$ with vertices $F(-1, 3)$, $G(-5, 1)$, $H(-3, 5)$
7. $\triangle CDE$ with vertices $C(2, 4)$, $D(5, 2)$, $E(6, 3)$
8. $\triangle JKL$ with vertices $J(-1, -5)$, $K(-2, -3)$, $L(-4, -6)$

Name ______________________ Class ______________ Date ______________

Review 185

Translations

OBJECTIVE: Using vectors to represent translations

MATERIALS: Graph paper, scissors, tracing paper

Example

What vector describes the translation of $ABCD$ to $A'B'C'D'$?

To get from A to A' (or from B to B' or C to C'), you move eight units left and seven units down. The vector that describes this translation is $\langle -8, 7 \rangle$.

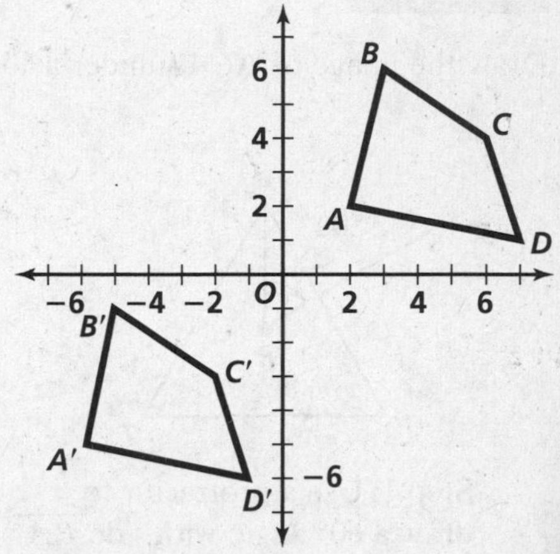

Exercises

- On graph paper, draw the x- and y-axes, and label Quadrants I–IV.
- Draw a quadrilateral in Quadrant I. Make sure that the vertices are on the intersection of grid lines.
- Trace the quadrilateral, and cut it out.
- Use the cutout to translate the figure to each of the other three quadrants.

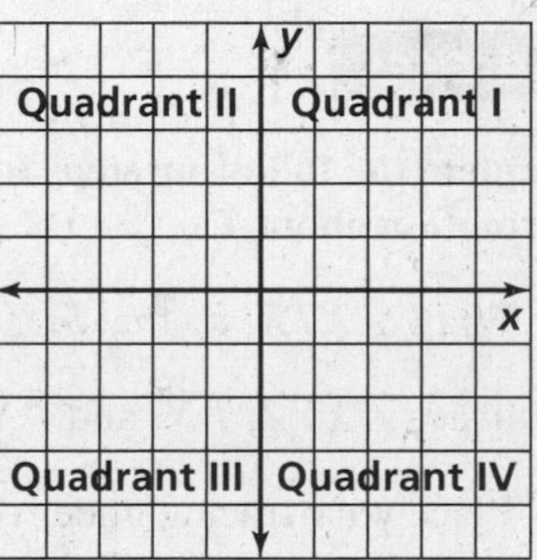

Name the vector that describes each translation of your quadrilateral.

1. from Quadrant I to Quadrant II

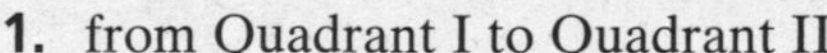

2. from Quadrant I to Quadrant III
3. from Quadrant I to Quadrant IV
4. from Quadrant II to Quadrant III
5. from Quadrant III to Quadrant I

Refer to *ABCD* in the example above.

6. Give the coordinates of the image of $ABCD$ under the translation $\langle -2, -5 \rangle$.
7. Give the coordinates of the image of $ABCD$ under the translation $\langle 2, -4 \rangle$.
8. Give the coordinates of the image of $ABCD$ under the translation $\langle 1, 3 \rangle$.

GEOMETRY TOPICS

Name ____________________ Class ____________ Date ____________

Review 186

OBJECTIVE: Locating rotation images of figures **MATERIALS:** Protractor, compass

Example

Draw the image of $\triangle CAT$ under a 60° rotation about P.

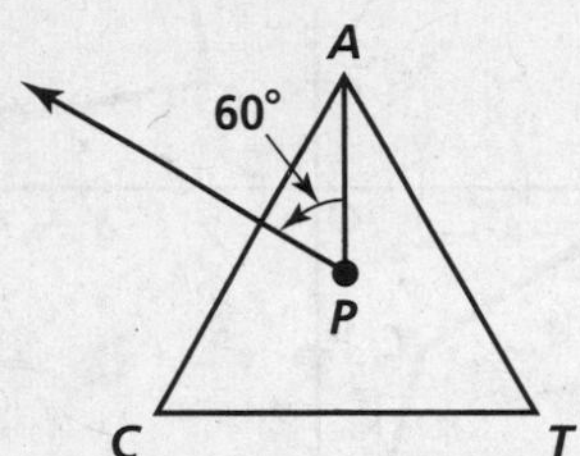

Step 1: Use a protractor to draw a 60° angle with side $\overline{PA}$.

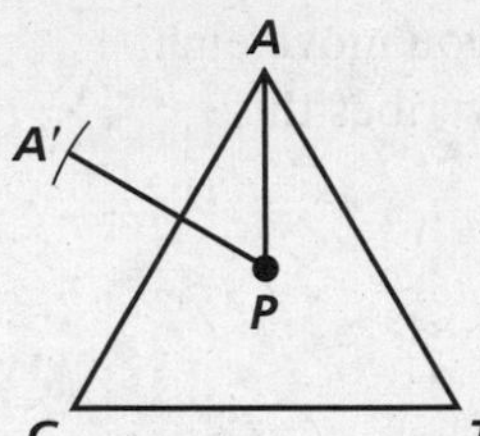

Step 2: Use a compass to construct $\overline{PA} \cong \overline{PA'}$.

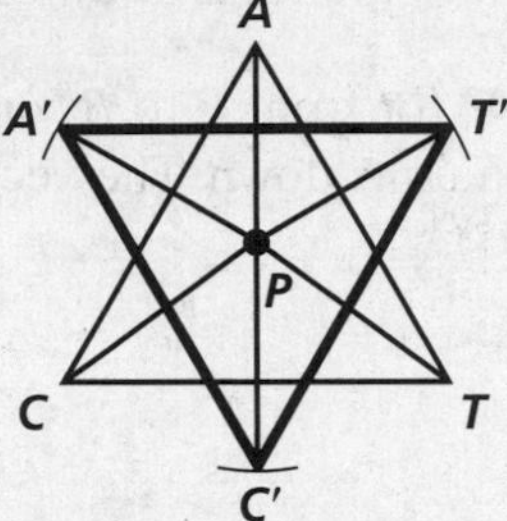

Step 3: Create C' and T' in a similar manner. Draw $\triangle C'A'T'$.

Exercises

Complete the following steps to draw the image of $\triangle XYZ$ under a 80° rotation about T.

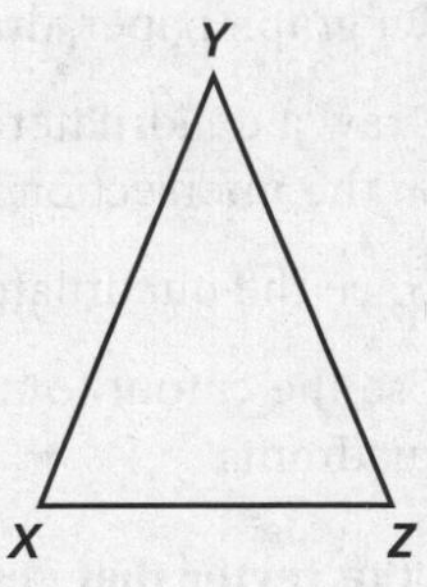

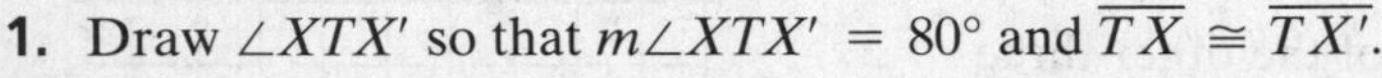

1. Draw $\angle XTX'$ so that $m\angle XTX' = 80°$ and $\overline{TX} \cong \overline{TX'}$.
2. Trace $\triangle XYZ$, $\overline{TX}$, and $\overline{TX'}$.
3. Place your tracing under the triangle at the right so that the two triangles and point T align.
4. With your pencil on T, rotate $\overline{TX'}$ on this paper until it is on top of $\overline{TX}$ on your tracing.
5. Trace the triangle from your tracing onto this paper, and label it $\triangle X'Y'Z'$.

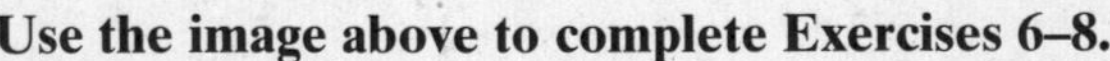

Use the image above to complete Exercises 6–8.

6. Draw the image of $\triangle XYZ$ under a 120° rotation about T.
7. Draw a point S inside $\triangle XYZ$. Draw the image of $\triangle XYZ$ under a 135° rotation about S.
8. Draw the image of $\triangle XYZ$ under a 90° rotation about Y.

Name ______________________________ Class ______________ Date ______________

Review 187

Compositions of Reflections

OBJECTIVE: Identifying reflections and their relation to other isometries

MATERIALS: None

Example

Name a transformation that maps the figure *ABCD* onto the figure *EFGH* shown at the right.

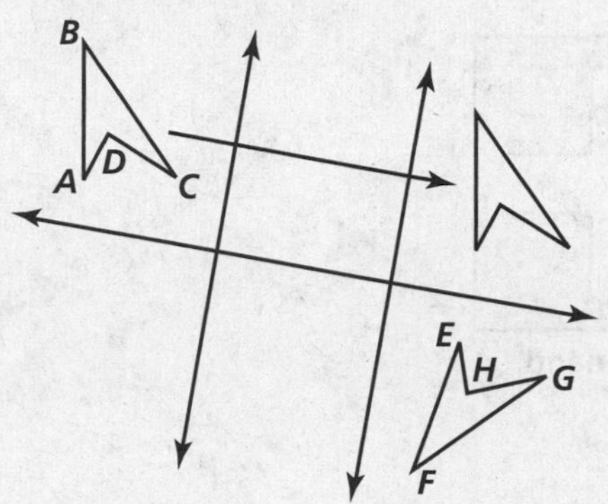

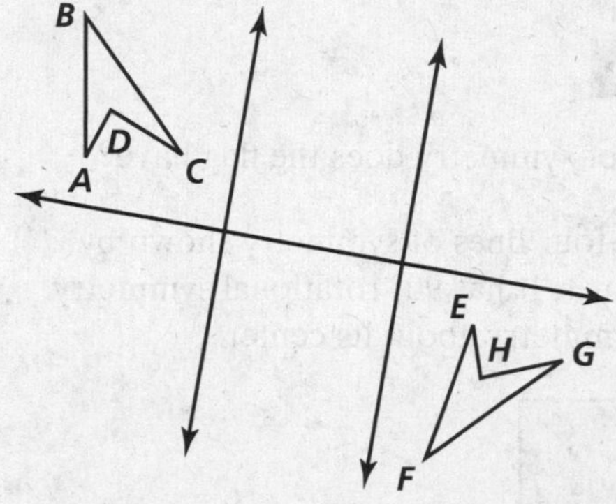

The transformation is a glide reflection. It involves a translation, or glide, followed by a reflection in a line parallel to the translation vector.

Exercises

- Draw two pairs of parallel lines that intersect as shown at the right.
- Draw a nonregular quadrilateral in the center of the four lines.
- Use paper folding and tracing to reflect the figure and its images so that there is a figure in each of the nine sections.
- Label the figures 1 through 9 as shown.

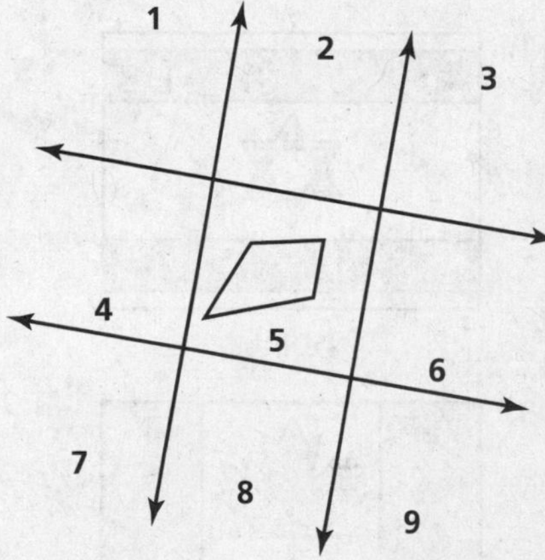

Describe a transformation that maps each of the following.

1. figure 4 onto figure 6
2. figure 1 onto figure 2
3. figure 7 onto figure 5
4. figure 2 onto figure 9
5. figure 1 onto figure 5
6. figure 6 onto figure 7
7. figure 8 onto figure 9
8. figure 2 onto figure 8

GEOMETRY TOPICS

Name ______________________ Class ______________ Date ______________

Review 188

OBJECTIVE: Identifying types of symmetry in figures

MATERIALS: None

Consider the following types of symmetry: rotational, point, line, and reflectional.

Example

What types of symmetry does the flag have?

Switzerland

The flag has four lines of symmetry shown by the dotted lines. It has 90° rotational symmetry and point symmetry about its center.

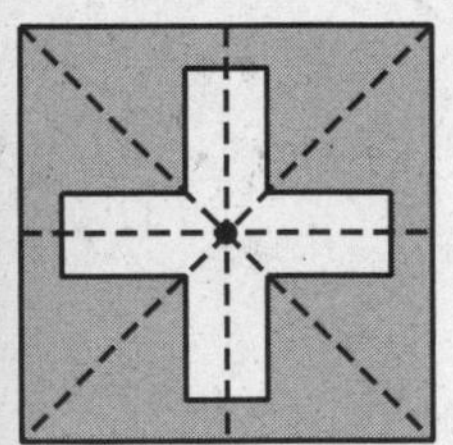

Exercises

Describe the symmetries in each flag.

1. 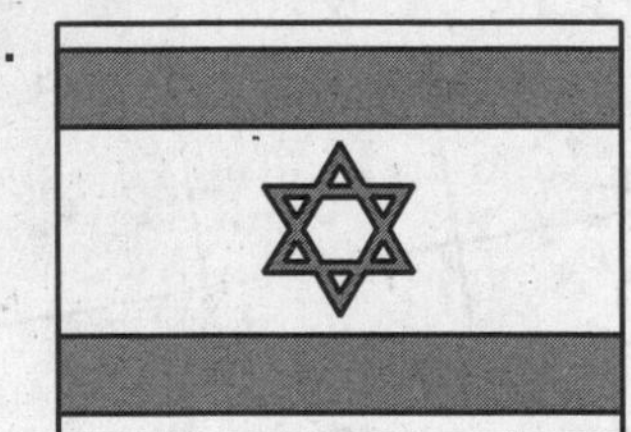

Israel

2. 

South Africa

3. 

Canada

4. 

United Kingdom

5. 

Honduras

6. 

Somalia

Name ______________________________ Class __________________ Date ______________

Review 189

OBJECTIVE: Identifying symmetries of tessellations	**MATERIALS:** Stiff paper or cardboard, scissors

Example

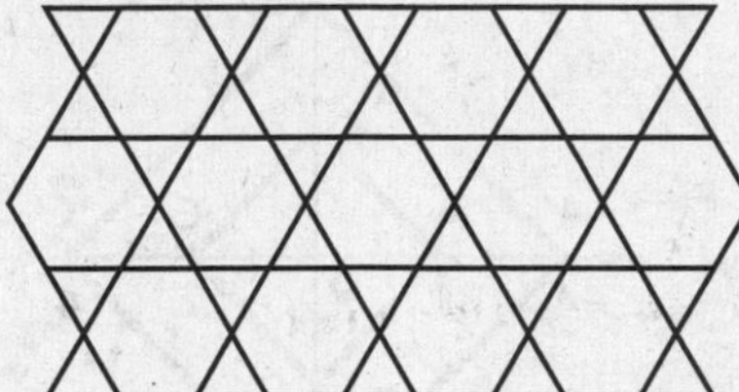

List the symmetries of the tessellation.

The tessellation has line symmetry as shown by the dotted lines below. It has rotational symmetry about the points shown. It has translational symmetry and glide reflection symmetry.

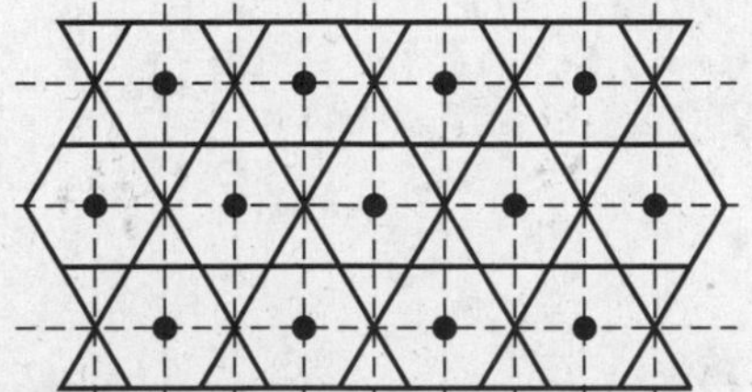

Exercises

Copy the figure at the right onto stiff paper or cardboard. Then cut it out.

1. Use the cutout to create a tessellation.
2. List the symmetries of the tessellation.

List the symmetries of each tessellation.

3. 

4. 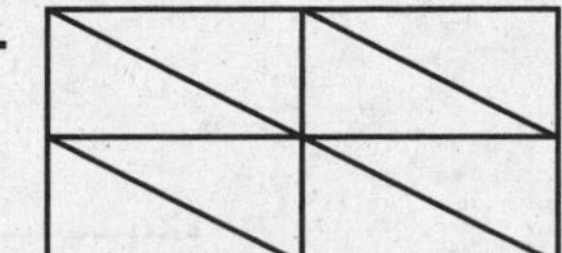

5. 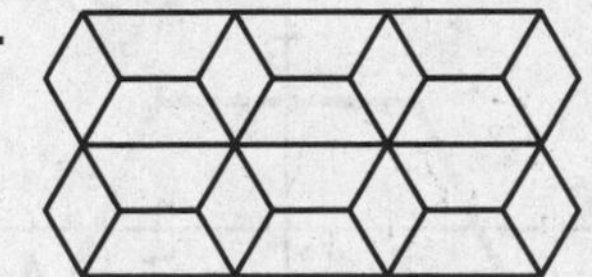

Name ______________________ Class ______________ Date ______________

Review 190

OBJECTIVE: Locating dilation images of figures **MATERIALS:** Graph paper

Example

Quadrilateral $ABCD$ has vertices $A(-2, 0)$, $B(0, 2)$, $C(2, 0)$, and $D(0, -2)$. Find the image of $ABCD$ under the dilation centered at the origin with scale factor 2. Then graph $ABCD$ and its image.

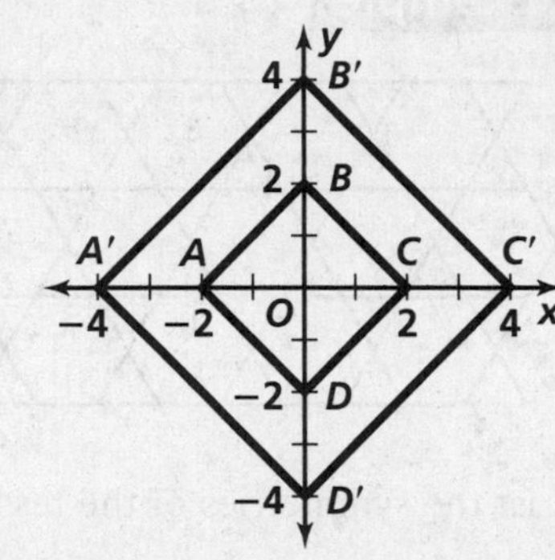

To find the image of the vertices of $ABCD$, multiply the x-coordinates and y-coordinates by 2.

$A(-2, 0) \rightarrow A'(-4, 0)$ $B(0, 2) \rightarrow B'(0, 4)$

$C(2, 0) \rightarrow C'(4, 0)$ $D(0, -2) \rightarrow D'(0, -4)$

Exercises

Use graph paper to complete Exercise 1.

1. **a.** Draw a quadrilateral in the coordinate plane.

   b. Draw the image of the quadrilateral under dilations centered at the origin with scale factors $\frac{1}{2}$, 2, and 4.

Draw the image of each figure under a dilation centered at the origin with the given scale factor.

2.

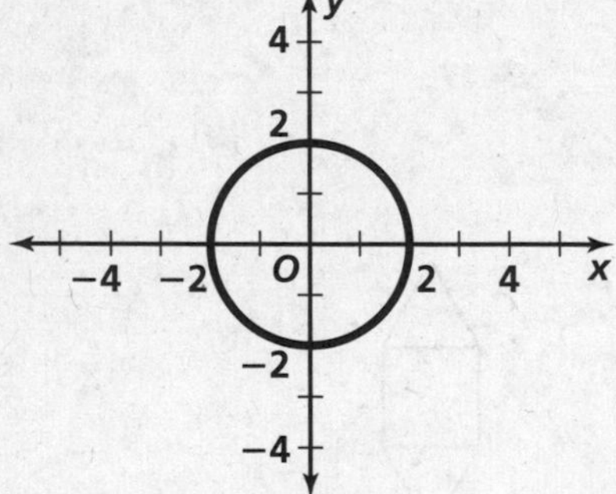

scale factor 2

3.

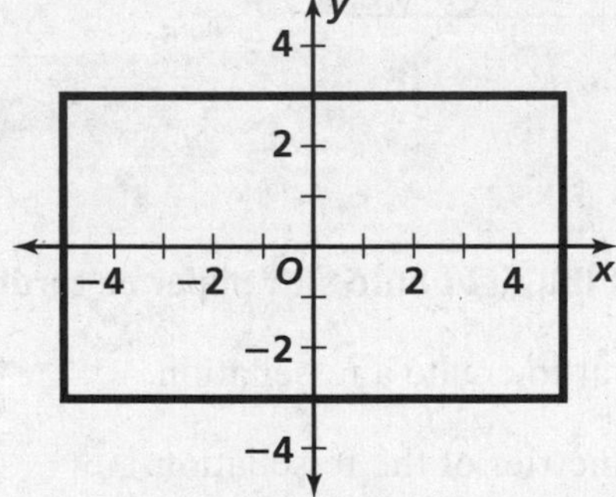

scale factor $\frac{1}{2}$

4.

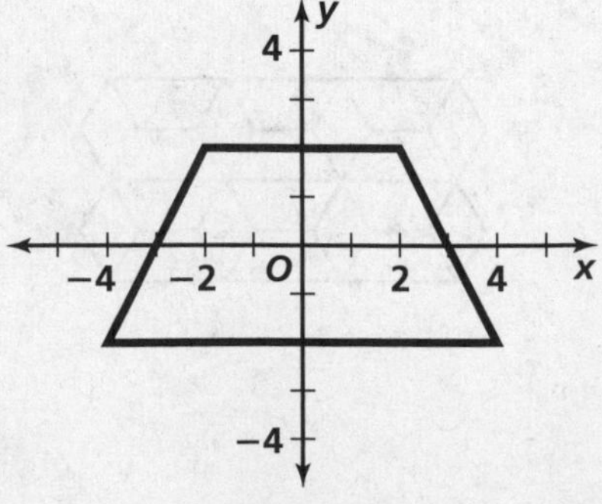

scale factor 3

5.

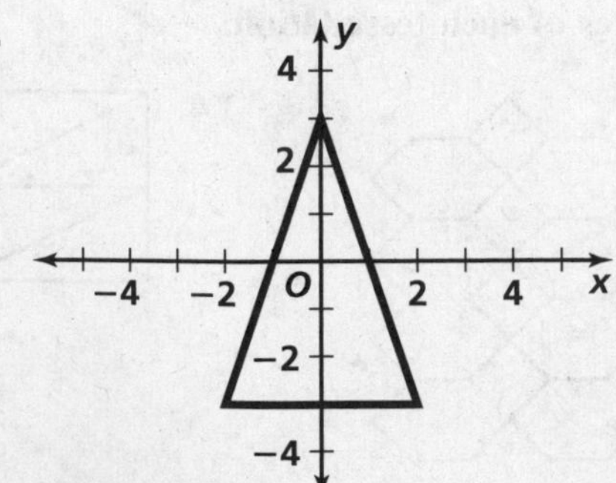

scale factor 4

Name ______________________ Class ______________ Date ______________

Review 191

Properties of Real Numbers

OBJECTIVE: Finding additive and multiplicative inverses	**MATERIALS:** None

The ***additive inverse*** of a number a is $-a$. The number $-a$ is also called the ***opposite*** of a. The sum of a number and its opposite, $a + (-a)$, is always 0.

The ***multiplicative inverse*** of a nonzero number a is $\frac{1}{a}$. The number $\frac{1}{a}$ is also called the reciprocal of a. The product of a nonzero number and its reciprocal, $a \cdot \frac{1}{a}$, is always 1. The number 0 does not have a multiplicative inverse.

Examples

Find the opposite and reciprocal of each number.

a. -7.4 **b.** $3\frac{1}{2}$

a. Opposite: $-(-7.4) = 7.4$

Reciprocal: $\frac{1}{-7.4} = \frac{10}{-74} = -\frac{10}{74} = -\frac{5}{37}$

b. Opposite: $-\left(3\frac{1}{2}\right) = -3\frac{1}{2}$

Reciprocal: $\frac{1}{3\frac{1}{2}} = \frac{1}{\frac{7}{2}} = \frac{2}{7}$

Exercises

Find the opposite and reciprocal of each number.

1. 3 **2.** -2 **3.** $-\frac{1}{6}$ **4.** $\frac{3}{5}$

5. -2.4 **6.** 0.6 **7.** $-5\frac{2}{3}$ **8.** $2\frac{1}{4}$

9. $\frac{\pi}{2}$ **10.** $-\frac{1}{\pi}$ **11.** -0.25 **12.** 1.3

13. $1\frac{2}{5}$ **14.** $-\sqrt{2}$ **15.** $\pi + 2$ **16.** $-\frac{9}{10}$

Name ______________________ Class ______________ Date ______________

Review 192

OBJECTIVE: Simplifying and evaluating algebraic expressions

MATERIALS: None

To simplify an algebraic expression, combine like terms using the basic properties of real numbers. Like terms have the same variables raised to the same powers.

To evaluate an algebraic expression, replace the variables in the expression with numbers and follow the order of operations.

Example

Simplify the algebraic expression $3(4x + 5y) - 2(3x - 7y)$. Then evaluate the simplified expression for $x = 3$ and $y = -2$.

Simplify the algebraic expression using the basic properties of real numbers.

$3(4x + 5y) - 2(3x - 7y) = 3(4x + 5y) + (-2)(3x + (-7)y)$ ⟵ **definition of subtraction**

$= 12x + 15y + (-6)x + 14y$ ⟵ **Distributive Property**

$= 12x + (-6)x + 15y + 14y$ ⟵ **Commutative Property of Addition**

$= (12 + (-6))x + (15 + 14)y$ ⟵ **Distributive Property**

$= 6x + 29y$

Now replace x with 3 and y with -2 in the simplified expression.

$6(3) + 29(-2) = 18 - 58 = -40$

Exercises

Simplify the algebraic expression. Then evaluate the simplified expression for the given values of the variable.

1. $(4x + 1) + 2x; x = 3$
2. $7(t + 3) - 11; t = 4$
3. $3y + 4z + 6y - 9z; y = 2, z = 1$
4. $2(u + v) - (u - v); u = 8, v = -3$
5. $5a^2 + 5a + a + 1; a = -2$
6. $6p^2 - (3p^2 + 2q^2); p = 1, q = 5$
7. $\frac{3}{4}(m + n) - \frac{1}{4}(m - n); m = 6, n = 2$
8. $\frac{r}{2} + \frac{s}{3} - \frac{r}{4} + \frac{1}{5}; r = -1, s = 0$

Name ______________________ Class ______________ Date ______________

Review 193

Solving Equations

OBJECTIVE: Solving an equation for one of its variables

MATERIALS: None

To solve an equation for one of its variables, rewrite the equation as an equivalent equation with the specified variable on one side of the equation by itself and an expression not containing that variable on the other side.

Example

Solve the equation $\frac{ax - b}{2} = x + 2b$ for x.

Use the properties of equality and the properties of real numbers to rewrite the equation as a sequence of equivalent equations.

$\frac{ax - b}{2} = x + 2b$

$2\left(\frac{ax - b}{2}\right) = 2(x + 2b)$ ⟵ **Multiply each side by 2.**

$ax - b = 2(x + 2b)$ ⟵ **Simplify.**

$ax - b = 2x + 4b$ ⟵ **Distributive Property**

$ax - 2x = 4b + b$ ⟵ **Add and subtract to get terms with x on one side and terms without x on the other side.**

$ax - 2x = 5b$ ⟵ **Simplify.**

$x(a - 2) = 5b$ ⟵ **Distributive Property**

$x = \frac{5b}{a - 2}$ ⟵ **Divide each side by $a - 2$.**

The final form of the equation has x on the left side by itself and an expression not containing x on the right side.

Exercises

Solve each equation for the indicated variable.

1. $3m - n = 2m + n$, for m
2. $2(u + 3v) = w - 5u$, for u
3. $ax + b = cx + d$, for x
4. $k(y + 3z) = 4(y - 5)$, for y
5. $\frac{1}{2}r + 3s = 1$, for r
6. $\frac{2}{3}f + \frac{5}{12}g = 1 - fg$, for f
7. $\frac{x + k}{j} = \frac{3}{4}$, for x
8. $\frac{a - 3y}{b} + 4 = a + y$, for y

ALGEBRA 2 TOPICS

Name ____________________ Class ____________________ Date ____________________

Review 194

OBJECTIVE: Solving and graphing inequalities **MATERIALS:** None

To solve an inequality, use the techniques used to solve an equation with one difference: when multiplying or dividing each side by a negative number, reverse the inequality.

Examples

Solve each inequality. Graph the solutions.

a. $2x - 5 \geq 13$ **b.** $4 + 3(1 - 2x) > 37$

Use the properties of real numbers and the properties of inequalities to rewrite each inequality in equivalent forms.

a. When dividing each side by a positive number, do not reverse the inequality.

$2x - 5 \geq 13$

$2x \geq 18$ ← **Add 5 to each side.**

$x \geq 9$ ← **Divide each side by 2.**

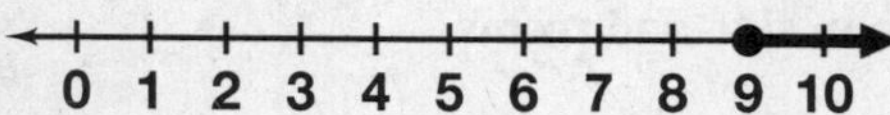

b. When dividing each side by a negative number, reverse the inequality.

$4 + 3(1 - 2x) > 37$

$4 + 3 - 6x > 37$ ← **Distributive Property**

$7 - 6x > 37$ ← **Simplify.**

$-6x > 30$ ← **Subtract 7 from each side.**

$x < -5$ ← **Divide each side by –6 and reverse the inequality.**

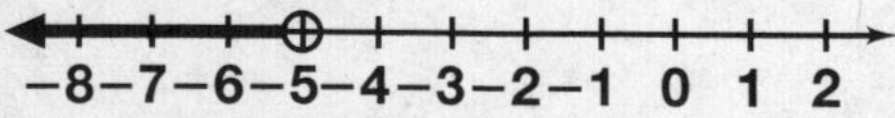

Exercises

Solve each inequality. Graph the solutions.

1. $3(y - 5) \leq 6$ **2.** $-4t > 2$ **3.** $3 - 4m < 11$ **4.** $7d \leq 2(d + 5)$

5. $-2(3 - h) + 2h \geq 0$ **6.** $3k - (1 - 2k) > 1$ **7.** $5p + 12 \leq 9p - 20$ **8.** $3 - 2r < 7 - r$

Name ____________________ Class ______________ Date ______________

Review 195

Absolute Value Equations and Inequalities

OBJECTIVE: Solving absolute value equations **MATERIALS:** None

For every positive real number a, both a and $-a$ satisfy the equation $|x| = a$.

To solve an absolute value equation, first rewrite the equation as an equivalent equation with the absolute value expression on the left side by itself. Then rewrite this equation as a compound equality using the rule that if $|x| = a$ then $x = a$ or $x = -a$.

Example

Solve the equation $2|x - 3| + 1 = 6x + 7$. Check for extraneous solutions.

Use the properties of equality to rewrite the equation as an equivalent equation with the absolute value expression on one side by itself. Then write that equation as a compound equality and solve each resulting equation.

$2|x - 3| + 1 = 6x + 7$

$2|x - 3| = 6x + 6$ ← **Subtract 1 from each side.**

$|x - 3| = 3x + 3$ ← **Divide each side by 2.**

$x - 3 = 3x + 3$ or $x - 3 = -(3x + 3)$ ← **Rewrite as a compound equality.**

$-2x = 6$ or $x - 3 = -3x - 3$ ← **Solve each equation.**

$x = -3$ or $4x = 0$

$x = -3$ or $x = 0$

To check for extraneous solutions, substitute each value for x in the original absolute value equation. Any value that does not satisfy the original equation must be discarded.

Check $2|-3 - 3| + 1 \stackrel{?}{=} 6(-3) + 7$ $\quad$ $2|0 - 3| + 1 \stackrel{?}{=} 6(0) + 7$

$2|-6| + 1 \stackrel{?}{=} -18 + 7$ $\quad$ $2|-3| + 1 \stackrel{?}{=} 0 + 7$

$2(6) + 1 \stackrel{?}{=} -11$ $\quad$ $2(3) + 1 \stackrel{?}{=} 7$

$13 \neq -11$ $\quad$ $7 = 7$

The only solution is 0; -3 is an extraneous solution.

Exercises

Solve each equation. Check for extraneous solutions.

1. $|2x + 7| = 5$ **2.** $|x - 3| = -1$ **3.** $|x + 7| = 2x + 8$ **4.** $|x - 0.5| + 0.3 = 1$

5. $3|2x + 5| = 15$ **6.** $|5x - 1| + 7 = 3x$ **7.** $2|x + 1| + x = 1$ **8.** $|x + 1| = 2x$

ALGEBRA 2 TOPICS

Name ________________ Class ________________ Date ________________

Review 196

Probability

OBJECTIVE: Finding theoretical probability **MATERIALS:** None

The possible results of an experiment are **outcomes.** If you want to find the theoretical probability of a particular event, or a **favorable outcome,** you use this formula:

$$P(\text{event}) = \frac{\text{number of outcomes in the event}}{\text{number of possible outcomes}}$$

Example

Find the theoretical probability of rolling a number cube and having an outcome of either 2 or 4.

$$P(2 \text{ or } 4) = \frac{(\text{number of times 2 or 4 are outcomes})}{(\text{total possible numbers on cube})} = \frac{2}{6}$$

$$= \frac{1}{3}$$

Exercises

Use the spinner at the right to determine the theoretical probability for each event.

1. P(the number is even)
2. P(5)
3. P(the number is prime)
4. P(the number is less than 6)
5. P(an odd number)
6. P(a number divisible by 2)
7. P(a multiple of 3)
8. P(an 11 or 15)
9. P(a composite number)
10. P(the number represents your age)
11. P(a perfect square)
12. P(the number represents your grade)
13. P(not a 5 or 7)

ALGEBRA 2 TOPICS

Name ______________________ Class ______________ Date ______________

Review 197

OBJECTIVE: Determining whether a relation is a function

MATERIALS: Number cube

- A **relation** is a set of ordered pairs.
- The **domain** is the set of the first numbers in each pair, or the *x*-values.
- The **range** is the set of the second numbers in each pair, or the *y*-values.
- A relation is a **function** if each input value *x* corresponds to exactly one output value *y*. In a set of ordered pairs for a function, an *x*-value cannot be repeated with two or more different *y*-values.

Example

Roll a number cube six times to get the *x*-values of six ordered pairs in a relation. Roll it six more times to get the *y*-values of the ordered pairs. Decide whether the relation is a function. Find the domain and the range of the relation.

$\{(6, 1), (2, 1), (5, 4), (2, 2), (1, 4), (4, 2)\}$ ← **Write the ordered pairs.**

$\{(6, 1), (⓶, 1), (5, 4), (⓶, 2), (1, 4), (4, 2)\}$ ← **Circle any *x*-values that repeat to determine whether the relation is a function.**

The *x*-value 2 is repeated with two different *y*-values so the relation is not a function.

The domain is the set of first numbers in each pair: $\{6, 2, 5, 1, 4\}$.
The range is the set of second numbers in each pair: $\{1, 4, 2\}$.

Exercises

Roll a number cube to find the indicated number of ordered pairs. Determine whether each set of ordered pairs is a function. Find the domain and range of each relation.

1. 5 ordered pairs **2.** 4 ordered pairs **3.** 6 ordered pairs **4.** 8 ordered pairs

Determine whether each relation is a function. Explain your answer. Find the domain and range of each relation.

5. $\{(1, 2), (1, 3), (1, 4), (1, 5), (1, 6)\}$

6. $\{(0, -1), (1, 2), (-1, -1), (-2, 5), (2, 9)\}$

7. $\{(A, B), (C, D), (E, F), (G, H)\}$

8. $\{(I, M), (N, P), (I, T), (I, P)\}$

9. $\{(0, 0)\}$

10. $\left\{\left(\frac{1}{2}, 3\right), (0.5, 4), (2, 1)\right\}$

Name ____________________ Class ____________ Date ____________

Review 198

OBJECTIVE: Using the slope-intercept form to write equations of lines

MATERIALS: None

- The slope-intercept formula is $y = mx + b$, where m represents the slope of the line, and b represents its y-intercept. The y-intercept is the point at which the line crosses the y-axis.
- The slope of a horizontal line is always zero, and the slope of a vertical line is always undefined.

Example

Find the equation of the line that contains the point $(3, -1)$ and has a slope of $-\frac{4}{3}$.

$-1 = \left(-\frac{4}{3}\right)(3) + b$ ← **To find b, substitute the values $-\frac{4}{3}$ for m, 3 for x, and -1 for y into the slope-intercept formula.**

$-1 = -4 + b$

$3 = b$

$y = -\frac{4}{3}x + 3$ ← **Substitute $-\frac{4}{3}$ for m and 3 for b into the slope-intercept formula.**

Exercises

Write the equation of each line.

1. $m = 4$; contains $(3, 2)$
2. $m = -2$; contains $(4, 7)$
3. $m = 0$; contains $(3, 0)$
4. $m = -1$; contains $(-5, -2)$
5. $m = 3$; contains $(-2, -4)$
6. $m = 0$; contains $(0, -7)$
7. $m = 8$; contains $(5, 0)$
8. $m = -1$; contains $(0, 7)$
9. $m = 0$; contains $(3, 8)$
10. $m = 4$; contains $(2, 5)$
11. $m = 7$; contains $(3, 2)$
12. $m = -1$; contains $(2, -6)$

Write the equation of each line.

13. 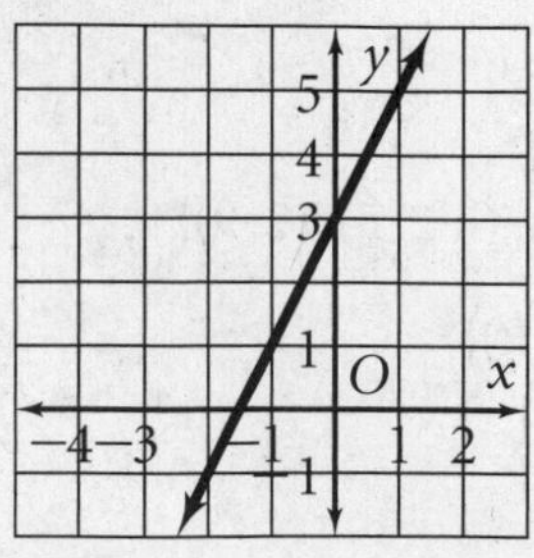

14. 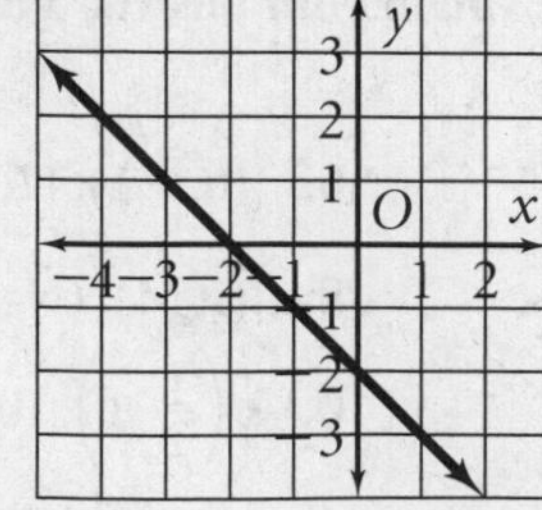

15. 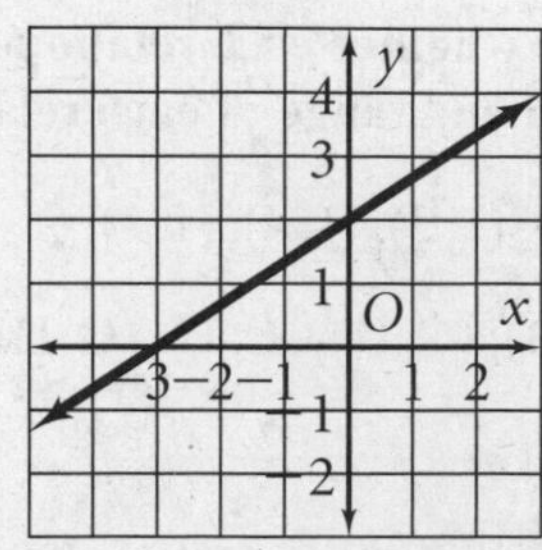

ALGEBRA 2 TOPICS

Name ____________ Class ____________ Date ____________

Review 199

Direct Variation

OBJECTIVE: Writing and interpreting direct variation equations

MATERIALS: None

A linear function defined by an equation of the form $y = kx$, where $k \neq 0$, represents *direct variation.* The constant k, the slope of the line, is called the *constant of variation.*

Given the value of y corresponding to a specific value of x, you can find the constant of variation k by substituting the given values of x and y into the equation $k = \frac{y}{x}$.

The equation $y = kx$ can be used to find the values of y that correspond to other values of x or vice versa.

Examples

Find the missing value for each direct variation.

a. If $y = 5$ when $x = 2$, find y when $x = 7$.

$k = \frac{y}{x} = \frac{5}{2}$ ⟵ **Use $y = 5, x = 2$, and $k = \frac{y}{x}$ to find the value of k.**

$y = \frac{5}{2}x$ ⟵ **Now use the form $y = kx$ and $k = \frac{5}{2}$ to write the equation of the direct variation.**

$y = \frac{5}{2}x = \frac{5}{2}(7) = \frac{35}{2} = 17\frac{1}{2}$ ⟵ **To find the value of y when $x = 7$, replace x with 7 in the direct variation equation and simplify to find y.**

b. If $y = 6$ when $x = -3$, find x when $y = -4$.

$k = \frac{y}{x} = \frac{6}{-3} = -2$ ⟵ **Use $y = 6, x = -3$, and $k = \frac{y}{x}$ to find the value of k.**

$y = -2x$ ⟵ **Now use the form $y = kx$ and $k = -2$ to write the equation of the direct variation.**

$-4 = -2x$
$2 = x$ ⟵ **To find the value of x when $y = -4$, replace y with -4 in the direct variation equation and solve for x.**

Exercises

Find the missing value for each direct variation.

1. If $y = 8$ when $x = 4$, find y when $x = 6$.

2. If $y = 12$ when $x = 3$, find y when $x = 5$.

3. If $y = 9$ when $x = 3$, find x when $y = 7$.

4. If $y = -6$ when $x = 2$, find x when $y = 9$.

5. If $y = \frac{3}{2}$ when $x = \frac{1}{4}$, find y when $x = \frac{2}{3}$.

6. If $y = 7$ when $x = 2$, find x when $y = 3$.

7. The height of an object varies directly with the length of its shadow. A person 6 ft tall casts an $8\frac{1}{2}$ ft shadow, while a tree casts a 38 ft shadow. How tall is the tree?

ALGEBRA 2 TOPICS

Name ______________________ Class ______________ Date ______________

Review 200

OBJECTIVE: Representing data graphically **MATERIALS:** Graph paper, ruler

- A trend line is a mathematical model that shows the relationship between two sets of data.
- A trend line can be used to make predictions.

Example

Use the data in the table to draw a scatter plot and a trend line. Then predict the expenditures on drugs and other medical nondurables in 2001.

U.S. Health Expenditures Drug and Other Medical Nondurables

Year	Expenditures (billions of dollars)
1995	8.9
1996	9.4
1997	10.0
1998	10.6

Source: *The World Almanac and Book of Facts, 2001*

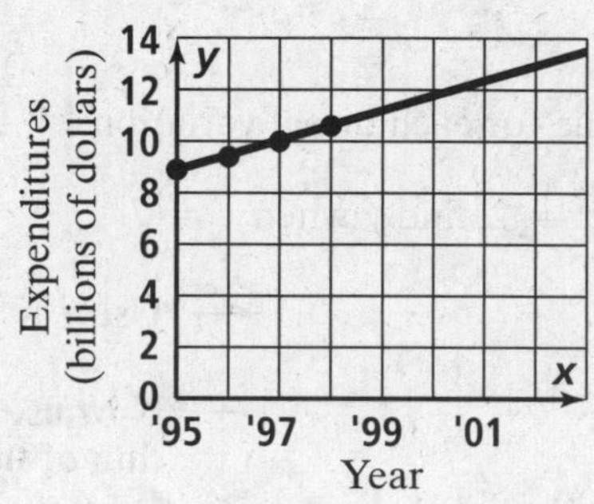

The model predicts expenditures of approximately 12.3 billion dollars in 2001.

Exercises

Use the data in the table.

Percent of U.S. Population Enrolled in HMOs

Year	Percent	Year	Percent
1992	14.3	1996	22.3
1993	15.1	1997	25.2
1994	17.3	1998	28.6
1995	19.4	1999	30.1

Source: *The World Almanac and Book of Facts, 2001*

1. Draw a scatter plot.
2. Draw a trend line and write its equation.
3. Use your model to predict the percent of the U.S. population enrolled in HMOs in 2006.

Name ________________ Class ________________ Date ________________

Review 201

OBJECTIVE: Graphing absolute value functions

MATERIALS: Graph paper, ruler

A function of the form $f(x) = |mx + b|$ is an *absolute value function.*

The graph of $f(x) = |mx + b|$ looks like an angle; its vertex is located at the point $\left(-\frac{b}{m}, 0\right)$.

Example

Graph $f(x) = |2x + 3|$.

First find the vertex. Using the form $\left(-\frac{b}{m}, 0\right)$ where $b = 3$ and $m = 2$, we obtain the vertex $\left(-\frac{3}{2}, 0\right)$.

Now find several points on the graph of $f(x) = |2x + 3|$. Choose values of x on both sides of the vertex.

x	−3	−2	−1	0	1
y	3	1	1	3	5

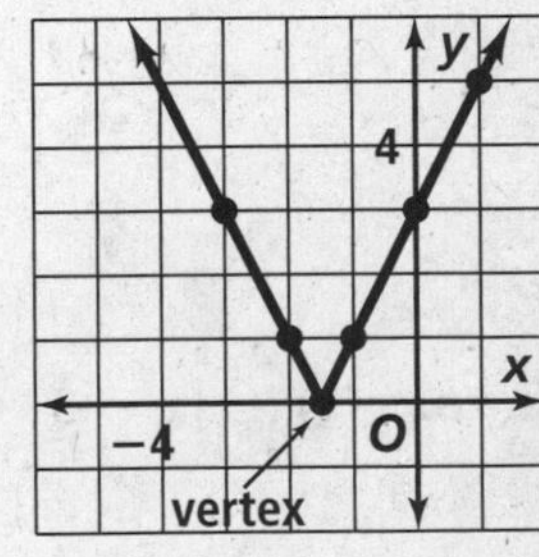

Plot the vertex and the points from the table in a rectangular coordinate system. Finish the graph by drawing two rays emanating from the vertex and passing through the other points.

Exercises

Find the vertex of each absolute value function.

1. $f(x) = |5x|$ **2.** $f(x) = |x + 3|$ **3.** $f(x) = |x - 4|$

4. $f(x) = |3x + 1|$ **5.** $f(x) = \left|\frac{1}{2}x - 3\right|$ **6.** $f(x) = \left|\frac{1}{4}x + 2\right|$

Find the vertex of each absolute value function. Then graph the function by plotting several other points.

7. $f(x) = |2x - 1|$ **8.** $f(x) = |3x - 1|$ **9.** $f(x) = |2x + 4|$

10. $f(x) = |x + 1|$ **11.** $f(x) = |x - 2|$ **12.** $f(x) = \left|2x - \frac{3}{2}\right|$

13. $f(x) = |3x|$ **14.** $f(x) = \left|\frac{1}{2}x + 1\right|$ **15.** $f(x) = \left|\frac{2}{3}x + 2\right|$

Name ________________________ Class ________________ Date ________________

Review 202

Vertical and Horizontal Translations

OBJECTIVE: Analyzing vertical, horizontal, and diagonal translations of the absolute value function

MATERIALS: Graph paper

If h and k are positive numbers, then

$g(x) = |x| + k$ shifts the graph of $f(x) = |x|$ up k units;

$g(x) = |x| - k$ shifts the graph of $f(x) = |x|$ down k units;

$g(x) = |x + h|$ shifts the graph of $f(x) = |x|$ left h units;

$g(x) = |x - h|$ shifts the graph of $f(x) = |x|$ right h units.

Examples

Graph each translation of $f(x) = |x|$.

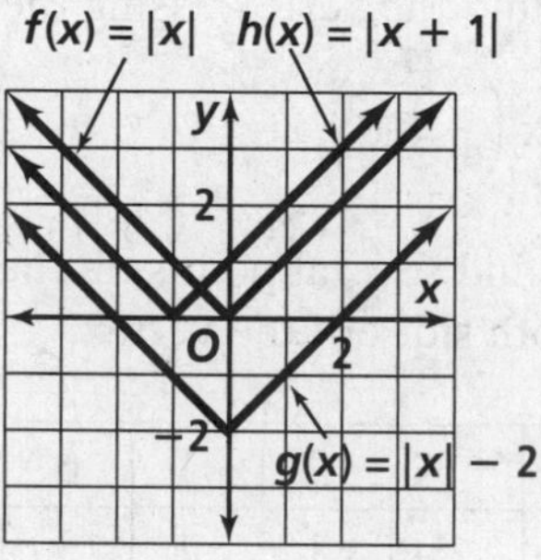

1. a. $g(x) = |x| - 2$ ⟵ **Shift the graph of $f(x) = |x|$ down 2 units.**

b. $h(x) = |x + 1|$ ⟵ **Shift the graph of $f(x) = |x|$ left 1 unit.**

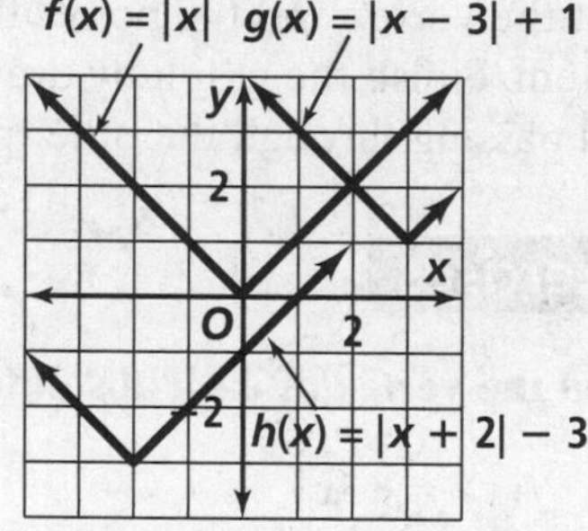

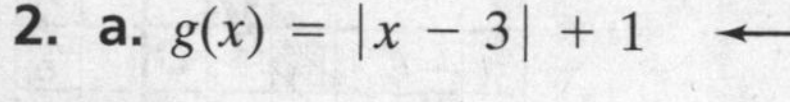

2. a. $g(x) = |x - 3| + 1$ ⟵ **Shift the graph of $f(x) = |x|$ right 3 units and up 1 unit.**

b. $h(x) = |x + 2| - 3$ ⟵ **Shift the graph of $f(x) = |x|$ left 2 units and down 3 units.**

Exercises

Complete each sentence. Then graph the translation of $f(x) = |x|$.

1. $g(x) = |x - 2|$ ⟵ Shift the graph of $f(x) = |x|$ ________ 2 units.

2. $g(x) = |x| + 1$ ⟵ Shift the graph of $f(x) = |x|$ ________ 1 unit.

3. $g(x) = |x| - 3$ ⟵ Shift the graph of $f(x) = |x|$ ________ 3 units.

4. $g(x) = |x + 3|$ ⟵ Shift the graph of $f(x) = |x|$ ________ 3 units.

5. $g(x) = |x - 1| - 5$ ⟵ Shift the graph of $f(x) = |x|$ ________ 1 unit and ________ 5 units.

6. $g(x) = |x + 4| + 2$ ⟵ Shift the graph of $f(x) = |x|$ ________ 4 units and ________ 2 units.

Name ______________________ Class ______________ Date ______________

Review 203

OBJECTIVE: Graphing inequalities with two variables

MATERIALS: Highlighting marker

Example

Graph the inequality $6x - 2y \leq 12$.

$6x - 2y \leq 12$

$y \geq 3x - 6$ ← **To graph the boundary line, write the inequality in slope-intercept form as if it were an equation.**

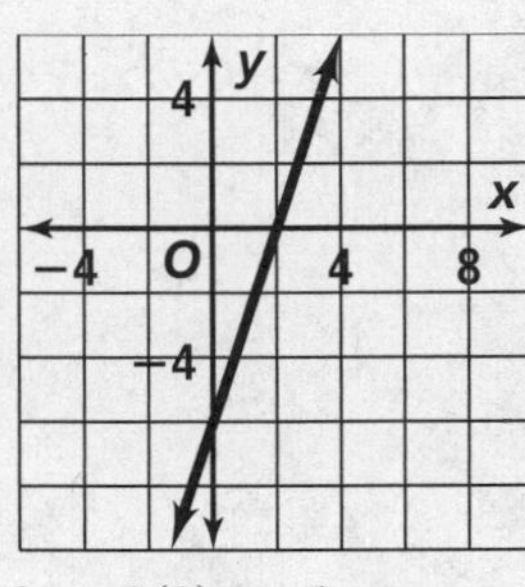

← **The boundary line is solid if the inequality contains $\leq$ or $\geq$. The boundary line is dashed if the inequality contains $<$ or $>$. Graph the boundary line $y = 3x - 6$ as a solid line.**

$0 \geq 3(0) - 6$ ← **Since the boundary line does not contain the origin, substitute the point (0, 0) into the inequality.**

$0 \geq -6$ ← **Simplify. The resulting inequality is true.**

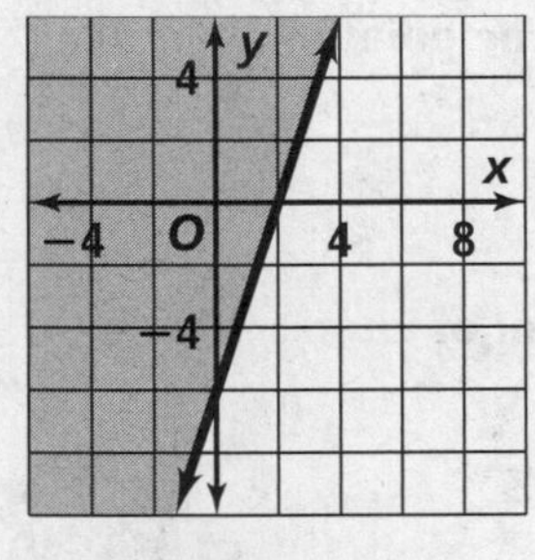

← **Use your highlighting marker to shade the region that contains the origin. If the resulting inequality were false, then you would shade the region that does not contain the origin.**

Exercises

Graph each inequality.

1. $y > 2x$

2. $x + y < 4$

3. $y < x + 1$

4. $y > x - 2$

5. $3x + 4y \leq 12$

6. $2y - 3x > 6$

7. $3x - 2 \leq 5x + y$

8. $x < -4$

9. $y \geq 5$

10. $x + 2y \geq 4$

11. $x + y < x + 2$

12. $3x - 3y < 3$

13. $x - 1 \geq 0$

14. $2y \leq 3$

15. $3x > 2 + y$

Name ______________________ Class ______________ Date ______________

Review 204

OBJECTIVE: Solving a system by graphing

MATERIALS: One blue and one yellow highlighter

As you solve a system of equations, remember the following ideas.

- Lines that have the same slopes but different y-intercepts are parallel and will never intersect. These systems are *inconsistent.*
- Lines that have both the same slope and the same y-intercept are the same line and will intersect at every point. These systems are *dependent.*
- Lines that have different slopes will intersect, and the system will have one solution. These systems are *independent.*

Example

Solve the system of equations by graphing. $\begin{cases} 2x + y = 8 \\ y - x = 2 \end{cases}$

$y = -2x + 8$ ⟵ **Write both equations in $y = mx + b$ form.**

$y = x + 2$

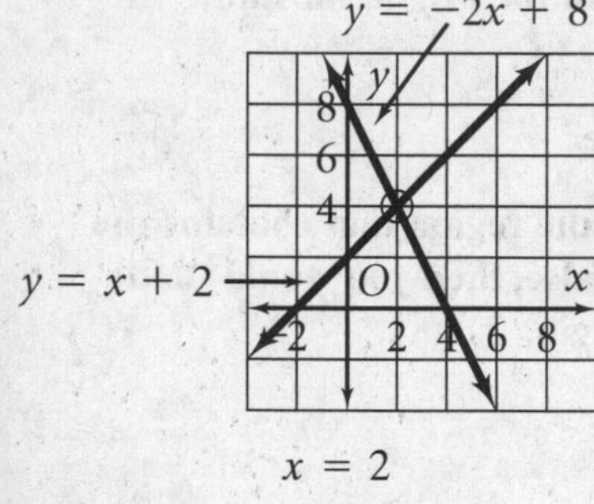

⟵ **Graph the line $y = -2x + 8$ with a blue highlighter. Graph the line $y = x + 2$ with a yellow highlighter. The point of intersection will be green. Circle it.**

$x = 2$ ⟵ **Determine the x- and y-coordinates of the point of intersection.**

$y = 4$

The solution is the ordered pair (2, 4).

$2(2) + 4 \stackrel{?}{=} 8$ ⟵ **Check by substituting the solution into both equations.**

$4 + 4 \stackrel{?}{=} 8$

$8 = 8$ ✔

$4 - 2 \stackrel{?}{=} 2$

$2 = 2$ ✔

Exercises

Use colored highlighters to solve each system of equations by graphing.

1. $\begin{cases} 3x + y = 6 \\ y = 3 \end{cases}$

2. $\begin{cases} -2x + y + 3 = 0 \\ x - 1 = y \end{cases}$

3. $\begin{cases} x + y = 3 \\ y = 3x - 1 \end{cases}$

4. $\begin{cases} y = 1 - x \\ 2x + y = 4 \end{cases}$

5. $\begin{cases} -x + 2y = 2 \\ 3x + 2y = -6 \end{cases}$

6. $\begin{cases} -x + y = -2 \\ -2x + 3y = -3 \end{cases}$

Name ______________________ Class ______________ Date ______________

Review 205

Solving Systems Algebraically

OBJECTIVE: Using elimination to solve a system **MATERIALS:** Graphing calculator (optional)

Follow these steps when using elimination to solve systems.

Step 1: Arrange the equations with like terms in columns.

Step 2: Circle the like terms for which you want to obtain coefficients that are opposites.

Step 3: Multiply each term of one or both equations by an appropriate number.

Step 4: Add the equations.

Step 5: Solve for the remaining variable.

Step 6: Substitute the value obtained in step 5 into either of the original equations, and solve for the other variable.

Step 7: Check the solution in the other original equation.

Example

Solve the system using the elimination method. $\begin{cases} 2x + 5y = 11 \\ 3x - 2y = -12 \end{cases}$

$$\begin{aligned} \textcircled{2x} + 5y &= 11 \\ \textcircled{3x} - 2y &= -12 \end{aligned}$$ ← **Circle the terms that you want to make opposite.**

$$\begin{aligned} 6x + 15y &= 33 \\ -6x + 4y &= 24 \end{aligned}$$ ← **Multiply each term of first equation by 3.** ← **Multiply each term of second equation by −2.**

$$19y = 57$$ ← **Add the equations.**

$$y = 3$$ ← **Solve for the remaining variable.**

$$\begin{aligned} 3x - 2(3) &= -12 \\ x &= -2 \end{aligned}$$ ← **Substitute 3 for *y* to solve for *x*.**

$$\begin{aligned} 2(-2) + 5(3) &\stackrel{?}{=} 11 \\ -4 + 15 &\stackrel{?}{=} 11 \\ 11 &= 11 \checkmark \end{aligned}$$ ← **Check using the other equation.**

The solution is $(-2, 3)$. You can also check the solution by using a graphing calculator.

Exercises

Solve each system of equations using elimination.

1. $\begin{cases} 3x + 2y = -17 \\ x - 3y = 9 \end{cases}$ **2.** $\begin{cases} 5f + 4m = 6 \\ -2f - 3m = -1 \end{cases}$ **3.** $\begin{cases} 3x - 2y = 5 \\ -6x + 4y = 7 \end{cases}$ **4.** $\begin{cases} -2x - 4y = 2 \\ 10x + 20y = -10 \end{cases}$

ALGEBRA 2 TOPICS

Name ____________________ Class ____________________ Date ____________________

Review 206

OBJECTIVE: Solving systems of inequalities

MATERIALS: Graph paper and a graphing calculator (optional)

Example

Solve the system $\begin{cases} 2x - y > 1 \\ x + y \geq 3 \end{cases}$ by graphing.

Step 1
Solve each inequality for y.

$2x - y > 1$
$-y > -2x + 1$
$y < 2x - 1$

and

$x + y \geq 3$
$y \geq -x + 3$

Step 2
Graph the boundary lines. Use a solid line for ≥ or ≤ inequalities. Use a dotted line for > and < inequalities.

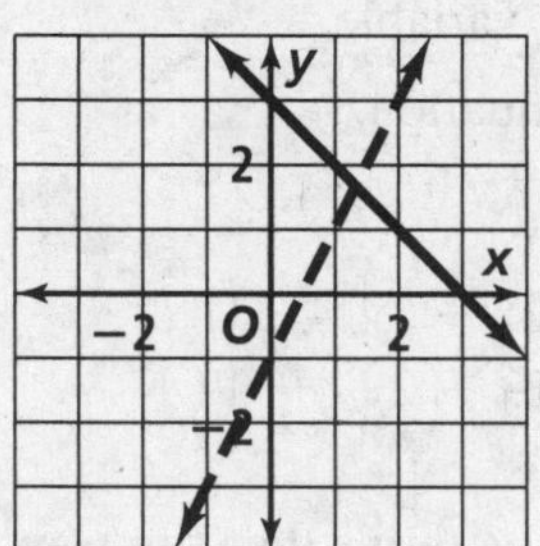

Step 3
Then shade on the appropriate side of each boundary line.

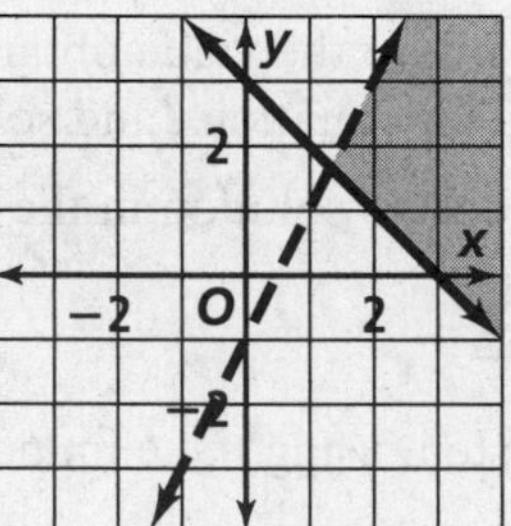

Exercises

Solve each system of inequalities by graphing.

1. $\begin{cases} y \leq x \\ y \geq 3x - 1 \end{cases}$

2. $\begin{cases} 2x + y > 3 \\ x - y < 2 \end{cases}$

3. $\begin{cases} x > 1 \\ y < x + 1 \end{cases}$

4. $\begin{cases} x + 3y \leq 9 \\ 2x - y > 1 \end{cases}$

5. $\begin{cases} y < -\frac{1}{3}x - 1 \\ y \geq 3x + 1 \end{cases}$

6. $\begin{cases} 4x + y \leq 1 \\ x + 2y \leq -1 \end{cases}$

7. $\begin{cases} y \leq 3 \\ y > 4x - 3 \end{cases}$

8. $\begin{cases} 2x + y < 3 \\ 3x - y < 2 \end{cases}$

9. $\begin{cases} y \geq -2 \\ 3x + y \leq 2 \end{cases}$

Name ____________________ Class ____________ Date ____________

Review 207

OBJECTIVE: Solving linear programming problems

MATERIALS: Graph paper

Example

Use linear programming. Find the values of x and y that maximize and minimize the objective function $P = 10x + 15y$.

$$\text{Restrictions}\begin{cases} x + y \leq 16 \\ 3x + 6y \leq 60 \\ x \geq 0 \\ y \geq 0 \end{cases}$$

Step 1
Graph the restrictions.

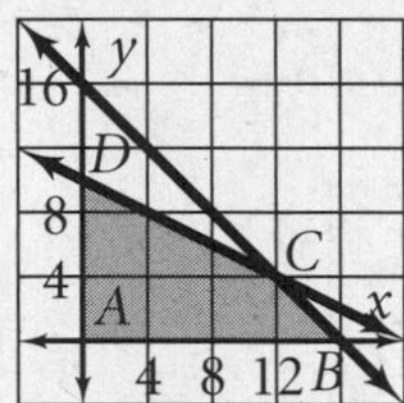

Step 2
Find coordinates of each vertex of the region.

VERTEX

$A(0, 0)$

$B(16, 0)$

$C(12, 4)$

$D(0, 10)$

Step 3
Evaluate P at each vertex.

$\mathbf{P = 10x + 15y}$

$P = 10(0) + 15(0) = 0$

$P = 10(16) + 15(0) = 160$

$P = 10(12) + 15(4) = 180$

$P = 10(0) + 15(10) = 150$

The maximum value of the objective function is 180. It occurs when $x = 12$ and $y = 4$.

The minimum value of the objective function is 0. It occurs when $x = 0$ and $y = 0$.

Exercises

Use linear programming. Find the values of x and y that maximize and minimize each objective function.

1. $\begin{cases} 5y + 4x \leq 35 \\ 5y + x \geq 20 \\ y \leq 6 \\ x \geq 1 \end{cases}$

$P = 8x + 2y$

2. $\begin{cases} x + y \geq 2 \\ x \geq y \\ x \leq 4 \\ y \geq 0 \end{cases}$

$P = x + 3y$

3. $\begin{cases} 3x + 4y \geq 12 \\ 5x + 6y \leq 30 \\ 1 \leq x \leq 3 \end{cases}$

$P = x - 2y$

Name ______________________ Class ______________ Date ______________

Review 208

OBJECTIVE: Graphing points in three dimensions

MATERIALS: Cardboard box

Use the inside corner of a cardboard box to model a three-dimensional coordinate system in which x, y, and z are all greater than 0.

- First label the bottom (or horizontal) edges of the box as the x-axis and the y-axis.
- Then the z-axis will be the vertical edge that passes through the origin or corner where the three edges meet.

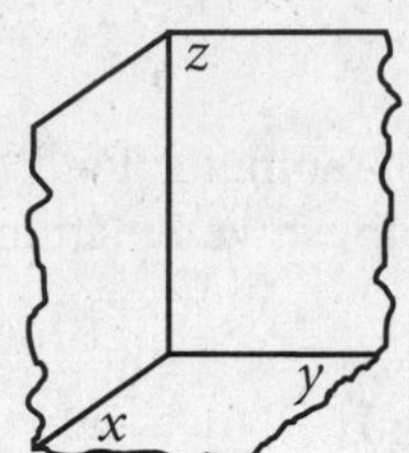

Example

Graph (3, 4, 5) in three dimensions. First, locate the point using the cardboard box. Start at the back left corner of the box. Move forward three units. Move right four units. Move up five units.

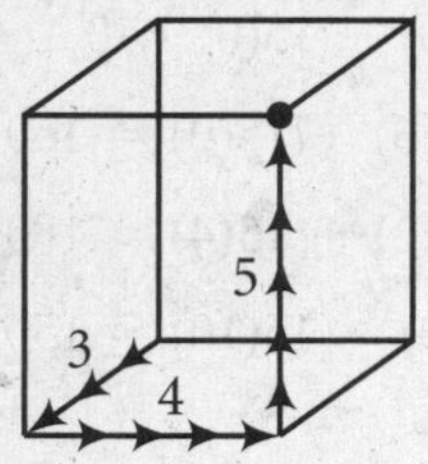

Then graph the point.

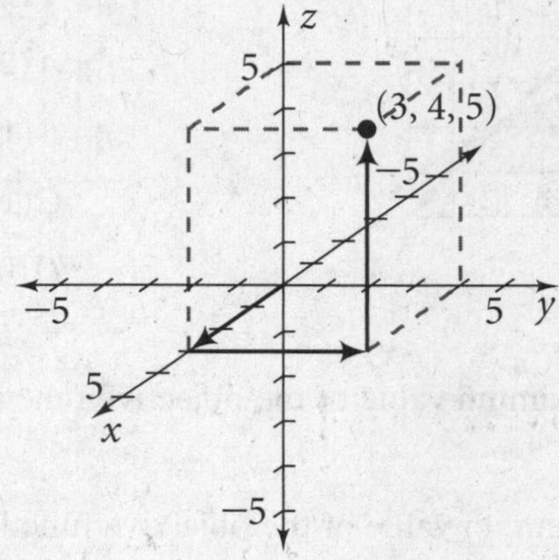

Exercises

Locate and graph each point in three dimensions by following the steps in the example.

1. (1, 2, 0)
2. (3, 2, 3)
3. (4, 0, 3)
4. (5, 1, 2)
5. (2, 5, 1)
6. (0, 0, 4)
7. (3, −1, −1)
8. (−3, −3, −3)
9. (5, 0, 1)
10. (0, 1, 3)
11. (1, 2, −5)
12. (5, 3, −4)
13. (2, 4, 6)
14. (−2, −2, −2)
15. (−1, −2, 5)
16. (1, 2, 8)
17. (−4, −5, 1)
18. (0, 0, 2)
19. (1, −4, −5)
20. (−6, 2, −4)

Name ______________________ Class ______________ Date ______________

Review 209

OBJECTIVE: Using elimination to solve systems with three variables

MATERIALS: Pink, yellow, and green highlighting markers

Example

Solve the system using elimination.

$$\begin{cases} x + y + z = 6 \\ 2x - y + 3z = 9 \\ -x + 2y + 2z = 9 \end{cases}$$

← **Use pink to highlight the first equation, yellow to highlight the second, and green to highlight the third.**

$$\begin{array}{r} x + y + z = 6 \\ -x + 2y + 2z = 9 \\ \hline \boxed{3y + 3z = 15} \end{array}$$

← **Add the pink and green to eliminate *x*. Circle the resulting sum.**

$$\begin{array}{r} 2x - y + 3z = 6 \\ -x + 2y + 2z = 9 \end{array}$$

← **Pair the yellow and green.**

$$\begin{array}{r} 2x - y + 3z = 9 \\ -2x + 4y + 4z = 18 \\ \hline \boxed{3y + 7z = 27} \end{array}$$

← **Multiply the green equation by 2 to eliminate *x* and add the two equations. Circle the resulting sum.**

$$\begin{array}{r} 3y + 3z = 15 \\ -3y + (-7z) = -27 \\ \hline -4z = -12 \\ z = 3 \end{array}$$

← **Pair the two circled equations. Subtract the second from the first to eliminate *y* and solve for *z*.**

$$3y + 3(3) = 15$$

← **Substitute the value of *z* into either of the circled equations.**

$$3y = 6$$

← **Solve for *y*.**

$$y = 2$$

$$x + 2 + 3 = 6$$

← **Substitute the values of *y* and *z* into any of the original equations. Solve for *x*.**

$$x = 1$$

The solution is (1, 2, 3).

Exercises

Solve each system using elimination.

1. $\begin{cases} 2x - y + 2z = 10 \\ 4x + 2y - 5z = 10 \\ x - 3y + 5z = 8 \end{cases}$

2. $\begin{cases} x - y + z = 6 \\ 2x + 3y + 2z = 2 \\ 3x + 5y + 4z = 4 \end{cases}$

3. $\begin{cases} 6x - 4y + 5z = 31 \\ 5x + 2y + 2z = 13 \\ x + y + z = 2 \end{cases}$

4. $\begin{cases} 3x + y + z = 2 \\ 4x - 2y + 3z = -4 \\ 2x + 2y + 2z = 8 \end{cases}$

5. $\begin{cases} 5x + 2y + z = 5 \\ 3x - 3y - 3z = 9 \\ x + 2y + 4z = 6 \end{cases}$

6. $\begin{cases} x + y + z = -1 \\ 4x + 3y + 2z = -10 \\ 2x - 4y - 2z = -6 \end{cases}$

Name Class Date

Review 210

Organizing Data into Matrices

OBJECTIVE: Organize data into matrices **MATERIALS:** Number cube

- The size, or order, of a matrix is specified by its dimensions. A 4 × 9 matrix has 4 rows and 9 columns.

Example

Roll the number cube to set up a 4 × 2 matrix. Each time, roll twice to produce a two-digit number. Use the left hand first, then the right.

	Left	Right
Trial 1	36	
Trial 2		
Trial 3		
Trial 4		

← **Roll the cube twice with your left hand. Suppose these rolls generate a 3 and a 6; in this case, write 36 in row 1.**

	Left	Right
Trial 1	36	
Trial 2	24	
Trial 3	26	
Trial 4	55	

← **Repeat, rolling with your left hand to fill in the first column.**

	Left	Right
Trial 1	36	15
Trial 2	24	43
Trial 3	26	22
Trial 4	55	46

← **Fill the second column for trials 1–4 by rolling with your right hand.**

Exercises

Use a number cube to produce the following matrix.

1. Create a 6 × 3 matrix. Label your columns left hand, right hand, and both hands. Let your rows represent six trials.

2. Rewrite the Example matrix as a 2 × 4 matrix.

3. Rewrite the matrix in Exercise 1 as a 3 × 6 matrix.

Name ____________________ Class ____________________ Date ____________________

Review 211

OBJECTIVE: Adding and subtracting matrices **MATERIALS:** Colored pencils

- To add or subtract matrices of the same size, circle the corresponding entries and their results with the same color pencils.

Example

Add the two matrices. Use a different color for each set of corresponding entries.

$$\begin{bmatrix} -3 & 5 \\ 9 & -2 \end{bmatrix} + \begin{bmatrix} 7 & -1 \\ 8 & -4 \end{bmatrix} =$$ ⟵ **Add the corresponding entries.**

$$\begin{bmatrix} -3 & 5 \\ 9 & -2 \end{bmatrix} + \begin{bmatrix} 7 & -1 \\ 8 & -4 \end{bmatrix} = \begin{bmatrix} 4 & \\ & \end{bmatrix}$$ ⟵ **(−3) + 7 = 4**

$$\begin{bmatrix} -3 & 5 \\ 9 & -2 \end{bmatrix} + \begin{bmatrix} 7 & -1 \\ 8 & -4 \end{bmatrix} = \begin{bmatrix} 4 & 4 \\ & \end{bmatrix}$$ ⟵ **5 + (−1) = 4**

$$\begin{bmatrix} -3 & 5 \\ 9 & -2 \end{bmatrix} + \begin{bmatrix} 7 & -1 \\ 8 & -4 \end{bmatrix} = \begin{bmatrix} 4 & 4 \\ 17 & \end{bmatrix}$$ ⟵ **9 + 8 = 17**

$$\begin{bmatrix} -3 & 5 \\ 9 & -2 \end{bmatrix} + \begin{bmatrix} 7 & -1 \\ 8 & -4 \end{bmatrix} = \begin{bmatrix} 4 & 4 \\ 17 & -6 \end{bmatrix}$$ ⟵ **(−2) + (−4) = (−6)**

Exercises

Circle the corresponding entries. Add or subtract the following matrices.

1. $\begin{bmatrix} -3 & 8 \\ 9 & -2 \end{bmatrix} + \begin{bmatrix} 1 & -5 \\ 5 & 0 \end{bmatrix}$

2. $\begin{bmatrix} 1 & -2 \\ 0 & -6 \end{bmatrix} - \begin{bmatrix} 6 & -3 \\ -1 & -8 \end{bmatrix}$

Add or subtract the following matrices.

3. $\begin{bmatrix} 1.5 & 0.5 \\ -2.5 & 2.5 \end{bmatrix} + \begin{bmatrix} -2.5 & -1.5 \\ 3.5 & -4.5 \end{bmatrix}$

4. $\begin{bmatrix} 3 & 1 & 4 \\ 0 & 2 & 1 \end{bmatrix} - \begin{bmatrix} 2 & 0 & 5 \\ 3 & 1 & 6 \end{bmatrix}$

5. $\begin{bmatrix} -9 & 2 & 0 \\ -1 & 0 & 3 \end{bmatrix} + \begin{bmatrix} -7 & -3 & -4 \\ 8 & -7 & -9 \end{bmatrix}$

6. $\begin{bmatrix} 7.5 & 4 \\ 3.5 & 5 \end{bmatrix} - \begin{bmatrix} 3 & -1.5 \\ 0.5 & -6.5 \end{bmatrix}$

7. $\begin{bmatrix} -1 & -4 \\ 0 & 5 \\ 9 & 0 \end{bmatrix} + \begin{bmatrix} -8 & -2 \\ 0 & -4 \\ -1 & 5 \end{bmatrix}$

8. $\begin{bmatrix} 0 & 1 \\ 5 & 2 \\ -9 & 0 \end{bmatrix} - \begin{bmatrix} -5 & -4 \\ -7 & -2 \\ 8 & 2 \end{bmatrix}$

9. $\begin{bmatrix} -2 & 5.5 \\ 9.5 & -4 \\ 0 & 3 \\ -7.5 & 6 \end{bmatrix} - \begin{bmatrix} 7 & -1.5 \\ 6 & 2.5 \\ -1.5 & 3 \\ -4 & 1 \end{bmatrix}$

10. $\begin{bmatrix} -4 & 0 & 2 \\ 1 & -7 & -5 \\ 2 & -4 & 9 \end{bmatrix} + \begin{bmatrix} -1 & -3 & 6 \\ 2 & 5 & 1 \\ 5 & -1 & -3 \end{bmatrix}$

Name ______________________ Class ______________ Date ______________

Review 212

OBJECTIVE: Multiplying matrices **MATERIALS:** Two pencils

- To multiply two matrices, the number of columns in the first matrix must be equal to the number of rows in the second matrix.
- The product matrix has the same number of rows as the first matrix and the same number of columns as the second matrix.

Example

Find the product AB.

$$AB = \begin{bmatrix} 3 & 1 & -1 \\ 2 & 0 & 3 \end{bmatrix}\begin{bmatrix} 1 & 4 \\ 3 & -1 \\ 2 & 5 \end{bmatrix}$$

Step 1: Check dimensions of matrices A and B to determine whether they can be multiplied. A has three columns and B has three rows.

$(3)(1) + (1)(3) + (-1)(2) = 4$

$$\begin{bmatrix} 4 & \\ & \end{bmatrix}$$

Step 2: Use two pencils to cover the second row of A and the second column of B so that only the first row of A and the first column of B can be seen. Multiply corresponding elements, and add the products. Place the result at $(AB)_{11}$.

$(3)(4) + (1)(-1) + (-1)(5) = 6$

$$\begin{bmatrix} 4 & 6 \\ & \end{bmatrix}$$

Step 3: Find $(AB)_{12}$ by multiplying the first row of A by the second column of B. Add the products, and enter the result. With your pencils, cover the rows and columns that you are not multiplying.

$(2)(1) + (0)(3) + (3)(2) = 8$

$$\begin{bmatrix} 4 & 6 \\ 8 & \end{bmatrix}$$

Step 4: Find $(AB)_{21}$ by multiplying the second row of A by the first column of B. Add the products, and enter the result.

$(2)(4) + (0)(-1) + (3)(5) = 23$

$$\begin{bmatrix} 4 & 6 \\ 8 & 23 \end{bmatrix}$$

Step 5: Find $(AB)_{22}$ by multiplying the second row of A by the second column of B. Add the products, and enter the result.

Exercises

Multiply the matrices.

1. $\begin{bmatrix} 1 & 2 \\ 4 & 3 \end{bmatrix}\begin{bmatrix} -3 & 5 \\ 2 & -1 \end{bmatrix}$

2. $\begin{bmatrix} 4 & 1 & 2 \\ -3 & 2 & 3 \\ 2 & 0 & 5 \\ 3 & 1 & 4 \end{bmatrix}\begin{bmatrix} 1 & 4 \\ 2 & 0 \\ -3 & 5 \end{bmatrix}$

3. $\begin{bmatrix} 4 & 1 & 0 & 2 \end{bmatrix}\begin{bmatrix} 1 & 0 & 1 \\ 2 & -1 & 0 \\ 3 & 5 & 1 \\ 1 & 3 & 0 \end{bmatrix}$

Name ______________________ Class ______________ Date ______________

Review 213

OBJECTIVE: Representing translations with matrices

MATERIALS: Graph paper and colored pencils

- A *translation* is a transformation that changes the location of a geometrical figure.

Example

A quadrilateral has vertices $A(0, 0)$, $B(-2, 3)$, $C(-5, 3)$, and $D(-5, 0)$. Use a matrix to translate the vertices 5 units right and 3 units down.

$$\begin{array}{cccc} A & B & C & D \end{array}$$
$$\begin{bmatrix} 0 & -2 & -5 & -5 \\ 0 & 3 & 3 & 0 \end{bmatrix}$$ ← **Write the vertices as a matrix.**

$$\begin{bmatrix} 5 & 5 & 5 & 5 \\ -3 & -3 & -3 & -3 \end{bmatrix}$$ ← **Write the translation matrix. Since the first row represents the *x*-coordinates, place 5 in each entry. Since the second row represents the *y*-coordinates, place −3 in each entry.**

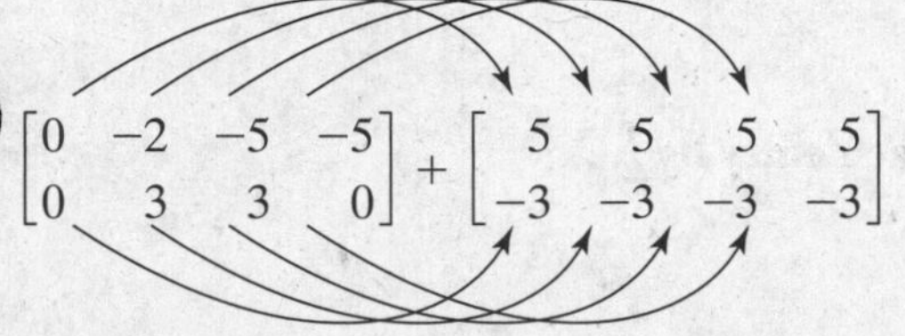

$$\begin{bmatrix} 0 & -2 & -5 & -5 \\ 0 & 3 & 3 & 0 \end{bmatrix} + \begin{bmatrix} 5 & 5 & 5 & 5 \\ -3 & -3 & -3 & -3 \end{bmatrix}$$ ← **Add the two matrices. Draw arrows connecting corresponding entries. Use a different colored pencil for each arrow.**

$$\begin{array}{cccc} A' & B' & C' & D' \end{array}$$
$$= \begin{bmatrix} 5 & 3 & 0 & 0 \\ -3 & 0 & 0 & -3 \end{bmatrix}$$ ← **Represent the translated points by A′, B′, C′, and D′ respectively.**

$A'(5, -3)$, $B'(3, 0)$, $C'(0, 0)$, $D'(0, -3)$ ← **Write the vertices as ordered pairs.**

← **Graph the original figure and its image. Label each point.**

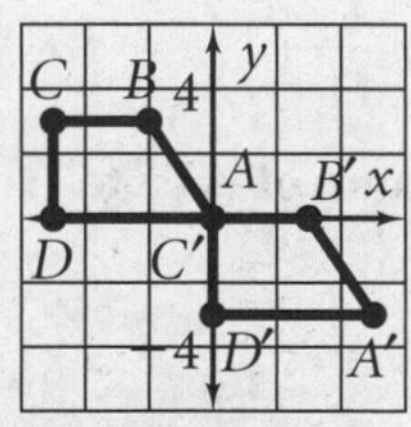

Exercises

A quadrilateral has vertices $A(0, 0)$, $B(-2, 3)$, $C(1, 4)$, and $D(3, 2)$. Use a matrix to translate the vertices according to the following. Graph the original figure and the image on graph paper.

1. a translation 1 unit right and 2 units down
2. a translation 3 units left and 1 unit down
3. a translation 4 units left and 3 units up
4. a translation 2 units right and 4 units up

Name ______________________ Class ______________ Date ______________

Review 214

2 × 2 Matrices, Determinants, and Inverses

OBJECTIVE: Finding and using the inverse of a 2 × 2 matrix

MATERIALS: None

- The inverse of a matrix A is the matrix A^{-1} such that the product $AA^{-1} = I$, the identity matrix. Suppose $A = \begin{bmatrix} a & b \\ c & d \end{bmatrix}$. If $ad - bc \neq 0$, then A has an inverse and $A^{-1} = \frac{1}{ad - bc}\begin{bmatrix} d & -b \\ -c & a \end{bmatrix}$.

Example

Write the inverse of the matrix $A = \begin{bmatrix} 2 & 4 \\ 1 & 3 \end{bmatrix}$.

$ad - bc = (2)(3) - (4)(1)$
$2 \neq 0$ ← **Calculate $ad - bc$. Since $ad - bc \neq 0$, the inverse does exist.**

$A^{-1} = \frac{1}{2}\begin{bmatrix} 3 & -4 \\ -1 & 2 \end{bmatrix}$ ← **Substitute values into the matrix inverse formula.**

$= \begin{bmatrix} \frac{3}{2} & -2 \\ -\frac{1}{2} & 1 \end{bmatrix}$ ← **Multiply each entry by $\frac{1}{2}$.**

$$\overset{A}{\begin{bmatrix} 2 & 4 \\ 1 & 3 \end{bmatrix}}\overset{A^{-1}}{\begin{bmatrix} \frac{3}{2} & -2 \\ -\frac{1}{2} & 1 \end{bmatrix}} = \overset{I}{\begin{bmatrix} 1 & 0 \\ 0 & 1 \end{bmatrix}}$$ ← **Check the results by verifying that $AA^{-1} = I$.**

because

$$\begin{bmatrix} 2\left(\frac{3}{2}\right) + 4\left(-\frac{1}{2}\right) & 2(-2) + 4(1) \\ 1\left(\frac{3}{2}\right) + 3\left(-\frac{1}{2}\right) & 1(-2) + 3(1) \end{bmatrix} = \begin{bmatrix} 1 & 0 \\ 0 & 1 \end{bmatrix}$$ ← **Multiply each row of A by each column of A^{-1} to calculate the product of A and A^{-1}.**

Exercises

Find the inverse of each 2 × 2 matrix. If it does not exist, write *no inverse*.

1. $\begin{bmatrix} 5 & -2 \\ -7 & 3 \end{bmatrix}$ **2.** $\begin{bmatrix} 9 & -2 \\ 5 & -1 \end{bmatrix}$ **3.** $\begin{bmatrix} 3 & 4 \\ 5 & 7 \end{bmatrix}$

4. $\begin{bmatrix} 6 & -3 \\ -2 & 1 \end{bmatrix}$ **5.** $\begin{bmatrix} -2 & 17 \\ 1 & 8 \end{bmatrix}$ **6.** $\begin{bmatrix} 7 & 4 \\ 3 & 2 \end{bmatrix}$

7. $\begin{bmatrix} 7 & -3 \\ -1 & 1 \end{bmatrix}$ **8.** $\begin{bmatrix} -9 & 3 \\ 6 & -2 \end{bmatrix}$ **9.** $\begin{bmatrix} 3 & 4 \\ 5 & 6 \end{bmatrix}$

Name ______________________ Class ______________ Date ______________

Review 215

3 × 3 Matrices, Determinants, and Inverses

OBJECTIVE: Finding the determinant of a 3 × 3 matrix

MATERIALS: Colored pencils

Like 2 × 2 matrices, a 3 × 3 matrix, $A = \begin{bmatrix} a_1 & b_1 & c_1 \\ a_2 & b_2 & c_2 \\ a_3 & b_3 & c_3 \end{bmatrix}$, has a determinant, det A.

$\det A = (a_1b_2c_3 + a_2b_3c_1 + a_3b_1c_2) - (a_1b_3c_2 + a_2b_1c_3 + a_3b_2c_1)$

Write matrix A, then copy matrix A to the right of the first matrix, aligning rows. In your first matrix, use three colored pencils and the first part of the formula to show what is being multiplied. In the second matrix, use other colors and the second part of the formula to show what is being multiplied. Do you see a pattern? This pattern will help you calculate the determinant of A.

Example

Find the determinant of A if $A = \begin{bmatrix} 3 & 2 & 1 \\ 4 & 3 & -2 \\ 5 & 0 & 0 \end{bmatrix}$.

$$\begin{aligned} \det A &= [3(3)(0) + 4(0)(1) + 5(2)(-2)] \\ &\quad - [3(0)(-2) + 4(2)(0) + 5(3)(1)] \end{aligned}$$ ⟵ **Use the definition.**

$$= [0 + 0 + -20] - [0 + 0 + 15]$$ ⟵ **Multiply.**

$$= -20 - 15 = -35$$ ⟵ **Simplify.**

Exercises

Evaluate the determinant of each matrix.

1. $\begin{bmatrix} 1 & -1 & -1 \\ -2 & 0 & 1 \\ 1 & -1 & 2 \end{bmatrix}$

2. $\begin{bmatrix} 0 & 1 & 2 \\ 3 & 2 & 1 \\ 4 & 0 & 3 \end{bmatrix}$

3. $\begin{bmatrix} 1 & 0 & 3 \\ 4 & 2 & -1 \\ -1 & 0 & 4 \end{bmatrix}$

4. $\begin{bmatrix} 3 & 1 & 12 \\ -2 & 0 & -6 \\ 3 & 5 & -1 \end{bmatrix}$

5. $\begin{bmatrix} 1 & 2 & -2 \\ -1 & 3 & 1 \\ 1 & -1 & 2 \end{bmatrix}$

6. $\begin{bmatrix} 1 & 2 & 3 \\ -4 & 5 & -4 \\ 2 & 6 & 7 \end{bmatrix}$

Name ____________________ Class ____________ Date ____________

Review 216

OBJECTIVE: Solving systems using inverse matrices

MATERIALS: Graphing calculator

- A system of linear equations can be solved by using inverse matrices when the system has exactly one solution.
- The determinant of $\begin{bmatrix} a & b \\ c & d \end{bmatrix}$ is $ad - bc$.
- If the determinant is zero, the matrix has no inverse.
- If the determinant is zero, the matrix equation has no solution or an infinite number of solutions. To solve, use another method.

Example

Use an inverse matrix to solve the linear system $\begin{cases} 4x + 3y = -4 \\ 3x - y = -3 \end{cases}$.

$$\overset{A}{\begin{bmatrix} 4 & 3 \\ 3 & -1 \end{bmatrix}} \overset{X}{\begin{bmatrix} x \\ y \end{bmatrix}} = \overset{B}{\begin{bmatrix} -4 \\ -3 \end{bmatrix}}$$

← **Write the system as a matrix equation**

```
MATRIX[A]    2 ×2
[4     3        ]
[3    -1        ]

2,2=−1
```

← **Store the coefficient matrix as matrix *A*.**

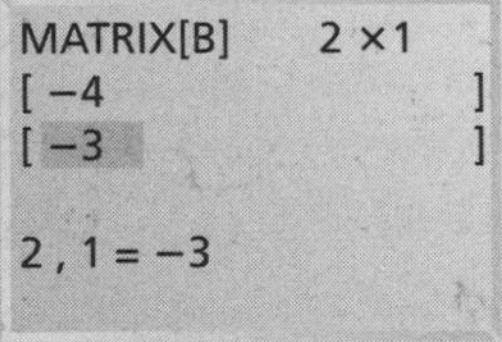

← **Store the constant matrix as matrix *B*.**

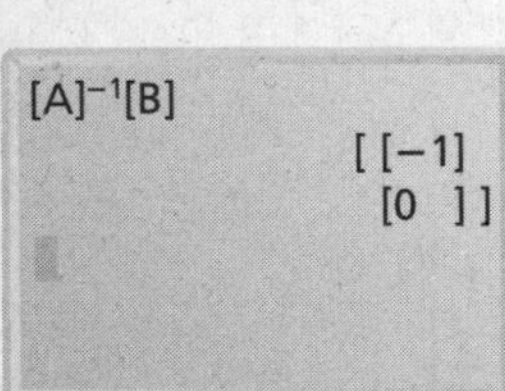

← **Multiply the matrices A^{-1} and *B*.**

Check the solution $(-1, 0)$ by substitution.

Exercises

Use a graphing calculator to solve each system. Check your solutions by substitution.

1. $\begin{cases} 2x - 7y = -3 \\ x + 5y = 7 \end{cases}$

2. $\begin{cases} x + 3y = 5 \\ x + 4y = 6 \end{cases}$

3. $\begin{cases} p - 3q = -1 \\ -5p + 16q = 5 \end{cases}$

4. $\begin{cases} 4m - 2n = -6 \\ -2m + n = 3 \end{cases}$

Name ________________________ Class ______________ Date ______________

Review 217

Augmented Matrices and Systems

OBJECTIVE: Using the augmented matrix to solve systems of equations

MATERIALS: None

Remember the row operations:

- Switch any two rows.
- Multiply a row by a constant.
- Add one row to another.
- Combine one or more of these steps.

Example

Use an augmented matrix to solve the system $\begin{cases} 2x + 4y = 8 \\ 3x + 5y = 15 \end{cases}$.

After the row operations, you want the system to be in the form $\left[\begin{array}{cc|c} 1 & 0 & m \\ 0 & 1 & n \end{array}\right]$. The solution to the system is (m, n).

Write the augmented matrix. $\longrightarrow$ $\left[\begin{array}{cc|c} 2 & 4 & 8 \\ 3 & 5 & 15 \end{array}\right]$

To make element a_{11} equal to 1, multiply Row 1 by $\frac{1}{2}$. Then replace Row 1 with the result.

$\frac{1}{2}(2\ \ 4\ \ 8) = (1\ \ 2\ \ 4)$ $\longrightarrow$ $\left[\begin{array}{cc|c} 1 & 2 & 4 \\ 3 & 5 & 15 \end{array}\right]$

To make element a_{21} equal to 0, multiply Row 1 by −3. Then add the result to Row 2, and replace Row 2 with this sum.

$-3(1\ \ 2\ \ 4) = (-3\ \ -6\ \ -12)$

$$\begin{array}{rrr} -3 & -6 & -12 \\ 3 & 5 & 15 \\ \hline 0 & -1 & 3 \end{array}$$

$\longrightarrow$ $\left[\begin{array}{cc|c} 1 & 2 & 4 \\ 0 & -1 & 3 \end{array}\right]$

To make element a_{22} equal to 1, multiply Row 2 by −1. Then replace Row 2 with the result.

$-1(0\ \ -1\ \ 3) = (0\ \ 1\ \ -3)$ $\longrightarrow$ $\left[\begin{array}{cc|c} 1 & 2 & 4 \\ 0 & 1 & -3 \end{array}\right]$

To make element a_{12} equal to 0, multiply Row 2 by −2. Then add the result to Row 1, and replace Row 1 with this sum.

$-2(0\ \ 1\ \ -3) = (0\ \ -2\ \ 6)$

$$\begin{array}{rrr} 0 & -2 & 6 \\ 1 & 2 & 4 \\ \hline 1 & 0 & 10 \end{array}$$

$\longrightarrow$ $\left[\begin{array}{cc|c} 1 & 0 & 10 \\ 0 & 1 & -3 \end{array}\right]$

The solution to the system is (10, −3). You can check the solution by substituting $x = 10$ and $y = -3$ into each of the original equations.

Exercises

1. $\begin{cases} x - 5y = 4 \\ -2x + y = 1 \end{cases}$

2. $\begin{cases} x - 3y = 5 \\ 3x - y = -1 \end{cases}$

3. $\begin{cases} 2x - y = 6 \\ 3x - y = 2 \end{cases}$

ALGEBRA 2 TOPICS

Name ______________________ Class ______________ Date ______________

Review 218

Modeling Data with Quadratic Functions

OBJECTIVE: Recognizing and using a quadratic function

MATERIALS: Graphing calculator

A quadratic function can be written in standard form:

$$f(x) = ax^2 + bx + c, \text{ where } a \neq 0.$$

ax^2 — quadratic term; bx — linear term; c — constant term

Example

Rewrite the function in standard form. Indicate whether the function is quadratic. Graph the function to check your answer.

$f(x) = (1 + x)(9 + x)$ ⟵ **Multiply and simplify to put in standard form.**

$f(x) = 9 + x + 9x + x^2$ ⟵ **Use the FOIL Method to apply the Distributive Property.**

$f(x) = x^2 + 10x + 9$ ⟵ **Combine like terms and simplify.**

Since it has a quadratic term, this is a quadratic function.

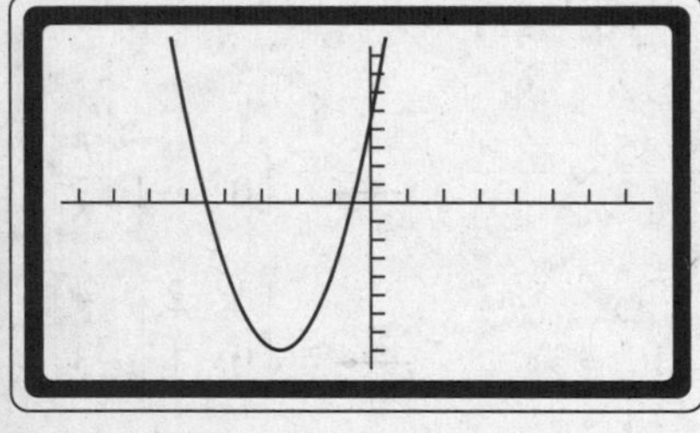

⟵ **Use a graphing calculator to check your answer. This is a quadratic function, since its graph is a parabola.**

Exercises

Rewrite each function in standard form. Indicate whether the function is quadratic. Then graph to check.

1. $f(x) = (-5x - 4)(-5x - 4)$

2. $y = 3(x - 1) + 3$

3. $y = x^2 + 24 - 11x - x^2$

4. $g(x) = (x - 7)(x + 7)$

5. $f(x) = (3 - x)(x + 3)$

6. $g(x) = x^2$

7. $f(x) = 3x(x + 1) - x$

8. $f(x) = (x + 4)(x - 4)$

9. $f(x) = 4x^2 + 5x$

10. $y = 2(x + 2)^2 - 2x^2$

Name ______________________ Class ______________ Date ______________

Review 219

OBJECTIVE: Graphing a parabola using the vertex and axis of symmetry

MATERIALS: Graph paper

- The graph of a quadratic function, $y = ax^2 + bx + c$, where $a \neq 0$, is a parabola.
- The axis of symmetry is the line $x = -\frac{b}{2a}$.
- The x-coordinate of the vertex is $-\frac{b}{2a}$. The y-coordinate of the vertex is $y = f\left(-\frac{b}{2a}\right)$, or the y-value when $x = -\frac{b}{2a}$.
- The y-intercept is $(0, c)$.

Example

Graph $y = 2x^2 - 8x + 5$.

$x = -\frac{b}{2a} = \frac{-(-8)}{2(2)} = \frac{8}{4} = 2$ ⟵ **Find the equation of the axis of symmetry.**

x-coordinate of vertex: 2 ⟵ $-\frac{b}{2a}$

$f\left(-\frac{b}{2a}\right) = f(2) = 2(2)^2 - 8(2) + 5$ ⟵ **Find the y-value when $x = 2$.**

$= 8 - 16 + 5$

$= -3$

y-coordinate of vertex: -3 ⟵ **The vertex is at $(2, -3)$.**

y-intercept: $(0, 5)$ ⟵ **The y-intercept is at $(0, c) = (0, 5)$.**

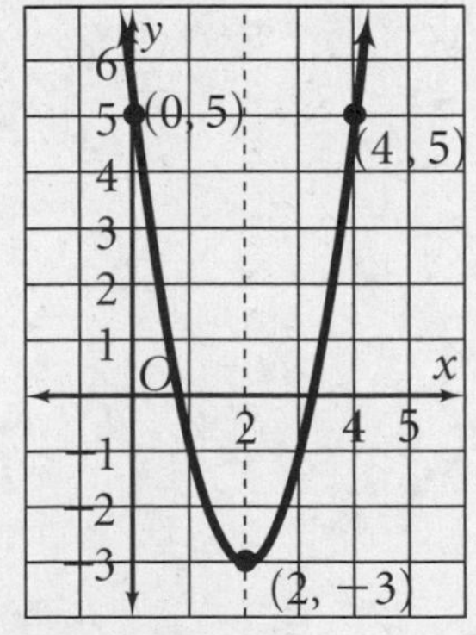

⟵ **Since a is positive, the graph opens upward, and the vertex is at the bottom of the graph. Plot the vertex and draw the axis of symmetry. Plot $(0, 5)$ and its corresponding point on the other side of the axis of symmetry.**

Exercises

Graph each parabola. Label the vertex and the axis of symmetry.

1. $y = x^2 - 4x + 7$
2. $y = x^2 + 8x + 11$
3. $y = -3x^2 + 6x - 9$
4. $y = -x^2 - 8x - 15$
5. $y = 2x^2 - 8x + 1$
6. $y = -2x^2 - 12x - 7$

Name ____________________ Class ____________ Date ____________

Review 220

Translating Parabolas

OBJECTIVE: Writing equations in vertex and standard forms

MATERIALS: None

- Standard form of a quadratic function is $y = ax^2 + bx + c$.
  Vertex form of a quadratic function is $y = a(x - h)^2 + k$.
- For a parabola in vertex form, the coordinates of the vertex are (h, k).

Example

Write $y = 3x^2 - 24x + 50$ in vertex form.

$y = ax^2 + bx + c$

$y = 3x^2 - 24x + 50$ ⟵ **Verify that the equation is in standard form.**

$b = -24, a = 3$ ⟵ **Find b and a.**

$x\text{-coordinate} = -\left(\frac{-24}{2(3)}\right)$ ⟵ **For an equation in standard form, the x-coordinate of the vertex can be found by using $x = -\frac{b}{2a}$. Substitute.**

$= 4$ ⟵ **Simplify.**

$y\text{-coordinate} = 3(4)^2 - 24(4) + 50$ ⟵ **Substitute 4 into the standard form to find the y-coordinate.**

$= 2$ ⟵ **Simplify.**

$y = 3(x - 4)^2 + 2$ ⟵ **Substitute (4, 2) for (h, k) into the vertex form.**

Once the conversion to vertex form is complete, check by multiplying.

$y = 3(x^2 - 8x + 16) + 2$

$y = 3x^2 - 24x + 50$

The result should be the standard form of the equation.

Exercises

Write each function in vertex form. Check.

1. $y = x^2 - 2x - 3$
2. $y = -x^2 + 4x + 6$
3. $y = x^2 + 3x - 10$
4. $y = x^2 - 9x$
5. $y = x^2 + x$
6. $y = x^2 + 5x + 4$
7. $y = 4x^2 + 8x - 3$
8. $y = \frac{3}{4}x^2 + 9x$
9. $y = -2x^2 + 2x + 1$

Write each function in standard form.

10. $y = (x - 3)^2 + 1$
11. $y = 2(x - 1)^2 - 3$
12. $y = -3(x + 4)^2 + 1$

Name ______________________ Class ______________ Date ______________

Review 221

Factoring Quadratic Expressions

OBJECTIVE: Factoring quadratic expressions **MATERIALS:** None

Example

Factor the expression $6x^2 - 5x - 4$.

$a = 6$, $b = -5$, and $c = -4$ ⟵ **Find a, b, and c; they are the coefficients of each term.**

$ac = -24$ and $b = -5$ ⟵ **We are looking for factors with product ac and sum b.**

Factors of −24	1, −24	−1, 24	2, −12	−2, 12	3, −8	−3, 8	4, −6	−4, 6
Sum of factors	−23	23	−10	10	−5	5	−2	2

The factors 3 and −8 are the combination whose sum is −5.

$\underbrace{6x^2 + 3x}\underbrace{- 8x - 4}$ ⟵ **Rewrite the middle term using the factors you found.**

$3x(2x + 1) - 4(2x + 1)$ ⟵ **Find common factors by grouping the terms in pairs.**

$(3x - 4)(2x + 1)$ ⟵ **Rewrite using the Distributive Property.**

Check: $(3x - 4)(2x + 1)$ ⟵ **You can check your answer by multiplying it back together.**

$6x^2 + 3x - 8x - 4$

$6x^2 - 5x - 4$

Remember that not all quadratic expressions are factorable.

Exercises

Factor each expression.

1. $x^2 + 6x + 8$ **2.** $x^2 - 4x + 3$ **3.** $2x^2 - 6x + 4$

4. $2x^2 - 11x + 5$ **5.** $2x^2 - 7x - 4$ **6.** $4x^2 + 16x + 15$

7. $x^2 - 5x - 14$ **8.** $7x^2 - 19x - 6$ **9.** $x^2 - x - 72$

10. $2x^2 + 9x + 7$ **11.** $x^2 + 12x + 32$ **12.** $4x^2 - 28x + 49$

13. $x^2 - 3x - 10$ **14.** $2x^2 + 9x + 4$ **15.** $9x^2 - 6x + 1$

16. $x^2 - 10x + 9$ **17.** $x^2 + 4x - 12$ **18.** $x^2 + 7x + 10$

19. $x^2 - 8x + 12$ **20.** $2x^2 - 5x - 3$ **21.** $x^2 - 6x + 5$

22. $3x^2 + 2x - 8$ **23.** $2x^2 + 11x + 5$ **24.** $x^2 + 3x - 28$

ALGEBRA 2 TOPICS

Name ______________________ Class ______________ Date ______________

Review 222

OBJECTIVE: Solving quadratic equations by graphing and factoring

MATERIALS: None

When graphing a quadratic equation, remember to use the formula $h = -\frac{b}{2a}$ to find the x-coordinate of the vertex of a parabola.
To complete the graph, plot the y-intercept $(0, c)$ and then make the parabola symmetrical.

Example

Solve the quadratic equation $x^2 + 6x + 8 = 0$ by graphing and factoring.

Graphing

Step 1
Graph the associated function $y = x^2 + 6x + 8$.

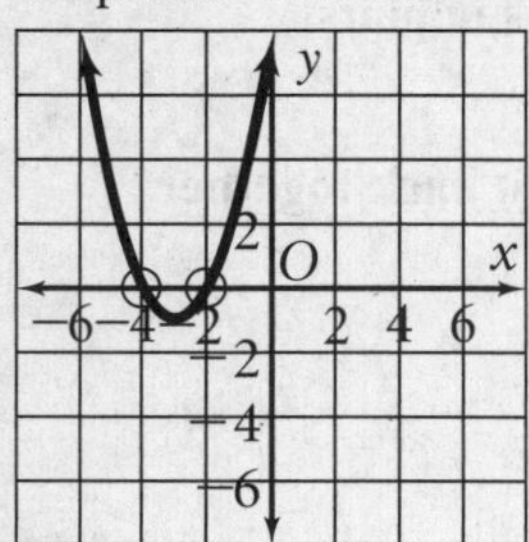

Step 2
Circle the place(s) where the graph crosses the x-axis.

Step 3
Find the values of x for the circled points.
$x = -4$ or $x = -2$

Factoring

Step 1
Factor the equation.
$(x + 4)(x + 2) = 0$

Step 2
Solve each factor for x.
$x + 4 = 0$ or $x + 2 = 0$
$x = -4$ or $x = -2$

The values for x are the same for each method.

Exercises

Solve each quadratic equation first by graphing and then by factoring.

1. $x^2 + 7x + 10 = 0$ **2.** $x^2 - 5x + 6 = 0$ **3.** $x^2 + 6x + 5 = 0$

4. $x^2 + 4x + 3 = 0$ **5.** $3x^2 + 10x + 3 = 0$ **6.** $0 = 2x^2 - 3x + 1$

Solve each quadratic equation by factoring.

7. $x^2 - 7x + 12 = 0$ **8.** $2x^2 + x - 15 = 0$ **9.** $x^2 + x - 2 = 0$

10. $3x^2 - 5x + 2 = 0$ **11.** $x^2 + 5x + 6 = 0$ **12.** $x^2 + x - 20 = 0$

Name ____________________ Class ____________ Date ____________

Review 223

Complex Numbers

OBJECTIVE: Adding, subtracting, and multiplying complex numbers

MATERIALS: None

- A *complex number* consists of a real part and an imaginary part. It is written in the form $a + bi$, where a and b are real numbers.
- When adding or subtracting complex numbers, you combine the real parts and then combine the imaginary parts.
- When multiplying complex numbers, use the Distributive Property.
- $i^2 = (\sqrt{-1})(\sqrt{-1}) = -1$ and $i = \sqrt{-1}$

Examples

Simplify $(3 - i) + (2 + 3i)$.

$(3 - i) + (2 + 3i)$

$= ③ - \boxed{i} + ② + \boxed{3i}$ ⟵ **Circle real parts. Put a square around imaginary parts.**

$= (3 + 2) + (-1 + 3)i$ ⟵ **Combine.**

$= 5 + 2i$

Simplify $(3 + 4i)(5 + 2i)$.

$(3 + 4i)(5 + 2i)$

$= 3(5) + 3(2i) + 4i(5) + 4i(2i)$ ⟵ **Use the Distributive Property.**

$= 15 + 6i + 20i + 8i^2$ ⟵ **Combine real parts and imaginary parts.**

$= 15 + 26i + 8(-1)$ ⟵ **Substitute $i^2 = -1$.**

$= 7 + 26i$

Exercises

Simplify each expression.

1. $2i + (-4 - 2i)$
2. $5i \cdot 12i$
3. $(2 + i)(2 - i)$
4. $(3 + i)(2 + i)$
5. $(4 + 3i)(1 + 2i)$
6. $3i(1 - 2i)$
7. $(6i)(-4i)$
8. $3i(4 - i)$
9. $3 - (-2 + 3i) + (-5 + i)$
10. $4i(6 - 2i)$
11. $2i + (3i)^2$
12. $(5 + 6i) + (-2 + 4i)$
13. $-14i(-4)$
14. $3i\sqrt{-6}$
15. $9(11 + 5i)$

Name ______________________ Class ______________ Date ______________

Review 224

OBJECTIVE: Solving quadratic equations by completing the square

MATERIALS: None

- Perfect square trinomials are equations in the form $x^2 + 2kx + k^2$, which can be factored into $(x + k)^2$. Completing the square produces a perfect square trinomial.
- To complete the square, you must write the equation so that the coefficient of the x^2 term equals 1.

Example

Complete the square to solve the quadratic equation.

$2x^2 + 20x - 22 = 0$

$2x^2 + 20x - 22 = 0$ ⟵ **Look to see whether the x^2 coefficient is 1.**

$x^2 + 10x - 11 = 0$ ⟵ **Divide each side by 2 to eliminate the x^2 coefficient.**

$x^2 + \textcircled{10}x - 11 = 0$ ⟵ **Circle the coefficient of the linear term.**

$x^2 + \textcircled{10}x = 11$ ⟵ **Add 11 to each side to get the variables on one side of the equal sign.**

$x^2 + \textcircled{10}x + 25 = 11 + 25$ ⟵ **Divide the circled number by 2, square it, and add the result to each side.**

$(x + 5)^2 = 36$ ⟵ **Factor the perfect square trinomial.**

$x + 5 = \pm 6$ ⟵ **Take the square root of each side.**

$x = -5 \pm 6$ ⟵ **Solve for x.**

$x = 1$ and -11 ⟵ **Simplify.**

Exercises

Solve each equation by completing the square.

1. $x^2 + 4x = 21$ **2.** $x^2 - 8x = 33$ **3.** $x^2 + 10x = -5$

4. $3x^2 + 10x + 3 = 0$ **5.** $3x^2 + 4x = 3$ **6.** $x^2 - 5x - 5 = 0$

7. $x^2 + 7x = 0$ **8.** $2x^2 - 7x - 4 = 0$ **9.** $x^2 - x - 7 = 0$

10. $x^2 - 8x + 4 = 0$ **11.** $x^2 - 6x + 6 = 0$ **12.** $x^2 + 2x = 15$

13. $x^2 + 2x - 5 = 0$ **14.** $2x^2 + 8x - 10 = 0$ **15.** $4x^2 + 4x = 3$

Name ________________ Class ________ Date ________

Review 225

The Quadratic Formula

OBJECTIVE: Solving quadratic equations by using the Quadratic Formula

MATERIALS: None

Follow each step below to solve any quadratic equation by using the Quadratic Formula.

1. Write the equation in the standard form $ax^2 + bx + c = 0$.
2. Substitute a-, b-, and c-values into the Quadratic Formula.
   $x = \frac{-b \pm \sqrt{b^2 - 4ac}}{2a}$
3. Simplify. Use imaginary numbers if necessary.
4. Check the solution(s) by substituting the values into the original equation.

Example

Use the Quadratic Formula to solve $x^2 + 2 = -2x$. Check your solution.

$$x^2 + 2 = -2x$$

$x^2 + 2x + 2 = 0$ ⟵ **Write in standard form.**

$\underline{1}x^2 + \textcircled{2}x + \boxed{2} = 0$ ⟵ **Underline a, circle b, and put a square around c.**

$x = \frac{-2 \pm \sqrt{2^2 - 4(1)(2)}}{2(1)}$ ⟵ **Substitute 1 for a, 2 for b, and 2 for c into the Quadratic Formula.**

$= \frac{-2 \pm \sqrt{-4}}{2}$ ⟵ **Simplify to find the values of x.**

$= \frac{-2 \pm 2i}{2}$

$= -1 \pm i$

Check:

$x^2 + 2 = -2x$	$x^2 + 2 = -2x$
$(-1 + i)^2 + 2 \stackrel{?}{=} -2(-1 + i)$	$(-1 - i)^2 + 2 \stackrel{?}{=} -2(-1 - i)$
$1 - 2i + i^2 + 2 \stackrel{?}{=} 2 - 2i$	$1 + 2i + i^2 + 2 \stackrel{?}{=} 2 + 2i$
$1 - 2i - 1 + 2 \stackrel{?}{=} 2 - 2i$	$1 + 2i - 1 + 2 \stackrel{?}{=} 2 + 2i$
$2 - 2i = 2 - 2i$ ✓	$2 + 2i = 2 + 2i$ ✓

Exercises

Solve each equation using the Quadratic Formula.

1. $x^2 - 3x + 2 = 0$
2. $-x^2 + 5x = 9$
3. $10x - 6 = 5x^2$
4. $x + 2x^2 + 1 = -1 - x$
5. $2x^2 + x = 10$
6. $2x + 1 = 2x^2$

ALGEBRA 2 TOPICS

Name ____________________ Class ____________________ Date ____________________

Review 226

OBJECTIVE: Comparing models of real data

MATERIALS: Graphing calculator

You can use your graphing calculator to model data and determine whether a linear, quadratic, or cubic model best fits the data. You can use the equation for that model to estimate values of data.

Example

The table shows winning times in the 400-meter run.

Men's Olympic Track and Field, 400-Meter Run

Year	1968	1972	1976	1980	1984	1988	1992	1996	2000
Seconds	43.86	44.66	44.26	44.60	44.27	43.87	43.50	43.49	43.84

Source: *The World Almanac and Book of Facts 2001*

a. Find and graph a linear model, a quadratic model, and a cubic model for the data.

Linear model

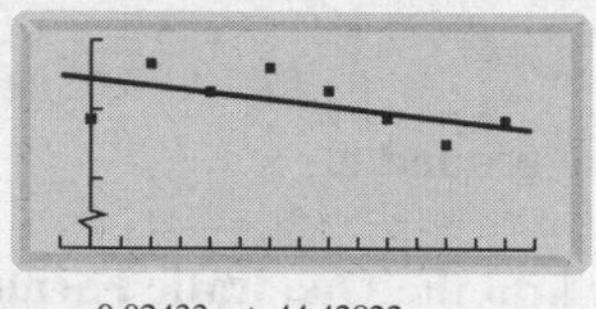

$y = -0.02433x + 44.42822$

Quadratic model

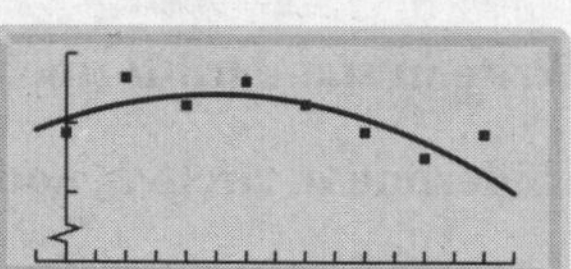

$y = -0.00127x^2 + 0.01640x + 44.23812$

Cubic model

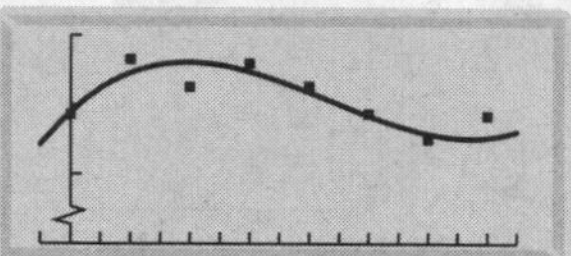

$y = 0.00032x^3 - 0.01665x^2 + 0.20197x + 43.89364$

b. The cubic model appears to be the best fit. Use it to estimate the winning time in 2004. Does your estimate seem reasonable?

Let $x =$ the years since 1968 and $y =$ the number of seconds. Substitute 36 for x and simplify.

$y = 0.00032(36)^3 - 0.01665(36)^2 + 0.20197(36) + 43.89364 = 44.51$

This estimate does not seem reasonable, since the times are generally decreasing. We would expect the time for the 2004 Olympic games to be less than the time for the 2000 Olympic games.

Exercises

Find a linear, quadratic, and cubic model for the data. Use the model that best fits the data to estimate the diving record in 2004.

Men's Olympic Springboard Diving Records

Year	1980	1984	1988	1992	1996	2000
Points	905.02	754.41	730.80	676.53	701.46	708.72

Source: *The World Almanac and Book of Facts 2001*

Name ______________________ Class ______________ Date ______________

Review 227

OBJECTIVE: Writing a polynomial function from its zeros

MATERIALS: None

- A polynomial function in factored form can be rewritten in standard form if you know its zeros.
- Use the Zero-Product Property to find values that will make the polynomial equal zero.

Example

Write a polynomial function in standard form with zeros at 0, 4, and −2.

$(x + 0)(x - 4)(x + 2)$ ⟵ **Write the factors using the zeros.**

$f(x) = x(x - 4)(x + 2)$ ⟵ **Write the polynomial function in factored form.**

$= x(x^2 - 2x - 8)$ ⟵ **Multiply $(x - 4)(x + 2)$ to convert to standard form.**

$= x^3 - 2x^2 - 8x$ ⟵ **Multiply by x using the Distributive Property.**

The polynomial function written in standard form is $f(x) = x^3 - 2x^2 - 8x$.

Exercises

Write a polynomial function with the given zeros.

1. $5, -1, 3$
2. $1, 7, -5$
3. $-1, 1, -6$
4. $2, -2, -3$
5. $2, 1, 3$
6. $2, 3, -3, -1$
7. $0, -8, 2$
8. $-10, 0, 2$
9. $-1, 1, -6$
10. $2, -2, -3$
11. $-2, 2, -\frac{3}{2}$
12. $-1, \frac{2}{3}$
13. $1, -3, -\frac{4}{3}$
14. $-2, -2, -3$
15. $4, -2$ (mult. 2)
16. $2, -1$ (mult. 2)

Find the zeros of each function.

17. $y = x(x + 8)(x - 2)$
18. $y = (x^2 - 4)(x^2 - 9)$
19. $y = (x - 3)(x + 3)$
20. $y = (3x + 2)(x - 5)$
21. $y = 6x(x - 8)$
22. $y = (x^2 - 1)(x^2 - 16)$
23. $y = x(x + 2)(x - 10)$
24. $y = (x^2 - 4)(x + 3)^2$
25. $y = (2x + 1)(x - 5)(x + 3)$
26. $y = 3x(x + 4)(2x - 3)$
27. $y = x^2(x^2 - 5)$
28. $y = 4x^2(x^2 - 36)$

Name ____________ Class ____________ Date ____________

Review 228

Dividing Polynomials

OBJECTIVE: Dividing polynomials **MATERIALS:** None

Example

Divide $2x^2 + 6x - 7$ by $x + 1$.

$$\begin{array}{r} 2x \\ \textcircled{x}+1 \overline{) \textcircled{2x^2} + 6x + 7} \end{array}$$

Step 1: To find the first term of the quotient, divide the highest- degree term of $2x2 + 6x + 7$ by the highest-degree term of the divisor, $x + 1$. Circle these terms before dividing.

$$\begin{array}{r} 2x \\ x+1 \overline{) 2x^2 + 6x + 7} \\ \underline{2x^2 + 2x} \end{array}$$

Step 2: Multiply $x + 1$ by the new term in the quotient. Align like terms.

$$\begin{array}{r} 2x \\ x+1 \overline{) 2x^2 + 6x + 7} \\ \underline{2x^2 + 2x} \\ 4x + 7 \end{array}$$

Step 3: Subtract. Bring down the next term.

$$\begin{array}{r} 2x + 4 \\ \textcircled{x}+1 \overline{) 2x^2 + 6x + 7} \\ \underline{2x^2 + 2x} \\ \textcircled{4x} + 7 \\ \underline{4x + 4} \\ 3 \end{array}$$

Step 4: Divide the highest-degree term of $4x + 7$ by the highest- degree term of $x + 1$. Circle these terms before dividing.

Step 5: Repeat Steps 2 and 3. The *remainder* is 3 because its degree is less than the degree of $x + 1$.

$2x^2 + 6x + 7$ divided by $x + 1$ is $2x + 4$, with a remainder of 3.

Exercises

Divide using long division.

1. $(3x^2 - 8x + 7) \div (x - 1)$
2. $x + 6\overline{)x^3 + 5x^2 - 3x - 4}$
3. $x - 5\overline{)x^2 + 3x - 8}$
4. $(x^2 + 6x + 14) \div (x + 3)$
5. $(x^3 - 7x^2 + 11x + 3) \div (x - 3)$
6. $x - 2\overline{)2x^3 - 3x^2 - x - 2}$
7. $(2x^2 - 4x + 7) \div (x - 3)$
8. $x + 7\overline{)x^3 + 2x^2 - 20x + 4}$
9. $x - 1\overline{)x^2 - 5x + 2}$
10. $(2x^3 + 3x^2 + x + 6) \div (x + 3)$

Name ______________________ Class ______________ Date ______________

Review 229

Solving Polynomial Equations

OBJECTIVE: Solving polynomial equations by factoring

MATERIALS: None

Example

Solve $2x^3 + 16 = 0$ by factoring. Find all complex roots.

$2x^3 + 16 = 0$

$2(x^3 + 8) = 0$ ⟵ **Since 2 is a common factor to each term, factor out 2.**

$2(x + 2)(x^2 - 2x + 4) = 0$ ⟵ **Factor the remaining cubic expression.**

$2 = 0$ or $(x + 2) = 0$ or $(x^2 - 2x + 4) = 0$ ⟵ **Use the Zero-Product Property.**

$x = -2$ or $x = \dfrac{2 \pm \sqrt{4 - 4(1)(4)}}{2(1)}$ ⟵ **Solve each equation for *x*. Use the Quadratic Formula when necessary.**

$x = -2$ or $x = \dfrac{2 \pm 2i\sqrt{3}}{2}$

$x = -2$ or $x = 1 \pm i\sqrt{3}$ ⟵ **Simplify.**

The solutions are -2 and $1 \pm i\sqrt{3}$.

Exercises

Solve each equation by factoring. Find all complex roots.

1. $x^3 - 8 = 0$

2. $4x^3 + 4 = 0$

3. $x^4 - x^2 - 72 = 0$

4. $x^4 + 9x^2 = -20$

5. $x^4 - 27x = 0$

6. $8x^3 = -1$

7. $7x^4 = -28x^2 - 21$

8. $x^3 = 64$

9. $8x^3 + 27 = 0$

10. $x^4 - 7x^2 = -12$

11. $2x^4 + 16x^2 = 40$

12. $2x^4 - 16x = 0$

13. $9x^4 - 25 = 0$

14. $2x^4 - x^2 = 3$

15. $x^4 + 5x^2 = -4$

16. $x^4 - 7x^2 - 8 = 0$

17. $2x^3 + 16 = 0$

18. $x^4 - 5x^2 - 24 = 0$

Name ______________________ Class ______________ Date ______________

Review 230

Theorems about Roots of Polynomial Equations

OBJECTIVE: Writing a polynomial equation from its roots

MATERIALS: None

Example

Find a third-degree polynomial equation with rational coefficients that has roots -4 and $2 - 3i$.

Roots: $-4, 2 - 3i, 2 + 3i$ ← **Since $2 - 3i$ is a root, its complex conjugate $2 + 3i$ is also a root.**

$(x + 4)\,[x - (2 - 3i)][x - (2 + 3i)]$ ← **Write the factored form of the polynomial.**

$(x + 4)[x^2 - x(2 + 3i) - x(2 - 3i) + (2 - 3i)(2 + 3i)]$ ← **Multiple the factors.**

$(x + 4)[x^2 - 2x - 3ix - 2x + 3ix + 4 + 6i - 6i - 9i^2]$

$(x + 4)[x^2 - 4x + 4 - 9i^2]$ ← **Simplify.**

$(x + 4)(x^2 - 4x + 13)$ ← **Multiply.**

$x^3 + 4x^2 - 4x^2 - 16x + 13x + 52$

$x^3 - 3x + 52$ ← **Simplify.**

A third-degree polynomial equation with rational coefficients and roots -4 and $2 - 3i$ is $x^3 - 3x + 52 = 0$.

Exercises

Find a third-degree polynomial equation with rational coefficients that has the given roots.

1. $1, 2 - i$

2. $5 + 2i, -2$

3. $3, 6 + i$

4. $-4, \sqrt{2}$

5. $2 - \sqrt{3}, -1$

6. $0, 3 - \sqrt{3}$

7. $3i, 7$

8. $2 + \sqrt{5}, 3$

9. $-3, i$

10. $1 - i, 8$

11. $1, 5i$

12. $2, 4 + i$

13. $3, -4i$

14. $0, 2 - i$

15. $-7, 1 - \sqrt{2}$

16. $-4, -\sqrt{7}$

Name ______________________ Class ______________ Date ______________

Review 231

The Fundamental Theorem of Algebra

OBJECTIVE: Finding all zeros of a polynomial function

MATERIALS: None

Example

Find all zeros of the function $f(x) = x^3 + 4x^2 - x - 10$.

The possible rational roots are ±1, ±2, ±5, ±10.

Use synthetic division to test each possible rational root until you get a remainder of zero.

$$\begin{array}{r|rrrr} 1 & 1 & 4 & -1 & -10 \\ & & 1 & 5 & 4 \\ \hline & 1 & 5 & 4 & -6 \end{array} \qquad \begin{array}{r|rrrr} -1 & 1 & 4 & -1 & -10 \\ & & -1 & -3 & 4 \\ \hline & 1 & 3 & -4 & -6 \end{array}$$

$$\begin{array}{r|rrrr} 2 & 1 & 4 & -1 & -10 \\ & & 2 & 12 & 22 \\ \hline & 1 & 6 & 11 & 12 \end{array} \qquad \begin{array}{r|rrrr} -2 & 1 & 4 & -1 & -10 \\ & & -2 & -4 & 10 \\ \hline & 1 & 2 & -5 & 0 \end{array}$$

So −2 is one of the roots.

$x^3 + 4x^2 - x - 10 = (x + 2)(x^2 + 2x - 5)$ ← **Use the coefficients from synthetic division to obtain the quadratic factor.**

$x = \dfrac{-b \pm \sqrt{b^2 - 4ac}}{2a}$ ← **Since $x^2 + 2x - 5$ cannot be factored, use the Quadratic Formula to solve $x^2 + 2x - 5 = 0$.**

$x = \dfrac{-2 \pm \sqrt{4 - 4(1)(-5)}}{2(1)}$

$x = \dfrac{-2 \pm \sqrt{24}}{2}$

$x = \dfrac{-2 \pm 2\sqrt{6}}{2}$

$x = -1 \pm \sqrt{6}$

The polynomial function $f(x) = x^3 + 4x^2 - x - 10$ has one rational zero, −2, and two irrational zeros, $-1 + \sqrt{6}$ and $-1 - \sqrt{6}$.

Exercises

Find all the zeros of each function.

1. $f(x) = x^3 - 2x^2 + 4x - 3$

2. $f(x) = x^3 - 3x^2 - 15x + 125$

3. $f(x) = 3x^3 - 2x^2 - 15x + 10$

4. $f(x) = x^4 - 4x^3 + 8x^2 - 16x + 16$

5. $f(x) = x^4 - 3x^2 + 2$

6. $f(x) = x^3 - 2x^2 - 17x - 6$

ALGEBRA 2 TOPICS

Name ______________________ Class ______________________ Date ______________________

Review 232

OBJECTIVE: Find permutations and combinations **MATERIALS:** Calculator

- A *permutation* of a set of items is an ordered arrangement of the items.
- If n and r are positive integers with $r \leq n$, then ${}_nP_r$ denotes the number of permutations of n distinct items taken r at a time.

$${}_nP_r = \frac{n!}{(n-r)!}$$

- A *combination* is a selection of items in which order does not matter.
- The number of combinations of n objects of a set chosen r objects at a time is given by the following formula:

$${}_nC_r = \frac{n!}{r!(n-r)!};\ \text{for } 0 \leq r \leq n$$

Example

If order is not important, in how many ways can five letters be chosen from the alphabet?

n = alphabet = 26 ← **Decide what number represents n and what number represents r.**
r = chosen letters = 5

${}_{26}C_5 = \frac{26!}{5!(21!)}$ ← **Use the formula to write the equation.**

$= \frac{7{,}893{,}600}{120}$ ← **Evaluate the factorials. Use the ! option of a calculator.**

$= 65{,}780$ ← **Simplify.**

There are 65,780 ways in which five letters can be chosen from the alphabet.

Exercises

1. How many permutations of six letters are there from A, E, B, L, N, O, S, T, and Y?

2. A chemist is making a solution of five chemicals in water. How many possible permutations are there in which to add the chemicals one at a time?

3. You have 12 CDs in your collection. You have time to listen to two CDs. How many combinations of CDs do you have to choose from?

4. Your biology teacher chooses six students from a class of 26 to do a special project. Find the total number of combinations.

5. In how many ways can a family of six line up for a photograph?

6. In how many ways can a president, vice president, secretary, and treasurer be elected from a club with 15 members?

7. A health food store offers ten toppings for yogurt. How many different three-topping yogurt sundaes can be formed with the ten toppings? (Assume that no topping is used twice.)

Name ______________________ Class ______________ Date ______________

Review 233

OBJECTIVE: Using the Binomial Theorem **MATERIALS:** None

- The *Binomial Theorem* states that for any binomial $(a + b)$ and any positive integer n,

  $(a + b)^n = {}_nC_0a^n + {}_nC_1a^{n-1}b + {}_nC_2a^{n-2}b^2 + \ldots + {}_nC_{n-1}ab^{n-1} + {}_nC_nb^n.$

- The theorem provides an effective method for expanding any power of a binomial.

Example

Use the Binomial Theorem to expand $(3x + 2)^3$.

Step 1
Determine a, b, and n.
$a = 3x, b = 2, n = 3$

Step 2
Use the formula to write the equation.
$(3x + 2)^3 = {}_3C_0(3x)^3 + {}_3C_1(3x)^2(2) + {}_3C_2(3x)(2)^2 + {}_3C_3(2)^3$

Step 3
Simplify.

$= 1(27x^3) + 3(9x^2)(2) + 3(3x)(4) + 1(8)$
$= 27x^3 + 54x^2 + 36x + 8$

Exercises

Fill in the correct coefficients, variables, and exponents for the expanded form of each binomial.

1. $(x + y)^4 = x^{\square} + \square x^3y + 6x^{\square}y^2 + \square xy^{\square} + \square^4$

2. $(z - y)^3 = z^{\square} - \square z^2y + \square zy^{\square} - \square^3$

3. $(x + z)^5 = x^{\square} + \square x^4z + 10x^{\square}z^2 + \square x^2z^{\square} + \square xz^4 + \square^5$

Use the Binomial Theorem to expand each binomial.

4. $(x + y)^5$
5. $(x - y)^5$
6. $(2x + y)^3$
7. $(x + 3y)^4$
8. $(x - 2y)^5$
9. $(2x - y)^5$
10. $(x - 3y)^4$
11. $(4x - y)^3$
12. $(x - 1)^5$
13. $(1 - x)^3$
14. $(x^2 + 1)^3$
15. $(y^2 + a)^4$

Name ______________________ Class ______________ Date ______________

Review 234

Roots and Radical Expressions

OBJECTIVE: Simplifying radical expressions	**MATERIALS:** None

- For any real numbers a and b, and any positive integer n, if $a^n = b$, then a is an nth root of b.
- For any negative real number a, $\sqrt[n]{a^n} = |a|$ when n is even.

Examples

Simplify $\sqrt[3]{1000x^3y^9}$.

$$\sqrt[3]{1000x^3y^9} = \sqrt[3]{10^3x^3(y^3)^3} \quad \longleftarrow \textbf{Write each factor as a cube.}$$

$$= \sqrt[3]{(10xy^3)^3} \quad \longleftarrow \textbf{Write as the cube of a product.}$$

$$= 10xy^3 \quad \longleftarrow \textbf{Simplify.}$$

Simplify $\sqrt[4]{\dfrac{256g^8}{h^4k^{16}}}$.

$$\sqrt[4]{\frac{256g^8}{h^4k^{16}}} = \sqrt[4]{\frac{4^4(g^2)^4}{h^4(k^4)^4}}$$

$$= \sqrt[4]{\left(\frac{4g^2}{hk^4}\right)^4} = \frac{4g^2}{|h|\,k^4}$$

The absolute value symbols are needed to ensure the root is positive when h is negative. Note that $4g^2$ and k^4 are never negative.

Exercises

Simplify. Use absolute value symbols when needed.

1. $\sqrt{36x^2}$
2. $\sqrt[3]{216y^3}$
3. $\sqrt{\dfrac{1}{100x^2}}$
4. $\dfrac{\sqrt{x^{20}}}{\sqrt{y^8}}$
5. $\sqrt[3]{\dfrac{(x+3)^3}{(x-4)^6}}$
6. $\sqrt[5]{x^{10}y^{15}z^5}$
7. $\sqrt[3]{\dfrac{27z^3}{(z+12)^6}}$
8. $\sqrt[4]{2401x^{12}}$
9. $\sqrt[3]{\dfrac{1331}{x^3}}$
10. $\sqrt[4]{\dfrac{(y-4)^8}{(z+9)^4}}$
11. $\sqrt[3]{\dfrac{a^6b^6}{c^3}}$
12. $\sqrt[3]{-x^3y^6}$

Name________________________ Class______________ Date____________

Review 235

Multiplying and Dividing Radical Expressions

OBJECTIVE: Rationalizing the denominator and simplifying	**MATERIALS:** None

- If $\sqrt[n]{a}$ and $\sqrt[n]{b}$ are real numbers and $b \neq 0$, then $\dfrac{\sqrt[n]{a}}{\sqrt[n]{b}} = \sqrt[n]{\dfrac{a}{b}}$.
- Rationalizing the denominator means that you are rewriting the expression so that no radicals appear in the denominator and there are no fractions inside the radical.

Example

Rationalize the denominator and simplify. Assume that all variables are positive.

$$\frac{\sqrt{9y}}{\sqrt{2x}} = \sqrt{\frac{9y}{2x}} \quad \longleftarrow \textbf{Rewrite as a square root of a fraction.}$$

$$= \sqrt{\frac{9y \cdot 2x}{2x \cdot 2x}} \quad \longleftarrow \textbf{Make the denominator a perfect square.}$$

$$= \sqrt{\frac{18xy}{4x^2}} \quad \longleftarrow \textbf{Simplify.}$$

$$= \frac{\sqrt{18xy}}{\sqrt{2^2 \cdot x^2}}$$

$$= \frac{\sqrt{18xy}}{2x}$$

$$= \frac{\sqrt{3^2 \cdot 2 \cdot x \cdot y}}{2x} \quad \longleftarrow \textbf{Simplify the numerator.}$$

$$= \frac{3\sqrt{2xy}}{2x}$$

Exercises

Rationalize the denominator of each expression. Assume that all variables are positive.

1. $\dfrac{\sqrt{5}}{\sqrt{x}}$

2. $\dfrac{\sqrt[3]{6ab^2}}{\sqrt[3]{2a^4b}}$

3. $\dfrac{\sqrt[4]{9y}}{\sqrt[4]{x}}$

4. $\dfrac{\sqrt{10xy^3}}{\sqrt{12y^2}}$

5. $\dfrac{4\sqrt[3]{k^9}}{16\sqrt[3]{k^5}}$

6. $\sqrt{\dfrac{3x^5}{5y}}$

7. $\dfrac{\sqrt[4]{10}}{\sqrt[4]{z^2}}$

8. $\sqrt[3]{\dfrac{19a^2b}{abc^4}}$

ALGEBRA 2 TOPICS

Name ______________________ Class ______________ Date ______________

Review 236

OBJECTIVE: Multiplying and dividing binomial radical expressions

MATERIALS: None

- Conjugates, such as $\sqrt{a} + \sqrt{b}$ and $\sqrt{a} - \sqrt{b}$, differ only in the sign of the second term. If a and b are rational numbers, then the product of conjugates produce a rational number:

$$\left(\sqrt{a} + \sqrt{b}\right)\left(\sqrt{a} - \sqrt{b}\right) = \left(\sqrt{a}\right)^2 - \left(\sqrt{b}\right)^2 = a - b.$$

- You can use the conjugate of a radical denominator to rationalize the denominator.

Examples

Multiply $\left(2\sqrt{7} - \sqrt{5}\right)\left(2\sqrt{7} + \sqrt{5}\right)$.

$\left(2\sqrt{7} - \sqrt{5}\right)\left(2\sqrt{7} + \sqrt{5}\right)$ ⟵ **These are conjugates.**

$= \left(2\sqrt{7}\right)^2 - \left(\sqrt{5}\right)^2$ ⟵ **Use the difference of squares formula.**

$= 28 - 5 = 23$ ⟵ **Simplify.**

Rationalize the denominator of $\dfrac{4\sqrt{2}}{1 + \sqrt{3}}$.

$\dfrac{4\sqrt{2}}{1 + \sqrt{3}}$

$= \dfrac{4\sqrt{2}}{1 + \sqrt{3}} \cdot \dfrac{1 - \sqrt{3}}{1 - \sqrt{3}}$ ⟵ **Use the conjugate of $1 + \sqrt{3}$ to rationalize the denominator.**

$= \dfrac{4\sqrt{2} - 4\sqrt{6}}{1 - 3}$ ⟵ **Multiply.**

$= \dfrac{4\sqrt{2} - 4\sqrt{6}}{-2} = -\dfrac{\left(4\sqrt{2} - 4\sqrt{6}\right)}{2}$ ⟵ **Simplify.**

$= \dfrac{-4\sqrt{2} + 4\sqrt{6}}{2}$

Exercises

Simplify. Rationalize all denominators.

1. $\left(3 + \sqrt{6}\right)\left(3 - \sqrt{6}\right)$

2. $\dfrac{2\sqrt{3} + 1}{5 - \sqrt{3}}$

3. $\left(4\sqrt{6} - 1\right)\left(\sqrt{6} + 4\right)$

4. $\dfrac{2 - \sqrt{7}}{2 + \sqrt{7}}$

5. $\left(2\sqrt{8} - 6\right)\left(\sqrt{8} - 4\right)$

6. $\dfrac{\sqrt{5}}{2 + \sqrt{3}}$

Name ______________________ Class ______________ Date ______________

Review 237

Rational Exponents

OBJECTIVE: Simplifying expressions with rational exponents

MATERIALS: None

- You can simplify a number with a rational exponent using the properties of exponents or by converting the expression to a radical expression.
- To write an expression with rational exponents in simplest form, write every exponent as a positive number using the following rules for $a \neq 0$.
  $a^{-n} = \frac{1}{a^n}$ and $\frac{1}{a^{-m}} = a^m$

Example

Write $(8x^9y^{-3})^{-\frac{2}{3}}$ in simplest form.

$(8x^9y^{-3})^{-\frac{2}{3}} = (2^3x^9y^{-3})^{-\frac{2}{3}}$ ← **Factor any numerical coefficients.**

$= (2^3)^{-\frac{2}{3}}(x^9)^{-\frac{2}{3}}(y^{-3})^{-\frac{2}{3}}$ ← **Use the property $(ab)^m = a^mb^m$.**

$= 2^{-2}x^{-6}y^2$ ← **Multiply exponents, using the property $(a^m)^n = a^{mn}$.**

$= \frac{y^2}{2^2x^6}$ ← **Write every exponent as a positive number.**

$= \frac{y^2}{4x^6}$ ← **Simplify.**

Exercises

Write each expression in simplest form. Assume that all variables are positive.

1. $y^{\frac{2}{3}}y^{\frac{3}{5}}$
2. $(16x^2y^8)^{-\frac{1}{2}}$
3. $(z^{-3})^{\frac{1}{9}}$
4. $(2x^{\frac{1}{4}})^4$
5. $\left(\frac{49x^{-6}}{9x^2}\right)^{\frac{1}{2}}$
6. $(25x^{-6}y^2)^{\frac{1}{2}}$
7. $\frac{x^{\frac{2}{3}}y^2}{x^{\frac{5}{3}}y^2}$
8. $(8a^{-3}b^9)^{\frac{2}{3}}$
9. $\left(\frac{16z^4}{25x^8}\right)^{-\frac{1}{2}}$
10. $a^{\frac{3}{4}} \cdot a^{\frac{3}{4}}$
11. $\left(\frac{x^2}{y^{-1}}\right)^{\frac{1}{5}}$
12. $(27m^9n^{-3})^{-\frac{2}{3}}$
13. $(2x^{\frac{1}{6}})(3x^{\frac{2}{6}})$
14. $\left(\frac{32r^2}{2s^4}\right)^{\frac{1}{4}}$
15. $(9z^{10})^{\frac{3}{2}}$

Name ____________________ Class ____________ Date ____________

Review 238

Solving Radical Equations

OBJECTIVE: Solving radical equations **MATERIALS:** None

- Equations containing radicals can be solved by isolating the radical on one side of the equation and then raising both sides to the same power that would undo the radical.
- An extraneous solution satisfies later equations in your work but does not make the original equation true.

Example

Solve $\sqrt{17 - x} - 3 = x$. Check your solution(s).

$$\sqrt{17 - x} - 3 = x$$

$$\sqrt{17 - x} = x + 3$$ ⟵ **Add 3 to each side to get the radical alone on one side of the equal sign.**

$$\left(\sqrt{17 - x}\right)^2 = (x + 3)^2$$ ⟵ **Square each side.**

$$17 - x = x^2 + 6x + 9$$

$$0 = x^2 + 7x - 8$$ ⟵ **Rewrite in standard form.**

$$0 = (x - 1)(x + 8)$$ ⟵ **Factor.**

$$x - 1 = 0 \text{ or } x + 8 = 0$$ ⟵ **Set each factor equal to 0 using the Zero Product Property.**

$$x = 1 \text{ or } x = -8$$

Check:

$\sqrt{17 - x} - 3 \stackrel{?}{=} x$	$\sqrt{17 - x} - 3 \stackrel{?}{=} x$
$\sqrt{17 - 1} - 3 \stackrel{?}{=} 1$	$\sqrt{17 - (-8)} - 3 \stackrel{?}{=} -8$
$\sqrt{16} - 3 \stackrel{?}{=} 1$	$\sqrt{25} - 3 \stackrel{?}{=} -8$
$1 = 1$ ✔	$2 \neq -8$

The only solution is 1.

Exercises

Solve. Check for extraneous solutions.

1. $x^{\frac{1}{2}} = 13$

2. $3\sqrt{2x} = 12$

3. $\sqrt{5x + 1} = \sqrt{4x + 3}$

4. $\sqrt{x^2 + 3} = x + 1$

5. $\sqrt{3x} = \sqrt{x + 6}$

6. $x = \sqrt{x + 7} + 5$

7. $x - 3\sqrt{x} - 4 = 0$

8. $\sqrt{x + 2} = x - 4$

9. $\sqrt[3]{5y + 2} - 3 = 0$

ALGEBRA 2 TOPICS

Name ______________________ Class ______________ Date ______________

Review 239

Function Operations

OBJECTIVE: Combining functions

MATERIALS: Highlighter pens of three different colors

- One way to combine two functions is by forming a composite.
- A composite is written $(g \circ f)$ or $g(f(x))$. The two different functions are g and f.
- Evaluate the inner function $f(x)$ first.
- Use this value, the first output, as the input for the second function, $g(x)$.

Example

Evaluate the expression $g(f(2))$ given the inner function, $f(x) = 3x - 5$ and the outer function, $g(x) = x^2 + 2$.

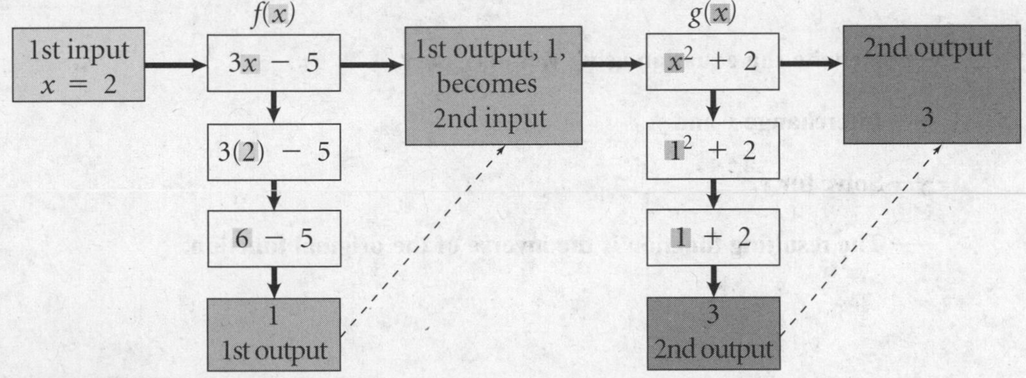

Exercises

Evaluate the expression $g(f(5))$ using the same functions for g and f as in the Example. Fill in blanks 1–8 on the chart.

Use one color highlighter to highlight the first input. Use a second color to highlight the first output and the second input. Use a third color to highlight the second output, which is the answer.

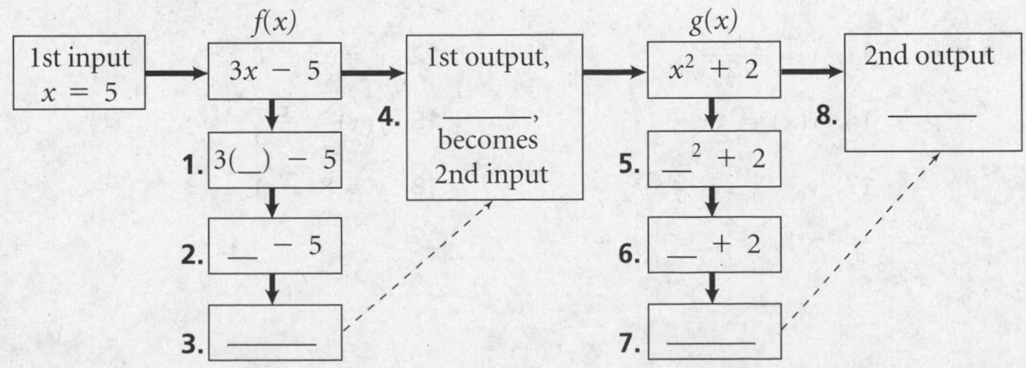

Given $f(x) = x^2 + 4x$ and $g(x) = 2x + 3$, evaluate each expression.

9. $f(g(2))$ **10.** $g(f(2.5))$ **11.** $g(f(-5))$ **12.** $f(g(-5))$

ALGEBRA 2 TOPICS

Name ______________________ Class ______________ Date ______________

Review 240

OBJECTIVE: Finding the inverse of a function **MATERIALS:** None

- Inverse operations "undo" each other. Addition and subtraction are inverse operations. So are multiplication and division. The inverse of cubing a number is taking its cube root.
- If two functions are inverses, they consist of inverse operations performed in the opposite order.

Example

Find the inverse of $f(x) = x + 1$.

$f(x) = x + 1$

$y = x + 1$ ← **Rewrite the equation using *y*, if necessary.**

$x = y + 1$ ← **Interchange *x* and *y*.**

$x - 1 = y$ ← **Solve for *y*.**

$y = x - 1$ ← **The resulting function is the inverse of the original function.**

So, $f^{-1}(x) = x - 1$.

Exercises

Find the inverse of each function.

1. $y = 4x - 5$
2. $y = 3x^3 + 2$
3. $y = (x + 1)^3$
4. $y = 0.5x + 2$
5. $f(x) = x + 3$
6. $f(x) = 2(x - 2)$
7. $f(x) = \frac{x}{5}$
8. $f(x) = 4x + 2$
9. $y = x$
10. $y = x - 3$
11. $y = \frac{x - 1}{2}$
12. $y = x^3 - 8$
13. $f(x) = \sqrt{x + 2}$
14. $f(x) = \frac{2}{3}x - 1$
15. $f(x) = \frac{x + 3}{5}$
16. $f(x) = 2(x - 5)^2$
17. $y = \sqrt{x} + 4$
18. $y = 8x + 1$

Name ______________________ Class ______________ Date ______________

Review 241

OBJECTIVE: Graphing radical functions **MATERIALS:** None

The graph of $y = a\sqrt{x - h} + k$ is a translation h units horizontally and k units vertically of $y = a\sqrt{x}$. The value of a determines a vertical stretch or compression of $y = \sqrt{x}$.

Example

Graph $y = 2\sqrt{x - 5} + 3$.

$$y = 2\sqrt{x - 5} + 3$$

$a = 2 \quad h = 5 \quad k = 3$

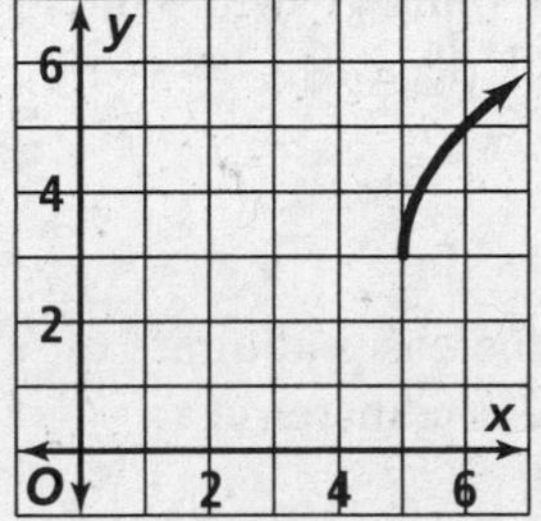

Translate the graph of $y = 2\sqrt{x}$ right five units and up three units. The graph of $y = 2\sqrt{x}$ looks like the graph of $y = \sqrt{x}$ with a vertical stretch by a factor of 2.

Exercises

Graph each function.

1. $y = \sqrt{x - 4} + 1$

2. $y = \sqrt{x} - 4$

3. $y = \sqrt{x + 1}$

4. $y = -\sqrt{x + 2} - 3$

5. $y = 2\sqrt{x - 1}$

6. $y = -2\sqrt{x + 3} + 4$

7. $y = -\sqrt{x} + 1$

8. $y = \sqrt{x + 3} - 4$

9. $y = 3\sqrt{x} + 2$

10. $y = -\sqrt{x - 2}$

11. $y = \sqrt{x - 1} - 2$

12. $y = -\sqrt{x + 4} - 1$

Name ______________________ Class ______________ Date ______________

Review 242

OBJECTIVE: Modeling exponential growth and decay

MATERIALS: None

- The general form of an exponential function is $y = ab^x$. This can model either growth or decay. When the value of b is greater than 1, the function models growth. When the value of b is between zero and 1, the function models decay.
- When you see words like *increase* or *appreciation*, think growth. When you see words like *decrease* and *depreciation*, think decay.

Example

Carl's weight at 12 yr is 82 lb. Assume that his weight increases at a rate of 16% each year. Write an exponential function to model the increase. Calculate his weight after 5 yr.

Step 1: Find a and b.

$a = 82$ ← ***a* is the original amount.**

$b = 1 + 0.16$ ← ***b* is the growth or decay factor. If you are modeling growth, *b* equals 1 plus the percent. If you are modeling decay, *b* equals 1 minus the percent. Carl's weight increases, so add.**

$= 1.16$

Step 2: Write the exponential function.

$y = ab^x$ ← **Use the formula.**

$y = 82(1.16)^x$ ← **Substitute.**

Step 3: Calculate.

$y = 82(1.16)^5$ ← **Substitute 5 for *x*.**

$y = 172.228$ ← **Use a calculator.**

If the model is correct, Carl will weigh about 172 lb in 5 yr.

Exercises

Write an exponential function to model each situation. Find each amount after the specified time.

1. A tree 3 ft tall grows 8% each year. How tall will the tree be at the end of 14 yr? Round the answer to the nearest hundredth.
2. The price of a new home is $126,000. The value of the home appreciates 2% each year. How much will the home be worth in 10 yr?
3. A motorcycle purchased for $9,000 today will be worth 6% less each year. For what can you expect to sell the motorcycle at the end of 5 yr?

Name ______________________ Class ______________ Date ______________

Review 243

Properties of Exponential Functions

OBJECTIVE: Graphing exponential functions **MATERIALS:** Graphing calculator, graph paper

Example

Sketch the graph of $y = 2\left(\frac{1}{3}\right)^{x+1} - 4$ as a translation of $y = 2\left(\frac{1}{3}\right)^{x}$.

Step 1: Detemine the base of the function $y = 2\left(\frac{1}{3}\right)^{x}$. Since $b < 1$, the graph will represent exponential decay.

Step 2: Make a table. Find more values if necessary to get a good picture of the graph.

x	$y = 2\left(\frac{1}{3}\right)^{x}$	y
−2	$2\left(\frac{1}{3}\right)^{-2} = 2(9)$	18
−1	$2\left(\frac{1}{3}\right)^{-1} = 2(3)$	6
0	$2\left(\frac{1}{3}\right)^{0} = 2(1)$	2
1	$2\left(\frac{1}{3}\right)^{1} = 2\left(\frac{1}{3}\right)$	$\frac{2}{3}$
2	$2\left(\frac{1}{3}\right)^{2} = 2\left(\frac{1}{9}\right)$	$\frac{2}{9}$

Step 3: Use the values for x and y from the table to graph the function.

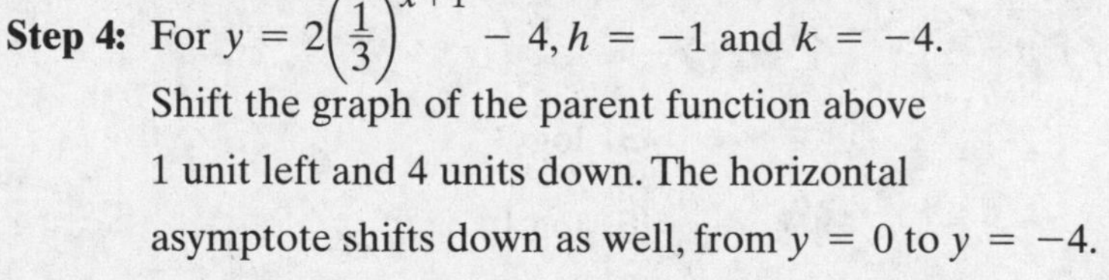

Step 4: For $y = 2\left(\frac{1}{3}\right)^{x+1} - 4$, $h = -1$ and $k = -4$. Shift the graph of the parent function above 1 unit left and 4 units down. The horizontal asymptote shifts down as well, from $y = 0$ to $y = -4$.

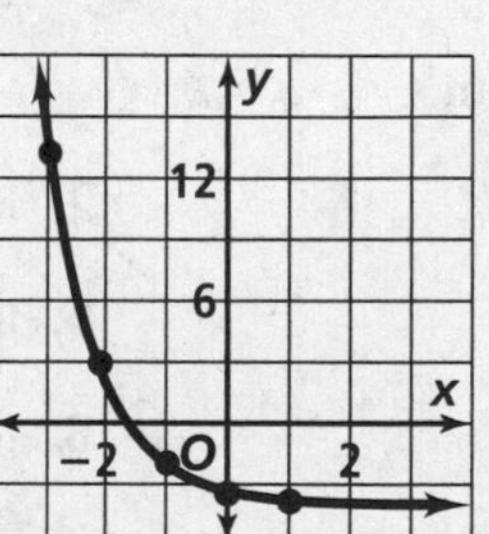

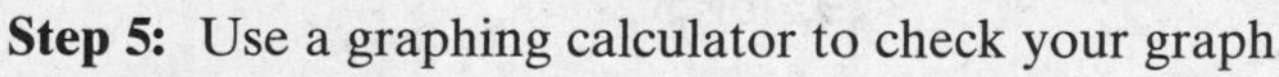

Step 5: Use a graphing calculator to check your graph.

Exercises

Graph each exponential function.

1. $y = \left(\frac{1}{5}\right)^{x}$
2. $y = 3^x + 1$
3. $y = 5^x$
4. $y = -\left(\frac{1}{2}\right)^{x}$
5. $y = -\left(\frac{1}{2}\right)^{x} + 4$
6. $y = \left(\frac{1}{4}\right)^{x}$
7. $y = \left(\frac{1}{4}\right)^{x-1}$
8. $y = 4^x + 1$
9. $y = -(2)^x$

Name ______________________ Class ______________ Date ______________

Review 244

OBJECTIVE: Evaluating logarithmic expressions **MATERIALS:** None

- A logarithmic function is the inverse or opposite of an exponential function.
- To evaluate logarithmic expressions, use the fact that $x = \log_b y$ means the same as $y = b^x$. Keep in mind that $x = \log y$ means $x = \log_{10} y$.

Example

Evaluate $\log_4 32$.

$x = \log_4 32$ ← **Write the equation in logarithmic form $x = \log_b y$.**

$32 = 4^x$ ← **Rewrite in exponential form $y = b^x$.**

$2^5 = (2^2)^x$ ← **Rewrite each side of the equation with like bases in order to solve the equation.**

$2^5 = 2^{2x}$ ← **Simplify.**

$5 = 2x$ ← **Set the exponents equal to each other.**

$x = \frac{5}{2}$ ← **Solve for x.**

$\log_4 32 = \frac{5}{2}$

Exercises

Evaluate the logarithm.

1. $\log_2 64$ **2.** $\log_4 64$ **3.** $\log_3 3^4$

4. $\log 10$ **5.** $\log 0.1$ **6.** $\log 1$

7. $\log_8 2$ **8.** $\log_{32} 2$ **9.** $\log_9 3$

Write each equation in exponential form.

10. $x = \log_3 8$ **11.** $2 = \log_5 25$ **12.** $\log 0.1 = -1$

13. $\log 7 = 0.845$ **14.** $\log 1000 = 3$ **15.** $-2 = \log 0.01$

16. $\log_3 81 = 4$ **17.** $\log_{49} 7 = \frac{1}{2}$ **18.** $\log_8 \frac{1}{4} = -\frac{2}{3}$

19. $\log_2 128 = 7$ **20.** $\log_5 \frac{1}{625} = -4$ **21.** $\log_6 36 = 2$

Name ______________________ Class ______________ Date ______________

Review 245

Properties of Logarithms

OBJECTIVE: Rewriting logarithmic expressions **MATERIALS:** None

- Logarithmic expressions can be rewritten using the **properties of logarithms.**

Product Property

$\log_b MN = \log_b M + \log_b N$

The log of a product is the sum of the logs of the factors.

Quotient Property

$\log_b \frac{M}{N} = \log_b M - \log_b N$

The log of a quotient is the difference of the logs of the numerator and denominator.

Power Property

$\log_b M^x = x \log_b M$

The log of an expression raised to an exponent is the exponent times the log of the expression.

Examples

Expand $\log_2 3x^4$.

$\log_2 3x^4 = \log_2 3 + \log_2 x^4 = \log_2 3 + 4\log_2 x$

Write $\log_5 6 - \log_5 4$ as a single logarithm.

$\log_5 6 - \log_5 4 = \log_5 \frac{6}{4} = \log_5 \frac{3}{2}$

Exercises

Use properties of logarithms to expand the following expressions.

1. $\log \frac{2}{3}$
2. $\log 6y$
3. $\log \frac{1}{5}$
4. $\log_3 x^3$
5. $\log_3 6xy$
6. $\log_6 36x^2$
7. $\log_5 xy$
8. $\log_3 \frac{x}{4}$
9. $\log_7 x^4$
10. $\log_3 x^2 y$
11. $\log_8 y^7$
12. $\log_5 x^4 y^3$

Use properties of logarithms to write each logarithmic expression as a single logarithm.

13. $\log_3 13 + \log_3 3$
14. $2 \log x + \log 5$
15. $\log_4 2 - \log_4 6$
16. $3 \log_3 3 - \log_3 3$
17. $\log_5 8 + \log_5 x$
18. $\log 2 - 2 \log x$
19. $\log_2 x + \log_2 y$
20. $3 \log_7 x - 5 \log_7 y$
21. $4 \log x + 3 \log x$
22. $\log_5 x + 3 \log_5 y$
23. $3 \log_2 x - \log_2 y$
24. $\log_2 16 - \log_2 8$

Name ______________________ Class ______________ Date ______________

Review 246

Exponential and Logarithmic Equations

OBJECTIVE: Using logarithms to solve exponential equations

MATERIALS: None

- When solving exponential equations, use inverse operations to isolate the variable. Remember that the inverse of raising to an exponent is taking the logarithm.

Example

Solve $7 - 5^{2x-1} = 4$.

$7 - 5^{2x-1} = 4$

$-5^{2x-1} = -3$ ⟵ **First isolate the term that has the variable in the exponent. Begin by subtracting 7 from each side.**

$5^{2x-1} = 3$ ⟵ **Multiply each side by −1.**

$\log_5 5^{2x-1} = \log_5 3$ ⟵ **Since the variable is in the exponent, use logarithms. Take $\log_5$ of each side since 5 is the base of the exponent.**

$(2x - 1)\log_5 5 = \log_5 3$ ⟵ **Use the Power Property of Logarithms.**

$2x - 1 = \log_5 3$ ⟵ **Simplify. (Recall that $\log_b b = 1$.)**

$2x - 1 = \frac{\log 3}{\log 5}$ ⟵ **Apply the Change of Base Formula.**

$2x = \frac{\log 3}{\log 5} + 1$ ⟵ **Add 1 to each side.**

$x = \frac{1}{2}\left(\frac{\log 3}{\log 5} + 1\right)$ ⟵ **Divide each side by 2.**

$x \approx 0.84$ ⟵ **Use a calculator to find a decimal approximation.**

Exercises

Solve each equation. Round the answer to the nearest hundredth.

1. $2^x = 5$

2. $10^{2x} = 8$

3. $5^{x+1} = 25$

4. $2^{x+3} = 9$

5 $3^{2x-3} = 7$

6. $4^x - 5 = 3$

7. $5 + 2^{x+6} = 9$

8. $4^{3x} + 2 = 3$

9. $1 - 3^{2x} = -5$

10. $2^{3x} - 2 = 13$

11. $5^{2x+7} - 1 = 8$

12. $7 - 2^{x+7} = 5$

Name ______________________ Class ______________ Date ______________

Review 247

Natural Logarithms

OBJECTIVE: Solving equations using natural logarithms	**MATERIALS:** Graphing calculator

- To solve equations that involve natural logarithms, use the following inverse properties:

  $\ln e^x = x$ $\quad$ $e^{\ln x} = x$

Example

Solve $4e^{2x} = 5$.

$4e^{2x} = 5$

$e^{2x} = \frac{5}{4}$ ⟵ **Divide each side by 4.**

$\ln e^{2x} = \ln 1.25$ ⟵ **Take the natural logarithm of each side since the base of the exponent is *e*.**

$2x = \ln 1.25$ ⟵ **Apply the inverse property $\ln e^x = x$.**

$x = \frac{\ln 1.25}{2}$ ⟵ **Divide each side by 2.**

$x \approx 0.112$ ⟵ **Use a calculator to approximate.**

The solution is $x \approx 0.112$.

Exercises

Solve each equation. Check your answers. Round answers to the nearest thousandth.

1. $2e^x = 4$

2. $e^{4x} = 25$

3. $e^x = 72$

4. $e^{3x} = 124$

5. $12e^{3x-2} = 8$

6. $\ln(x - 3) = 2$

7. $\ln 2x = 4$

8. $1 + \ln x^2 = 2$

9. $\ln(2x - 5) = 3$

Use the formula $A = Pe^{rt}$ to solve.

10. If $5000 is invested in a savings account that pays 7.85% interest compounded continuously, how much money will be in the account after 12 yr?

11. If $10,000 is invested in a savings account that pays 8.65% interest compounded continuously, in how many years will the balance be $250,000? Round to the nearest tenth.

Name ______________________ Class ______________ Date ______________

Review 248

OBJECTIVE: Identifying and solving inverse variations

MATERIALS: None

- In a direct variation, $y = kx$, as the value of one variable increases, so does the other. For inverse variation, $y = \frac{k}{x}$, as the value of one variable increases, the value of the other decreases.

Example

The time t that is necessary to complete a task varies inversely as the number of people p working. If it takes 4 h for 12 people to paint the exterior of a house, how long would it take for 3 people to do the same job?

$t = \frac{k}{p}$ ⟵ **Write an inverse variation. Since time is dependent on people, t is the dependent variable and p is the independent variable.**

$4 = \frac{k}{12}$ ⟵ **Substitute 4 for t and 12 for p.**

$48 = k$ ⟵ **Multiply both sides by 12 to solve for k, the constant of variation.**

$t = \frac{48}{p}$ ⟵ **Substitute 48 for k. This is the equation of the inverse variation.**

$t = \frac{48}{3} = 16$ ⟵ **Substitute 3 for p. Simplify to solve the equation.**

It would take 3 people 16 h to paint the exterior of the house.

Exercises

1. The time t needed to complete a task varies inversely as the number of people p. It takes 5 h for seven men to install a new roof. How long would it take ten men to complete the job?

2. The time t needed to drive a certain distance varies inversely as the speed r. It takes 7.5 h at 40 mi/h to drive a certain distance. How long would it take to drive the same distance at 60 mi/h?

3. The cost of each item bought is inversely proportional to the number of items when spending a fixed amount. When 42 items are bought, each costs $1.46. Find the number of items when each costs $2.16 each.

4. The length ℓ of a rectangle of a certain area varies inversely as the width w. The length of a rectangle is 9 cm when its width is 6 cm. Determine its length if its width is 8 cm.

Name ______________________ Class ______________ Date ______________

Review 249

Graphing Inverse Variations

OBJECTIVE: Identifying asymptotes and graphing inverse variations

MATERIALS: None

- An inverse variation equation has the form $y = \frac{k}{x}$. Its graph has vertical and horizontal asymptotes on the x- and y-axes.
- When an equation is of the form $y = \frac{k}{x - b} + c$, it is a translation of the inverse variation graph $y = \frac{k}{x}$. This means that the graph is moved b units to the left or right and c units up or down. The asymptotes are found at $x = b$ and $y = c$.

Example

Sketch the graph of $y = -\frac{6}{x - 3} + 2$, and include any asymptotes.

$y = -\frac{6}{x - 3} + 2$ ⟵ **Check to see that the equation is in $y = \frac{k}{x - b} + c$ form.**

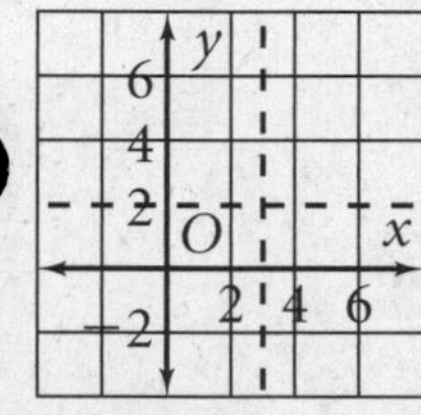

⟵ **Because $b = 3$ and $c = 2$, the vertical asymptote will occur at $x = 3$ and the horizontal asymptote at $y = 2$.**

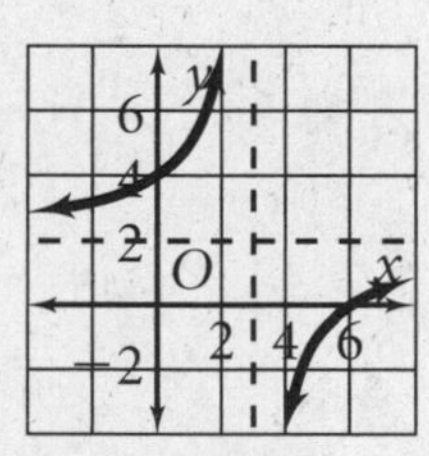

⟵ **Because k is negative, the branches occur in the upper–left and lower–right regions. When k is positive, the branches occur in the upper–right and lower–left regions.**

Exercises

Sketch the asymptotes and the graph of each function.

1. $y = \frac{8}{x}$
2. $y = -\frac{4}{x}$
3. $xy = 2$
4. $y = \frac{2}{x + 4}$
5. $y = -\frac{4}{x - 8}$
6. $y = -\frac{2}{x} + 3$
7. $y = \frac{1}{x} - 4$
8. $y = -\frac{2}{x + 3} - 3$
9. $y = \frac{2}{x - 3} + 4$
10. $y = \frac{3}{x - 2} - 4$
11. $y = \frac{2}{3x} + \frac{3}{2}$
12. $y = -\frac{2}{x + 2} + 3$

Name ______________________ Class ______________ Date ______________

Review 250

Rational Functions and Their Graphs

OBJECTIVE: Finding and classifying points of discontinuity

MATERIALS: None

Rational functions may have two different types of points of discontinuity.

- A hole is present at $x = a$ when a is a zero of both the numerator and the denominator.
- A vertical asymptote is present at $x = a$ when a is a zero of the denominator only.
- Find points of discontinuity before attempting to graph the function.

Example

Find and classify any points of discontinuity for $y = \frac{x^2 + x - 6}{3x^2 - 12}$.

$$y = \frac{x^2 + x - 6}{3x^2 - 12}$$

$$y = \frac{(x - 2)(x + 3)}{3(x - 2)(x + 2)}$$ ← **Factor the numerator and denominator completely.**

$$y = \frac{(x - 2)(x + 3)}{3(x - 2)(x + 2)}$$ ← **Circle common factors in the numerator and denominator to indicate holes.**

$$x - 2 = 0$$ ← **Use the Zero-Product Property to find the point of discontinuity.**

$$x = 2$$

$$x + 2 = 0$$
$$x = -2$$ ← **Use the Zero-Product Property with any remaining factors in the denominator to find the asymptotes.**

There is a hole at $x = 2$ and a vertical asymptote at $x = -2$.

ALGEBRA 2 TOPICS

Exercises

Find and classify any points of discontinuity.

1. $y = \frac{x}{x^2 - 9}$

2. $y = \frac{3x^2 - 1}{x^3}$

3. $y = \frac{6x^2 + 3}{x - 1}$

4. $y = \frac{5x^3 - 4}{x^2 + 4x - 5}$

5. $y = \frac{7x}{x^3 + 1}$

6. $y = \frac{12x^4 + 10x - 3}{3x^4}$

7. $y = \frac{12x + 24}{x^2 + 2x}$

8. $y = \frac{x^2 - 1}{x^2 + 3x + 2}$

9. $y = \frac{x^2 - 1}{x^2 - 2x - 3}$

Name ____________________ Class ____________ Date ____________

Review 251

Rational Expressions

OBJECTIVE: Multiplying and dividing rational expressions

MATERIALS: None

Example

Divide $\frac{x^2-2x-35}{2x^3-3x^2}$ by $\frac{7x-49}{4x^3-9x}$.

$$\frac{x^2-2x-35}{2x^3-3x^2} \div \frac{7x-49}{4x^3-9x}$$

$$= \frac{x^2-2x-35}{2x^3-3x^2} \cdot \frac{4x^3-9x}{7x-49}$$ ⟵ **Multiply by the reciprocal of the second expression.**

$$= \frac{(x-7)(x+5)}{x \cdot x(2x-3)} \cdot \frac{x(2x-3)(2x+3)}{7(x-7)}$$ ⟵ **Factor expressions completely.**

$$= \frac{\cancel{(x-7)}(x+5)}{\cancel{x} \cdot x\cancel{(2x-3)}} \cdot \frac{\cancel{x}\cancel{(2x-3)}(2x+3)}{7\cancel{(x-7)}}$$ ⟵ **Divide out common factors.**

$$= \frac{2x^2+13x+15}{7x}$$ ⟵ **Multiply remaining factors.**

Exercises

Multiply or divide. Write the result in simplest form.

1. $\frac{x^2-y^2}{(x-y)^2} \cdot \frac{1}{x+y}$
2. $\frac{a^2-a-6}{a^2-7a+12} \cdot \frac{a^2-2a-8}{a^2-3a-10}$
3. $\frac{3x+12}{2x-8} \div \frac{x^2+8x+16}{x^2-8x+16}$
4. $\frac{2x}{3x-12} \div \frac{x^2-2x}{x^2-6x+8}$
5. $\frac{4x^2-4x}{x^2+2x-3} \cdot \frac{x^2+x-6}{4x}$
6. $\frac{x^2+3x}{x^2+6x+8} \cdot \frac{-(x^2+x-2)}{4x^3+12x^2}$
7. $\frac{2x^2-16x}{x^2-9x+8} \div \frac{2x}{5x-5}$
8. $\frac{x-3}{x^2-5x-14} \div \frac{x^2-x-6}{x-7}$
9. $\frac{2x-10}{3x-21} \div \frac{x-5}{4x-28}$
10. $\frac{x^2-9x+14}{x^3+2x^2} \div \frac{x-2}{x+2}$
11. $\frac{x^2+2x-8}{x^2} \cdot \frac{x^2-3x}{x^2+x-12}$
12. $\frac{x^2+3x}{x^2-3x+2} \cdot \frac{x^2+x-2}{3x^2+9x}$
13. $\frac{4x-16}{4x} \div \frac{x^2-2x-8}{3x+6}$
14. $\frac{3x-12}{2x^2-8x} \div \frac{x^2+x-6}{x^3-4x}$
15. $\frac{x^4-9x^2}{x^3+3x^2} \cdot \frac{3x}{x^2-3x}$
16. $\frac{1}{x^4-x^3-2x^2} \cdot \frac{x^2-x-2}{x^2}$

ALGEBRA 2 TOPICS

Name ______________ Class ______________ Date ______________

Review 252

Adding and Subtracting Rational Expressions

OBJECTIVE: Adding and subtracting rational expressions

MATERIALS: None

- To find the sum or difference of two rational expressions with like denominators, simply add or subtract their numerators. Then write the answer over the common denominator.
- To find the sum or difference of two rational expressions with unlike denominators, first find the least common denominator. Then multiply each fraction by the factors needed to get the least common denominator. Remember, the factor(s) multiplied should always be in fraction form and equivalent to 1—for example, $\frac{x+1}{x+1}$.

Example

Subtract: $\frac{2x}{3x+5} - \frac{14}{x+7}$. Simplify, if possible.

$$\frac{2x}{3x+5} - \frac{14}{x+7}$$

$$\frac{2x}{(3x+5)} - \frac{14}{(x+7)}$$ ← **Circle the factors multiplied to get the least common denominator.**

$$= \frac{2x(x+7)}{(3x+5)(x+7)} - \frac{14(3x+5)}{(3x+5)(x+7)}$$ ← **Multiply as necessary to rewrite with the least common denominator.**

$$= \frac{(2x^2+14x)}{(3x+5)(x+7)} - \frac{(42x+70)}{(3x+5)(x+7)}$$ ← **Use the Distributive Property in the numerator.**

$$= \frac{2x^2+14x-42x-70}{(3x+5)(x+7)}$$ ← **Subtract the numerators of the fractions.**

$$= \frac{2x^2-28x-70}{(3x+5)(x+7)}$$ ← **Combine like terms.**

The difference is $\frac{2x^2-28x-70}{(3x+5)(x+7)}$.

ALGEBRA 2 TOPICS

Exercises

Add or subtract. Simplify, if possible.

1. $\frac{3}{2a+3} + \frac{2a}{2a+3}$

2. $\frac{y}{y-1} + \frac{2}{1-y}$

3. $\frac{3}{x+2} + \frac{2}{x^2-4}$

4. $\frac{y}{y^2-y-20} + \frac{2}{y+4}$

5. $\frac{x}{x^2+5x+6} - \frac{2}{x^2+3x+2}$

6. $\frac{4x+1}{x^2-4} - \frac{3}{x-2}$

7. $-\frac{2}{7x} - \frac{5}{4x}$

8. $\frac{12x^2-x+9}{3x+33} - \frac{16}{x+11}$

9. $\frac{4}{x^2+3x} + \frac{5}{x^3-2x^2}$

Name ____________________ Class ____________ Date ____________

Review 253

Solving Rational Equations

OBJECTIVE: Solving rational equations **MATERIALS:** None

- When one side of a rational equation has a sum or difference, multiply each side by the LCD. This eliminates the fractions.

Example

Solve the equation.

$$\frac{6}{x} + \frac{x}{2} = 4$$

$2x\left(\frac{6}{x}\right) + 2x\left(\frac{x}{2}\right) = 2x(4)$ ← **Multiply the LCD, 2x, by each term.**

$2\cancel{x}\left(\frac{6}{\cancel{x}}\right) + \cancel{2}x\left(\frac{x}{\cancel{2}}\right) = 2x(4)$ ← **Cancel where possible.**

$12 + x^2 = 8x$ ← **Simplify.**

$x^2 - 8x + 12 = 0$ ← **Write the equation in standard form.**

$(x - 2)(x - 6) = 0$ ← **Factor.**

$x - 2 = 0 \quad x - 6 = 0$ ← **Use the Zero-Product Property to solve for x.**

$x = 2 \quad x = 6$

Exercises

Solve each equation. Check each solution.

1. $\frac{10}{x+3} + \frac{10}{3} = 6$

2. $-\frac{1}{x-3} = \frac{x-4}{x^2-27}$

3. $\frac{6}{x-1} + \frac{2x}{x-2} = 2$

4. $\frac{7}{3x-12} - \frac{1}{x-4} = \frac{2}{3}$

5. $\frac{2x}{5} = \frac{x^2-5x}{5x}$

6. $\frac{8(x-1)}{x^2-4} = \frac{4}{x-2}$

7. $x + \frac{4}{x} = \frac{25}{6}$

8. $\frac{2}{x} + \frac{6}{x-1} = \frac{6}{x^2-x}$

9. $\frac{2}{x} + \frac{1}{x} = 3$

10. $\frac{4}{x-1} = \frac{5}{x-1} + 2$

11. $\frac{1}{x} = \frac{5}{2x} + 3$

12. $\frac{x+6}{5} = \frac{2x-4}{5} - 3$

13. Quinn can refinish hardwood floors four times as fast as Jack. They have to refinish 100 ft^2 of flooring. Working together, Quinn and Jack can finish the job in 3 hours. How long would it take each of them working alone?

Name ______________________ Class ______________ Date ______________

Review 254

Probability of Multiple Events

OBJECTIVE: Finding probabilities of multiple events

MATERIALS: Colored pencils

Example

Find the probability. A cage at the pet store contains ten white mice. Out of the ten, there are four females and six males. There are also ten black mice, of which six are female and four are male. Suppose you reach into the cage and randomly pick one mouse. What is the probability that the one you selected is female or black?

Step 1: Make a table of possibilities. These are events that can happen at the same time. The events are not mutually exclusive.

Step 2: Find *P*(female) by putting a circle around each female mouse.

$$P(\text{female}) = \frac{10}{20} = \frac{1}{2}$$

Step 3: Find *P*(black) by putting an "X" through each black mouse.

$$P(\text{black}) = \frac{10}{20} = \frac{1}{2}$$

Step 4: Find the events that have both a circle and an "X."

$$P(\text{female and black}) = \frac{6}{20} = \frac{3}{10}$$

Step 5: Use the formula $P(A \text{ or } B) = P(A) + P(B) - P(A \text{ and } B)$ to find *P*(female or black).

$$\frac{10}{20} + \frac{10}{20} - \frac{6}{20} = \frac{14}{20} = \frac{7}{10}, \text{ or } 70\%$$

The probability that you select a mouse that is female or black is 70%.

(f) w	(f) w	(f) w	(f) w
m w	m w	m w	m w
m w	m w	(f) b̸	(f) b̸
(f) b̸	(f) b̸	(f) b̸	(f) b̸
m b̸	m b̸	m b̸	m b̸

Exercises

Find the probability of each event.

1. Use the information from the example above to find the probability of selecting a mouse that is either white or male. Use the same table, but use a pencil of a different color.

2. A bag of marbles contains 13 marbles that are opaque and 32 marbles that are translucent. Of the opaque marbles, 3 are red, 5 are blue, and 5 are green. Of the translucent marbles, 8 are red, 12 are blue and 12 are green. What is the probability that you randomly pick a marble that is red or opaque?

3. Use the table you constructed for Exercise 2 and a different color marker to find the probability that you randomly pick a marble that is green or translucent.

ALGEBRA 2 TOPICS

Name ______________________ Class ______________ Date ______________

Review 255

OBJECTIVE: Graphing conic sections **MATERIALS:** Graph paper

- To graph a conic section, make a table of values, and plot the points associated with those values.
- In the case of a circle or ellipse, connect the points with a smooth curve.
- In the case of hyperbola, connect the points with two smooth curves.
- Determine the lines of symmetry, the domain, and the range from the graph.

Example

Graph the equation $4x^2 + 9y^2 = 36$. Identify the conic section and its lines of symmetry. Then find the domain and range.

Make a table of values.

x	−3	−2	−1	0	1	2	3
y	0	±1.5	±1.9	±2	±1.9	±1.5	0

← **Substitute each *x*-value into the equation. Solve for *y*.**

Plot the points, and connect them with a smooth curve.

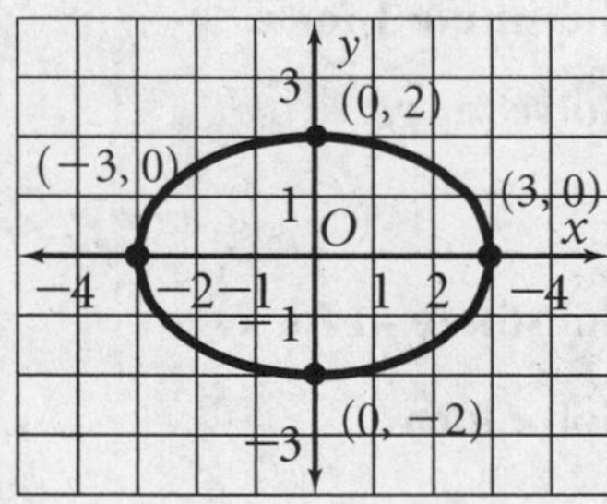

← **The graph should be symmetric.**

The graph shows that the equation is an ellipse. It has two lines of symmetry: the *x*-axis and the *y*-axis.

The domain is $\{x \mid -3 \le x \le 3\}$. The range is $\{y \mid -2 \le y \le 2\}$.

Exercises

Graph each equation. Identify the conic section and its lines of symmetry. Then find the domain and range.

1. $25x^2 + 4y^2 = 100$ **2.** $x^2 + y^2 = 36$ **3.** $4x^2 - y^2 = 16$

4. $3x^2 + 3y^2 = 27$ **5.** $9x^2 + 4y^2 = 36$ **6.** $5x^2 - 4y^2 = 80$

Name ____________________ Class ____________ Date ____________

Review 256

OBJECTIVE: Graphing parabolas **MATERIALS:** Graph paper

Example

Graph the equation $y = -\frac{1}{2}x^2$. Include the vertex, focus, and directrix on your graph.

Step 1:

Identify information from the given equation.

$y = -\frac{1}{2}x^2$

$a < 0$ ← ***a* is negative.**

opens downward ← **When *a* is negative, the parabola has these characteristics.**

focus: $(0, -c)$

directrix: $y = c$

Step 2:

Find c.

$|a| = \frac{1}{4c}$ ← **True for all parabolas.**

$\left|-\frac{1}{2}\right| = \frac{1}{4c}$ ← **Substitute $-\frac{1}{2}$ *a*.**

$(2c)\left|-\frac{1}{2}\right| = (2c)\frac{1}{4c} = \frac{1}{2}$ ← **Solve for *c*.**

Step 3:

Find the vertex, the focus, and the equation of the directrix.

$(0, 0)$ ← **The parabola is of the form $y = ax^2$, so the vertex is at the origin.**

$\left(0, -\frac{1}{2}\right)$ ← **The focus is always $(0, -c)$.**

$y = \frac{1}{2}$ ← **The directrix is at $y = c$.**

Step 4:

Locate two more points on the parabola.

$y = -\frac{1}{2}(1)^2$

$y = -\frac{1}{2}$ ← **Substitute 1 for *x*.**

$\left(1, -\frac{1}{2}\right)$ ← **Solve for *y*.**

$y = -\frac{1}{2}(-1)^2$

$y = -\frac{1}{2}$ ← **Substitute –1 for *x*.**

$\left(-1, -\frac{1}{2}\right)$ ← **Solve for *y*.**

Step 5:

Graph the parabola using the information you found.

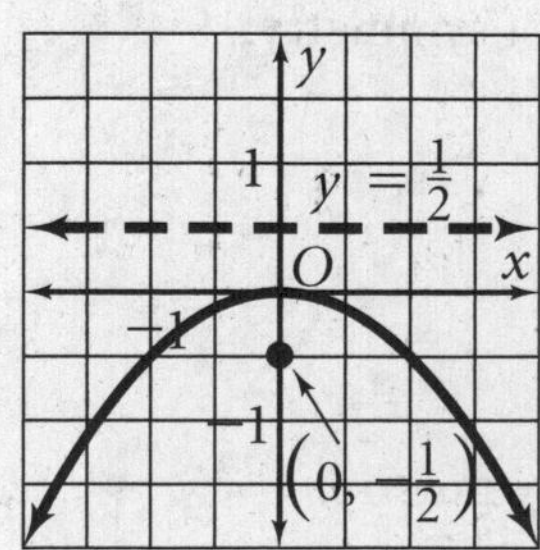

Exercises

Graph each equation. Include the vertex, focus, and directrix on each graph.

1. $y = \frac{1}{4}x^2$
2. $y = -\frac{1}{6}x^2$
3. $x = -\frac{1}{3}y^2$
4. $x = \frac{3}{4}y^2$
5. $y = x^2$
6. $x = \frac{1}{2}y^2$

Name ______________________ Class ______________ Date ______________

Review 257

OBJECTIVE: Finding the center and radius of a circle

MATERIALS: None

- When working with circles, begin by writing the equation in standard form:

$$(x - h)^2 + (y - k)^2 = r^2$$

- Unlike equations of parabolas, which include either x^2 or y^2, the equation of a circle will include both x^2 and y^2.

Example

Find the radius and center of the circle with equation $(x - 2)^2 + (x + 3)^2 = 16$.

$(x - 2)^2 + (y + 3)^2 = 16$	← **The given equation is in standard form.**
$(x - 2)^2 + (y - (-3))^2 = 16$	← **Because standard form has $(y - k)$, change the addition to subtraction.**
$h = 2, k = -3$	← **Find h and k.**
$(2, -3)$	← **The center is (h, k).**
$r^2 = 16$	← **Find r.**
$r = 4$	← **Take the square root of each side. Since radius is a distance, ignore the negative value.**

The center is $(2, -3)$ and the radius is 4.

Exercises

Find the radius and center of each circle.

1. $(x - 5)^2 + (y - 2)^2 = 9$

2. $(x + 8)^2 + (y - 4)^2 = 8$

3. $(x - 4)^2 + (y + 3)^2 = 20$

4. $(x - 3)^2 + y^2 = 6$

5. $x^2 + (y - 5)^2 = 25$

6. $(x + 6)^2 + (y + 7)^2 = 1$

7. $(x + 1)^2 + (y + 2)^2 = 36$

8. $(x - 2)^2 + (y - 5)^2 = 4$

9. $x^2 + y^2 = 4$

10. $(x - 1)^2 + (y + 3)^2 = 9$

11. $(x - 2)^2 + (y - 3)^2 = 12$

12. $(x + 1)^2 + (y - 3)^2 = 25$

13. $x^2 + (y + 3)^2 = 45$

14. $(x + 4)^2 + y^2 = 63$

15. $(x + 2)^2 + (y - 6)^2 = 75$

16. $(x - 7)^2 + (y + 3)^2 = 18$

17. $(x - 4)^2 + (y + 1)^2 = 24$

18. $(x + 9)^2 + (y - 9)^2 = 81$

Name ____________ Class ____________ Date ____________

Review 258

OBJECTIVE: Writing the equation of an ellipse **MATERIALS:** None

To find the standard form of the equation of an ellipse with center at (0, 0), major axis of length $2a$, and minor axis of length $2b$, where $a > b$, use the following:

- When the width is greater than the height, use $\frac{x^2}{a^2} + \frac{y^2}{b^2} = 1$.
- When the height is greater than the width, use $\frac{x^2}{b^2} + \frac{y^2}{a^2} = 1$.

Example

Find the equation of an ellipse that is 10 units wide and 8 units high. Assume that the center is (0, 0).

$\frac{x^2}{a^2} + \frac{y^2}{b^2} = 1$ ⟵ **Since the width is greater than the height, use the standard form of a horizontal ellipse.**

$2a = 10 \quad 2b = 8$ ⟵ **Find *a* and *b*.**

$a = 5 \quad b = 4$

$a^2 = 25 \quad b^2 = 16$ ⟵ **Find a^2 and b^2.**

$\frac{x^2}{25} + \frac{y^2}{16} = 1$ ⟵ **Substitute 25 for a^2 and 16 for b^2.**

Exercises

Find the equation of the ellipse given the height and width. Assume that the center of the ellipse is (0, 0).

1. height 26 ft, width 24 ft
2. height 12 ft, width 4 ft
3. height 10 ft, width 6 ft
4. height 6 ft, width 18 ft
5. height 20 m, width 50 m
6. height 10 ft, width 22 ft
7. height 16 m, width 18 m
8. height 20 ft, width 3 ft
9. height 3 cm, width 6 cm
10. height 14 m, width 30 m
11. height 12 ft, width 9 ft
12. height 12 in., width 4 in.
13. height 7 m, width 8 m
14. height 2 in., width 10 in.
15. height 16 cm, width 9 cm

16. Australian Rules Football is played on an elliptical field. One of the fields used for this sport is 174 meters long and 148 meters wide. Find an equation of the ellipse.

Name ____________ Class ____________ Date ____________

Review 259

OBJECTIVE: Graphing hyperbolas **MATERIALS:** Graph paper

- Because the equation of a hyperbola involves subtraction, there are two possibilities for standard form. Put the positive variable first, and the result is either $\frac{x^2}{a^2} - \frac{y^2}{b^2} = 1$ or $\frac{y^2}{a^2} - \frac{x^2}{b^2} = 1$. Note that the a^2 is always the denominator of the first term.
- When the x^2-term is positive, the hyperbola opens to the left and to the right. When the y^2-term is positive, the hyperbola opens upward and downward.

Example

Graph $16y^2 - 9x^2 = 144$.

$\frac{y^2}{9} - \frac{x^2}{16} = 1$ ⟵ **Divide by 144 on both sides of the equation.**

$\frac{y^2}{3^2} - \frac{x^2}{4^2} = 1$ ⟵ **Convert to standard form $\frac{y^2}{a^2} - \frac{x^2}{b^2} = 1$.**

$a = 3$ and $b = 4$ ⟵ **Find a and b.**

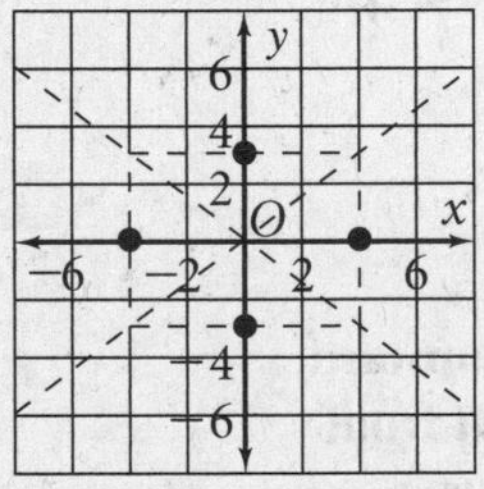

⟵ **Put points at ±3 on the y-axis and at ±4 on the x-axis. Use these to draw a central rectangle and the asymptotes.**

$3^2 + 4^2 = c^2$ ⟵ **Use $a^2 + b^2 = c^2$ to find c. Simplify.**

$c = \pm 5$

The foci are $(0, 5)$ and $(0, -5)$. ⟵ **Find the foci using $(0, c)$ and $(0, -c)$.**

⟵ **Sketch the hyperbola using the vertices $(0, \pm 3)$.**

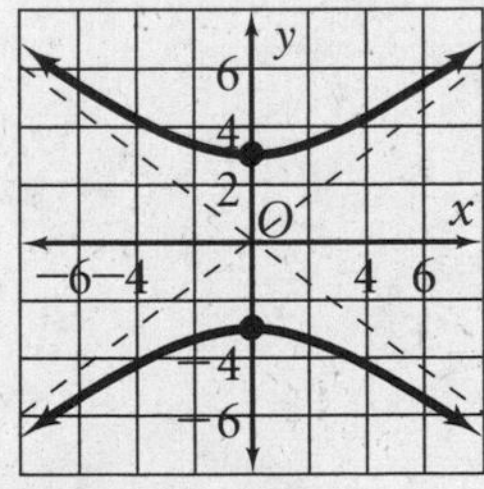

Exercises

Find the foci of each hyperbola. Then draw the graph.

1. $\frac{x^2}{9} - \frac{y^2}{1} = 1$

2. $\frac{y^2}{16} - \frac{x^2}{4} = 1$

3. $4x^2 - y^2 = 4$

4. $y^2 - 4x^2 = 4$

5. $x^2 - y^2 = 3$

6. $9y^2 - 25x^2 = 225$

Name ______________________ Class ______________ Date ______________

Review 260

OBJECTIVE: Writing and identifying the equation of a translated conic section

MATERIALS: Graph paper

Example

Identify the conic section $4x^2 + 4y^2 + 20x - 16y + 37 = 0$.
Rewrite the equation in standard form. Then sketch the graph.

$$4x^2 + 4y^2 + 20x - 16y + 37 = 0$$

$$4x^2 + 20x + 4y^2 - 16y + 37 = 0$$ ← **Group the *x*- and *y*-terms.**

$$4x^2 + 20x + 4y^2 - 16y = -37$$ ← **Subtract 37 from each side.**

$$4(x^2 + 5x) + 4(y^2 - 4y) = -37$$ ← **Factor out coefficients of the x^2- and the y^2-terms.**

$$4\left(x^2 + 5x + \frac{25}{4}\right) + 4(y^2 - 4y + 4) = -37 + 25 + 16$$ ← **Complete the square.**

$$4\left(x + \frac{5}{2}\right)^2 + 4(y - 2)^2 = 4$$ ← **Simplify.**

$$\left(x + \frac{5}{2}\right)^2 + (y - 2)^2 = 1$$ ← **Divide each side by 4.**

There are no denominators, and both x and y have squared terms.
The equation fits the standard form of a circle. The center of the circle is $\left(-\frac{5}{2}, 2\right)$ and the radius of the circle is 1.

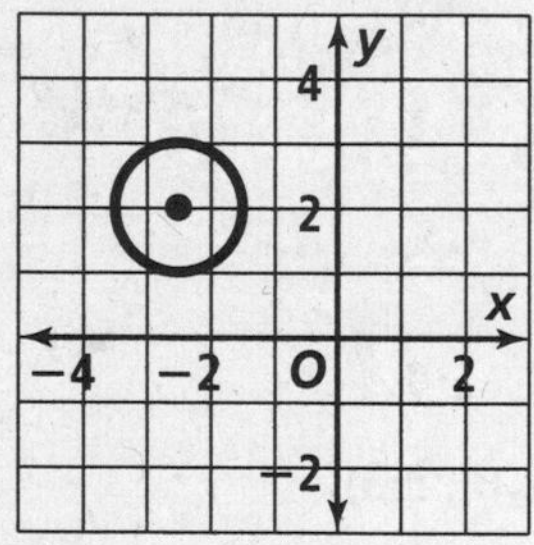

← **Graph the center. Plot points 1 unit upward, downward, to the right and to the left from the center. Connect with a smooth curve.**

Exercises

Identify the conic section represented by each equation by writing the equation in standard form. Then sketch the graph.

1. $x^2 - 2x + 4y - 3 = 0$

2. $x^2 + 4y^2 + 6x - 8y + 9 = 0$

3. $9x^2 - 4y^2 + 18x + 16y - 43 = 0$

4. $x^2 + y^2 + 10x - 6y + 18 = 0$

5. $y^2 - 8x - 6y + 9 = 0$

6. $4x^2 + y^2 + 64x - 12y + 288 = 0$

7. $y^2 - 4x - 4y + 16 = 0$

8. $x^2 - 4y^2 - 2x - 8y - 7 = 0$

Review 261

OBJECTIVE: Finding the *n*th term in a sequence **MATERIALS:** None

Some patterns are much easier to determine than others. Here are some tips that can help with unfamiliar patterns.

- If the terms become progressively smaller, subtraction or division may be involved.
- If the terms become progressively larger, addition or multiplication may be involved.

Example

Find the next term in this sequence: 6, 8, 11, 15, 20, . . .

6 8 11 15 20	⟵	**Spread the numbers in the sequence apart, leaving space between numbers.**
+2 +3 +4 +5	⟵	**Beneath each space, write what can be done to get the next number in the sequence.**
In each term, the number that is added to the previous term increases by one.	⟵	**Find a pattern.**

If the pattern is continued, the next term is 20 + 6, or 26.

Exercises

Describe the pattern that is formed. Find the next three terms.

1. 38, 33, 28, 23, . . .

2. 7, 14, 28, 56, . . .

3. −5, −7, −9, −11, . . .

4. 2, 6, 18, 54, . . .

5. 4.5, 5, 5.5, 6, . . .

6. 17, 19, 23, 29, . . .

Match each sequence on the left with a statement on the right.

7. 9, 15, 21, 27, . . .

8. 9, 10.5, 13.5, 19.5, . . .

9. 3, 2.5, 1.5, 0, . . .

10. −4, 4, 12, 20, . . .

11. 32, 16, 8, 4, . . .

12. 2, 4, 8, 16, . . .

A. The next term in the sequence is −2.

B. The sixth term is 39.

C. Each term is one half of the previous term.

D. Each term is two times the previous term.

E. The fifth term is 31.5.

F. The eighth term is 52.

Name ______________ Class ______________ Date ______________

Review 262

Arithmetic Sequences

OBJECTIVE: Finding the nth term of an arithmetic sequence

MATERIALS: None

Example

Find the 15th term of an arithmetic sequence whose first three terms are 20, 16.5, and 13.

$20 - 16.5 = 3.5$
$16.5 - 13 = 3.5$ ← **First, find the common difference. The difference between consecutive terms is 3.5. The sequence decreases. The common difference is −3.5.**

$a_n = a_1 + (n - 1)d$ ← **Use the explicit formula.**

$a_{15} = 20 + (15 - 1)(-3.5)$ ← **Substitute $a_1 = 20$, $n = 15$, and $d = -3.5$.**

$= 20 + (14)(-3.5)$ ← **Subtract within parentheses.**

$= 20 + -49$ ← **Multiply.**

$= -29$ ← **The 15th term is −29.**

Check the answer. Write $a_1, a_2, \ldots, a_{15}$ down the left side of your paper. Start with $a_1 = 20$. Subtract 3.5 and record 16.5 next to a_2. Continue until you find a_{15}.

Exercises

Find the 25th term of each sequence.

1. 20, 18, 16, 14, . . .

2. 0.0057, 0.0060, 0.0063, . . .

3. 4, 0, −4, −8, . . .

4. 0.2, 0.7, 1.2, 1.7, . . .

5. −10, −8.8, −7.6, −6.4, . . .

6. 22, 26, 30, 34, . . .

7. Suppose you begin to work selling ads for a newspaper. You will be paid \$50.00/wk plus a minimum of \$7.50 for each potential customer you contact. What is the least amount of money you earn after contacting eight businesses in 1 wk?

8. In March, Jaime starts a savings account for a mountain bike. He initially deposits \$15.00. He decides to increase each deposit by \$8.00. How much is his seventeenth deposit?

9. Sue is knitting a blanket for her infant niece. Each day, she knits four more rows than the day before. She knitted seven rows on Sunday. How many rows did she knit on the following Saturday?

Name ______________________ Class ______________ Date ______________

Review 263

OBJECTIVE: Finding the nth term of a geometric sequence

MATERIALS: None

- A geometric sequence has a constant ratio between consecutive terms. This ratio is the common ratio.
- A geometric sequence formula can be written as a recursive formula, $a_n = a_{n-1} \cdot r$, or as an explicit formula, $a_n = a_1 \cdot r^{n-1}$.

Example

Find the 12th term of the geometric sequence 5, 15, 45, ...

5, 15, 45, . . .

$r = \frac{15}{5} = \frac{45}{15} = 3$ ⟵ **Find r by calculating the common ratio between consecutive terms. This is a geometric sequence because there is a common ratio between consecutive terms.**

$a_n = 5(3)^{n-1}$ ⟵ **Substitute $a_1 = 5$ and $r = 3$ into the explicit formula to find a formula for the nth term of the sequence.**

$a_{12} = 5(3)^{11}$ ⟵ **Substitute $n = 12$ to find the 12th term of the sequence.**

$a_{12} = 885{,}735$ ⟵ **Remember to first calculate 3^{11}, then multiply by 5.**

Exercises

Find the indicated term of the geometric sequence.

1. $4, 2, 1, \ldots$ Find a_{10}.

2. $5, \frac{15}{2}, \frac{45}{4}, \ldots$ Find a_8.

3. $6, -2, \frac{2}{3}, \ldots$ Find a_{12}.

4. $1, -\frac{2}{3}, \frac{4}{9}, \ldots$ Find a_7.

5. $100, 200, 400, \ldots$ Find a_9.

6. $8, 32, 128, \ldots$ Find a_4.

Write the explicit formula for each sequence. Then generate the first five terms.

7. $a_1 = 1, r = \frac{1}{2}$

8. $a_1 = 2, r = 3$

9. $a_1 = 12, r = 3$

10. $a_1 = 1, r = \frac{1}{4}$

11. $a_1 = 5, r = \frac{1}{10}$

12. $a_1 = 1, r = \frac{1}{3}$

13. $a_1 = 5, r = 2$

14. $a_1 = 1, r = 3$

15. $a_1 = 3, r = 6$

16. $a_1 = 3, r = 3$

17. $a_1 = 2, r = 2$

18. $a_1 = 2, r = \frac{1}{2}$

19. $a_1 = 1, r = \frac{1}{5}$

20. $a_1 = 3, r = 4$

21. $a_1 = 5, r = \frac{1}{4}$

Name ______________________ Class ______________ Date ____________

Review 264

OBJECTIVE: Finding the sum of a given number of terms of a series

MATERIALS: None

Example

Evaluate the series $\sum_{n=2}^{4}(5-2n)$.

$\sum_{n=②}^{④}\boxed{(5-2n)}$ ← **Circle the upper and lower limits. Box the explicit formula.**

(n = 2) (n = 3) (n = 4) ← **In circles, write all possible values of *n*, beginning with the lower limit and ending with the upper limit.**

(n = 2) (n = 3) (n = 4)

$\boxed{5-2(2)}$ $\boxed{5-2(3)}$ $\boxed{5-2(4)}$ ← **Under each circle, draw a box; copy the explicit formula, substituting the value in the circle above the box for the value of *n*.**

(n = 2) (n = 3) (n = 4)

$\sum_{n=2}^{4}(5-2n) = \boxed{5-2(2)} + \boxed{5-2(3)} + \boxed{5-2(4)}$ ← **The value of the series is the sum of the values in the boxes.**

$= 1 + (-1) + (-3)$ ← **Evaluate each expression.**

$= -3$ ← **Find the sum of the terms.**

The sum of the series is −3.

Exercises

Evaluate each series.

1. $\sum_{n=1}^{3}(n-4)$

2. $\sum_{n=1}^{4}\frac{1}{3n}$

3. $\sum_{n=3}^{8}(3n-1)$

4. $\sum_{n=3}^{8}\frac{2n}{3}$

5. $\sum_{n=3}^{9}(4-2n)$

6. $\sum_{n=1}^{5}8n$

7. $\sum_{n=2}^{7}4n$

8. $\sum_{n=1}^{7}(3-2n)$

9. $\sum_{n=2}^{5}(5n+1)$

10. An outdoor amphitheater has 45 rows of seats. The first row has 89 seats. The last row has 177 seats. Each row has 2 more seats than the previous row. Write an explicit formula representing the number of seats in the *n*th row. Then find the sum of the 45 rows of seats.

Name ______________________ Class ______________ Date ______________

Review 265

Geometric Series

OBJECTIVE: Finding the sum of a finite and of an infinite geometric series	**MATERIALS:** None

- The sum of a finite geometric series is the sum of the terms of a geometric sequence. This sum can be found by using the formula $S_n = \frac{a_1(1 - r^n)}{1 - r}$, where a_1 is the first term, r is the common ratio, and n is the number of terms.
- The sum of an infinite geometric series with $|r| < 1$ is found by using the formula $S = \frac{a_1}{1 - r}$, where a_1 is the first term and r is the common ratio. If $|r| \geq 1$, then the series has no sum.

Example

Find the sum of the first ten terms of the series $8 + 16 + 32 + 64 + 128 + \ldots$

$a_1 = 8$ ⟵ **a_1 is the first term in the series.**

$r = \frac{16}{8} = \frac{32}{16} = \frac{64}{32} = \frac{128}{64} = 2$ ⟵ **Simplify the ratio formed by any two consecutive terms to find r.**

$n = 10$ ⟵ **n is the number of terms in the series to be added together.**

$S_{10} = \frac{8(1 - 2^{10})}{1 - 2}$ ⟵ **Substitute $a_1 = 8$, $r = 2$, and $n = 10$ into the formula for the sum of a finite geometric series.**

$= \frac{8(-1023)}{-1}$ ⟵ **Simplify inside the parentheses.**

$= 8184$ ⟵ **Simplify.**

Exercises

Evaluate the series to the given term.

1. $3 + 12 + 48 + 192 + \ldots; S_6$

2. $8 + 2 + \frac{1}{2} + \frac{1}{8} + \ldots; S_5$

3. $-10 - 5 - 2.5 - 1.25 - \ldots; S_7$

4. $10 + (-5) + \frac{5}{2} + \left(-\frac{5}{4}\right) + \ldots; S_{11}$

Evaluate each infinite geometric series.

5. $10 + 5 + 2.5 + \ldots$

6. $-1 + \frac{2}{11} - \frac{4}{121} + \ldots$

7. $\frac{1}{4} + \frac{7}{32} + \frac{49}{256} + \ldots$

8. $\frac{1}{2} - \frac{1}{5} + \frac{2}{25} - \ldots$

9. $-\frac{1}{6} + \frac{1}{12} - \frac{1}{24} + \ldots$

10. $20 + 16 + \frac{64}{5} + \ldots$

11. $12 + 4 + \frac{4}{3} + \ldots$

12. $\frac{1}{4} - \frac{1}{8} + \frac{1}{16} - \ldots$

13. $\frac{2}{3} + \frac{2}{15} + \frac{2}{75} + \ldots$

Name ______________________ Class ______________ Date ______________

Review 266

Area Under a Curve

OBJECTIVE: Developing area under a curve as a series

MATERIALS: Graph paper, colored pencils

You can use rectangles to approximate the area under the curve $f(x)$. You can use summation notation to represent the sum of the areas of these rectangles.

$$A = \sum_{n=1}^{b} (w)f(a_n)$$

b ← number of rectangles

width of each rectangle (w) function value at a_n

Example

Graph $f(x) = x^2 + 2$. Use inscribed rectangles 0.5 units wide to approximate the area under the curve for $0 \le x \le 2$.

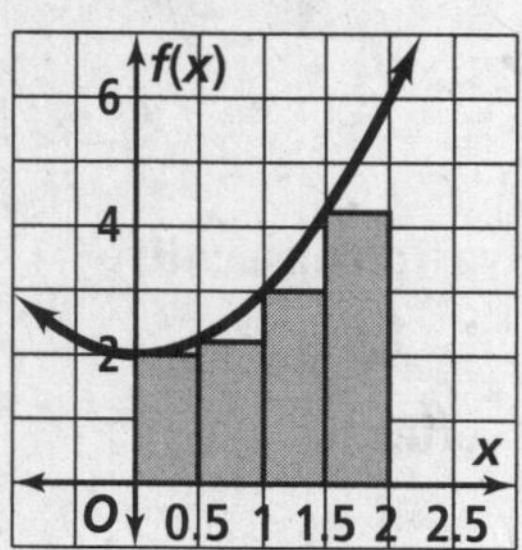

← **Draw the curve on the grid.**

← **Determine and label the interval endpoints. Counting from 0 to 2 by 0.5 units, we get 4 intervals with endpoints at 0, 0.5, 1, 1.5, and 2.**

← **Draw segments from these endpoints on the x-axis to the graph of f. When using inscribed rectangles, the shortest of each consecutive pair of segments represents the height of the rectangle. Draw and shade these 4 rectangles.**

$A = \sum_{n=1}^{b} (w)f(a_n)$ ← **Write the formula.**

$= \sum_{n=1}^{4} (0.5)f(a_n)$ ← **Substitute $b = 4$ since there are 4 rectangles, and $w = 0.5$ since each rectangle is 0.5 units wide.**

$= (0.5)f(a_1) + (0.5)f(a_2) + (0.5)f(a_3) + (0.5)f(a_4)$ ← **Expand the summation.**

$= (0.5)(2) + (0.5)(2.25) + (0.5)(3) + (0.5)(4.25)$ ← **$f(a_1)$ is the height of the first rectangle. This corresponds to $f(0)$ which is 2. Similarly determine the heights of the remaining rectangles: $f(0.5) = 2.25$, $f(1) = 3$, and $f(1.5) = 4.25$.**

$= 0.5(2 + 2.25 + 3 + 4.25)$ ← **Use the Distributive Property.**

$= 5.75$ ← **Simplify.**

The area is approximately 5.75 units^2.

Exercises

Use the method shown in the Example to approximate the area under each curve for the interval $0 \le x \le 2$. Use inscribed rectangles 0.5 unit wide.

1. $f(x) = 2x^2$

2. $f(x) = -x^2 + 4$

3. $y = 2x + 3$

4. $y = -x + 2$

5. $f(x) = x^2 + 1$

6. $f(x) = -x^2 + 6$

Name ______________________ Class ______________ Date ______________

Review 267

Probability Distributions

OBJECTIVE: Making a probability distribution **MATERIALS:** None

Example

Create a frequency table and a probability distribution to report the probability that a student in a class carries more than $1 in coins.

Step 1:

Ask each student to find the dollar amount of coins that they are carrying and record the data.

Student #	1	2	3	4	5	6	7	8	9	10	11	12	13	14	15
Amount	0.00	0.25	0.50	1.25	0.00	0.78	0.80	1.49	0.50	0.00	0.75	1.00	0.00	1.05	0.00

Step 2:
Organize the data into a frequency table.

Dollar amount of coins carried by students

Amount	**No. of students**
Less than $1.00	11
Exactly $1.00	1
More than $1.00	3
Total	15

Step 3:
Give the probability for each possibility.

P(less than $1.00) $= \frac{11}{15}$

P(exactly $1.00) $= \frac{1}{15}$

P(more than $1.00) $= \frac{3}{15}$

Check that the sum of the probabilities is 1.

$$\frac{11}{15} + \frac{1}{15} + \frac{3}{15} = \frac{15}{15} = 1$$

The probability that a student carries more than $1.00 in change is $\frac{3}{15}$ or $\frac{1}{5}$.

Exercises

Create a frequency table. Find the probability distribution for the following.

1. Average rainfall in inches for the month of April over the past 13 years in a city is as follows:
1.7 1.7 1.0 2.1 2.7 0.2 2.4 1.9 0.4 0.8 1.4 2.5 1.2
Report the probability that this city will have less than 1 in. of rain in April.

2. The status of professors in a university math department is as follows: tenured, nontenured, nontenured, tenured, beginning, nontenured, tenured, nontenured, nontenured, beginning, tenured, nontenured, beginning, nontenured, tenured
Report the probability that a professor in this department is tenured.

Name ______________________ Class ______________ Date ______________

Review 268

Conditional Probability

OBJECTIVE: Finding conditional probabilities **MATERIALS:** None

Example

A college computer lab has 100 computers. Some of these computers are personal computers (PCs), and others are Macintoshes (Macs). Some of the computers are new, and others are used. A student enters the lab and picks a computer at random. Find each probability.

Types of Computers in Lab

	PCs	Macs	Total
New	40	30	70
Used	20	10	30
Total	60	40	100

$P(\text{computer is new}) = \frac{70}{100}$ ⟵ **Write the probability as a ratio.**

$= \frac{7}{10}$ ⟵ **Reduce.**

$P(\text{computer is a PC}) = \frac{60}{100}$ ⟵ **Write *P* as a ratio.**

$= \frac{3}{5}$ ⟵ **Reduce.**

$P(\text{computer is new and a PC}) = \frac{40}{100}$ ⟵ **Write *P* as a ratio.**

$= \frac{2}{5}$ ⟵ **Reduce.**

Given that the computer is new, what is the probability that it is a Mac?

$P(\text{Mac} \mid \text{new}) = \frac{30}{70}$ ⟵ **Write *P* as a ratio.**

$= \frac{3}{7}$ ⟵ **Reduce.**

Given that the computer is used, what is the probability that it is a PC?

$P(\text{PC} \mid \text{used}) = \frac{20}{30}$ ⟵ **Write *P* as a ratio.**

$= \frac{2}{3}$ ⟵ **Reduce.**

Exercises

A bag contains 20 red balls with a blue dot and 15 red balls without the dot. In addition, the bag contains 30 white balls with a blue dot and 25 white balls without the dot. Use a table similar to the one above to find each probability.

1. $P(\text{red})$ **2.** $P(\text{white})$ **3.** $P(\text{with a dot})$

4. $P(\text{no dot})$ **5.** $P(\text{red and with a dot})$ **6.** $P(\text{white and no dot})$

7. $P(\text{red} \mid \text{with a dot})$ **8.** $P(\text{white} \mid \text{no dot})$ **9.** $P(\text{no dot} \mid \text{white})$

Name ______________________ Class ______________ Date ______________

Review 269

Analyzing Data

OBJECTIVE: Analyzing statistical data

MATERIALS: Number cube, two different-colored pencils

- When finding central tendencies, use these clues: The mode is the number that occurs most often. The median is the number that occurs in the middle. The mean is the average of data values.

Example

Find the mean, median, and mode for the values below.
2 2 5 5 1 4 6 6 3 5 3 4 3 2 4 4 5 2 4 1
3 5 4 3 5 3 4 3 5 3 3 1 5 6 3 1 1 4 4 1

Step 1: To find the mode, rewrite the data in numerical order from least to greatest. Draw circles around like data using one colored pencil. Record the frequency of each.
1 1 1 1 1 1 2 2 2 2 3 3 3 3 3 3 3 3 3 3 4 4 4 4 4 4 4 4 4
5 5 5 5 5 5 5 5 6 6 6
The mode is 3 because it occurs most often.

Step 2: To find the median, put a box around the middle value(s) with a different colored pencil.
1 1 1 1 1 1 2 2 2 2 3 3 3 3 3 3 3 3 3 3 4 4 4 4 4 4 4 4 4
5 5 5 5 5 5 5 5 6 6 6
Since there are two middle values, find their mean, or average.

$$\frac{(3 + 4)}{2} = \frac{7}{2} = 3.5$$

The median is 3.5.

Step 3: To find the mean, add all values and divide by the number of values.
$138 \div 40 = 3.45$.
The mean is 3.45.

Exercises

Find the mean, median, and mode for each set of values.

1. 872 888 895 870 882 878 891 890 888

2. 0.5 0.5 0.4 1.2 0.0 0.9 1.4 1.0 2.1 0.7 0.5 1.7

3. 2020 2040 2068 2120 2015 2301 2254

4. 322 101 245 289 135 409 375 185 340

5. 25 27 26 33 28 26 24 30 26 28 24 27

6. 8 9 21 12 7 24 14 21 10 14 18 21 16

7. 4.4 5.6 1.5 2.1 3.8 1.9 4.7 2.5 4.7 2.8

8. 6371 6378 6372 6371 6379 6380 6374

9. 194 502 413 768 986 616 259 351 825

10. 85 84 81 81 85 82 86 84 83 86 90 81

Name ______________________ Class ______________ Date ______________

Review 270

OBJECTIVE: Determining standard deviation **MATERIALS:** None

The standard deviation of a collection of numbers $(x_1, x_2, x_3, \ldots, x_n)$,

$$\sigma = \sqrt{\frac{(x_1 - \overline{x})^2 + (x_2 - \overline{x})^2 + \ldots + \ldots + (x_n - \overline{x})^2}{n}}$$, where $\overline{x}$ is the mean of $x_1, x_2, \ldots, x_n$.

Example

Find the standard deviation for 100, 158, 170, 192.

$$\overline{x} = \frac{100 + 158 + 170 + 192}{4}$$ ← **Find the mean.**

$$\overline{x} = 155$$

$$(100 - 155)^2 = 3025$$
$$(158 - 155)^2 = 9$$
$$(170 - 155)^2 = 225$$
$$(192 - 155)^2 = 1369$$

← **Subtract the mean from each value in the data set. Square each difference.**

$$\sigma = \sqrt{\frac{3025 + 9 + 255 + 1369}{4}}$$ ← **Find the standard deviation.**

$$= \sqrt{1157}$$

$$\approx 34$$

Exercises

Find the standard deviation of each set of values.

1. 6.5 7.0 9.0 8.0 7.5

2. 5.6 5.8 5.9 6.1

3. 201 203 208 210 211

4. 12 14 15 17 19

A family goes grocery shopping every week. In a month the costs of the groceries are \$72.42, \$91.50, \$58.99, and \$69.02.

5. What is the mean?

6. What is the standard deviation?

7. Within how many standard deviations of the mean is a cost of \$50.00?

8. Within how many standard deviations of the mean is a cost of \$102.00?

The distances driven by eight different vehicles using 12 gal of gasoline were 174 mi, 271 mi, 208 mi, 196 mi, 340 mi, 214 mi, 236 mi, and 385 mi.

9. Find the mean and the standard deviation for the distances traveled.

10. How many items in the data set fall within one standard deviation of the mean? Within two standard deviations?

Name ______________________ Class ______________ Date ______________

Review 271

Working with Samples

OBJECTIVE: Finding the margin of error	**MATERIALS:** None

- A random sample cannot be entirely accurate. The margin of error allows you to find the likely range for the true population proportion. The margin of error is $\pm\frac{1}{\sqrt{n}}$ for a sample of size n.

Example

A random sample of 784 high school students reports that 38% of them choose math as their favorite subject. Find the margin of error. Use it to find the likely range for the true population proportion.

The margin of error $= \pm\frac{1}{\sqrt{784}}$ ⟵ **Use the margin of error formula.**

$= \pm\frac{1}{28}$ ⟵ **Simplify.**

$\approx \pm 0.036$ ⟵ **Convert the fraction to a decimal.**

$= \pm 3.6\%$ ⟵ **Convert the decimal to a percent.**

$38\% + 3.6\% = 41.6\%$ ⟵ **Use the result from the sample. Add and subtract the margin of error.**

$38\% - 3.6\% = 34.4\%$

The proportion of students who say math is their favorite subject is likely to be between 34.4% and 41.6%.

Exercises

Find the margin of error. Find an interval that is likely to contain the true population proportion for the following. Round to the nearest tenth of a percent.

1. In a random sample of 1296 high school football players, 72% have purchased a brand of shoes based on the type worn by their favorite NFL player.
2. In a survey of 576 math students, 86% report having used up the eraser of their pencil before the pencil is half gone.
3. In a certain part of the country, only 12% of the 324 dogs sampled suffered from fleas.
4. In a poll of 1460 voters, 54% voted for the Republican candidate.
5. In a survey of 2891 high school students, 78% report having seen the music video made for a song before they purchased a recording of the song.

Name ______________________ Class ______________ Date ______________

Review 272

OBJECTIVE: Finding binomial probabilities **MATERIALS:** None

- Suppose you have repeated independent trials, each with a probability of success p and a probability of failure q (with $p + q = 1$). Then the probability of x successes in n trials is ${}_nC_x p^x q^{n-x}$.

Example

Find the probability of two successes in five trials with a probability of success of 0.2 for each trial.

$q = 1 - p$ ← **Find q.**

$q = 0.8$

${}_nC_x = \frac{5!}{2!(5-2)!}$ ← **Find ${}_nC_x$.**

$= 10$

${}_nC_x p^x q^{n-x} = {}_5C_2(0.2)^2(0.8)^{5-2}$ ← **Substitute x, n, p, and q values.**

$= 10(0.2)^2(0.8)^3$ ← **Substitute 10 for ${}_nC_x$.**

$= 10(0.04)(0.512)$ ← **Simplify.**

$= 0.2048$

The probability is about 20%.

Exercises

Find the probability of x successes in n trials for the given probability of success p on each trial. Round to the nearest tenth of a percent.

1. $x = 3, n = 4, p = 0.3$

2. $x = 4, n = 6, p = 0.1$

3. $x = 7, n = 9, p = 0.4$

4. $x = 5, n = 6, p = 0.3$

5. A light fixture contains six light bulbs. With normal use, each bulb has a 95% chance of lasting for 2 yr. What is the probability that all six bulbs last for 2 yr?

6. Use the information from Exercise 5. What is the probability that five of the six bulbs will last for 2 yr?

7. Suppose the bulbs have an 80% chance of lasting for 2 yr. Find the probability that three of the six bulbs will last for 2 yr.

Name ______________________ Class ______________ Date ______________

Review 273

OBJECTIVE: Using a normal curve to describe data distribution

MATERIALS: None

- The standard deviation tells how each data value in the set differs from the mean.
- Because normal curves contain the same probability distribution, they can easily be used to make predictions on a set of data.

Example

The length of life of a particular battery is normally distributed with the mean equal to 500 h. The standard deviation is equal to 50 h. Out of 250 batteries tested, find the number of batteries that are still working after 550 h.

Step 1: Sketch the normal curve. Label the mean 500. Label the standard deviations using intervals of 50.

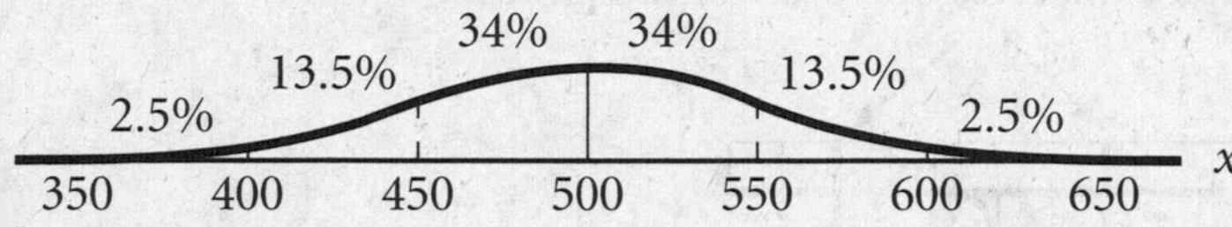

Step 2: A battery that is still going after 550 h falls more than one standard deviation above the mean. Calculate the percent of batteries at least one standard deviation above the mean.

$13.5\% + 2.5\% = 16\%$ ← **Add the percentages that fall more that one standard deviation above the mean.**

$0.16(250) = 40$ ← **Find 16% of the 250 original batteries.**

About 40 of the 250 batteries are still working after 550 h.

Exercises

Sketch and label the normal curve for the following data. Make a prediction based on the curve.

1. A light bulb lasts an average of 219 h. Out of 1000 bulbs, how many will not last 79 h if the standard deviation is 70 h?
2. In a math class of 26 students, a series of 100 multiplication problems can be completed in a mean time of 4 min. The standard deviation is 1 min. How many math students will still be working after 5 min?
3. A group of 71 frogs had a mean hopping distance of 66 in. and a standard deviation of 3 in. How many frogs will hop more than 72 in.?

Name ______________________ Class ______________ Date ______________

Review 274

OBJECTIVE: Recognizing periodic graphs and their features	**MATERIALS:** Yellow, pink, and green highlighting markers

- The graph of a *periodic function* shows a repeating pattern. The distance from one point on the graph to the point where the pattern begins repeating is called the *period.*
- To find the amplitude, use $A = \frac{1}{2}$ (maximum value – minimum value).

Example

Determine if the graph represents a periodic function. If it is periodic, calculate the period and amplitude of the function.

The repeating pattern determines that the function is periodic.

Draw a vertical line on the graph with the yellow marker. Draw another vertical line at the point where the graph completes one cycle of the pattern.

Draw a horizontal line with a green marker from the *y*-axis to the highest points on the graph.

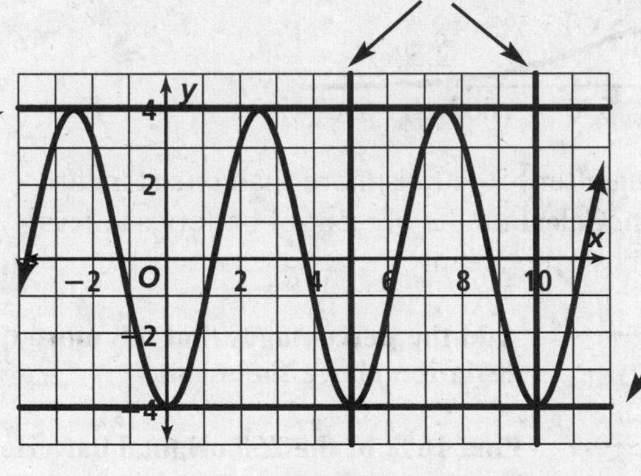

Draw a horizontal line with the pink marker from the *y*-axis to the lowest points on the graph.

Period = 10 − 5 = 5 ⟵ **Calculate the period by determining the distance from one yellow line to the other.**

Amplitude $= \frac{1}{2}(4 - (-4)) = \frac{1}{2}(8) = 4$ ⟵ **Calculate the amplitude using the formula with the maximum being the *y*-value at the green marker and the minimum value the *y*-value at the pink marker.**

Exercises

For each graph of a periodic function, calculate the period and amplitude of the function.

1. 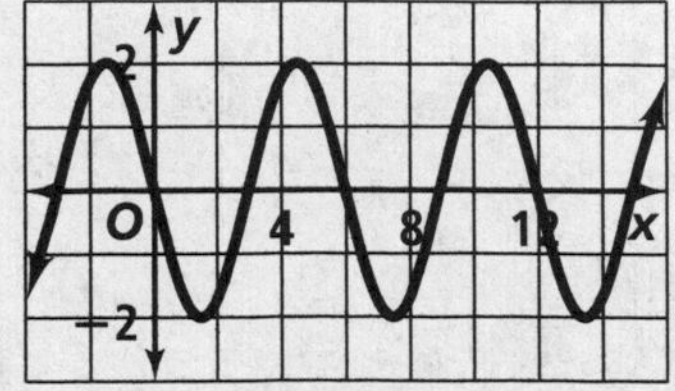

2. 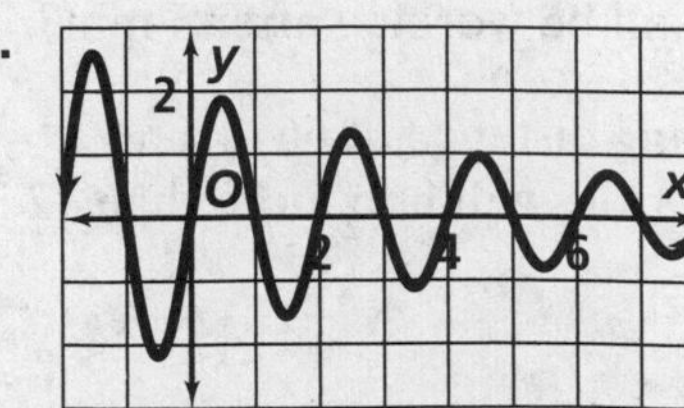

3. 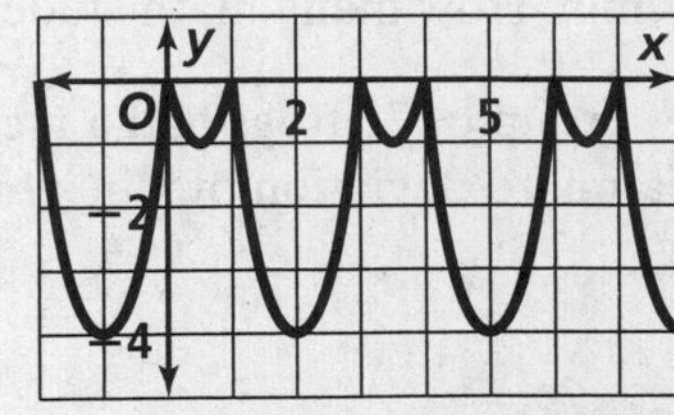

Name ______________________ Class ______________ Date ______________

Review 275

Angles and the Unit Circle

OBJECTIVE: Finding the coordinates of points on the unit circle

MATERIALS: Ruler, protractor, compass, and calculator

Example

Find the coordinates of the point where the terminal side of a 315° angle intersects the unit circle.

Step 1: Use a compass to draw a unit circle. Use a protractor to sketch the angle. Have the terminal side of the angle intersect the circle.

Step 2: Since the terminal side is in the fourth quadrant, *x* is positive and *y* is negative.

Step 3: Use a ruler to draw the horizontal leg of the right triangle. The terminal side of the angle is its hypotenuse. The negative *y*-axis is the other leg.

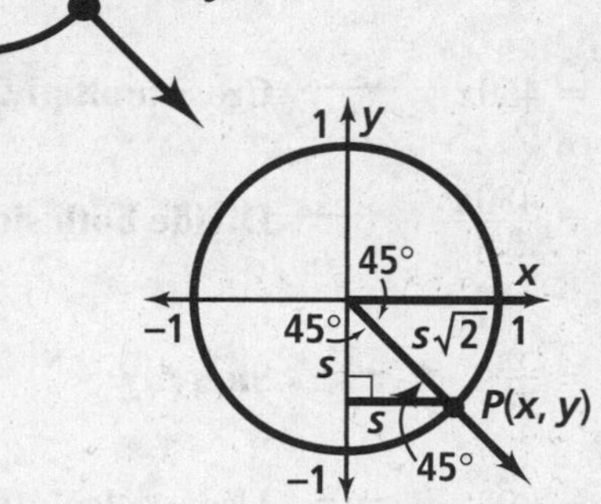

Step 4: Since 360 − 315 = 45, you can label the acute angles of the triangle as 45°. Use properties of special right triangles. The length of the hypotenuse is $\sqrt{2}$ times the length of a leg. Label each leg *s*.

hypotenuse = 1 — **Step 5: The unit circle has a radius of 1 unit.**

$s\sqrt{2} = 1$ — **Substitute $s\sqrt{2}$ for the length of the hypotenuse.**

$s = \dfrac{1}{\sqrt{2}}$ — **Divide both sides by $\sqrt{2}$.**

$s = \dfrac{\sqrt{2}}{2}$ — **Rationalize the denominator by multiplying the fraction by $\dfrac{\sqrt{2}}{\sqrt{2}}$.**

each leg $= \dfrac{\sqrt{2}}{2}$

The coordinates of the point of intersection are $\left(\dfrac{\sqrt{2}}{2}, -\dfrac{\sqrt{2}}{2}\right)$.

Exercises

Find the coordinates of the point where the terminal side of each angle intersects the unit circle.

1. −150° **2.** 30° **3.** −330° **4.** −45° **5.** 120° **6.** 225°

Name ______________________ Class ______________ Date ______________

Review 276

OBJECTIVE: Using radian measure for angles **MATERIALS:** None

- When converting radians to degrees or degrees to radians, use the proportion $\frac{\text{degree measure}}{360} = \frac{\text{radian measure}}{2\pi}$.

Example

Write the measure of 225° in radians.

$\frac{225}{360} = \frac{x}{2\pi}$ ⟵ **Substitute 225 for degree measure and a variable for radian measure.**

$360x = 450\pi$ ⟵ **Cross multiply.**

$x = \frac{450\pi}{360}$ ⟵ **Divide both sides by 360.**

$x = \frac{5\pi}{4}$ ⟵ **Simplify.**

$x \approx 3.93$ ⟵ **Use a calculator.**

$\frac{\theta}{360} = \frac{\frac{5}{4}\pi}{2\pi}$ ⟵ **Check by substituting the radians into the proportion and solving for degrees.**

$\frac{\theta}{360} = \frac{\frac{5}{4}\not{\pi}}{2\not{\pi}}$ ⟵ **Cancel π since it is in the numerator and denominator.**

$2\theta = 450$ ⟵ **Cross multiply.**

$\theta = 225$ ⟵ **Divide both sides by 2. This gives the degree measure.**

An angle of 225° measures about 3.93 radians.

Exercises

Write each measure in radians and check.

1. 20° **2.** 150° **3.** 45°

4. −110° **5.** 315° **6.** 320°

Write each measure in degrees and check.

7. $-\frac{3\pi}{2}$ **8.** $\frac{5\pi}{3}$ **9.** $\frac{\pi}{12}$

10. $\frac{8\pi}{5}$ **11.** $-\frac{7\pi}{6}$ **12.** $\frac{9\pi}{2}$

Review 277

The Sine Function

OBJECTIVE: Graphing sine curves	**MATERIALS:** Graph paper, colored pencils, and string

Example

Graph at least two cycles of the function $y = 2 \sin \frac{1}{2}\theta$.

$|a| = 2$ — **Step 1:** **Find the amplitude.**

$b = \frac{1}{2}$ — **Find the number of cycles in the interval from 0 to 2π.**

$\frac{2\pi}{b} = \frac{2\pi}{\frac{1}{2}}$ — **Find the period of the curve.**

$= 4\pi$

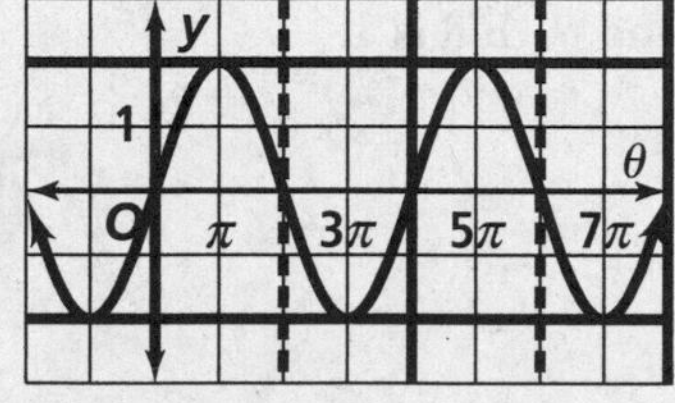

Step 2: **Draw a horizontal and vertical axis. Label $\pi, 2\pi, 3\pi \ldots, 8\pi$. Draw a red solid vertical line at 0, 4π, and 8π to denote the end of each cycle. Draw a blue dotted vertical line at 2π and 6π to denote one-half cycle. Draw a green solid horizontal line at $y = 2$ and $y = -2$ to denote the amplitude.**

Step 3: **Use string to form the graph. Then draw the graph.**

Exercises

Graph each function.

1. $y = \sin \frac{1}{2}\theta$

2. $y = 2 \sin 3\theta$

3. $y = 5 \sin \theta$

4. $y = 2 \sin 2\theta$

5. $y = \sin \frac{1}{3}\theta$

6. $y = \frac{1}{2} \sin \theta$

7. $y = -2 \sin \frac{1}{2}\theta$

8. $y = -\sin 3\theta$

9. $y = -\frac{1}{4} \sin \theta$

Name ______________________ Class ______________ Date ______________

Review 278

OBJECTIVE: Graphing cosine curves **MATERIALS:** None

- The basic equation for a cosine function is $y = a \cos b\theta$. The amplitude is $|a|$ and the period is $\frac{2\pi}{b}$.

Example

Identify the amplitude and period for the function $y = 4 \cos 2\pi\theta$. Graph the function.

$y = 4 \cos 2\pi\theta$

$|a| = |4| = 4$ ⟵ **Find the amplitude of the function.**

$\frac{2\pi}{b} = \frac{2\pi}{2\pi} = 1$ ⟵ **Calculate the period of the function.**

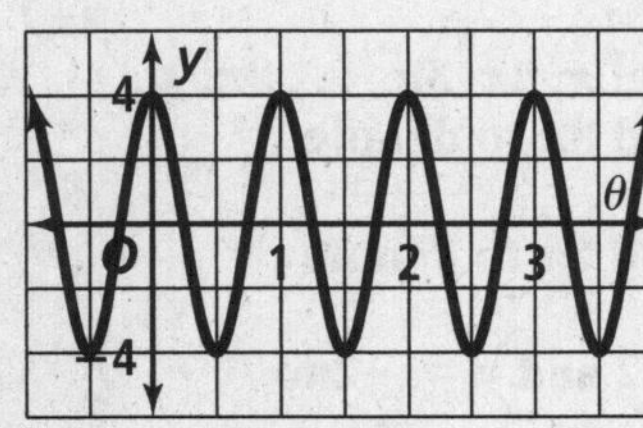

⟵ **Since the amplitude is 4, start the graph at (0, 4). Complete one cycle between 0 and 1 since the period is 1.**

Exercises

Identify the amplitude and period. Graph each function.

1. $y = \frac{1}{2} \cos 2\theta$
2. $y = 3 \cos \frac{1}{2}\theta$
3. $y = \cos 3\theta$
4. $y = \frac{1}{4} \cos \pi\theta$
5. $y = -2 \cos \frac{1}{2}\theta$
6. $y = 2 \cos 6\pi\theta$
7. $y = -2 \cos \theta$
8. $y = \cos \frac{1}{5}\theta$
9. $y = 2 \cos 2\theta$

Name ______________________ Class ______________ Date ______________

Review 279

OBJECTIVE: Graphing tangent curves **MATERIALS:** None

The tangent function is a discontinuous periodic function. Its equation in standard form is $y = \tan b\theta$. For the tangent function, b, represents the number of cycles from 0 to π, and its period is $\frac{\pi}{b}$. One cycle occurs in the interval from $-\frac{\pi}{2b}$ to $\frac{\pi}{2b}$, and vertical asymptotes occur at the end of each cycle.

Example

Graph the function $y = 3 \tan \pi\theta$.

$\frac{\pi}{b} = \frac{\pi}{\pi} = 1$ ← **Calculate the period of the function. One cycle occurs in the interval $-\frac{1}{2}$ to $\frac{1}{2}$.**

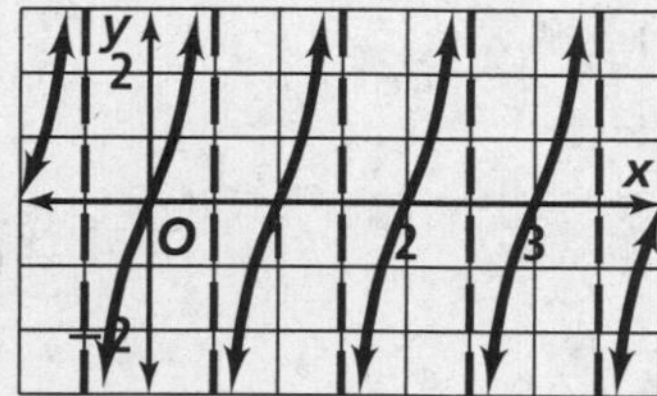

← **Because the period is 1, asymptotes occur every 1 unit—at . . . , $-\frac{1}{2}, \frac{1}{2}, \frac{3}{2}, \frac{5}{2}, \frac{7}{2}$, ...**

Plot three points in each cycle. Sketch the curve.

Exercises

Identify the period and tell where the asymptotes occur between 0 and 2π. Graph each function.

1. $y = 3 \tan 2\theta$
2. $y = -2 \tan \frac{1}{2}\theta$
3. $y = -2 \tan \theta$
4. $y = 2 \tan 2\theta$
5. $y = -\tan \frac{\pi}{2}\theta$
6. $y = \frac{1}{2} \tan \theta$
7. $y = \tan 3\theta$
8. $y = -2 \tan \frac{1}{2}\pi\theta$
9. $y = 2 \tan \frac{\pi}{4}\theta$

Name ______________________ Class ______________ Date ______________

Review 280

Translating Sine and Cosine Functions

OBJECTIVE: Graphing translations of trigonometric curves

MATERIALS: None

A horizontal translation of a periodic function is a phase shift. When $g(x) = f(x-h)$, the value of h is the amount of the shift left or right. If $h > 0$, the shift is to the right. If $h < 0$, the shift is to the left.

A vertical translation can occur as well. When $g(x) = f(x) + k$, the value of k is the amount of the shift up or down. If $k > 0$, the shift is up. If $k < 0$, the shift is down.

Example

Sketch the graph of $y = 2 \sin 3\left(x - \frac{\pi}{3}\right) + 1$ in the interval from 0 to 2π.

Since $a = 2$ and $b = 3$, the graph is a translation of $y = 2 \sin 3x$.

Step 1: Sketch one cycle of $y = 2 \sin 3x$. Use five points in the pattern zero–max–zero–min–zero.

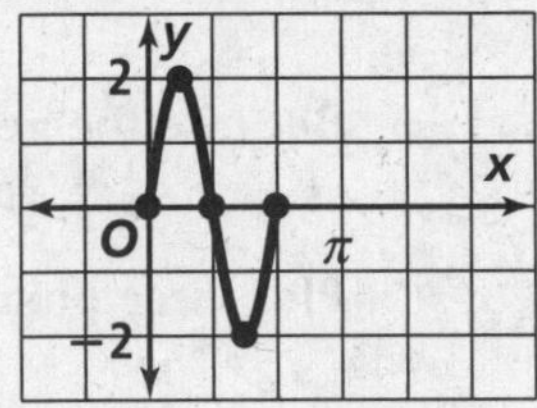

Step 2: Since $h = \frac{\pi}{3}$ and $k = 1$, translate the graph $\frac{\pi}{3}$ units to the right and 1 unit up. Extend the periodic pattern throughout the interval from 0 to 2π. Sketch the graph.

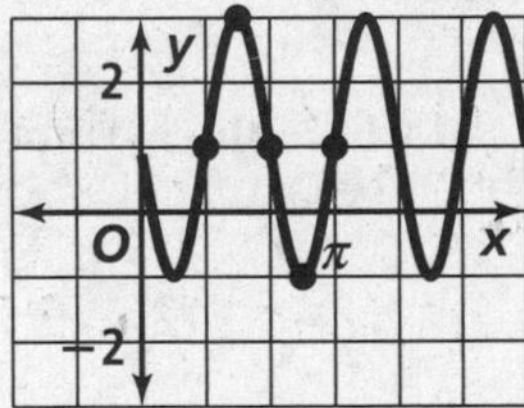

ALGEBRA 2 TOPICS

Exercises

Sketch each graph in the interval from 0 to 2π.

1. $y = \cos 3\left(x + \frac{\pi}{2}\right)$
2. $y = -2 \sin \frac{1}{2}x - 1$
3. $y = -2 \cos (x + \pi) - 2$
4. $y = \frac{1}{2} \sin 2(x - 2)$
5. $y = -\sin 2x + 3$
6. $y = \frac{1}{2} \cos \left(x - \frac{\pi}{3}\right)$
7. $y = \sin 3x + \frac{1}{2}$
8. $y = -2 \cos \frac{1}{2}(x + \pi)$
9. $y = 2 \cos \frac{\pi}{4}x + 2.5$

Name ______________________ Class ______________ Date ______________

Review 281

Reciprocal Trigonometric Functions

OBJECTIVE: Graphing reciprocal trigonometric functions

MATERIALS: None

The cosecant (csc), secant (sec), and cotangent (cot) functions are defined as reciprocals of the sine (sin), cosine (cos), and tangent (tan) functions, respectively. Their domains include all real numbers except those that make a denominator zero.

$\csc\theta = \frac{1}{\sin\theta}$ $\qquad \sec\theta = \frac{1}{\cos\theta}$ $\qquad \cot\theta = \frac{1}{\tan\theta}$

Example

Sketch the graph of $y = \cos\theta$ and $y = \sec\theta$ in the interval from 0 to 2π.

Step 1: Make a table of values. The graph of $y = \sec\theta$ has asymptotes where $\cos\theta$ is equal to zero.

θ	0	$\frac{\pi}{4}$	$\frac{\pi}{2}$	$\frac{3\pi}{4}$	π	$\frac{5\pi}{4}$	$\frac{3\pi}{2}$	$\frac{7\pi}{4}$	2π
$\cos\theta$	1	0.71	0	−0.71	−1	−0.71	0	0.71	1
$\sec\theta$	1	1.41	—	−1.41	−1	−1.41	—	1.41	1

Step 2: Plot the points and sketch the graphs.

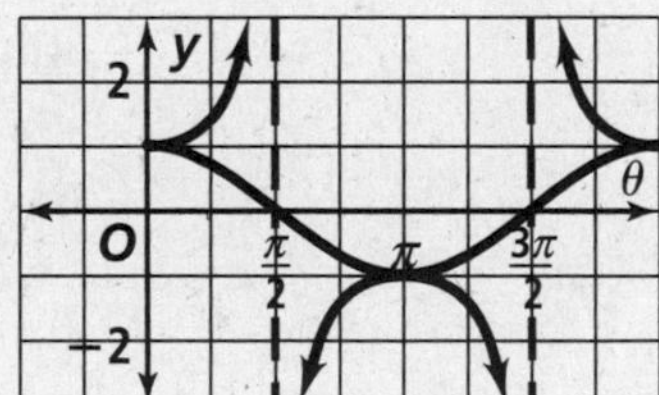

Exercises

Sketch each graph in the interval from 0 to 2π.

1. $y = \cot 3\,\theta$

2. $y = -2\sec\frac{1}{2}\theta$

3. $y = -2\csc(\theta + \pi) - 2$

4. $y = \frac{1}{2}\csc 2(\theta - 2)$

5. $y = -\sec 2\,\theta$

6. $y = \frac{1}{2}\cot\left(\theta - \frac{\pi}{2}\right)$

7. $y = \cot 3\theta + \frac{1}{2}$

8. $y = -2\csc\frac{1}{2}\theta$

9. $y = 2\cot\frac{\pi}{4}\theta$

ALGEBRA 2 TOPICS

Name ____________________ Class ____________ Date ____________

Review 282

OBJECTIVE: Verifying trigonometric identities **MATERIALS:** None

To verify an identity, you should transform one side of the equation until it is the same as the other side. It is sometimes helpful to write all the functions in terms of sine and cosine.

Example

Verify the identity $1 + \cot^2 \theta = \csc^2 \theta$.

$$1 + \cot^2 \theta = 1 + \left(\frac{\cos \theta}{\sin \theta}\right)^2$$ ← **Cotangent identity**

$$= 1 + \frac{\cos^2 \theta}{\sin^2 \theta}$$ ← **Simplify.**

$$= \frac{\sin^2 \theta}{\sin^2 \theta} + \frac{\cos^2 \theta}{\sin^2 \theta}$$ ← **Write the fractions with common denominators.**

$$= \frac{\sin^2 \theta + \cos^2 \theta}{\sin^2 \theta}$$ ← **Add.**

$$= \frac{1}{\sin^2 \theta}$$ ← **Pythagorean identity**

$$= \csc^2 \theta$$ ← **Reciprocal identity**

Exercises

Verify each identity.

1. $\cot \theta \tan \theta = 1$

2. $\cos \theta \sec \theta = 1$

3. $\csc \theta \tan \theta + \cot^2 \theta = \csc^2 \theta$

4. $\sin \theta (1 + \cot^2 \theta) = \csc \theta$

5. $\sec \theta \cot \theta = \csc \theta$

6. $\sec^2 \theta - \sec^2 \theta \cos^2 \theta = \tan^2 \theta$

7. $\cot \theta \tan \theta + \tan^2 \theta = \sec^2 \theta$

8. $\csc^2 \theta - \cot^2 \theta = 1$

9. $\sin \theta + \cos \theta \cot \theta = \csc \theta$

10. $\dfrac{\sec \theta - \cos \theta}{\sec \theta} = \sin^2 \theta$

11. $\cot \theta \sec \theta \sin \theta = 1$

12. $\tan \theta (\sin \theta - \csc \theta) = -\cos \theta$

Name ______________________ Class ______________ Date ______________

Review 283

Solving Trigonometric Equations Using Inverses

OBJECTIVE: Solving trigonometric equations using inverses

MATERIALS: Calculator

Example

Solve $4 \sin \theta - \sqrt{3} = 2 \sin \theta$ for $0 \leq \theta < 2\pi$.

$4 \sin \theta - \sqrt{3} = 2 \sin \theta$

$2 \sin \theta - \sqrt{3} = 0$ ← **Subtract $2 \sin \theta$ from each side.**

$2 \sin \theta = \sqrt{3}$ ← **Add $\sqrt{3}$ to each side.**

$\sin \theta = \frac{\sqrt{3}}{2}$ ← **Divide each side by 2.**

$\sin^{-1} \frac{\sqrt{3}}{2} = \frac{\pi}{3}$ ← **Use the inverse function to find one value of θ.**

The sine function is also positive in Quadrant II. So another value of θ is $\pi - \frac{\pi}{3} = \frac{2\pi}{3}$.

The two solutions between 0 and 2π are $\frac{\pi}{3}$ and $\frac{2\pi}{3}$.

Exercises

Solve each equation for $0 \leq \theta < 2\pi$.

1. $\sin \theta + 2 \sin \theta \cos \theta = 0$
2. $2 \sin \theta - 4 = -2 \sin \theta$
3. $2 \cos^2 \theta + \cos \theta - 1 = 0$
4. $\cos \theta - 2 \sin \theta \cos \theta = 0$
5. $\sqrt{3} + 5 \sin \theta = 3 \sin \theta$
6. $3 \sin \theta = 1$
7. $2 \tan \theta - 4 = 0$
8. $4 \sin^2 \theta - 1 = 0$
9. $2 \sin^2 \theta + 3 \sin \theta = -1$
10. $\tan \theta(\sin \theta - 1) = 0$
11. $3 \tan \theta = -\sqrt{3}$
12. $-5 \cos \theta = \cos \theta - 3\sqrt{3}$

Name ______________________ Class ______________ Date ______________

Review 284

OBJECTIVE: Using trigonometric ratios to find missing measures of right triangles

MATERIALS: Calculator

To apply a trigonometric formula correctly, label the triangle's adjacent leg, opposite leg, and hypotenuse first. Follow these steps:

Step 1: Place an index finger on the right angle. Place your other index finger on the side opposite the right angle. Label it the *hypotenuse.*

Step 2: Place an index finger on the given angle. Place your other index finger on the leg touching the given angle. Label it *adjacent.*

Step 3: Keep the index finger on the given angle. Place your other index finger on the leg opposite the given angle. Label it *opposite.*

Example

In right $\triangle ABC$, $m\angle A = 42°$ and $c = 28$. Find the lengths of a and b. Round to the nearest tenth.

B, $c = 28$, a, $42°$, A, b, C

$\sin\theta = \frac{\text{opp}}{\text{hyp}}$ ⟵ **To find a, the opposite leg, use sine.**

$\sin 42° = \frac{a}{28}$ ⟵ **Substitute values.**

$28(\sin 42°) = a$ ⟵ **Multiply each side by 28.**

$28(0.6691) = a$ ⟵ **Use a calculator.**

$18.7 = a$ ⟵ **Label $a = 18.7$ on the triangle.**

$\cos\theta = \frac{\text{adj}}{\text{hyp}}$ ⟵ **To find b, the adjacent leg, use cosine.**

$\cos 42° = \frac{b}{28}$ ⟵ **Substitute values.**

$28(\cos 42°) = b$ ⟵ **Multiply each side by 28.**

$28(0.7431) = b$ ⟵ **Use a calculator.**

$20.8 = b$ ⟵ **Label $b = 20.8$ on the triangle.**

Exercises

In $\triangle ABC$, $\angle C$ is a right angle. Two measures are given. Find the remaining sides and angles to the nearest tenth.

1. $m\angle B = 20°, a = 6$

2. $m\angle B = 60°, c = 14$

3. $m\angle A = 10°, a = 10$

4. $b = 7, c = 10$

5. $a = 35, b = 21$

6. $m\angle A = 36.5°, c = 28.2$

Name ____________________ Class ____________ Date ____________

Review 285

Area and the Law of Sines

OBJECTIVE: Using the Law of Sines to find the measures of the sides or angles of a triangle

MATERIALS: None

Law of Sines: $\frac{\sin A}{a} = \frac{\sin B}{b} = \frac{\sin C}{c}$

Use the Law of Sines when you are given the measure of two angles of a triangle and the length of any side or the measure of two sides and the measure of the angle opposite one of them.

Example

Based on the given information, use the Law of Sines to find side b in the triangle.

$A = 30°, B = 70°, a = 8$ ⟵ **Because we know two angles and a side, use the Law of Sines.**

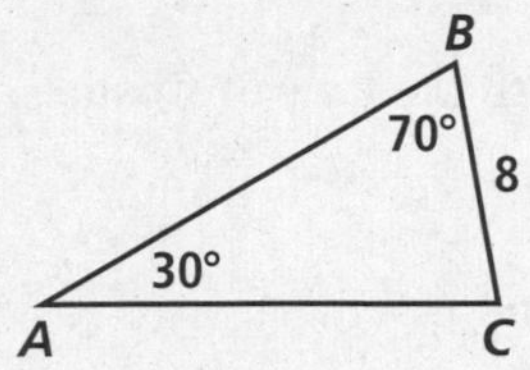

⟵ **Draw a triangle, and label *A*, *B*, and *a*.**

$\frac{\sin 30°}{8} = \frac{\sin 70°}{b}$ ⟵ **Substitute values into the Law of Sines formula.**

$\frac{0.5}{8} = \frac{0.9397}{b}$ ⟵ **Use a calculator to find sin 30° and sin 70°.**

$0.5b = 7.52$ ⟵ **Multiply each side by 8*b*.**

$b = 15.04$ ⟵ **Solve for *b*.**

Exercises

Find the unknown side measure or angle for each triangle. Round to the nearest tenth.

1. Find a if $A = 18°, B = 28°$, and $b = 100$.
2. Find c if $B = 18°, C = 152°$, and $b = 4$.
3. Find a if $C = 16°, A = 92°$, and $c = 32$.
4. Find B if $C = 95°, b = 5$, and $c = 6$.
5. Find B if $A = 40°, b = 6$, and $a = 12$.
6. Find c if $A = 50°, C = 60°$, and $a = 36$.
7. Find c if $B = 110°, C = 40°$, and $b = 18$.
8. Find a if $A = 5°, C = 125°$, and $c = 510$.

Name ____________________ Class ____________ Date ____________

Review 286

OBJECTIVE: Using the Law of Cosines to find the measures of the sides or angles of a triangle

MATERIALS: None

- To determine whether to use the Law of Sines or the Law of Cosines, look at the given information.
- If given the measure of two sides for a triangle and the angle between them or the measure of all three sides, use the Law of Cosines.
- If given the measure of two angles of a triangle and the length of any side or the measure of two sides and the measure of the angle opposite one of them, use the Law of Sines.

Example

Based on the given information, use the Law of Cosines to find the third side of the triangle.

$B = 20°, a = 120, c = 100$ ⟵ **Because B is between a and c, use the Law of Cosines.**

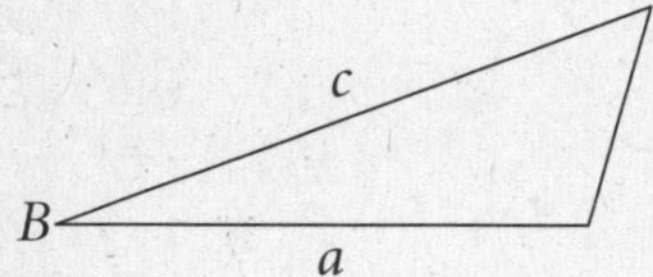

⟵ **Draw a triangle and label a, c, and B.**

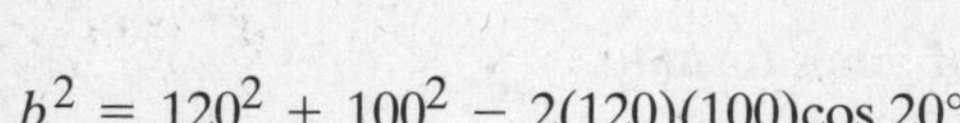

$b^2 = 120^2 + 100^2 - 2(120)(100)\cos 20°$ ⟵ **Insert the values into the Law of Cosines formula. Note that the side you are finding the length of and that side's opposite angle are on opposite ends of the equation.**

$b^2 = 14400 + 10000 - (24000)(0.93969)$ ⟵ **Use a calculator to find cos 20°.**

$b^2 = 1847.4$ ⟵ **Simplify.**

$b = 42.98$ ⟵ **Find the square root of each side.**

Exercises

Find the unknown side measure or angle for each triangle. Round to the nearest tenth.

1. Find a if $A = 18°$, $c = 72$, and $b = 100$.
2. Find c if $a = 15$, $C = 152°$, and $b = 4$.
3. Find A if $B = 45°$, $a = 9$, and $c = 19$.
4. Find a if $A = 16°$, $b = 92$, and $c = 32$.
5. Find B if $a = 9$, $b = 3$, and $c = 11$.
6. Find c if $C = 30°$, $a = 15$, and $b = 15$.
7. Find C if $B = 95°$, $a = 5$, and $c = 6$.
8. Find B if $a = 18$, $b = 26$, and $c = 15$.

Name ______________________ Class ______________ Date ______________

Review 287

Angle Identities

OBJECTIVE: Finding exact trigonometric values using angle sum and difference identities

MATERIALS: None

We can use the following identities to find exact values for some trigonometric functions.

Angle Difference Identities

$\sin(A - B) = \sin A \cos B - \cos A \sin B$

$\cos(A - B) = \cos A \cos B + \sin A \sin B$

$\tan(A - B) = \dfrac{\tan A - \tan B}{1 + \tan A \tan B}$

Angle Sum Identities

$\sin(A + B) = \sin A \cos B + \cos A \sin B$

$\cos(A + B) = \cos A \cos B - \sin A \sin B$

$\tan(A + B) = \dfrac{\tan A + \tan B}{1 - \tan A \tan B}$

Example

Find the exact value of sin 75°.

$75° = 45° + 30°$ ← **We know exact values for the trigonometric functions at 45° and 30°, so we can use the sum identity for sine.**

$\sin(A + B) = \sin A \cos B + \cos A \sin B$ ← **Sine Angle Sum Identity**

$\sin(45° + 30°) = \sin 45° \cos 30° + \cos 45° \sin 30°$ ← **Substitute 45° for *A* and 30° for *B*.**

$= \dfrac{\sqrt{2}}{2} \cdot \dfrac{\sqrt{3}}{2} + \dfrac{\sqrt{2}}{2} \cdot \dfrac{1}{2}$ ← **Replace with exact values.**

$= \dfrac{\sqrt{6}}{4} + \dfrac{\sqrt{2}}{4}$ ← **Simplify.**

$= \dfrac{\sqrt{6} + \sqrt{2}}{4}$

So $\sin 75° = \dfrac{\sqrt{6} + \sqrt{2}}{4}$.

Exercises

Find each exact value. Use a sum or difference identity if needed.

1. sin 150° **2.** cos 195° **3.** cos 150°

4. sin 165° **5.** cos (−75°) **6.** sin (−75°)

7. tan (−300°) **8.** tan 120° **9.** sin (−45°)

Name ____________________ Class ____________________ Date ____________________

Review 288

Double-Angle and Half-Angle Identities

OBJECTIVE: Using double-angle and half-angle identities to verify other identities

MATERIALS: None

Double-Angle Identities

$\cos 2\theta = \cos^2 \theta - \sin^2 \theta$

$\cos 2\theta = 2\cos^2 \theta - 1$

$\cos 2\theta = 1 - 2\sin^2 \theta$

$\sin 2\theta = 2 \sin \theta \cos \theta$

$\tan 2\theta = \dfrac{2 \tan \theta}{1 - \tan^2 \theta}$

Half-Angle Identities

$\sin \dfrac{\theta}{2} = \pm\sqrt{\dfrac{1 - \cos \theta}{2}}$

$\cos \dfrac{\theta}{2} = \pm\sqrt{\dfrac{1 + \cos \theta}{2}}$

$\tan \dfrac{\theta}{2} = \pm\sqrt{\dfrac{1 - \cos \theta}{1 + \cos \theta}}$

You can use the double-angle and half-angle identities to verify other identities.

Example

Verify the identity $\sin^2 \theta = \dfrac{1 - \cos 2\theta}{2}$

$\sin^2 \theta = \dfrac{1 - \cos 2\theta}{2}$

$\sin^2 \theta = \dfrac{1 - (1 - 2\sin^2 \theta)}{2}$ ⟵ **Use the double-angle identity for cos 2*θ*.**

$\sin^2 \theta = \dfrac{2\sin^2 \theta}{2}$ ⟵ **Simplify.**

$\sin^2 \theta = \sin^2 \theta$ ⟵ **Simplify.**

Exercises

Verify each identity.

1. $2 \cot 2\theta = \cot \theta - \tan \theta$

2. $\cos^2 \theta = \dfrac{1 + \cos 2\theta}{2}$

3. $\csc \theta - 2 \sin \theta = \dfrac{\cos 2\theta}{\sin \theta}$

4. $\sin^2 \dfrac{\theta}{2} = \dfrac{\csc \theta - \cot \theta}{2 \csc \theta}$

5. $\cot \theta = \dfrac{\sin 2\theta}{1 - \cos 2\theta}$

6. $\sin^2 \dfrac{\theta}{2} = \dfrac{\tan \theta - \sin \theta}{2 \tan \theta}$

ALGEBRA 2 TOPICS

Answers

Pre-Algebra Topics

Review 1

1. 4(5), 20 **2.** 4(8), 32 **3.** 4(6), 24 **4.** 4(*d*), 4*d*
5. $\frac{h}{7}$ **6.** $j - 9$ **7.** $2x$ **8.** $y + 2$ **9.** $\frac{42}{s}$ **10.** $16d$

Review 2

1. 22 **2.** 3 **3.** 4 **4.** 1 **5.** 9 **6.** 9 **7.** 37 **8.** 1 **9.** 35 **10.** 7 **11.** 5 **12.** 42 **13.** 10 **14.** 3 **15.** 3 **16.** 8 **17.** 18 **18.** 23

Review 3

1. 9 **2.** 40 **3.** 5 **4.** 10 **5.** 2 **6.** 9 **7.** 26 **8.** 16 **9.** 29 **10.** 2 **11.** 14 **12.** 7 **13.** 16 **14.** 54

Review 4

1. 9, 11, 13; 2, 2, 2, 2, 2 **2.** Phillipe won 13 games on the sixth day. **3.** 13, 18; 1, 2, 3, 4, 5 **4.** Jennifer rode 18 miles in the sixth week. Jennifer rode 5 miles more in week 6 than in week 5.

Review 5

1. 515 **2.** 27 **3.** 700 **4.** 60 **5.** 21 **6.** 360 **7.** 24 **8.** 1,425 **9.** 1,300 **10.** 276 **11.** 45 **12.** 353,000

Review 6

1. 14.5, 14.45, none **2.** 5.6, 6, 7 **3.** 38.8, 37, none **4.** 2.0, 1.85, 1.8 and 2.6 **5.** 803.6 ft **6.** 802 ft **7.** None

Review 7

1. 3, 4, 14; $350 **2.** 9, 9; 90, 180; 326, 978; 1,167 digits **3.** 12

Review 8

1. 17 **2.** 10, 25 **3.** 2, 4 **4.** 2, 4, 12 **5.** 1, 5, 11, 55 **6.** 1, 2, 4, 5, 8, 10, 20, 40 **7.** 1, 2, 3, 6, 7, 14, 21, 42 **8.** 1, 2, 3, 4, 6, 8, 12, 16, 24, 48

Review 9

1. steak, fries, beans; steak, fries, peas; chicken, mashed, beans; chicken, mashed, peas; chicken, fries, beans; chicken, fries, peas; hamburger, mashed, beans; hamburger, mashed, peas; hamburger, fries, beans; hamburger, fries, peas; 12 meals
2. $1.19

Review 10

1.a. $3 **b.** $4 **c.** $8 **d.** $15 **2.** $44 **3.** $\frac{1}{8}$ of the pie

Review 11

1. $x = \frac{y-b}{m}$ **2.** $m = \frac{y-b}{x}$ **3.** $s = \frac{p}{6}$
4. $h = \frac{2A}{B+b}$ **5.** $P = \frac{I}{rt}$ **6.** $x = \frac{3(y+5)}{2}$
7. $p = \frac{t}{0.05}$ **8.** $w = \frac{V}{lh}$ **9.** $m = \frac{2k}{v^2}$
10. $V = \frac{W + pL}{p}$ **11.** $G = \frac{Fr^2}{m_1m_2}$
12. $L = \frac{pV - W}{p}$ **13.** $e = \frac{hv - E}{V}$
14. $m = \frac{Mu}{v - u}$

Review 12

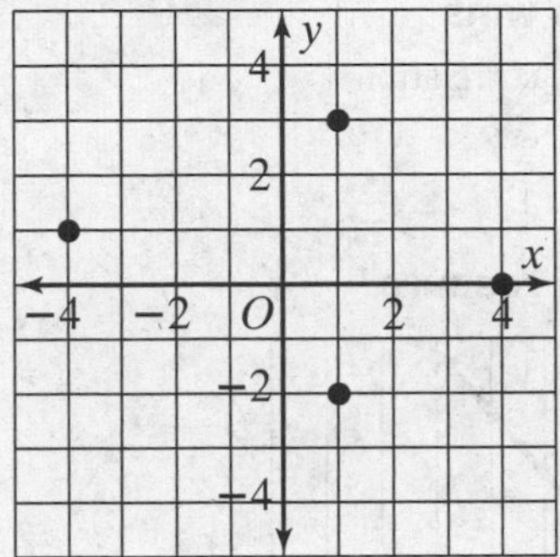

No; a pencil held vertically would pass through both (1, 3) and (1, −2).

Review 13

1. $y = 7x$ **2.** $y = x - 8$ **3.** $y = -2x + 9$
4. $y = \frac{1}{3}x + 9$ **5.** $y = -\frac{1}{4}x - 7$ **6.** $y = 6x - 11$

Review 14

1.

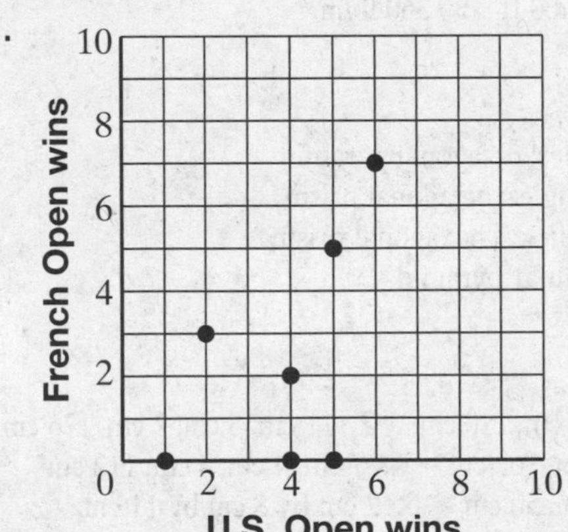

ANSWERS

Review 14 *(continued)*

2.

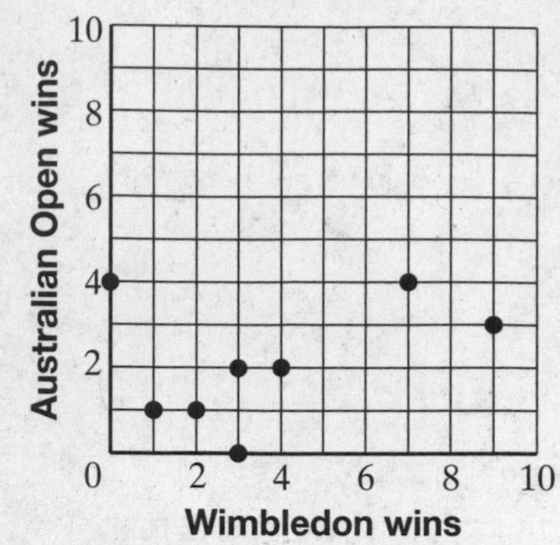

3. no correlation **4.** positive correlation

Review 15

1–2.

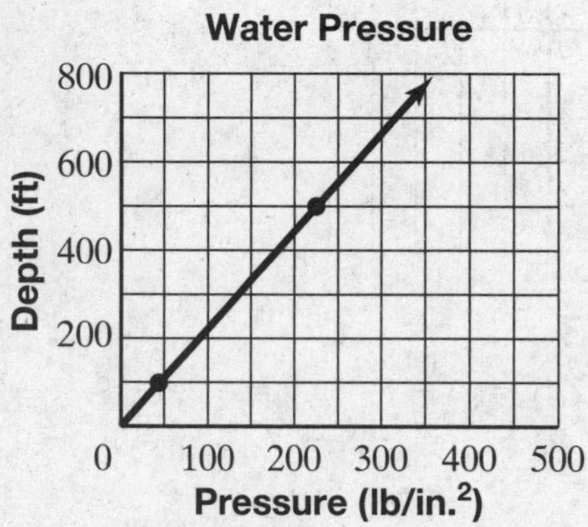

3. $y = \frac{20}{9}x$ **4.** 400 ft **5.** 360 lb/in.^{2}

Review 16

1. octagon, triangles; octagonal pyramid
2. octagons, rectangles; octagonal prism
3. hexagons, rectangles; hexagonal prism
4. triangles; triangular pyramid

Review 17

1. 13 cm, 10 cm, 1 cm, 130 cm^3 **2.** 11 cm, 8 cm, 2 cm, 176 cm^3
3. 9 cm, 6 cm, 3 cm, 162 cm^3 **4.** 7 cm, 4 cm, 4 cm, 112 cm^3
5. 5 cm, 2 cm, 5 cm, 50 cm^3 **6.** 2 cm by 8 cm by 11 cm

Review 18

1. (4), 5 **2.** 7, (8) **3.** (−3), −2 **4.** (9), 10 **5.** (6), 7
6. (−5), −4 **7.** 11, (12) **8.** (−11), −10 **9.** 7 **10.** 9 **11.** 11
12. 12 **13.** 8 **14.** 10 **15.** 2 **16.** 4 **17.** 3 **18.** −2
19. 6 **20.** −5 **21.** −10 **22.** −6 **23.** 7

Review 19

1.

Inches	3	4	5	6	7
Frequency	5	3	1	1	2

Charleston Rainfall

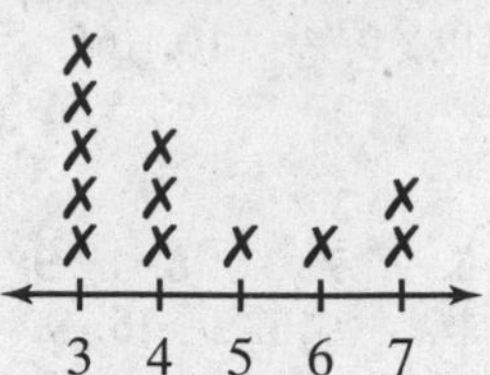

2.

Inches	0	1	2	3	4
Frequency	5	2	0	4	1

San Francisco Rainfall

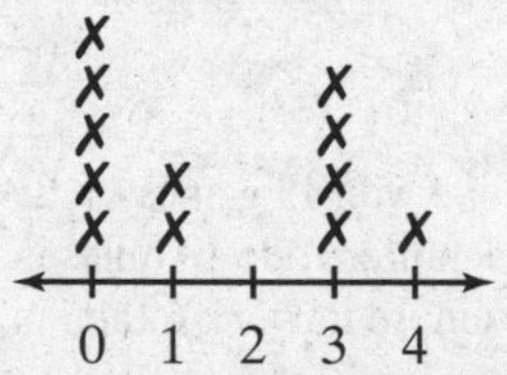

3.

Inches	3	4
Frequency	8	4

Wilmington Rainfall

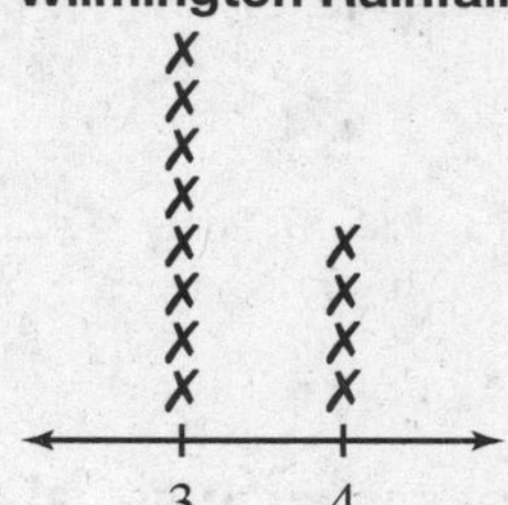

Review 20

1. 98, 80.5, 118

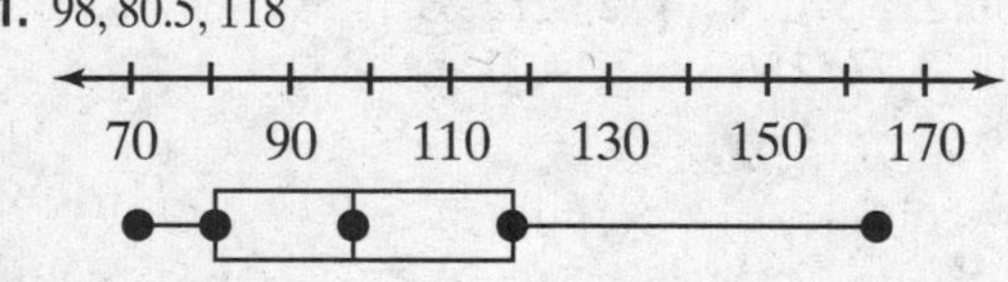

2. 13, 4, 21

0 10 20 30 40

ANSWERS

Review 21

1.

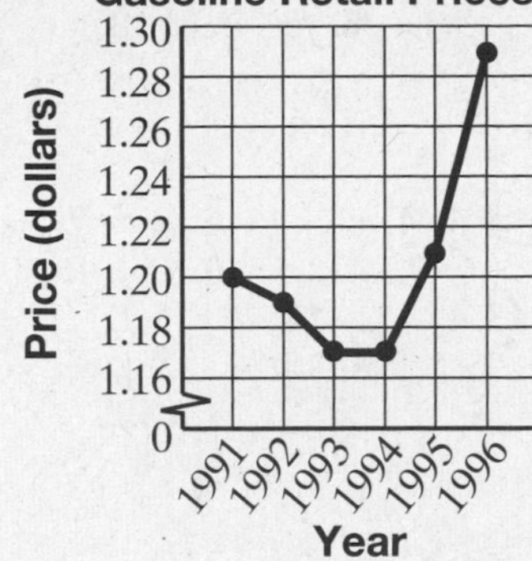

2.

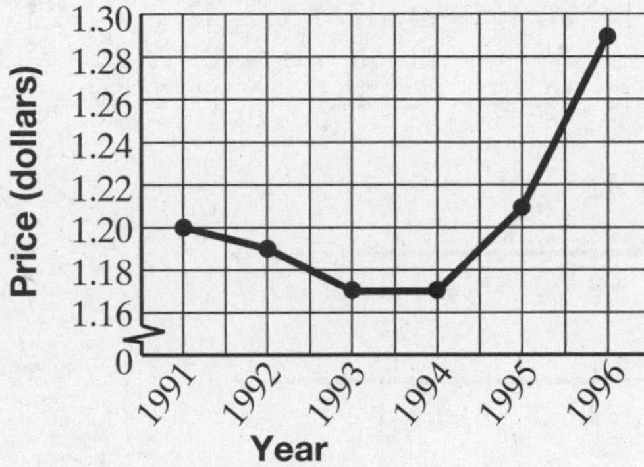

3. The first graph implies that prices decreased rapidly from 1991 to 1993 and increased rapidly from 1994 to 1996. The second graph implies slower changes.

Review 22

1. 160 shirts, $\frac{8}{400} = \frac{x}{8{,}000}$ **2.** 144 shirts, $\frac{9}{500} = \frac{x}{8{,}000}$
3. 480 games, $\frac{16}{400} = \frac{x}{12{,}000}$ **4.** 450 games, $\frac{30}{800} = \frac{x}{12{,}000}$
5. 456 games, $\frac{19}{500} = \frac{x}{12{,}000}$ **6.** 459 games, $\frac{65}{1{,}700} = \frac{x}{12{,}000}$

Review 23

1. 1, 5, 4, 0 **2.** 50% **3.** 40% **4.** 90% **5.** 40% **6.** 60%

Review 24

1. 37 (1 and 36) **2.** 49 (7 and 7) **3.** 16 and 4

Algebra 1 Topics

Review 25

1. $n + 5$ **2.** $n - 8$ **3.** $\frac{n}{9}$ **4.** $5n - 3$ **5.** $12n = 84$
6. $n - 7 = 22$ **7.** $8x = 72$ **8.** $\frac{n}{3} = 18$

Review 26

1. Check students' work. **2.** Check students' work.
3. Check students' work. **4.** Check students' work.
5. −3 **6.** −75 **7.** 2 **8.** 28 **9.** 3 **10.** −1
11. −20 **12.** −56

Review 27

1. rational, real **2.** rational, real **3.** whole, integer, rational, real **4.** rational, real **5.** irrational, real **6.** integers, rational, real **7.** rational, real **8.** natural, whole, integers, rational, real **9.** natural, whole, integers, rational, real **10.** integers, rational, real **11.** rational, real **12.** irrational, real
13.–18. Check students' work.

Review 28

1. −7 **2.** 17 **3.** 3 **4.** −10 **5.** −5 **6.** −3 **7.** 2 **8.** −1
9. −3.8 **10.** 7.6 **11.** −2.3 **12.** 21.2 **13.** 0.2 **14.** −10.3
15. −20 **16.** −6.3 **17.** −1 **18.** −9 **19.** 1 **20.** 9
21. 5.9 **22.** 0.9 **23.** −0.9 **24.** −5.9 **25.** 10.5 **26.** 3.7
27. −3.7 **28.** −10.5

Review 29

1. −5 **2.** −3 **3.** 9 **4.** 10 **5.** −10 **6.** −9 **7.** −1 **8.** 7
9. 2.3 **10.** 3.2 **11.** −14.4 **12.** −7.3 **13.** 6.2 **14.** −1.6
15. −1.2 **16.** −13.7 **17.** −7 **18.** 1 **19.** −1 **20.** 7 **21.** 13
22. −3 **23.** 7 **24.** −5 **25.** $\begin{bmatrix} -6 & -3 \\ -2 & -3 \end{bmatrix}$ **26.** $\begin{bmatrix} -\frac{1}{6} \\ 2 \end{bmatrix}$

Review 30

1.–8. Check students' work. **9.** −8 **10.** −72 **11.** 10
12. −88 **13.** 49 **14.** 50

Review 31

1. $10x + 8$ **2.** $3x - 2$ **3.** $28x - 12$ **4.** $20 + 10x$
5. $30 - 18x$ **6.** $3x - 5$ **7.** $6x - 12$ **8.** $21x + 28$
9. $8x + 8y$ **10.** $-4x - 3$ **11.** $2x - 1$ **12.** $6x + 3$
13. $-14x + 3$ **14.** $7x + 1$ **15.** $-3x - 4$

Review 32

1. Assoc. Prop. of Add. **2.** Distributive Prop.
3. Comm. Prop. of Mult. **4.** Assoc. Prop. of Mult.
5. Distributive Prop. **6.** Comm. Prop. of Add. **7.** 12 **8.** 8
9. 9; 9 **10.** 8 **11.** 6 **12.** 7; 7

Review 33

1. (−8, 4) **2.** (−4, 0) **3.** (−2, 2) **4.** (0, 3) **5.** (2, 1)
6. (7, 4) **7.** (8, −3) **8.** (5, −6) **9.** (−3, −5) **10.** (−6, −8)

Answers

Review 33 *(continued)*

11.–16.

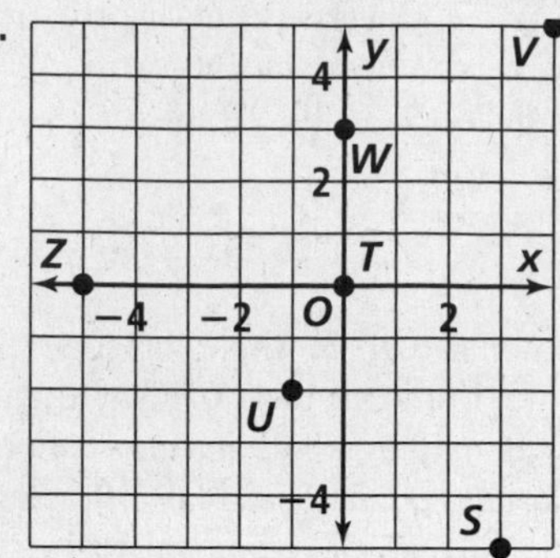

Review 34

1.–9. Check students' models.
1. 7 **2.** 6 **3.** −2 **4.** 3 **5.** 3 **6.** 2 **7.** 9 **8.** 3 **9.** −2
10. 25 **11.** −2 **12.** 4 **13.** −4.9 **14.** 7 **15.** 2.5

Review 35

1. 5, subtracted, inverse; add, each; divided, dividing; side, 6; −18 **2.** 4 **3.** 28 **4.** −3

Review 36

1. $a + 6x + 5$ **2.** $13a - 3x - 5$ **3.** $-b - 3x + 5$
4. $-10m + t + 4$ **5.** $-3r + 3s$ **6.** $2p - 9x + 4$
7. $9k - 2x + 5$ **8.** $2a - 2x + 5.5$ **9.** $-a + 2y - 4$
10. $-5c + 6x - 3$ **11.** $2b - x + 6$ **12.** $2c - 9$
13. -5 **14.** $2y + 0.5z - 0.5$ **15.** $4a + 3b + 4$
16. $\frac{1}{3}a - 2$ **17.** $4x - 10$ **18.** $5x - 4y + z$ **19.** $\frac{1}{2}x + 1$
20. $8y - 3x - 3$

Review 37

1. subtract; from; 4 **2.** $4b$; add; to **3.–5.** Check students' work. **3.** 3.5 **4.** 2 **5.** 17 **6.** 8 **7.** −3 **8.** 2

Review 38

1. 8:00 P.M. **2.** 2:00 P.M.

Review 39

1. ○ = ▲ − ❐ **2.** ○ = $\frac{●❐}{▲}$ **3.** Check students' work.

4. $a = y - 5x$ **5.** $q = \frac{m - 6p}{6}$ **6.** $x = \frac{8 - 3y}{2}$

7. $z = \frac{xy}{3}$ **8.** $y = \frac{w - 3x - 3z}{3}$ **9.** $y = \frac{2w - z}{8}$

Review 40

1. \$915.60; \$900; no mode **2.** 5.375; 5; no mode
3. 12; 9; no mode **4.** 73.5; 73; 72 **5.** 70; 70; 70

Review 41

1. yes **2.** yes **3.** yes **4.** yes **5.** no **6.** yes **7.** no **8.** no

Review 42

1. $y < 6$ **2.** $x < 5$ **3.** $w > 5$ **4.** $x > 16$ **5.** $y \geq 2$
6. $a < 4$ **7.** $h \leq 3$ **8.** $s > 5$ **9.** $b < 5$ **10.** $x < 15$
11. $a > 12$ **12.** $b < 14$ **13.** $c > 2$ **14.** $d < 5$
15. $f > 19$ **16.** $x + 35 \geq 75$; at least \$40

Review 43

1. <; > **2.** <; > **3.** >; < **4.** >; < **5.** <; >
6. >; < **7.** $a < 6$ **8.** $b < -7$ **9.** $c < 4$
10. $x < -14$ **11.** $y > -4$ **12.** $f > 7$ **13.** $d \leq -2.5$
14. $m \geq -15$ **15.** $x < 20$ **16.** $n \leq -20$ **17.** $k > -1.6$
18. $p \geq -15$ **19.** $t > -3.5$ **20.** $z > -10$ **21.** $w \geq 7.2$

Review 44

1. $x < 2$; −3 −2 −1 0 1 2 3

2. $x < 3$; −3 −2 −1 0 1 2 3

3. $x < 2$; −3 −2 −1 0 1 2 3

4. $x < 2$; −3 −2 −1 0 1 2 3

5. $x > -1$; −3 −2 −1 0 1 2 3

6. $x > -3$; −3 −2 −1 0 1 2 3

Review 45

1. $x \leq -3$ or $x \geq 2$;

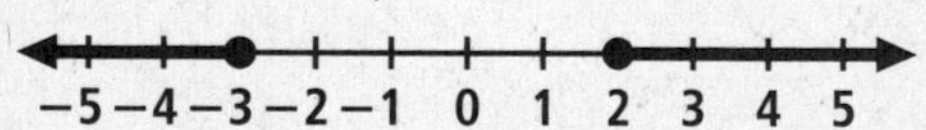

2. $x \leq -1$ or $x > 3$;

−2 −1 0 1 2 3 4

3. $-4 \leq x < 2$;

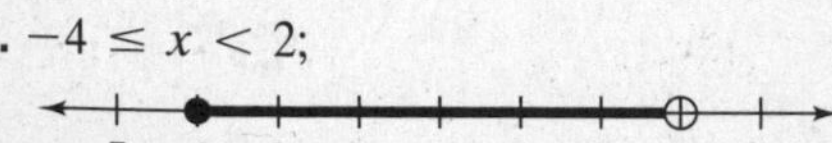

4. $x \leq -4$ or $x > 2$;

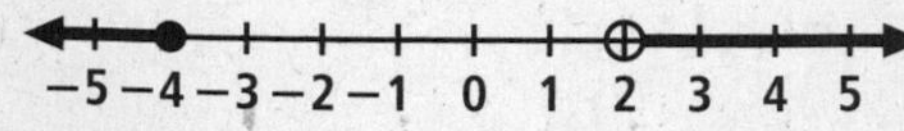

Review 45 *(continued)*

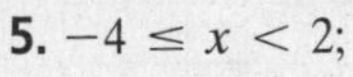

5. $-4 \le x < 2$;

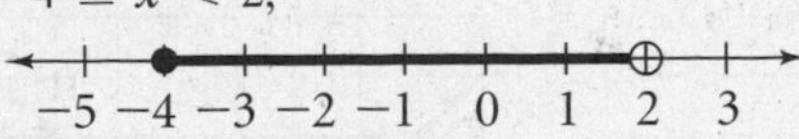

6. $-4 < x \le 6$;

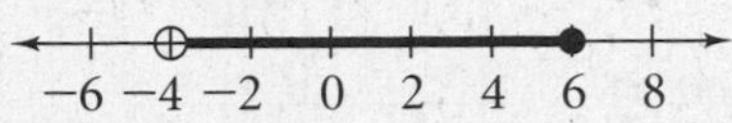

7. $-2 \le x < 4$;

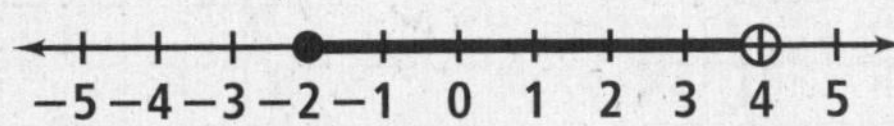

8. $x < -2$ or $x \ge 3$;

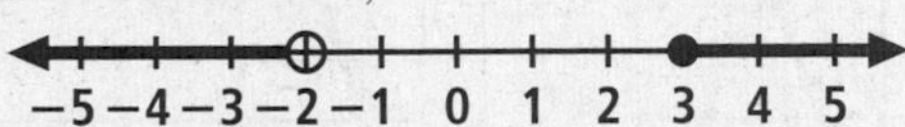

9. $x \le -5$ or $x > -3$;

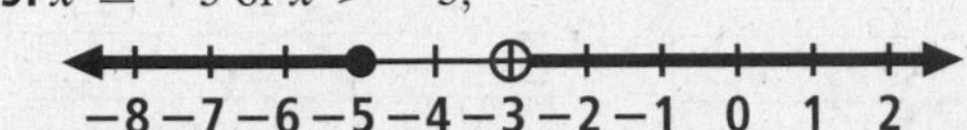

10. $-4 \le x < -2$;

−8 −7 −6 −5 −4 −3 −2 −1 0 1 2

11. $x < -5$ or $x \ge 3$;

−6 −5 −4 −3 −2 −1 0 1 2 3 4

12. $-2 < x \le 8$;

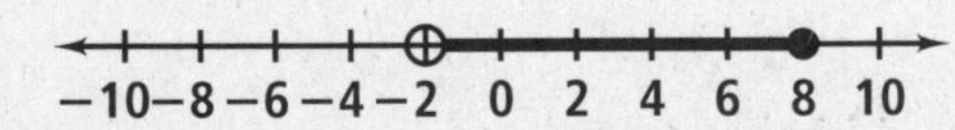

Review 46

1. $-5 < c < 5$;

−5 −4 −3 −2 −1 0 1 2 3 4 5

2. $u \le -1$ or $u \ge 1$;

−5 −4 −3 −2 −1 0 1 2 3 4 5

3. $-3 \le a \le 1$;

−5 −4 −3 −2 −1 0 1 2 3 4 5

4. $m < \frac{1}{3}$ or $m > 1$;

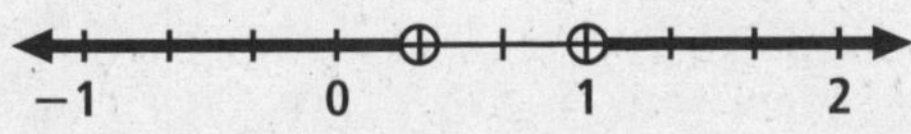

5. $y \le 5$ or $y \ge 7$;

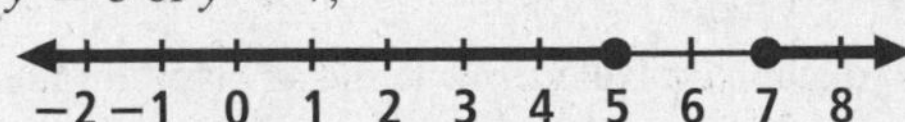

6. $-4 < n < 3$;

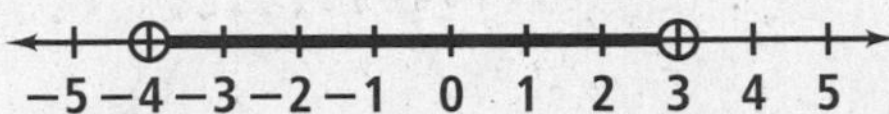

7. $-2 \le u \le 6$;

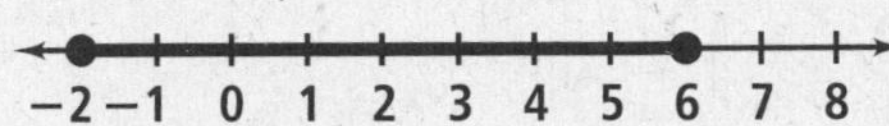

8. $g < -4$ or $g > -1$;

−8 −7 −6 −5 −4 −3 −2 −1 0 1 2

9. $y \le -4$ or $y \ge 5$;

−5 −4 −3 −2 −1 0 1 2 3 4 5

Review 47

1. yes **2.** no **3.** yes **4.** 1 **5.** 3 **6.** 9 **7.** 12 **8.** 24 **9.** 1 **10.** 3 **11.** 2 **12.** 1

Review 48

1. 3 **2.** 13.5 **3.** 7.5 **4.** 9

Review 49

1. 5 **2.** 20 **3.** 25% **4.** 20% **5.** 15 **6.** 12 **7.** 50% **8.** 6.25 **9.** $\frac{1}{7}$ or 0.14 **10.** 75% **11.** 48 h **12.** $3.30

Review 50

1. 50% increase **2.** 29% decrease **3.** 33% increase **4.** 100% increase **5.** Answers may vary. Sample: For a classroom with 20 students there is a 40% decrease. **6.** 42% increase **7.** 13% decrease

Review 51

1. $\frac{3}{5}$ **2.** $\frac{1}{10}$ **3.** $\frac{2}{25}$ **4.** $\frac{41}{50}$ **5.** 0 **6.** $\frac{2}{5}$ **7.** $\frac{9}{50}$ **8.** $\frac{7}{10}$ **9.** $\frac{2}{25}$ **10.** $\frac{9}{50}$

Review 52

1.–2. Check students' work.

Review 53

1. It shows total distance traveled. **2.** It shows elapsed time.
3.

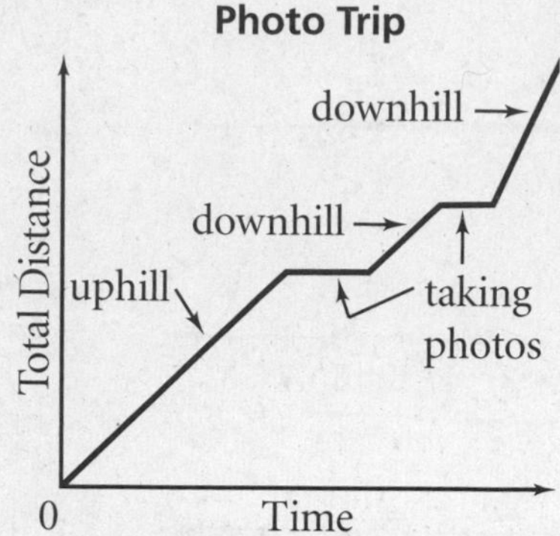

4. The flat part of the graph. When you are taking pictures, you are not moving. **5.** The ride down Lookout Knoll. When you ride down, you go faster and cover the distance in a shorter amount of time.
6.

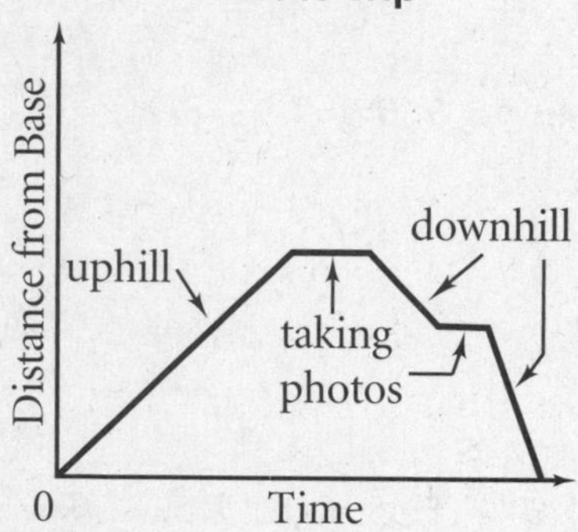

Review 54

1. $d = \{-4, -2, 0, 1, 2\}$; $r = \{-1, 0, 3, 4, 6\}$
2. $d = \{-6, -3, 1, 2, 3\}$; $r = \{-4, -1, 2, 4, 7\}$ **3.** no
4. yes **5.** -8 **6.** 6 **7.** -4 **8.** 5 **9.** 1 **10.** 5 **11.** $\{0, 4\}$
12. $\{-3, 0, -1\}$ **13.** $\{2, 3, 7\}$ **14.** $\{-2, 0, 4\}$ **15.** $\{4, 6\}$
16. $\{-7, -5\}$

Review 55

1.

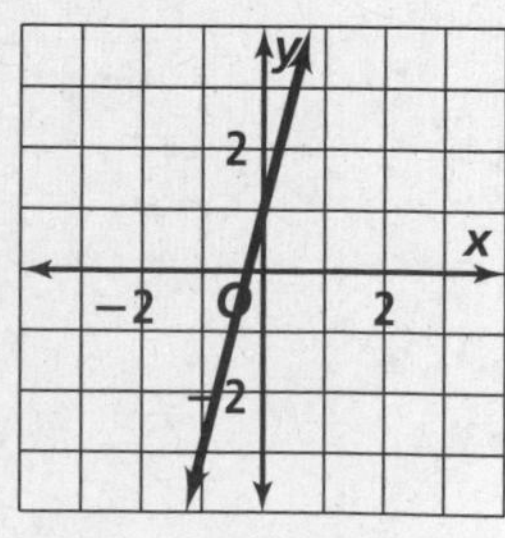

2.

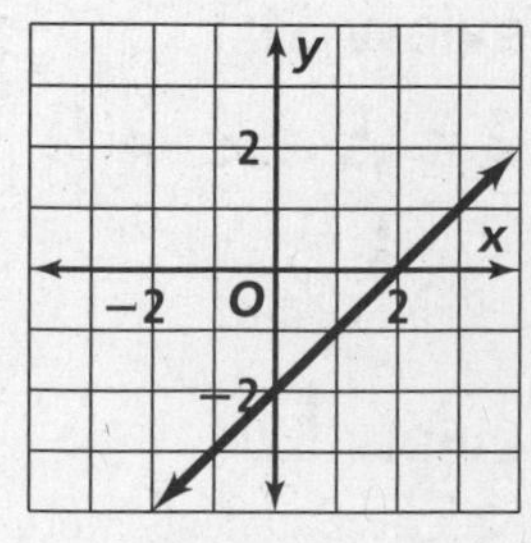

3.

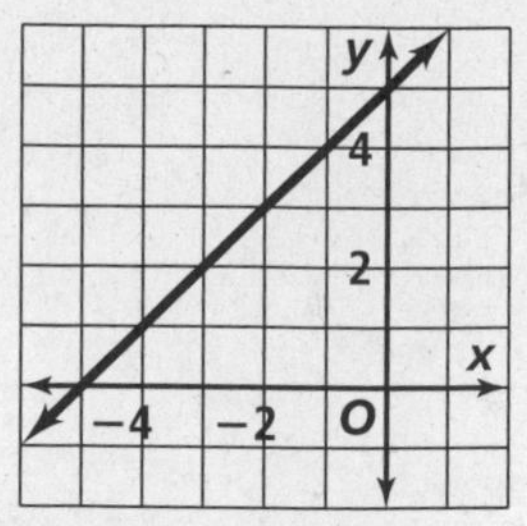

4.

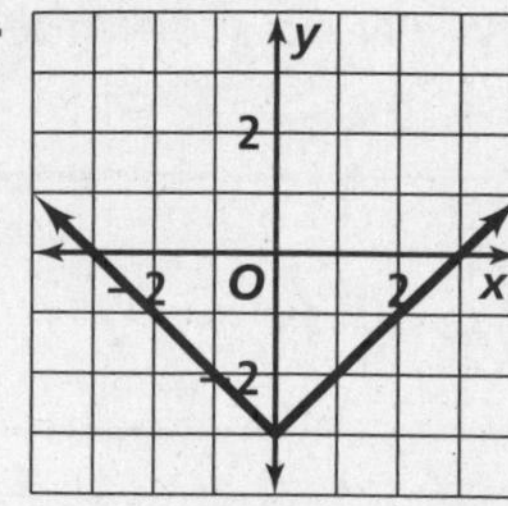

5.

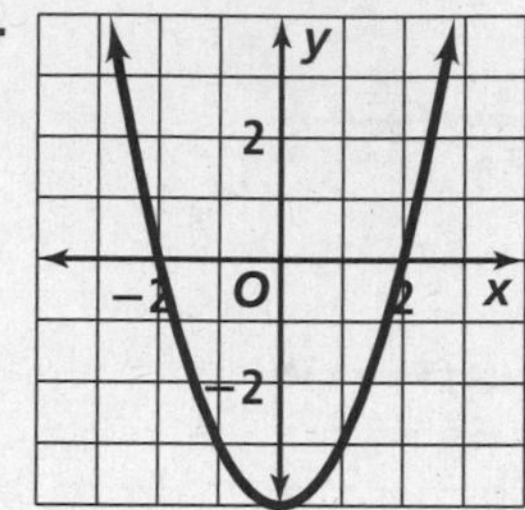

6.

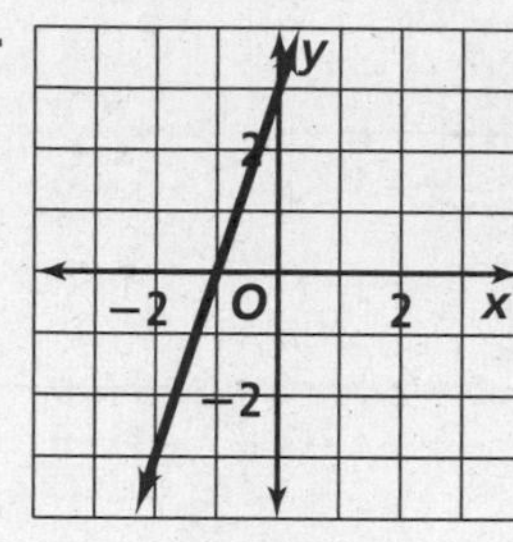

7.

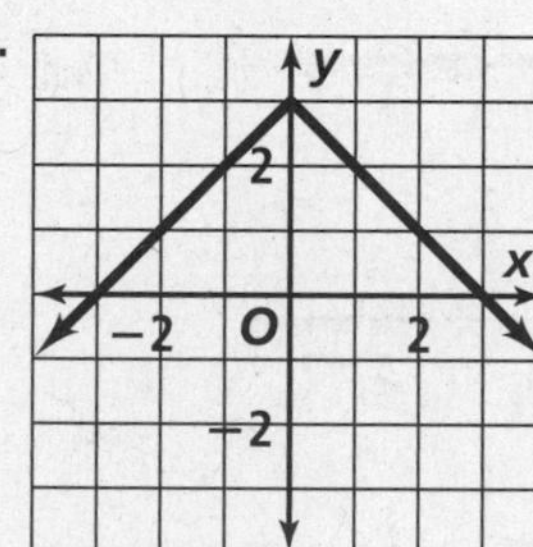

8.

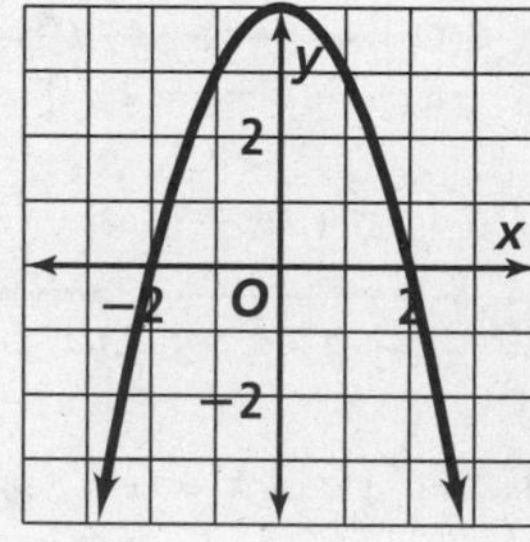

Review 56

1. $f(x) = 3x$ **2.** $f(x) = x - 1$ **3.** $f(x) = x^2$
4. $\ell(w) = 4w + 2$ **5.** $w(\ell) = \frac{1}{2}\ell$ **6.** $c(a) = 0.99a$
7. $d(t) = 65t$ **8.** $v(q) = 0.25q$ **9.** $e(n) = 8.25n$ **10.** $f(d) = 3d$

Review 57

1. yes; -3 **2.** no **3.** yes; -2 **4.** yes; 1 **5.** yes; 2 **6.** no

Review 58

1. 7 **2.** -4 **3.** 11 **4.** $-6, -8$ **5.** 8, 11
6. $-37, -42$ **7.** $A(n) = 2 + 7(n - 1)$; 30; 65
8. $A(n) = 5 - 4(n - 1)$; -11; -31
9. $A(n) = -52 + 11(n - 1)$; -8; 47

Review 59

1. 1 **2.** $\frac{1}{2}$ **3.** -4 **4.** 0 **5.** undefined

Review 60

1. Check students' work. **2.** Check students' work.
3. $y = 3x + 1$ **4.** $y = -2x + 3$ **5.** $y = x - 1$

Review 61

1. 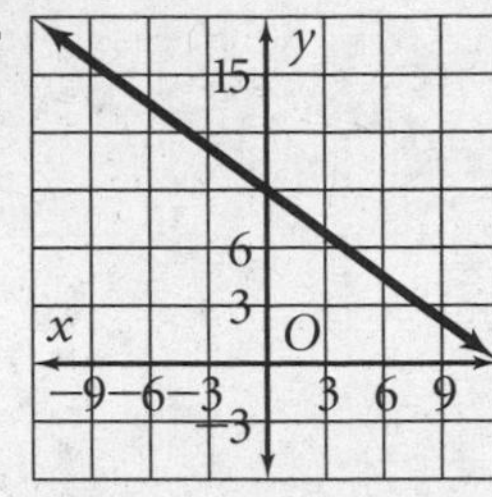

2. 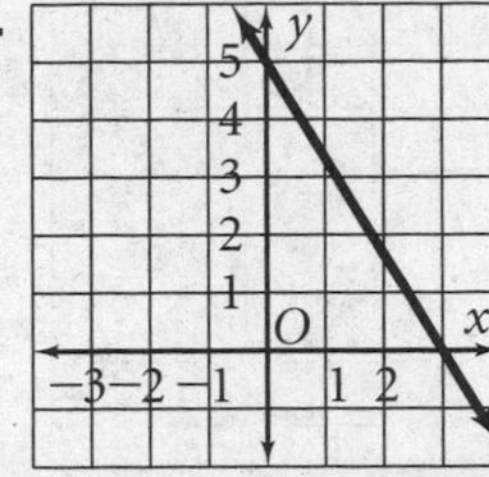

3. 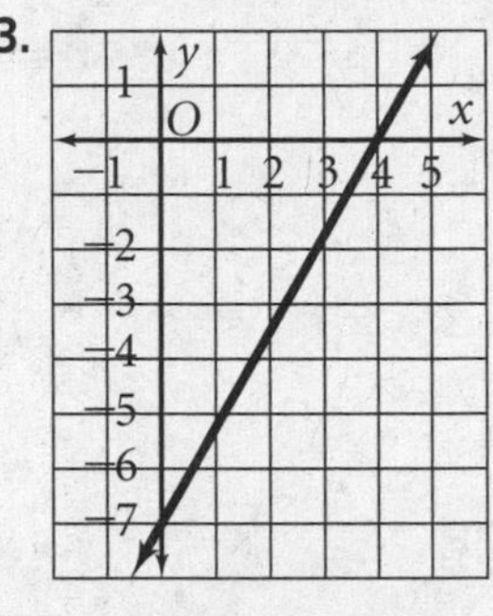

4. 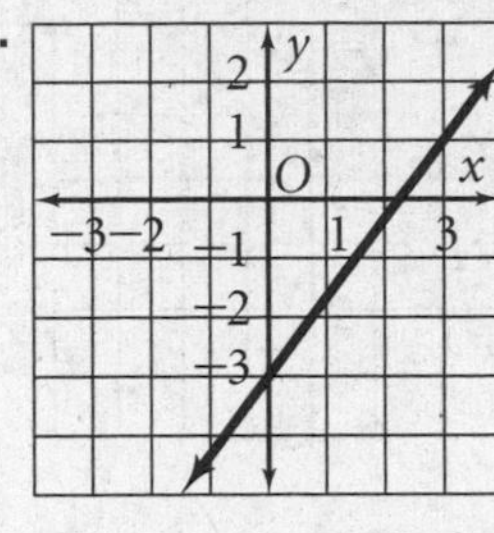

5. 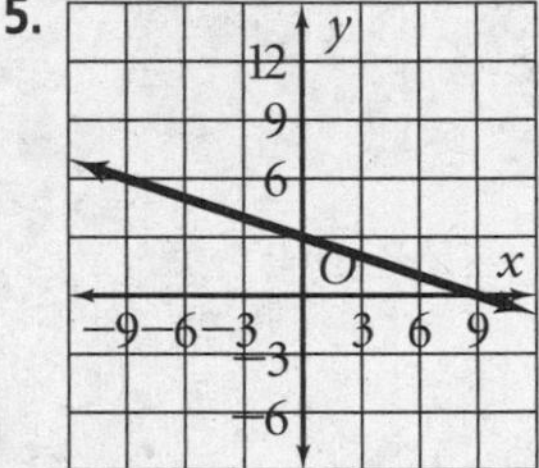

6. 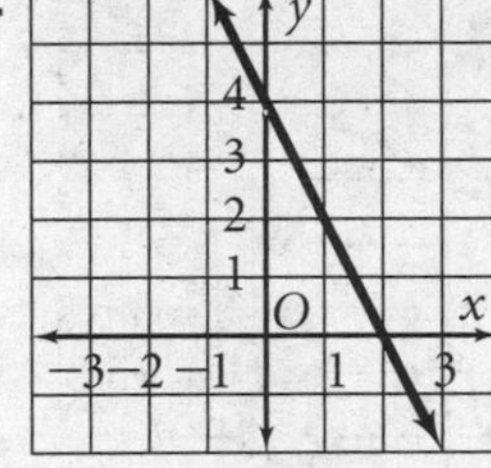

Review 62

Note: One possible form of the answer is given.

1. $y - 3 = \frac{1}{2}(x - 4)$ **2.** $y - 2 = 4(x - 5)$

3. $y - 2 = -2(x + 4)$ **4.** $y = 5$ **5.** $y + 5 = x - 2$

6. $y - 3 = 5(x - 4)$ **7.** $y + 1 = -3(x - 2)$

8. $y - 4 = \frac{2}{3}(x + 3)$ **9.** $y + 1 = -\frac{1}{4}(x - 4)$

10. $y = -2$ **11.** $y - 4 = x - 8$ **12.** $y - 1 = \frac{1}{2}(x + 4)$

13. $y + 6 = \frac{2}{3}(x - 6)$ **14.** $y = \frac{7}{8}x$ **15.** $y + 2 = -\frac{1}{2}x$

16. $y - 7 = \frac{3}{2}(x - 2)$ **17.** $y + 10 = 2(x + 1)$

18. $y - 7 = -x$ **19.** $y - 1 = -2x$

Review 63

1. $y = 5x - 1; y = -\frac{1}{5}x - 1$

2. $y = -3x + 4; y = \frac{1}{3}x + 4$

3. $y = 2x - 3; y = -\frac{1}{2}x - 3$

4. $y = -\frac{1}{4}x + 2; y = 4x + 2$

5. $y = \frac{1}{2}x - 1; y = -2x - 1$

6. $y = -\frac{1}{2}x + 2; y = 2x + 2$

7. $y = -3x + 2; y = \frac{1}{3}x + 2$

8. $y = \frac{2}{3}x - 2; y = -\frac{3}{2}x - 2$

9. $y = 3x + 6; y = -\frac{1}{3}x + 6$

Review 64

1. Answers may vary. Sample: $y = -0.075x + 21$
2. Answers may vary. Sample: $y = 4x + 20$
3. Answers may vary. Sample: $y = 0.12x - 1.2$

Review 65

1. up 12 units **2.** down 15 units
3. left 13 units **4.** right 15 units

5. 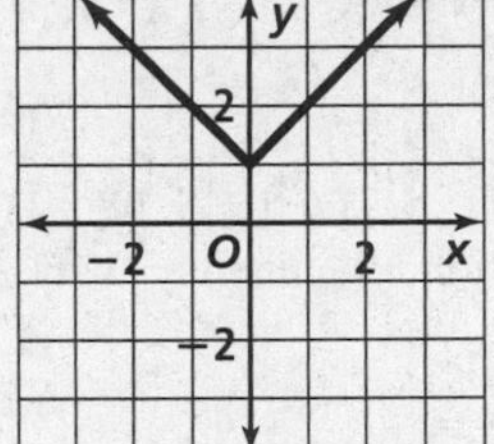

6. 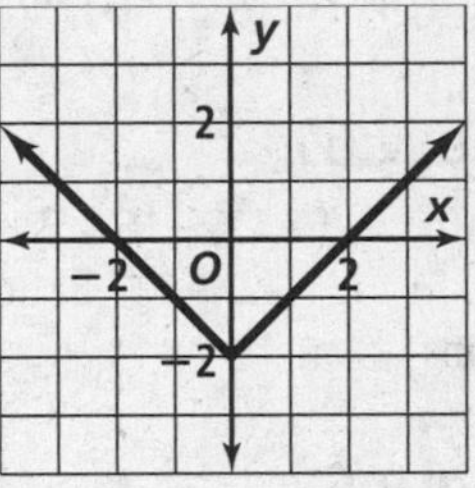

7. 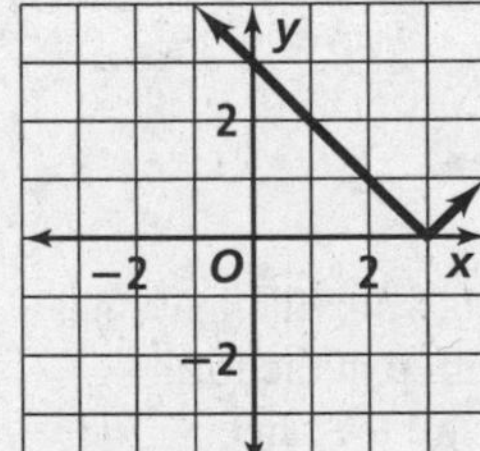

8. 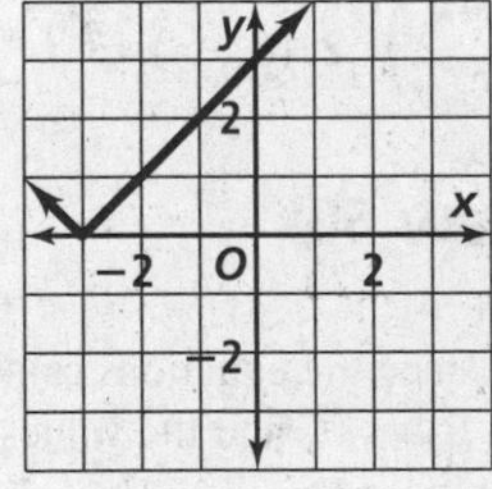

Review 66

1. (2, 8);

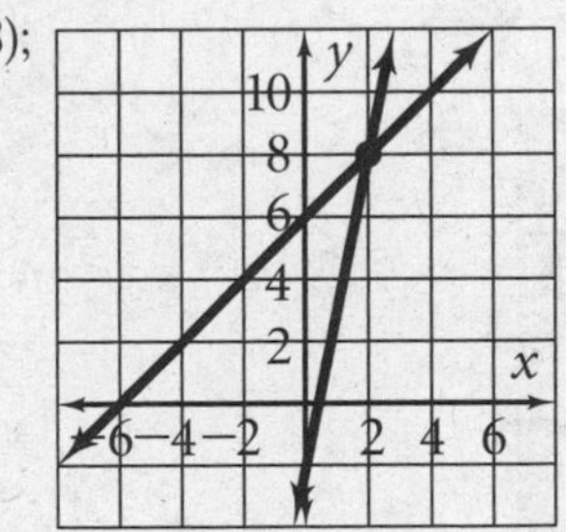

ANSWERS

Review 66 *(continued)*

2. (6, 8);

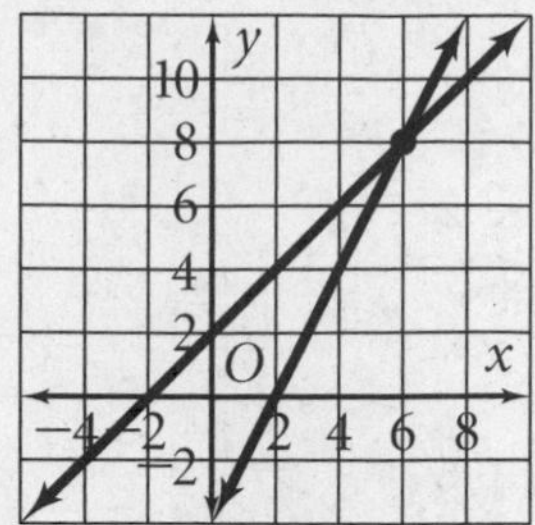

3. (0, 2);

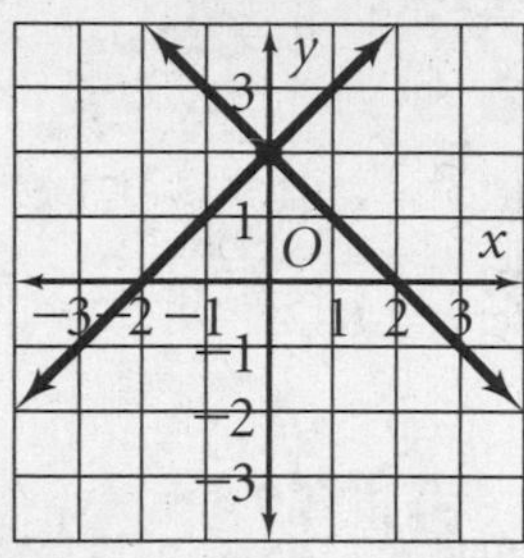

4. no solution **5.** infinite number of solutions **6.** (3, 0) **7.** (−1, −4) **8.** (−2, −7) **9.** no solution

Review 67

1. (4, 10) **2.** (−12, −16) **3.** (−1, 1) **4.** (1.5, 1) **5.** (2, −1) **6.** (3, 0.5) **7.** (−2, −1) **8.** no solution **9.** infinitely many solutions

Review 68

1. $\left(-\frac{4}{3}, 2\right)$ **2.** (6, −4) **3.** (−1, 1)

Review 69

1. $5x + 4y = 7, 4x + 4y = 6$; \$1.00, \$.50; Elimination is easiest since the equations can be written in the form $Ax + By = C$ and the values of B are the same.
2. $82 - 5x = y, 37 - 2x = y$; \$15.00, \$7.00; Use substitution since the equations are in $y = mx + b$ form.

Review 70

1.

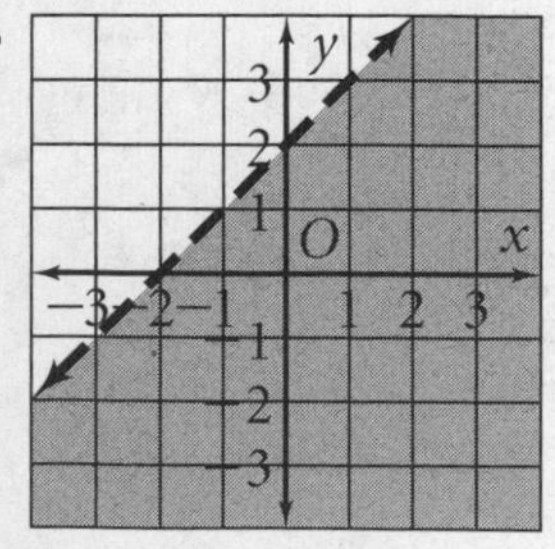

2.

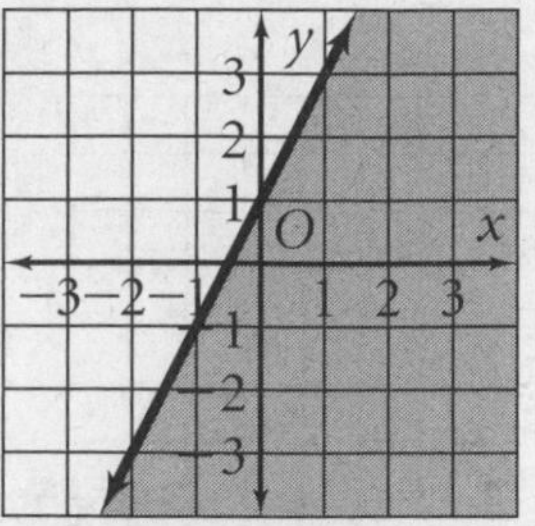

3.

Review 71

1.

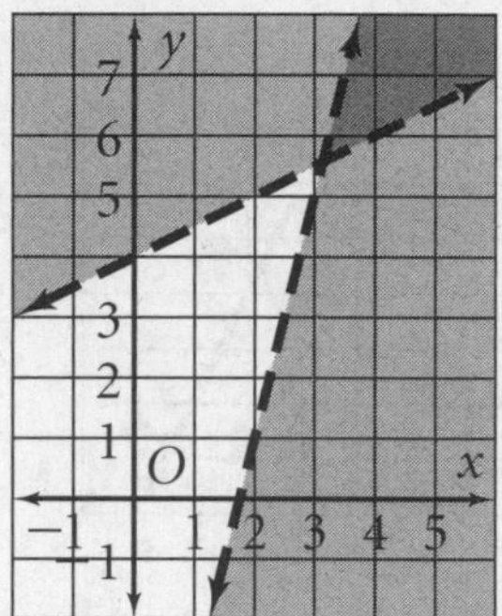

2.

3.

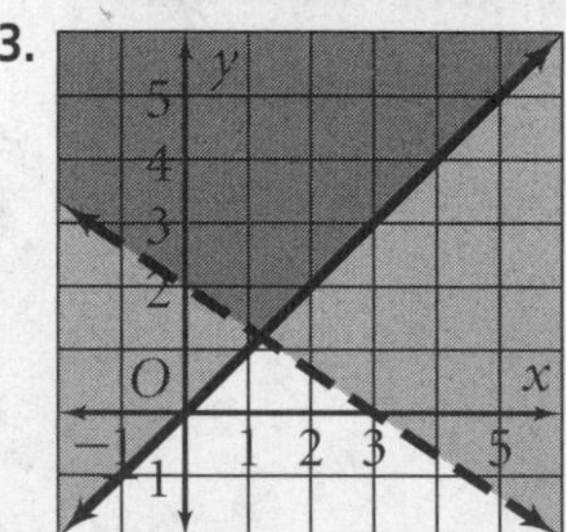

Review 72

1. $\frac{1}{1000}$ **2.** 1 **3.** $\frac{1}{625}$ **4.** $\frac{1}{343}$ **5.** $\frac{4}{9}$ **6.** $\frac{1}{625x^4}$ **7.** $\frac{1}{4}$ **8.** 1

9. $\frac{1}{b^5}$ **10.** $\frac{2401}{16}$ **11.** $3a$ **12.** $-\frac{1}{64}$ **13.** $\frac{1}{a^3b^4}$ **14.** $\frac{3}{x^2y}$

Review 72 *(continued)*

15. $\frac{12x}{y^3}$ **16.** 128 **17.** $\frac{1}{12x}$ **18.** $\frac{y}{12x^2}$ **19.** $\frac{1}{2x^2}$ **20.** $\frac{9a^2}{b}$
21. 1000

Review 73

1. 4.2×10^5 **2.** 5.1×10^9 **3.** 2.6×10^{11}
4. 8.3×10^8 **5.** 7.5×10^{-4} **6.** 4.005×10^{-3}
7. 634,500,000 **8.** 0.000032 **9.** 4,081,000 **10.** 0.002581
11. 0.0307 **12.** 1,526,000 **13.** 0.000804 **14.** 762,500
15. 68,250 **16.** 0.00003081 **17.** 838.47 **18.** 0.036245

Review 74

1. 5 **2.** 3 **3.** 3 **4.** 1 **5.** −1 **6.** −2 **7.** 12 **8.** 18 **9.** −9
10. $24x^6$ **11.** $\frac{18m^6}{a^2}$ **12.** $\frac{p^5}{q^9}$ **13.** $120x^7$ **14.** $8x^7y^3$
15. $189x^2y^2$ **16.** $24y^9$ **17.** x^3 **18.** x^4y **19.** $12ab$
20. $\frac{r^4}{s^2}$ **21.** $3pq$

Review 75

1. 390,625 **2.** a^{20} **3.** 64 **4.** $64x^3$ **5.** $49a^8$ **6.** $27g^6$
7. $g^{10}h^{15}$ **8.** s^{12} **9.** x^6y^{12} **10.** 1 **11.** g^2 **12.** c^{28} **13.** 1
14. $512a^3b^{18}$ **15.** x^4y^6 **16.** x^{14} **17.** $9x^4y^2$ **18.** $-8x^6$
19. x^9y^{12} **20.** $27x^6y^3$ **21.** $-64x^6y^9$ **22.** 1 **23.** $\frac{1}{x^2}$

Review 76

1. z^3 **2.** $\frac{729}{64}$ **3.** m **4.** $\frac{1}{5}$ **5.** b^6 **6.** $\frac{a^3}{3}$ **7.** $\frac{1}{8}$ **8.** d^5 **9.** x^2
10. 10^{18} **11.** $2x$ **12.** $\frac{2x^3}{3}$ **13.** x^7 **14.** $\frac{3x^2}{2}$ **15.** $\frac{1}{x^5}$ **16.** x^8

Review 77

1. 512, 2048, 8192 **2.** −48, 96, −192 **3.** 1, −1, 1
4. $\frac{3}{4}, \frac{3}{8}, \frac{3}{16}$ **5.** $\frac{5}{4}, -\frac{5}{8}, \frac{5}{16}$ **6.** 0.01, 0.001, 0.0001
7. 1875, 9375, 46,875 **8.** −40.5, −60.75, −91.125
9. 121.5, 364.5, 1093.5 **10.** $\frac{8}{81}, -\frac{8}{243}, \frac{8}{729}$
11. 112, −224, 448 **12.** 6.25, 3.125, 1.5625
13. 2048, 8192, 32,768 **14.** 4.75, −2.375, 1.1875

Review 78

1. 328,050 cans **2.** 67,500 **3.** $16,000
4. 1200 cells; 76,800 cells

Review 79

1. $y = 5{,}000 \cdot 1.03^{10}$; 6720 **2.** $y = 100 \cdot 1.08^5$; $147
3. $y = 2 \cdot 1.1^8$; 4 ft **4.** $y = 1000 \cdot 0.90^5$; $590
5. $y = 5000 \cdot 0.865^8$; $1567
6. $y = 20{,}000 \cdot 0.875^{10}$; $5262

Review 80

1. $6x + 2y - 4$ **2.** $a^2 + 8a + 3$ **3.** $9x^2 - 2x - 3$
4. $7x^2 + 8x - 9$ **5.** $14z^3 + 2z^2 - 3$ **6.** $7x^2 + 1$
7. $5x^2 - x + 1$ **8.** $6x^3 - x^2 - 3x + 3$ **9.** $7y^2 + 1$
10. $2x^2 - 17$ **11.** $5x^3 + 3$ **12.** $4x^3 - 2x^2 + 6x - 5$
13. $x^3 + 4x^2 + 6x - 7$ **14.** $x^2 - x + 10$

Review 81

1. $7(3x - 2)$ **2.** $5y(y^2 - 2y + 3)$ **3.** $x(x^2 + 3x + 1)$
4. $3x^2(1 + 2x^2)$ **5.** $6x(3x^2 - x + 4)$ **6.** $z^2(z - 3)$
7. $6k(2k^2 + k - 3)$ **8.** $2x(3x^2 - 2x + 4)$
9. $4p(2p^3 + 3p + 1)$ **10.** $18x(2x - 1)$ **11.** $6x(x + 3)$
12. $2x(3x^2 - x + 4)$ **13.** $6x(x^2 + x - 1)$ **14.** $5x^2(x + 1)$
15. $3(x + 1)(x + 1)$ **16.** $5x(2x + 7)$ **17.** $8x^3(x^2 + 2x - 1)$
18. $3x(3x - 5)(x + 1)$

Review 82

1. $x^2 + 4x - 12$ **2.** $x^2 - 12x + 32$ **3.** $x^2 + 6x - 27$
4. $x^2 - 5x - 14$ **5.** $2x^2 + 11x + 12$ **6.** $2x^2 + 13x + 20$
7. $14x^2 - 20x - 16$ **8.** $9x^2 + 12x + 4$ **9.** $5x^2 + 6x + 1$
10. $2x^2 + 3x + 1$ **11.** $8x^2 - 2x - 1$ **12.** $3x^2 + 5x - 2$

Review 83

1. $x^2 - 14x + 49$ **2.** $x^2 + 2x + 1$ **3.** $x^2 - 8x + 16$
4. $x^2 - 2xy + y^2$ **5.** $4x^2 + 12x + 9$ **6.** $9x^2 - 30x + 25$
7. $4x^2 + 4x + 1$ **8.** $25x^2 - 40x + 16$ **9.** $x^2 - 49$
10. $x^2 - 64$ **11.** $x^2 - 9$ **12.** $x^2 - y^2$ **13.** $16x^2 - 9$
14. $4x^2 - 25$ **15.** $9x^2 - 4$ **16.** $49x^2 - 1$

Review 84

1. $(y + 9)(y + 2)$ **2.** $(x - 3)(x - 5)$ **3.** $(x - 9)(x - 2)$
4. $(y - 1)(y - 4)$ **5.** $(x + 4)(x + 2)$
6. $(y - 6)(y - 2)$ **7.** $(r + 12)(r + 1)$
8. $(x - 3)(x - 13)$ **9.** $(x - 2)(x - 8)$
10. $(x - 2)(x + 1)$ **11.** $(x - 8)(x + 4)$
12. $(x - 9)(x + 2)$ **13.** $(x + 2)(x + 5)$
14. $(x - 3)(x - 8)$ **15.** $(x + 7)(x + 9)$

Review 85

1. $(2x + 7)(x + 2)$ **2.** $(2x - 5)(2x - 1)$
3. $(x - 2)(6x - 1)$ **4.** $(3x - 4)(2x + 5)$
5. $(x + 2)(3x - 2)$ **6.** $(8x - 3)(x + 2)$
7. $(x - 1)(2x - 3)$ **8.** $(5x + 4)(x - 6)$
9. $(3x + 1)(2x - 3)$ **10.** $(2x + 3)(3x - 1)$
11. $(4x + 3)(2x - 1)$ **12.** $(3x - 1)(5x - 2)$

Review 86

1. $(a + 2)(a - 1)$ **2.** $(x + 8)(x - 8)$
3. $(y + 7)(y - 7)$ **4.** $(2x + 5)(2x - 5)$
5. $(3y + 4)(3y - 4)$ **6.** $(5x + 8)(5x - 8)$
7. $3(x + 2)(x - 2)$ **8.** $2(x + 3)(x - 3)$
9. $4(x - 2)(x + 2)$ **10.** $(x + 15)(x - 15)$
11. $(x - 12)(x + 12)$ **12.** $(4x + 7)(4x - 7)$
13. $6(x - 3)(x + 3)$ **14.** $7(x - 4)(x + 4)$
15. $5(x - 5)(x + 5)$

Review 87

1. $(x + 2)(2x^2 + 1)$ **2.** $(x + 3)(2x^2 + 3)$
3. $(x - 5)(5x^2 + 2)$ **4.** $(x + 6)(2x^2 - 5)$
5. $(7x - 4)(x^2 + 1)$ **6.** $(3x - 4)(3x^2 - 6)$
7. $(x + 1)(3x - 2)$ **8.** $(x + 1)(2x - 3)$
9. $(5x - 1)(x + 7)$

Review 88

1. upward, zero

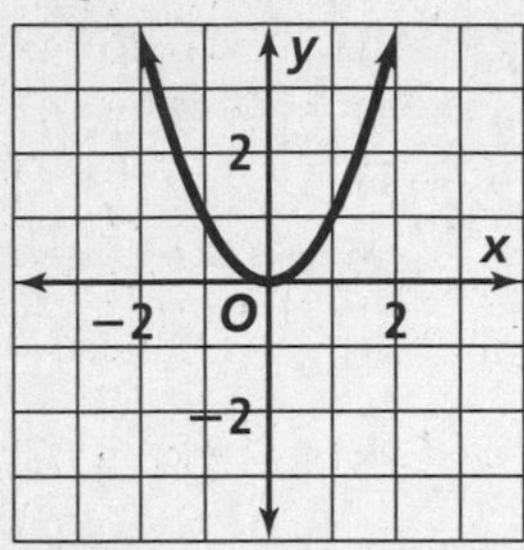

2. upward, up one

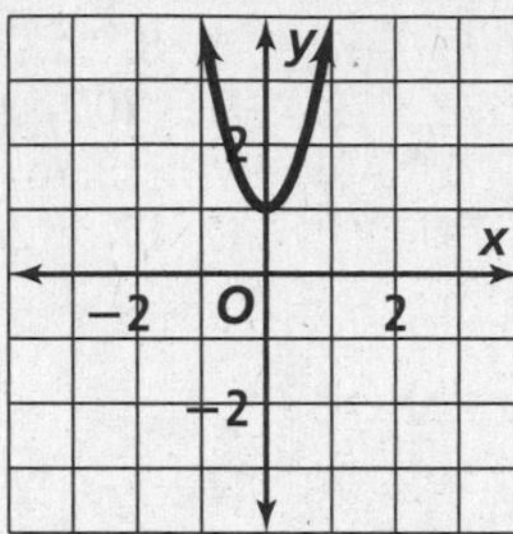

3. downward, zero

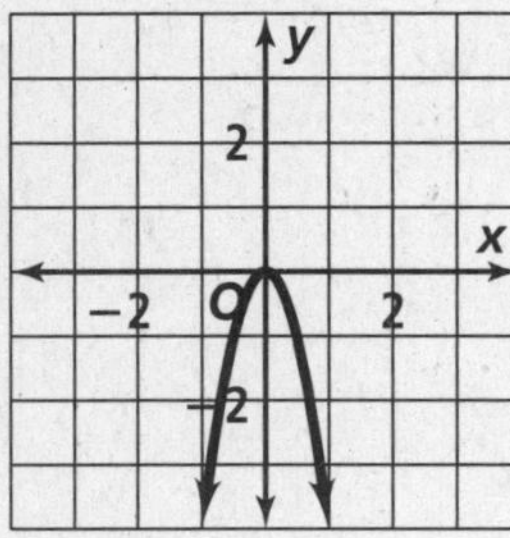

4. upward, zero

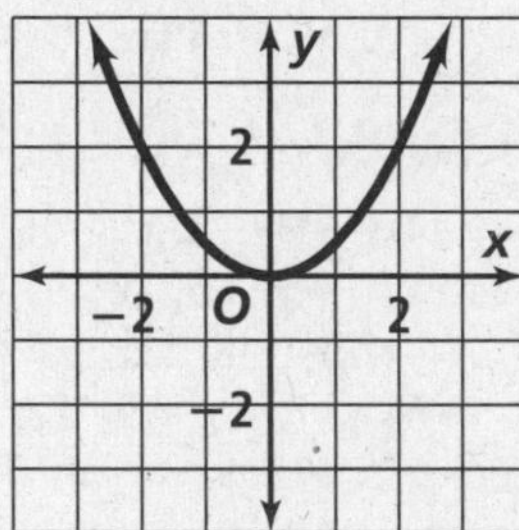

5. downward, down three

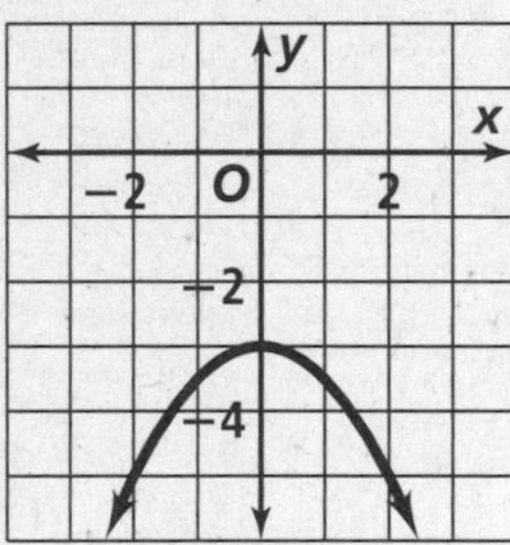

6. upward, up one-half

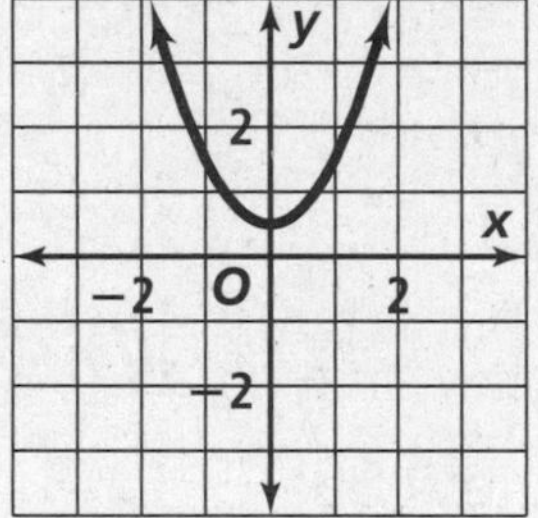

7. upward, down four

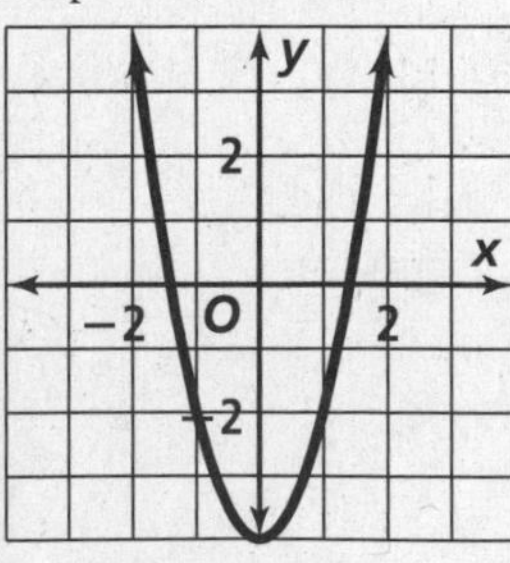

8. downward, down three

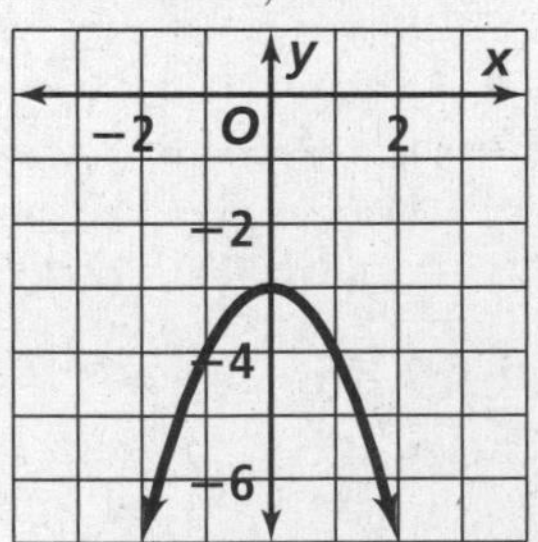

9. downward, up seven

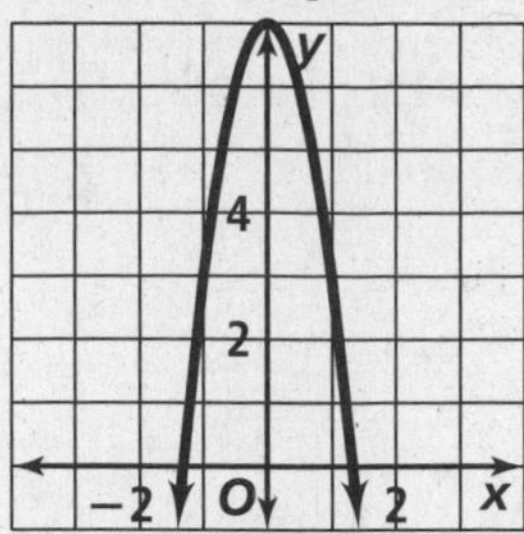

10. upward, down two

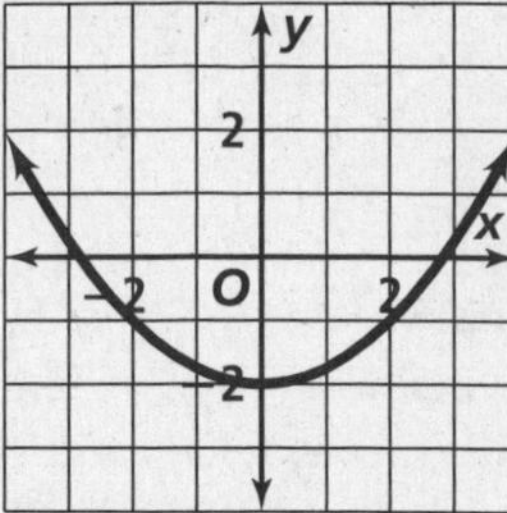

Review 89

1. $y = -x^2 + 4x + 16$ **2.** $x = 2$ **3.** $(2, 20)$
4. Answers may vary.
5.

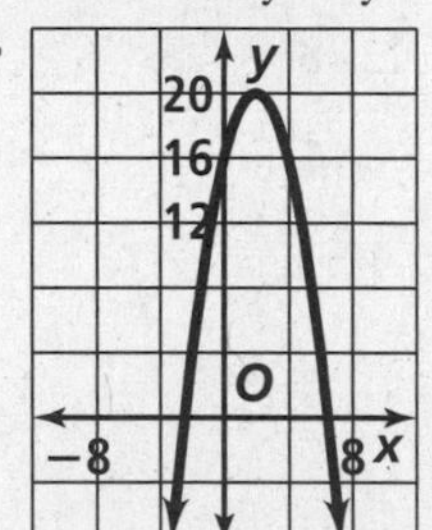

6.

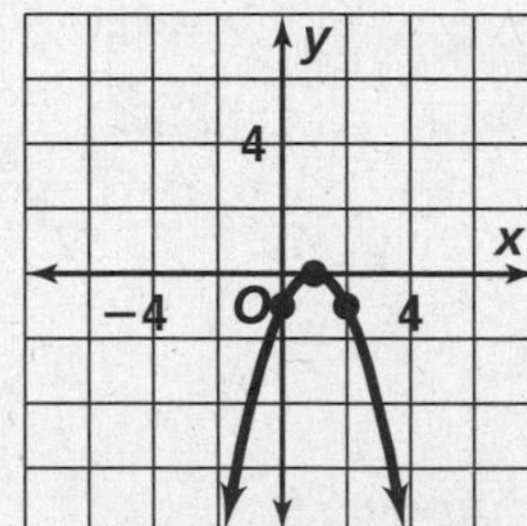

7.

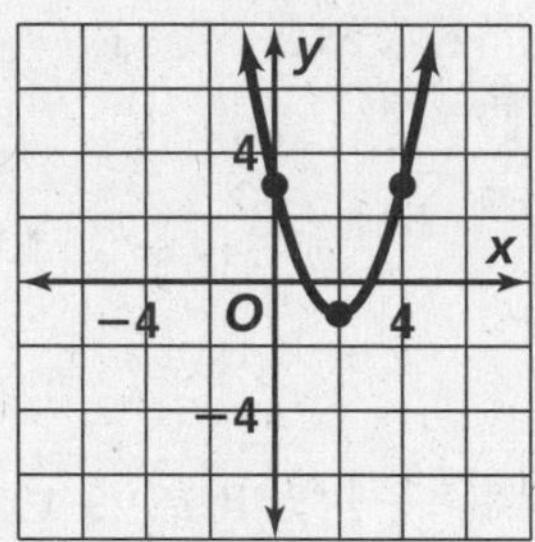

Review 90

1.

Number	Principal Square Root	Negative Square Root	Rational/ Irrational	Perfect Square or $\sqrt{\ }$ Between Which Two Consecutive Integers
$\frac{1}{64}$	$\frac{1}{8}$	$-\frac{1}{8}$	rational	perfect square
26	5.099 . . .	−5.099 . . .	irrational	between 5 and 6
23	4.795 . . .	−4.795 . . .	irrational	between 4 and 5
−36	undefined	undefined	undefined	undefined
$\frac{81}{324}$	$\frac{1}{2}$	$-\frac{1}{2}$	rational	perfect square

2. 10; rational **3.** 3.464 . . . ; irrational **4.** undefined **5.** 7.937 . . . ; irrational **6.** 0; rational **7.** $-\frac{1}{3}$; rational

Review 91

1. $4x^2 = 100$	**2.** $2x^2 = 6$	**3.** $x^2 = -4$	**4.** $81x^2 = 25$
$x^2 = 25$	$x^2 = 3$	$x^2 = -4$	$x^2 = \frac{25}{81}$
$x = \pm\sqrt{25}$	$x = \pm\sqrt{3}$	$x = \pm\sqrt{-4}$	$x = \pm\sqrt{\frac{25}{81}}$
$x = \pm 5$	$x = \pm\sqrt{3}$	no solution	$x = \pm\frac{5}{9}$

Review 92

1. −2, −5 **2.** 4, −3 **3.** 2, 3 **4.** 4, 2 **5.** −1.5, −1 **6.** $\frac{4}{3}$, −2
7. −4, 7 **8.** 2.5, −2 **9.** $\frac{2}{3}$, −1

Review 93

1a. Divide both sides by 3. **1b.** Add 15 to both sides.
1c. Square $\frac{1}{2}$ the coefficient of x, and add to both sides.
1d. Write the right side as a square. **1e.** Take the square root of both sides. **1f.** Simplify and solve for x. **1g.** Write two equations. **1h.** Solve. **2.** 8, 2 **3.** 8, 4 **4.** 0.26, 11.74
5. 0.58, −8.58

Review 94

1. $-\frac{1}{3}$, −2 **2.** −2 , −1 **3.** 0.44 , −1.69 **4.** 2 , $\frac{1}{5}$
5. −6, 1 **6.** 1.47, −1.14 **7.** 4, −1 **8.** 1.45, −1.20

Review 95

1. −15; none; none **2.** −12; none; none **3.** 0; one; one
4. 0; one **5.** 7; two **6.** −56; none

Review 96

1. Linear; $y = 3x - 1$ **2.** Quadratic; $y = -2x^2$
3. Linear; $y = \frac{1}{2}x + 2$ **4.** Exponential; $y = -2 \cdot 3^x$
5. Quadratic; $y = \frac{1}{4}x^2$

Review 97

1. $2\sqrt{6}$ **2.** 30 **3.** $16\sqrt{5}$ **4.** $6\sqrt{3}$ **5.** $3\sqrt{2}$ **6.** $\frac{5\sqrt{3}}{3}$
7. $4\sqrt{7}$ **8.** $\frac{4\sqrt{5}}{5}$ **9.** $\frac{\sqrt{14}}{5}$ **10.** $\frac{\sqrt{5}}{8}$ **11.** $\frac{\sqrt{6}}{2}$ **12.** $\frac{4}{3}$

Review 98

1. 8 **2.** 9.2 **3.** 13 **4.** 4.9 **5.** 8.1 **6.** 8.5 **7.** 10.9 **8.** 15 **9.** 10
10. 7 **11.** 5 **12.** 12

Review 99

1. 7.2 **2.** 8.5 **3.** 9.9 **4.** 7.1 **5.** (1, 5) **6.** $\left(-1, -1\frac{1}{2}\right)$
7. (−4, 6) **8.** (−4, 3)

Review 100

1. $4\sqrt{6}$ **2.** $10\sqrt{3}$ **3.** $4\sqrt{3}$ **4.** $4\sqrt{3}$ **5.** $7\sqrt{6}$ **6.** $4\sqrt{7}$
7. $5 + 2\sqrt{5}$ **8.** 1 **9.** $2 - \sqrt{6}$ **10.** $17 + 4\sqrt{15}$
11. $14 + 2\sqrt{10}$ **12.** $6 + \sqrt{3}$

Review 101

1. 27 **2.** 11 **3.** no solution **4.** 4 **5.** 2 **6.** 5 **7.** $\frac{35}{3}$ **8.** 5
9. 12

Review 102

1.

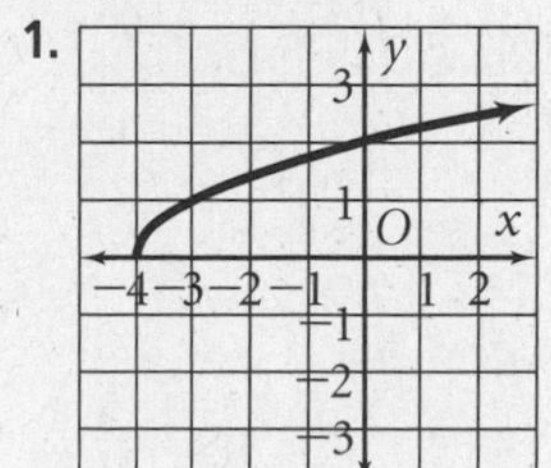

2.

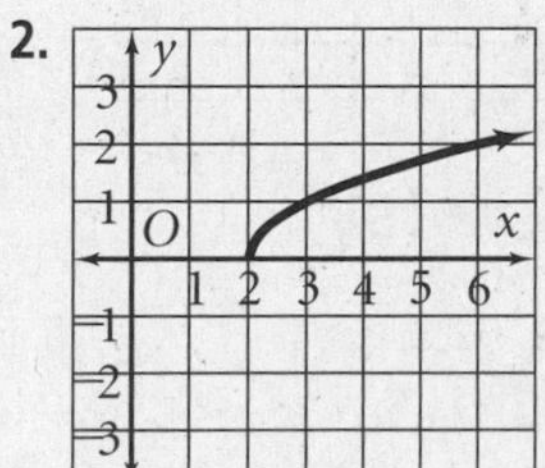

ANSWERS

Review 102 *(continued)*

3. 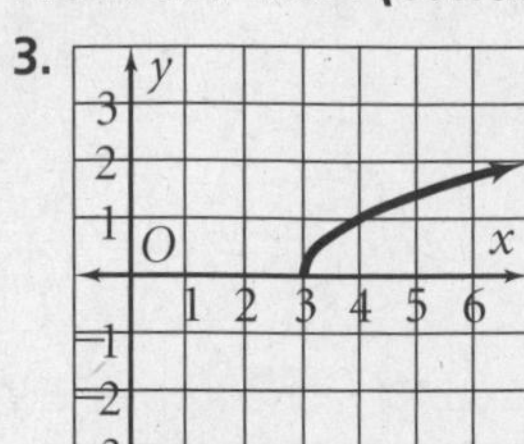

4. 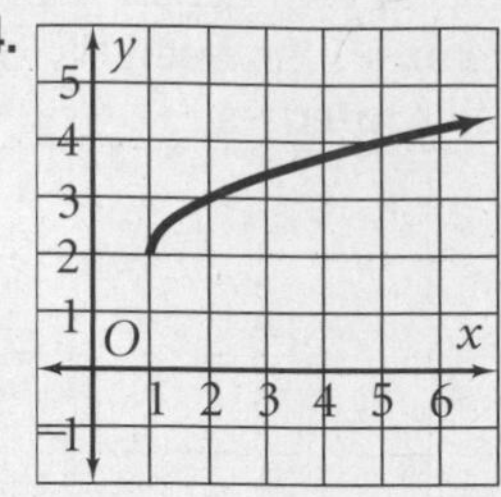

5. 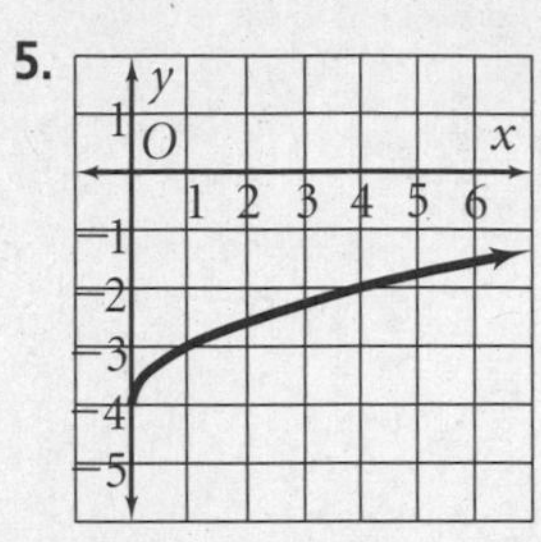

6. 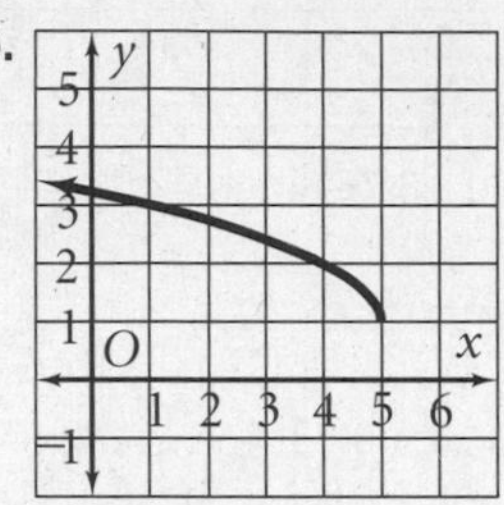

7. 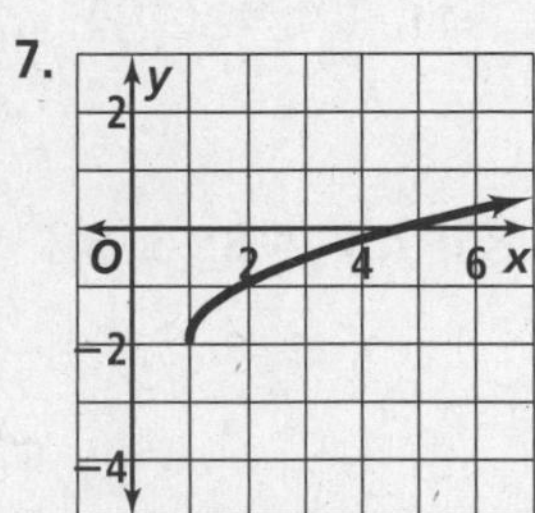

8. 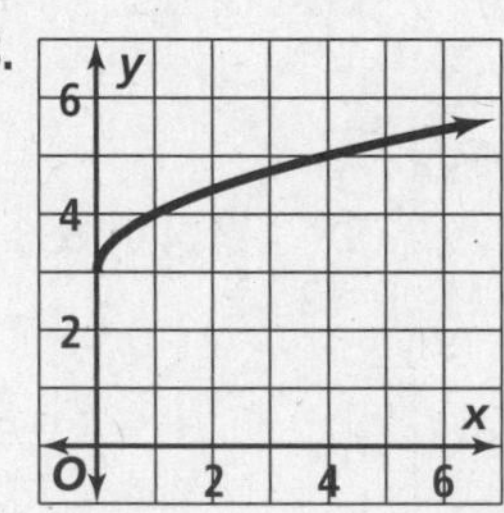

9. 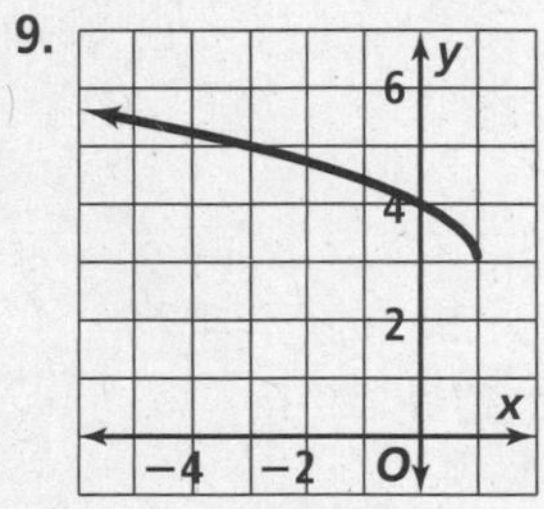

10. 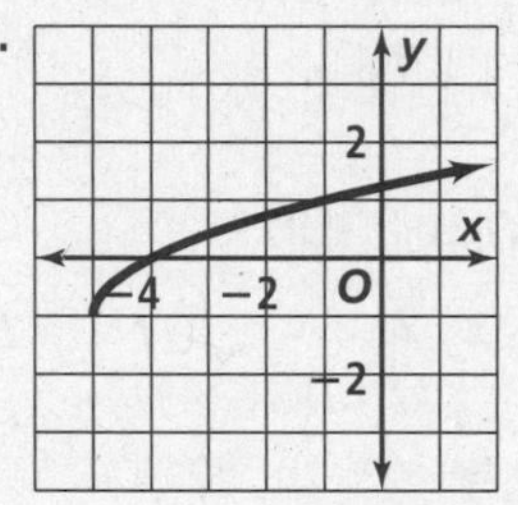

11. 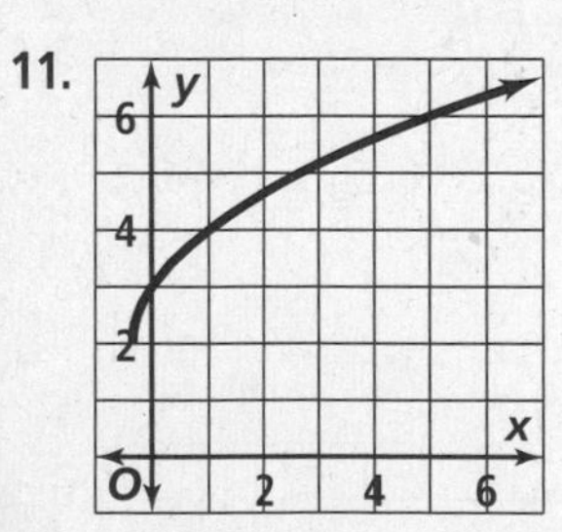

12. 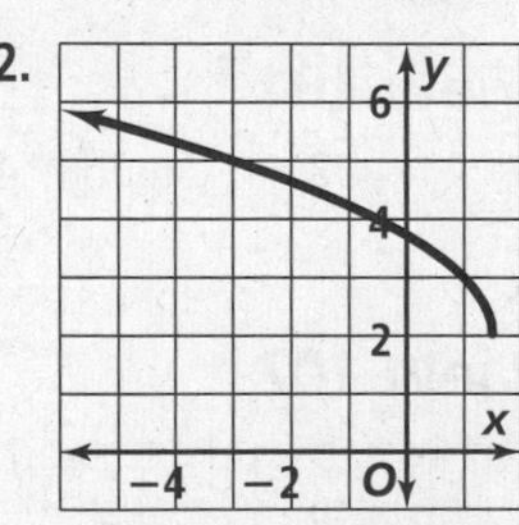

Review 103

1. $\frac{3}{5}$ **2.** $\frac{4}{5}$ **3.** $\frac{3}{4}$ **4.** $\frac{4}{5}$ **5.** $\frac{4}{3}$ **6.** $\frac{4}{5}$

Review 104

1. 151; 132 **2.** $10.22

3.

Price	No. Sold
$12.50	132
$12.00	138
$11.50	144
$11.00	151
$10.22	162

Review 105

1. 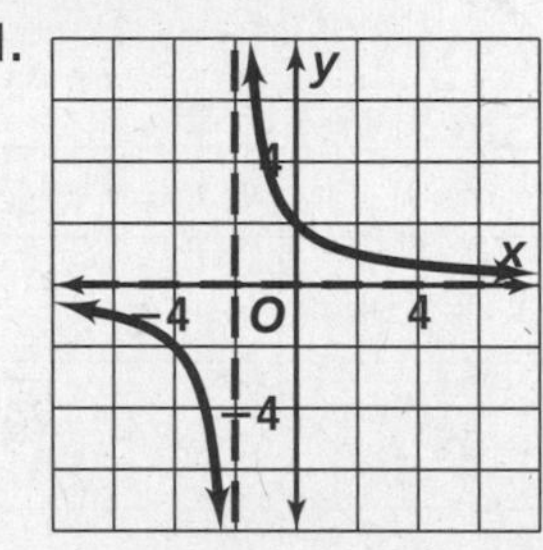

2. 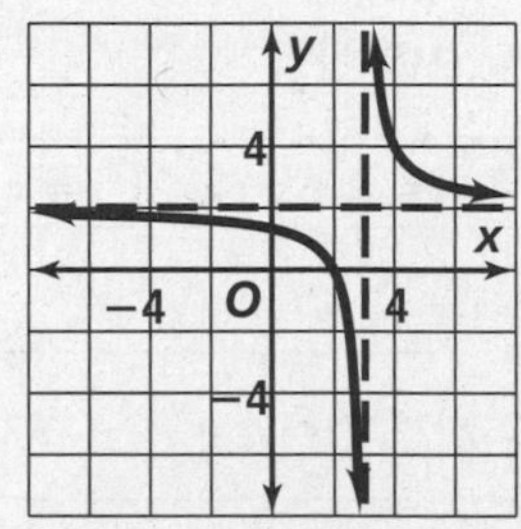

3. 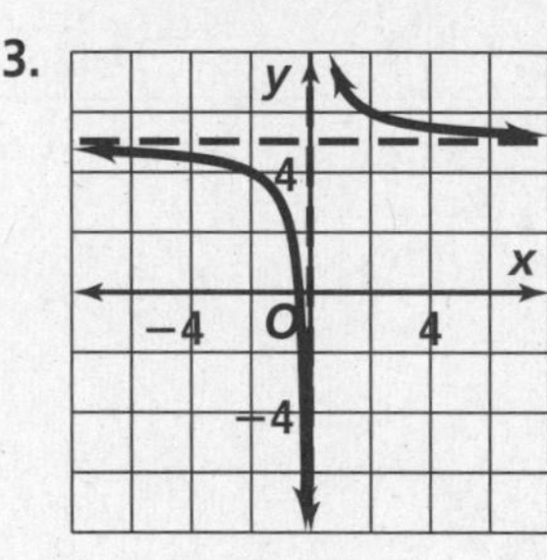

4. 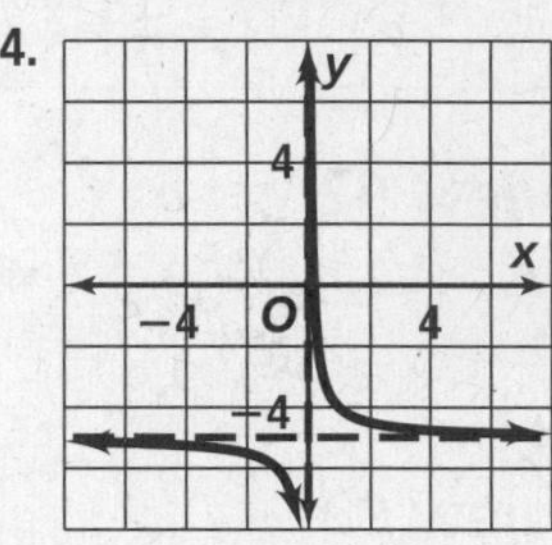

5. 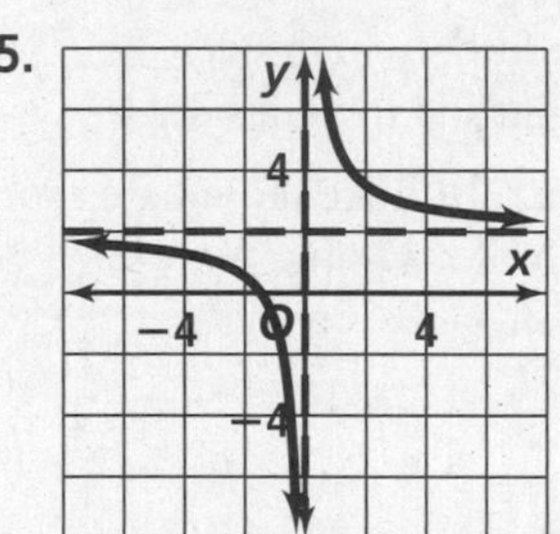

6. 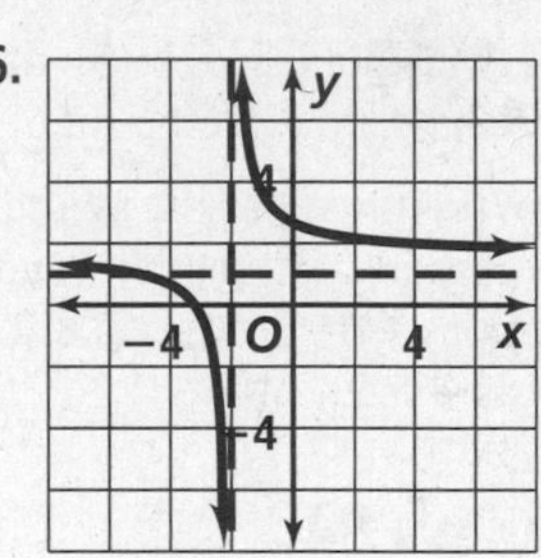

Review 106

1. $\frac{5}{3}$ **2.** $\frac{1}{2}$ **3.** 2 **4.** $\frac{5}{x + 4}$ **5.** $\frac{x - 8}{x - 3}$ **6.** $\frac{3x}{x + 5}$

Review 107

1. $\frac{x - 1}{2}$ **2.** x **3.** $x - 1$ **4.** $\frac{x + 3}{5}$ **5.** $\frac{x}{30}$ **6.** $\frac{x - 3}{x - 2}$

Review 108

1. $x + 2$ **2.** $x + 3 + \frac{2}{2x - 1}$ **3.** $x^2 - 2x + 4 - \frac{16}{x + 2}$
4. $x^2 + x - 1$ **5.** $x - 4$ **6.** $6x + 18 - \frac{12}{x + 4}$
7. $2x - 8$ **8.** $2x^2 + 7x + 3$ **9.** $x^2 + 9x + 26 + \frac{36}{x - 2}$
10. $4x^2 + 10x + 6$

ANSWERS

Review 109

1. $\frac{3x^2 + x - 11}{(x + 2)(x - 2)}$ 2. $\frac{6x - 1}{(x + 1)(x + 2)}$

3. $\frac{-10}{(z - 4)(-z - 4)}$ 4. $\frac{x^2 + 2x - 4}{(x + 5)(x + 1)}$

5. $\frac{4x - 11}{(x - 3)(x + 3)}$ 6. $\frac{3}{x + 2}$

Review 110

1. $\frac{12}{35}$ **2.** $\frac{25}{24}$ **3.** $\frac{15}{16}$ **4.** $-\frac{2}{7}$ **5.** -2 **6.** 5 **7.** 2 **8.** 0, 4 **9.** 2

10. 4 **11.** No solution **12.** 2 **13.** $\frac{1}{9}$ **14.** $\frac{5}{17}$ **15.** $\frac{1}{4}$

16. $-\frac{3}{2}$ **17.** 8 **18.** $\frac{3}{5}$ **19.** -4 **20.** $-\frac{3}{2}$ **21.** 15

Review 111

1. 11! **2.** 11^{11} **3.** 14! **4.** 14^{14}

Review 112

1. 10 **2.** 924 **3a.** 462 **3b.** 126 **4.** 38,760 **5.** 10

Geometry Topics

Review 113

1.

2.

3.

4.

5.

6.  , 

Review 114

1.–6. Check students' work.

7.

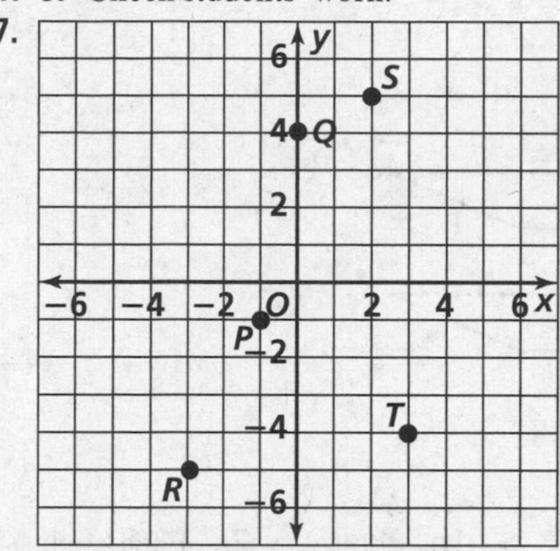

8. Sample: *R, Q, T* **9.** *P, R, S*

10. Sample: $\overleftrightarrow{RS}$ and $\overleftrightarrow{QT}$

Review 115

Samples:

1. $\overleftrightarrow{AB}$ and $\overleftrightarrow{EF}$ **2.** $\overleftrightarrow{AB}$ and $\overleftrightarrow{DH}$ **3.** $\overleftrightarrow{AC}$ and $\overleftrightarrow{AE}$

4. plane *ABD* and plane *EFH* **5.** plane *CDH* and plane *BFD* **6.** plane *CDH*, plane *ACG*, and plane *ABD*

7. $\overleftrightarrow{EG}$ and $\overleftrightarrow{BF}$

8.

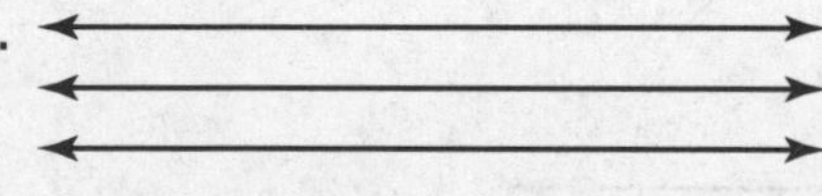

9.

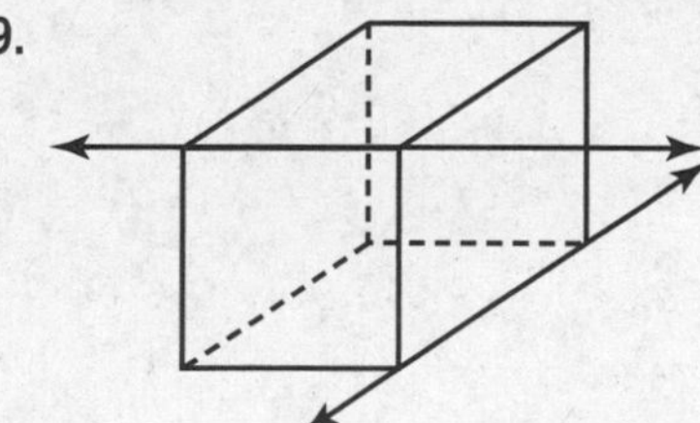

10.

11.

ANSWERS

Review 115 *(continued)*

12.

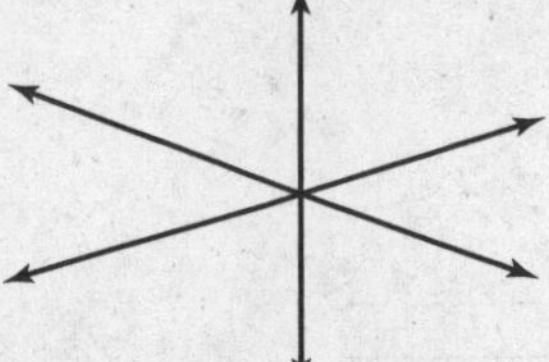

13.

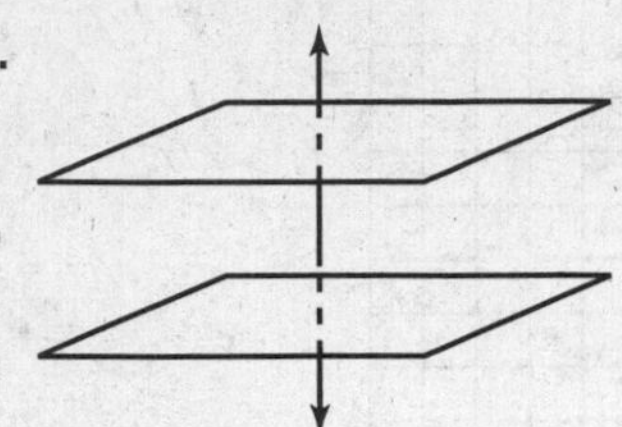

Review 116

1a. Each angle is 108°. **1b.** obtuse **2a.** Each angle is 72°. **2b.** acute **3a.** Each angle is 108°. **3b.** obtuse **4.** 90°, right **5.** 55°, acute **6.** 110°, obtuse **7.** 50°, acute **8.** 90°, right **9.** 100°, obtuse

Review 117

Samples:

1.

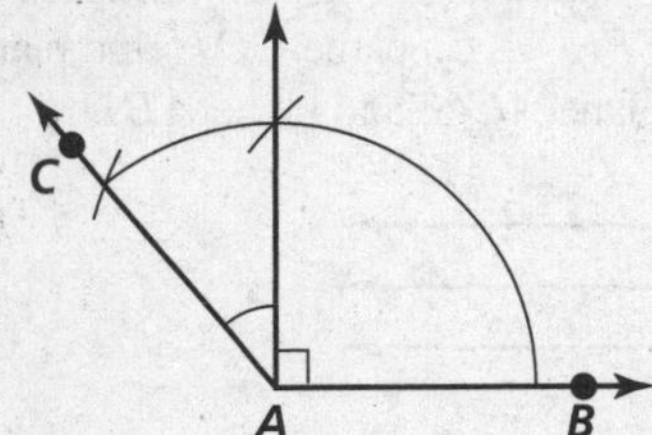

2.

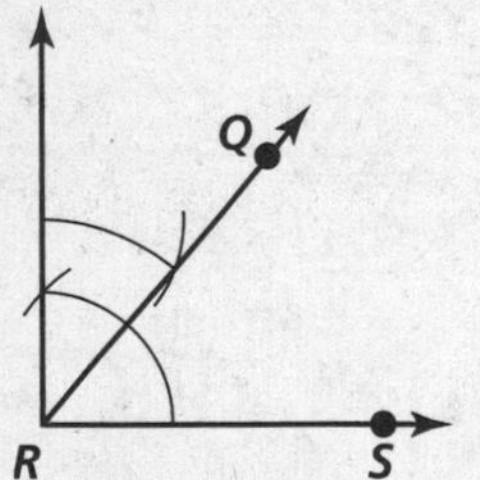

3.

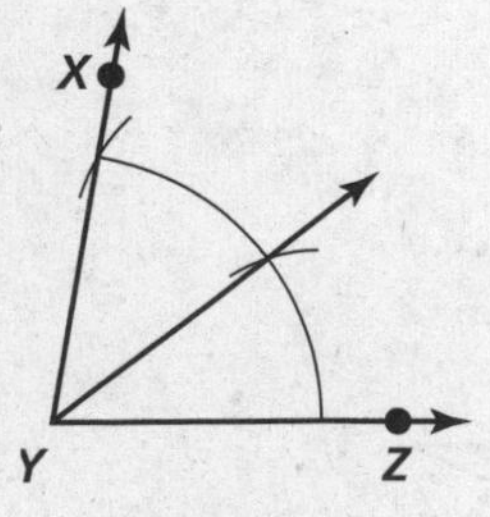

4.

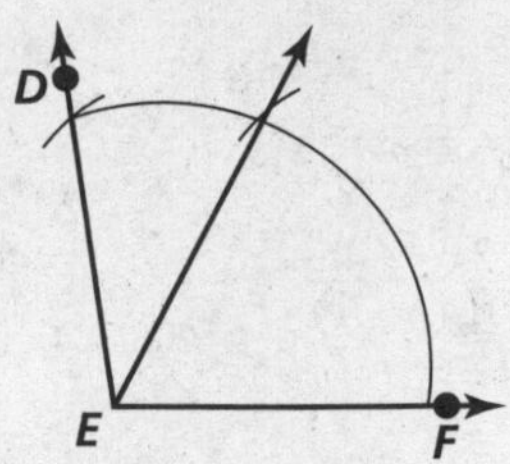

5.

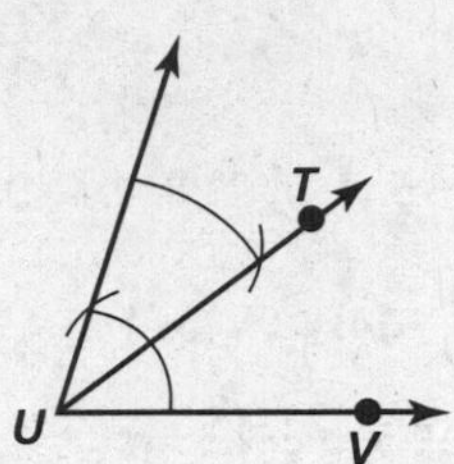

6.

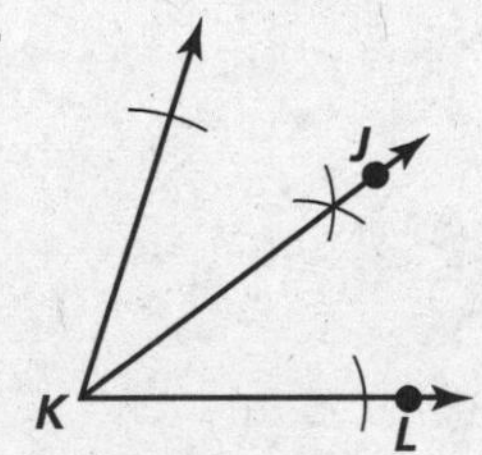

Review 118

1.

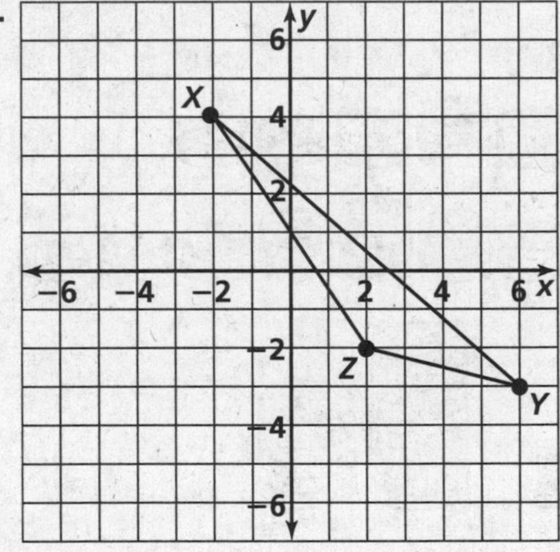

2. $XY \approx 10.6, YZ \approx 4.1, XZ \approx 7.2$
3. $4.1 + 7.2 = 11.3, 11.3 > 10.6$ **4.** 12.2
5. 8.1 **6.** 9.9 **7.** 11.4 **8.** 9.2 **9.** 8.5
10. 18.0 **11.** 8.5 **12.** 17

Review 119

1a. 1 by 60, 2 by 30, 3 by 20, 4 by 15, 5 by 12, and 6 by 10; Check students' drawings. **1b.** 122, 64, 46, 38, 34, and 32 **2a.** 1 by 36, 2 by 18, 3 by 12, 4 by 9 and 6 by 6; Check students' drawings. **2b.** 1 by 36 **3.** 3 cm by 6 cm

Review 119 *(continued)*

4. Sample:

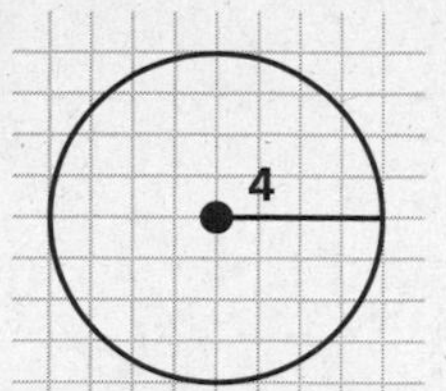

5. Sample: 50 units^2 **6.** Sample: 50.3 units^2
7. They are close.

Review 120

1.–3. Check students' work. **4.** If you hear thunder, then you see lightning; statement: false; converse: false. **5.** If your pants are jeans, then they are blue; statement: false; converse: false. **6.** If you are eating a tangerine, then you are eating an orange fruit; statement: false; converse: true. **7.** If a number is an integer, then it is a whole number; statement: true; converse: false. **8.** If a triangle has one angle greater than 90°, then it is an obtuse triangle; statement: true; converse: true. **9.** If $n^2 = 64$, then $n = 8$; statement: true; converse: false. **10.** If you got an A for the quarter, then you got an A on the first test; statement: false; converse: false. **11.** If a figure has four sides, then it is a square; statement: true; converse: false. **12.** If $x = 144$, then $\sqrt{x} = 12$; statement: true; converse: true.

Review 121

1. If $n = 15$ or n $= -15$, then $|n| = 15$. If $|n| = 15$, then $n = 15$ or $n = -15$. **2.** If two segments are congruent, then they have the same measure. If two segments have the same measure, then they are congruent. **3.** If you live in California, then you live in the most populated state in the United States. If you live in the most populated state in the United States, then you live in California. **4.** If an integer is a multiple of 10, then its last digit is 0. If an integer's last digit is 0, then it is a multiple of 10. **5.** No; counterexamples may vary. Sample: A giraffe is a large animal. **6.** Yes; two planes intersect if and only if they form a line. **7.** Yes; a number is an even number if and only if it ends in 0, 2, 4, 6, or 8. **8.** Yes; a triangle is a three-sided figure if and only if the angle measures sum to 180°.

Review 122

1. Law of Detachment; the police officer will give Darlene a ticket. **2.** Law of Syllogism; if two planes do not have any points in common, then they are parallel. **3.** Law of Detachment; Landon has a broken arm. **4.** Not possible; a conclusion cannot be drawn from a conditional and its confirmed conclusion. (Brad may live in Peoria, Illinois.) **5.** Law of Detachment; the circumference is π.

Review 123

1. Addition Property of Equality **2.** Symmetric Property of Equality **3.** Distributive Property **4.** Subtraction Property of Equality **5.** Addition Property of Equality **6.** Multiplication Property of Equality **7.** Substitution **8.** Transitive Property of Equality **9.** 4, 5, 1, 3, 2

Review 124

1.–7. 5, 2, 4, 1, 6, 3, 7 or 5, 2, 1, 4, 6, 3, 7
8. Sample: $m\angle 10 + m\angle 6 = 180$ by the Angle Addition Postulate. $m\angle 6 + m\angle 7 + m\angle 8 = 180$ by the Angle Addition Postulate. $m\angle 10 + m\angle 6 = m\angle 6 + m\angle 7 + m\angle 8$ by the Transitive Property of Equality. Subtract from both sides, and you get $m\angle 10 = m\angle 7 + m\angle 8$. Because $\angle 10$ is a right angle, $m\angle 7 + m\angle 8 = 90$. It is given that $m\angle 7 = m\angle 8$. By Substitution, $2m\angle 8 = 90$. Divide both sides by 2, and $m\angle 8 = 45$. **9.** Sample: Because $\angle 9$ and $\angle 10$ form a straight angle, $m\angle 9 + m\angle 10 = 180$ by the Angle Addition Postulate. By the definition of supplementary angles, $\angle 9$ and $\angle 10$ are supplementary. **10.** Sample: Because $\angle 10$ and $\angle 6$ form a straight angle, $m\angle 10 + m\angle 6 = 180$ by the Angle Addition Postulate. $\angle 10$ is a right angle, so $90 + m\angle 6 = 180$. Subtract 90 from both sides, and you get $m\angle 6 = 90$. So $m\angle 6$ is a right angle by the definition of right angles.

Review 125

1a.–1b. Sample:

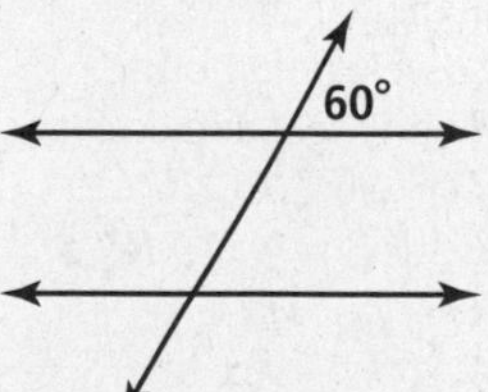

1c.–1d. Sample:

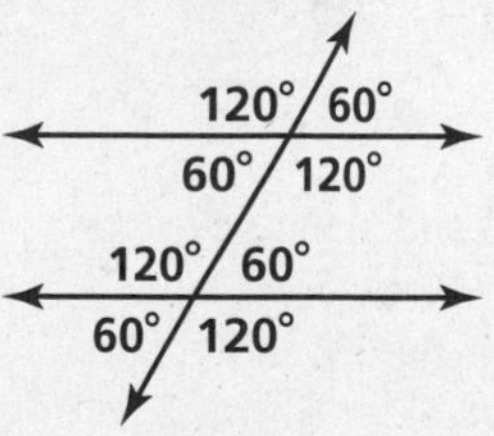

2. 110 **3.** 70 **4.** 110 **5.** 110 **6.** 70 **7.** 70
8. 110

Review 126

1.

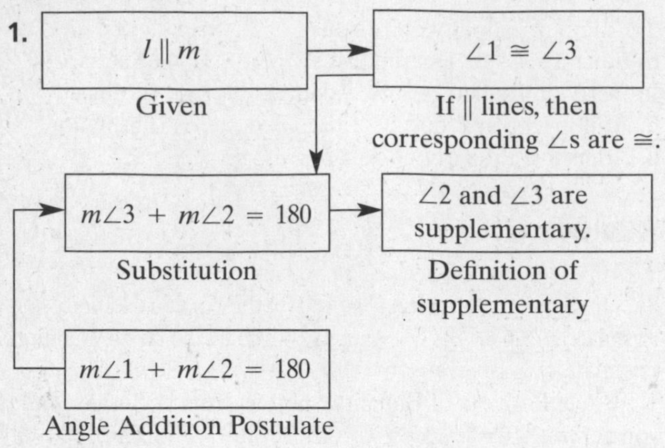

2.

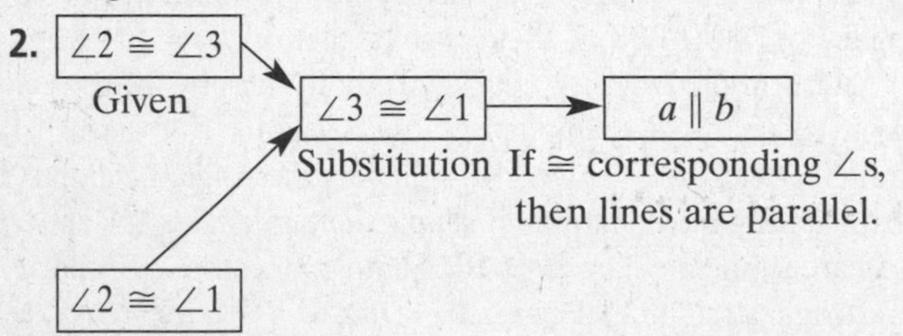

Review 127

1. $\triangle ABD$: $m\angle ABD = 120$, $m\angle ADB = 30$; $\triangle CBE$: $m\angle CBE = 120$, $m\angle CEB = 30$, $m\angle BCE = 30$; $\triangle BDE$: $m\angle BDE = 60$, $m\angle DBE = 60$, $m\angle BED = 60$
2. $\triangle DBE$ and $\triangle ABC$ are acute, equiangular, and equilateral; $\triangle ABD$ and $\triangle CBE$ are isosceles and obtuse; $\triangle ACE$, $\triangle ADE$, $\triangle CED$, and $\triangle CAD$ are right and scalene.
3. $\triangle PQT$: $m\angle PTQ = 45$, $m\angle PQT = 90$; $\triangle PQR$: $m\angle PQR = 90$, $m\angle QPR = 45$, $m\angle QRP = 45$; $\triangle RQS$: $m\angle RQS = 90$, $m\angle QSR = 45$; $\triangle SQT$: $m\angle SQT = 90$, $m\angle QST = 45$, $m\angle STQ = 45$ **4.** $PT = TS = RS = PR = 40$ mm; $PQ = QT = QR = QS = 28$ mm
5. $\triangle PQT$, $\triangle PQR$, $\triangle RQS$, $\triangle SQT$, $\triangle PRS$, $\triangle PTS$, $\triangle PRT$, and $\triangle RST$ are right and isosceles.

Review 128

1. $\angle 1$ and $\angle 2$ are interior angles; $\angle 3$ and $\angle 4$ are exterior angles. **2.** $m\angle 1 = 135$; $m\angle 2 = 90$; $m\angle 3 = 45$; $m\angle 4 = 90$ **3.** $\angle 1$ is an interior angle; $\angle 2$ and $\angle 4$ are exterior angles; $\angle 3$ is neither. **4.** $m\angle 1 = 60$; $m\angle 2 = 120$; $m\angle 3 = 60$; $m\angle 4 = 120$

Review 129

Check students' graphs.
1. $y = 2x - 6$ **2.** $y = \frac{1}{3}x$ **3.** $y = -x - 3$
4. $y = \frac{5}{6}x + 2$ **5.** $y = -\frac{1}{2}x + 1$ **6.** $y = 1$
7. $y = -\frac{7}{2}x + 10$ **8.** $y = -x + 1$ **9.** $y = \frac{2}{5}x + 1$
10. $y = 1$ **11.** $y = -2x - 6$ **12.** $x = -3$
13. $y = -3x + 10$ **14.** $y = 3x - 10$
15. $y = \frac{1}{4}x + \frac{1}{2}$ **16.** $y = -\frac{3}{4}x + 4$
17. $y = -x + 1$ **18.** $y = 1$

Review 130

1a. -2 **1b.** $\frac{1}{2}$ **2a.** $\frac{1}{4}$ **2b.** -4 **3a.** undefined
3b. 0 **4a.** $y = -2x + 4$ **4b.** $y = \frac{1}{2}x + \frac{3}{2}$
4c.

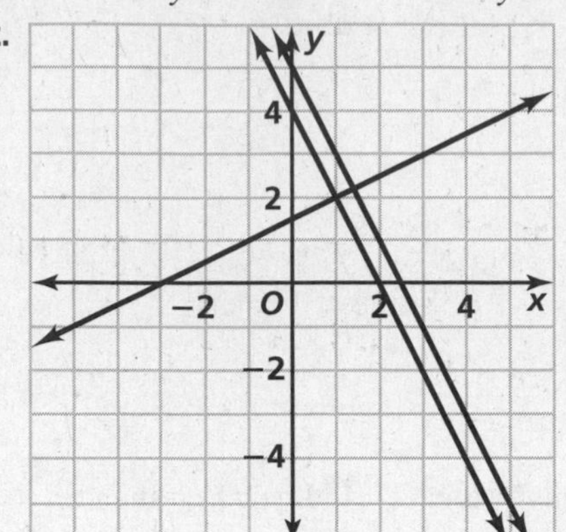

5a. $y = -\frac{2}{3}x - 4$ **5b.** $y = \frac{3}{2}x - 4$
5c.

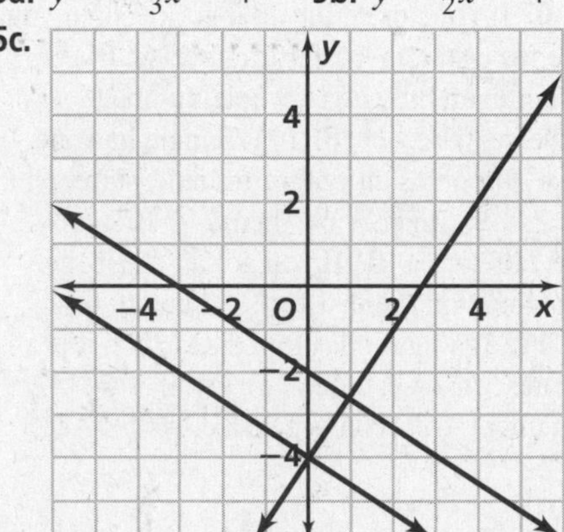

6a. $y = 3x + 7$ **6b.** $y = -\frac{1}{3}x - 3$
6c.

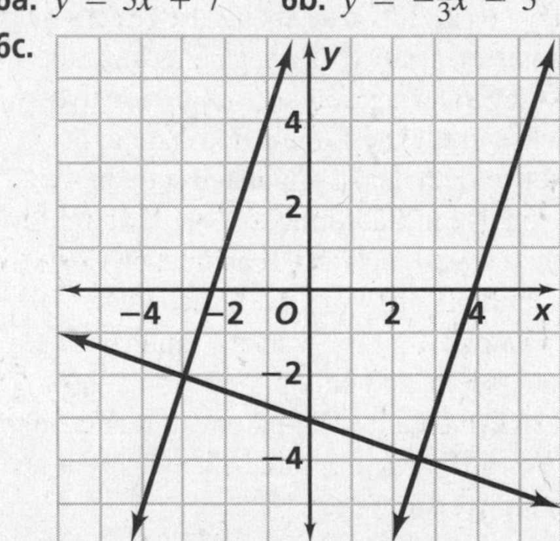

7. $m_{JK} = -1$; $m_{LM} = -1$; parallel **8.** $m_{JK} = \frac{2}{3}$; $m_{LM} = -\frac{3}{2}$; perpendicular **9.** $m_{JK} = -\frac{1}{6}$; $m_{LM} = -\frac{1}{5}$; neither **10.** $m_{JK} = -\frac{3}{2}$; $m_{LM} = \frac{4}{5}$; neither **11.** $m_{JK} = 2$; $m_{LM} = -\frac{1}{2}$; perpendicular **12.** $m_{JK} = \frac{1}{5}$; $m_{LM} = 5$; neither **13.** $m_{JK} = \frac{1}{4}$; $m_{LM} = -\frac{1}{4}$; parallel **14.** m_{JK} undefined; $m_{LM} = 0$; perpendicular

Review 131

1. Sample:

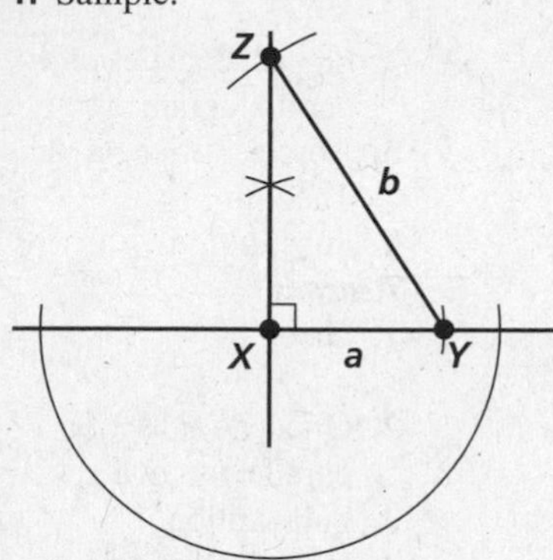

2.–4. Check students' work.

Review 132

1. b **2.** c **3.** a **4.** 117 **5.** 119

Review 133

1.–2. Check students' work. **3.** SSS; $\triangle AEB \cong \triangle CDB$ **4.** SAS; $\triangle MNQ \cong \triangle ONP$ **5.** SSS; $\triangle PRQ \cong \triangle VUT$ **6.** SSS: $\triangle JMK \cong \triangle LMK$ **7.** SAS; $\triangle QSP \cong \triangle QSR$ **8.** SAS; $\triangle YTX \cong \triangle WXT$

Review 134

1.

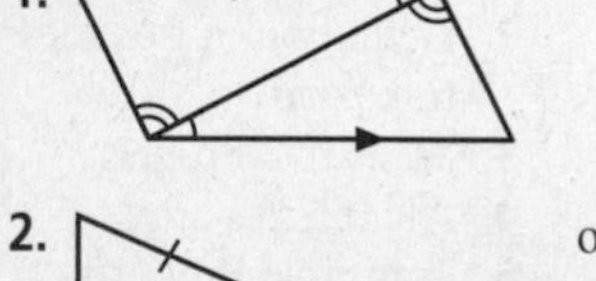

2.

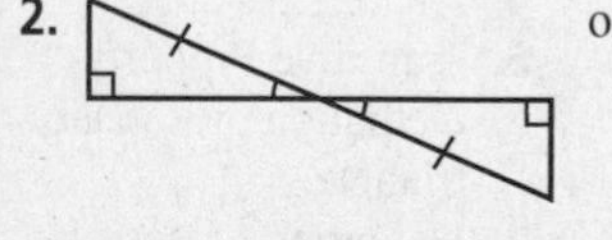

or

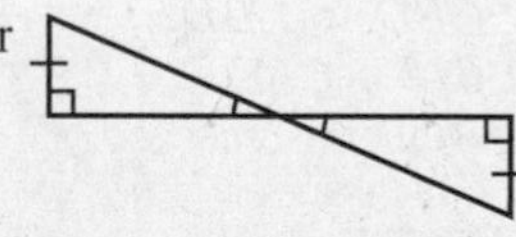

3. Check students' work. **4.** $\angle ABD \cong \angle CBD$ **5.** $\angle JMK \cong \angle LKM$ or $\angle JKM \cong \angle LMK$ **6.** $\overline{UZ} \cong \overline{YZ}$ **7.** $\overline{DY} \cong \overline{DO}$ **8.** $\angle P \cong \angle A$ **9.** $\angle CYL \cong \angle ALY$

Review 135

1a. $\overline{QK} \cong \overline{QA}$; $\overrightarrow{QB}$ bisects $\angle KQA$ **1b.** definition of bisector **1c.** $\overline{BQ} \cong \overline{BQ}$ **1d.** SAS Postulate **1e.** CPCTC

2.

Statements	***Reasons***
1. $\overline{MN} \cong \overline{MP}$, $\overline{NO} \cong \overline{PO}$	1. Given
2. $\overline{MO} \cong \overline{MO}$	2. Reflexive Property of $\cong$
3. $\triangle MPO \cong \triangle MNO$	3. SSS Postulate
4. $\angle N \cong \angle P$	4. CPCTC

3.

Statements	***Reasons***
1. $\overline{ON}$ bisects $\angle JOH$, $\angle J \cong \angle H$	1. Given
2. $\angle JON \cong \angle HON$	2. Definition of bisector
3. $\overline{ON} \cong \overline{ON}$	3. Reflexive Property of $\cong$
4. $\triangle JON \cong \triangle HON$	4. AAS Theorem
5. $\overline{JN} \cong \overline{HN}$	5. CPCTC

Review 136

1. Each angle is 60°. **2.** 120 **3.** 120 **4.** 50 **5.** 70 **6.** 60 **7.** 65 **8.** 115 **9.** 55 **10.** 120 **11.** 60

Review 137

1. Sample: $RS = 1.3$ cm, $ST = 1.6$ cm, $QT = 2.5$ cm, $QR = 2.3$ cm; not congruent **2.** Sample: $NT = 2.3$ cm, $TG = 2.3$ cm, $AT = 1.9$ cm; $\triangle NAT \cong \triangle GAT$ **3.** Sample: $TO = 3.3$ cm, $TR = 2.8$ cm, $MO = 2.8$ cm; $\triangle TOM \cong \triangle OTR$ **4.** HL Theorem can be applied; $\triangle BDA \cong \triangle CAD$. **5.** HL Theorem cannot be applied. **6.** HL Theorem can be applied; $\triangle MUN \cong \triangle MLN$. **7.** HL Theorem can be applied; $\triangle THF \cong \triangle FET$ or $\triangle THF \cong \triangle TEF$. **8.** HL Theorem can be applied; $\triangle OKR \cong \triangle AHR$. **9.** HL Theorem cannot be applied.

Review 138

1.

Statements	***Reasons***
1. $\angle PSR$ and $\angle PQR$ are right $\angle$s; $\angle QPR$ and $\angle SRP$	1. Given
2. $\angle PSR$ and $\angle PQR$	2. Right $\angle$s are congruent.
3. $\overline{PR} \cong \overline{PR}$	3. Reflexive Property of $\cong$
4. $\triangle QPR \cong \triangle SRP$	4. AAS Theorem
5. $\angle STR \cong \angle QTP$	5. Vertical $\angle$s are $\cong$.
6. $\overline{PQ} \cong \overline{RS}$	6. CPCTC
7. $\triangle STR \cong \triangle QTP$	7. AAS Theorem

2. Sample: Prove $\triangle MLP \cong \triangle QPL$ by the AAS Theorem. Then use CPCTC and vertical angles to show $\triangle MLN \cong \triangle QPN$ by the AAS Theorem. **3.** Sample: Prove $\triangle ACD \cong \triangle ECB$ by the SAS Postulate. Then use CPCTC and vertical angles to show $\triangle ABF \cong \triangle EDF$ by the AAS Theorem.

Review 139

Triangles will vary.

1a. $PQ = 8$ **1b.** $MN = 16$ **1c.** $YZ = 32$
2a. $NO = 2.5$ **2b.** $ST = 10$ **2c.** $UV = 20$
3a. $QR = 4$ **3b.** $ST = 8$ **3c.** $UV = 16$

Review 140

1. no **2.** yes **3.** yes **4.** no **5.** B **6.** C

Review 141

1. Sample:

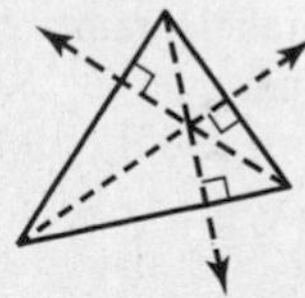

Review 141 *(continued)*

2. Sample:

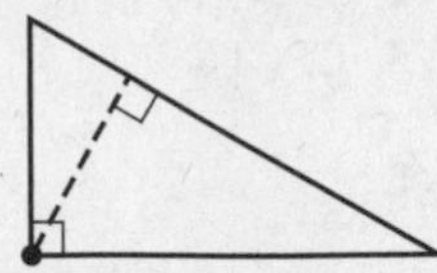

Review 142

1. Step 1: B; Step 2: D; Step 3: F; Step 4: E; Step 5: A; Step 6: C **2.** Step 1: Assume $\overline{EF} \cong \overline{DE}$. Step 2: If $\overline{EF} \cong \overline{DE}$, then by the Isosceles Triangle Theorem, $\angle D \cong \angle F$. Step 3: But $\angle D \ncong \angle F$. Step 4: Therefore, $\overline{EF} \ncong \overline{DE}$.

Review 143

1. Check students' work. The longest side will be opposite the largest angle. The shortest side will be opposite the smallest angle. **2.** largest: $\angle DEF$; smallest: $\angle DFE$ **3.** largest: $\angle PQR$; smallest: $\angle PRQ$ **4.** largest: $\angle ACB$; smallest: $\angle CBA$ **5.** longest: $\overline{DF}$; shortest: $\overline{FE}$ **6.** longest: $\overline{PQ}$; shortest: $\overline{RQ}$ **7.** longest: $\overline{SV}$; shortest: $\overline{ST}$

Review 144

1.–4. Samples:

1.

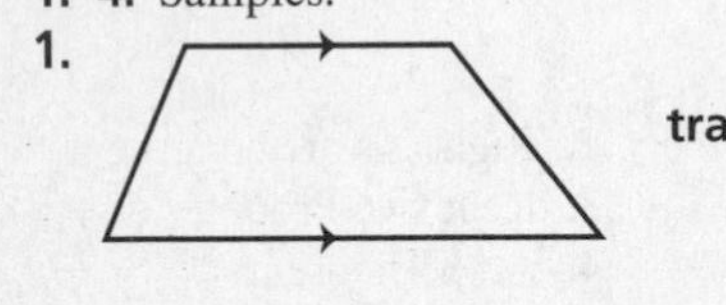

trapezoid

2.

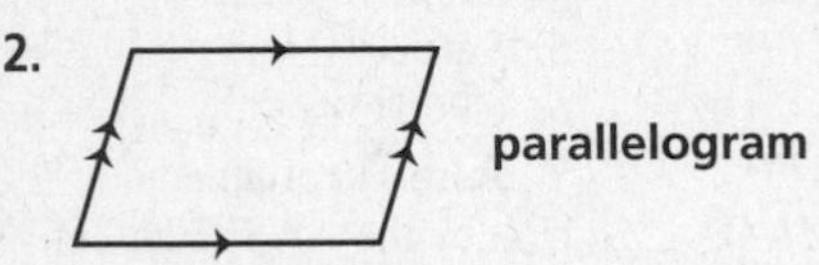

parallelogram

3.

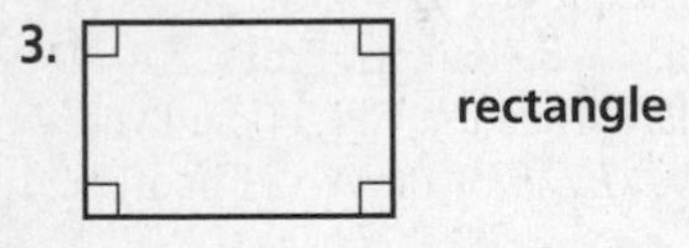

rectangle

4.

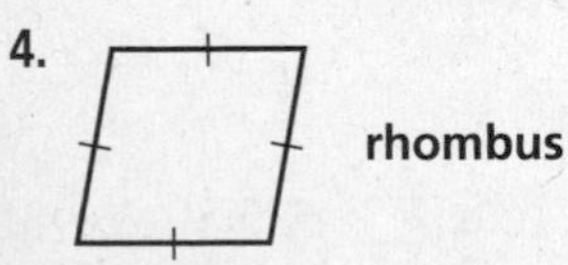

rhombus

5. parallelogram **6.** rectangle **7.** isosceles trapezoid **8.** rhombus **9.** trapezoid **10.** kite **11.** rectangle **12.** square

Review 145

1.

Statements	*Reasons*
1. Parallelogram $ABCD$	**1.** Given
2. $\overline{AB} \cong \overline{CD}$, $\overline{BC} \cong \overline{DA}$	**2.** Opposite sides of a parallelogram are congruent.
3. $\overline{BD} \cong \overline{DB}$	**3.** Reflexive Prop. of $\cong$
4. $\triangle ABD \cong \triangle CDB$	**4.** SSS
5. $\angle A \cong \angle C$	**5.** CPCTC

2.

Statements	*Reasons*
1. Parallelogram $ACDE$; $\overline{CD} \cong \overline{BD}$	**1.** Given
2. $\angle C \cong \angle E$	**2.** Opposite angles of a parallelogram are $\cong$.
3. $\angle CBD \cong \angle C$	**3.** Isosceles Triangle Theorem
4. $\angle CBD \cong \angle E$	**4.** Substitution

3.

Statements	*Reasons*
1. Parallelogram $ACDE$; $\overline{AE} \cong \overline{BD}$	**1.** Given
2. $\overline{AE} \cong \overline{CD}$	**2.** Opposite sides of a parallelogram are $\cong$.
3. $\overline{CD} \cong \overline{BD}$	**3.** Substitution
4. $\angle CBD \cong \angle C$	**4.** Isosceles Triangle Theorem

4.

Statements	*Reasons*
1. Parallelogram $ACDE$; $\angle CBD \cong \angle E$	**1.** Given
2. $\angle E \cong \angle C$	**2.** Opposite angles of a parallelogram are $\cong$.
3. $\angle CBD \cong \angle C$	**3.** Substitution
4. $\overline{CD} \cong \overline{BD}$	**4.** If 2 $\angle$s of a $\triangle$ are $\cong$, sides opposite them are $\cong$.
5. $\triangle BDC$ is isosceles.	**5.** Def. of isosceles triangle

5.

Statements	*Reasons*
1. Isosceles trap. $ABDE$; $\angle C \cong \angle E$	**1.** Given
2. $\overline{AE} \cong \overline{BD}$; $\angle E \cong \angle BDE$	**2.** Definition of isosceles trapezoid
3. $\angle C \cong \angle BDE$	**3.** Transitive Property
4. $\angle CBD \cong \angle BDE$	**4.** Alt. int. $\angle$'s are $\cong$.
5. $\angle C \cong \angle CBD$	**5.** Transitive Property
6. $\triangle BCD$ is isosceles.	**6.** Definition of isosceles triangle
7. $\overline{BD} \cong \overline{CD}$	**7.** Definition of isosceles triangle
8. $\overline{AE} \cong \overline{CD}$	**8.** Transitive Property

Review 146

1. no **2.** no **3.** no **4.** yes

5.

Statements	*Reasons*
1. $\overline{BD} \cong \overline{CD}$, $\overline{AE} \cong \overline{BD}$, $\overline{AE} \parallel \overline{CD}$	**1.** Given
2. $\overline{AE} \cong \overline{CD}$	**2.** Substitution
3. $ACDE$ is a parallelogram.	**3.** If one pair of opposite sides is both congruent and parallel, then the quadrilateral is a parallelogram.

6.

Statements	*Reasons*
1. $\angle CBD \cong \angle C$, $\overline{AE} \cong \overline{BD}$, $\overline{AC} \cong \overline{ED}$	**1.** Given
2. $\overline{BD} \cong \overline{CD}$	**2.** If 2 $\angle$s of a $\triangle$ are $\cong$, sides opposite them are $\cong$.

ANSWERS

Review 146 *(continued)*

3. $\overline{AE} \cong \overline{CD}$	3. Substitution
4. $ACDE$ is a parallelogram.	4. If both pairs of opposite sides are $\cong$, then the quad. is a parallelogram.

Review 147

1. $m\angle 1 = 60; m\angle 2 = 30; m\angle 3 = 90$ **2.** $m\angle 1 = 80; m\angle 2 = 50; m\angle 3 = 50; m\angle 4 = 100$ **3.** $m\angle 1 = 80; m\angle 2 = 100; m\angle 3 = 40; m\angle 4 = 40$ **4.** $m\angle 1 = 60; m\angle 2 = 60; m\angle 3 = 60$ **5.** $m\angle 1 = 75; m\angle 2 = 75; m\angle 3 = 15; m\angle 4 = 90$ **6.** $m\angle 1 = 45; m\angle 2 = 45$

Review 148

1. 90 **2.** 52 **3.** 90 **4.** 38 **5.** 52 **6.** 90
7. 27 **8.** 63 **9.** 27
10. Sample:

Statements	***Reasons***
1. $\overline{LP} \cong \overline{MN}$	1. Given
2. $\angle LPN \cong \angle MNP$	2. Theorem 6-15
3. $\overline{PN} \cong \overline{PN}$	3. Reflexive Prop. of $\cong$
4. $\triangle LNP \cong \triangle MPN$	4. SAS Postulate
5. $\overline{PM} \cong \overline{LN}$	5. CPCTC
6. $\overline{LM} \cong \overline{LM}$	6. Reflexive Prop. of $\cong$
7. $\triangle PLM \cong \triangle NML$	7. SSS Postulate
8. $\angle LPQ \cong \angle MNQ$	8. CPCTC
9. $\angle LQP \cong \angle MQN$	9. Vertical angles are $\cong$.
10. $\triangle LQP \cong \triangle MQN$	10. AAS Theorem

11. 87 **12.** 48 **13.** 45 **14.** 48 **15.** 24
16. 24 **17.** 132 **18.** 24 **19.** 132 **20.** Sample: Both $\triangle LMQ$ and $\triangle PNQ$ have the same angle measures, but their sides have different lengths.

Review 149

1. $Q(x + k, m)$ **2.** $X(-a, 0); W(0, -b)$ **3.** $S(a, -a); T(0, -a)$ **4.** Each side has length $a\sqrt{2}$, so it is a rhombus. One pair of opposite sides has slope of 1, and the other pair has slope of -1. Therefore, because $(1)(-1) = -1$, the rhombus has four right angles and is a square. **5.** Each side has length of $\sqrt{2a^2 + 2a + 1}$. Therefore, the figure is a rhombus. **6.** $C(x - k, m)$

Review 150

1. Each diagonal has length $\sqrt{c^2 + (b + a)^2}$. **2.** The midpoints are $(\frac{b}{2}, \frac{c}{2})$ and $(\frac{b + a}{2}, \frac{c}{2})$. The line connecting the midpoints has slope of 0 and is therefore parallel to the third side. **3.** The midpoints are $(\frac{a}{2}, 0)$, $(a, \frac{b}{2})$, $(\frac{a}{2}, b)$ and $(0, \frac{b}{2})$. The segments joining the midpoints each have length $\frac{1}{2}\sqrt{a^2 + b^2}$. **4.** The midpoints are $(\frac{a}{2}, \frac{b}{2})$, $(-\frac{a}{2}, \frac{b}{2})$, $(-\frac{a}{2}, -\frac{b}{2})$, and $(\frac{a}{2}, -\frac{b}{2})$. The quadrilateral formed by these points has sides with slopes of 0, 0, undefined, and undefined. Therefore, the sides are vertical and horizontal, and consecutive sides are perpendicular. **5.** The median meets the base at (0, 0), the midpoint of the base. Therefore, the median has undefined slope; i.e., it is vertical. Because the base is a horizontal segment, the median is perpendicular to the base. **6.** The midpoints are $(\frac{a}{2}, 0)$, $(\frac{a + d}{2}, \frac{e}{2})$, $(\frac{b + d}{2}, \frac{c + e}{2})$, and $(\frac{b}{2}, \frac{c}{2})$. One pair of opposite sides has slope of $\frac{e}{d}$, and the other pair of opposite sides has slope of $\frac{c}{b - a}$. Therefore, the figure is a parallelogram because opposite sides are parallel.

Review 151

1. Samples:

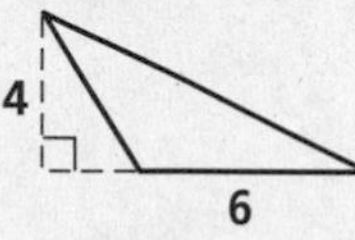

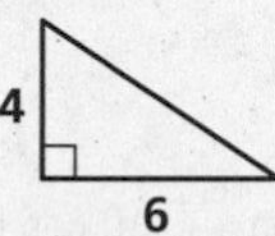

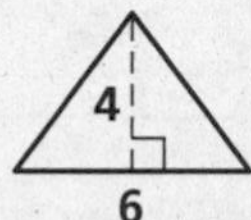

2. Samples:

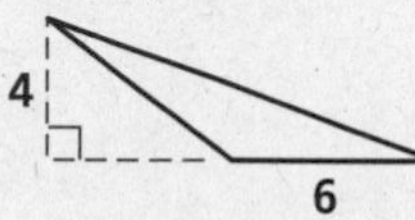

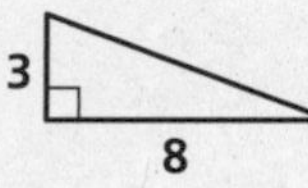

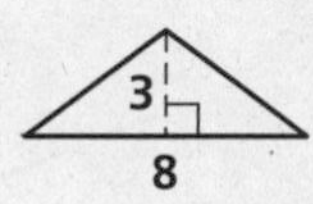

3. 20 cm^2 **4.** 55 in.^{2} **5.** 6 m **6.** 8 ft **7.** 4 in.
8. Samples:

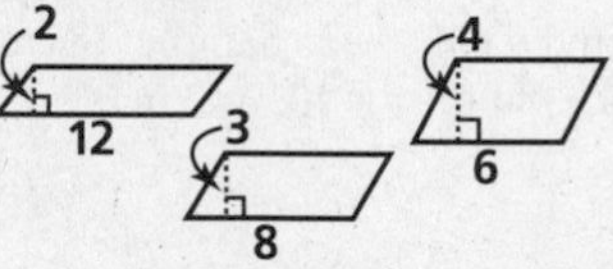

9. 5 in. **10.** 23 cm **11.** 9 ft

Review 152

1.–2. Sample:

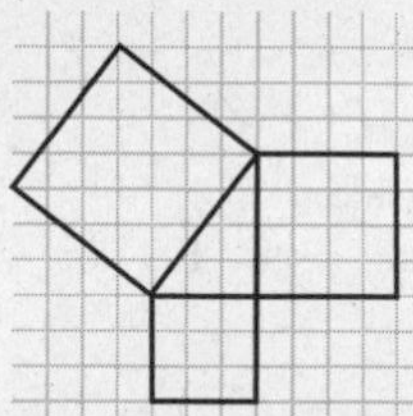

3. Sample: 9, 16, and 25 **4.** They are equal. **5.** The sum of the squares of the two legs equals the square of the hypotenuse. **6.** $4\sqrt{5}$ **7.** $7\sqrt{2}$ **8.** 8 **9.** 6

Review 153

1.–2. Sample:

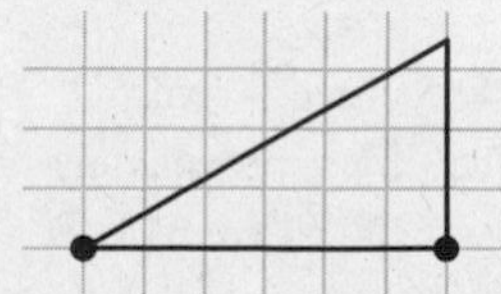

ANSWERS

Review 153 *(continued)*

3. Sample: 3.5 and 7 **4.** Sample: 3.5 and 7
5. Sample: They are approximately equal.
6. Check students' work. **7.** $d = 2\sqrt{3}; e = 4$
8. $f = \frac{4\sqrt{3}}{3}; g = \frac{8\sqrt{3}}{3}$ **9.** $x = 3\sqrt{3}; y = 3$
10. $u = 6\sqrt{3}; v = 12$

Review 154

1. Sample:

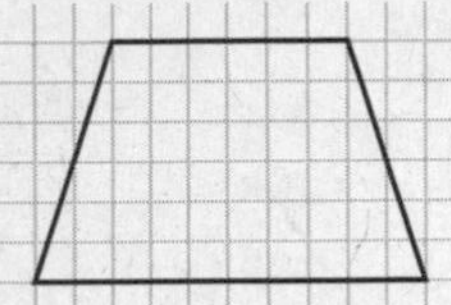

2. Sample: bases = 6 cm and 10 cm, height = 6 cm
3. Sample: 48 cm^2 **4.** Check students' work.
5. Sample:

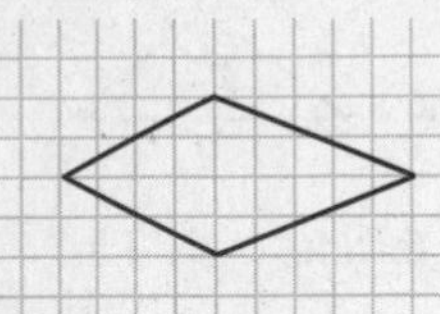

6. Sample: diagonals = 4 cm and 9 cm **7.** Sample: 18 cm^2
8. Check students' work. **9.** 144 ft^2 **10.** 112 in.^{2}
11. 75 m^2 **12.** 98.4 cm^2

Review 155

1.–2. Sample:

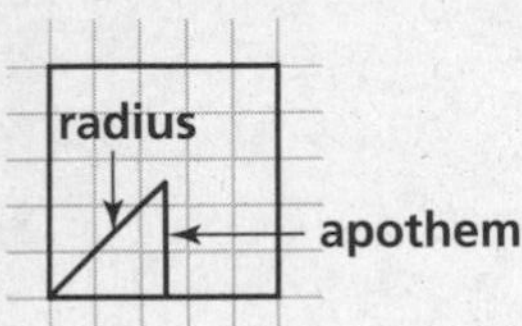

3. Sample: apothem = 2.5, radius = 3.5, side = 5
4. yes **5.** They are approximately equal. **6.** 100 in.^{2}
7. 200 ft^2 **8.** 72 cm^2 **9.** 8 m^2

Review 156

1. Sample:

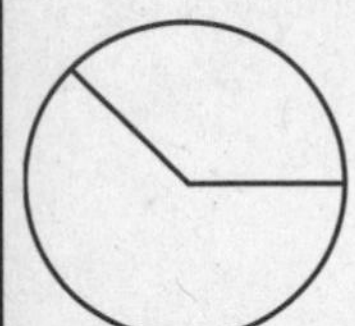

2. Sample: 135° **3.** Sample: 2 cm **4.** Sample: $\frac{3\pi}{2}$ cm ≈ 4.7 cm **5.** Sample: 4.5 cm **6.** They are approximately equal. **7.** $\frac{5\pi}{6}$ **8.** $\frac{10\pi}{3}$ **9.** 5π **10.** $\frac{20\pi}{3}$ **11.** $\frac{5\pi}{2}$
12. $\frac{25\pi}{6}$ **13.** $\frac{15\pi}{2}$

Review 157

1.–2. Sample:

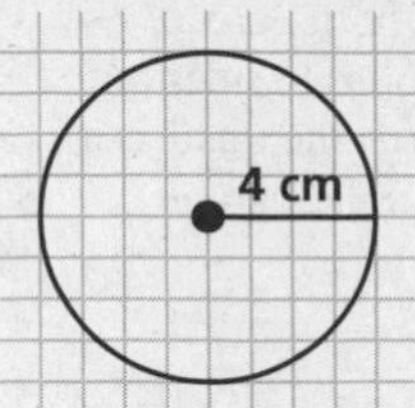

3. Sample: 50 cm^2 **4.** Sample: 50.3 cm^2 **5.** They are approximately equal. **6.** Check students' work.
7. 25π ft^2 **8.** 4π in.^{2} **9.** 64π m^2 **10.** 20.25π ft^2
11. 324π cm^2 **12.** 64π in.^{2} **13.** 14 cm **14.** 615 cm^2

Review 158

1. Check students' work. **2.** ≈ 21% **3.** Check students' work. **4.** Sample: They are approximately equal.
5. Sample: The ratio would tend to be close to 21%.
6. ≈ 43%

Review 159

1. 534 apples **2.** 768 gallons **3.** 4627 employees
4. about 4800 picture frames **5.** 90 **6.** 2450 **7.** 85
8. 560 **9.** 58 **10.** 7308 **11.** 12 **12.** 20,250
13. 2500

Review 160

1. $\triangle KLM \sim \triangle QRS$; 5 : 3 **2.** $\triangle ABC \sim \triangle XYZ$; 10 : 7
3. not similar **4.** not similar **5.** $LMPR \sim QICK$; 1 : 1
6. not similar **7.** similar with ratio 10 : 11 **8.** not similar **9.** similar with ratio 4 : 9

Review 161

1. $\triangle ABC \sim \triangle ZYX$ by AA ~ **2.** not similar
3. $\triangle QEU \sim \triangle SIO$ by SSS ~ **4.** $\triangle ABC \sim \triangle RST$ by AA ~ **5.** not similar **6.** $\triangle BAC \sim \triangle XQR$ by SAS ~ **7.** yes; by SSS ~ or by AA ~ **8.** No; the vertex angles may differ in measure. **9.** All congruent triangles are similar with ratio 1 : 1. Similar triangles are not necessarily congruent.

Review 162

1. $x = \frac{25}{13}; y = \frac{144}{13}; z = \frac{60}{13}$ **2.** $x = \frac{400}{29}; y = \frac{441}{29}; z = \frac{420}{29}$ **3.** $x = 4.8; y = 8$ **4.** $x = 12; y = 16$
5. $x = \sqrt{2}; y = \sqrt{3}; z = \sqrt{6}$ **6.** $x = 2\sqrt{10}; y = \sqrt{15}; z = 2\sqrt{6}$ **7.** $\frac{120}{13}$ **8.** $\frac{42}{\sqrt{85}} = \frac{42\sqrt{85}}{85}$
9. $\frac{ab}{\sqrt{a^2 + b^2}}$

Review 163

1. $x = 4.5$ **2.** $x = \frac{8}{3}$ **3.** $x = 7.2; y = 4.8$

ANSWERS

Review 163 *(continued)*

4. $x = \frac{15}{8}; y = \frac{25}{8}$ **5.** $x = 9$ **6.** $x = \frac{3}{2}; y = \frac{5}{2}$
7. $BN = \frac{16}{5}; CN = \frac{24}{5}$ **8.** $BY = \frac{3}{2}$

Review 164

1. 4 : 3; 16 : 9 **2.** 8 : 5; 64 : 25 **3.** 9 : 5; 81 : 25
4. 4 : 3 **5.** 4 : 5 **6.** 3 : 5 **7.** 16 : 9 **8.** 16 : 25
9. 9 : 25

Review 165

1. 26.6 **2.** 76.0 **3.** 80.5 **4.** 26.6
5. 8.1 **6.** 0.8 **7.** $m\angle A = 53.1; m\angle B = 36.9$
8. $m\angle A = 67.4; m\angle B = 22.6$ **9.** $m\angle A = 70.5;$ $m\angle B = 19.5$ **10.** $m\angle A = 63.4; m\angle B = 26.6$
11. 26.6 **12.** 63.4 **13.** 49.4

Review 166

1. $DF = 2.7, EF = 7.5$ **2.** $XZ = 8.7, YZ = 10$
3. $RS = 8.4, ST = 13.1$ **4.** 5.8 **5.** 30; 60 **6.** 16.6; 73.4 **7.** 23.6; 66.4 **8.** 2.1; 3.4 **9a.** 7.1 **9b.** $\sqrt{51}$

Review 167

1. 42.9 ft **2.** 1113.8 ft **3.** 2.2° **4.** 42.0 ft
5. 76.1 ft **6.** 19.1 ft

Review 168

1. 12.8 mi/h at 51.3° off directly across **2a.** 10 mi
2b. 36.9° west of due north **3.** The bird's path shifts 31.0° east of due south. **4.** 4 mi/h

Review 169

1. 19.3 in.^{2} **2.** 123.1 cm^2 **3.** 86.6 in.^{2} **4.** 172.0 in.^{2}
5. 363.3 in.^{2} **6.** 126.3 in.^{2} **7a.** 81 in.^{2} **7b.** area of square $= s^2$

Review 170

1. Sample:

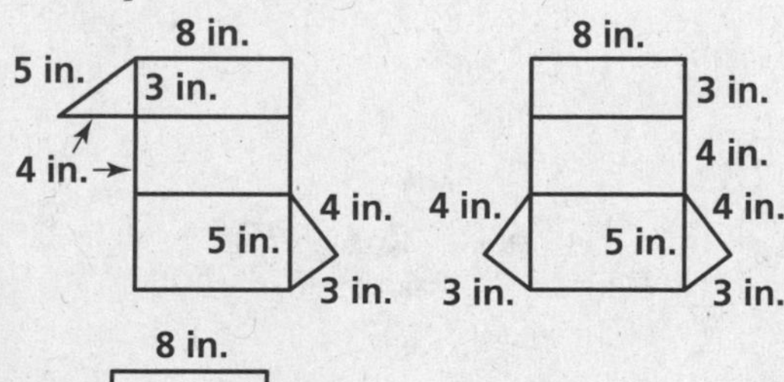

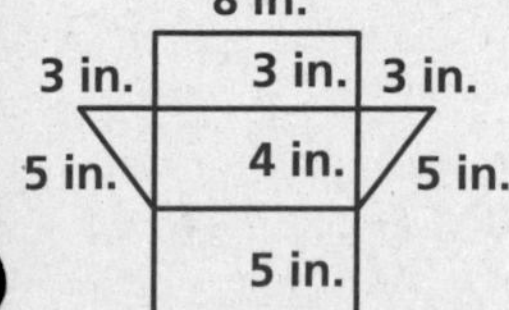

2. Check students' work. **3.** vertices = 6; faces = 5; edges = 9 **4.** $E = V + F - 2; 9 \stackrel{?}{=} 6 + 5 - 2; 9 = 9$

5.

6.

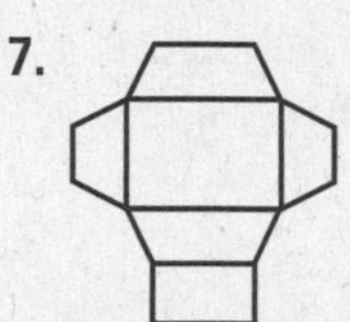

7.

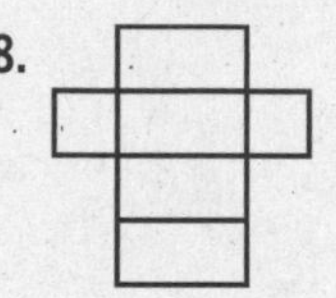

8.

Review 171

1a.

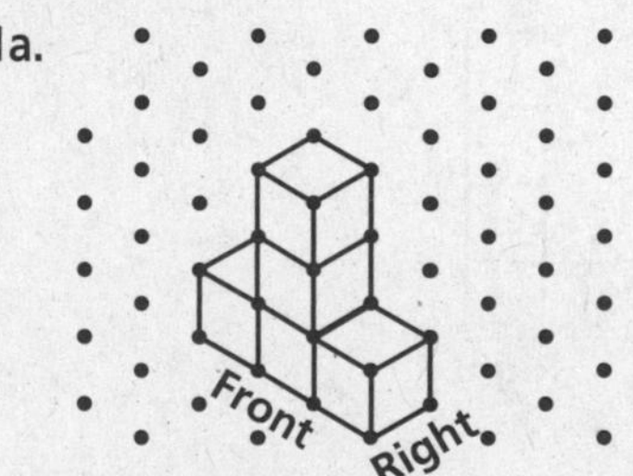

1b.

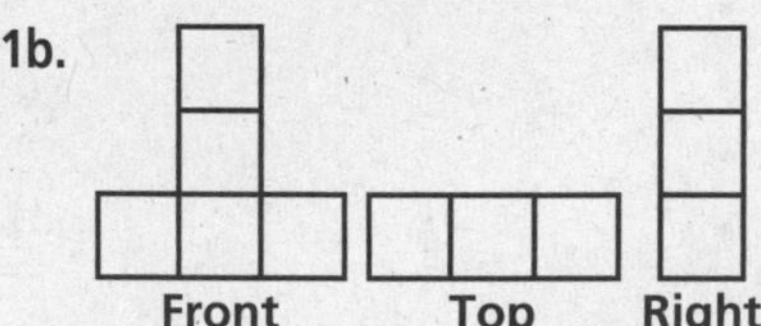

2a.

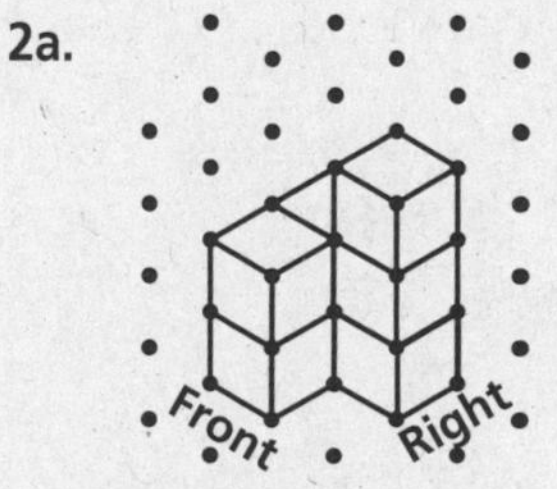

2b.

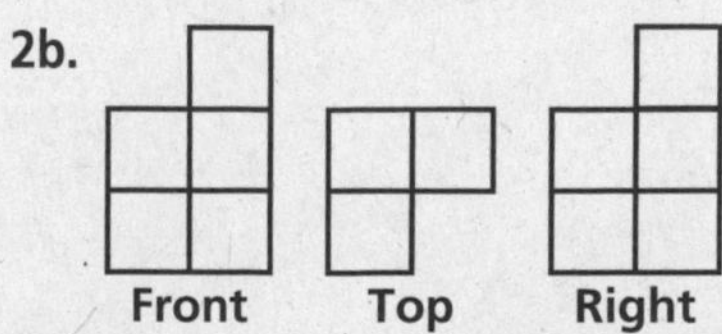

Review 171 *(continued)*

3a.

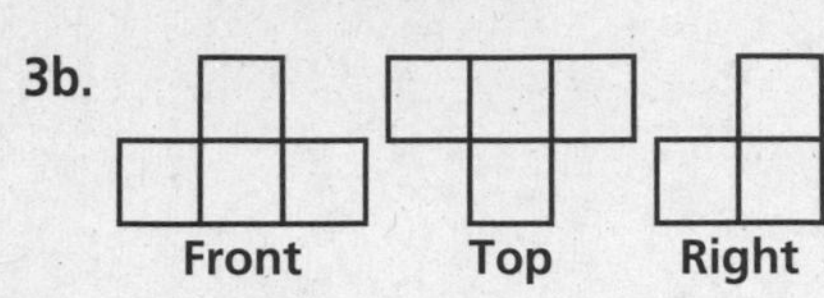

3b.

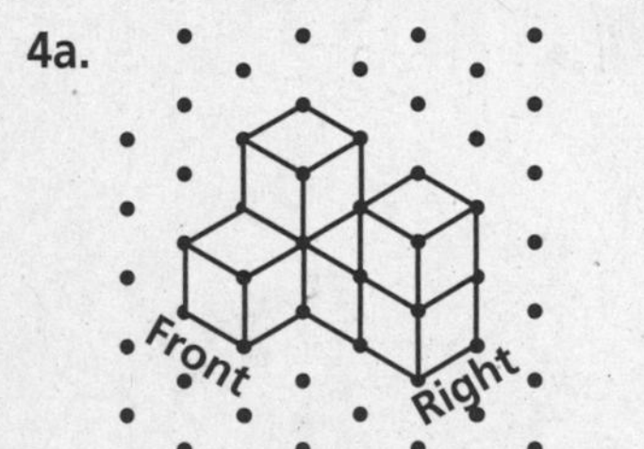

4a.

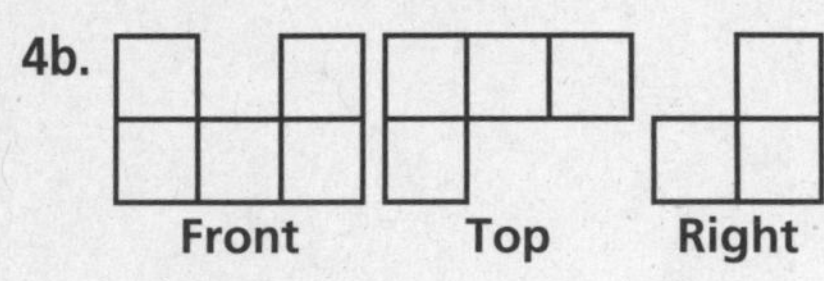

4b.

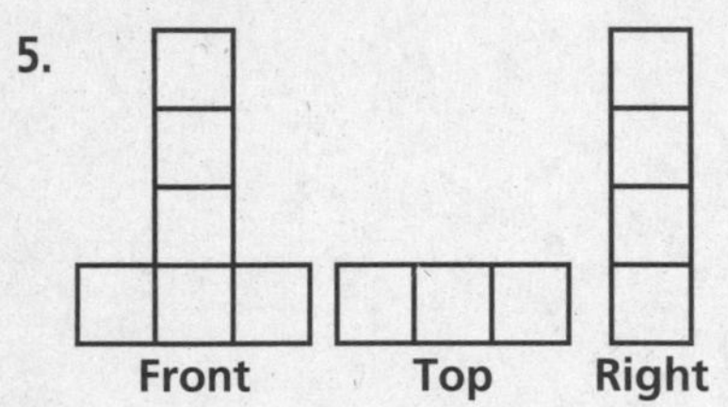

5.

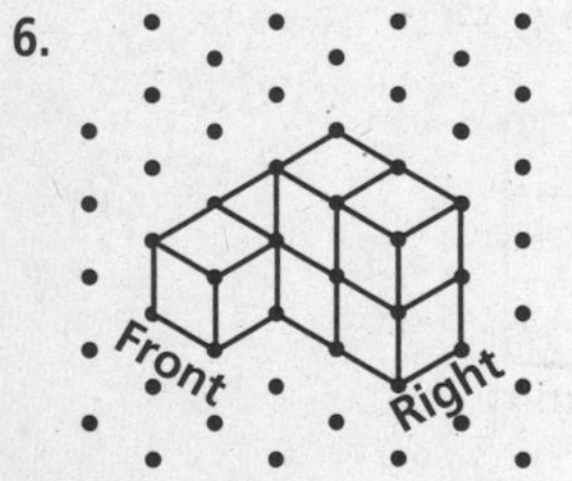

6.

Front Right

Review 172

1.–2. Check students' work. **3.** L.A. = 300 cm^2; S.A. = 350 cm^2 **4.** 722.6 cm^2 **5.** 864 $in.^2$ **6.** 153.3 m^2

Review 173

1. Sample:

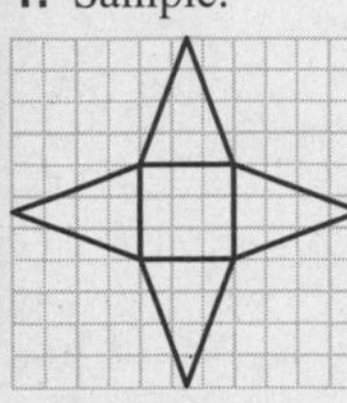

2. Check students' work. **3.** Sample: base = 3 cm, slant height = 4 cm **4.** Sample: 33 cm^2 **5.** 896 cm^2 **6.** 314.2 m^2 **7.** 416.2 $in.^2$ **8.** 349.3 ft^2

Review 174

1. 490 cm^3 **2.** 242.5 cm^3 **3.** 735 m^3 **4.** 2544.7 $in.^3$ **5.** 756 ft^3 **6.** 2261.9 cm^3

Review 175

1. B **2.** 301.6 cm^3 **3.** 1296 ft^3 **4.** 48 $in.^3$ **5.** 211.6 m^3

Review 176

1.–4. Check students' work. **5.** four circles **6.** They are the same. **7.** V = 113.1 $in.^3$; S.A. = 113.1 $in.^2$ **8.** V = 523.6 cm^3; S.A. = 314.2 cm^2 **9.** V = 7238.2 m^3; S.A. = 1809.6 m^2 **10.** V = 8181.2 ft^3; S.A. = 1963.5 ft^2 **11.** V = 1047.4 $in.^3$; S.A. = 498.8 $in.^2$ **12.** V = 310.3 mm^3; S.A. = 221.7 mm^2

Review 177

1. 2 : 1 **2.** 3 : 2 **3.** 64 : 125 **4.** 512 : 125 **5.** $250\sqrt{2} : 27$ **6.** 16 : 9 **7.** 49 : 25

Review 178

1. $\sqrt{157}$ **2.** $\sqrt{741}$ **3.** $\sqrt{2}$ **4.** 7.5

Review 179

1. $5\sqrt{5}$ **2.** $12\sqrt{2}$ **3.** $2\sqrt{14}$ **4.** 11.83 cm **5.** 2.54 cm **6.** 8.66 in. **7.** 2.78 in.

Review 180

1. 87 **2.** 40 **3.** 60 **4.** 55 **5.** $x = 94, y = 80$ **6.** 120 **7.** 40 **8.** 20 **9.** 70

Review 181

1. 93 **2.** 156 **3.** 42 **4.** 35 **5.** 60 **6.** 55 **7.** $x = 36; y = 60; z = 48$ **8.** $x = 64; y = 64; z = 52$ **9.** $x = 46; y = 90; z = 44$

Review 182

1. $(x - 3)^2 + (y - 11)^2 = 4$ **2.** $(x + 5)^2 + y^2 = 225$
3. $(x - 6)^2 + (y + 6)^2 = 7$ **4.** $x^2 + y^2 = 20$
5. $(x + 2)^2 + (y + 2)^2 = 4$
6. $(x - 3)^2 + (y - 1)^2 = 50$
7. $(x - 5)^2 + (y - 2)^2 = 36$
8. $(x - 4)^2 + (y - 2)^2 = 25$
9. $(x + 2)^2 + (y - 3)^2 = 25$ **10.** $C(-3, -5); r = 5$
11. $C(0, 0); r = 0.2$ **12.** $C(4, 0); r = \sqrt{6}$
13. $C(3, 5); r = 4$

Review 183

1.–5. Check students' work. **6.** the line perpendicular to $\overline{AB}$ at its midpoint **7.** one, the midpoint of $\overline{AB}$

Review 184

1.–5. Check students' work. **6.** reflection over x-axis: $F'(-1, -3), G'(-5, -1), H'(-3, -5)$; reflection over y-axis: $F'(1, 3), G'(5, 1), H'(3, 5)$ **7.** reflection over x-axis: $C'(2, -4), D'(5, -2), E'(6, -3)$; reflection over y-axis: $C'(-2, 4), D'(-5, 2), E'(-6, 3)$ **8.** reflection over x-axis: $J'(-1, 5), K'(-2, 3), L'(-4, 6)$; reflection over y-axis: $J'(1, -5), K'(2, -3), L'(4, -6)$

Review 185

1.–5. Check students' work. **6.** $A'(0, -3), B'(1, 1), C'(4, -1), D'(5, -4)$ **7.** $A'(4, -2), B'(5, 2), C'(8, 0), D'(9, -3)$ **8.** $A'(3, 5), B'(4, 9), C'(7, 7), D'(8, 4)$

Review 186

1.–5.

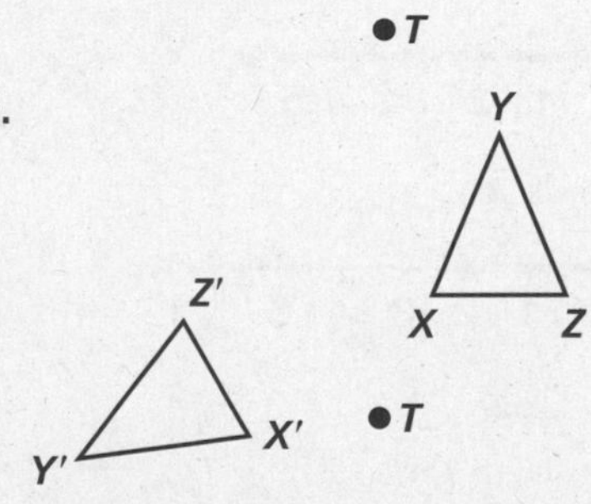

6.

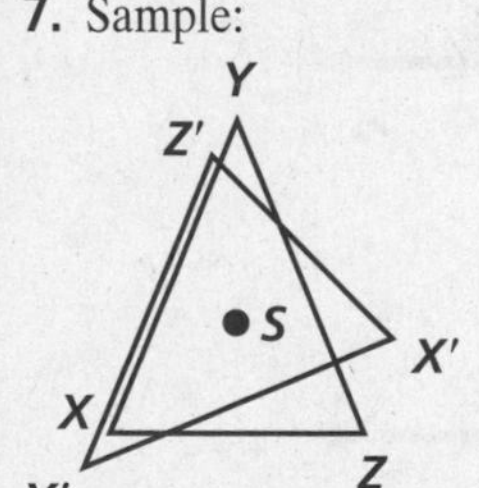

7. Sample:

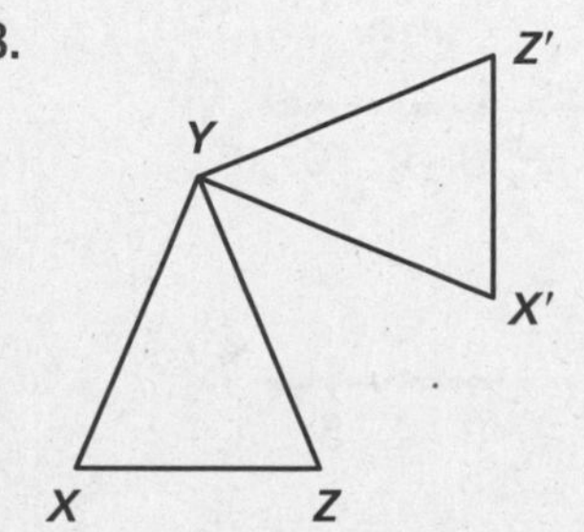

8.

Review 187

1. translation **2.** reflection **3.** rotation **4.** glide reflection **5.** rotation **6.** glide reflection **7.** reflection **8.** translation

Review 188

1. two lines of symmetry (vertical and horizontal), 180° rotational symmetry (point symmetry) **2.** one line of symmetry (horizontal) **3.** one line of symmetry (vertical) **4.** two lines of symmetry (vertical and horizontal), 180° rotational symmetry (point symmetry) **5.** one line of symmetry (vertical) **6.** one line of symmetry (vertical)

Review 189

1.

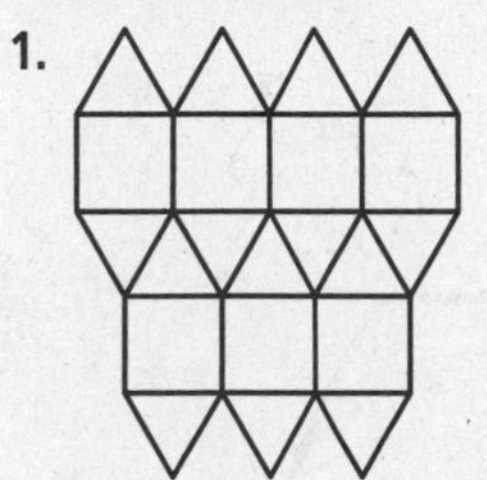

2. Sample:

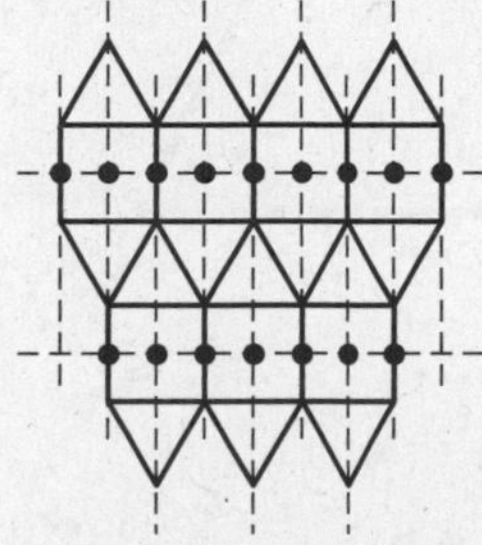

line symmetry in the dashed lines, rotational symmetry around points, translational symmetry, glide reflectional symmetry

3.

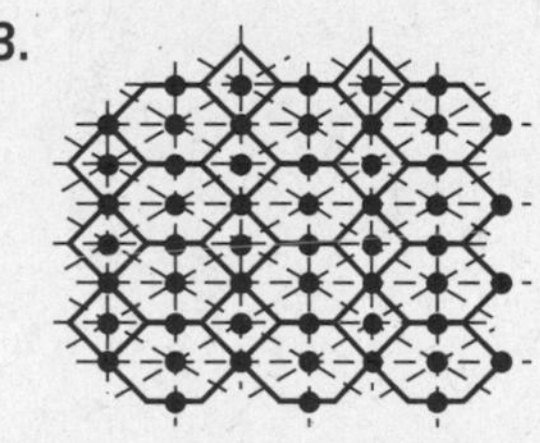

line symmetry in the dashed lines, rotational symmetry around points, translational symmetry, glide reflectional symmetry

4.

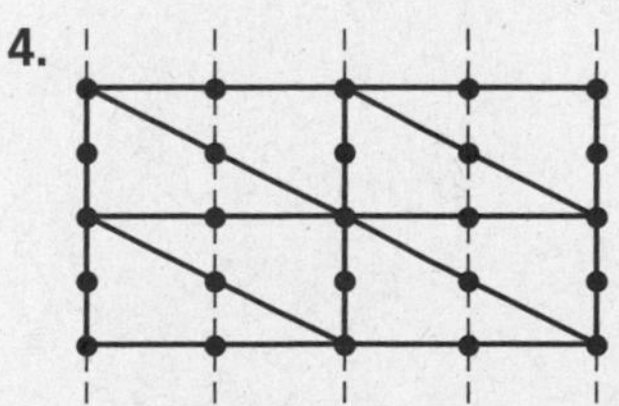

rotational symmetry around points, translational symmetry

5.

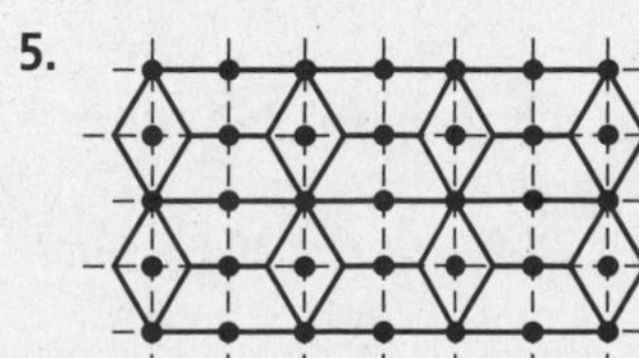

line symmetry in the dashed lines, rotational symmetry around points, translational symmetry, glide reflectional symmetry

ANSWERS

Review 190

1. Check students' work.

2.

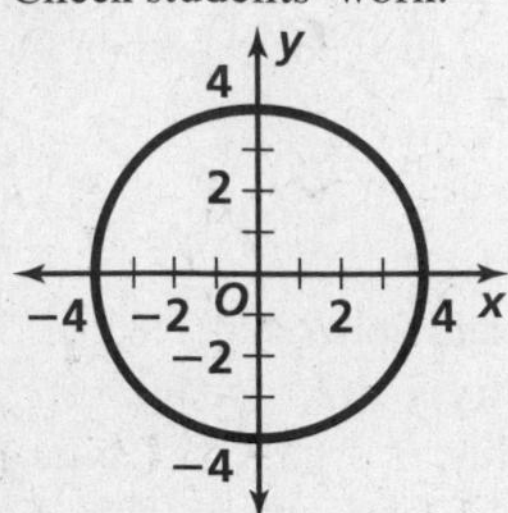

3.

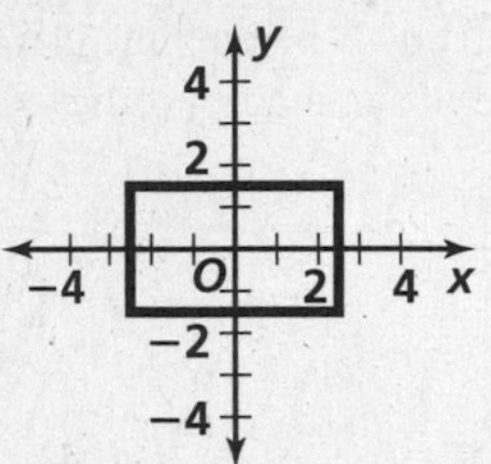

4.

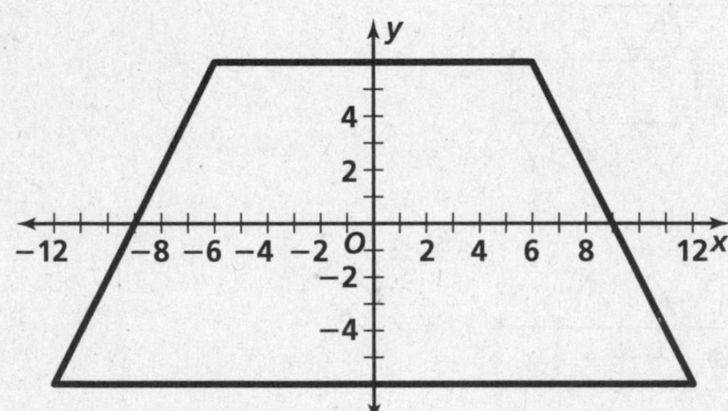

5.

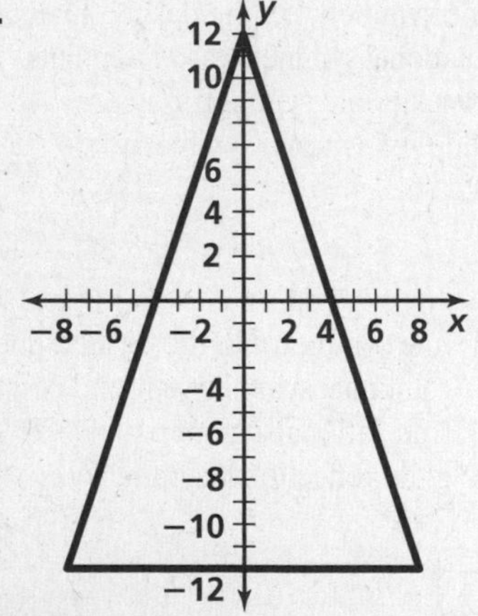

Algebra 2 Topics

Review 191

1. $-3; \frac{1}{3}$ **2.** $2; -\frac{1}{2}$ **3.** $\frac{1}{6}; -6$ **4.** $-\frac{3}{5}; \frac{5}{3}$ **5.** $2.4; -\frac{5}{12}$ **6.** $-0.6; \frac{5}{3}$ **7.** $5\frac{2}{3}; -\frac{3}{17}$ **8.** $-2\frac{1}{4}; \frac{4}{9}$ **9.** $-\frac{\pi}{2}; \frac{2}{\pi}$ **10.** $\frac{1}{\pi}; -\pi$ **11.** $0.25; -4$ **12.** $-1.3; \frac{10}{13}$ **13.** $-1\frac{2}{5}; \frac{5}{7}$ **14.** $\sqrt{2}; -\frac{\sqrt{2}}{2}$ **15.** $-\pi - 2; \frac{1}{\pi + 2}$ **16.** $\frac{9}{10}; -\frac{10}{9}$

Review 192

1. $6x + 1; 19$ **2.** $7t + 10; 38$ **3.** $9y - 5z; 13$ **4.** $u + 3v; -1$ **5.** $5a^2 + 6a + 1; 9$ **6.** $3p^2 - 2q^2; -47$ **7.** $\frac{1}{2}m + n; 5$ **8.** $\frac{r}{4} + \frac{s}{3} + \frac{1}{5}; -\frac{1}{20}$

Review 193

1. $m = 2n$ **2.** $u = \frac{w - 6v}{7}$ **3.** $x = \frac{d - b}{a - c}$ **4.** $y = -\frac{3kz + 20}{k - 4}$ **5.** $r = 2 - 6s$ **6.** $f = \frac{12 - 5g}{8 + 12g}$ **7.** $x = \frac{3j - 4k}{4}$ **8.** $y = \frac{a + 4b - ab}{b + 3}$

Review 194

1. $y \leq 7$

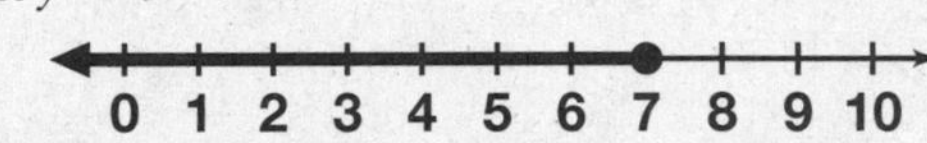

2. $t < -\frac{1}{2}$

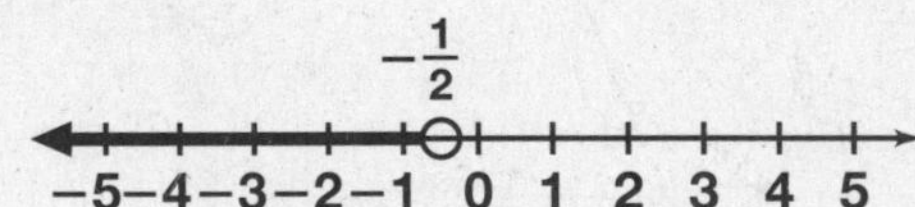

3. $m > -2$

−5 −4 −3 −2 −1 0 1 2 3 4 5

4. $d \leq 2$

−5 −4 −3 −2 −1 0 1 2 3 4 5

5. $h \geq 1\frac{1}{2}$

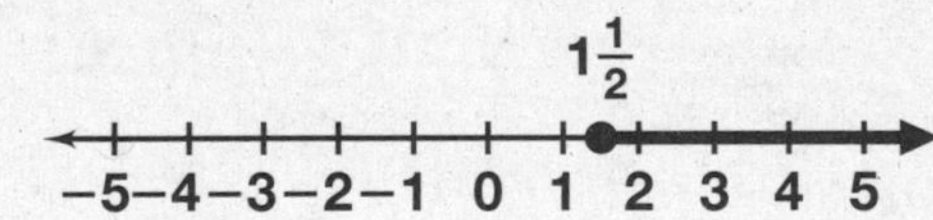

6. $k > \frac{2}{5}$

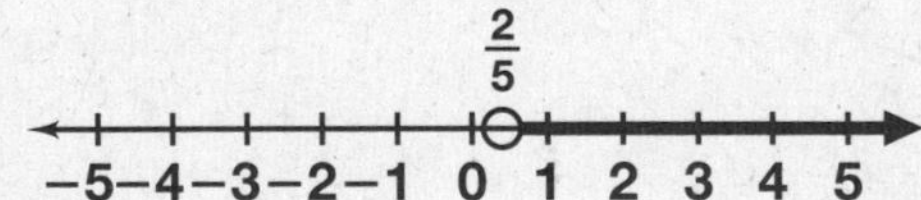

7. $p \geq 8$

0 1 2 3 4 5 6 7 8 9 10

8. $r > -4$

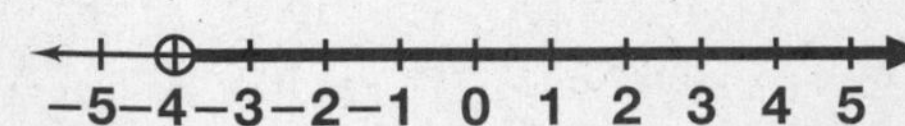

Review 195

1. $-6, -1$ **2.** no solution **3.** -1 **4.** $-0.2, 1.2$
5. $-5, 0$ **6.** no solution **7.** $-3, -\frac{1}{3}$ **8.** 1

Review 196

1. $\frac{5}{12} \approx 0.42$, or 42% **2.** $\frac{1}{12} \approx 0.08$, or 8%
3. $\frac{5}{12} \approx 0.42$, or 42% **4.** $\frac{1}{3} \approx 0.33$, or 33%
5. $\frac{7}{12} \approx 0.58$, or 58% **6.** $\frac{5}{12} \approx 0.42$, or 42%
7. $\frac{1}{3} \approx 0.33$, or 33% **8.** $\frac{1}{6} \approx 0.17$, or 17%
9. $\frac{1}{2}$, or 50% **10.** Answers may vary. **11.** $\frac{1}{4}$, or 25%
12. Answers may vary. **13.** $\frac{5}{6} \approx 0.83$, or 83%

Review 197

1.–4. Check students' work. **5.** No; the x-value 1 is repeated with different y-values; domain: {1}; range: {2, 3, 4, 5, 6}
6. Yes; no x-value is repeated; domain: {0, 1, −1, −2, 2}; range: {−1, 2, 5, 9}
7. Yes; no x-value is repeated; domain: {A, C, E, G}; range: {B, D, F, H} **8.** No; the x-value I is repeated with different y-values; domain: {I, N}; range: {M, P, T} **9.** Yes; no x-value is repeated; domain: {0}; range: {0} **10.** No; the x-value $\frac{1}{2} = 0.5$ is repeated with different y-values; domain: $\left\{\frac{1}{2}, 2\right\}$; range: {3, 4, 1}

Review 198

1. $y = 4x - 10$ **2.** $y = -2x + 15$ **3.** $y = 0$
4. $y = -x - 7$ **5.** $y = 3x + 2$ **6.** $y = -7$
7. $y = 8x - 40$ **8.** $y = -x + 7$ **9.** $y = 8$
10. $y = 4x - 3$ **11.** $y = 7x - 19$ **12.** $y = -x - 4$
13. $y = 2x + 3$ **14.** $y = -x - 2$ **15.** $y = \frac{2}{3}x + 2$

Review 199

1. 12 **2.** 20 **3.** $\frac{7}{3}$ **4.** -3 **5.** 4 **6.** $\frac{6}{7}$ **7.** $26\frac{14}{17}$ ft

Review 200

1.

2.

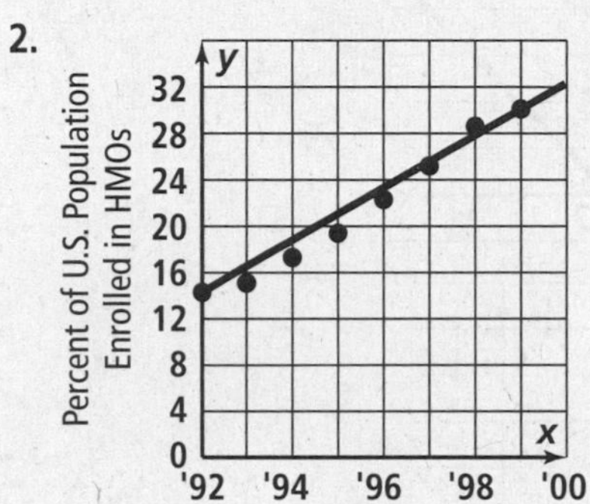

; using (0, 14.3) and (7, 30.1): $y = 2.26x + 14.3$

3. about 45.9%

Review 201

1. (0, 0) **2.** (−3, 0) **3.** (4, 0) **4.** $\left(-\frac{1}{3}, 0\right)$
5. (6, 0) **6.** (−8, 0)
7. $\left(\frac{1}{2}, 0\right)$;

8. $\left(\frac{1}{3}, 0\right)$;

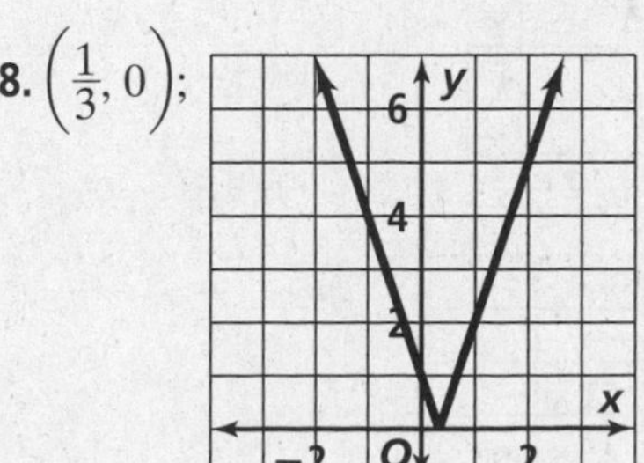

ANSWERS

Review 201 *(continued)*

9. $(-2, 0)$;

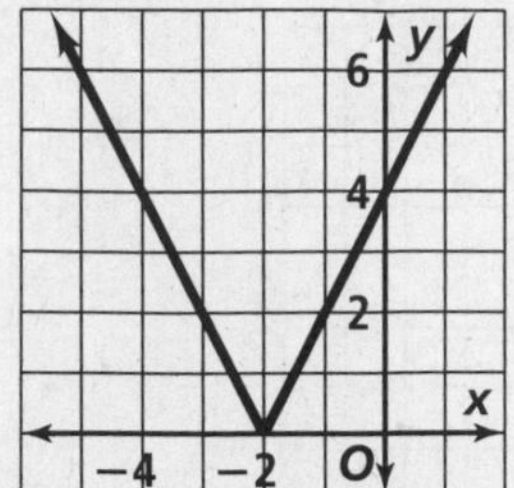

10. $(-1, 0)$;

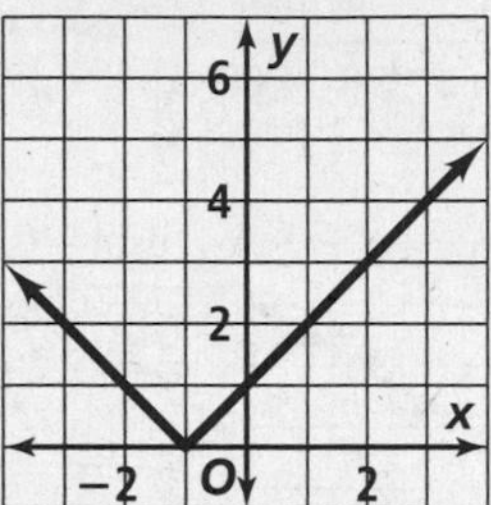

11. $(2, 0)$;

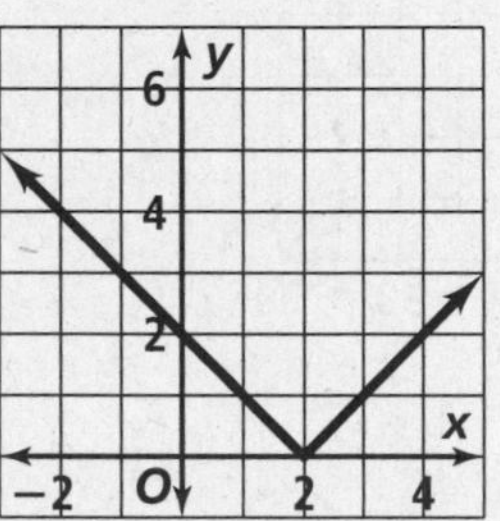

12. $\left(\frac{3}{4}, 0\right)$;

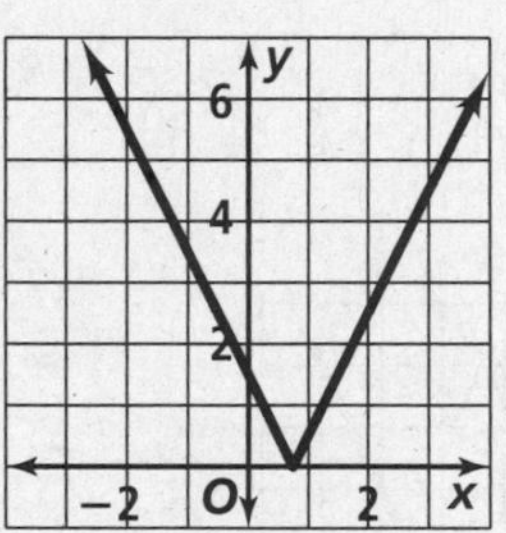

13. $(0, 0)$;

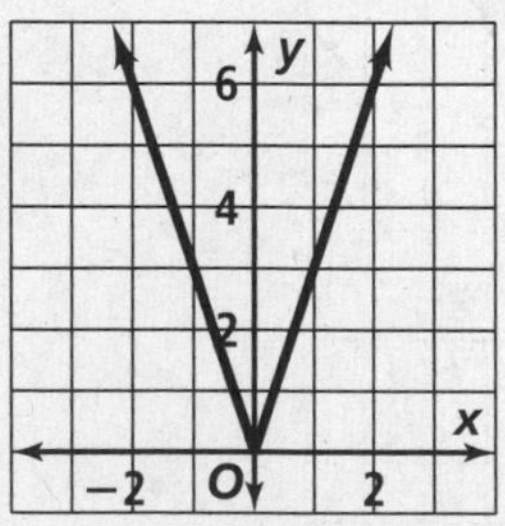

14. $(-2, 0)$;

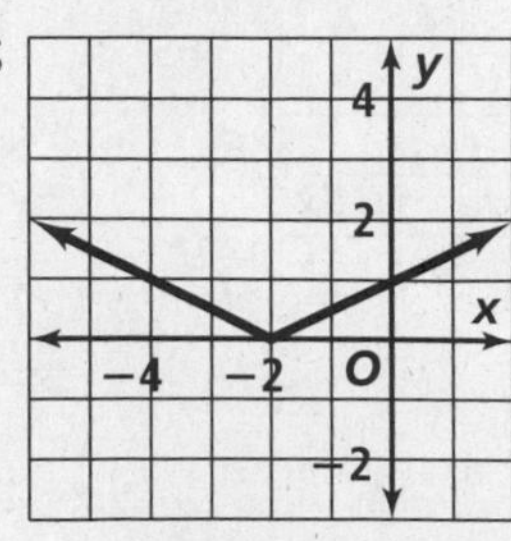

15. $(-3, 0)$;

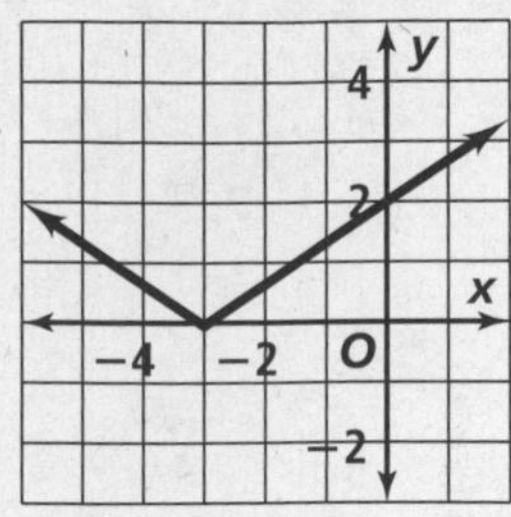

Review 202

1. right;

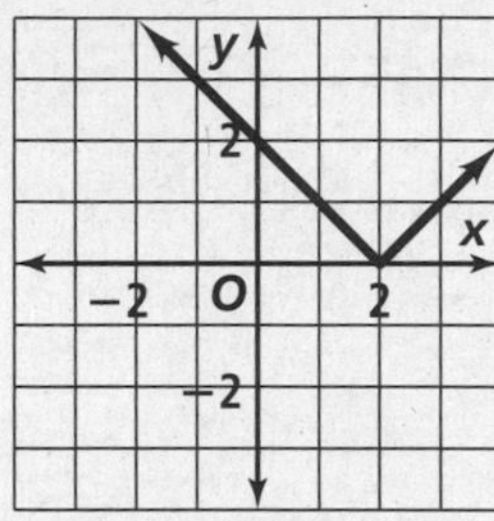

2. up;

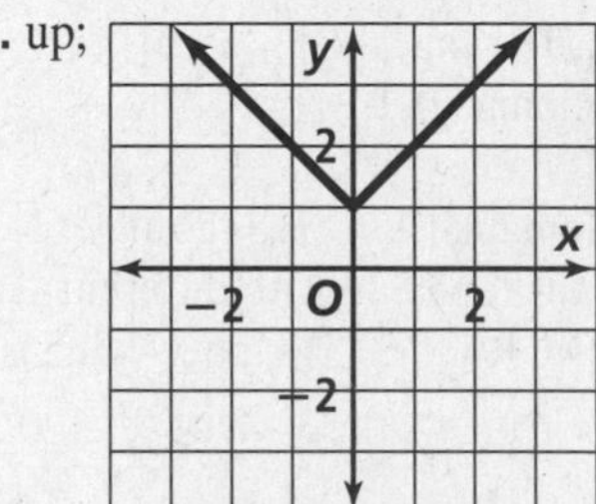

3. down;

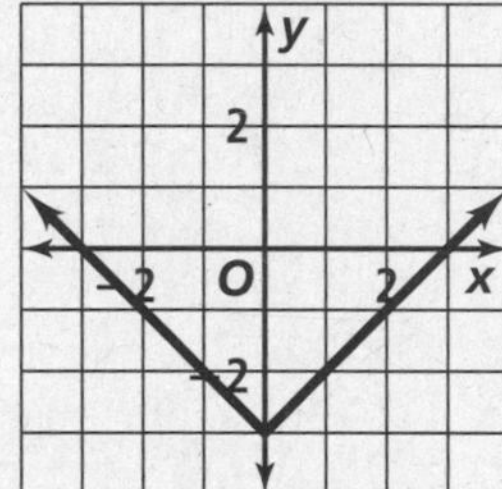

4. left;

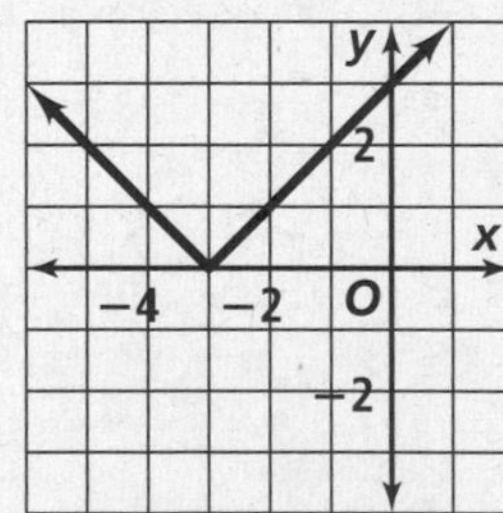

5. right; down;

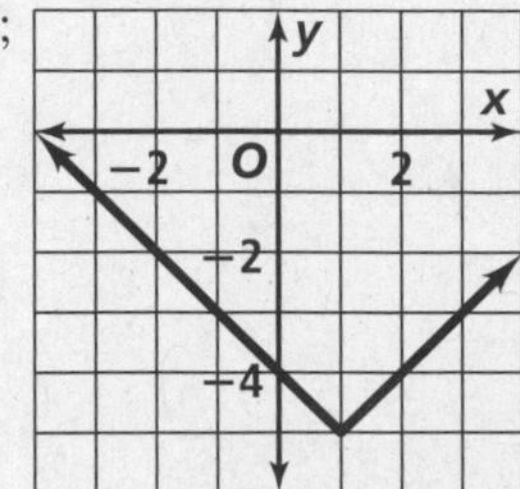

ANSWERS

Review 202 *(continued)*

6. left; up;

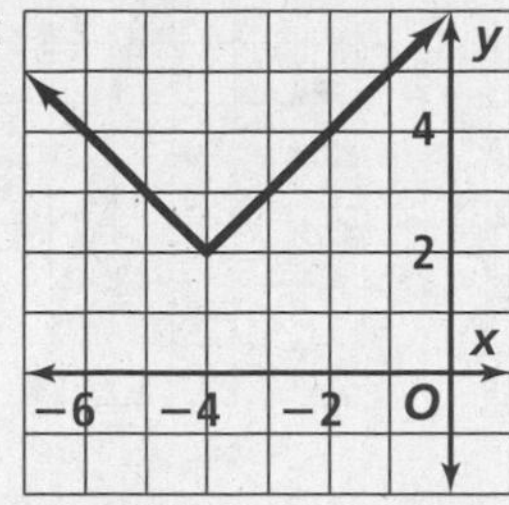

Review 203

1.

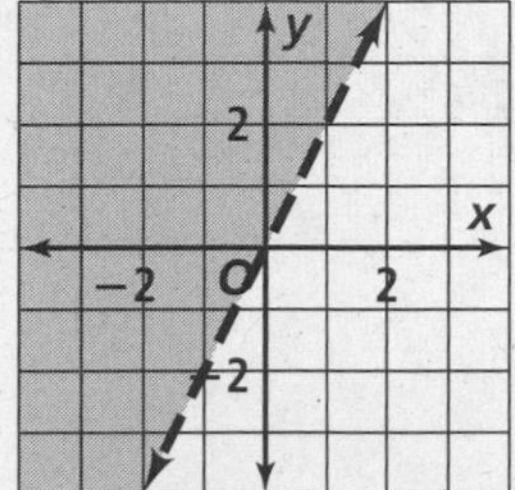

2.

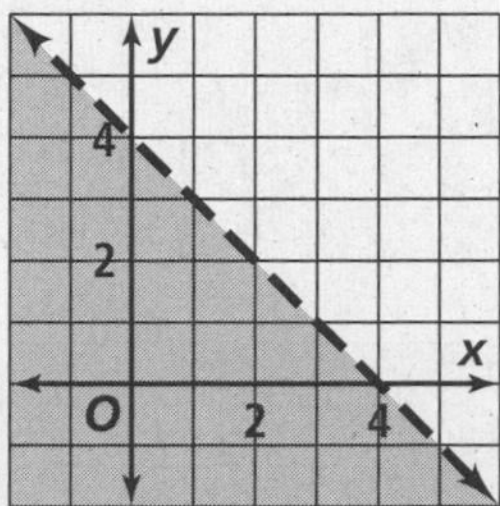

3.

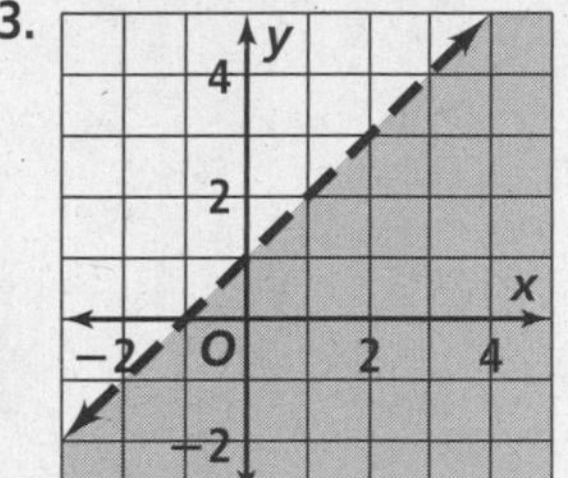

4.

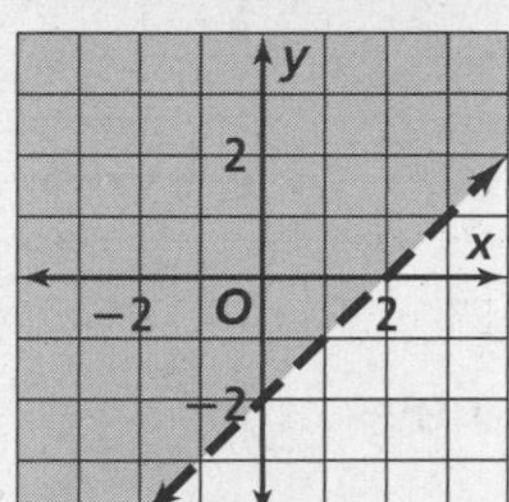

5.

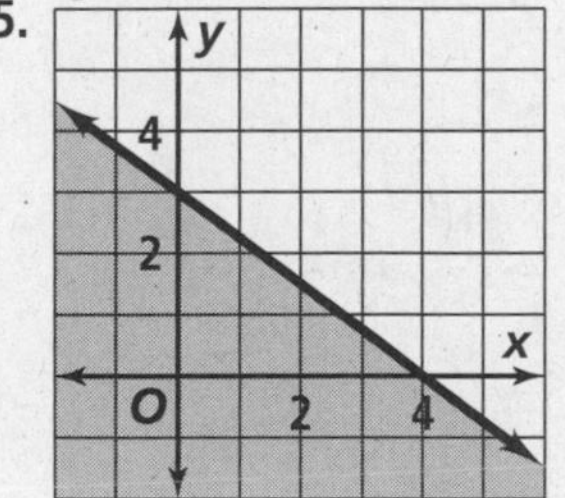

6.

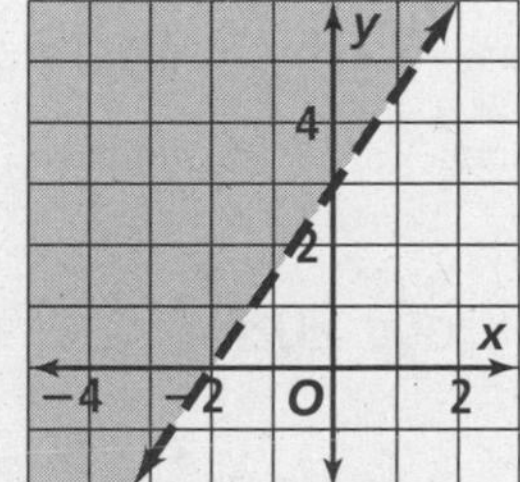

7.

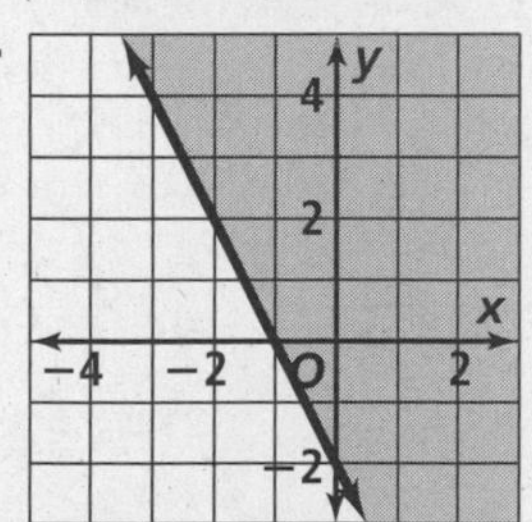

8.

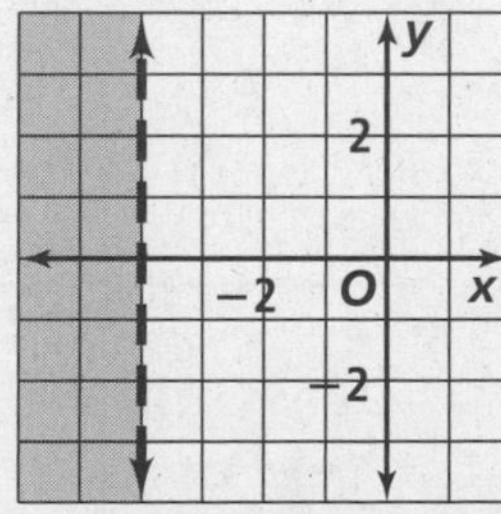

9.

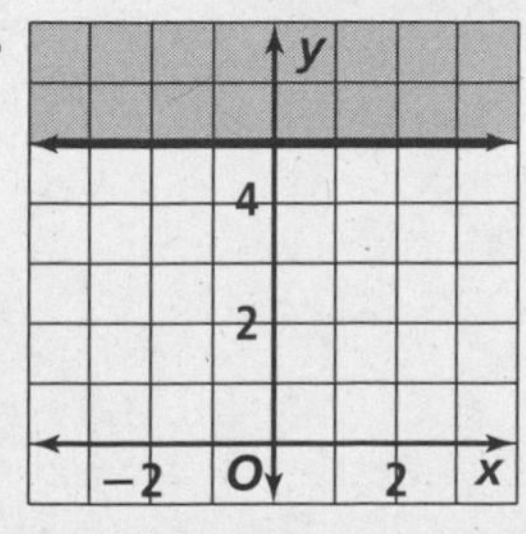

10.

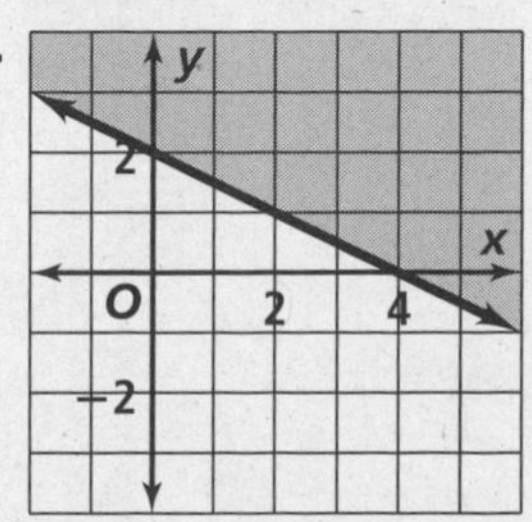

11.

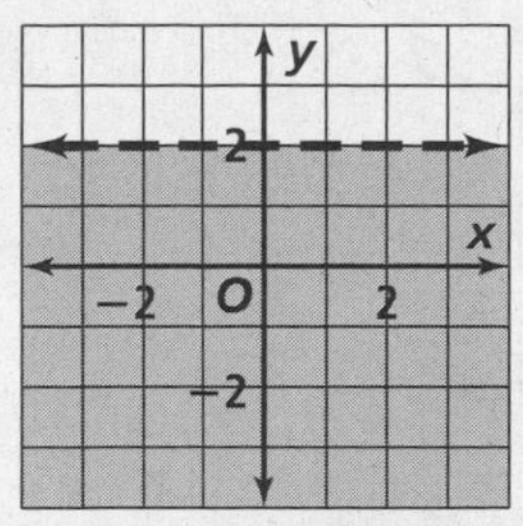

12.

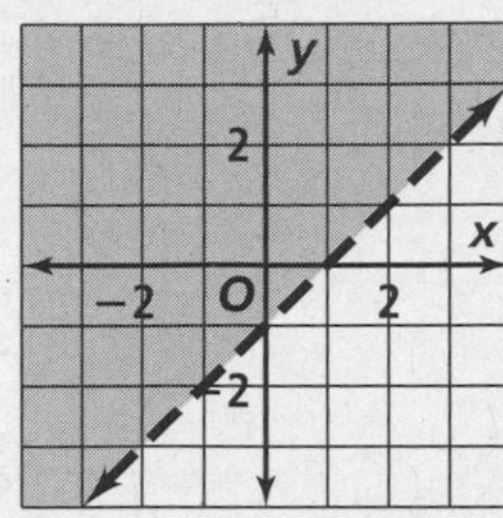

13.

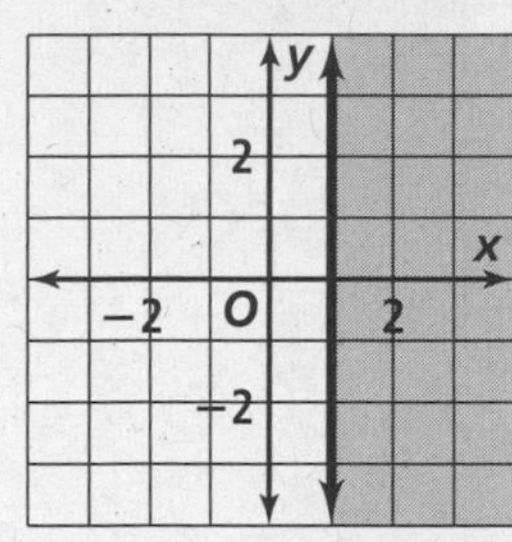

14.

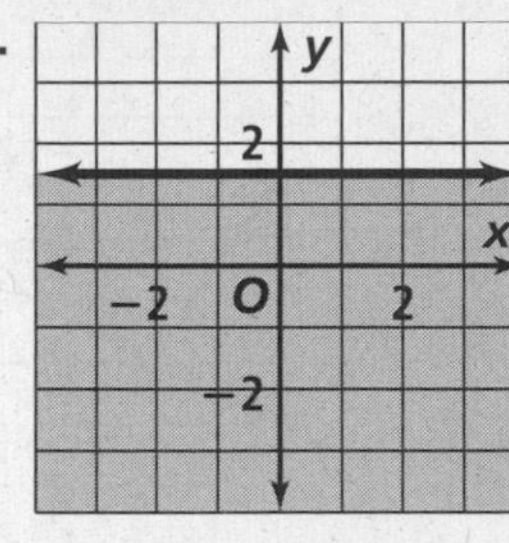

15.

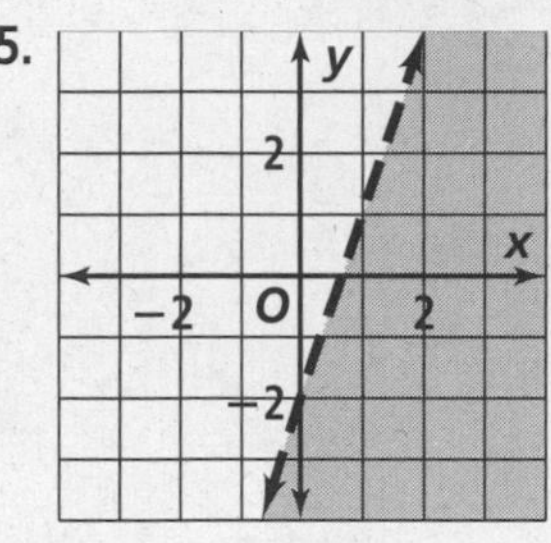

Review 204

1. (1, 3);

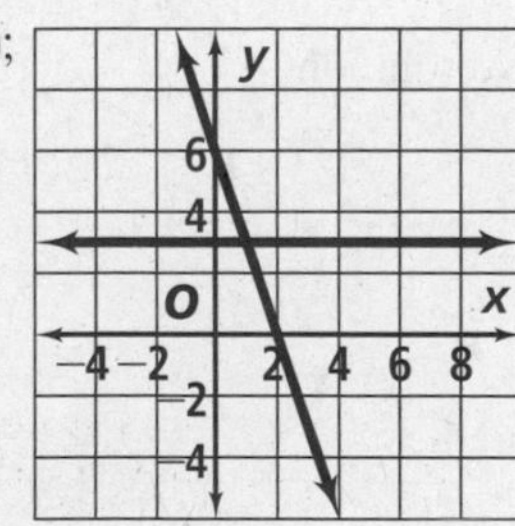

2. (2, 1);

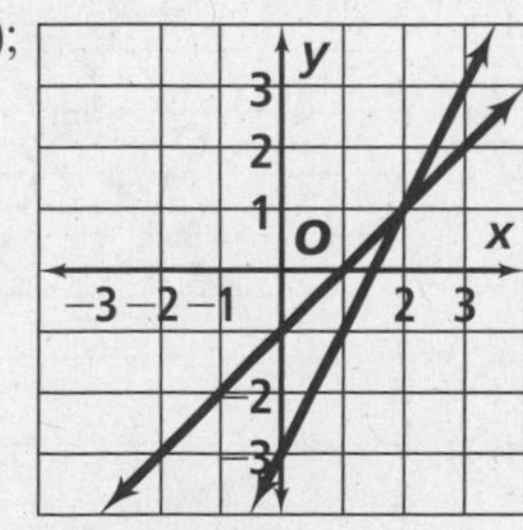

3. (1, 2);

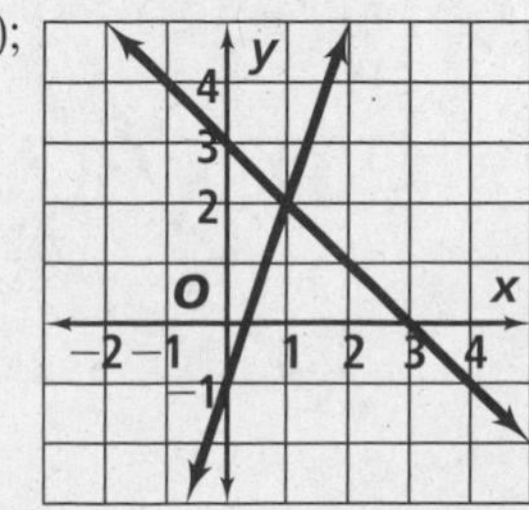

Review 204 *(continued)*

4. (3, −2);

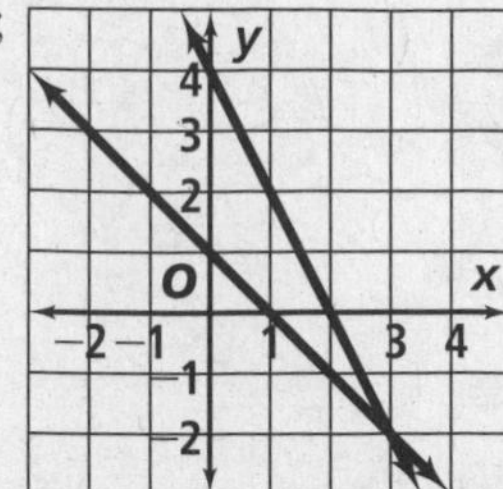

5. (−2, 0);

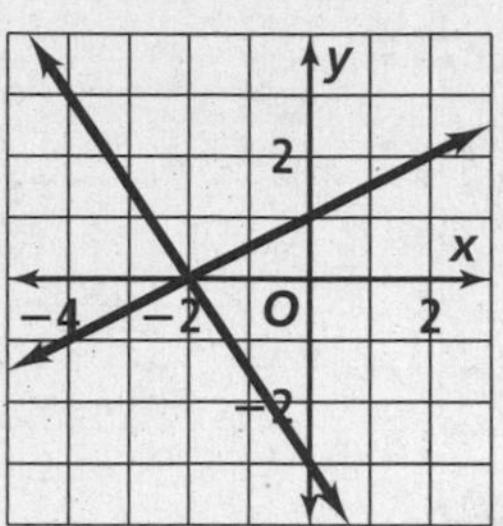

6. (3, 1);

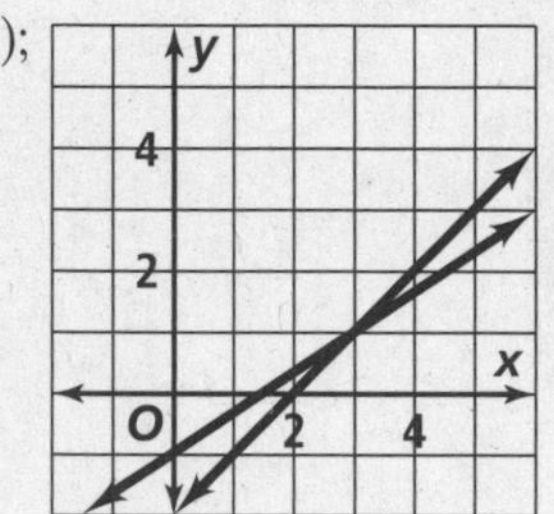

Review 205

1. (−3, −4) **2.** (2, −1) **3.** No solution

4. $\left\{ (x, y) \mid y = -\frac{1}{2}x - \frac{1}{2} \right\}$

Review 206

1.

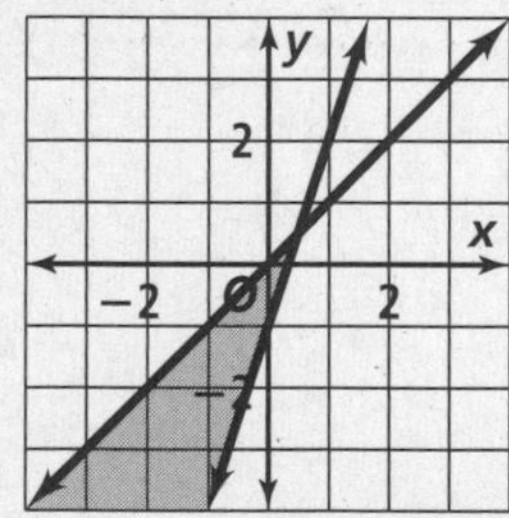

2.

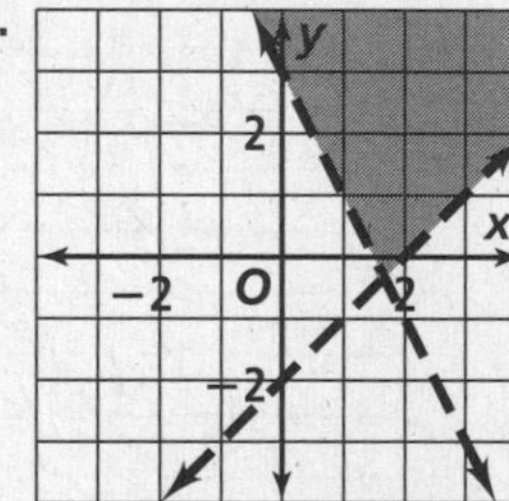

3.

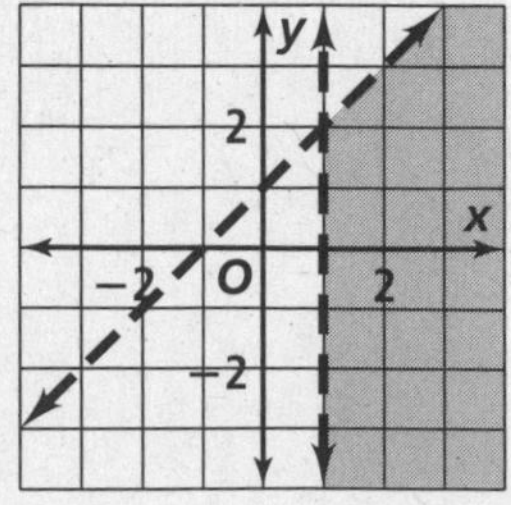

4.

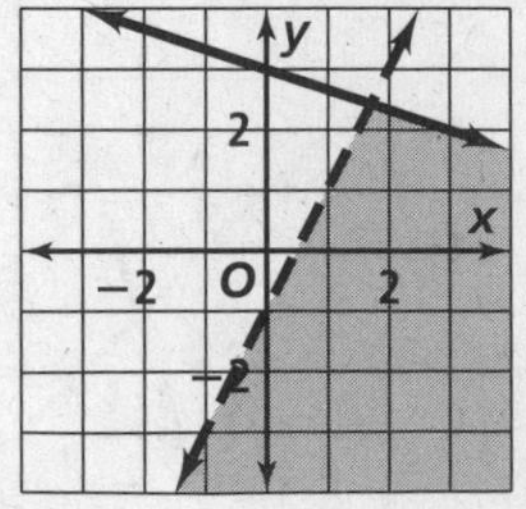

5.

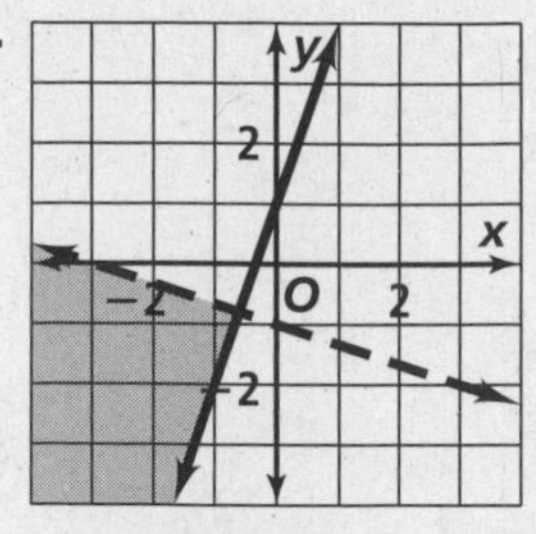

6.

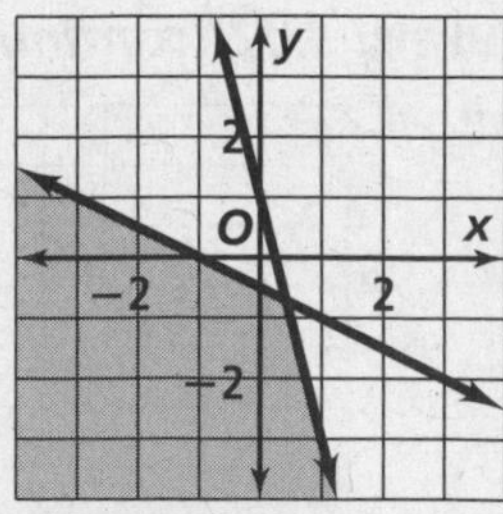

7.

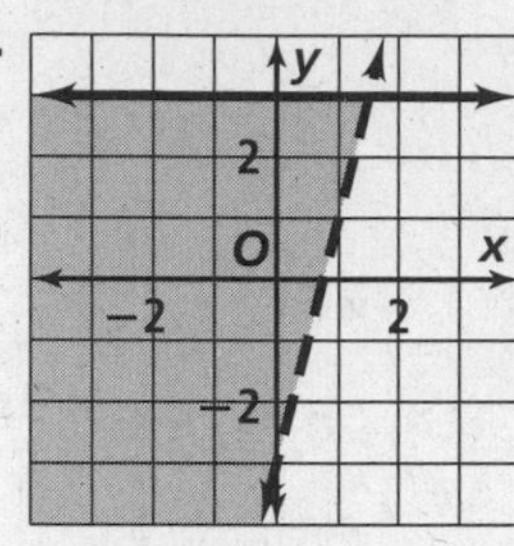

8.

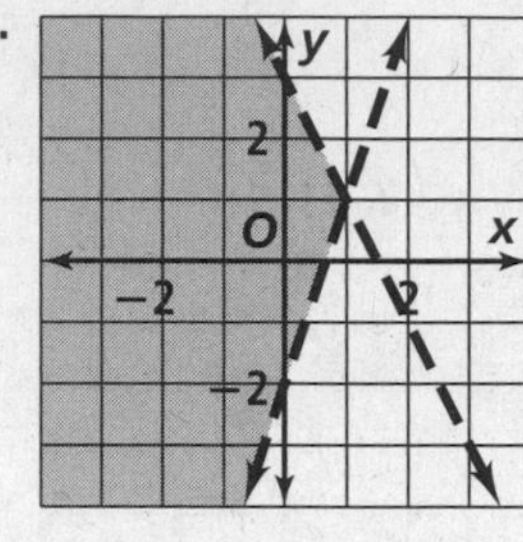

9.

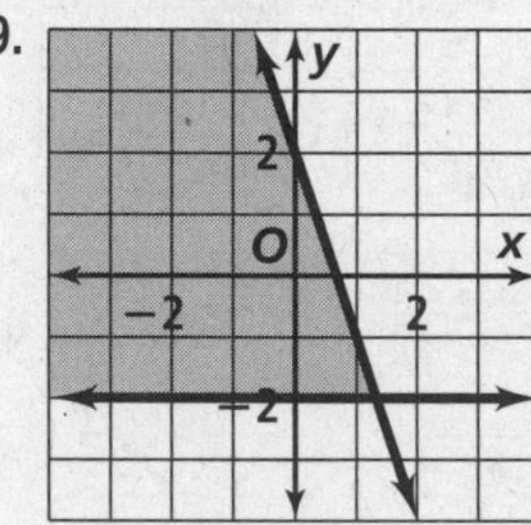

Review 207

1. max: 46 at (5, 3); min: $\frac{78}{5}$ at $\left(1, \frac{19}{5}\right)$

2. max: 16 at (4, 4); min: 2 at (2, 0)

3. max: $\frac{3}{2}$ at $\left(3, \frac{3}{4}\right)$; min. $-\frac{22}{3}$ at $\left(1, \frac{25}{6}\right)$

Review 208

1.

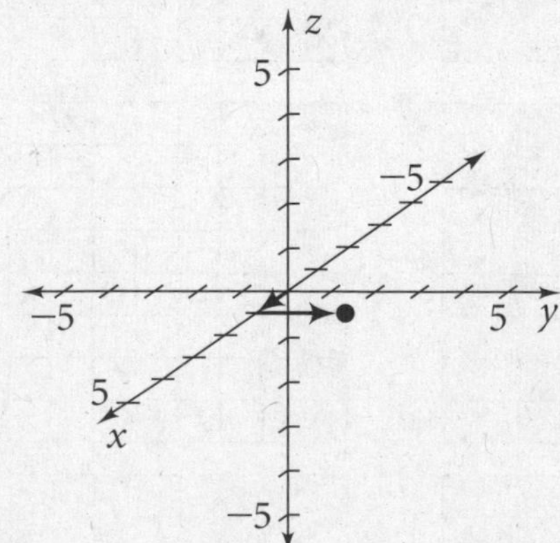

ANSWERS

Review 208 *(continued)*

2.

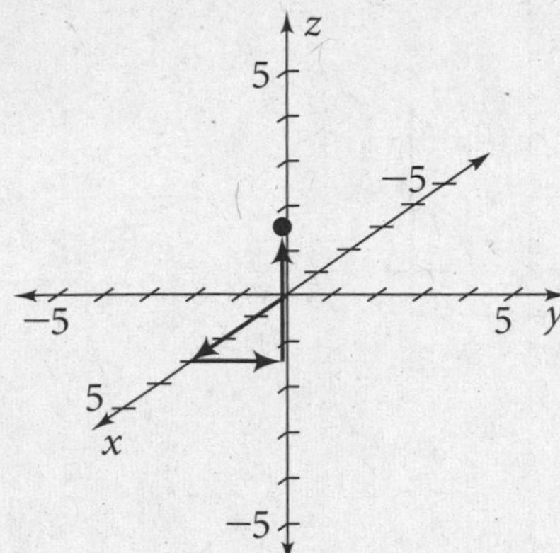

3.

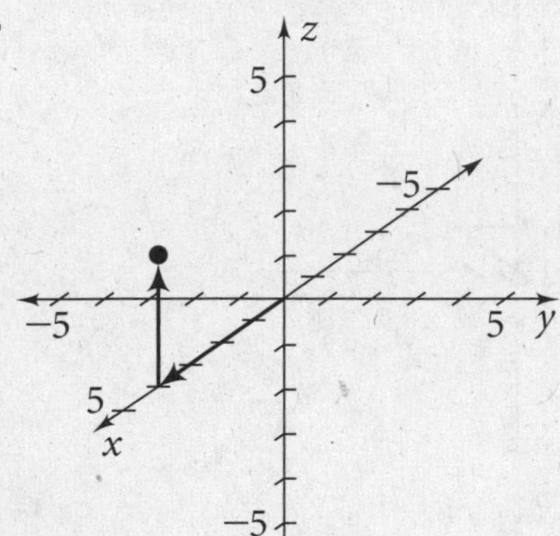

4.

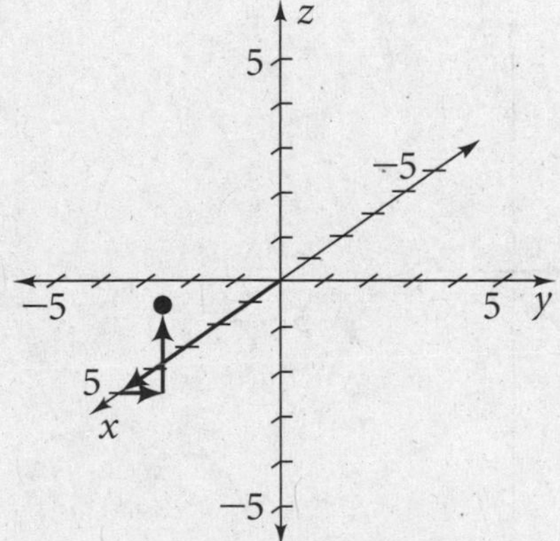

5.

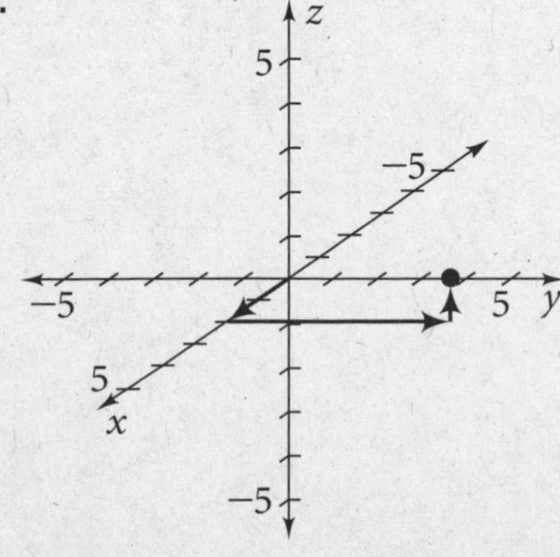

6.

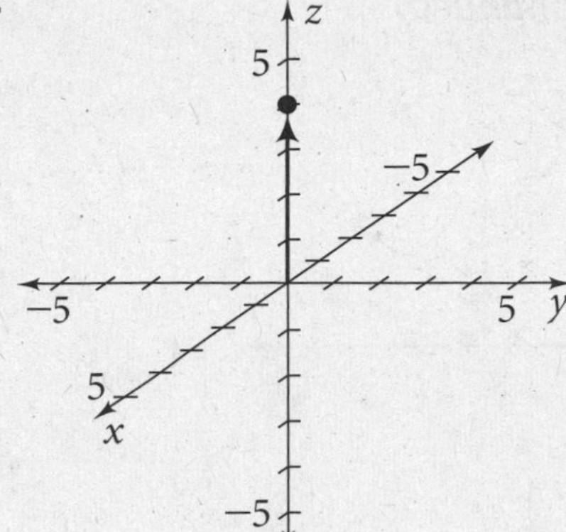

7.

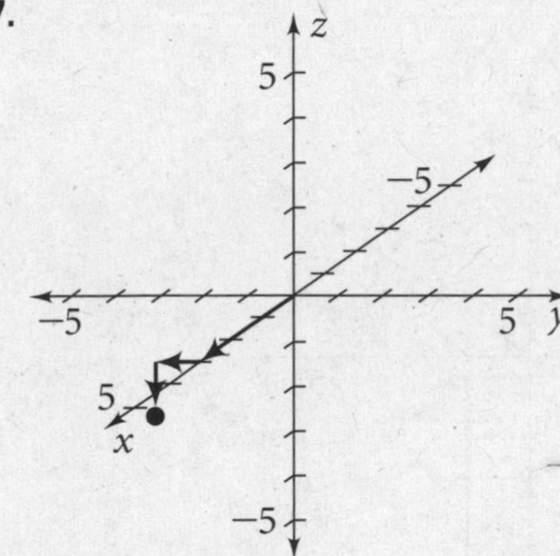

8.

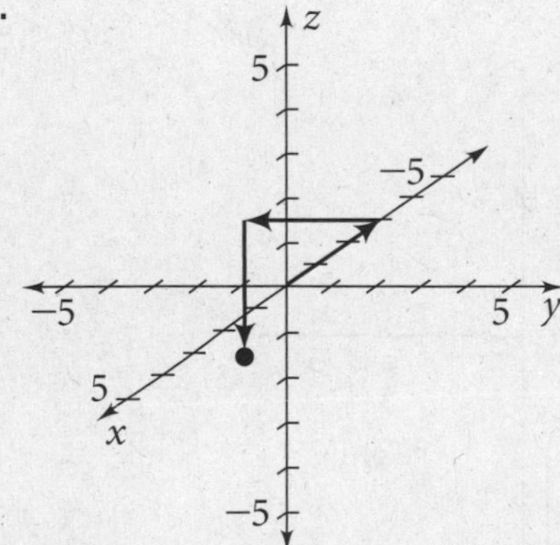

9.

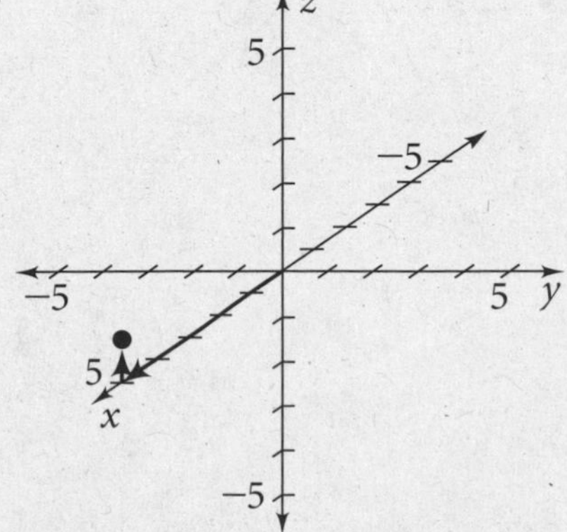

Review 208 *(continued)*

10.

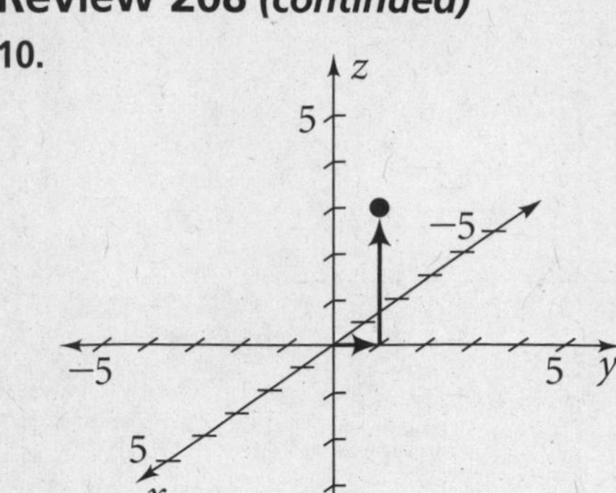

11.

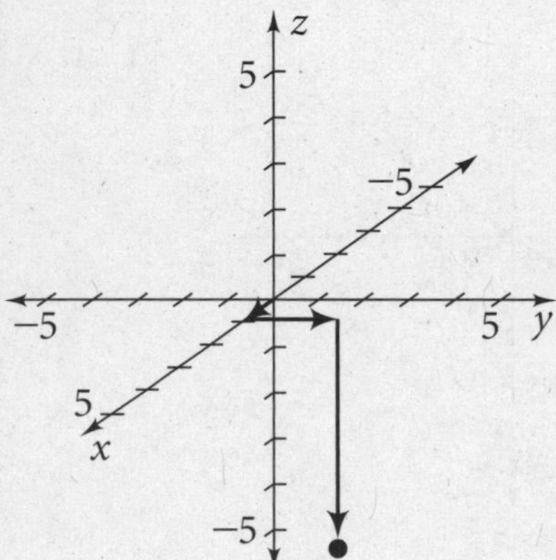

12.

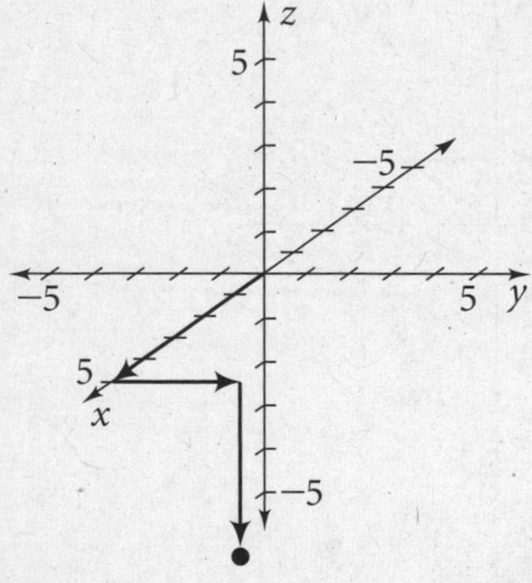

13.

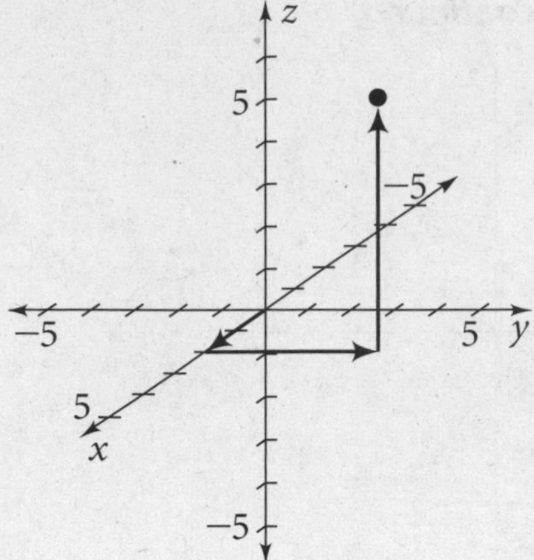

14.

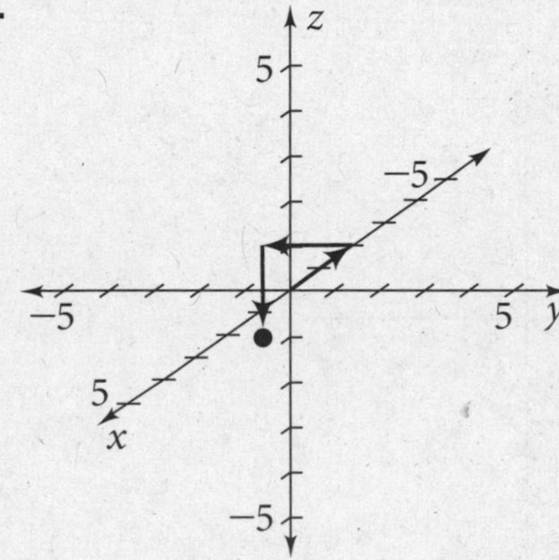

15.

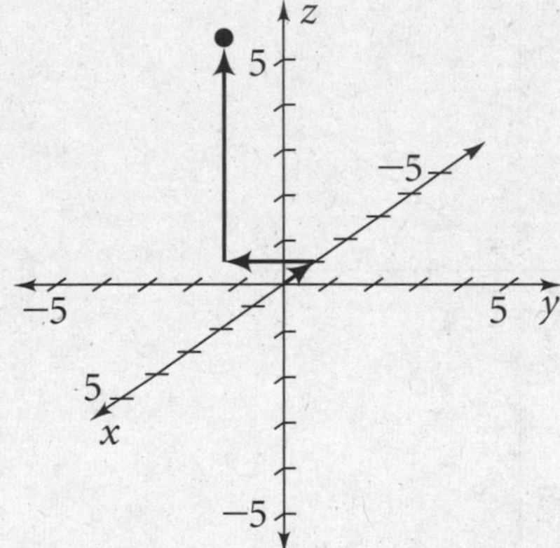

ANSWERS

Review 208 *(continued)*

16.

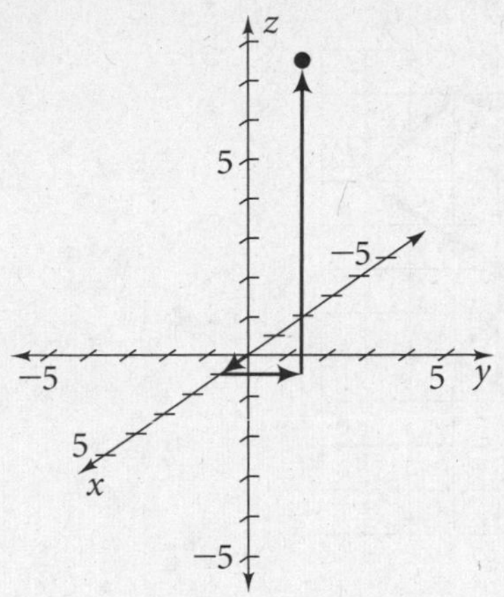

17.

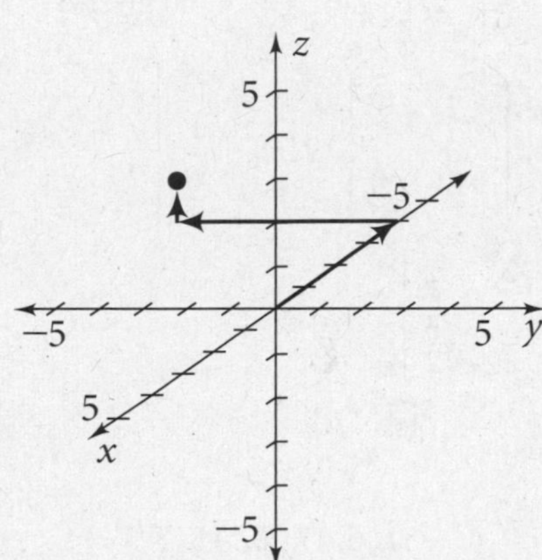

18.

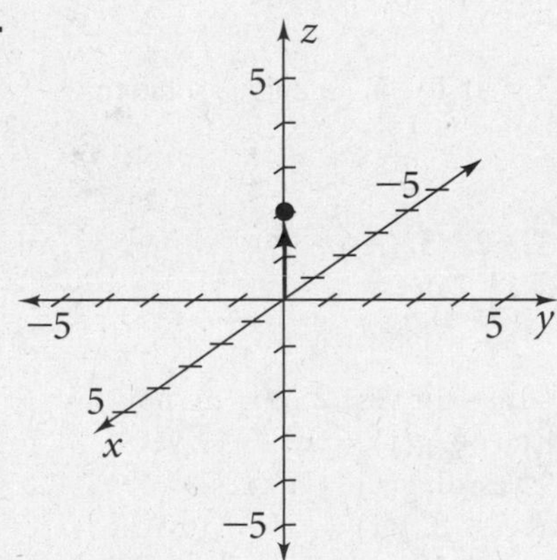

19.

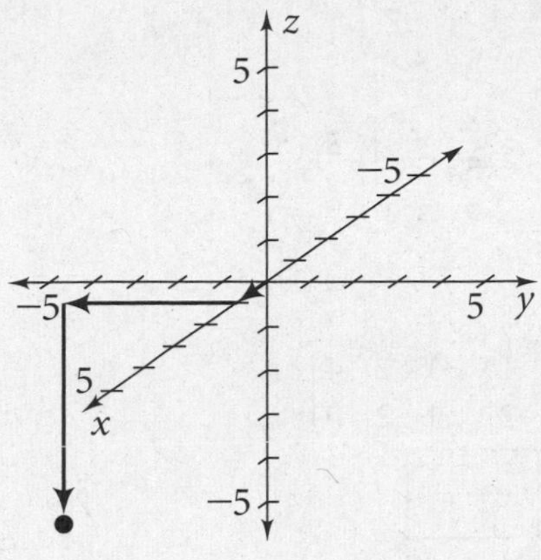

20.

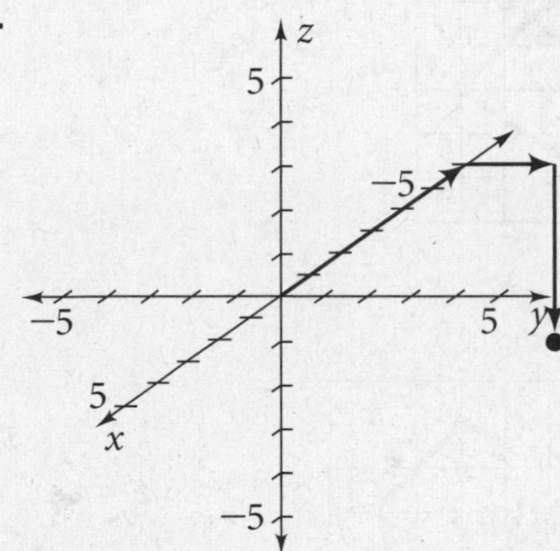

Review 209

1. $(4, 2, 2)$ **2.** $(2, -2, 2)$ **3.** $(3, -2, 1)$ **4.** $(-1, 3, 2)$
5. $(2, -4, 3)$ **6.** $(-3, -2, 4)$

Review 210

1. Answers may vary. Check students' work.

2.
$$\begin{array}{r c} \text{Trial} & \begin{matrix} 1 & 2 & 3 & 4 \end{matrix} \\ \begin{matrix} \text{Left} \\ \text{Right} \end{matrix} & \begin{bmatrix} 36 & 24 & 26 & 55 \\ 15 & 43 & 22 & 46 \end{bmatrix} \end{array}$$

3. Check students' work.

Review 211

1. $\begin{bmatrix} -2 & 3 \\ 14 & -2 \end{bmatrix}$ **2.** $\begin{bmatrix} -5 & 1 \\ 1 & 2 \end{bmatrix}$ **3.** $\begin{bmatrix} -1 & -1 \\ 1 & -2 \end{bmatrix}$

4. $\begin{bmatrix} 1 & 1 & -1 \\ -3 & 1 & -5 \end{bmatrix}$ **5.** $\begin{bmatrix} -16 & -1 & -4 \\ 7 & -7 & -6 \end{bmatrix}$ **6.** $\begin{bmatrix} 4.5 & 5.5 \\ 3 & 11.5 \end{bmatrix}$

7. $\begin{bmatrix} -9 & -6 \\ 0 & 1 \\ 8 & 5 \end{bmatrix}$ **8.** $\begin{bmatrix} 5 & 5 \\ 12 & 4 \\ -17 & -2 \end{bmatrix}$ **9.** $\begin{bmatrix} -9 & 7 \\ 3.5 & -6.5 \\ 1.5 & 0 \\ -3.5 & 5 \end{bmatrix}$

10. $\begin{bmatrix} -5 & -3 & 8 \\ 3 & -2 & -4 \\ 7 & -5 & 6 \end{bmatrix}$

Review 212

1. $\begin{bmatrix} 1 & 3 \\ -6 & 17 \end{bmatrix}$ **2.** $\begin{bmatrix} 0 & 26 \\ -8 & 3 \\ -13 & 33 \\ -7 & 32 \end{bmatrix}$ **3.** $[8 \;\; 5 \;\; 4]$

Review 213

1. $A'B'C'D' = \begin{bmatrix} 1 & -1 & 2 & 4 \\ -2 & 1 & 2 & 0 \end{bmatrix}$

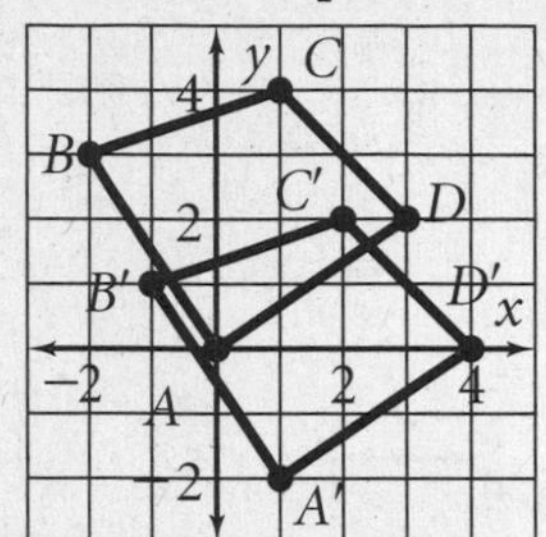

2. $A'B'C'D' = \begin{bmatrix} -3 & -5 & -2 & 0 \\ -1 & 2 & 3 & 1 \end{bmatrix}$

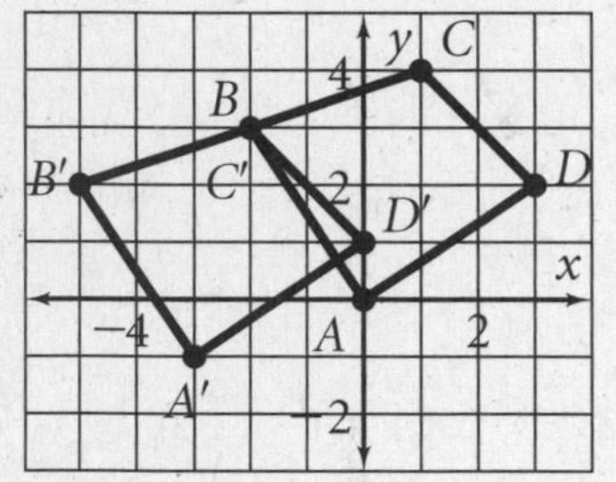

3. $A'B'C'D' = \begin{bmatrix} -4 & -6 & -3 & -1 \\ 3 & 6 & 7 & 5 \end{bmatrix}$

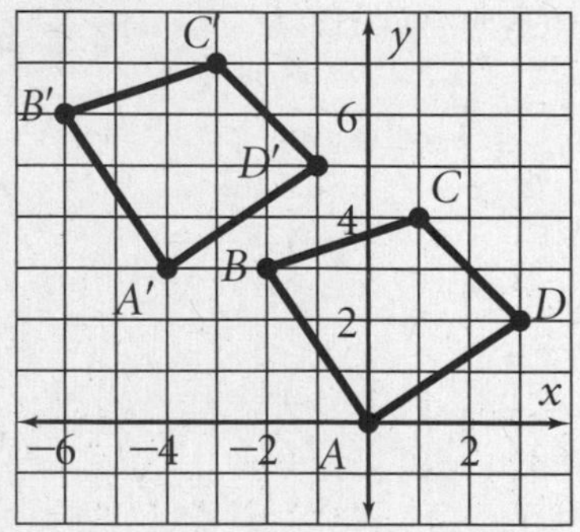

4. $A'B'C'D' = \begin{bmatrix} 2 & 0 & 3 & 5 \\ 4 & 7 & 8 & 6 \end{bmatrix}$

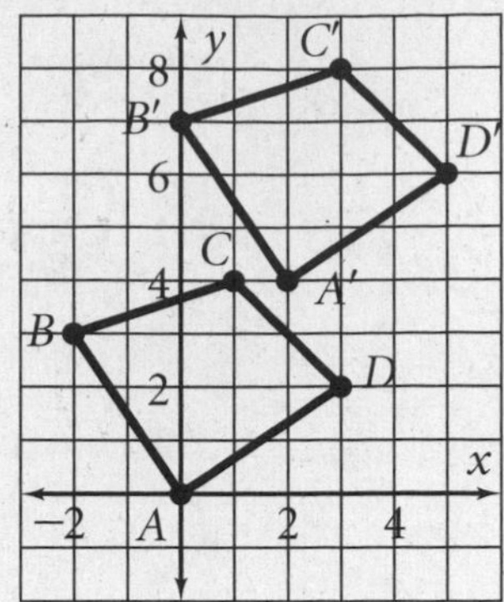

Review 214

1. $\begin{bmatrix} 3 & 2 \\ 7 & 5 \end{bmatrix}$ **2.** $\begin{bmatrix} -1 & 2 \\ -5 & 9 \end{bmatrix}$ **3.** $\begin{bmatrix} 7 & -4 \\ -5 & 3 \end{bmatrix}$ **4.** no inverse

5. $\begin{bmatrix} -\frac{8}{33} & \frac{17}{33} \\ \frac{1}{33} & \frac{2}{33} \end{bmatrix}$ **6.** $\begin{bmatrix} 1 & -2 \\ -\frac{3}{2} & \frac{7}{2} \end{bmatrix}$ **7.** $\begin{bmatrix} \frac{1}{4} & \frac{3}{4} \\ \frac{1}{4} & \frac{7}{4} \end{bmatrix}$

8. no inverse **9.** $\begin{bmatrix} -3 & 2 \\ \frac{5}{2} & -\frac{3}{2} \end{bmatrix}$

Review 215

1. −6 **2.** −21 **3.** 14 **4.** −50 **5.** 17 **6.** −3

Review 216

1. (2, 1) **2.** (2, 1) **3.** (−1, 0) **4.** no unique solution

Review 217

1. (−1, −1) **2.** (−1, −2) **3.** (−4, −14)

Review 218

1. $f(x) = 25x^2 + 40x + 16$; yes **2.** $y = 3x$; no
3. $y = -11x + 24$; no **4.** $g(x) = x^2 - 49$; yes
5. $f(x) = -x^2 + 9$; yes **6.** $g(x) = x^2$; yes
7. $f(x) = 3x^2 + 2x$; yes **8.** $f(x) = x^2 - 16$; yes
9. $f(x) = 4x^2 + 5x$; yes **10.** $y = 8x + 8$; no

Review 219

1. 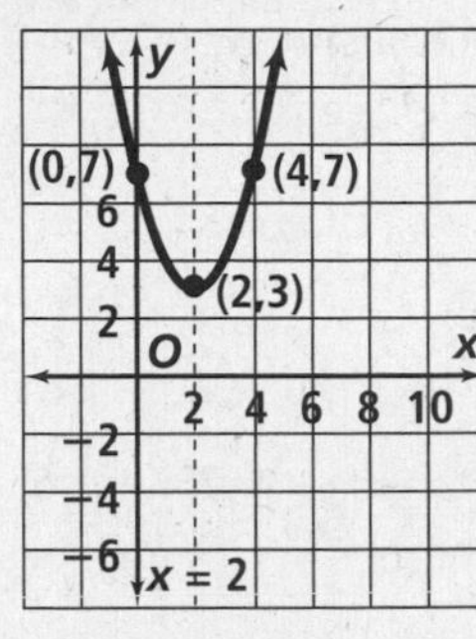

2. 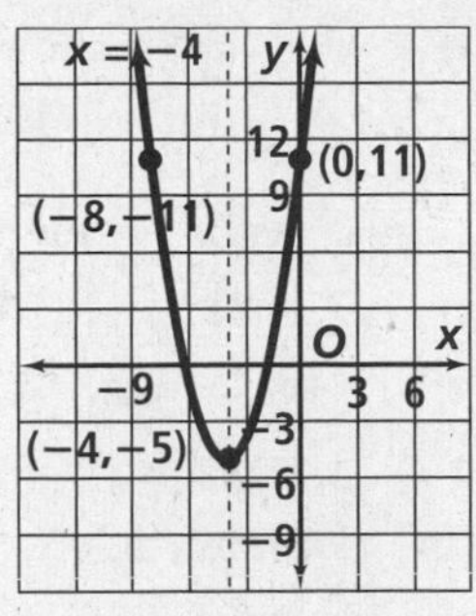

3. 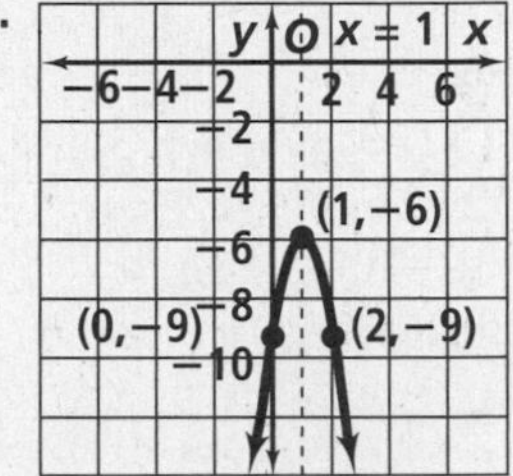 

4. 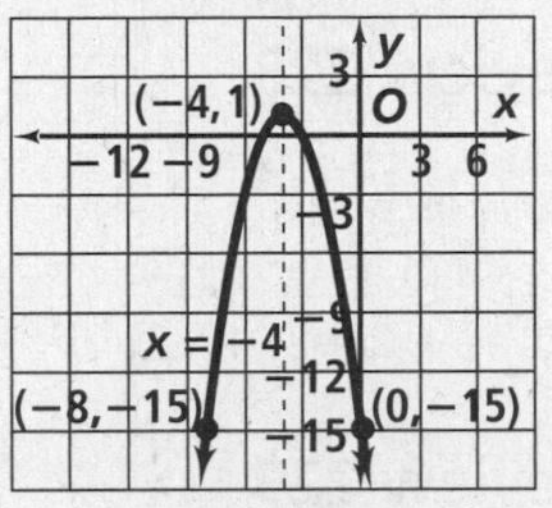

5. 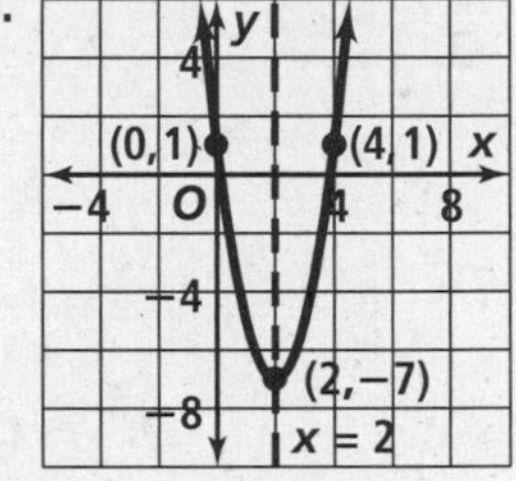

6. 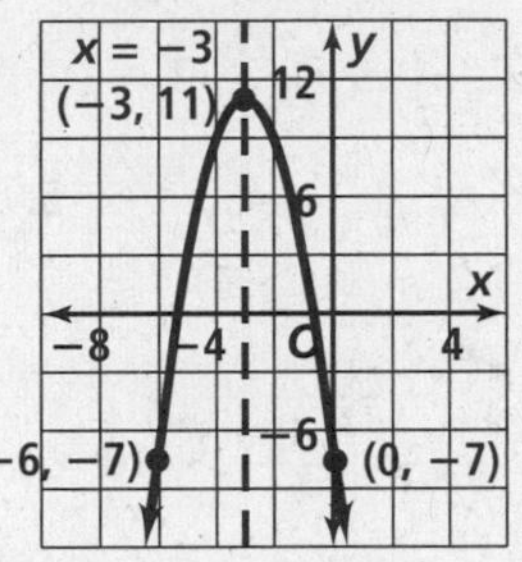

Review 220

1. $y = (x - 1)^2 - 4$ **2.** $y = -(x - 2)^2 + 10$

3. $y = \left(x + \frac{3}{2}\right)^2 - \frac{49}{4}$ **4.** $y = \left(x - \frac{9}{2}\right)^2 - \frac{81}{4}$

5. $y = \left(x + \frac{1}{2}\right)^2 - \frac{1}{4}$ **6.** $y = \left(x + \frac{5}{2}\right)^2 - \frac{9}{4}$

7. $y = 4(x + 1)^2 - 7$ **8.** $y = \frac{3}{4}(x + 6)^2 - 27$

9. $y = -2\left(x - \frac{1}{2}\right)^2 + \frac{3}{2}$ **10.** $y = x^2 - 6x + 10$

11. $y = 2x^2 - 4x - 1$ **12.** $y = -3x^2 - 24x - 47$

Review 221

1. $(x + 4)(x + 2)$ **2.** $(x - 3)(x - 1)$ **3.** $2(x - 2)(x - 1)$
4. $(2x - 1)(x - 5)$ **5.** $(2x + 1)(x - 4)$ **6.** $(2x + 5)(2x + 3)$
7. $(x + 2)(x - 7)$ **8.** $(7x + 2)(x - 3)$ **9.** $(x - 9)(x + 8)$
10. $(2x + 7)(x + 1)$ **11.** $(x + 4)(x + 8)$
12. $(2x - 7)(2x - 7)$ **13.** $(x - 5)(x + 2)$
14. $(2x + 1)(x + 4)$ **15.** $(3x - 1)(3x - 1)$
16. $(x - 1)(x - 9)$ **17.** $(x + 6)(x - 2)$
18. $(x + 5)(x + 2)$ **19.** $(x - 6)(x - 2)$
20. $(2x + 1)(x - 3)$ **21.** $(x - 1)(x - 5)$
22. $(3x - 4)(x + 2)$ **23.** $(2x + 1)(x + 5)$
24. $(x - 4)(x + 7)$

Review 222

1. 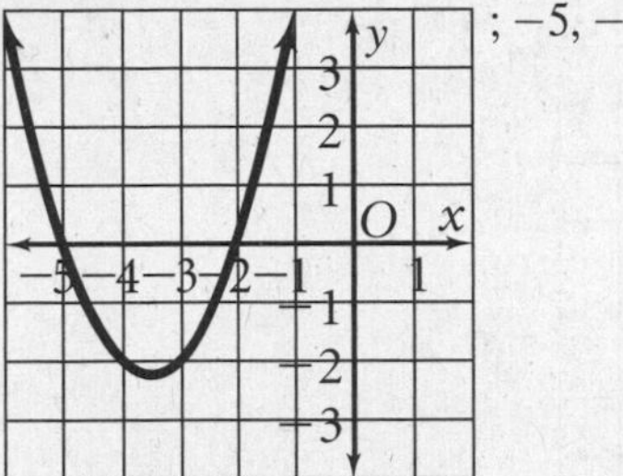

; −5, −2

2. 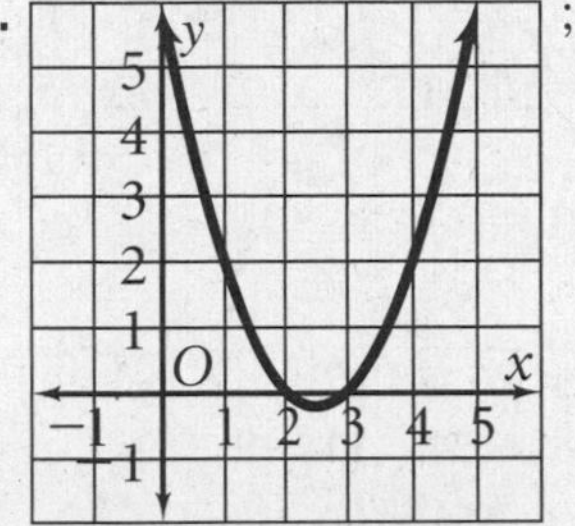

; 3, 2

3. 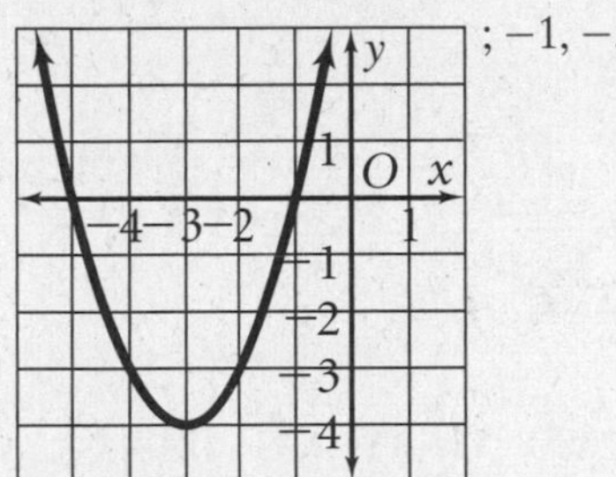

; −1, −5

4. 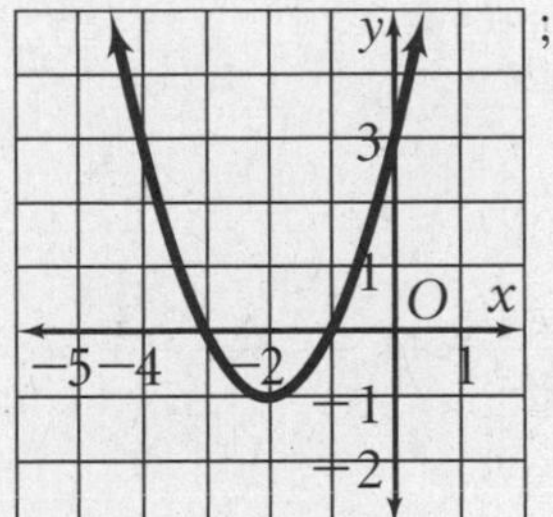

; −3, −1

5. 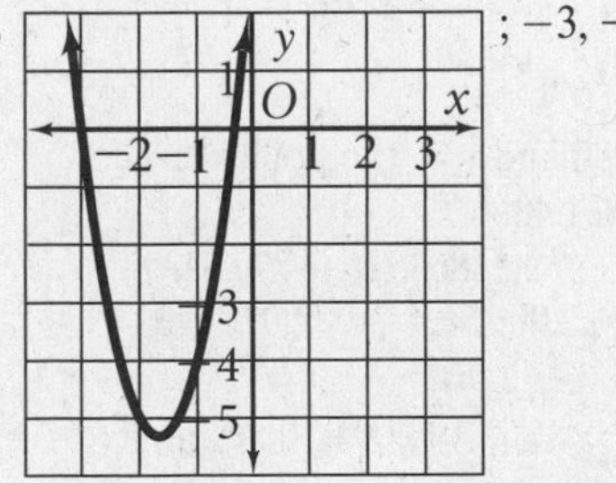

; $-3, -\frac{1}{3}$

ANSWERS

Review 222 *(continued)*

6. 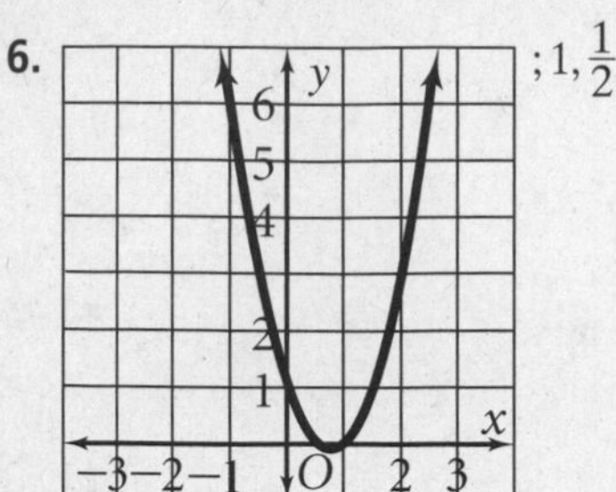

; $1, \frac{1}{2}$

7. 3, 4 **8.** $-3, \frac{5}{2}$ **9.** −2, 1 **10.** $\frac{2}{3}, 1$ **11.** −3, −2 **12.** −5, 4

Review 223

1. −4 **2.** −60 **3.** 5 **4.** $5 + 5i$ **5.** $-2 + 11i$ **6.** $6 + 3i$
7. 24 **8.** $3 + 12i$ **9.** $-2i$ **10.** $8 + 24i$ **11.** $-9 + 2i$
12. $3 + 10i$ **13.** $56i$ **14.** $-3\sqrt{6}$ **15.** $99 + 45i$

Review 224

1. −7, 3 **2.** −3, 11 **3.** $-5 \pm 2\sqrt{5}$ **4.** $-3, -\frac{1}{3}$

5. $\frac{-2 \pm \sqrt{13}}{3}$ **6.** $\frac{5 \pm 3\sqrt{5}}{2}$ **7.** −7, 0 **8.** $-\frac{1}{2}, 4$

9. $\frac{1 \pm \sqrt{29}}{2}$ **10.** $4 \pm 2\sqrt{3}$ **11.** $3 \pm \sqrt{3}$ **12.** −5, 3

13. $-1 \pm \sqrt{6}$ **14.** −5, 1 **15.** $\frac{1}{2}, -\frac{3}{2}$

Review 225

1. 2, 1 **2.** $\frac{5 \pm i\sqrt{11}}{2}$ **3.** $\frac{5 \pm i\sqrt{5}}{5}$ **4.** $\frac{-1 \pm i\sqrt{3}}{2}$

5. $2, -\frac{5}{2}$ **6.** $\frac{1 \pm \sqrt{3}}{2}$

Review 226

Let x = the years since 1980 and y = the points earned.
Linear: $y = -8.533x + 831.48667$
Quadratic: $y = 1.09767x^2 - 30.48635x + 890.02893$
Cubic: $y = -0.05697x^3 + 2.80674x^2 - 42.97396x + 900.96698$
The cubic model gives the best fit. In 2004, the estimated diving record is 698.72 points.

Review 227

1. $f(x) = x^3 - 7x^2 + 7x + 15$
2. $f(x) = x^3 - 3x^2 - 33x + 35$
3. $f(x) = x^3 + 6x^2 - x - 6$ **4.** $f(x) = x^3 + 3x^2 - 4x - 12$
5. $f(x) = x^3 - 6x^2 + 11x - 6$
6. $f(x) = x^4 - x^3 - 11x^2 + 9x + 18$
7. $f(x) = x^3 + 6x^2 - 16x$ **8.** $f(x) = x^3 + 8x^2 - 20x$
9. $f(x) = x^3 + 6x^2 - x - 6$
10. $f(x) = x^3 + 3x^2 - 4x - 12$
11. $f(x) = x^3 + \frac{3}{2}x^2 - 4x + 6$ **12.** $f(x) = x^2 + \frac{1}{3}x - \frac{2}{3}$
13. $f(x) = x^3 + \frac{10}{3}x^2 - \frac{1}{3}x - 4$
14. $f(x) = x^3 + 7x^2 + 16x + 12$
15. $f(x) = x^3 - 12x - 16$ **16.** $f(x) = x^3 - 3x - 2$
17. 0, −8, 2 **18.** 2, −2, 3, −3 **19.** 3, −3 **20.** $-\frac{2}{3}, 5$ **21.** 0, 8
22. −4, 4, −1, 1 **23.** 0, −2, 10 **24.** 2, −2, −3 **25.** $-\frac{1}{2}, 5, -3$
26. $0, -4, \frac{3}{2}$ **27.** $0, \sqrt{5}, -\sqrt{5}$ **28.** 0, 6, −6

Review 228

1. $3x - 5$, R 2 **2.** $x^2 - x + 3$, R −22 **3.** $x + 8$, R 32
4. $x + 3$, R 5 **5.** $x^2 - 4x - 1$ **6.** $2x^2 + x + 1$
7. $2x + 2$, R 13 **8.** $x^2 - 5x + 15$, R −101
9. $x - 4$, R −2 **10.** $2x^2 - 3x + 10$, R −24

Review 229

1. $2, -1 \pm i\sqrt{3}$ **2.** $-1, \frac{1 \pm i\sqrt{3}}{2}$ **3.** $-3, 3, -2i\sqrt{2}, 2i\sqrt{2}$

4. $-2i, 2i, -i\sqrt{5}, i\sqrt{5}$ **5.** $0, 3, \frac{-3 \pm 3i\sqrt{3}}{2}$

6. $-\frac{1}{2}, \frac{1 \pm i\sqrt{3}}{4}$ **7.** $-i, i, -i\sqrt{3}, i\sqrt{3}$ **8.** $4, -2 \pm 2i\sqrt{3}$

9. $-\frac{3}{2}, \frac{3 \pm 3i\sqrt{3}}{4}$ **10.** $-2, 2, -\sqrt{3}, \sqrt{3}$

11. $-\sqrt{2}, \sqrt{2}, -i\sqrt{10}, i\sqrt{10}$ **12.** $0, 2, -1 \pm i\sqrt{3}$

13. $-\frac{\sqrt{15}}{3}, \frac{\sqrt{15}}{3}, -i\frac{\sqrt{15}}{3}, i\frac{\sqrt{15}}{3}$ **14.** $-\frac{\sqrt{6}}{2}, \frac{\sqrt{6}}{2}, -i, i$

15. $-i, i, -2i, 2i$ **16.** $-2\sqrt{2}, 2\sqrt{2}, -i, i$ **17.** $-2, 1 \pm i\sqrt{3}$
18. $-2\sqrt{2}, 2\sqrt{2}, -i\sqrt{3}, i\sqrt{3}$

Review 230

1. $x^3 - 5x^2 + 9x - 5 = 0$ **2.** $x^3 - 8x^2 + 9x + 58 = 0$
3. $x^3 - 15x^2 + 73x - 111 = 0$ **4.** $x^3 + 4x^2 - 2x - 8 = 0$
5. $x^3 - 3x^2 - 3x + 1 = 0$ **6.** $x^3 - 6x^2 + 6x = 0$
7. $x^3 - 7x^2 + 9x - 63 = 0$ **8.** $x^3 - 7x^2 + 11x + 3 = 0$
9. $x^3 + 3x^2 + x + 3 = 0$ **10.** $x^3 - 10x^2 + 18x - 16 = 0$
11. $x^3 - x^2 + 25x - 25 = 0$
12. $x^3 - 10x^2 + 33x - 34 = 0$
13. $x^3 - 3x^2 + 16x - 48 = 0$ **14.** $x^3 - 4x^2 + 5x = 0$
15. $x^3 + 5x^2 - 15x - 7 = 0$
16. $x^3 + 4x^2 - 7x - 28 = 0$

Review 231

1. $1, \frac{1 \pm i\sqrt{11}}{2}$ **2.** $-5, 4 \pm 3i$ **3.** $\frac{2}{3}, -\sqrt{5}, \sqrt{5}$

4. $2, -2i, 2i$ **5.** $-1, 1, -\sqrt{2}, \sqrt{2}$ **6.** $-3, \frac{5 \pm \sqrt{33}}{2}$

Review 232

1. 60,480 **2.** 120 **3.** 66 **4.** 230,230 **5.** 720 **6.** 32,760 **7.** 120

Review 233

1. 4; 4; 2; 4; 3; y **2.** 3; 3; 3; 2; y **3.** 5; 5; 3; 10; 3; 5; z
4. $x^5 + 5x^4y + 10x^3y^2 + 10x^2y^3 + 5xy^4 + y^5$
5. $x^5 - 5x^4y + 10x^3y^2 - 10x^2y^3 + 5xy^4 - y^5$
6. $8x^3 + 12x^2y + 6xy^2 + y^3$ **7.** $x^4 + 12x^3y + 54x^2y^2 + 108xy^3 + 81y^4$ **8.** $x^5 - 10x^4y + 40x^3y^2 - 80x^2y^3 + 80xy^4 - 32y^5$ **9.** $32x^5 - 80x^4y + 80x^3y^2 - 40x^2y^3 + 10xy^4 - y^5$ **10.** $x^4 - 12x^3y + 54x^2y^2 - 108xy^3 + 81y^4$ **11.** $64x^3 - 48x^2y + 12xy^2 - y^3$ **12.** $x^5 - 5x^4 + 10x^3 - 10x^2 + 5x - 1$ **13.** $1 - 3x + 3x^2 - x^3$
14. $x^6 + 3x^4 + 3x^2 + 1$ **15.** $y^8 + 4y^6a + 6y^4a^2 + 4y^2a^3 + a^4$

Review 234

1. $6|x|$ **2.** $6y$ **3.** $\frac{1}{10|x|}$ **4.** $\frac{x^{10}}{y^4}$ **5.** $\frac{x+3}{(x-4)^2}$ **6.** x^2y^3z

7. $\frac{3z}{(z+12)^2}$ **8.** $7|x^3|$ **9.** $\frac{11}{x}$ **10.** $\frac{(y-4)^2}{|z+9|}$ **11.** $\frac{a^2b^2}{c}$

12. $-xy^2$

Review 235

1. $\frac{\sqrt{5x}}{x}$ **2.** $\frac{\sqrt[3]{3b}}{a}$ **3.** $\frac{\sqrt[4]{9x^3y}}{x}$ **4.** $\frac{\sqrt{30xy}}{6}$ **5.** $\frac{k\sqrt[3]{k}}{4}$

6. $\frac{x^2\sqrt{15xy}}{5y}$ **7.** $\frac{\sqrt[4]{10z^2}}{z}$ **8.** $\frac{\sqrt[3]{19ac^2}}{c^2}$

Review 236

1. 3 **2.** $\frac{\sqrt{3}+1}{2}$ **3.** $20 + 15\sqrt{6}$ **4.** $\frac{-11+4\sqrt{7}}{3}$

5. $40 - 28\sqrt{2}$ **6.** $2\sqrt{5} - \sqrt{15}$

Review 237

1. $y^{\frac{19}{15}}$ **2.** $\frac{1}{4xy^4}$ **3.** $\frac{1}{z^{\frac{1}{3}}}$ **4.** $16x$ **5.** $\frac{7}{3x^4}$ **6.** $\frac{5y}{x^3}$ **7.** $\frac{1}{x}$

8. $\frac{4b^6}{a^2}$ **9.** $\frac{5x^4}{4z^2}$ **10.** $a^{\frac{3}{2}}$ **11.** $x^{\frac{2}{5}}y^{\frac{1}{5}}$ **12.** $\frac{n^2}{9m^6}$ **13.** $6x^{\frac{1}{2}}$

14. $\frac{2r^{\frac{1}{2}}}{s}$ **15.** $27z^{15}$

Review 238

1. 169 **2.** 8 **3.** 2 **4.** no solution **5.** 3 **6.** 9 **7.** 16 **8.** 7 **9.** 5

Review 239

1. 5 **2.** 15 **3.** 10 **4.** 10 **5.** 10 **6.** 100 **7.** 102 **8.** 102
The first input should be one color. Answers 3 and 4 should be a second color. Answers 7 and 8 should be a third color.
9. 77 **10.** 35.5 **11.** 13 **12.** 21

Review 240

1. $y = \frac{x+5}{4}$ **2.** $y = \sqrt[3]{\frac{x-2}{3}}$ **3.** $y = \sqrt[3]{x} - 1$

4. $y = 2x - 4$ **5.** $f^{-1}(x) = x - 3$ **6.** $f^{-1}(x) = \frac{x+4}{2}$

7. $f^{-1}(x) = 5x$ **8.** $f^{-1}(x) = \frac{x-2}{4}$ **9.** $y = x$

10. $y = x + 3$ **11.** $y = 2x + 1$ **12.** $y = \sqrt[3]{x+8}$

13. $f^{-1}(x) = x^2 - 2$ **14.** $f^{-1}(x) = \frac{3}{2}(x+1)$

15. $f^{-1}(x) = 5x - 3$ **16.** $f^{-1}(x) = 5 \pm \sqrt{\frac{x}{2}}$

17. $y = (x-4)^2$ **18.** $y = \frac{x-1}{8}$

Review 241

1.

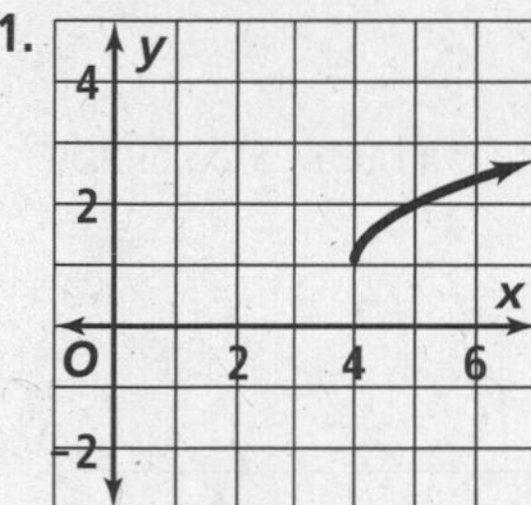

2.

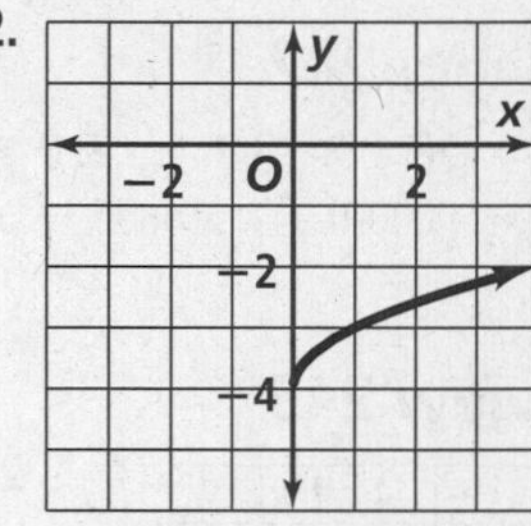

3.

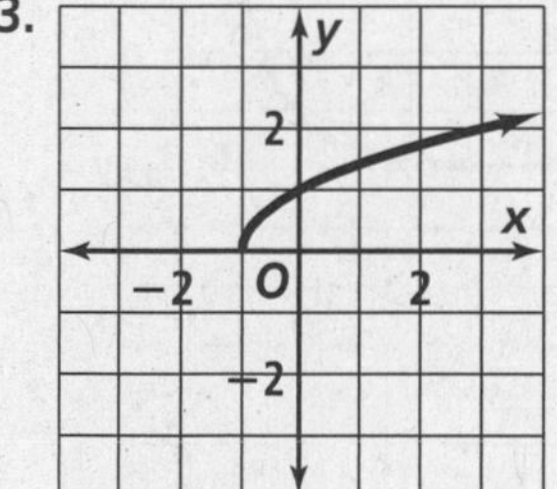

4.

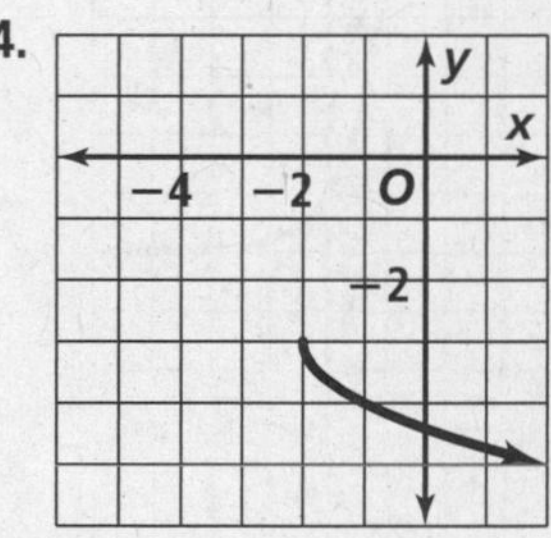

5.

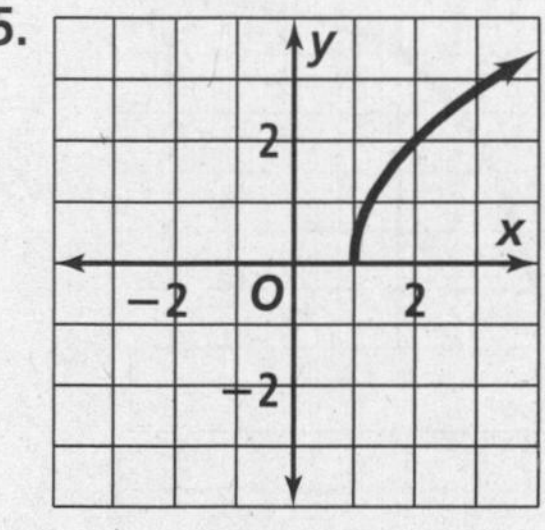

6.

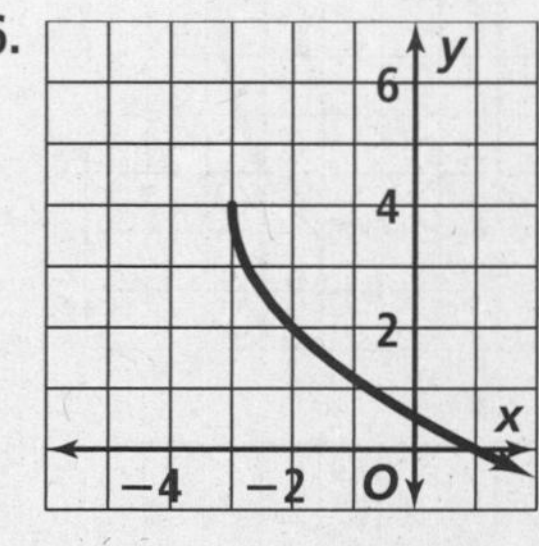

7.

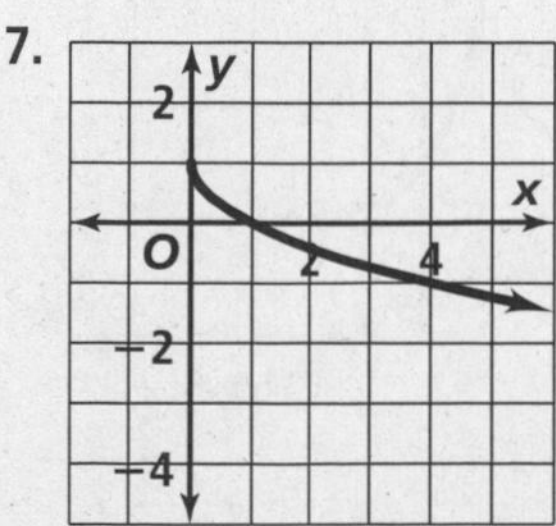

8.

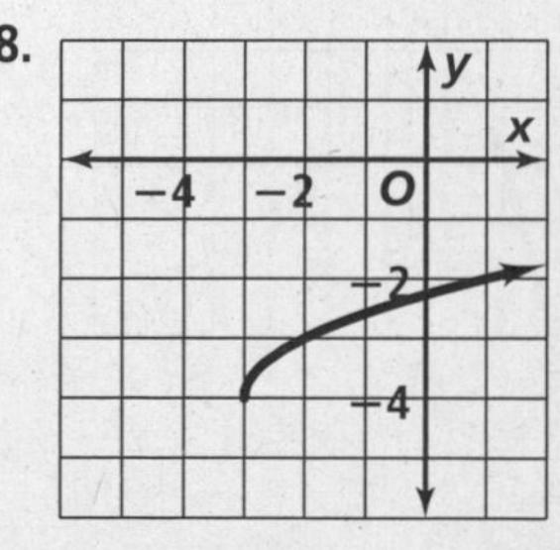

ANSWERS

Review 241 *(continued)*

9.

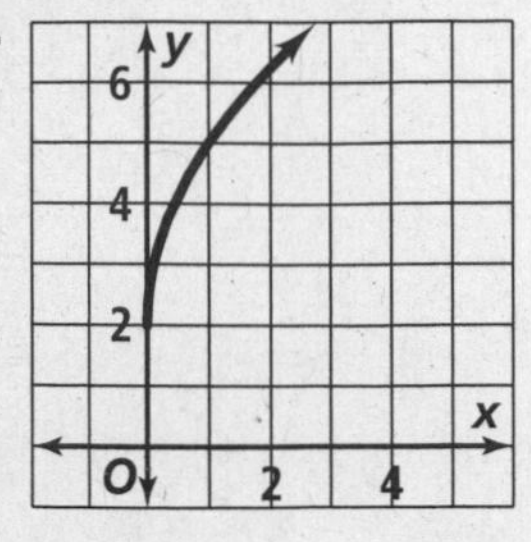

10.

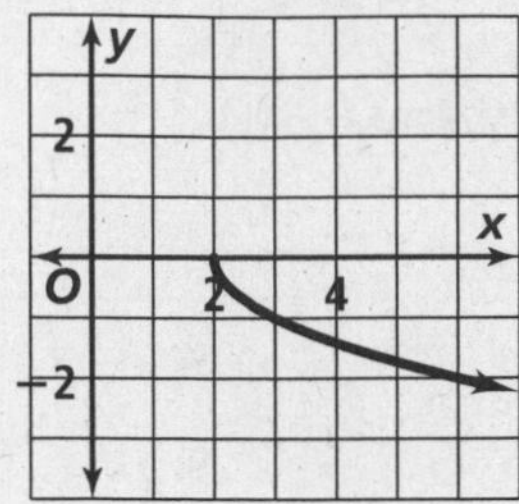

11.

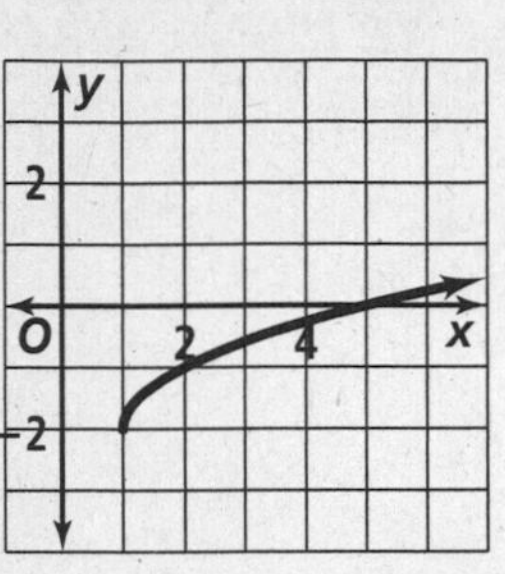

12.

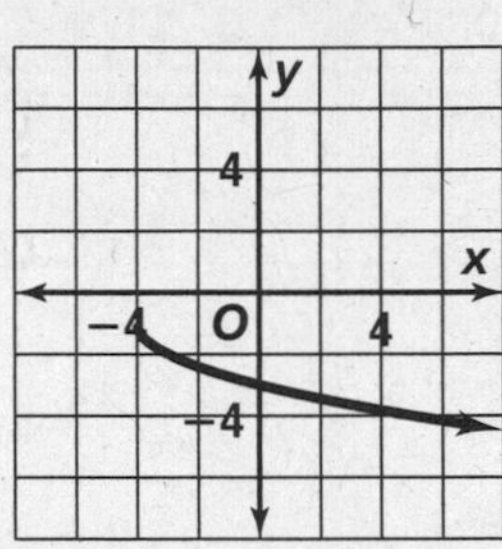

Review 242

1. $y = 3(1.08)^x$; 8.81 ft **2.** $y = 126{,}000(1.02)^x$; \$153,593.30
3. $y = 9000(0.94)^x$; \$6605.14

Review 243

1.

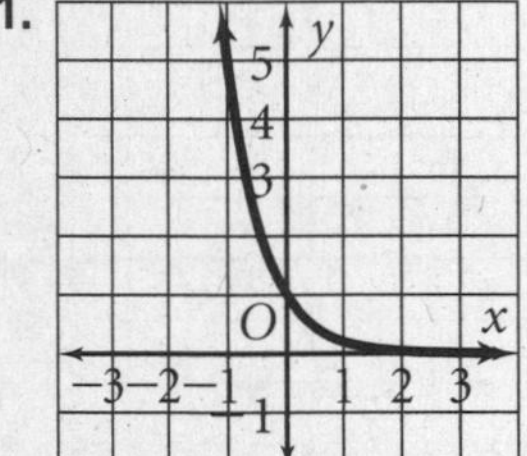

2.

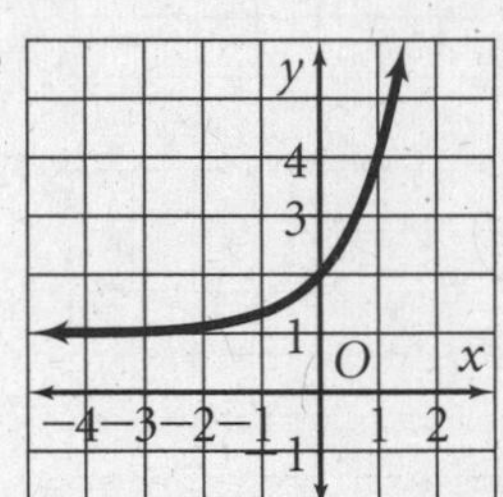

3.

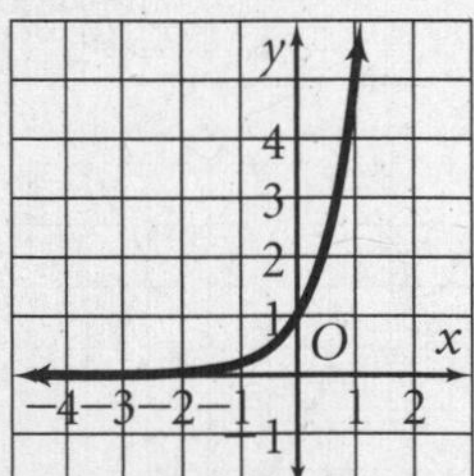

4.

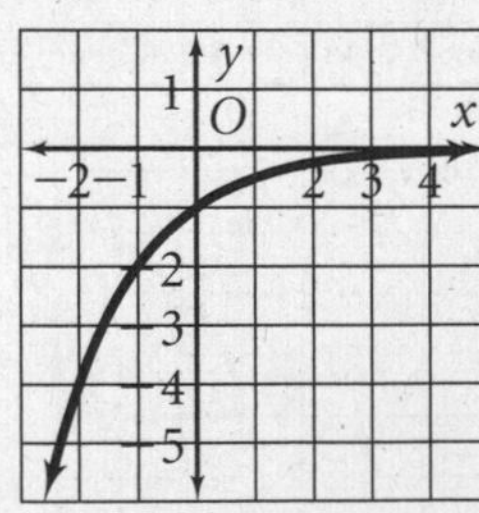

5.

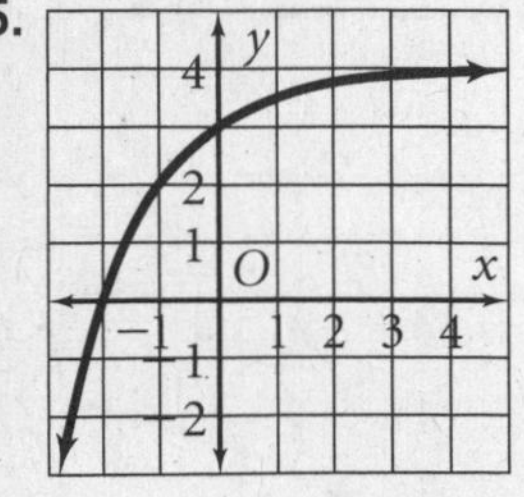

6.

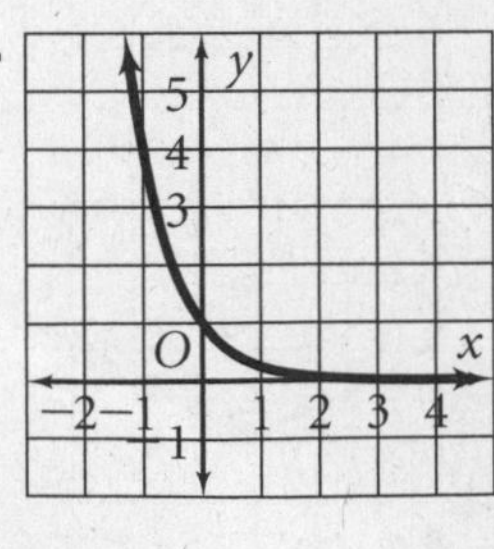

7.

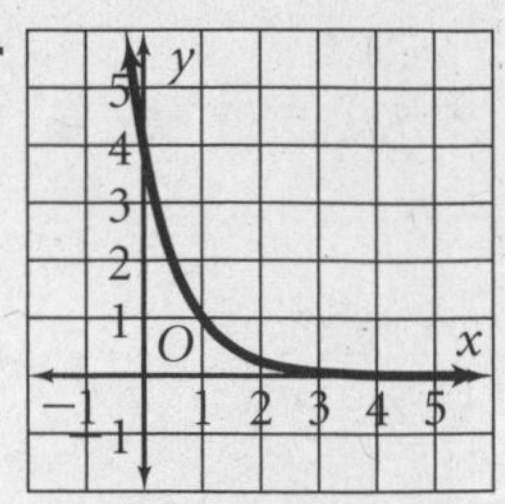

8.

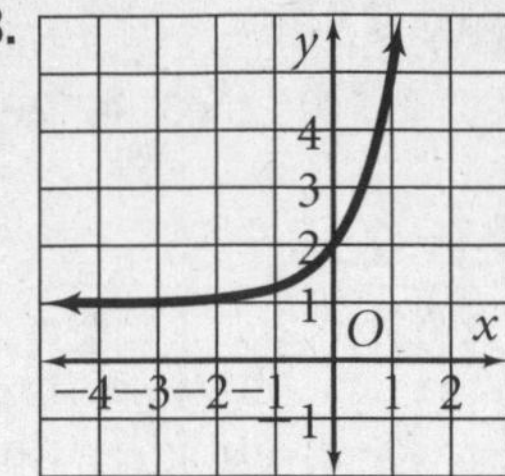

9.

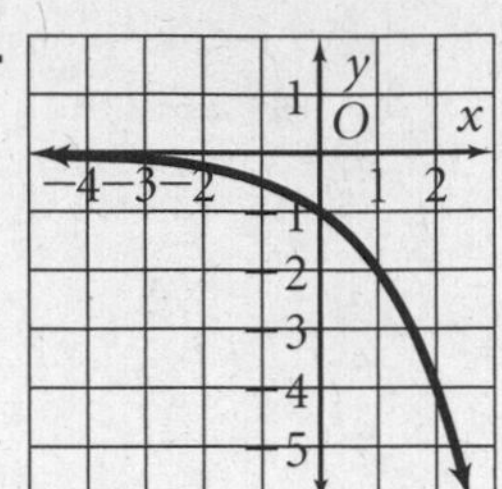

Review 244

1. 6 **2.** 3 **3.** 4 **4.** 1 **5.** −1 **6.** 0 **7.** $\frac{1}{3}$ **8.** $\frac{1}{5}$ **9.** $\frac{1}{2}$
10. $3^x = 8$ **11.** $5^2 = 25$ **12.** $10^{-1} = 0.1$
13. $10^{0.845} = 7$ **14.** $10^3 = 1000$ **15.** $10^{-2} = 0.01$
16. $3^4 = 81$ **17.** $49^{\frac{1}{2}} = 7$ **18.** $8^{-\frac{2}{3}} = \frac{1}{4}$ **19.** $2^7 = 128$
20. $5^{-4} = \frac{1}{625}$ **21.** $6^2 = 36$

Review 245

1. $\log 2 - \log 3$ **2.** $\log 6 + \log y$
3. $\log 1 - \log 5$, or $-\log 5$ **4.** $3 \log_3 x$
5. $\log_3 6 + \log_3 x + \log_3 y$
6. $\log_6 36 + 2 \log_6 x$, or $2 + 2\log_6 x$ **7.** $\log_5 x + \log_5 y$
8. $\log_3 x - \log_3 4$ **9.** $4 \log_7 x$ **10.** $2 \log_3 x + \log_3 y$
11. $7 \log_8 y$ **12.** $4 \log_5 x + 3 \log_5 y$ **13.** $\log_3 39$ **14.** $\log 5x^2$
15. $\log_4 \frac{1}{3}$ **16.** $\log_3 9$, or 2 **17.** $\log_5 8x$ **18.** $\log \frac{2}{x^2}$
19. $\log_2 xy$ **20.** $\log_7 \frac{x^3}{y^5}$ **21.** $\log x^7$ **22.** $\log_5 xy^3$
23. $\log_2 \frac{x^3}{y}$ **24.** $\log_2 2$, or 1

Review 246

1. 2.32 **2.** 0.45 **3.** 1 **4.** 0.17 **5.** 2.39 **6.** 1.50 **7.** −4 **8.** 0
9. 0.82 **10.** 1.30 **11.** −2.82 **12.** −6

Review 247

1. 0.693 **2.** 0.805 **3.** 4.277 **4.** 1.607 **5.** 0.532 **6.** 10.389
7. 27.299 **8.** ±1.649 **9.** 12.543 **10.** \$12,825.53 **11.** 37.2 yr

Review 248

1. 3.5 h **2.** 5 h **3.** about 28 items **4.** 6.75 cm

Review 249

1. 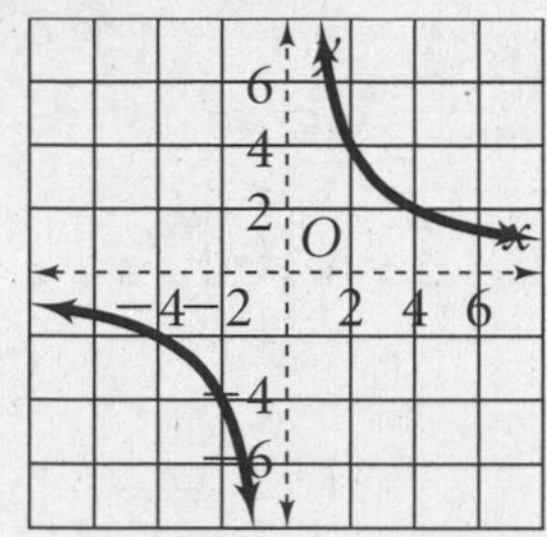
; $x = 0, y = 0$

2. 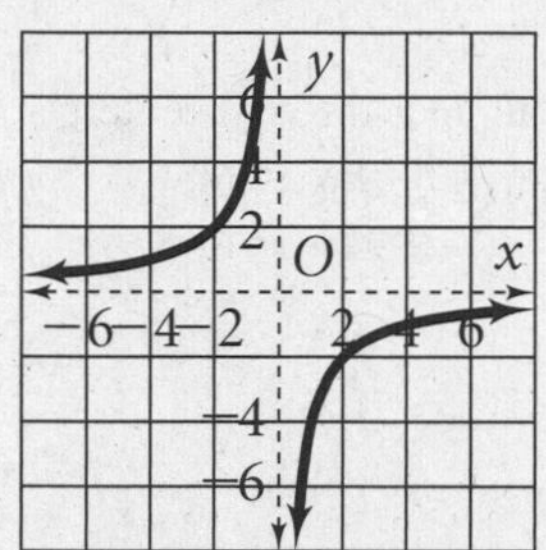
; $x = 0, y = 0$

3. 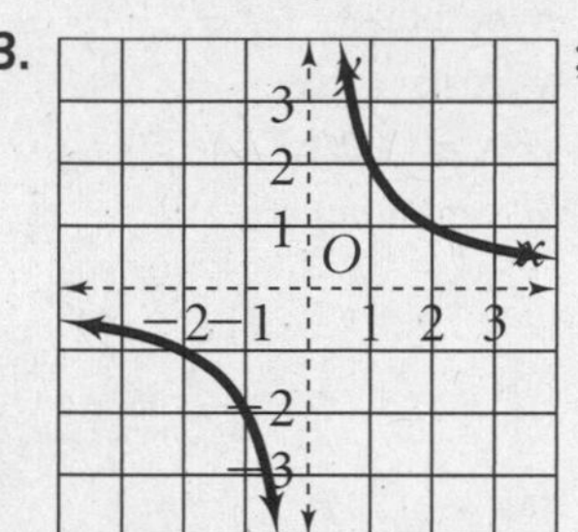
; $x = 0, y = 0$

4. 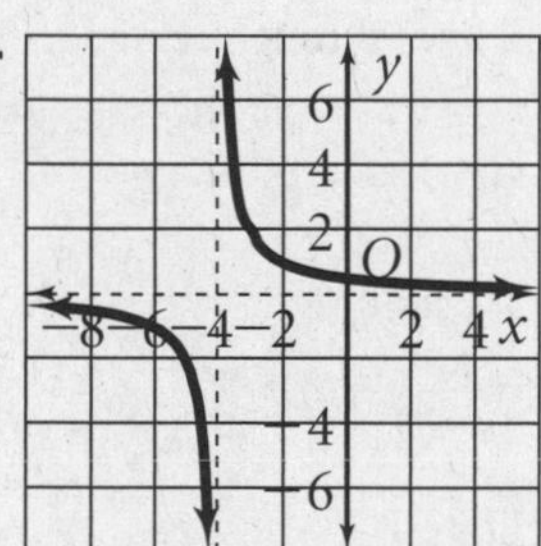
; $x = -4, y = 0$

5. 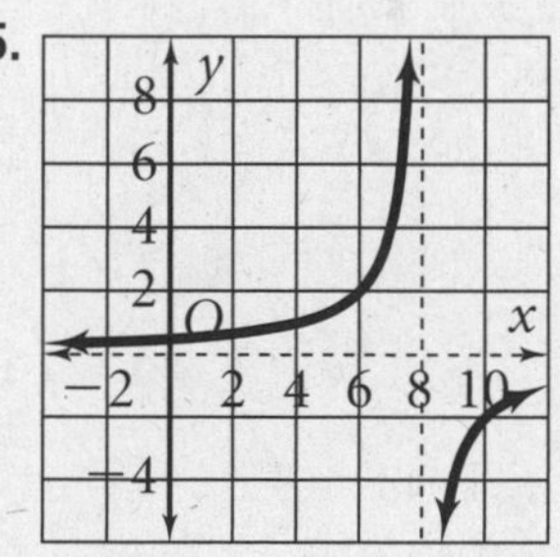
; $x = 8, y = 0$

6. 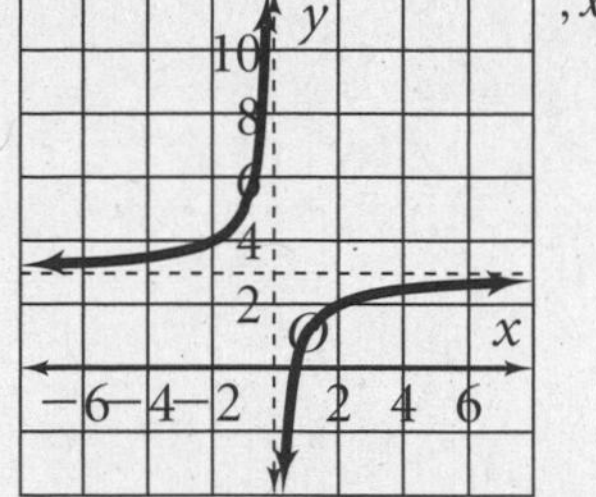
; $x = 0, y = 3$

7. 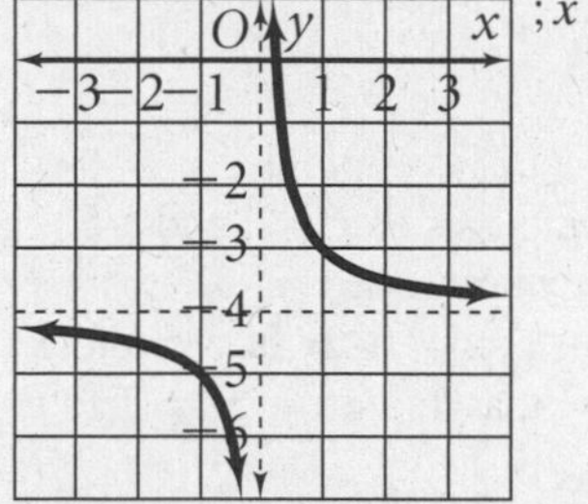
; $x = 0, y = -4$

8. 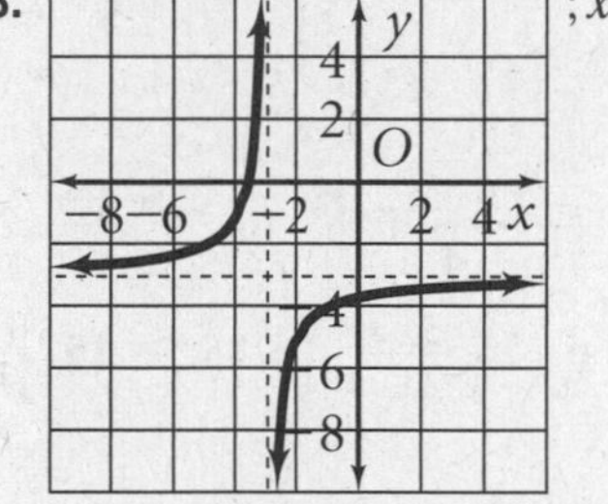
; $x = -3, y = -3$

9. 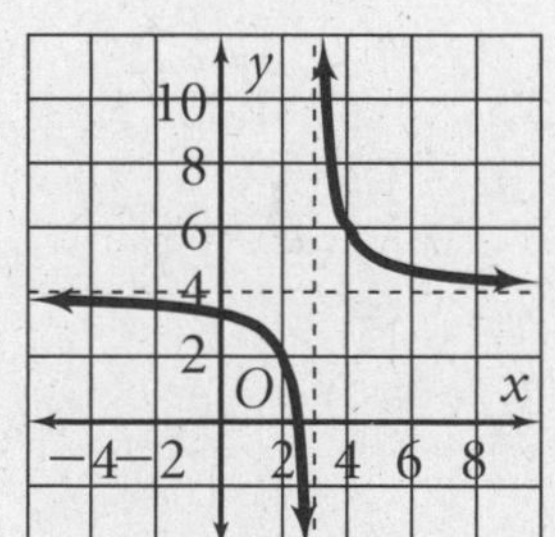
; $x = 3, y = 4$

10. 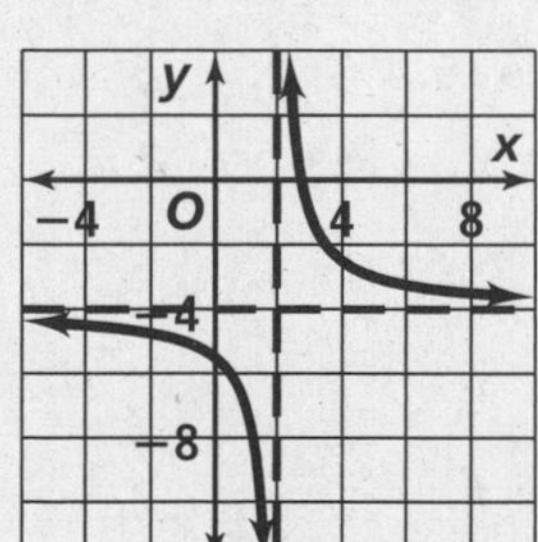
; $x = 2, y = -4$

11. 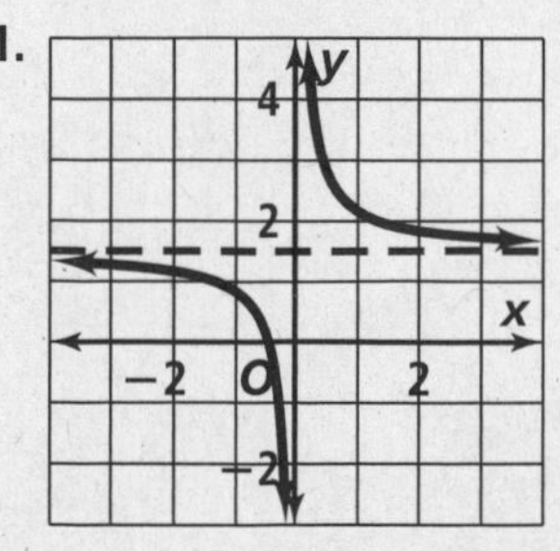
; $x = 0, y = \frac{3}{2}$

ANSWERS

Review 249 *(continued)*

12. 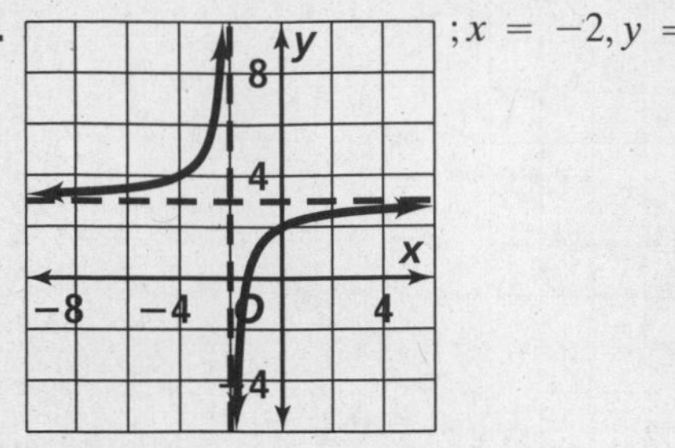

$; x = -2, y = 3$

Review 250

1. asymptotes at $x = 3$ and -3 **2.** asymptote at $x = 0$ **3.** asymptote at $x = 1$ **4.** asymptotes at $x = 1$ and -5 **5.** asymptote at $x = -1$ **6.** asymptote at $x = 0$ **7.** asymptote at $x = 0$ and hole at $x = -2$ **8.** asymptote at $x = -2$ and hole at $x = -1$ **9.** asymptote at $x = 3$ and hole at $x = -1$

Review 251

1. $\frac{1}{x - y}$ **2.** $\frac{a + 2}{a - 5}$ **3.** $\frac{3x - 12}{2x + 8}$ **4.** $\frac{2}{3}$ **5.** $x - 2$ **6.** $\frac{1 - x}{4x^2 + 16x}$ **7.** 5 **8.** $\frac{1}{x^2 + 4x + 4}$ **9.** $\frac{8}{3}$ **10.** $\frac{x - 7}{x^2}$ **11.** $\frac{x - 2}{x}$ **12.** $\frac{x + 2}{3x - 6}$ **13.** $\frac{3}{x}$ **14.** $\frac{3x + 6}{2x + 6}$ **15.** 3 **16.** $\frac{1}{x^4}$

Review 252

1. 1 **2.** $\frac{y - 2}{y - 1}$ **3.** $\frac{3x - 4}{(x + 2)(x - 2)}$ **4.** $\frac{3y - 10}{(y - 5)(y + 4)}$ **5.** $\frac{x - 3}{(x + 1)(x + 3)}$ **6.** $\frac{x - 5}{(x + 2)(x - 2)}$ **7.** $-\frac{43}{28x}$ **8.** $\frac{12x^2 - x - 39}{3(x + 11)}$ **9.** $\frac{4x^2 - 3x + 15}{x^2(x + 3)(x - 2)}$

Review 253

1. $\frac{3}{4}$ **2.** $5, -\frac{3}{2}$ **3.** $\frac{8}{5}$ **4.** 6 **5.** −5 **6.** 4 **7.** $\frac{3}{2}, \frac{8}{3}$ **8.** no solution **9.** 1 **10.** 0.5 **11.** −0.5 **12.** 25 **13.** Quinn: 3.75 h, Jack: 15 h

Review 254

1. $\frac{7}{10}$ **2.** $\frac{7}{15}$ **3.** $\frac{37}{45}$

Review 255

1. 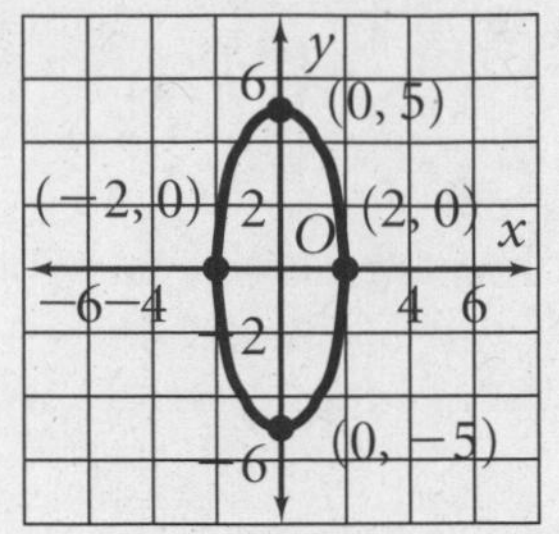

; ellipse; x-axis, y-axis; $\{x \mid -2 \le x \le 2\}$, $\{y \mid -5 \le y \le 5\}$

2. 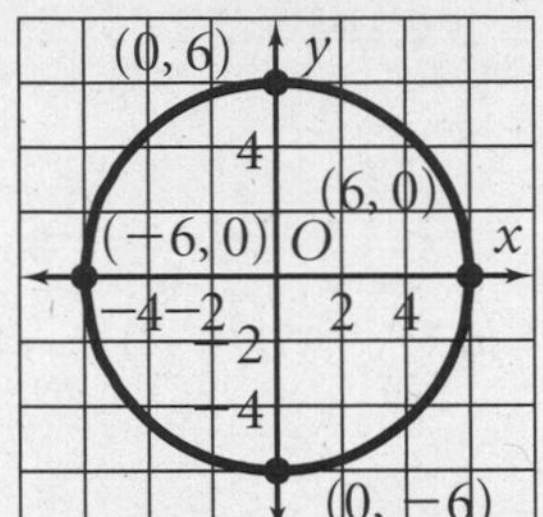

; circle; all lines through center; $\{x \mid -6 \le x \le 6\}$, $\{y \mid -6 \le y \le 6\}$

3. 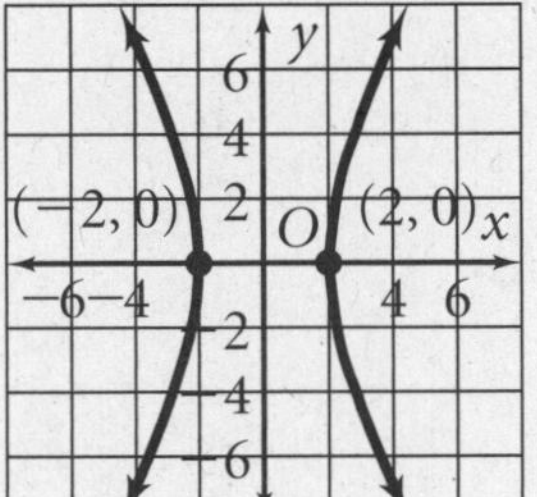

; hyperbola; x-axis, y-axis; $\{x \mid x \le -2$ or $x \ge 2\}$, all real numbers

4. 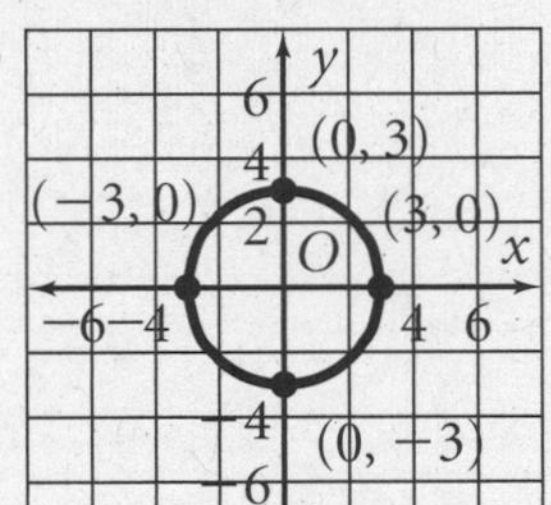

; circle; all lines through center, $\{x \mid -3 \le x \le 3\}$; $\{y \mid -3 \le y \le 3\}$

5. 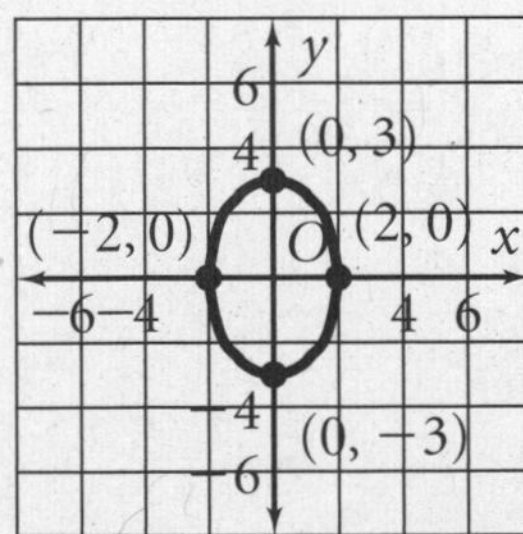

; ellipse; x-axis, y-axis; $\{x \mid -2 \le x \le 2\}$, $\{y \mid -3 \le y \le 3\}$

6. 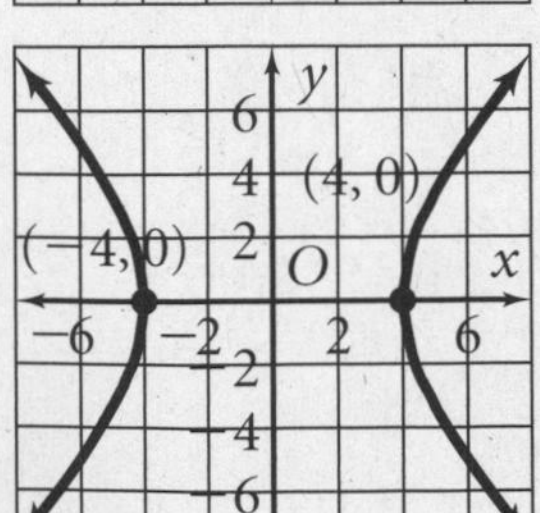

; hyperbola; x-axis, y-axis; $\{x \mid x \le -4$ or $x \ge 4\}$, all real numbers

Review 256

1.
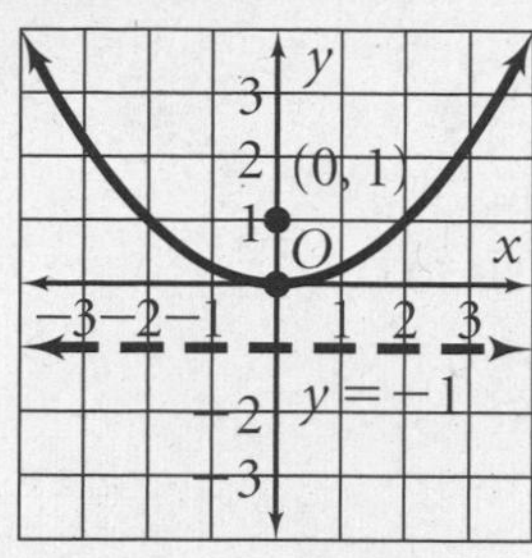

2.
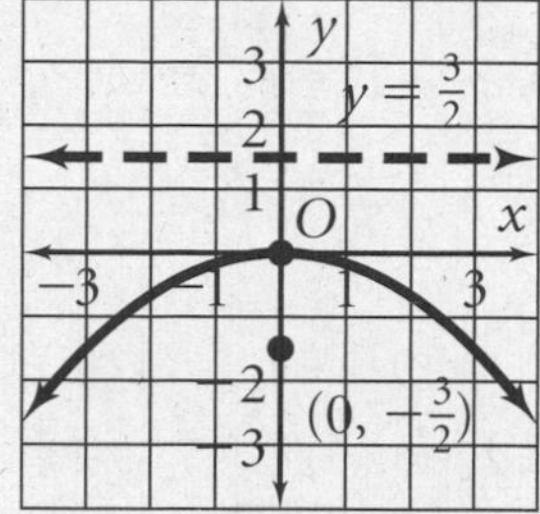

3.
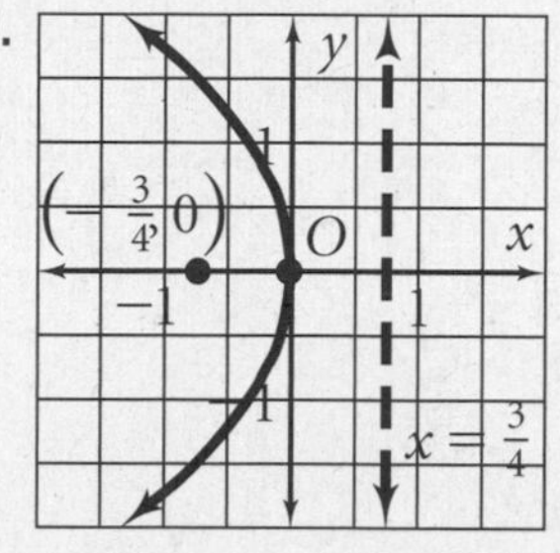

4.
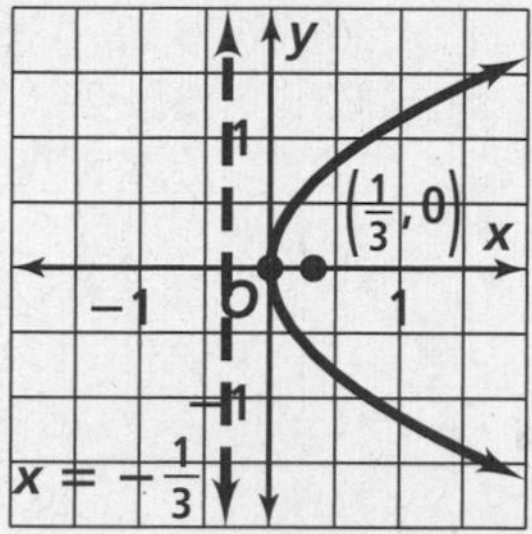

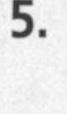

5.
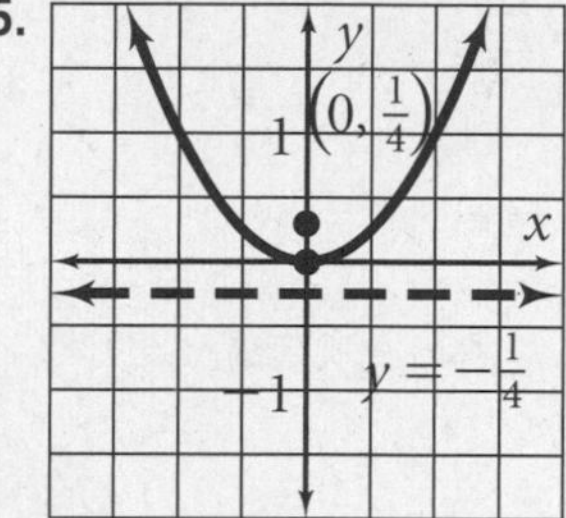

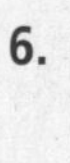

6.
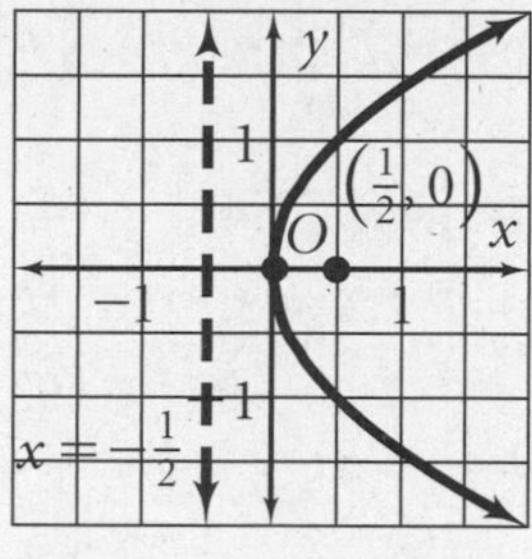

Review 257

1. 3; (5, 2) **2.** $2\sqrt{2}$; (−8, 4) **3.** $2\sqrt{5}$; (4, −3) **4.** $\sqrt{6}$; (3, 0) **5.** 5; (0, 5) **6.** 1; (−6, −7) **7.** 6; (−1, −2) **8.** 2; (2, 5) **9.** 2; (0, 0) **10.** 3; (1, −3) **11.** $2\sqrt{3}$; (2, 3) **12.** 5; (−1, 3) **13.** $3\sqrt{5}$; (0, −3) **14.** $3\sqrt{7}$; (−4, 0) **15.** $5\sqrt{3}$; (−2, 6) **16.** $3\sqrt{2}$; (7, −3) **17.** $2\sqrt{6}$; (4, −1) **18.** 9; (−9, 9)

Review 258

1. $\frac{x^2}{144} + \frac{y^2}{169} = 1$ **2.** $\frac{x^2}{4} + \frac{y^2}{36} = 1$ **3.** $\frac{x^2}{9} + \frac{y^2}{25} = 1$

4. $\frac{x^2}{81} + \frac{y^2}{9} = 1$ **5.** $\frac{x^2}{625} + \frac{y^2}{100} = 1$ **6.** $\frac{x^2}{121} + \frac{y^2}{25} = 1$

7. $\frac{x^2}{81} + \frac{y^2}{64} = 1$ **8.** $\frac{x^2}{2.25} + \frac{y^2}{100} = 1$ **9.** $\frac{x^2}{9} + \frac{y^2}{2.25} = 1$

10. $\frac{x^2}{225} + \frac{y^2}{49} = 1$ **11.** $\frac{x^2}{20.25} + \frac{y^2}{36} = 1$

12. $\frac{x^2}{4} + \frac{y^2}{36} = 1$ **13.** $\frac{x^2}{16} + \frac{y^2}{12.25} = 1$

14. $\frac{x^2}{25} + y^2 = 1$ **15.** $\frac{x^2}{20.25} + \frac{y^2}{64} = 1$

16. $\frac{x^2}{7569} + \frac{y^2}{5476} = 1$

Review 259

1. $(\pm\sqrt{10}, 0)$;

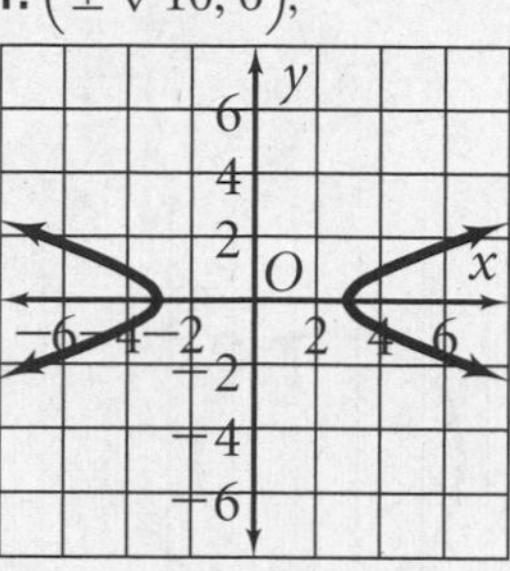

2. $(0, \pm 2\sqrt{5})$;

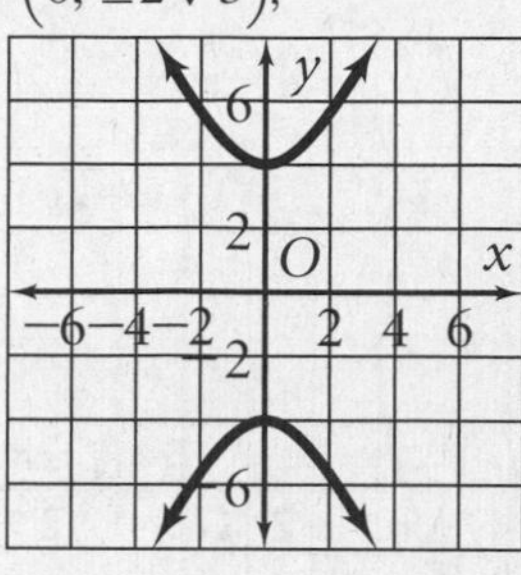

3. $(\pm\sqrt{5}, 0)$;

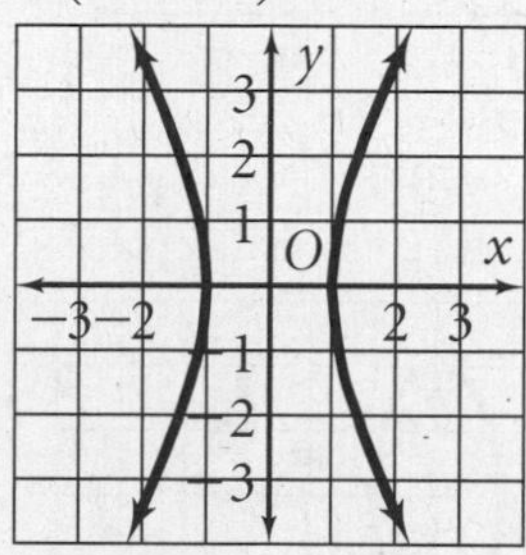

4. $(0, \pm\sqrt{5})$;

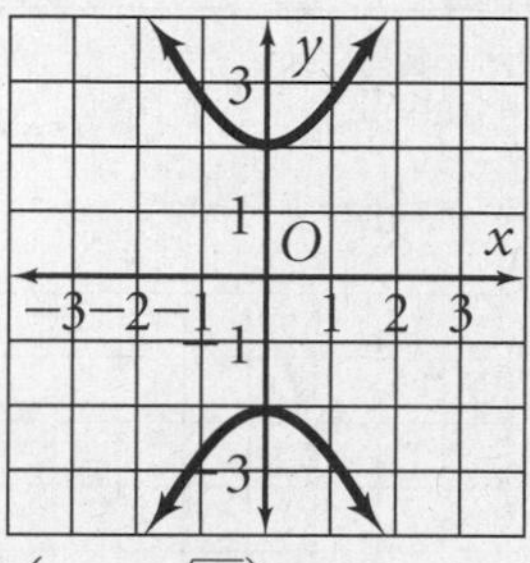

5. $(\pm\sqrt{6}, 0)$;

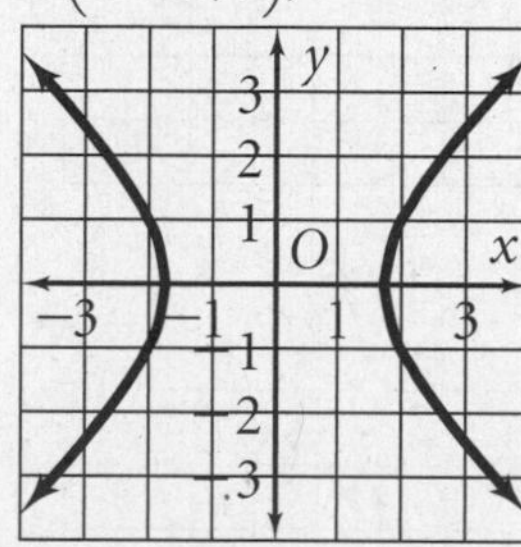

6. $(0, \pm\sqrt{34})$;

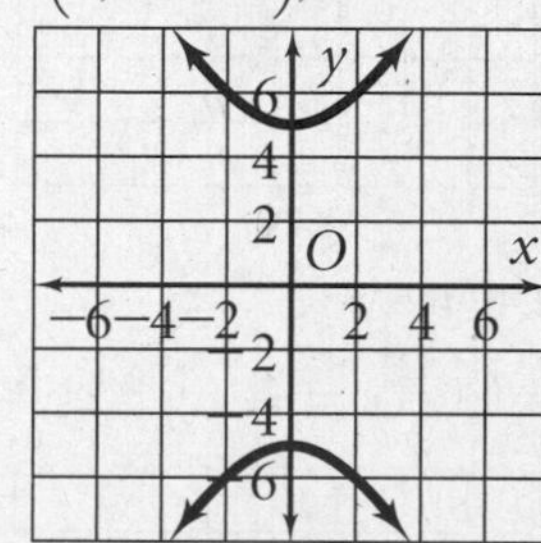

Review 260

1. parabola;

$y = -\frac{1}{4}(x - 1)^2 + 1$

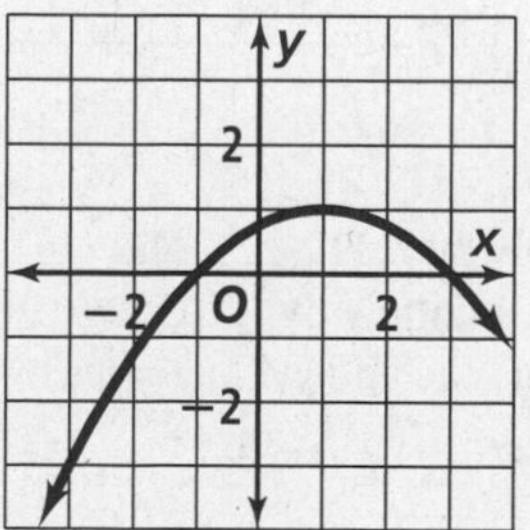

2. ellipse;

$\frac{(x + 3)^2}{4} + \frac{(y - 1)^2}{1} = 1$

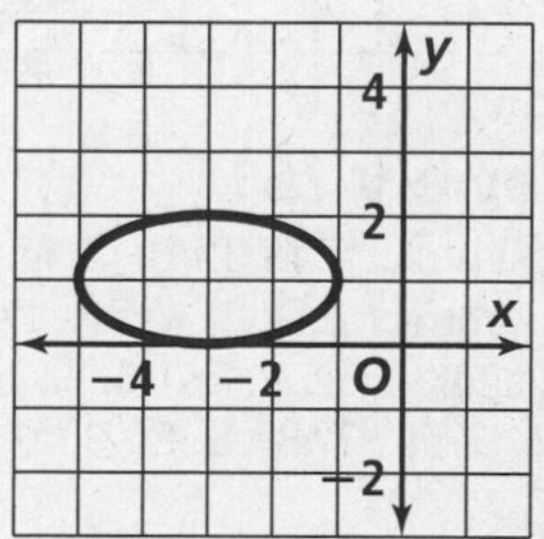

ANSWERS

Review 260 *(continued)*

3. hyperbola; $\frac{(x+1)^2}{4} - \frac{(y-2)^2}{9} = 1$

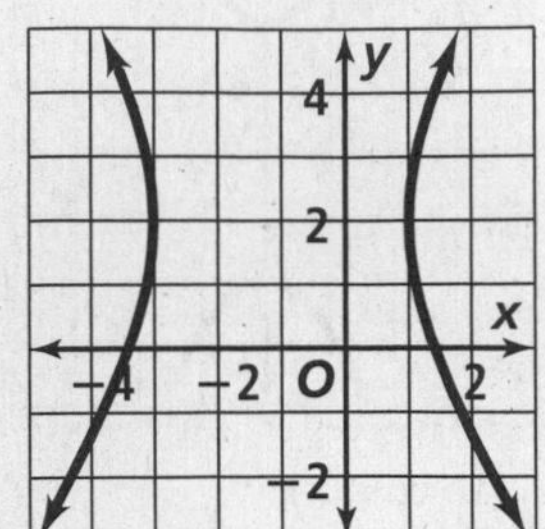

4. circle; $(x+5)^2 + (y-3)^2 = 16$

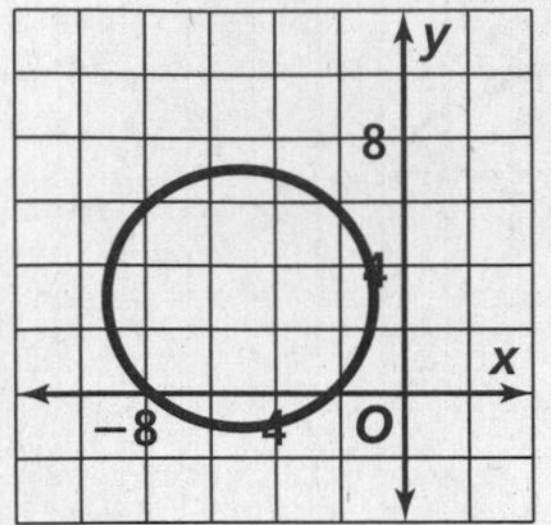

5. parabola; $x = \frac{1}{8}(y-3)^2$

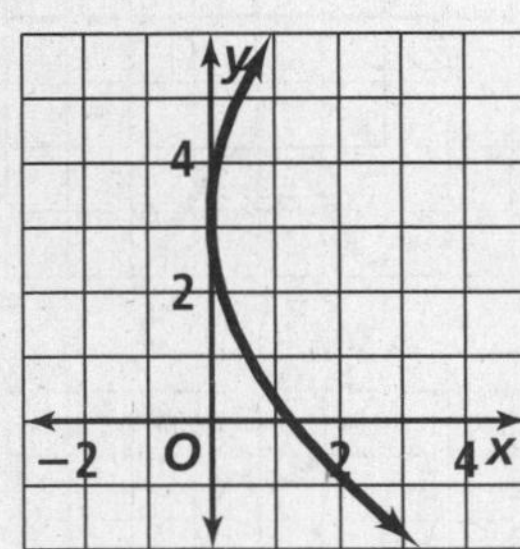

6. ellipse; $\frac{(x+8)^2}{1} + \frac{(y-6)^2}{4} = 1$

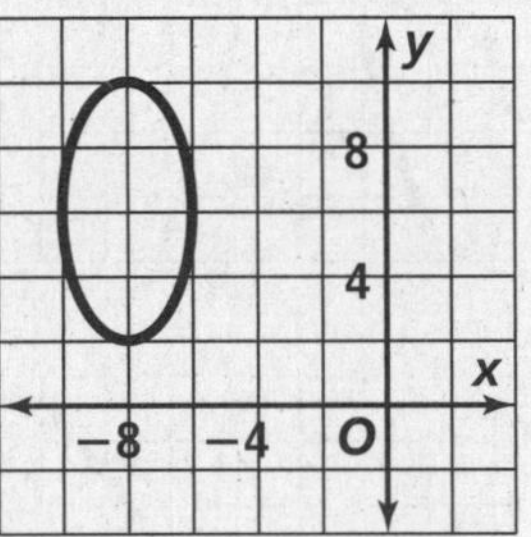

7. parabola; $x = \frac{1}{4}(y-2)^2 + 3$

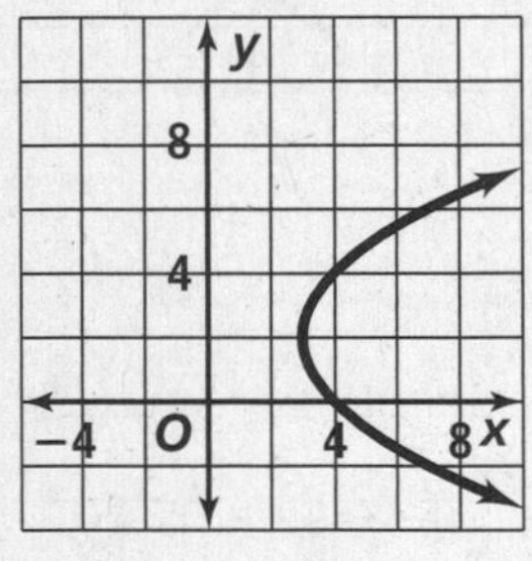

8. hyperbola; $\frac{(x-1)^2}{4} - \frac{(y+1)^2}{1} = 1$

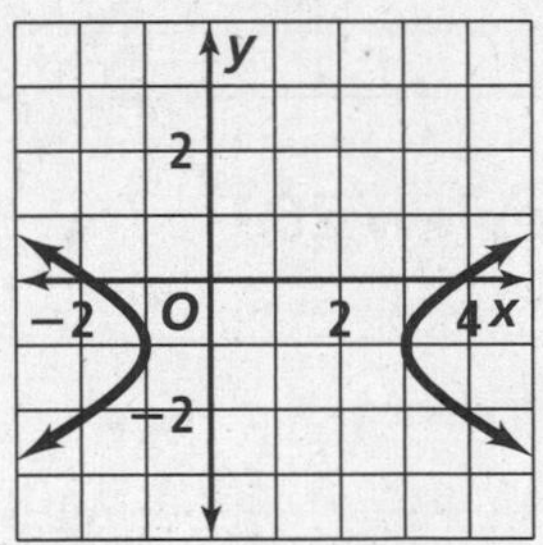

Review 261

1. subtract 5; 18, 13, 8 **2.** multiply by 2; 112, 224, 448 **3.** subtract 2; −13, −15, −17 **4.** multiply by 3; 162, 486, 1458 **5.** add 0.5; 6.5, 7, 7.5 **6.** each time the addend increases by 2; 37, 47, 59 **7.** B **8.** E **9.** A **10.** F **11.** C **12.** D

Review 262

1. −28 **2.** 0.0129 **3.** −92 **4.** 12.2 **5.** 18.8 **6.** 118 **7.** \$110 **8.** \$143 **9.** 31 rows

Review 263

1. $\frac{1}{128}$ **2.** $\frac{10,935}{128}$ **3.** $-\frac{2}{59,049}$ **4.** $\frac{64}{729}$ **5.** 25,600 **6.** 512

7. $a_n = 1\left(\frac{1}{2}\right)^{n-1}$; $1, \frac{1}{2}, \frac{1}{4}, \frac{1}{8}, \frac{1}{16}$

8. $a_n = 2(3)^{n-1}$; 2, 6, 18, 54, 162

9. $a_n = 12(3)^{n-1}$; 12, 36, 108, 324, 972

10. $a_n = 1\left(\frac{1}{4}\right)^{n-1}$; $1, \frac{1}{4}, \frac{1}{16}, \frac{1}{64}, \frac{1}{256}$

11. $a_n = 5\left(\frac{1}{10}\right)^{n-1}$; $5, \frac{1}{2}, \frac{1}{20}, \frac{1}{200}, \frac{1}{2000}$

12. $a_n = 1\left(\frac{1}{3}\right)^{n-1}$; $1, \frac{1}{3}, \frac{1}{9}, \frac{1}{27}, \frac{1}{81}$

13. $a_n = 5(2)^{n-1}$; 5, 10, 20, 40, 80

14. $a_n = 1(3)^{n-1}$; 1, 3, 9, 27, 81

15. $a_n = 3(6)^{n-1}$; 3, 18, 108, 648, 3888

16. $a_n = 3(3)^{n-1}$; 3, 9, 27, 81, 243

17. $a_n = 2(2)^{n-1}$; 2, 4, 8, 16, 32

18. $a_n = 2\left(\frac{1}{2}\right)^{n-1}$; $2, 1, \frac{1}{2}, \frac{1}{4}, \frac{1}{8}$

19. $a_n = 1\left(\frac{1}{5}\right)^{n-1}$; $1, \frac{1}{5}, \frac{1}{25}, \frac{1}{125}, \frac{1}{625}$

20. $a_n = 3(4)^{n-1}$; 3, 12, 48, 192, 768

21. $a_n = 5\left(\frac{1}{4}\right)^{n-1}$; $5, \frac{5}{4}, \frac{5}{16}, \frac{5}{64}, \frac{5}{256}$

Review 264

1. −6 **2.** $\frac{25}{36}$ **3.** 93 **4.** 22 **5.** −56 **6.** 120 **7.** 108 **8.** −35 **9.** 74 **10.** $a_n = 87 + 2n$; 5985 seats

Review 265

1. 4095 **2.** $\frac{341}{32}$ **3.** $-\frac{635}{32}$ **4.** $\frac{3415}{512}$ **5.** 20 **6.** $-\frac{11}{13}$ **7.** 2 **8.** $\frac{5}{14}$ **9.** $-\frac{1}{9}$ **10.** 100 **11.** 18 **12.** $\frac{1}{6}$ **13.** $\frac{5}{6}$

Review 266

Answers are in units^2.

1. 3.5 **2.** 4.25 **3.** 9 **4.** 1.5 **5.** 3.75 **6.** 8.25

Review 267

1.

Amount of Rain	No. of years
Less than 1 in.	3
Exactly 1 in.	1
More than 1 in.	9
Total	13

; $\frac{3}{13}$

2.

Status	No. of Professors
Beginning	3
Tenured	5
Nontenured	7
Total	15

; $\frac{1}{3}$

ANSWERS

Review 268

1. $\frac{7}{18}$ **2.** $\frac{11}{18}$ **3.** $\frac{5}{9}$ **4.** $\frac{4}{9}$ **5.** $\frac{2}{9}$ **6.** $\frac{5}{18}$ **7.** $\frac{2}{5}$ **8.** $\frac{5}{8}$ **9.** $\frac{5}{11}$

Review 269

1. about 883.8; 888; 888 **2.** about 0.9; 0.8; 0.5
3. about 2116.9; 2068; no mode **4.** about 266.8; 289; no mode
5. 27; 26.5; 26 **6.** 15; 14; 21 **7.** 3.4; 3.3; 4.7 **8.** 6375; 6374; 6371
9. 546; 502; no mode **10.** 84; 84; 81

Review 270

1. about 0.86 **2.** about 0.18 **3.** about 3.93 **4.** about 2.42
5. \$72.98 **6.** \$11.78 **7.** 2 **8.** 3 **9.** 253 mi; 69.5 mi **10.** 5; 8

Review 271

1. ±2.8%; 69.2% to 74.8% **2.** ±4.2%; 81.8% to 90.2%
3. ±5.6%; 6.4% to 17.6% **4.** ±2.6%; 51.4% to 56.6%
5. ±1.9%; 76.1% to 79.9%

Review 272

1. 7.6% **2.** 0.1% **3.** 2.1% **4.** 1.0% **5.** about 73.5%
6. about 23.2% **7.** about 8.2%

Review 273

1.

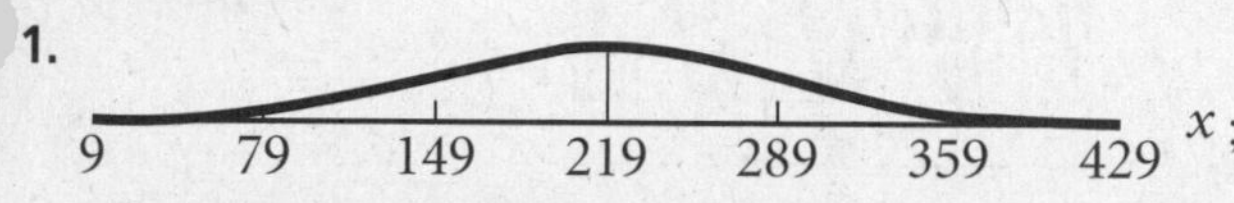

About 25 light bulbs will not last 79 h.

2.

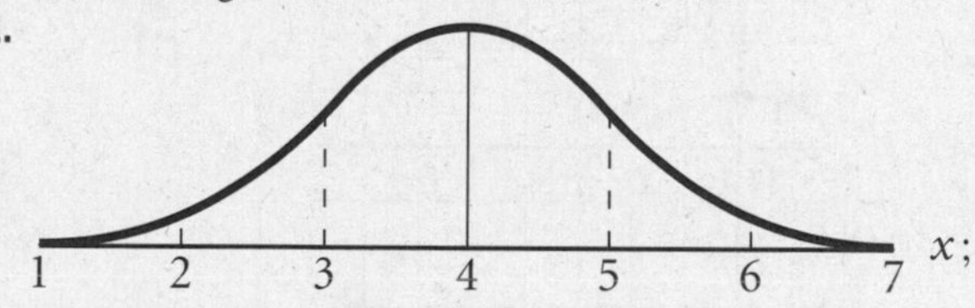

About 4 students would still be working after 5 min.

3.

About 2 frogs will hop more than 72 in.

Review 274

1. 6; 2 **2.** not periodic **3.** 3; 2

Review 275

1. $\left(-\frac{\sqrt{3}}{2}, -\frac{1}{2}\right)$ **2.** $\left(\frac{\sqrt{3}}{2}, \frac{1}{2}\right)$ **3.** $\left(\frac{\sqrt{3}}{2}, \frac{1}{2}\right)$
4. $\left(\frac{\sqrt{2}}{2}, -\frac{\sqrt{2}}{2}\right)$ **5.** $\left(-\frac{1}{2}, \frac{\sqrt{3}}{2}\right)$ **6.** $\left(-\frac{\sqrt{2}}{2}, -\frac{\sqrt{2}}{2}\right)$

Review 276

1. $\frac{\pi}{9} \approx 0.35$ **2.** $\frac{5\pi}{6} \approx 2.62$ **3.** $\frac{\pi}{4} \approx 0.79$

4. $-\frac{11\pi}{18} \approx -1.92$ **5.** $\frac{7\pi}{4} \approx 5.50$ **6.** $\frac{16\pi}{9} \approx 5.59$

7. −270° **8.** 300° **9.** 15° **10.** 288° **11.** −210° **12.** 810°

Review 277

1.

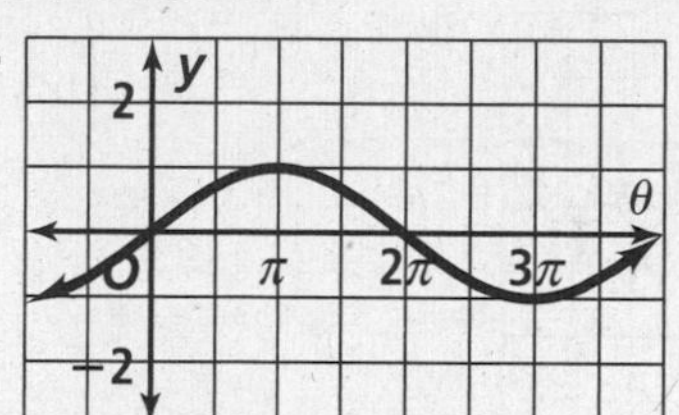

2.

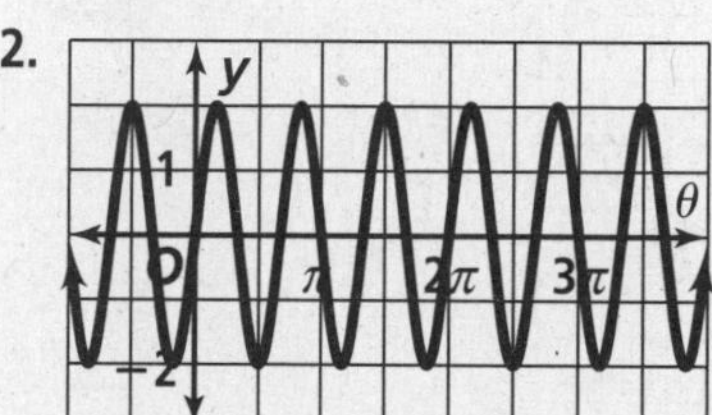

3.

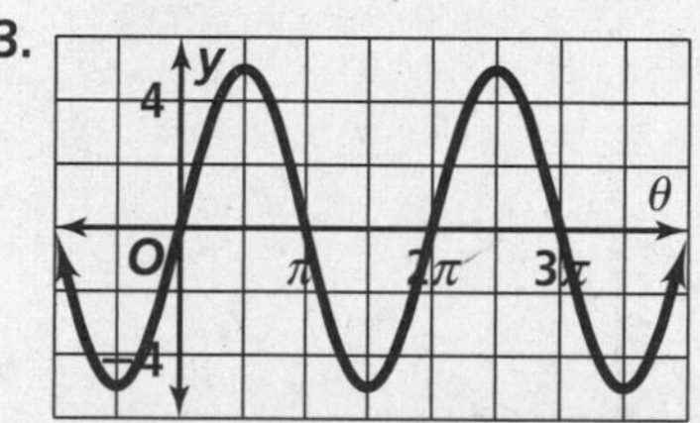

4.

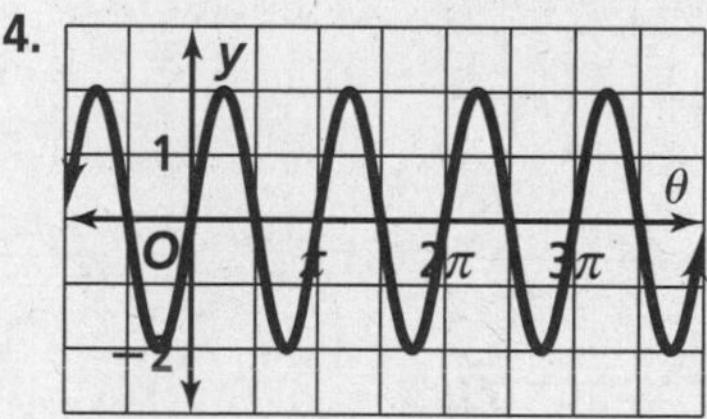

5.

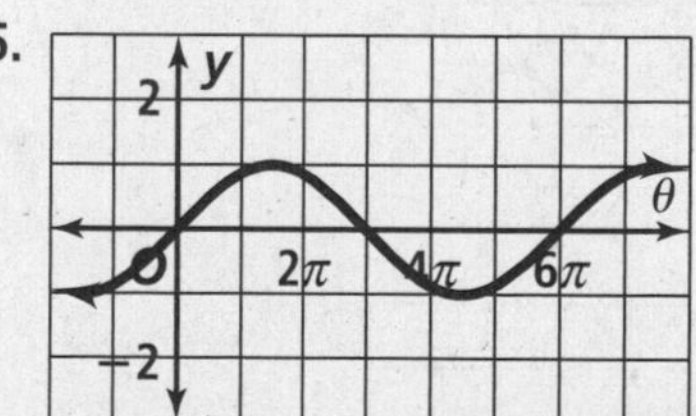

6.

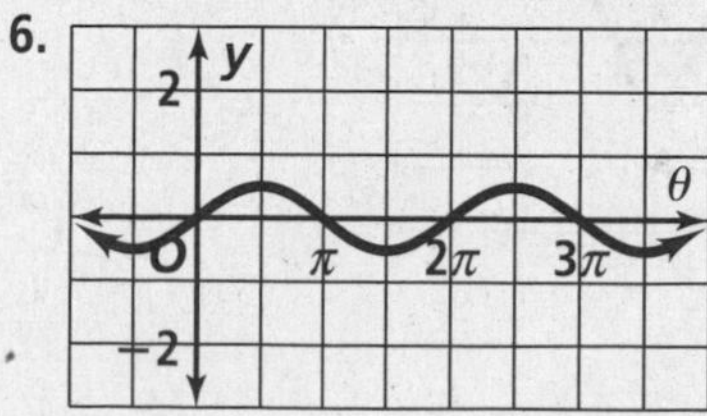

ANSWERS

Review 277 *(continued)*

7. 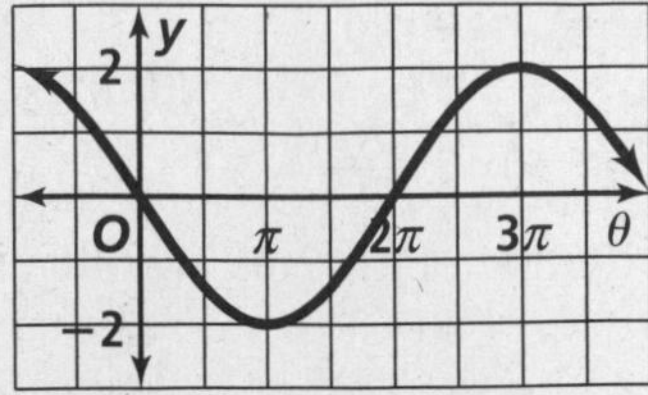

8. 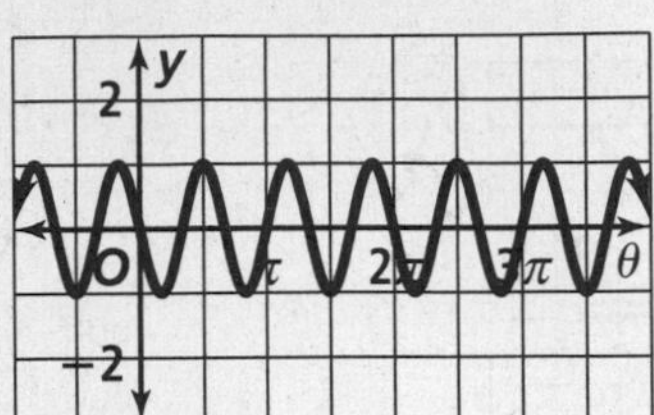

9. 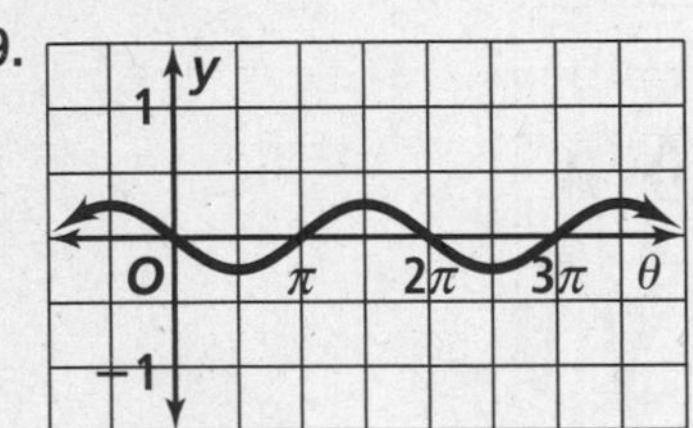

Review 278

1. $\frac{1}{2}$; π; 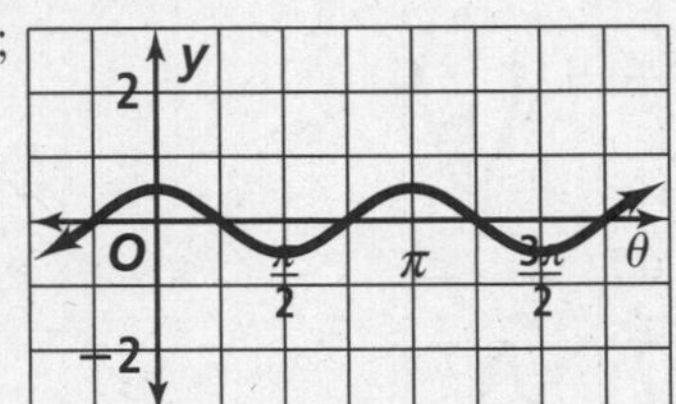

2. 3; 4π; 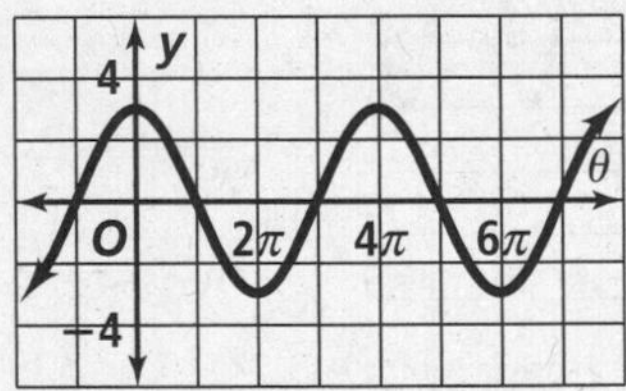

3. 1; $\frac{2}{3}\pi$; 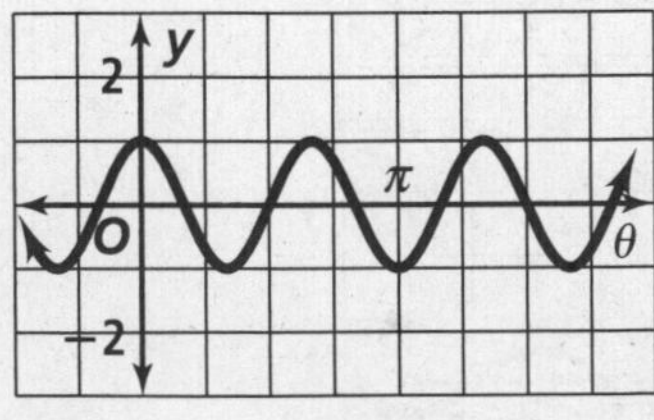

4. $\frac{1}{4}$; 2; 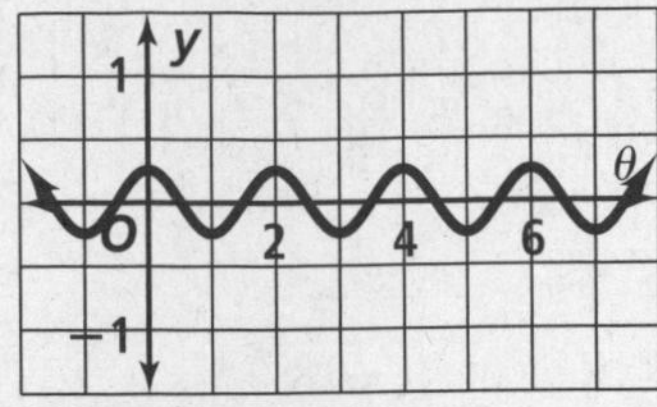

5. 2; 4π; 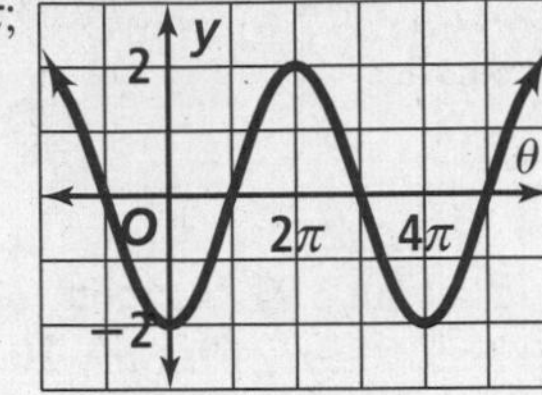

6. 2; $\frac{1}{3}$; 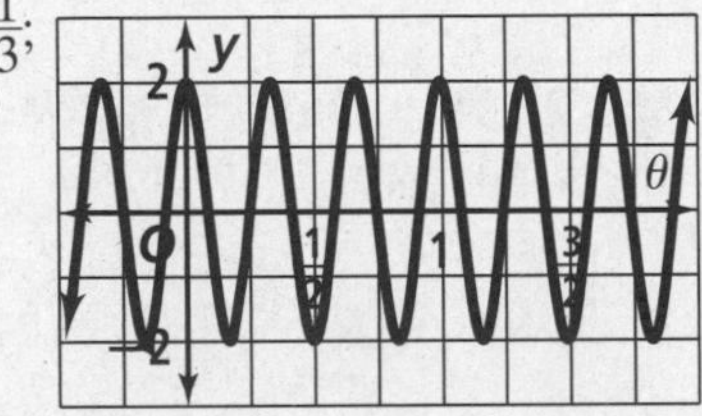

7. 2; 2π; 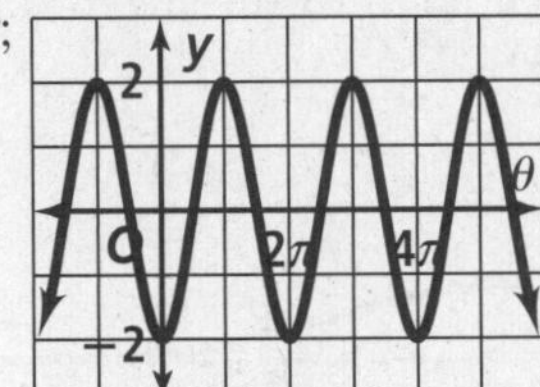

8. 1; 10π; 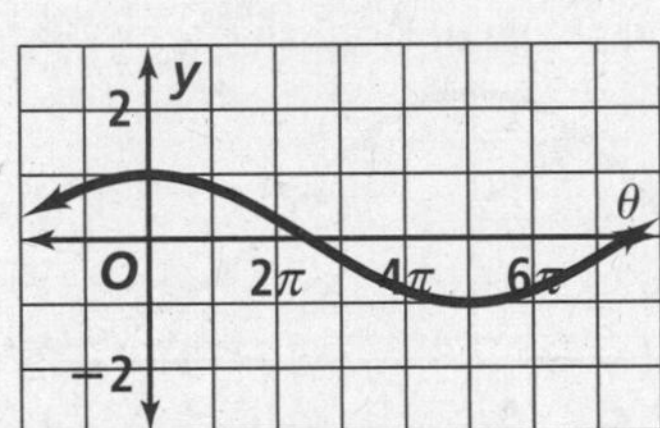

9. 2; π; 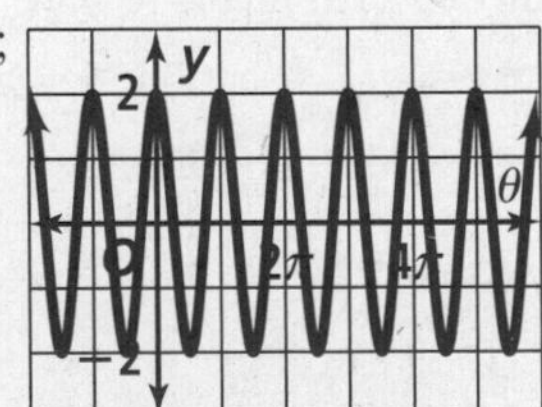

Review 279

1. $\frac{\pi}{2}$; $\frac{\pi}{4}$, $\frac{3\pi}{4}$, $\frac{5\pi}{4}$, $\frac{7\pi}{4}$; 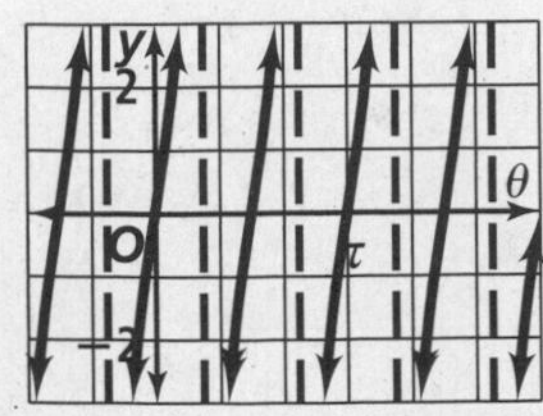

ANSWERS

Review 279 *(continued)*

2. 2π; π;

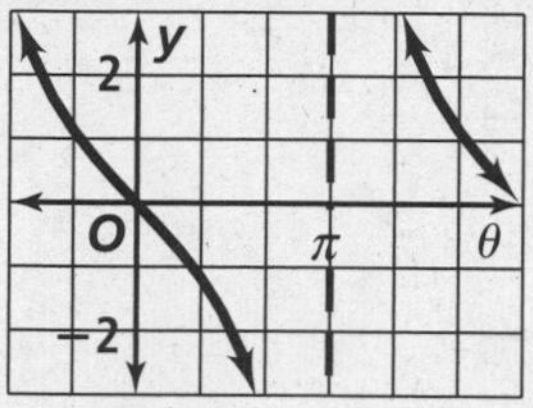

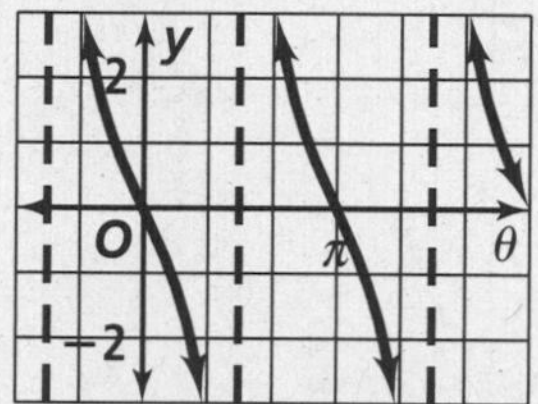

3. π; $\frac{\pi}{2}, \frac{3\pi}{2}$;

4. $\frac{\pi}{2}$; $\frac{\pi}{4}, \frac{3\pi}{4}, \frac{5\pi}{4}, \frac{7\pi}{4}$;

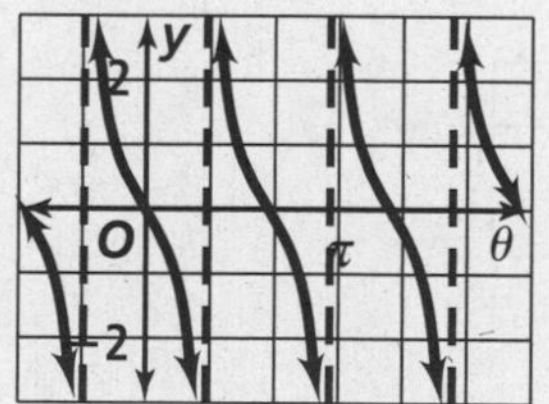

5. 2; 1, 3, 5;

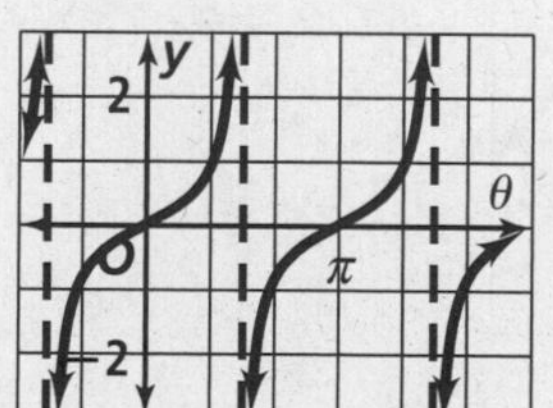

6. π; $\frac{\pi}{2}, \frac{3\pi}{2}$;

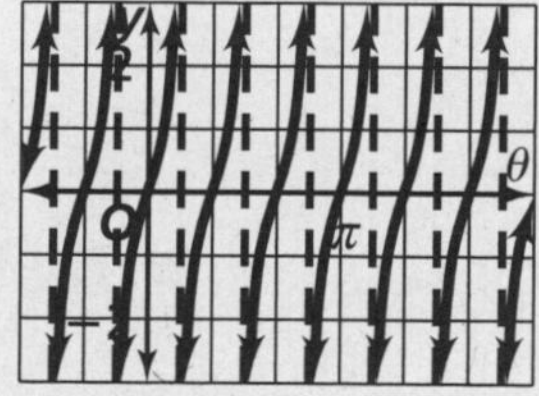

7. $\frac{\pi}{3}$; $\frac{\pi}{6}, \frac{\pi}{2}, \frac{5\pi}{6}, \frac{7\pi}{6}, \frac{3\pi}{2}, \frac{11\pi}{6}$;

8. 2; 1, 3, 5;

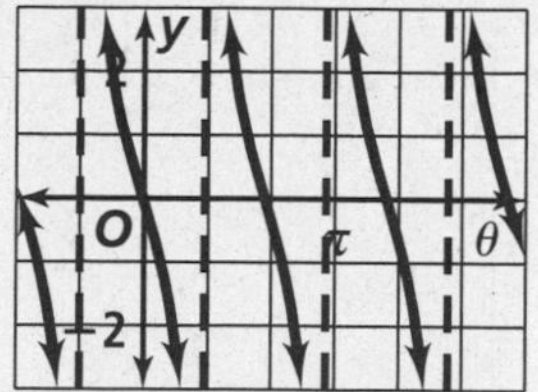

9. 4; 2, 6;

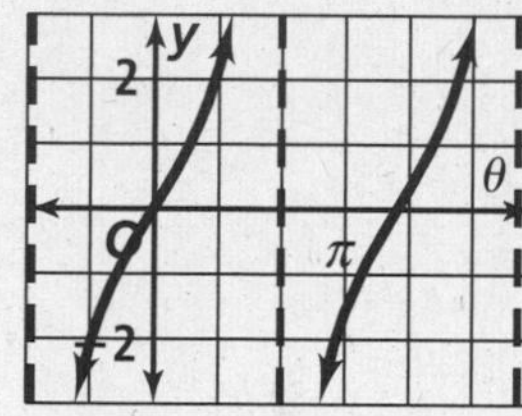

Review 280

1.

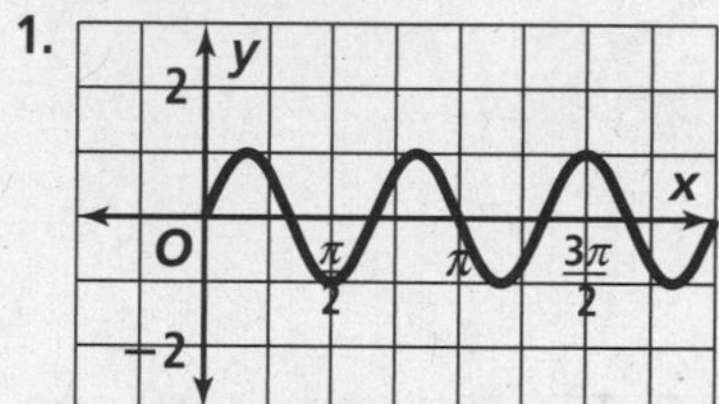

2.

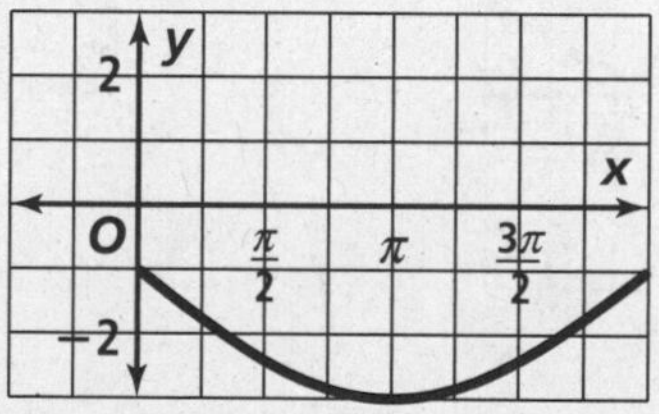

3.

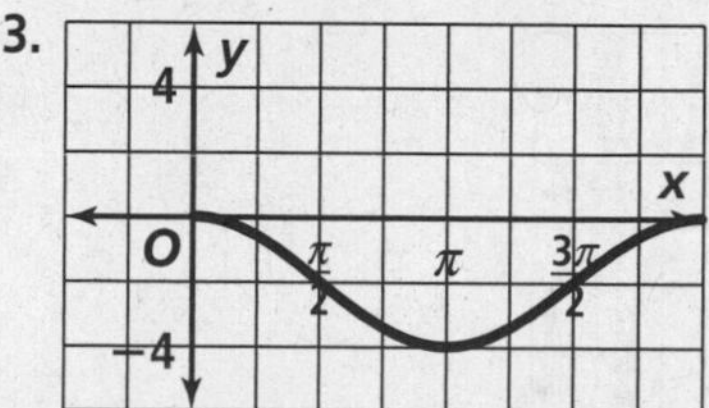

4.

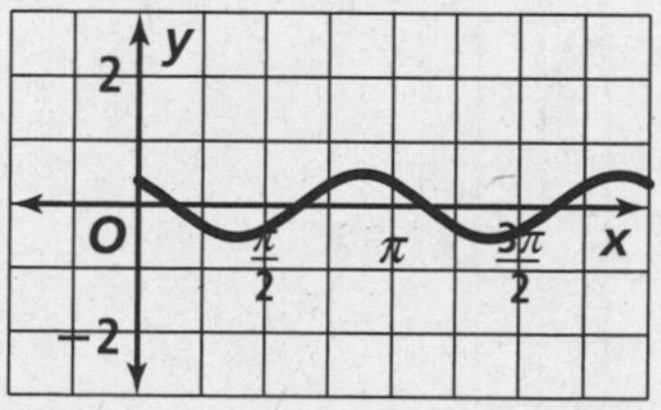

5.

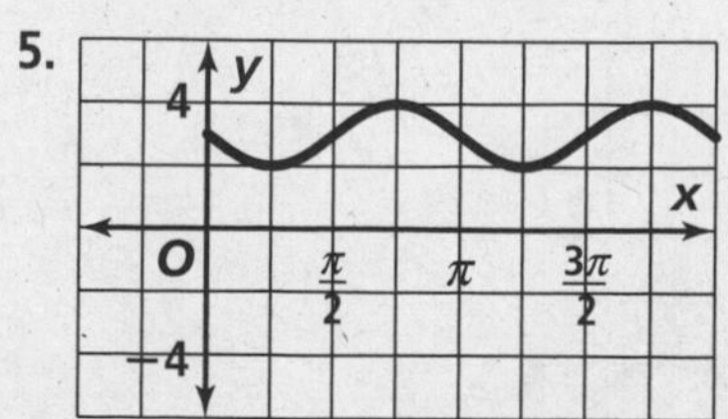

ANSWERS

Review 280 *(continued)*

6.

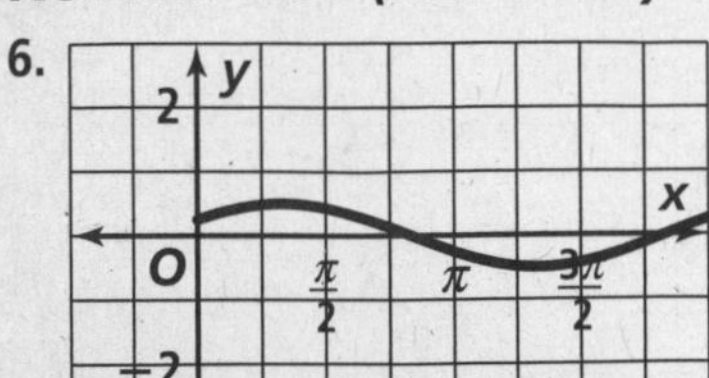

7.

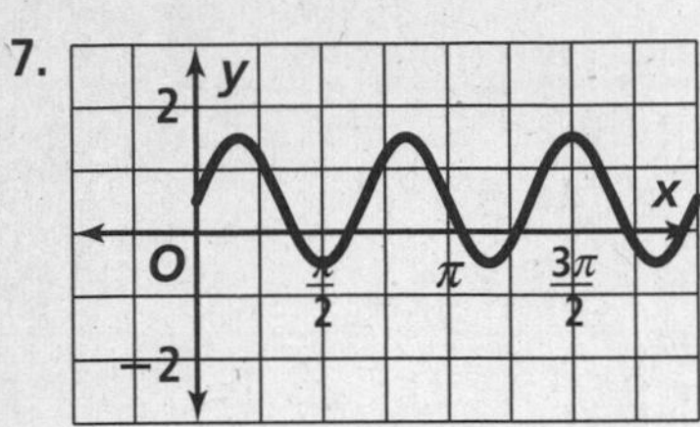

8.

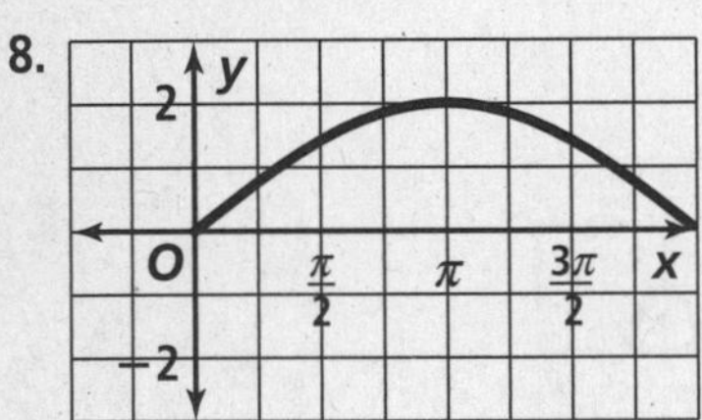

9.

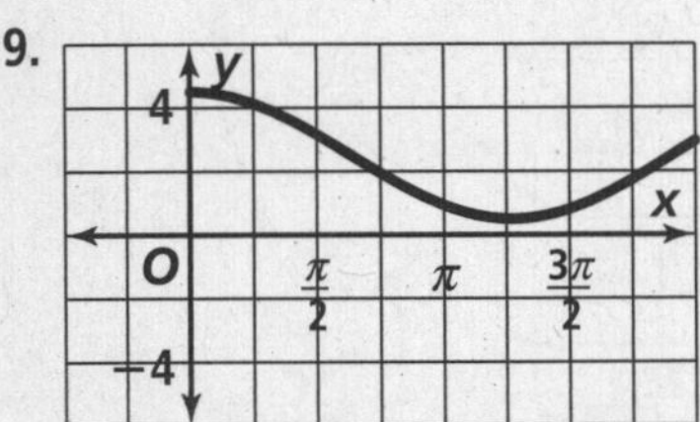

Review 281

1.

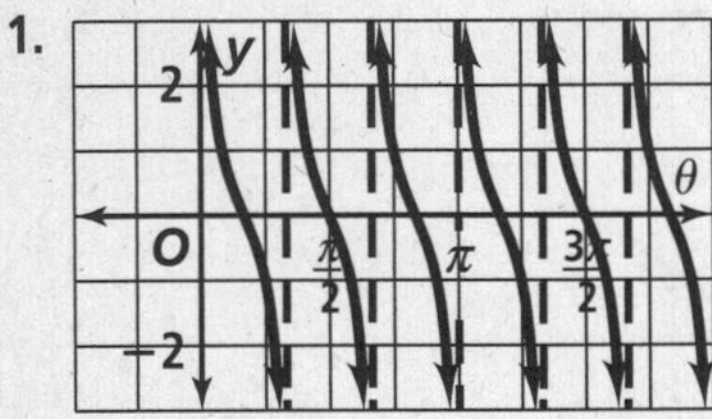

2.

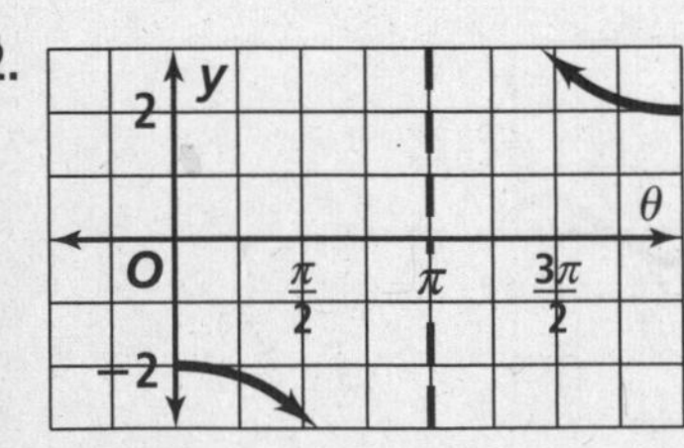

3.

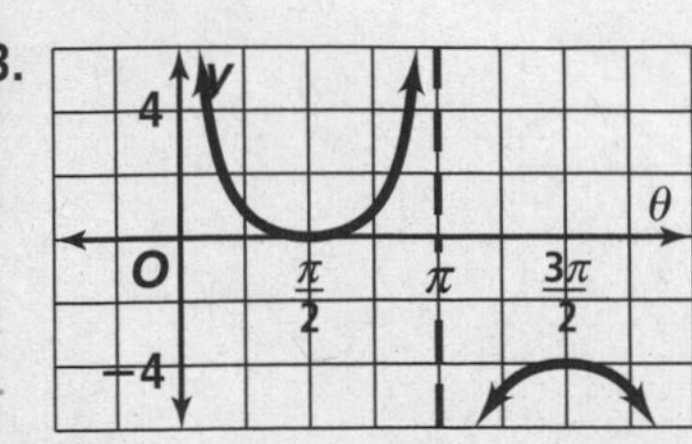

4.

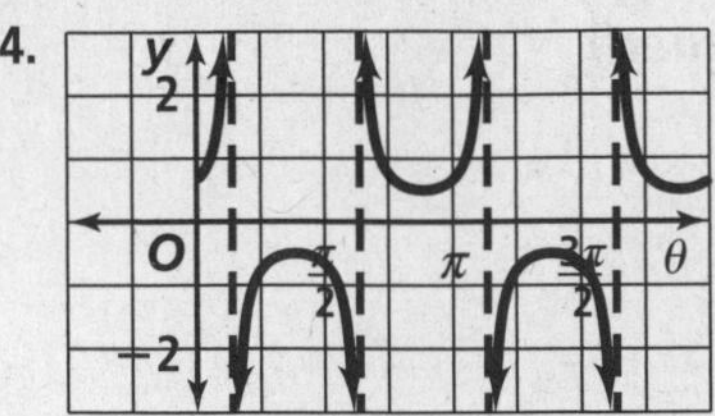

5.

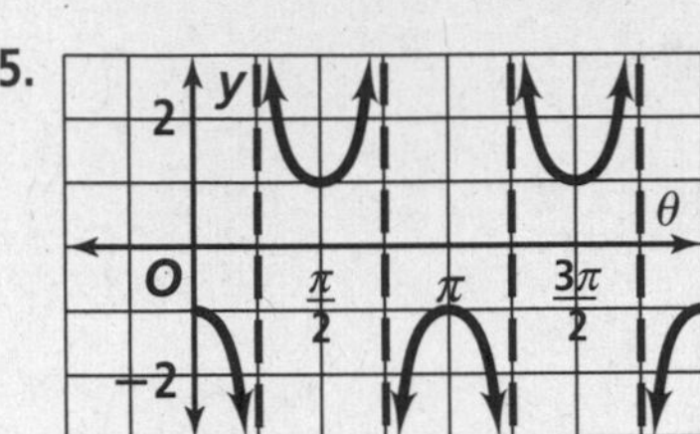

6.

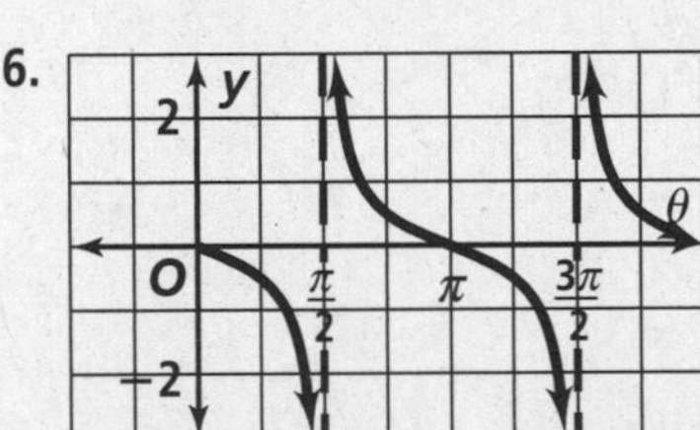

7.

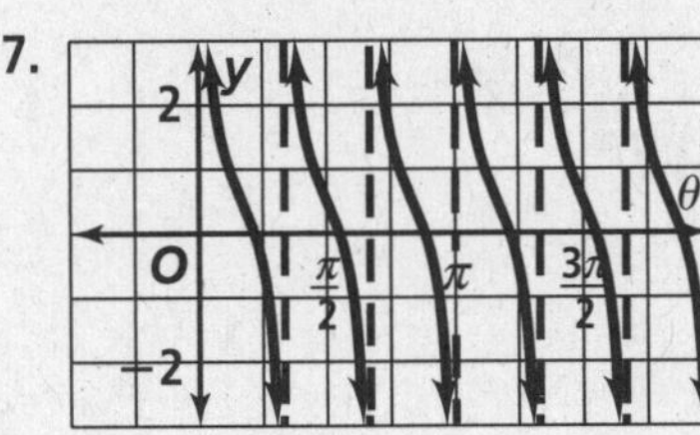

8.

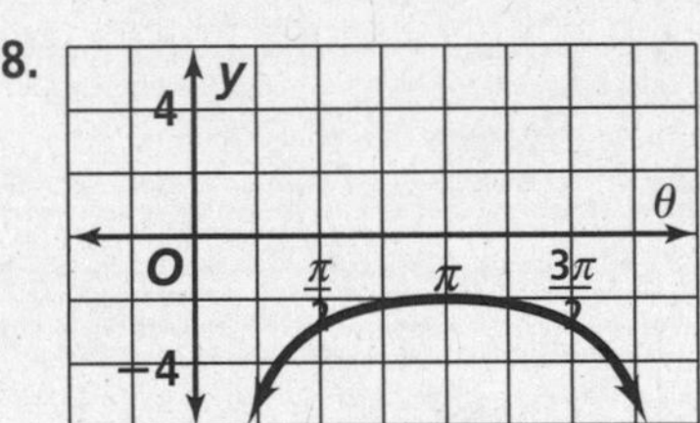

9.

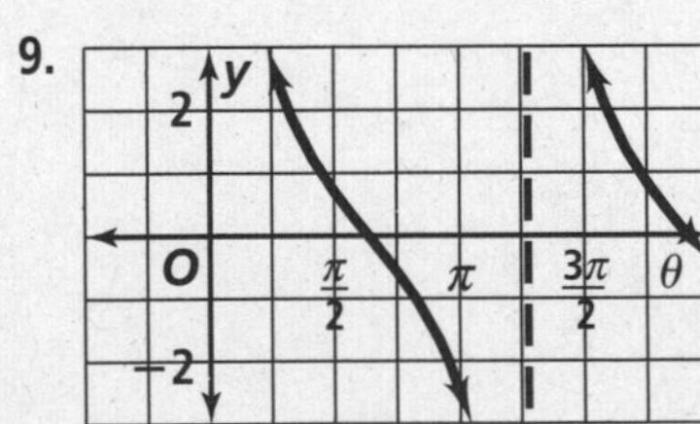

Review 282

1.–12. Answers will vary.

Review 283

1. $0, \frac{2\pi}{3}, \pi, \frac{4\pi}{3}$ **2.** $\frac{\pi}{2}$ **3.** $\frac{\pi}{3}, \frac{5\pi}{3}, \pi$ **4.** $\frac{\pi}{2}, \frac{3\pi}{2}, \frac{\pi}{6}, \frac{5\pi}{6}$

5. $\frac{5\pi}{3}, \frac{4\pi}{3}$ **6.** 0.34, 2.80 **7.** 1.11, 4.25 **8.** $\frac{\pi}{6}, \frac{5\pi}{6}, \frac{7\pi}{6}, \frac{11\pi}{6}$

Review 283 *(continued)*

9. $\frac{7\pi}{6}, \frac{3\pi}{2}, \frac{11\pi}{6}$ **10.** $0, \pi$ **11.** $\frac{5\pi}{6}, \frac{11\pi}{6}$ **12.** $\frac{\pi}{6}, \frac{11\pi}{6}$

Review 284

1. $m\angle A = 70°; c = 6.4, b = 2.2$
2. $m\angle A = 30°; b = 12.1, a = 7$
3. $m\angle B = 80°; b = 56.7, c = 57.6$
4. $m\angle A = 45.6°; a = 7.1, m\angle B = 44.4°$
5. $m\angle A = 59°; m\angle B = 31°, c = 40.8$
6. $m\angle B = 53.5°; a = 16.8, b = 22.7$

Review 285

1. 65.8 **2.** 6.1 **3.** 116.0 **4.** 56.1° **5.** 18.7° **6.** 40.7
7. 12.3 **8.** 54.3

Review 286

1. 38.6 **2.** 18.6 **3.** 26.8° **4.** 61.9 **5.** 12.9° **6.** 7.8
7. 47.3° **8.** 103.6°

Review 287

1. $\frac{1}{2}$ **2.** $\frac{-\sqrt{6} - \sqrt{2}}{4}$ **3.** $-\frac{\sqrt{3}}{2}$ **4.** $\frac{\sqrt{6} - \sqrt{2}}{4}$
5. $\frac{\sqrt{6} - \sqrt{2}}{4}$ **6.** $\frac{-\sqrt{6} - \sqrt{2}}{4}$ **7.** $\sqrt{3}$
8. $-\sqrt{3}$ **9.** $-\frac{\sqrt{2}}{2}$

Review 288

1.–6. Answers may vary.

ANSWERS